D1272162

American Literary Scholarship

1980

American Literary Scholarship

An Annual / 1980

Edited by J. Albert Robbins

Essays by Wendell Glick, David B. Kesterson, G. R. Thompson, Hershel Parker, Jerome Loving, Louis J. Budd, Robert L. Gale, George Bornstein and Stuart Y. McDougal, Karl F. Zender, Scott Donaldson, William J. Scheick, Kermit Vanderbilt, David Stouck, Jack Salzman, Jerome Klinkowitz, Richard Crowder, Lee Bartlett, Winifred Frazer, John M. Reilly, Jonathan Morse, F. Lyra, Marc Chénetier, Hans Galinsky, Gaetano Prampolini, Hiroko Sato, Rolf Lundén

Duke University Press, Durham North Carolina, 1982

6 130/82 pel. 37.75

Foreword

The chief announcement about persons associated with this annual is that James L. Woodress plans to retire as principal editor after next year's volume, *ALS 1981*. I plan to edit *ALS 1982* and the following volume, covering 1983, will have Warren G. French as editor.

It was James Woodress who saw how scholarship in American literature grew and grew, threatening each who strove to "keep up" with his specialties and be an informed "generalist" as well. Each year that effort became harder. Jim Woodress decided to do something about it. As he explains in the first sentence of the foreword in the first volume (*ALS 1963*), "The idea for this book originated when I returned from a year in Europe and was overwhelmed by the quantity of scholarship produced during my absence." And so the series began. *ALS 1981* will be the nineteenth volume. Of these Jim will have edited eleven, and in all nineteen of them his advice and guidance have been essential. *American Literary Scholarship* has become a constantly useful research and teaching resource and many, I'm sure, would agree with the cliché, I don't know what we would do without it. Thanks to Jim's vision and year in Europe, we haven't had to.

I want to thank G. R. Thompson for helping us out with the Poe chapter this year. The chapter next year will be done by Donald B. Stauffer (SUNY, Albany), who has handled the Chapter 3 assignment for us in the past. Replacing Hershel Parker, a veteran of the Melville chapter for nine years, will be Robert Milder (Washington University, St. Louis). After seven years covering Fiction: 1900 to the 1930s, David Stouck will be replaced by John Murphy (Merrimack College, North Andover, Mass.). And this is Winifred Frazer's fifth and final year of reviewing Drama for us. Her successor, a former author of that chapter, is Walter J. Meserve, Department of Theatre and Drama, Indiana University, Bloomington. Among the foreign scholars, coverage of Japanese Contributions will alternate, Hiroko Sato as author this year and Keiko Beppu next year. Professor Rolf Lundén has covered Scandinavian Contributions for the past eight years, since we instituted the chapter on Foreign Scholarship in the *ALS 1973* volume. Next year that portion of Chapter 21 will be prepared by Mona Pers, of the University College of Västerås, Sweden. Warm thanks to these retirees for their long and faithful service.

We have touched upon some of these matters before, but it may be useful to remind readers of our procedures. Taking the present volume as illustration, we have followed this pattern. (1) We have received batches of 1980 citations of current festschriften and essay collections during 1980 and 1981 from James L. Harner (Bowling Green State University), head of that portion of the *MLA International Bibliography* (*MLAB*). The editor distributed these to concerned chapter authors. (2) During 1981 the off-year editor (James Woodress) researched and distributed article citations. Each chapter author, of course, made his own search for materials, especially in obvious journals relevant to his topic. Richard Crowder—at work on Chapter 16, Poetry: 1900 to the 1940s—for example, learned of critical and biographical works in that area, wrote for review copies, and read them. He also routinely covered such standard journals as *American Literature* and *Concerning Poetry* and such author journals as the *Robinson Jeffers Newsletter*, *William Carlos Williams Review*, and *Wallace Stevens Journal*. He worked on article leads sent him by Professor Woodress. (3) Target date for completed manuscripts was August 15, 1981. On July 13 I received from the New York office of MLA an advance printout of the 1980 *MLAB* and I cut out and sorted items for distribution to chapter authors. In most cases, the chapter author had seen these items, but the few he was unaware of, he read and added to his manuscript. (4) The printed *MLA Bibliography* reached members on or around October 31, 1981, after many authors had finished and mailed manuscripts to me. The published *MLAB*, too late to be of primary use, was a final checklist, alerting a chapter author to the occasional item which escaped his net.

The point I wish to make is this: for all practical purposes we operate independently of *MLAB*. If we waited for the printed volume to appear in the fall of 1981, it would take us close to an extra year to read, compose, edit, and print *ALS*.

One might well ask, Does *ALS* turn up a significant number of items not in the corresponding *MLAB*? To get some sense of this,

I ran a test check of the first 30 of the 72 typescript pages in Jerome Klinkowitz' chapter 15, Fiction: The 1950s to the Present. What I found was that *MLAB* does a splendid job in reporting articles and a not-so-splendid job in citing books. Though *MLAB* covers *MELUS, Descant,* and *Commentary,* the bibliography staff missed three articles which Professor Klinkowitz cites. Klinkowitz also cites articles which impressed him as significant in the following journals not covered by *MLAB: New Republic, Granta* (a revived British journal), *Fiction International,* the *Ohio Library Association Bulletin, Harper's* and *Atlantic Monthly. MLAB* fails to cite John Barth's important essay in the January *Atlantic,* "The Literature of Replenishment."

The oversight by *MLAB* of important books is more striking. Professor Klinkowitz cites the following titles not recorded in the 1980 *MLAB*: James M. Mellard, *The Exploded Form: The Modernist Novel in America;* Sanford Pinsker, *Between Two Worlds: The American Novel in the 1960s;* Ihab Hassan, *The Right Promethean Fire: Imagination, Science, and Cultural Change;* John Griffiths' *Three Tomorrows: American, British, and Soviet Science Fiction;* Richard Kostelanetz, *Text-Sound Texts,* Jerome Klinkowitz's *The American 1960s: Imaginative Acts in a Decade of Change* and the enlarged editions of his *Literary Disruptions* and his *The Practice of Fiction in America;* James E. Kibler, Jr.'s *American Novelists Since World War II,* 2nd series.

As we have advised readers of *ALS* repeatedly, this annual is selective and no substitute for the *MLA Bibliography.* Our chapter authors cannot cover "everything." Now, if the above sample is valid, I can advise readers of *ALS*: In your search for materials, be sure to look at both *MLAB* and *ALS. ALS* provides some citations you won't find in the *Bibliography* for the same subject year.

J. Albert Robbins

Indiana University

Table of Contents

Key to Abbreviations

Festschriften, Essay Collections, and Books Discussed in More Than One Chapter

Affairs of the Mind / Peter Quennell, ed., *Affairs of the Mind: The Salon in Europe and America from the 18th to the 20th Century* (Washington: New Republic)

American Bypaths / Robert G. Collmer and Jack W. Herring, eds., *American Bypaths: Essays in Honor of E. Hudson Long* (Waco: Baylor Univ. Press)

American Hieroglyphics / John T. Irwin, *American Hieroglyphics: The Symbol of the Egyptian Hieroglyphics in the American Renaissance* (Yale)

The American South / Louis D. Rubin, Jr., ed., *The American South: Portrait of a Culture* (LSU)

Amérique, Ecriture, Argent / Jacques Darras, ed., *Amérique, Ecriture, Argent* (Amiens: Centre d'Etudes Americaines, Univ. de Picardie)

At Last / Kathleen Woodward, *At Last, The Real Distinguished Thing: The Late Poems of Eliot, Pound, Stevens, and Williams* (Ohio State)

The Binding of Proteus / Marjorie W. McCune, Tucker Orbison, and Philip M. Withim, eds., *The Binding of Proteus: Perspectives on Myth and the Literary Process* (Bucknell)

Black Fiction / A. Robert Lee, ed., *Black Fiction: New Studies in the Afro-American Novel Since 1945* (Barnes and Noble)

The Comedy of Language / Fred Miller Robinson, *The Comedy of Language: Studies in Modern Comic Literature* (Mass.)

Corps Création / Jean Guillaumin, ed., *Corps Création* (Presses Universitaires de Lyon)

The David Myth / Raymond-Jean Frontain and Jan Wojcik, eds., *The David Myth in Western Literature* (Purdue)

Development of American Romance / Michael Davitt Bell, *The Development of American Romance: The Sacrifice of Relation* (Chicago)

Le Discours de la Violence / Régis Durand, ed., *Le Discours de la Violence dans la Culture Americaine* (Presses Universitaires de Lille, 1979)

The Exploded Form / James M. Mellard, *The Exploded Form: The Modernist Novel in America* (Illinois)

Le Facteur Religieux / Jean Béranger, ed., *Le Facteur Religieux en Amerique du Nord* (Bordeaux: Maison des Sciences Humaines d'Aquitaine)

A Fair Day / Jack D. Durant and M. Thomas Hester, eds., *A Fair Day in the Affections: Literary Essays in Honor of Robert B. White, Jr.* (Raleigh, N. C.: Winston Press)

Fiction as Wisdom / Irvin Stock, *Fiction as Wisdom from Goethe to Bellow* (Penn. State)

Fifty Years of Yoknapatawpha / Doreen Fowler and Ann J. Abadie, eds., *Fifty Years of Yoknapataw-*

pha: Faulkner and Yoknapatawpha, 1979 (Miss.)

Figures in a Ground / Diane Bessai and David Jackel, eds., *Figures in a Ground: Canadian Essays on Modern Literature Collected in Honor of Sheila Watson* (Saskatoon: Western Producer Prairie Books, 1978)

The Forms of Autobiography / William C. Spengemann, *The Forms of Autobiography: Episodes in the History of a Literary Genre* (Yale)

Harlekinade / Kordula Rose-Werle, *Harlekinade—Genealogie und Metamorphose: Struktur und Deutung des Motivs bei J. D. Salinger und V. Nabokov*, Trier Studien zur Literatur 3 (Lang)

Kleinstück Festschrift / Hans-Heinrich Freitag and Peter Hühn, eds. *Literarische Ansichten der Wirklichkeit: Studien zur Wirklichkeitskonstitution in englischsprachiger Literatur: To Honour Johannes Kleinstück* (Lang)

Medicine and Literature / Enid Rhodes Peschel, ed., *Medicine and Literature* (New York: Neale Watson Academic Publications)

Mid-America Linguistics Conf. / Donald M. Lance and Daniel E. Gulstad, eds., *Papers from the 1977 Mid-America Linguistics Conference* (Missouri)

Minority Literature / George E. Carter and James R. Parker, eds., *Minority Literature and the Urban Experience.* Selected Proc. of the 4th Annual Conf. on Minority Studies (Univ. of Wisconsin–La Crosse, 1978)

Money Talks / Roy R. Male, ed., *Money Talks: Language and Lucre in American Fiction* (Oklahoma)

Narrative Strategies / Syndy M. Conger and Janice R. Welsch, eds., *Narrative Strategies: Original Essays in Film and Prose Fiction* (Macomb: Western Ill. Univ.)

Poetic Knowledge / Roland Hagenbüchle and Joseph T. Swann, eds.,

Poetic Knowledge: Circumference and Center: Papers from the Wuppertal Symposium, 1978 (Schriftenreihe Literaturwissenschaft, Gesamthochschule Wuppertal, 18 [Bonn: Bouvier])

The Practice of Fiction / Jerome Klinkowitz, *The Practice of Fiction in America: Writers from Hawthorne to the Present* (Iowa State)

Proceedings of the 7th Congress / Milan V. Dimić and Juan Ferraté, eds., *Proceedings of the 7th Congress of the International Comparative Literature Association* (Stuttgart: Bieber, 1979)

Prodigal Sons / David Wyatt, *Prodigal Sons: A Study in Authorship and Authority* (Johns Hopkins)

Regards sur la Littérature / Michel Fabre, ed., *Regards sur la Littérature Noire Americaine / French Approaches to Black American Literature* (Paris: Publications de la Sorbonne Nouvelle)

Seasoned Authors / Louis Filler, ed., *Seasoned Authors for a New Season: The Search for Standards in Popular Writing* (Bowling Green, Ohio: Popular)

Second Black Renaissance / C. W. E. Bigsby, *The Second Black Renaissance: Essays in Black Literature* (Greenwood)

A Southern Renaissance / Richard H. King, *A Southern Renaissance, The Cultural Awakening of the American South, 1930–1955* (Oxford)

Stürzl Festschrift / James Hogg, ed., *Essays in Honour of Erwin Stürzl on his Sixtieth Birthday* (Univ. Salzburg)

Toward a New American Literary History / Louis J. Budd, Edwin H. Cady, and Carl L. Anderson, eds., *Toward a New American Literary History: Essays in Honor of Arlin Turner* (Duke)

Unappeased Imagination / Glenn O. Carey, ed., *Faulkner: The Unap-*

peased Imagination, A Collection of Critical Essays (Whitston)

The Unsounded Centre / Martin Bickman, The Unsounded Centre: Jungian Studies in American Romanticism (N. Car.)

Violence and Culture / Dickson D. Bruce, Violence and Culture in the Antebellum South (Texas, 1979)

Women, Women Writers, and the West / L. L. Lee and Merrill Lewis, eds., Women, Women Writers, and the West (Whitston, 1979)

Women's Autobiography / Estelle C. Jelinek, ed., Women's Autobiography: Essays in Criticism (Indiana)

Yugoslav Perspectives / James L. Thorson, ed., Yugoslav Perspectives on American Literature (Ann Arbor, Mich.: Ardis Publishers)

The Law of the Heart / Sam B. Girgus, The Law of the Heart: Individualism and the Modern Self in American Literature (Texas, 1979)

Periodicals, Annuals, Series

AAAH / Acta Academiae Aboensis Humaniora (Abo, Finland)

AAus / Americana-Austriaca

ABBW / AB Bookman's Weekly

ABC / American Book Collector

AF / Anglistische Forschungen

AH / American Heritage

AHumor / American Humor

AI / American Imago

AL / American Literature

ALR / American Literary Realism

ALS / American Literary Scholarship

AmerS / American Studies

AmerSS / American Studies in Scandinavia

Amst / Amerikastudien

AN&Q / American Notes and Queries

Anglia: Zeitschrifte für Englische Philologie

APR / American Poetry Review

AQ / American Quarterly

ArAA / Arbeiten aus Anglistik und Amerikanistik

Arcadia: Zeitschrift für Vergleichende Literaturwissenschaft

Archiv für das Studium der Neuren Sprachen und Literaturen

ArielE / Ariel: A Review of International English Literature

ArmD / Armchair Detective

ArQ / Arizona Quarterly

Artes (Stockholm)

ASch / The American Scholar

AtM / Atlantic Monthly

ATQ / American Transcendental Quarterly

ASInt / American Studies International

BALF / Black American Literature Forum

BB / Bulletin of Bibliography

BCM / Book Collector's Market

BI / Books at Iowa

BLRev / Bluegrass Literary Review (Midway, Ky.)

Boundary / Boundary 2: A Journal of Post-modern Literature

BRH / Bulletin of Research in the Humanities

BSUF / Ball State Univ. Forum

Calamus: Walt Whitman Quarterly International (Tokyo)

Caliban (Toulouse, France)

Callaloo: A Black South Journal of Arts and Letters

CB / Classical Bulletin (Wilmore, Ky.)

CCR / Claflin College Review

CE / College English

CEA / CEA Critic

CentR / Centennial Review

CHAL / Cambridge History of American Literature

ChiR / Chicago Review

CHSB / Conn. Hist. Soc. Bulletin

Cithara: Essays in the Judaeo-Christian Tradition

CJAS / Canadian Journal of African Studies

CL / Comparative Literature

CLAJ / College Language Association Journal

ClioI / CLIO: A Journal of Literature, History and Philosophy of History
CLQ / Colby Library Quarterly
CLS / Comparative Literature Studies
CollL / College Literature
Commentary
CompD / Comparative Drama
ConL / Contemporary Literature
CP / Concerning Poetry
CRCL / Canadian Review of Canadian Literature
CRevAS / Canadian Review of American Studies
Crit / Critique: Studies in Modern Fiction
CritI / Critical Inquiry
CritQ / Critical Quarterly
Criticism: A Quarterly for Literature and the Arts
CS / Concord Saunterer
CSE / Center for Scholarly Editions
DAI / Dissertation Abstracts International
DeltaES / Delta: Revue du Centre d'Etudes et de Recherche sur les Ecrivains du Sud aux Etats-Unis (Montpellier, France)
Descant: Texas Christian Univ. Literary Journal
DicS / Dickinson Studies (formerly Emily Dickinson Bulletin)
Dismisura
DR / Dalhousie Review
DrN / Dreiser Newsletter
DSN / Dickens Studies Newsletter
DUJ / Durham University Journal
EA / Etudes Anglaises
EAL / Early American Literature
EAS / Essays in Arts and Sciences
Edda: Nordisk Tidskrift for Litteraturforskning
EGN / Ellen Glasgow Newsletter
EIC / Essays in Criticism
EIHC / Essex Institute Historical Collections
ELH [formerly English Literary History]
ELN / English Language Notes
ELS / English Literary Studies
ELWIU / Essays in Literature (Western Ill. Univ.)
English (London)

EON / Eugene O'Neill Newsletter
ESA / English Studies in Africa
ESC / English Studies in Canada
ESQ: A Journal of the American Renaissance
ESRS / Emporia State Research Studies
EurH / Europäische Hochschulschriften
Europe: Revue Littéraire Mensuelle
EuWN / Eudora Welty Newsletter
Expl / Explicator
Extrapolation
FAR / French-American Review
FaSt / Faulkner Studies, An Annual of Research, Criticism, and Reviews (Coral Gables, Fla.)
FInt / Fiction International
Genre
GissingN / Gissing Newsletter
GL&L / German Life and Letters
Gothic
Granta (Cambridge, Eng.)
GRENA / Groupe d'Etudes et de Recherches Nord-Américaines (Aix-en-Provence)
HC / Hollins Critic
HJR / Henry James Review (Baton Rouge, La.)
HLB / Harvard Library Bulletin
HN / Hemingway Notes
HNH / Historical New Hampshire
HSE / Hungarian Studies in English
HSL / Univ. of Hartford Studies in Literature
HTR / Harvard Theological Review
HudR / Hudson Review
IFR / International Fiction Review
IJAS / Indian Journal of American Studies
IllQ / Illinois Quarterly
IQ / Italian Quarterly
JAAR / Journal of the American Academy of Religion
JAmS / Journal of American Studies
JBS / Journal of Black Studies
JEGP / Journal of English and Germanic Philology
JEthS / Journal of Ethnic Studies
JHI / Journal of the History of Ideas
JL / Journal of Linguistics
JLN / Jack London Newsletter

JML / Journal of Modern Literature
JNT / Journal of Narrative Technique
JOHJ / John O'Hara Journal
JPC / Journal of Popular Culture
JQ / Journalism Quarterly
KAL / Kyushu American Literature (Fukuoka, Japan)
KFR / Kentucky Folklore Record
KPAB / Kentucky Philological Association Bulletin
KR / Kenyon Review
KRev / Kentucky Review (Lexington)
L&P / Literature and Psychology
LArb / Linguistische Arbeiten
LetA / Letterature d'America (Rome)
LFQ / Literature/Film Quarterly
LGJ / Lost Generation Journal
LHY / Literary Half-Yearly
LitR / Literary Review (Fairleigh-Dickinson Univ.)
LJGG / Literaturwissenschaftliches Jahrbuch im Auftrage der Görres-Gesellschaft
LOS / Literary Onomastics Studies
LRN / Literary Research Newsletter
MarkhamR / Markham Review
McNR / McNeese Review
MD / Modern Drama
Meanjin
MELUS: The Journal of the Society for the Study of the Multi-ethnic Literature of the United States
Merkur: Deutsche Zeitschrift für Europäisches Denken
MFS / Modern Fiction Studies
MHLS / Mid-Hudson Language Studies
Mid-America: The Yearbook of the Society for the Study of Midwestern Literature
MissQ / Mississippi Quarterly
MLA / Modern Language Association
MLS / Modern Language Studies
MMisc / Midwestern Miscellany
MMN / Marianne Moore Newsletter
ModA / Modern Age
Monatshefte
Mosaic: A Journal for the Interdisciplinary Study of Literature
MP / Modern Philology
MPS / Modern Poetry Studies
MQ / Midwest Quarterly

MQR / Michigan Quarterly Review
MR / Massachusetts Review
MSE / Massachusetts Studies in English
MSEx / Melville Society Extracts
MSpr / Moderna Språk (Stockholm)
MTJ / Mark Twain Journal
MV / Minority Voices
N&Q / Notes and Queries
NAR / North American Review
NConL / Notes on Contemporary Literature
NCTR / Nineteenth Century Theatre Research
NDEJ / Notre Dame English Journal
NDQ / North Dakota Quarterly
NEQ / New England Quarterly
NER / New England Review
NewL / New Letters
NewRep / New Republic
NHJ / Nathaniel Hawthorne Journal
NMAL: Notes on Modern American Literature
NMW / Notes on Mississippi Writers
Novel: A Forum on Fiction
NSAA / Neue Studien zur Anglistik und Amerikanistik
NYH / New York History
NYRB / New York Review of Books
Obsidian: Black Literature in Review
Ody / Odyssey: A Journal of the Humanities
OJES / Osmania Journal of English Studies
OL / Orbis Litterarum: International Review of Literary Studies
OntarioR / Ontario Review
Paideuma: A Journal Devoted to Ezra Pound Scholarship
Paragone: Rivista Mensile di Arte Figurativa e Letteratura
Parnassus: Poetry in Review
PBSA / Papers of the Bibliographical Society of America
PCL / Perspectives on Contemporary Literature
PLL / Papers on Language and Literature
PMHS / Proceedings of the Massachusetts Historical Society
PMLA: Publications of the Modern Language Association of America

PN / *Poe Newsletter*
PNotes / *Pynchon Notes* (Brentwood, N. Y.)
PoeS / *Poe Studies*
PoT / *Poetics Today: Theory and Analysis of Literature & Communications* (Tel Aviv)
PR / *Partisan Review*
Prospects: An Annual Journal of American Cultural Studies
Publishing Hist / *Publishing History*
QH / *Quaker History*
RALS / *Resources for American Literary Study*
RANAM / *Recherches Anglaises et Américaines*
Renascence: Essays on Value in Literature
RES / *Review of English Studies*
RFEA / *Revue Française d'Etudes Américaines*
RFI / *Regionalism and the Female Imagination*
RJN / *Robinson Jeffers Newsletter*
RLC / *Revue de Littérature Comparée*
RLMC / *Rivista di Letterature Moderne e Comparate* (Florence)
RomN / *Romance Notes*
RS / *Research Studies*
SA / *Studi Americani* (Rome)
SAB / *South Atlantic Bulletin*
SAF / *Studies in American Fiction*
SAJL / *Studies in American Jewish Literature*
Salmagundi
SAP / *Studia Anglica Posnaniensia: An International Review of English Studies*
SAQ / *South Atlantic Quarterly*
SB / *Studies in Bibliography*
SBHC / *Studies in Browning and his Circle*
SDR / *South Dakota Review*
SenR / *Seneca Review*
SFS / *Science-Fiction Studies*
SGym / *Siculorum Gymnasium*
Shenandoah
SHR / *Southern Humanities Review*
Signs: Journal of Women in Culture and Society
SJS / *San Jose Studies*

SLitI / *Studies in the Literary Imagination*
SLJ / *Southern Literary Journal*
SNNTS / *Studies in the Novel* (North Tex. State Univ.)
SoQ / *Southern Quarterly*
SoR / *Southern Review*
SoSt / *Southern Studies*
Soundings: A Journal of Interdisciplinary Studies
SovL / *Soviet Literature*
SpM / *Spicilegio Moderno* (Bologna)
SR / *Sewanee Review*
SS / *Scandinavian Studies*
SSF / *Studies in Short Fiction*
SSL / *Studies in Scottish Literature*
SSMLN / *Society for the Study of Midwestern Literature Newsletter*
StAR / *St. Andrews Review*
StHum / *Studies in the Humanities*
StQ / *Steinbeck Quarterly*
Style
Sub-Stance: A Review of Theory and Literary Criticism
SuL / *Sprache und Literatur* (Stuttgart, Germany)
SWR / *Southwest Review*
TCL / *Twentieth-Century Literature*
TDR / *The Drama Review*
Thalia: Studies in Literary Humor
ThS / *Theatre Survey*
TJ / *Theatre Journal*
TJQ / *Thoreau Journal Quarterly*
TLS / *[London] Times Literary Supplement*
TSLL / *Texas Studies in Literature and Language*
TUSAS / Twayne United States Author Series
TWAS / Twayne World Authors Series
TWN / *Thomas Wolfe Newsletter*
TWNew / *Tennessee Williams Newsletter*
UDR / *Univ. of Dayton Review*
UMSE / *Univ. of Mississippi Studies in English*
USP / *Under the Sign of Pisces: Anaïs Nin and her Circle*
UTQ / *Univ. of Toronto Quarterly*
VQR / *Virginia Quarterly Review*
VNRN / *Vladimir Nabokov Research Newsletter*

WAL / Western American Literature
WCWN / William Carlos Williams Newletter
WCWR / William Carlos Williams Review (formerly *William Carlos Williams Newsletter*)
WHR / Western Humanities Review
WiF / William Faulkner: Materials, Studies, and Criticism (Tokyo)
WilsonQ / Wilson Quarterly
WIRS / Western Illinois Regional Studies
WMQ / William and Mary Quarterly

WS / Women's Studies
WSJour / Wallace Stevens Journal
WVUPP / West Virginia Univ. Philological Papers
WWR / Walt Whitman Review
WWS / Western Writers Series (Boise State Univ.)
YER / Yeats Eliot Review
YFS / Yale French Studies
YR / Yale Review
YULG / Yale Univ. Library Gazette
ZAA / Zeitschrift für Anglistik und Amerikanistik

Publishers

Atheneum / New York: Atheneum Publishers
Arizona / Tucson: Univ. of Arizona Press
Athlone / London: Athlone Press
Assoc. Univ. / East Brunswick, N.J.: Associated Univ. Presses
Barnes and Noble / New York: Barnes and Noble
Bilingual Press / Ypsilanti, Mich.: Bilingual Press
Black Sparrow Press / Santa Barbara, Calif.: Black Sparrow Press
Bobbs-Merrill / Indianapolis: Bobbs-Merrill Company
Boise State / Boise, Idaho: Boise State Univ.
Bucknell / Lewisburg, Pa.: Bucknell Univ. Press
Calif. / Berkeley: Univ. of California Press
Cambridge / Cambridge, Eng.: Cambridge Univ. Press
Capra Press / Santa Barbara, Calif.: Capra Press
Chelsea House / New York: Chelsea House
Chicago / Chicago: Univ. of Chicago Press
City Lights / San Francisco: City Lights Books
Clarendon / Oxford: Clarendon Press
Clarkson N. Potter / New York: Clarkson N. Potter

Columbia / New York: Columbia Univ. Press
Cornell / Ithaca, N.Y.: Cornell Univ. Press
David R. Godine / Boston: David R. Godine
Delaware / Newark: Univ. of Delaware Press
Dodd, Mead / New York: Dodd, Mead and Co.
Doubleday / New York: Doubleday & Co.
Dutton / New York: E. P. Dutton
Eden Press / Westmount, Canada: Eden Press
Eerdmans / Grand Rapids, Mich.: Wilham B. Eerdmans Pub. Co.
Elizabeth Press / New Rochelle, N.Y.: Elizabeth Press
Exposition / Hicksville, N.Y.: Exposition Press
Fairleigh Dickinson / Rutherford, N.J.: Fairleigh Dickinson Univ. Press
Farrar / New York: Farrar, Straus & Giroux
Fawcett / New York: Fawcett Book Groups
Fordham / Bronx, N.Y.: Fordham Univ. Press
Fortress / Philadelphia: Fortress Press
Four Seasons / San Francisco: Four Seasons Foundation
Free Press / New York: Free Press
Gale / Detroit: Gale Research Co.

Garland / New York: Garland Publishing Co.

Gay Sunshine / San Francisco: Gay Sunshine Press

Georgia / Athens: Univ. of Georgia Press

Greenwood / Westport, Conn.: Greenwood Press

Grey Fox / Bolinas, Calif.: Grey Fox Press

Grilled Flower / Durango, Colo.: Grilled Flower Press

Grove / New York: Grove Press

Hall / Boston: G. K. Hall and Co.

Harcourt / New York: Harcourt Brace Jovanovich

Harper / New York: Harper & Row

Harvard-Belknap / Cambridge, Mass.: Belknap Press of Harvard Univ. Press

Harvard / Cambridge, Mass.: Harvard Univ. Press

Holmes & Meier / New York: Holmes & Meier Publishers

Holt / New York: Holt, Rinehart & Winston

Hopkins / Baltimore: Johns Hopkins Univ. Press

Houghton Mifflin / Boston: Houghton Mifflin Co.

Howard / Washington, D.C.: Howard Univ. Press

Howard Fertig / New York: Howard Fertig

Humanities Press / Atlantic Highlands, N.J.: Humanities Press

Idaho State / Pocatello: Idaho State Univ. Press

Illinois / Urbana: Univ. of Illinois Press

Indiana / Bloomington: Indiana Univ. Press

Iowa State / Ames: Iowa State Univ. Press

Johns Hopkins / Baltimore: Johns Hopkins Univ. Press

Kansas / Lawrence: Regents Press of Kansas

Kennikat / Port Washington, N.Y.: Kennikat Press

Kent State / Kent, Ohio: Kent State Univ. Press

Kentucky / Lexington: Univ. Press of Kentucky

Knopf / New York: Alfred A. Knopf

Lang / Frankfurt, Germany: Peter Lang

Little, Brown / Boston: Little, Brown

Liveright / New York: Liveright Pub. Corp.

LSU / Baton Rouge: Louisiana State Univ. Press

Lyle Stuart / Secaucus, N.J.: Lyle Stuart

Mass. / Amherst: Univ. of Massachusetts Press

McFarland / Jefferson, N.C.: McFarland and Co.

Memphis / Memphis: Memphis State Univ. Press

Methuen / London: Methuen

Michigan / Ann Arbor: Univ. of Michigan Press

Mich. State / East Lansing: Michigan State Univ. Press

Minnesota / Minneapolis: Univ. of Minnesota Press

Miss. / Jackson: Univ. Press of Mississippi

Missouri / Columbia: Univ. of Missouri Press

MIT / Cambridge, Mass.: MIT Press

Monitor / Beverly Hills, Calif.: Monitor Book Co.

Morrow / New York: William Morrow and Co.

Mouton / The Hague: Mouton Publishers

Neale Watson / New York: Neale Watson Academic Publications

Nebraska / Lincoln: Univ. of Nebraska Press

N. Car. / Chapel Hill: Univ. of North Carolina Press

New Directions / New York: New Directions Publishing Corp.

New Rep. / New York: New Republic Books

Northeastern / Boston: Northeastern Univ. Press

Norton / New York: W. W. Norton & Co.

NYU / New York: New York Univ. Press

Ohio / Athens: Ohio Univ. Press

Ohio State / Columbus: Ohio State Univ. Press

Oklahoma / Norman: Univ. of Oklahoma Press

Oxford / New York: Oxford Univ. Press

Penn. State / University Park: Pennsylvania State Univ. Press

Pittsburgh / Pittsburgh: Univ. of Pittsburgh Press

Popular / Bowling Green, Ohio: Popular Press

Potter / New York: Clarkson N. Potter

Prentice-Hall / Englewood Cliffs, N.J.: Prentice-Hall

Presido Press / Novato, Calif.: Presido Press

Princeton / Princeton, N.J.: Princeton Univ. Press

Quintessence Publ. / Amador City, Calif.: Quintessence Publications

Random House / New York: Random House

Routledge / London: Routledge and Kegan Paul

Rutgers / New Brunswick, N.J.: Rutgers Univ. Press

S. Car. / Columbia: Univ. of South Carolina Press

S. Chand / New Delhi: S. Chand and Co.

St. Martin's / New York: St. Martin's

Scarecrow / Metuchen, N.J.: Scarecrow Press

Scribner's / New York: Charles Scribner's Sons

Shambhala / Boulder, Colo.: Shambhala Publications

Sierra Club / San Francisco: Sierra Club Books

Simon & Schuster / New York: Simon and Schuster

Slavica Publishers / Columbus, Ohio: Slavica Publishers

So. Calif. / Los Angeles: Univ. of Southern California Press

So. Ill. / Carbondale: Southern Illinois Univ. Press

Stanford/ Stanford, Calif.: Stanford Univ. Press

Star Rover / Oakland, Calif.: Star Rover House

SUNY / Albany: State Univ. of New York Press

Swallow / Chicago: Swallow Press

Syracuse / Syracuse, N.Y.: Syracuse Univ. Press

Taplinger / New York: Taplinger Publishing Co.

Tenn. / Knoxville: Univ. of Tennessee Press

Texas / Austin: Univ. of Texas Press

Texas Tech / Lubbock, Texas: Texas Tech Press

Townsend / Nashville, Tenn.: Townsend Press

Twayne / Boston: Twayne Publishers

Ungar / New York: Frederick Ungar Publishing Co.

Univ. Microfilms / Ann Arbor, Mich.: University Microfilms International

Univ. Press / Lanham, Md.: Univ. Press of America

Urizen Books / New York: Urizen Books

Viking / New York: Viking Press

Virginia / Charlottesville: Univ. Press of Virginia

Wayne / Detroit: Wayne State Univ. Press

Weidenfeld & Nicolson / London: Weidenfeld and Nicolson

Whitston / Troy, N.Y.: Whitston Publishing Co.

Wis. / Madison: Univ. of Wisconsin Press

Yale / New Haven, Conn.: Yale Univ. Press

Yoknapatawpha Press / Oxford, Miss.: Yoknapatawpha Press

Part I

1. Emerson, Thoreau, and Transcendentalism

Wendell Glick

Critical interest in the American transcendentalists continued to expand in 1980, with Margaret Fuller's becoming a palpable presence, and such minor figures as the Alcotts, Ripley, Judd, Lydia Child, Hedge, Cranch, Brownson, and others rising, however dimly, from the shade. It was an expansive year, moreover, for Emerson and Thoreau. In all, I have examined 20 books and more than 100 articles, wondering in some instances whether the search for truth is as compelling as the search for tenure. Something in the cultural ethos of these times probably accounts for some of this interest, while in some cases the motivation is clearly the availability of new critical tools, often thrust upon the texts, in my view, with crippling rigor. One would like to think that what is going on is the centennial reexamination that T. S. Eliot advised in *The Use of Poetry and the Use of Criticism*: every 100 years it is criticism's task to review the past of our literature and set the writers and their works in a new order.

i. General Studies, Textual Studies, Bibliography

I opened Roger Asselineau's *The Transcendentalist Constant in American Literature* (N.Y.U.) with the hope of encountering an analysis of the penetration of our literature by transcendentalist ideology, as promised in the title. I found nothing of the sort. Defining "Transcendental Constant" loosely as a belief in something "beyond appearances" (p. 129) and a way of seeing the world characterized by awe and wonder (p. 166), Asselineau has a license to discover

Once more this year I acknowledge the substantial aid of Professor Roger Lips and of Ms. Mara Smith in preparing this essay.—W.G.

the "Constant" in whatever writers he happens to have an interest—Whitman, Dreiser, O'Neill, Sherwood Anderson, Hemingway, Williams, and Lowenfels, whom he views as "the closest approximation to Walt Whitman in the twentieth century" (p. 163). Closer than Hart Crane, one wonders? The title of this book seems a post hoc device for justifying gathering essays written at various times into one volume. There is no mention of such writers as Robinson, Frost, Faulkner, and Stevens (to name only a few) in whom one would expect the "Transcendental Constant" to be prominent. Alfred Rosa's *Salem, Transcendentalism, and Hawthorne* (Fairleigh Dickinson) is precisely what the title says it is, a study of the transcendental movement in a local setting, its invasion of an essentially conservative community, and the community's reaction. A long and somewhat separate essay deals with Hawthorne's relation to the transcendentalists. The most useful general study of the year is Joel Myerson's *The New England Transcendentalists and the* Dial (Fairleigh Dickinson), a thoroughly researched, meticulously documented study of the *Dial*'s genesis in the Transcendental Club and its periods of editorship under Emerson and Margaret Fuller. For each volume of the *Dial* Myerson traces the editorial and pecuniary difficulties, and for each volume cites the responses of the reviewers, conservative (e.g., Andrews Norton) and liberal. Myerson's history of the periodical is followed by thumbnail biographies of the 40 identifiable contributors and an appendix that includes tables of contents for each *Dial* number, the contributions of each author, and an extensive bibliography. David Robinson in "Culture and Religion in the American Renaissance" (*ESQ* 26:38–51) solidifies his position as perhaps our most knowledgeable interpreter of the interpenetration of American romanticism by religious belief. In his review essay of books by Welter, Douglas, and Bercovitch he demonstrates how religious thought provided in America "categories of political individualism" [Welter] and "the liberal and sentimental ethos to balance that atomism" [Douglas], and fused "ideas of self-sufficiency and liberal progress into a national symbol and cultural hegemony" [Bercovitch] (p. 50). In "The Agitator and the Intellectuals: William Lloyd Garrison and the New England Transcendentalists" (*Midamerica* 62: 173–87) Patsy S. and Billy Ledbetter bring together the familiar facts of Garrison's acquaintanceships with ten or so transcendentalists, without probing into the subtleties of the relationships.

Interest of literary theorists in the transcendentalists' views of the relation of language and symbol to empirical fact and meaning continued in 1980. John T. Irwin's *American Hieroglyphics* is a distant corollary to the promising philological studies of Philip Gura and Michael West, which build upon each other (*ALS 1979*, p. 12). Irwin's book opens with a brief and informative history of the interest of Emerson and Thoreau in Egyptian pictographs (an interest widely shared by their contemporaries), and claims centrality for the hieroglyphical emblem to the thought and style of both men. The influence of the Egyptologist Champollion is traced through Sampson Reed and Edward Everett to Emerson and Thoreau, for whom the hieroglyphical emblem allegedly came to represent "a basic understanding of the nature of the universe" (p. 13), dictating the form their writing had to take in treating that universe. But the transcendentalists in this book are only starters for a phallic leap into Poe, Hawthorne, and Melville: Irwin views Hawthorne's expulsion from the customhouse, for example, as "a symbolic decapitation/castration" by means of which Hawthorne carried out "an ironic revenge upon his Puritan forefathers" (p. 280). The comment upon Bulkington's "phallic six-inch chapter" may illuminate *Moby Dick* for some readers; for this one, however, it exemplifies how critics become tools of their tools. Mason I. Lowance, Jr.'s *The Language of Canaan: Metaphor and Symbol in New England from the Puritans to the Transcendentalists* (Harvard) builds a convincing case for the great debt of "the utopian design of much nineteenth- and twentieth-century American writing . . . to the symbolic language of New England Puritanism" (p. ix). Though the bulk of this book deals with New England figurative language of the 17th and 18th centuries, its final chapter, "From Edwards to Emerson and Thoreau: A Reevaluation" (pp. 277–95) authoritatively links the figurative prophetic language of the 17th-century Puritans as reshaped by Edwards to *Walden* and *A Week*. Rather than claiming (as did Perry Miller) a direct linkage of ideology between Puritans and transcendentalists, Lowance argues for the continuity of their "epistemological science of perceiving nature and the symbolic expression of that perception" (p. 278). Lowance is convincing because he works close to his texts, integrating his argument carefully at the same time with the work of Bercovich (for the Puritans), and Moldenhauer, Lorch, and Paul for the transcendentalists. The book is an impressive study of American discourse, but on a broader plane it is a study of the American character itself. It deserves to be widely read, and not by students of language alone.

The year saw the publication of the fifth volume in the authoritative Princeton series of the works of Thoreau. *A Week on the Concord and Merrimack Rivers* was edited by Carl F. Hovde; the text, textual introduction, and editorial apparatus were reviewed and verified by William Howarth, Elizabeth Witherell, and Joseph Moldenhauer in consultation with Hovde. Linck C. Johnson, a long-time student of *A Week*, wrote the historical introduction. The considerable interest in *A Week* over the past several years will now have the support of a scholarly text, which should prove a stimulus to further research. The seal of the Center for Editions of American Authors attests to the rigor with which the staff of the edition challenges textual and editorial decisions. Hovde's text is based upon an exhaustive study of all existing authoritative autograph and printed forms, and it now becomes definitive. The Princeton format sets a high standard for attractiveness. Margaret Fuller's *Woman in the Nineteenth Century* appeared during the year in a facsimile of the 1845 edition (S. Car.) with an historical and critical introduction by Madeleine B. Stern and textual apparatus by Joel Myerson. The rare first edition, the only edition over which Fuller exercised control in publication, will now be readily available to scholars, who should no longer be tempted to use the corrupt Fuller-Greeley edition of 1855. *Henry David Thoreau: The Natural History Essays*, edited by Robert Sattelmeyer, appeared in the "Literature of the American Wilderness" series (Layton, Utah: Peregrine Smith), with an introduction by the editor that gives a coherent picture of Thoreau as naturalist. Included in the collection, which spans Thoreau's lifetime, is the essay "Huckleberries" as edited by the late Leo Stoller and first printed by Iowa and the New York Public Library in 1970. *Walden and Other Writings*, edited by William Howarth and issued by Modern Library, contains a good general survey of Thoreau's writing career.

Two useful reference works appearing this year are Alma J. Payne's *Louisa May Alcott: A Reference Guide* (G. K. Hall) and *The New Thoreau Handbook* (NYU) edited by Walter Harding and Michael Meyer. I am amazed to discover from Payne's *Guide* that Alcott wrote 42 books and hundreds of pieces of short fiction and nonfiction. Items in the *Guide* are listed chronologically in two categories for easy access and reference: "Writings by Louisa May Alcott" and "Writings About Louisa May Alcott." The index is complete. *The New Thoreau Handbook* is a revision and updating of *The Thoreau Handbook* (N.Y.U.) compiled by Harding in 1959. Though the original volume attempted completeness in its listings of Thoreau scholarship, the revised volume is limited "to particularly significant works and to works generally available in a good university library" (p. viii). The distinctly original dimension of the new handbook is an added chapter, "Thoreau's Art"; its inclusion as a discrete category bears testimony to the direction Thoreau scholarship has taken in the past 20 years. When deletions must be made and annotations kept brief, Thoreau scholars will disagree as to inclusions and length of annotation merited by particular studies. These constitute value judgments. I confess to puzzlement as to the treatment of some of the entries, e.g. (p. 84): "By far the most thoughtful analysis of the book [*Walden*] is Stanley Cavell, *The Senses of Walden* [*ALS 1972*, pp. 12–13], though it is not always an easy book to read." That Cavell's book is immensely insightful is for me not debatable. I happen to agree that it is the best study of *Walden* ever published. But if Annie Russell Marble's *Thoreau: His Home, Friends, and Books* deserves a half page of comment (pp. 18–19), "by far the most thoughtful analysis" of *Walden* deserves more than this one sentence and a brief later sentence that asserts that Cavell's book discusses "Thoreau's efforts to invest his language with scriptural meanings" (p. 196). Questions of differing judgments aside, however, the bibliographical resources of this book alone make it indispensable.

The 1980 *Studies in the American Renaissance* (Twayne) continues the policy of issuing primary source material hitherto unpublished. Given its attractive permanent format, this is most appropriate. Frederick Wagner's "Eighty-Six Letters (1814–82) of A. Bronson Alcott (Part Two)" (pp. 183–228) adds 45 additional letters to the 41 published in *SAR* in 1979 (*ALS 1979*, p. 5). Wagner's copious annotations add to the interest and usefulness of these letters for readers not familiar with the Alcott circle of acquaintances. Also continued in *SAR* 1980 is Gary L. Collison's "A Calendar of the Letters of Theodore Parker" (pp. 317–408), bringing the total number of entries to 1999. In all, 77 of the Parker letters are to Emerson. Scholars working on any of the New England transcendentalists will find Collison's catalog of the locations and recipients of these letters very timesaving. Still an additional useful reference tool in the 1980 *SAR* is William Brennan's "An Index to Quotations in Thoreau's *A Week on the Concord and Merrimack Rivers*" (pp. 259–90), keyed to and compiled in conjunction with Carl F. Hovde's edition of *A Week* in the Princeton series. A separate bibliography of Thoreau's sources (pp. 282–90) testifies to the breadth and variety of Thoreau's reading. Kevin P. Van Anglen's "The Sources for Thoreau's Greek Translations" (pp. 291–300), also a spin-off of the editorial work on the Princeton Edition, is a corrective to the pioneer work of Ethel Seybold on Thoreau's use and knowledge of Greek and Roman classics, in particular with respect to the editions Thoreau used as a basis for his translations.

Finally, several new items were added during the year to the Very, Emerson, and Thoreau canons. David Robinson in "Four Early Poems of Jones Very" (*HLB* 28:146–51) prints four hitherto unknown poems discovered in papers once in the possession of Charles Stearns Wheeler, the Harvard friend of Thoreau and Very. They are stiff, mannered poems unlike the lyrical verse Very was to write later. Francis B. Dedmond reprinted in *ATQ* (41:13–16) an intriguing letter Emerson contributed by request to a pamphlet advertising a protest meeting held in Faneuil Hall on 24 September 1846 to object to the forced return by Boston merchants of an escaped New Orleans slave. Emerson was not yet ready to accept invitations to attend antislavery protest meetings, and did not attend this one, but his letter expresses his moral outrage that commerce tolerates and abets inhumanity. The letter is not in Rusk. The most current Thoreau bibliography, students of transcendentalism should be reminded, is published in each issue of the *Thoreau Society Bulletin* edited by Walter Harding; and Thomas Blanding continues to unearth Thoreau manuscript material that finds its way into the *Concord Saunterer*. Two previously unpublished Thoreau letters, one a first draft the final form of which has disappeared, appeared in the Spring issue (15:19–22).

ii. Emerson

a. **Life and Thought.**　Ellen Tucker Emerson's biography of her mother, *The Life of Lidian Jackson Emerson* (Twayne), ed. Dolores

Bird Carpenter, is a pleasant surprise; it has the ring of objectivity. Lidian emerges from the shadow of her famous husband as an interesting person in her own right, a polemicist for social causes, deserving attention as a microcosm of the experience of 19th-century women. The mass of anecdotal information on members of the Emerson family, the Thoreaus, Hosmers, Alcotts, and other citizens of Concord congeals into a convincing picture of 19th-century small-town domestic life. In reading the book I found myself attempting to assess the extent of Lidian's influence on her husband, so unlike her in many respects. Carpenter's introduction is bland, but her footnotes are generous and useful. "Lidian Emerson's 'Transcendental Bible'" by Carpenter (*SAR*, 91–96) extracts from *The Life* (pp. 81–83) a collection of satirical maxims formulated by Lidian ostensibly to spoof her husband's transcendentalism: they deserve a more analytical study than Carpenter provides. "Emerson and his Children: Their Childhood Memories" (*HLB* 28:407–30) by Edith Emerson Webster Gregg is comprised of recollections of their father by the Emerson children, Ellen, Edith, and Edward. Gregg has selected from her manuscripts and we do not have the complete documents or any information as to what she edited out. Yet the picture of Emerson that develops out of family testimony is of a warm, loving, firm father, willing to spend much time with his children. Little of the material is new, however; Cabot, Holmes, and Rusk had access to it. Robert Loewenberg in "Emerson or Inference: Could Emerson Read Greek?" (*ELN* 18:27–30) makes a convincing case for Emerson's having had only a superficial knowledge of the Greek tongue, in spite of recent opinions to the contrary. Edith Emerson, however (according to Gregg, p. 413), spoke of Emerson's helping his children with elementary Greek. Owen Hawley's "The Marietta Lecture Series of 1866–1867" (*SAR*, pp. 425–44) is a well researched piece; but since this series was in no way unique, the essay adds nothing to our knowledge of Emerson the lecturer. A more appropriate place of publication might have been a journal of local Ohio history.

The single book-length analysis of Emerson's thought to appear during the year, Lewis Leary's *Ralph Waldo Emerson: An Interpretative Essay* (Twayne), offers little that is new. Indeed, "those who know Emerson well" (p. ix) are pointedly excluded by Leary from his audience. David Robinson's "Emerson's Natural Theology and the Paris Naturalists: Toward a Theory of Animated Nature" (*JHI* 41:

69–88) is a clearly written article firmly grounded upon a thorough study of primary and secondary sources. Robinson's thesis is that "Emerson was not entirely ready to abandon revealed theology until his experience at Paris [in 1833], and he had no clear vision of how nature might support the moral sense until he had worked through this experience" (p. 71). To the common knowledge that the Paris experience influenced Emerson's break with New England theology Robinson has added a clear and convincing explanation of how this happened, and why. Ulrich Horstmann in "Mythos der Bemächtigung: Anmerkungen zur Ästhetik des Ralph Waldo Emerson" (*Amst* 25:175–97) challenges the "orthodox assumption" that Emerson's transcendentalism is the product of "*philosophical* thinking." Instead, Horstmann suggests, Emerson was a mythmaker, and his transcendentalism "is nothing else but an *artificial myth*." Since my German is no better than Emerson's Greek, I have been unable to follow the nuances of Horstmann's argument; but Leonard Neufeldt's study of Emerson and science (*ALS 1977*, pp. 6–7) makes me skeptical of the claim that Emerson in his mythmaking employed "the selfsame principles of power, compulsion, and exploitation that he deplored" in the natural sciences (p. 175 *passim*). Richard Lee Francis' contention in "Morn at Mid Noon: The Emerging Emersonian Method" (*PCP* 15,ii:1–8) is that in Emerson's brief, 1835 journal which he called "Ro MIND" we have "a principal link between the style and structure of the sermons and the style and structure of the great Essays as they were to crystalize first in *Nature*" (p. 2). This is a considerable claim, and though there is support for Francis' point that Emerson in these two brief essays comprising "Ro MIND" for the first time takes a position midway between spirit and sense, the importance of this slight matter (six pages in the published *Journals*) seems to me less crucial than Francis makes it out to be. Glen M. Johnson's approach to "Emerson's Craft of Revision: The Composition of the *Essays* (1841)" (*SAR*, 51–72) is to draw textual matter from the journals and lectures for comparison with the finished versions Emerson published in the essays. Many of the "types" of revision seem to me less generic than they are to Johnson: I am less confident than he of the "principles" of revision that lay in the back of Emerson's mind as he adapted early textual forms for the essays. Johnson believes that Emerson's alterations were as a rule not substantive, but were made with brevity, sound, and clarity in mind, in the hope that he would thus "move a reader to mental and moral action" (p. 71). Proof of such intention is lacking.

b. **Criticism of Individual Works.** Foremost in this grouping for the year I place Merton Sealts's *Emerson's* Nature: *Origin, Growth, Meaning* (So. Ill.), the second edition of the volume edited in 1969 by Sealts and the late Alfred R. Ferguson. To this original edition (see *ALS 1969*, p. 18) have been added an important essay by Barry Wood, first published elsewhere, and original essays by Barbara Packer and Sealts: "The Instructed Eye: Emerson's Cosmogony in 'Prospects' " and "The Composition of *Nature*," respectively. The new essay by Sealts is alone worth the price of the book. Packer's thesis is that Emerson's reading a book by David Brewster on Newton led him to change his cosmogony. It is a closely argued, carefully written essay, launched by an explication of a difficult crux in "Prospects" that throws light on the position Emerson at that time was taking that "the axis of vision is not coincident with the axis of things, and so they appear not transparent but opake" (p. 220). My skepticism is deepened somewhat by the absence of proof that Emerson actually read Brewster. The Sealts essay gives the reader far more than the title promises: bringing an impressive knowledge of Emerson to bear upon the struggle to compose *Nature*, Sealts provides a painstaking section-by-section critique of the book that illuminates many facets of Emerson's thought in 1836. I cannot summarize an essay of such density without distortion, but its general purpose is to examine in depth Emerson's attitude toward nature and show how he dealt with this question in *Nature*.

The two essays appearing this year on *The Conduct of Life* seem to me to have limited value. Richard Lee Francis' "Necessitated Freedom: Emerson's *The Conduct of Life*" (*SAR*, 73–89) moves quickly through the essays that comprise the book, allegedly discovering "a hierarchical structure" beginning with "Fate" and "culminating" in "the pivotal essay," "Considerations by the Way" (p. 74). J. Russell Reaver in "Emerson's Focus in *The Conduct of Life*" (*SAB* 45:78–89) begins with the assumption that Emerson wrote his books with dominant images in mind, that the shape of *The Conduct of Life* is that of an hourglass, and that the "pivotal essay" (to use Francis' term) is "Behavior" (p. 78). If one of these interpretations is correct, the other isn't. Before writing "The Under-

lying Structure of the Divinity School Address: Emerson as Jeremiah"
(*SAR* 41–49) Carol Johnson could profitably have read Buell, Hei-
mert, and particularly Perry Miller's "The Jeremiad" in *From Colony
to Province*. She seizes a few connections between Jeremiah and
Emerson, ignoring most of the differences. "The Task of Amphion in
Emerson's 'Politics' " by Christine E. Wharton and James S. Leonard
(*PLL* 16:161–73) suffers from a lack of systematic analysis of "Politics" and lack of a firm knowledge of what other scholars (e.g., Gray)
have had to say about Emerson's debt to Plato. It is cavalier to dismiss
them with the casual remark that "Previous studies . . . have tended
to be conjectural in method and general in conclusion" (p. 163). The
importance of Amphion to "Politics" is as a result overstated. David
Bromwich's "Emerson's 'Ode to W. H. Channing' " (*HudR* 33:210–
22) is a careful and cautious explication of this poem against a somewhat general grasp of Emerson's turmoil with respect to his responsibility for social activism.

c. Emerson and Other Writers.   Interest in drawing parallels between Emerson and other writers continues unabated. Predictably,
several of these involve Thoreau. Fritz Oehlschlaeger's "Whitman on
Thoreau and Emerson: A Correction and Speculation" (*WWR* 26:
156–58) theorizes that Franklin Sanborn's presumed ranking of
Thoreau above Emerson at Whitman's Concord visit in 1881 should
be viewed as a "significant revelation of Whitman's regard for
Thoreau" (p. 158). Leonard N. Neufeldt in "Emerson, Thoreau, and
Daniel Webster" (*ESQ* 26:26–37) contrasts the high esteem held
for Webster by Emerson with the low estimate of Webster held by
Thoreau, and discerns in the difference one reason for the strain in
the Emerson-Thoreau relationship that developed in the mid-1840s.
Gay Wilson Allen in "How Emerson, Thoreau, and Whitman Viewed
the 'Frontier' " (*Toward a New American Literary History*, pp. 111–
28) sees close parallels between the revulsion of Emerson and that
of Thoreau for the predatory white American pioneers who were
destroying the natural resources of the country. The two concur,
Allen believes, in attributing the shortcomings and failures of men
to their lack of harmony with nature. Whitman's mythologizing of
the western pioneer's felling the forests to create a great people
Allen finds less prescient than the ecological warnings of Emerson

and Thoreau. A German study by Rudiger C. Schlicht which I missed in 1977, *Die Padagogischen Ansatze Amerikanischer Transcendentalisten: Erziehungswissenschaftliche Studien zu Amos Bronson Alcott, Ralph Waldo Emerson und Henry David Thoreau 1830–1840* (Bern: Peter Lang) compares the pedagogical theories of the three transcendentalists.

Lisa Steinman calls attention to Alfred Kreymborg's detection of the strong influence of Emerson upon Marianne Moore's poetry, in particular "The Monkeys" ("Moore, Emerson and Kreymborg: The Use of Lists in 'The Monkeys'" [*MMN* 4:7–10]). Carren O. Kaston in "Emersonian Consciousness and *The Spoils of Poynton*" (*ESQ* 26: 88–99) attempts to tie Fleda Vetch to Emerson, disclaiming however a "direct" influence. Kaston's principal interest in this essay is Fleda Vetch as a "character of consciousness," and Emerson seems to me to intrude. Even if one grants that, in creating Fleda Vetch, James "in effect socialized Emerson's visionary eyeball self" (p. 91), one must remember that loss of the personal self for Emerson and for James are two different things. "Melville and Emerson's Rainbow" (*ESQ* 26:53–78) by Merton M. Sealts, Jr. demonstrates what the critic can do who begins with a thorough knowledge of the authors he is juxtaposing; Sealts's 76 extended footnotes testify to his firm grasp of both Melville and Emerson. Sealts conjectures astutely as to what Melville actually knew of Emerson, the nature of his response to Emerson, and what Emerson meant to Melville "from the time of *Pierre* to the time of *Billy Budd*" (p. 57). Finally, Martin Bickman's *The Unsounded Center* includes two sections on Emerson. The first (pp. 28–31) suggests that Emerson's "Plato" reflects an awareness of the key problem of relating the two poles of thought, identity and otherness, much as Poe recognizes the problem in *Eureka*; and the second, "The Double Consciousness Revisited" (pp. 80–94), posits that both Jung and Emerson were "deliberately unsystematic thinkers" who viewed artistic activity as the bridge for "joining the conscious and the unconscious" (p. 80). Bickman's stated purpose is to "deepen the connections between Jung and Emerson" (p. 81), but his argument drifts. After some clichés on the reason and the understanding and scattered allusions to "The Poet," "The Oversoul," "Circles," and other essays he launches into an extended explication of "Experience" in which Jung gradually disappears, and a somewhat forced "revisiting" of Emerson's double consciousness takes place. Bickman presumably believes that Emerson would have been a Jungian if he had had the chance.

iii. Thoreau

a. **Life and Thought.** The single new book dealing with Thoreau in 1980 is Mary Elkins Moller's *Thoreau in the Human Community* (Mass.). Moller undertakes to restore Thoreau as a palpable human being, capable of friendship and believing in the human need for close relations with other persons. She disclaims writing "a strictly biographical study" (p. xii), focusing instead on "those passages [in his writings] which reveal his varying attitudes toward other persons and toward Humanity, which reveal his need for communication and intimate relationships" (p. xii). I gather that the intent is to treat Thoreau the theorist of community rather than Thoreau the active person. But doer and sayer are one, as Emerson put it, and disclaimers notwithstanding, this book becomes largely biographical as such chapter titles as "Thoreau, le Misanthrope," "Seven Friendships," and "Other Relationships" testify. I sense that Moller's motivation in writing may have been her need to free herself from Perry Miller's disparagements of Thoreau—to exorcise her private daemon—for in almost every chapter, as the notes reveal, she tries to neutralize Miller's bias, alleging that he ignored Thoreau's "generous, yearning" impulses, emphasizing instead his "sometimes perverse, misanthropic ones" (p. xiv). As a result, she goes on to say, Miller "has continued to exert an unfortunate influence." Upon whom, she does not reveal, and certainly not upon recent Thoreau scholarship. What Moller has done in this book is to cull from Thoreau's writings passages testifying to his sense of community, his need for friendships, his sense of social obligation, as they ameliorate his disparagements of mass man. William Bronk's *The Brother in Elysium: Ideas of Friendship and Society in the United States* (New Rochelle, N.Y.: Elizabeth Press) contains a long and sensitive essay on Thoreau. "Silence and Henry Thoreau" consists of three sections: "Friendship," which defines with more subtlety than does Moller's book Thoreau's thoughts about community and social relations; "Freedom," which Thoreau achieved (according to Bronk) by identifying himself "with whatever in the present most embodied the things of eternity" (p. 68), and "Social Action," the least original of the three sections, which develops (often in Thoreau's own words) Thoreau's rationale for declining to relate to reform movements, philanthropies, and the state. Bronk's lyric prose suggests its author's deep personal engagement with Thoreau's thought. The lead article in this year's SAR (pp. 1–35), "A Thoreau Iconography" by Thomas Blanding and Walter Harding, is an informative essay of permanent value. Blanding and Harding have gathered and printed all of the known and conjectured information about likenesses of Thoreau, those of certain authenticity and those probably spurious, reproducing them in the text. Michael Meyer's "Thoreau's Rescue of John Brown from History" (*SAR*, 301–16) examines Thoreau's response to the Harper's Ferry episode in the context of the newspaper reports of the event, raising again the question as to what Thoreau knew of Brown's ruthlessness at Pottawatomie River, Kansas. Meyer concludes that Thoreau refused "to recognize or admit anything that would divert his transcendental tracking of Brown" (p. 312). Louis Simon's "Pour Henry-David Thoreau" (*Europe* 58:190–92) reviews briefly the progress of Thoreau studies in France in the past five years. Two significant articles connecting Thoreau with the theory and practice of the American luminist painters of the mid-19th century should be read together: Barton Levi St. Armand's "Luminism in the Work of Henry David Thoreau: The Dark and the Light" (*CRevAS* 11:13–30) and John Conron's " 'Bright American Rivers': The Luminist Landscapes of Thoreau's *A Week on the Concord and Merrimack Rivers*" (*AQ* 32:144–66). St. Armand supports the view of John I. H. Baur that luminism was "A Neglected Aspect of the Realist Movement in Nineteenth-Century Painting" (p. 28), and makes a strong case for its being "in fact the missing link between late Romantic idealism and early literary Naturalism" (p. 27). Both *Walden* and *Cape Cod* in their sharply etched pictorial passages thus prefigure a new vision and way of seeing that was to become dominant later in the works of Stephen Crane, Dreiser, and Norris. Conron's treatment of the luminist painters is less full than St. Armand's, but by reproducing the paintings of Martin Heade he ties Thoreau's *Week* convincingly to the luminist school. If these two essays are any criterion, the interpretation of Thoreau by the methods of art criticism is promising indeed. Robert Sattelmeyer quotes in "Thoreau and Melville's *Typee*" (*AL* 52:462–68) an unpublished journal notebook comment by Thoreau on Melville's book, which Thoreau read at the time when he was pondering the differences between civilized and primitive man. Sattelmeyer suggests that the book led Thoreau into his serious study of primitive cultures. John D. Margolis in *Joseph Wood Krutch: A Writer's Life* (Tenn.), pp. 150–56, details the influence of Thoreau upon Krutch's philosophy.

b. Studies of Individual Works. Two studies of *Walden* deserve note. John C. Hirsh's "Thoreau's *Walden*" (*Expl* 39:15–16) ties Thoreau's allusion to *Ranz des Vaches* in chapter 6 of *Walden* directly to Schiller's song of the same name in *Wilhelm Tell*. Peter A. Fritzell in "*Walden* and Paradox: Thoreau as Self-Conscious Ecologist" (*NER* 3:51–67) views *Walden* as a book approachable from three perspectives: that of the environmentalist, the idealist, and the self-conscious ecologist (p. 51). The style of the self-conscious ecologist is "dialectic," he argues, "designed to explore the competing claims of the environmentalist and the personalist" (p. 63). Paradox in *Walden* becomes a tool, therefore, for Thoreau's mediating among his multiple personae. The one essay of the year to deal with *Cape Cod*, Richard J. Schneider's "*Cape Cod*: Thoreau's Wilderness of Illusion" (*ESQ* 26:184–96), does much to relate this work to Thoreau's attempted resolution of the tension between nature and the self. Schneider argues that Thoreau took his Ktaadn dilemma to the sea and the wild coast of Cape Cod, to an Eastern surrogate for the wildness of the West, only to discover that, like Ktaadn, the ocean is unknowable. *Cape Cod* thus construed is Thoreau's counterresponse to his own optimistic belief expressed in chapter 2 of *Walden* that nature and man are in harmony, that there is a "hard bottom and rocks in place, which we can call *reality*." Frederick Garber's essay, "A Space for Saddleback: Thoreau's *A Week on the Concord and Merrimack Rivers*" (*CentR* 24:322–37) adds to the swelling literature that argues for a unity of meaning and purpose in *A Week*. Garber sees the text as leading the reader in two directions at once, "down the river and into the mind" (p. 326), observation and meditation ("two kinds of travelling" [p. 328]) taking place simultaneously. In his inclusion of the climb up Saddleback in *A Week*, though the experience actually took place five years after the trip on the river with John, Thoreau made explicit, Garber feels, his "attitude toward the world around him and the world up there. He was never quite able

to reconcile the performances of the mind with those of the body"
(p. 337), the "desire of the one to ascend and the other to remain below." Eberhard Alsen in " 'Light-winged Smoke': Thoreau's Apology
for his Poetry" (*ESQ* 26:197–201) argues that this poem is an autobiographical statement reflecting as early as 1843 Thoreau's "doubts
about his ability to express his intimations of the Absolute in his
poems" (p. 200). And finally, Robert Sattelmeyer in "Thoreau's
Projected Work on the English Poets" (*SAR*, pp. 239–57) educes
sufficient external evidence from primary sources to show that almost surely the four early notebooks containing English poetry that
we have assumed to be commonplace books (including the Library
of Congress Notebook) were actually collections of material Thoreau
copied with the intention of writing a book of some kind on the
English poets.

   Limitations of space, to my regret, preclude mention of the many
short articles in *Thoreau Society Bulletin,* the *Concord Saunterer,*
and *Thoreau Journal Quarterly.* The lead articles in *TSB* are often
important contributions; and it is a rare issue of *CS* that fails to include one or two significant essays in addition to an original Thoreau
letter or other unpublished manuscript. In *TJQ* scholarly pieces are
occasional. *TJQ* will terminate publication with the Fall 1981 issue.
It will be supplanted by the *Thoreau Quarterly,* a scholarly literary
and philosophical journal to be published at the Philosophy Department of the University of Minnesota beginning in 1982.

iv. Minor Transcendentalists

Seven book-length biographies and collections of criticism in one year
are unheard of for this group, and these are over and above textual
editions. *Margaret Fuller's* Woman in the Nineteenth Century: A
Literary Study of Form and Content, of Sources and Influence by
Marie Mitchell Olesen Urbanski (Greenwood) is the first book to
deal critically with Margaret Fuller's best-known work. The attraction of Fuller's dramatic life has led most Fuller scholars into biographical studies, and despite her stated intention, "to examine
Fuller's *Woman in the Nineteenth Century* as a literary work" (p. 4),
Urbanski is not able wholly to resist the temptation. Much of this
material is not new; the background information on American feminism and transcendentalism, for example, is well known. Nearly all

of Fuller's male associates and peers emerge from this study as chauvinists—Emerson, Thoreau, Hawthorne, Holmes, Lowell among them. What Fuller seems to have done in *Woman*, as I understand Urbanski, was to extend the transcendentalist doctrine of the deification of man to include woman, employing such standard transcendental rhetorical techniques as the Puritan sermon and the symbol of circularity. I regret that Urbanski chose to base her study of *Woman* on the second edition, edited in 1855 by Arthur Fuller and Horace Greeley, which according to Joel Myerson (see "Textual Studies," above) has no authority. Urbanski's lengthy bibliography does not mention the standard (1845) edition. Myerson's judicious selection of Fuller criticism for *Critical Essays on Margaret Fuller* (G. K. Hall) includes chapter 5 of Urbanski's book as its terminal piece, and gives a full sense of the major attitudes toward Fuller from her death to the present. Madeleine B. Stern's "Margaret Fuller and the Phrenologist-Publishers" (*SAR*, pp. 229–37) traces the interest of the publisher Fowler and Wells in Fuller from 1837 when Orson Fowler did a phrenological reading on Fuller's head to 1894 when the *Phrenological Journal* published a portrait of Fuller to demonstrate the faculty of "ideality." Madelon Bedell's *The Alcotts: Biography of a Family* (New York: Clarkson N. Potter) dramatizes the relationships among Bronson, his wife Abby, and their four daughters. Though the focus is ostensibly upon Bronson, the dramatic center of the book for many will be Abby's struggle to live with the "Tedious Archangel," humoring his vagaries and egocentricities, all the while mired in poverty. Bedell has winnowed painstakingly the voluminous manuscript residue left by members of the family that chronicle their daily lives and struggles, ending her book somewhat abruptly with the Dred Scott case in 1854. Her conjectures as to Bronson's state of mind in times of crisis are just that (e.g., see p. 299), and her delineations of the crosscurrents of American thought in the '30s and '40s are very broad. One pauses also at such judgments as that Bronson Alcott "inspired such peers as Ralph Waldo Emerson to the heights of philosophical speculation in his famous essay *Nature*" (p. 288). But the sense Bedell gives of the Alcott family and the New England setting is a living one. In a reprint of *Louisa May Alcott* (1889) by Ednah D. Cheney (New York: Chelsea House) Ann Douglas provides a useful introduction which puts both Cheney and Louisa in perspective. *George Ripley*

(TUSAS 281) by Henry L. Golemba, which I missed in 1977, assigns to Ripley the central role in the rise of the transcendental movement before 1838: following the pattern set by most biographers of minor figures, Golemba proposes "to rescue from obscurity the biography of Ripley" (p. 9). For me he does not succeed, though he develops a consistent pattern in Ripley's thought through the successive stages of Unitarian minister, militant reformer, polemicist and opponent of Andrews Norton, founder of the Brook Farm Community, and literary critic, influencing the country's estimates of Melville, Emerson, Thoreau, Poe, Hawthorne, James, and others. Golemba's accounting for Ripley's "near obscurity" on the grounds chiefly of his having been overshadowed by Emerson (p. 151) is surely debatable. Francis B. Dedmond's *Sylvester Judd* (TUSAS 365) is more modest in its claims: Dedmond's careful analysis of *Margaret* and *Philo* leads me to conclude that all that should be done by literary scholars toward resuscitating Judd has now been done, and we can hand him over to the historians of Unitarian theology. Judd's life aim was obviously identical with his announced aim for his novel, *Margaret*: "to promote the course of liberal Christianity" (p. 63). His was not a creative mind. For those who feel unease at their ignorance of Judd, this short book will dispel the discomfort with very little pain, for Dedmond has done our reading for us and has in effect removed Judd from the category of minor transcendentalists. I mention in passing two books on Orestes Brownson, who, if he was a minor transcendentalist, was not one for long. *No Divided Allegiance*, ed. Leonard Gilhooley (Fordham), contains two essays linking Brownson with American transcendentalism, "Orestes Brownson: Jacksonian Literary Critic" by C. Carroll Hollis (pp. 51–83), and "Brownson's Significance for American Democracy Today" (pp. 175–93) by Alvan S. Ryan. *Contradiction and Dilemma: Orestes Brownson and the American Idea* (Fordham), also by Gilhooley, suggests in its title a conflict with *No Divided Allegiance*, title of the essay collection. These two books leave Brownson as little more than a footnote in the history of American transcendentalism, despite Brownson's early association with Ripley and his brush with Emerson and Thoreau.

Articles appeared during the year on Hedge, Sanborn, and Cranch. Doreen Hunter in "Frederic Henry Hedge, What Say You?" (*AQ* 32:186–201) argues that Hedge's rift with Emerson did not result from growing conservatism in Hedge, but that the differences

between the two were present from the very beginning of the relationship. Instead of an evolution toward conservatism in Hedge, she
sees rather in Emerson's "Experience" evidence that Emerson in 1843
had moved toward Hedge's position that the Reason is at times not
to be relied upon. This is a worthwhile essay in its delineating clearly
the poles of the Transcendentalist movement. "F. B. Sanborn and
the Lost New England World of Transcendentalism" by D. R. Wilmes
(*CLQ* 16:237–47) pictures the young Sanborn as "Transcendental
only in the light of after-glows" (p. 239), as ideologically shallow
and superficial in his perceptions of the philosophies of Emerson
and Thoreau, and upon his death in 1917, as the last flicker of a movement that had survived regionally in Concord alone. Francis B. Dedmond's "Christopher Pearse Cranch: Emerson's Self-Appointed De-
fender Against the Philistines" (*CS* 15:6–19) calls attention to the
irony of Cranch's being remembered as a caricaturist of Emerson's
Nature, particularly of the "transparent eyeball" passage, when
Cranch for 50 years from 1837 to 1877 was unremitting in his defense
of Emerson's thought and person. Dedmond's evidence is unassail-
able. I wish, however, that he had undertaken an explanation of the
conflict between the apparent ridicule in the caricatures and Cranch's
praise of Emerson in print.

University of Minnesota, Duluth

2. Hawthorne

David B. Kesterson

This year's essay is dedicated to the memory of Arlin Turner, who died in April of 1980 and whose stellar biography of Hawthorne was published just a few weeks before his death. Arlin Turner was friend and helpmate to all Hawthorneans. Known for his kindness, generosity, and perspicacity, he is greatly missed. It is some comfort, however, that we shall continue to appreciate and profit from the impeccable scholarly legacy he leaves behind.

The year was a busy and important one for Hawthorne studies. The trend was obviously biographical, with two major full-scale biographies seeing print and a third volume appearing that focuses in detail on Hawthorne's years abroad. Numerous articles probed various aspects of Hawthorne's life and career. Textually, the long-awaited edition of *The French and Italian Notebooks* added its mark to the year's rapid progress toward the establishment of a full complement of updated biographical and textual material on Hawthorne. The *Nathaniel Hawthorne Journal, 1977* appeared in 1980, containing nearly 40 articles, notes, checklists, reports, and book reviews; and there were two issues of the *Hawthorne Society Newsletter*, featuring bibliography, short articles and notes, abstracts and lists of conference papers on Hawthorne, and other Hawthorneana. The fall number, the "Arlin Turner Memorial Issue," carries tributes to the late Professor Turner by Rita K. Gollin, C. E. Frazer Clark, Jr., and Terence Martin.

Doctoral dissertations continued in steady flow (close to 20 this year), a large number of which are devoted to Hawthorne and interdisciplinary subjects or Hawthorne in relation to other writers, trends which were noted in last year's *ALS* review and which accelerated this year. In keeping with current strong interest in Hawthorne and the arts, John L. Idol, Jr. and Sterling K. Eisiminger published another installment of their ongoing work, "Operas Based on Hawthorne" (*HSN* 6,ii:7), while Betty E. Chmaj in "Sonata for American Studies: Perspectives on Charles Ives" (*Prospects* 4[1979]: 1–58) reexamines Ives's interpretation of Hawthorne both in his essay and the second movement of the sonata. Studies on Hawthorne and art are covered in section *ii.*

Finally, if 1979 boasted a prime Hawthorne media event in the public television production of *The Scarlet Letter*, 1980 answered with Calvin Scaggs's PBS showing of "Rappaccini's Daughter," the Hawthorne contribution to the American Short Story Series.

i. Texts, Editions, Bibliography, Biography

The major effort in texts and editions is the monumental (in both importance and size—1,045 pages) *French and Italian Notebooks,* ed. Thomas Woodson (Ohio State), volume 14 of the Centenary Edition. Here for the first time in published form are Hawthorne's complete continental notebooks and also the invaluable pocket diaries for 1858 and 1859. Heavily indebted to the late Norman Holmes Pearson's 1941 Yale dissertation, "The French and Italian Notebooks by Nathaniel Hawthorne," this edition nevertheless reflects further editing by the Centenary staff and the gathering of new information from a number of sources not available to Pearson. Of the usual Centenary editorial apparatus, most helpful is a section of cross-references to *The Marble Faun.* Overall, the significance of having the intact French-Italian journals and diaries in print can hardly be overemphasized. Offering the "most sustained and detailed journalizing of Hawthorne's life," they fill in the details of Hawthorne's last years abroad.

Of greatly lessened scope but still important is the text of a letter by Hawthorne attesting to his general malaise during his final months of life (George Monteiro, "The First Publication of One of Hawthorne's Last Letters," *NHJ* 1977, pp. 349–50). And there is a Hungarian edition of 17 Hawthorne stories and sketches, *Nathaniel Hawthorne: A Lelkipásztor Fekete Fatyla* (Budapest, 1979), edited by Csaba Tóth.

Four pieces of textual criticism deserve brief mention. Philip

Gaskell's "Hawthorne, *The Marble Faun*, 1860" in *From Writer to Reader: Studies in Editorial Method* (Oxford, 1978), pp. 183–95, criticizes the philosophy, methods, and techniques of the CEAA (now CSE) by using the Centenary *Marble Faun* as test case, his main quarrel being with the method of establishing definitive copy-texts. Hershel Parker's "Aesthetic Implications of Authorial Excisions: Examples from Nathaniel Hawthorne, Mark Twain, and Stephen Crane" in *Editing Nineteenth-Century Fiction* (Garland, 1978), pp. 99–119, is not so much an attack on the CEAA/CSE as a challenge to the revered editorial notion started by W. W. Greg that an author's last text is "best." Parker points to Hawthorne's occasional excisions between first and later collected printings of stories, changes which cause passages to read obscurely. A more positive reaction to the work of the CEAA/CSE is Michael Holzman's, John Holland's, and Cora Agatucci's "Hawthorne's 'Uncollected Tales': The Problem of Attribution" (*RALS* 9[1979]:133–39). Using computer analysis to identify certain common words in Hawthorne's writings, these scholars basically confirm J. Donald Crowley's more subjective selection of attributed tales in volume 11 of the Centenary edition. Completely removed from Centenary concerns, Gloria C. Erlich's probing "Who Wrote Hawthorne's First Diary" (*NHJ 1977*, pp. 37–70) deals with the old question of this mystifying little book's authenticity. After examining all the available evidence, the editorial methods of Samuel T. Pickard, and emphasizing the absence of a manuscript, Erlich concludes that the diary is probably a forgery, and she is astonished at the way "scholars have handled the questionable text." Despite her good sleuth work, it is doubtful that the case is closed on the "first diary."

Several checklists of criticism brought Hawthorne secondary bibliography up to date, the most current and thorough being Buford Jones's two installments of "Current Hawthorne Bibliography" (*HSN* 6,i:10–12; 6,ii:8–12). Jones lists bibliographies, books wholly or partially on Hawthorne, articles, dissertations, and miscellany. Wayne Allen Jones's "A Checklist of Recent Hawthorne Scholarship" (*NHJ 1977*, pp. 373–89) reaches back to 1973 and ends with 1977 in listing editions and reprints of Hawthorne's works, critical books, articles and essays, and dissertations. More specialized is Fumio Ano's "A Checklist of Theses on Hawthorne in Japan: 1964–1976" (*NHJ 1977*, pp. 337–40), a listing of 38 theses from Japanese graduate schools. The checklist is designed to reflect "the remarkable increase of scholarly interest in Hawthorne since 1964" in Japan.

The major breakthrough in the year's scholarship, however, was in biographical study. *Annus Mirabilis* is hardly an inflated term, for there were two comprehensive biographies, by Arlin Turner and James R. Mellow, a detailed look at Hawthorne's years abroad by Raymona E. Hull, and several findings of lesser scope about particular aspects of Hawthorne's life and work.

Arlin Turner's impressive *Nathaniel Hawthorne: A Biography* (Oxford) is the scholarly biography that has been needed for years. Making use of the most recent findings, Turner fills in gaps and illuminates once-obscured corners in Hawthorne lore. Weight of fact never endangers the book's readability, however. With steady, low-keyed style, Turner involves the reader in a captivating study of Hawthorne's character and personality as well as the shifts and turns of his career. If somewhat short on interpretation of detail and intentionally sparse in criticism of Hawthorne's works, the biography succeeds admirably in presenting Hawthorne as a man of his times, one whose life was tightly interwoven with the people and events of his day. Turner demonstrates to what a major degree Hawthorne was a public and political figure. The book is a judicious, balanced, carefully tooled piece of work and should serve scholars and general readers well for years.

Just as concerned with Hawthorne and his milieu is James Mellow's more popularly pitched, yet scholarly based *Nathaniel Hawthorne in His Times* (Houghton Mifflin). This book is the first of a promised quartet of "interlocking" biographies on Hawthorne, Margaret Fuller, Emerson, and Thoreau, Mellow's purpose being not only to explore in depth the lives of major authors but also to focus on the many "major and minor personalities" with whom they associated. He succeeds in this first volume with admirable eclecticism, providing both an intensive, well-researched view of Hawthorne's life and career and a large dose of personalities and events that filled Hawthorne's life. The long, multipart chapters are replete with historical and biographical vignettes. Unlike Turner, Mellow renders judgments and suppositions about various problematic aspects of Hawthorne's life, and he indulges in more criticism of the works, frequently relating fictive events and themes of the works to Hawthorne's own experiences (perhaps questionably so at times) and sampling contemporary critical reaction to Hawthorne's writings.

Raymona Hull's *Nathaniel Hawthorne: The English Experience, 1853–1864* (Pittsburgh) broadens the English interlude to include the later years abroad as well as Hawthorne's final four years back home. Expounding a thesis that the English experience shaped the remainder of Hawthorne's life, the book is a highly detailed examination of the personal and social lives of the Hawthornes abroad, from sketches of places they lived and their household routines to descriptions of each community they inhabited. Straightforward in her presentation of fact, Hull indulges in little speculation, refusing even to add to the wealth of conjecture surrounding Hawthorne's final years and cause of death. The book fills a gap in our previous understanding of Hawthorne's foreign interlude. What with John R. Byers' selected edition of Hawthorne's consular despatches (*EIHC*, 1977) and Mark F. Sweeney's annotated edition of all the despatches (*SAR*, 1978, 1979) all that is now needed to complete the picture of Hawthorne in England is a thorough study of his consulship (and one is in the making).

Several articles round out the year's extensive work in biography, two of them dealing with Hawthorne and his maternal relatives. Gloria Erlich in "Hawthorne and the Mannings" (*SAR*, 97–117) demonstrates, as does Arlin Turner in the biography, just how close to the Manning world Hawthorne actually was as a youth and young man and how that world influenced him throughout his life, especially in his involvement in "worldly affairs." Reacting to Hawthorne's 1852 statement to R. H. Stoddard that after leaving college he enjoyed "some slender means of supporting" himself, Wayne Allen Jones's "Hawthorne's 'Slender Means'" (*NHJ 1977*, pp. 1–34) takes close inventory of the funding that sustained Hawthorne during these postcollege days of writing and reading. James Mellow discusses Hawthorne's and Sophia's culinary habits during their "honeymoon" years in Concord (*Gourmet* 40,xi:47–48,128,130,132). Finally, Patrick Brancaccio in "'The Black Man's Paradise': Hawthorne's Editing of *The Journal of an African Cruiser*" (*NEQ* 53:23–41) discusses the extent of Hawthorne's involvement with his friend Horatio Bridge's literary enterprise, concluding persuasively that Hawthorne was much more than an editor: he had "a major influence on the shaping of the manuscript and the thematic emphasis of the work."

ii. General Studies

The year saw two classic studies reprinted: George E. Woodberry's
Nathaniel Hawthorne (Chelsea House) and Harry Levin's *The
Power of Blackness: Hawthorne, Poe, Melville* (Ohio). The Woodberry volume, part of the American Men and Women of Letters
Series, is a paperback issue of the 1902 study but with an added
introduction by Richard Poirier that reassesses (favorably, in general) Woodberry's late Victorian approach to Hawthorne. Levin's
book, also paperback, is reprinted just as issued in 1958.

A good many studies concentrated on Hawthorne and the various
traditions, literary and cultural, that influenced him. Probably the
best article in this regard is Edward Stone's "The 'Many Morals' of
The Scarlet Letter" (*NHJ 1977*, pp. 215–38), which, despite the title,
treats Hawthorne's short fiction as well as the novels. Stone depicts
Hawthorne as caught in an uncomfortable position between moralist
and artist. Unable to determine his own ultimate stance toward
either calling, Hawthorne "vacillated, now priest, now heretic."
Stone's article insightfully relates Hawthorne's dilemma to the context of the moralistic tradition and reader expectations of his times.
In his chapter "Puritan Romance: Nathaniel Hawthorne" in *From
Wilderness to Wasteland: The Trial of the Puritan God in the American Imagination* (Kennikat, 1979), pp. 121–45, Charles Berryman
traces Hawthorne's relationship to Puritanism, transcendentalism,
and Shakespearean tragedy. He views Hawthorne as a Hester figure
trapped by unresolvable conflicts, his fiction reflecting the themes of
Renaissance tragedy. Though the discussion of Hawthorne's religious
dilemma is not new, Berryman's Renaissance context is informative
and the parallels between Hawthorne's and Hester's positions telling.

Transcendentalism is the touchstone for Alfred Rosa's chapter
"Nathaniel Hawthorne" in his dissertation-based *Salem, Transcendentalism and Hawthorne* (Fairleigh Dickinson), pp. 114–45 and
passim. Unfortunately, Rosa's study offers little that is new to Hawthorne scholarship beyond tracing Salem's reaction to transcendentalism and bringing together in one place nearly everything that has
been said about Hawthorne's personal and literary relationship to the
movement. Noteworthy for its ambitious undertaking, but likewise
less than wholly successful, is John T. Irwin's "Hawthorne" in

American Hieroglyphics, pp. 239–84. Irwin's attempts to illustrate the impact of the discovery of the Rosetta stone and the decipherment of Egyptian hieroglyphics on major American romantics results in his taking a new slant on Hawthorne's ambiguity—that of the hieroglyphics as ambiguous symbols in themselves—and establishing other relationships between Hawthorne and the Egyptian symbols. Irwin's discussion of dual identity and veil imagery is fruitful, but his insights often remain purely speculative and his perspective on Hawthorne's relationship to the hieroglyphics is obscured by overly complicated symbolic analysis. More rewarding is a fresh reappraisal of gothicism, *The Gothic Tradition in Fiction* (Columbia, 1979), pp. 171–79 and passim, in which Elizabeth MacAndrew discusses selected Hawthorne stories plus *The House of the Seven Gables* and *The Marble Faun* in light of various gothic motifs. She focuses mainly on Hawthorne's evil scientists, some of them "ambiguous grotesques."

Burgeoning interest in Hawthorne and art brought three contributions in addition to discussions of the subject in the three biographies and the edition of *The French and Italian Notebooks* (see section *i.*). Rita K. Gollin in " 'Getting a Taste for Pictures': Hawthorne at the Manchester Exhibition" (*NHJ 1977*, pp. 80–97) recounts Hawthorne's visits to see the art treasures of Great Britain in 1857. She concludes perceptively that the experience prepared Hawthorne for his multiple encounters with art in Italy, developed his interest in the character of the artist, sensitized him to art as "interchange between the painter and the spectator," and—above all—taught him that art could involve him "emotionally, intellectually, and spiritually." In "Transcendental Admirers: Turner's American Friends" (*Art News* 79,x:80–83) James Mellow depicts Hawthorne as the most lukewarm of the Concord writers toward the romantic works of J. M. W. Turner. After several years of study, however, Hawthorne came to show "a steady, if erratic, growth in appreciation," surprising in a man who preferred the representational in art. A quite different view of Hawthorne and art is advanced by Sarah I. Davis in "Hawthorne and the Revision of American Art History" (*NHJ 1977*, pp. 125–36). Her thesis is that by writing "Drowne's Wooden Image," a story about "eclectic art,"—crafts rather than "ideal" art—Hawthorne was expressing his appreciation of the craft tradition as the seed bed from which American sculpture developed,

a view promulgated by some current art historians. The point is
well made, though perhaps somewhat restricted in its perspective on
Hawthorne and "ideal" art.

Other general appraisals touched on topics ranging from Hawthorne and the critics to Hawthorne and the Civil War. In "Hawthorne Debunkers Examined" (*NHJ* 1977, pp. 99–107) B. Bernard
Cohen uses Hawthorne for a look at the status of modern criticism.
Reacting against the subjective negative criticism of Hawthorne by
Martin Green and Lionel Trilling, Cohen argues that such approaches
have not advanced literary criticism "significantly beyond the type
practiced in Hawthorne's own time." He calls for criticism to develop
as "a sound and objective discipline," a state in which Hawthorne's
reputation will only survive. Robert E. Morsberger's "Hawthorne:
The Civil War as the Unpardonable Sin" (*NHJ* 1977, pp. 111–22)
holds that Hawthorne was the one major writer of his time "to challenge the necessity and justice of the War" because he thought it
always wrong to uphold abstract causes over individual concerns.
He finds Hawthorne's antiwar sentiments consistent with the views
expressed in such works as *Grandfather's Chair*, "Earth's Holocaust,"
and *Septimius Felton*. Jeffrey J. Mayhook makes a case for the importance of heraldry in selected stories and *The Scarlet Letter* in
"'Bearings Unknown to English Heraldry' in *The Scarlet Letter*"
(*NHJ* 1977, pp. 173–214). Reviewing the history of heraldry and
examining image clusters associated with that tradition, Mayhook
shows how Hawthorne—after all an American Democrat—employs
devices of heraldry often with irony and new meanings "unknown in
the Old World."

iii. Novels and Longer Works

The year's work on the novels was christened by the reprinting of
Richard Chase's well-known 1957 chapter "Hawthorne and the Limits
of Romance" in his *American Novel and Its Tradition* (Johns Hopkins). Chase's concentration on *The Scarlet Letter* seems to prefigure
the favorite subject of the year's criticism on Hawthorne's works, for
there are noticeably more articles on this novel than in any of the last
few years. Approaches range from historical and linguistic to biographical and ascetic. There were, of course, the usual attempts to
reconcile once and for all the disparate elements of "The Custom-

House" and the novel proper. Though not without its share of conventional treatments, the year can boast of an assortment of innovative, even radical, readings of *The Scarlet Letter*. Unsurprisingly, only a few make significant contributions to our understanding of the novel.

One of the more engaging articles is Michel Small's "Hawthorne's *The Scarlet Letter*: Arthur Dimmesdale's Manipulation of Language" (*AI* 37:113–23), a linguistic approach. Small sees Dimmesdale as using language in two ways—to recover self-esteem and, paradoxically, to release "libidinal" impulses. Thus language reveals the central tension in him. An otherwise rewarding discussion is somewhat marred by the final section which changes the emphasis to the question of Hawthorne's own guilt and alienation. Trying to broaden historical perspective on the novel, Earl R. Hutchison, Sr., in "Antiquity and Mythology in *The Scarlet Letter*: The Primary Sources" (*ArQ* 36:197–210) unconvincingly asserts that certain characters and story motifs in classical mythology are the chief sources of the novel. (Could the "A" actually stand for Aphrodite?!) The argument is reductive. Gary Lane's "Structural Dynamics and the Unknowable in *The Scarlet Letter*" (*NHJ* 1977, pp. 323–30) examines the interrelationships of the four major characters to demonstrate a "patterned ambivalence" that underscores the blurring of illusion and reality.

Clearly the most innovative, if problematical, studies of *The Scarlet Letter* are William C. Spengemann's chapter "Poetic Biography" in *The Forms of Autobiography: Episodes in the History of a Literary Genre* (Yale), pp. 132–65, and Viola Sachs's "The Gnosis of Hawthorne and Melville: An Interpretation of *The Scarlet Letter* and *Moby-Dick*" (*AQ* 32,ii:123–43). The more fruitful is Spengemann's argument that *The Scarlet Letter* represents a special kind of anti-Augustinian poetic biography—one that transfers Hawthorne's own most inner concerns and tensions to the complex natures and roles of his characters. Although Hawthorne only "half knew it," he did find "his true being, his true society, and his immortality in *The Scarlet Letter*." Sachs's article claims that the novel's "third dimension" is a "hidden center . . . where the revelation of the Spirit occurs." To reach that center, readers have to wend their way patiently "through a labyrinth of symbols, key words, signs," and if they do they undergo a "rite of initiation leading to *gnosis*." Though highly imaginative and provocative, the central point is ultimately strained and farfetched.

In quality of criticism "The Custom-House" fared better than the novel proper. The most significant study is John G. Bayer's "Narrative Techniques and the Oral Tradition in *The Scarlet Letter* (*AL* 52: 250–63), which cogently suggests that in the preface Hawthorne borrows on "oral modes of composition" in order to win over his audience and make them sympathetic. If "The Custom-House" is understood as an "exordium for the romance proper," confusion over its purpose "can be allayed." A sense of ancient history and "immemorial tradition" in both preface and novel handily links the two pieces, according to Jane Donahue Eberwein in " 'The Scribbler of Bygone Days': Perceptions of Time in Hawthorne's 'Custom-House' " (*NHJ* 1977, pp. 239–47). By mingling history with contemporary events, Hawthorne presents time as neither "linear or even cyclic" but "eschatological," like that of the early Puritans. The preface as discrete work is the tenor of Carlanda Green's "The Custom-House: Hawthorne's Dark Wood of Error" (*NEQ* 53:184–95), her thesis being that Hawthorne's journey is one to hell and self-discovery on the order of Dante's, Virgil's, and Odysseus' trips to the underworld. "The Custom-House" foreshadows the theme of the novel in that it deals with journeys "through the dark sins of the human heart to salvation or lack of it."

The House of the Seven Gables was viewed during the year by Jeffrey L. Meikle as a "consciously structured . . . alchemical drama" reflecting changes wrought on the Pyncheons by "time and the elements," in "Hawthorne's Alembic: Alchemical Images in *The House of the Seven Gables* (*ESQ* 26:173–83), a provocative article that nevertheless errs in insisting that all parallels mentioned are consciously drawn from alchemy. Jan Cohn's brief treatment of the novel in *The Palace or the Poorhouse: The American House as a Cultural Symbol* (Mich. State, 1979), pp. 57–60, is an interesting view of the Pyncheon house caught between Holgrave and Clifford's destructive wishes and Phoebe's protective feelings. In Cohn's view the "double thrust of property and hearth" becomes "a sexual conflict, one that woman necessarily wins." One wishes Cohn had included other Hawthorne houses in this intriguing book. From property to lack of, Patrick K. Dooley in "Genteel Poverty: Hepzibah in *The House of the Seven Gables*" (*MarkhamR* 9:33–35) dwells on Hepzibah in context of Thorstein Veblen's economic thesis of work and the leisure class.

The Blithedale Romance prompted two new articles on Coverdale, one cultural, one Freudian. From an interesting international perspective, Noriaki Nakai in "Coverdale's Narrative—a Portrait of the Artist as a Nineteenth-Century American in *The Blithedale Romance*" (*American Review* [Tokyo] 14:141–62) views Coverdale's situation and efforts at Blithedale as paralleling Hawthorne's challenge as an artist in young America. Thus the "real" or "inmost Me" of Hawthorne is the author "determined to participate in the making of American history by means of writing literature." Coverdale's love and sexuality are the sole interest of Richard VanDeWeghe's "Hawthorne's *The Blithedale Romance*: Miles Coverdale, His Story" (*NHJ* 1977, pp. 289–303). With something of a new twist, VanDeWeghe interprets Coverdale's aloofness as a sign of his being incapable of understanding his sexuality both while at Blithedale and as he relates his story in retrospect. Coverdale actually loves both Priscilla and Zenobia, just in different ways.

Though the publication of *The French and Italian Notebooks* will undoubtedly spawn a host of articles on *The Marble Faun*, this year brought only three that are noteworthy. Not surprisingly, two dealt with the novel and art. The more theoretical and speculative is Jonathan Auerbach's innovative, if sometimes belabored and obscure, "Executing the Model: Painting, Sculpture, and Romance-Writing in Hawthorne's *The Marble Faun*" (*ELH* 47:102–20). Auerbach extolls the murder of Miriam's model as the central metaphor of the novel, one that represents a purgation that must occur in Hawthorne's own artistic process so he can be free of the conscious burden of novel-writing to create effectively in the realm where the actual and imaginary meet. Louise K. Barnett's focus in "American Novelists and the Portrait of Beatrice Cenci" (*NEQ* 53:168–83) is on how Guido's portrait influenced not only *The Marble Faun* but also Melville's *Pierre* and Edith Wharton's *The House of Mirth* and *The Mother's Recompense* and how in all four novels its presence underscores the theme of incest. Barnett concludes that the portrait provided Hawthorne with the focus and symbol for his concerns about sin, guilt, remorse, and expiation, presenting an antithesis (evil versus good) of the Faun image. The most rewarding article of the year on Hawthorne's Italian novel is Samuel Coale's "*The Marble*

Faun: 'A Frail Structure of Our Own Reading' " (*ELWIU* 7:55–65). Coale sees *The Marble Faun* as Janus-faced, looking back to older traditions and ahead to modern conventions in fiction, presenting unresolved tensions and conflicts as a result. Coale does an admirable job of earmarking the special characteristics and difficulties of this novel, even satisfactorily explaining the problems with Hilda's characterization as stemming from Hawthorne's own confusion over the ultimate nature and direction of his novel. Especially cogent is his view of *The Marble Faun* as "pre-modernist," even Bergsonian in its emphasis on subective responses.

One last article on the longer works takes a holistic approach to a collection of tales. Stephen Adams' "Unifying Structures in *Mosses from an Old Manse*" (*SAF* 8:147–63) theorizes that the individual tales and sketches are closely interrelated by recurrent images and themes dealing with a quest for the "new Eden" and a "network of relationships" in which the pieces "shed light on each other and confront the reader with multiple points of view." Insightful and certainly new, the article nevertheless insists on too intricate a "network" among tales that after all were not originally written with collective publication in mind.

iv. Short Works

A wealth of criticism concerns the short fiction in general as well as particular stories, sketches, and essays. Though the more important stories continued to draw most of the commentary, a few that are rarely treated likewise invited critical response.

Three scholars address the short works in general. Starting with the premise that Hawthorne's sketches have never been appreciated "at their full value as compositions," Richard Harter Fogle in "Hawthorne's Sketches and the English Romantics" in *Towards a New American Literary History*, pp. 129–39, asserts that not only are the sketches "strongly unified" and "securely moored to actuality," but also more than the stories they are "speculations, explorations in the world of mind and spirit, and thus are exercises in imagination." The key term "imagination" allows Fogle to relate the sketches to romantic themes and techniques of Wordsworth, Coleridge, Keats, and Shelley, his comparisons making clearer Hawthorne's relationship with English romanticism. Verisimilitude in Hawthorne's tales is the subject of Shannon Burns's "Hawthorne's Literary Theory in the Tales" (*NHJ 1977*, pp. 261–77), while Nancy Bunge in "Dreams in Hawthorne's Tales" (*NHJ 1977*, pp. 279–87) sets out to prove that a Jungian rather than Freudian reading of Hawthorne's dream works is more pertinent. Her point is well made, though it is unfortunate she could not have access to Rita K. Gollin's *Nathaniel Hawthorne: The Truth of Dreams* (1979) when the article was written. Evan Carton's "Hawthorne and the Province of Romance" (*ELH* 47: 331–54) asserts that the warfare between art and history throughout Hawthorne's works is clearly dramatized in the four tales comprising "Legends of the Province House." Art manages to subsume history in these pieces, with a triumph that prefigures what happens in all of Hawthorne's romances.

Criticism on individual tales begins with Hawthorne's earliest extant productions. "Alice Doane's Appeal" and "The Hollow of the Three Hills" are the main focus of David Downing's "Beyond Convention: The Dynamics of Imagery and Response in Hawthorne's Early Sense of Evil" (*AL* 51:463–76). Downing posits that even early in his career Hawthorne was transcending traditional gothic and romantic conventions as well as the Calvinist belief in natural depravity and was developing new psychological themes of evil that account for the complex "Oedipal and sexual dimensions" of a later story like "My Kinsman, Major Molineux." Roberta F. Weldon in "Hawthorne's Old Apple-Dealer and Wordsworth's Leechgatherer" (*NHJ 1977*, pp. 249–59) detects specific parallels between the protagonists of Hawthorne's sketch and Wordsworth's poem in "subject, imagery, theme, and in the critical theory that informs them." The strength of Weldon's article is in the comparison of two similar "solitaries" and the contrast of Wordsworth's and Hawthorne's romanticism. Another influence study is R. Lamar Bland's "William Austin's 'The Man with the Cloaks: A Vermont Legend': An American Influence on Hawthorne's 'The Man of Adamant'" (*NHJ 1977*, pp. 138–45). Bland argues plausibly that Hawthorne's probable reading of Austin's story while he was composing "The Man of Adamant" caused him to reshape his own story structurally and symbolically.

Two studies of "Roger Malvin's Burial" probe the story's historical and environmental undercurrents. John Samson's "Hawthorne's Oak Trees" (*AL* 52:457–61) relates the oak tree under which Reuben Bourne leaves Malvin to die to the historic Charter Oak, thus concluding that the tree-top is ultimately blighted not just by Bourne's personal guilt but—since he was an Indian fighter—by guilt resulting from the "frontiersman's subversion of the values symbolized by the Charter Oak." More productive is Arthur E. Robinson's reading of the complex setting of the story, in " 'Roger Malvin's Burial': Hawthorne and the American Environment" (*NHJ* 1977, pp. 147–66). Recognizing a "social and ecological thrust" that complements the story's main psychological and moralistic import, Robinson views the natural setting of the story as dualistic (inviting versus repelling) and as suggesting a subtheme of virgin wilderness as opposed to desecration of nature by encroaching civilization. The central ambiguity in the forest imagery echoes that in the story as a whole. Surprisingly, the only separate contribution on "My Kinsman, Major Molineux" is Jesse Bier's addition to the store of ample name sources for "Molineux." In "Hawthorne's 'My Kinsman, Major Molineux' " (*Expl* 38,iv:42–44) Bier claims that the root "mol," French for "soft," is fitting since Robin's challenge is to "come into his own by finally giving up all hard doctrinaire ideas of what maturity is." It is doubtful Bier's proposal will inhibit the search for further sources of one of Hawthorne's most puzzling choices of name.

Harold F. Mosher, Jr.'s "The Sources of Ambiguity in Hawthorne's 'Young Goodman Brown': A Structuralist Approach" (*ESQ* 26:16–25) makes some cogent points about the importance of Hawthorne's methodology and the artistic distance between Brown's and Hawthorne's points of view, but becomes entangled in Lévi-Straussean jargon ("syntagmatic sequence," "superposable segments," "binary oppositions"). Two studies of "The Minister's Black Veil" are more rewarding. Elaine Barry's "Beyond the Veil: A Reading of Hawthorne's 'The Minister's Black Veil' " (*SSF* 17:15–20) refreshingly concentrates on the secondary characters of the story, detecting the same ambiguities at work in them as in Mr. Hooper. The veil, then, represents a paradox outside Hooper: the other characters' limitations in judgment (of him) and also their understandable humanness. Another study, based on the assumption that Hooper is Hawthorne's "most difficult 'case' of Puritan conscience," is Michael J. Colacurcio's "Parson Hooper's Power of Blackness: Sin and Self in 'The Minister's Black Veil' " (*Prospects* 5:331–411). Ambitious and multifaceted, if overly long, the article offers a dual purpose for investigating the story: to arrive at the "approximate depth and drift of Hooper's meaning" and to see if his "career of exacerbated subjectivity contains any clues to his historical configuration." The article's main strengths are the placing of Hooper in the context of American religious history, and the relating of the veil to the Puritan concept of self as hell.

Of Hawthorne's later stories, "The Birthmark" attracted most of the attention. Two articles are particularly noteworthy. Robert Micklus' "Hawthorne's Jekyll and Hyde: The Aminadab in Aylmer" (*L&P* 29 [1979]:148–59) argues convincingly that Aminadab is the "repressed, 'lower' half of Aylmer's composite nature" and that this nagging awareness of an inner flaw disillusions Aylmer and urges him on to remove the imperfection from Georgiana. Shannon Burns in "Alchemy and 'The Birth-Mark'" (*ATQ* 42 [1979]:147–58) focuses on the spiritual, unifying aspects of alchemical science, concluding that Aylmer's error as alchemist is in losing sight of the desired union of body and spirit. In removing Georgiana's birthmark he thwarts the possibility for that blend since he has actually removed "essential parts of her personality." Burns's reading can be faulted only for its overemphasis on Aylmer's drive for spiritual perfection. C. T. Walters' "Ritual, Process and Definition: Hawthorne's 'The Artist of the Beautiful' and the Creative Dilemma" in *Rituals and Ceremonies in Popular Culture* (Bowling Green), pp. 282–95, discusses Owen Warland's success and failure as a reflection of the cultural challenge Hawthorne believed faced all artists of his time: "the creation of an object of Beauty that still demonstrated practical use." A mixed piece that wavers between analysis of the story and 19th-century art (and shortchanges both), the article nevertheless makes some cogent points along the way, especially about Owen's failure to be "rejuvenated by the salutary effects of environment." Last, Christopher Brown's "'Ethan Brand': A Portrait of the Artist" (*SSF* 17:171–74) reiterates the interpretation of Brand as an artist figure whose sin involves "the process of artistic creation" and its attendant dangers. Brown insists too much on similarities between Hawthorne and Brand.

v. Hawthorne and Others

Influence and parallel studies continue to proliferate. Subjects treated this year are about equally divided between American and British/

Continental authors. The most interesting and meaningful work done is on Hawthorne and Melville and Hawthorne and James.

While not trying to prove a direct influence of Hegel's thought on Hawthorne, John Carlos Rowe's "The Internal Conflict of Romantic Narrative: Hegel's *Phenomenology* and Hawthorne's *The Scarlet Letter*" (*MLN* 95:1203–31) does point to close parallels between Hawthorne's concept of romance and Hegel's view of spirit. The romanticism of both men, Rowe believes, is best expressed "in their anguished struggles to maintain the harmony of the universal and the particular, the abstract and the sensuous." Verbose and ponderous with philosophical terminology, Rowe's statement is not as illuminating on *The Scarlet Letter* as on the esoteric aspects of romance. On a more material topic, O. M. Brack, Jr. in "Hawthorne and Johnson at Uttoxeter" (*American Bypaths*, pp. 1–18) explores Hawthorne's compelling interest in Dr. Johnson—especially his guilt and public penance—and posits that Hawthorne's perception of Johnson's character informs the "language throughout his career." Though interesting, the similarities between Hawthorne and Johnson are more likely products of kindred minds than direct influence.

Hawthorne and the English romantics as a group have already been discussed in section *iv.* in connection with Richard Fogle's "Hawthorne's Sketches and the English Romantics." A case of particular likeness is discerned by Janet Harris in "Hawthorne and the Byronic Hero" (*NHJ* 1977, pp. 305–17). A comparison of characters from four of Hawthorne's novels and several tales with protagonists from Byron's works leads Harris to conclude that "these two Romantics observed the same aspects of human nature and described these traits artistically." Turning the tables on the usual pattern of influence are two studies that declare Hawthorne's influence on 19th-century English writers. Rita K. Gollin's "Hester, Hetty, and the Two Arthurs" (*NHJ* 1977, pp. 319–22) convincingly traces the possible impact of *The Scarlet Letter* on George Eliot's *Adam Bede* in "plot, setting, and character," an influence made all the more probable by Eliot's attesting to Hawthorne's being "'a grand favourite of mine.'" And Kerry Powell in "Hawthorne, Arlo Bates, and *The Picture of Dorian Gray*" (*PLL* 16:403–16) perceptively relates Hawthorne, Bates, and Oscar Wilde to the "magic-portrait tradition of Gothic fiction" and believes that Hawthorne's "Prophetic Pictures" and "Edward Randolph's Portrait" probably influenced Wilde's novel. Though some speculation enters in, the case is made more likely by Wilde's known interest in Hawthorne.

In their respective biographies Arlin Turner and James Mellow add to the corpus of material on the Hawthorne-Melville relationship. Hyatt H. Waggoner's "Hawthorne's Presence in *Moby-Dick* and in Melville's Tales and Sketches" (*NHJ 1977*, pp. 73–79) appears in his 1979 book *The Presence of Hawthorne* and was reviewed in last year's *ALS.*

Arlin Turner's portrayal of Hawthorne's association with Melville in chapter 18, "In the Berkshires," is expectedly restrained and balanced. The friendship between the two men generally held sway, Turner believes, until Melville overstepped with his exuberant letter to Hawthorne of 17 November 1851, the suggestive imagery of which caused Hawthorne to withdraw. In characteristic understatement, Turner summarizes, "Following this letter, the two met only twice, a year later in Concord and five years later in Liverpool, and the intimately personal element is absent from Melville's subsequent letters." Mellow's more extensive portrait of the relationship in his chapter "The Citizen of Somewhere Else" is accompanied by an elucidation of the 19th-century concept of "higher love," Emerson's essay "Love" serving as basic resource. Mellow largely rules out an explicit homosexual yearning in Melville for Hawthorne, though he believes the record suggests some possible ambivalent feelings on the part of the younger man toward his handsome neighbor and idol. Though both Turner and Mellow adhere fairly closely to the record, charting the course of the friendship from the Monument Mountain Excursion to Hawthorne's departure from the Berkshires some 15 months later, Mellow's account is more speculative and interpretative than Turner's straightforward, almost terse treatment.

In other work on Hawthorne and 19th-century American authors, Scott A. Dennis in "The World of Chance: Howells's Hawthornian Self-Parody" (*AL* 52:279–93) points to Howells' echoing Hawthorne's "characters, plots, and themes," especially from *The Blithedale Romance,* in his 1893 bathetic romance *The World of Chance.* The article is well done and convincing, though it has more bearing on Howells than Hawthorne studies. Another successful influence study is Robert E. Hogan's "*Dr. Heidenhoff's Process* and *Miss Ludington's*

Sister: Edward Bellamy's Romances of Immortality" (*SAF* 8:51–
68). Hogan demonstrates that in Bellamy's two novels the influence
of Hawthorne "is evident in certain names, character types, and
themes," especially the themes of "guilt, moral responsibility, and
immortality." In addition, he addresses Bellamy's references to Hawthorne and his works, and Bellamy's notebook passages that bear
striking resemblance to Hawthorne's.

Though far from the bonanza 1979 brought in Hawthorne-James
studies, the subject is advanced by Thaddeo K. Babiiha's *The James-
Hawthorne Relation: Bibliographic Essays* (G. K. Hall). A valuable
book that treats a wealth of material on the relationship, it is composed of six bibliographic essays dealing with the pieces in which
James wrote about or referred to Hawthorne or his works, studies
which have considered the general relationship between the two
authors, and specific influence on James by Hawthorne's works. The
book is well organized, the appraisals judicious. The only serious
drawback is Babiiha's limited parameters: few works after 1974 are
reviewed (the original study was a 1977 dissertation). Thus there is
no discussion of such important contributions to the Hawthorne-
James question as Robert E. Long's *The Great Succession* (1979),
Hyatt Waggoner's discussion in the final chapter of *The Presence of
Hawthorne* (1979), or articles by Richard Ruland and Jesse Bier.
Would that there had been a final updating before publication.

Hawthorne's "presence," to use Hyatt Waggoner's term, is de-
tectable in the thoughts or works of several 20th-century American
writers, according to other studies. John L. Idol, Jr. in "Nathaniel
Hawthorne and Thomas Wolfe" (*HSN* 6,i:6–7) briefly recounts
Wolfe's interest in Hawthorne and his works and emphasizes Wolfe's
placement of Hawthorne among writers of " 'the first mark.' " Like
Melville, Wolfe was "fixed and fascinated by Hawthorne's penetration of the blackness in mankind." Hisao Tanaka's "Hawthorne and
Faulkner" (*SALit* 15[1979]:17–35) is an interesting charting of
Hawthorne-Faulkner parallels, though it is little more than a re-
minder of what established scholarship has already addressed. Fi-
nally, arriving at the most contemporary stop, Joan D. Winslow discerns telling, if unsurprising, parallels in the psychological fiction of
Hawthorne and Joyce Carol Oates, in "The Stranger Within: Two
Stories by Oates and Hawthorne" (*SSF* 17,iii:263–68). Her focus is

on "Young Goodman Brown" and "Where Are You Going, Where Have You Been," stories whose protagonists "encounter their devils because they have tried to avoid a recognition of the disturbing character of human nature."

North Texas State University

3. Poe

G. R. Thompson

Returning to the Poe chapter after six years produces a curiously blurred sense of *déjà vu*. Poe criticism seems simultaneously to have advanced—especially in the examination of narrative strategies and in revealing patterns of self-reflexive encodings of artistic process—while overall remaining the same. I note that the "scholars" and the "critics" are still at odds—the scholars complaining about overly imaginative critical interpretations and many critics (especially those who wish to be thought avant garde) unconcerned with traditional secondary scholarship. None of this is confined to Poe studies, of course. Hershel Parker has been railing against a lack of hardcore scholarship in Melville criticism for years, in *ALS* and elsewhere, calling for rejection of both narrow New Critical searches for textual "unity" and fancy poststructuralist and deconstructionist wordgames. Parker wants (as I read him) criticism to be based on the stable "factual" world of textual scholarship, bibliography, and biography. Whereas some ten years ago I was excited by the possibilities of the newer critical methodologies making their first inroads on American critical praxis (see the "Themes and Criticism" chapter of *ALS 1969* and *ALS 1971*), now I too cast a skeptical eye on what seems a self-indulgent, self-promoting criticism in America. But the "New Scholarship" as envisioned by Parker may be a simplistic overreaction. I'm afraid the concept of "New Scholarship" embraces illusions—the illusions that somehow if we can possess the "facts" of the text we will understand it, that biographical facts lead to "proper" critical interpretations, that perceptions of textual unity or mythic amplifications have no value divorced from such "facts." What is the text? This seemingly simple question has complex implications. By the very

I wish to acknowledge the help of Laura A. Hoelscher, a teaching assistant at Purdue University, who also served as my research assistant in 1981.—G.R.T.

act of extending the concept of a "text" into biographical matters, into the printed text's "place" in an author's canon and in an author's career, we move toward subjectivity, into the unstable world of interpretation. Biography is a subgenre of fiction. Our textual decisions are interpretations that to some extent make the canon of an author ultimately a fiction.

i. Hardcore Scholarship: Texts and Bibliography

The disturbing fictiveness even of oldstyle "textual" scholarship is made evident by a small, more-or-less biographical text focused not on Poe but upon his major editor, upon a scholarly tradition that is in fact an extension of the concept of the text. Thomas Ollive Mabbott's Harvard edition of Poe's *Poems* and *Tales and Sketches* was to be major event in Poe studies in the '70s. His widow, Maureen Cobb Mabbott, has produced a portrait of *Mabbott as a Poe Scholar* (Baltimore: Enoch Pratt Free Library, Edgar Allan Poe Society, and the Library of the Univ. of Baltimore) that is more central to the problems of Poe scholarship than would appear at first glance. It is in two parts: an informal history of "TOM" as a scholar whose "hobby" was Poe; followed by a commentary on seeing Poe's *Tales and Sketches* through the Press after Mabbott's death. Mabbott's principal scholarly outlet and his basic model was *Notes & Queries*: "Neither then nor later was he interested in working up long theoretical articles. I do not think he ever had anything in *PMLA* . . . at heart he was a scientist and was interested in discovering facts and presenting them concisely" (p. 5). His emphasis was on "sources and records rather than on his own opinions" (p. 22). Of course, the Harvard Poe is shot through with Mabbott's opinions, which range from judgments on semicrossed *t*'s and the dots over *i*'s, to decisions on copy-text, to the debunking of both fanciful and "unimaginative" critical interpretations; Mabbott insisted on a largely biographical way of reading, of interpreting the works *and* their sources, especially for the poems. Much of the basis for Mabbott's opinions is unspecified, and his wife describes the rejection of one major textual theory as follows: it was from his "long background of study and proven 'rightness' that he made the decision not to follow for his Poe texts the Greg-Bowers textual methodology" (p. 29). He chose each text on its "individual merits." What these merits are is

unclear, but they have something to do with the author's latest revisions, though Mabbott's actual selections are inconsistent (again,
especially in the poems). We are asked, then, to *believe* in Mabbott's
"scientific" subjectivity or "proven 'rightness.'"

If we in fact are inclined to accord Mabbott a high degree of
rightness, what are we to make of the fact that the *Tales and Sketches*
ends up printing a large number of texts from R. W. Griswold's edition of Poe's works? The matter is not simple or one-sided. For
within his biases Mabbott's judgments are expert and his extensive
scholarship impeccable. Certainly Mabbott did not blindly follow
Griswold. Writing to his fiancée in 1924, he remarked on the ad-
vantages that New York afforded to scholars (in the days before
microfilm and Xerox) for examination of Mss. at sales; his inspection
of a particular Ms. made "more complex the whole relation of Poe's
Literati text to that of Griswold's. That G. botched the job is certain
anyway" (p. 12). But how much did Griswold "botch"? Maureen
Mabbott notes that R. A. Stewart in his textual notes to the 1902
Harrison edition claimed that "Griswold is very defective in typography" but that Mabbott had marked in the margin of his copy,
"Not so!" The general assumption is that "because Griswold was
unreliable and vindictive in some cases, he must be in all," but "a
close comparison of the texts where Harrison uses the *Broadway
Journal* and Mabbott the Griswold texts reveals that the typographical errors in the *Broadway Journal* add up to 129, and those in Griswold to 93" (pp. 30–31). Presumably then, Griswold's altered *Broadway Journal* texts of Poe, as filtered through the Mabbotts, may be
a reliable text, possibly reflecting the author's last revisions. But
textual and bibliographical scholars have widely differing ideas about
what constitutes the "best" or "preferred" copy-text, and Mabbott's
choices have been severely criticized by Joseph J. Modenhauer (see
ALS 1978, p. 30) and others.

There is only one bibliographical study of note this year, Burton
R. Pollin's extensive list in *Poe Studies* (13:17–28), "Poe 'Viewed and
Reviewed': An Annotated Checklist of Contemporaneous Notices."
The checklist "provides an index to and brief description of all
known contemporary reviews and notices of Poe's separately published works" (p. 17); it is limited to items that appeared before his
death and excludes notices of periodical publications. The list has
what seem to be expertly summarized annotations (though they are

inescapably interpretative) and reveals the extent to which Poe was noticed by his contemporaries and the variety of opinion (largely favorable) about his works.

ii. Semihardcore: Biography, Sources, Analogues, Parallels

Problems similar to those of texts and bibliography plague biographical and source studies, an area obviously more open to "interpretation." How often does a "life" of an author need "revision"? An author's life is a text, dependent on the various, changing conventions of its genre. The history of early Poe studies revolves around what is essentially a biographical conflict of texts. After all the decades of "criticism," the nearest thing we have to a definitive biography is still the critically weak work of A. H. Quinn, now forty years old. This year's major effort in biography is disappointing. John Evangelist Walsh's *Poe the Detective* (see *ALS 1968*, p. 168) was a fascinating and responsible piece of detective work. The same cannot be said of his *Plumes in the Dust: The Love Affair of Edgar Allan Poe and Fanny Osgood* (Chicago: Nelson-Hall). This work is essentially a novelistic invention in which the notes and appendices attempt to assemble evidence that Poe was the father of Frances Osgood's child, Fanny Fay; but what Walsh offers us is primarily unsubstantiated speculation on the possibility of a liaison in Providence in July 1845.

A bibliographical and source oriented scholar who is tired of fashionable criticism and longs for a return to a more old-fashioned mode is J. Lasley Dameron in *Popular Literature: Poe's Not-so-soon Forgotten Lore* (Baltimore: Enoch Pratt Free Library, the Edgar Allan Poe Society, and the Library of the Univ. of Baltimore). Dameron calls Ruth L. Hudson's 1935 dissertation (Univ. of Va.), which lists over 100 "analogues" to Poe's tales a "breath of fresh air in Poe criticism" (p. 2). Despite the sense of time warp this statement provokes, perhaps given some of the willfully obfuscatory criticism now current, one can sympathize with Dameron's desire to return to a simpler mode of source and analogue study. He relates three of Poe's tales, "Balloon-Hoax," "Man of the Crowd," and "Usher," to the kind of fiction he has found in British and American periodicals from 1820 to 1840 (why 1840?) and finds two "widely diverging facets" of American popular taste: preference for "classical" form and tone, and appetite for the "scientific" (mainly pseudosciences like phrenology and mesmerism). In his understanding of American popular taste, Dameron rather too severely restricts Poe's tastes and reading, asserting for one thing that Poe in his preface to *Tales of the Grotesque and Arabesque* (1840) "flatly denied" any "affinity" with German writers of Gothic tales. Dameron quotes from the preface but omits Poe's comments about the "pseudo-horror" of "some of the secondary names" of German literature and fails to fill in the biographical context that reveals part of the motivation for the preface. This suppression of the full facts constitutes a distortion. Presumably Dameron does this because to admit Poe's interest in German literature (what about French?) would make him too "romantic," less "classical." Admitting some few romantic proclivities in Poe, however, he attempts to show that Poe principally sought to "blend the sensational theme with the dictates of a traditional classical taste" (p. 5). When Dameron presents "sources" for the three tales, mainly unnoticed until now, he is interesting and clear, especially, I would say, when he offers evidence from Robert Macnish's *An Introduction of Phrenology* (1836) and John Reid's *Essays Hypochondriacal and Other Nervous Affections* (1817) that in their state of "terror" and especially of "wonder" both "the narrator and Roderick Usher may be said to be in a condition which might induce a spectral illusion . . ." (p. 13). But that this constitutes an implicit "opinion" on a major critical controversy of interpretation will be clear to every student of Poe.

If Dameron has in mind the kind of loose and muddled study of Poe's affinities with German romantic writers that J. Wolff presents in "Romantic Variations of Pygmalion Motifs by Hoffmann, Eichendorff and Edgar Allan Poe" (*GL&L* 33[1979]:53–60), I can certainly understand his weariness. Perhaps more to his taste would be Edward W. Pitcher's "From Hoffmann's 'Das Majorat' to Poe's 'Usher' via 'The Robber's Tower': Poe's Borrowings Reconsidered" (*ATQ* 39:231–36). Pitcher questions the standard assumption that the influence of Hoffmann's tale is through Sir Walter Scott's summary of the work in the *Foreign Quarterly Review*; he makes a case for inclusion of John Hardman's "The Robber's Tower" (1828) in the line of influence. Hardman's "improvements" on Hoffmann's devices parallel

Poe's technique. Among features present in Hardman but absent from Hoffmann are: "an expanded variant" of the story-within-the-story device in which the inner narrative is interrupted three times by sounds outside the room which in turn correspond to sounds reported in the narrative; the presence of a young maiden recently buried in a vault placed immediately below the chamber of the narrator; and the theme of anxiety over premature burial. This seems to me a first-rate example of a straightforward, responsible source study that adds to our critical understanding of how Poe worked.

I hope that those who think that I have overemphasized Poe's affinities for German romantic writers and thinkers will believe that I am disinterested in my judgment of the pure beauty of the scholarly argument of Glen A. Omans' lengthy study of the influence of Immanuel Kant on Poe; it is to my taste one of the best, if not the best, articles of the year. As to its "truth," readers will have to judge for themselves. In "Intellect, Taste, and the Moral Sense: Poe's Debt to Kant" (*SAR 1980*, pp. 123–68), Omans observes that Poe's division of the mind into the three areas indicated by the title is Kantian—and only Kantian—a direct borrowing from the "Introduction" to Kant's *Critique of Judgment*. The first part of Omans' essay surveys every reference Poe made to Kant in his fiction; there follows a step-by-step survey of Poe's development of the three-faculty model in his essays and reviews, along with a careful and lucid summary of Kant's categories of *Verstand, das Geschmacksurteil*, and *Vernunft*, the middle term usually translated as *Taste*, indicating aesthetic judgment. His summary of Kant's principles of "disinterestedness" in aesthetic judgment and the distinction between truth and beauty clarify Poe's use of similar terms. Omans demonstrates the differences among several tripartite theories of the mind beginning with Aristotle and continuing through Addison, Gerard, Akenside, Reid, Blair, and others. "Poe and Kant use 'taste' or the aesthetic faculty rather than 'imagination' and locate it between the reasoning power and the moral will, rather than between the physical senses and the moral sense" (p. 157, n. 12). He distinguishes between Kant's terms and those of Schelling and his followers in the English-speaking world: Coleridge, Shelley, Keats, Carlyle, Emerson, Longfellow, Bryant. The middle part of the essay surveys Coleridge and shows that despite heavy borrowings from Kant, Coleridge did not embrace the three-faculty model of the mind and its mediating function of *Taste* as Kant outlined it. Poe's usage of Kantian terms is always closer to Kant than is that of Coleridge, who fused Kant's ideas with those of Fichte and Schelling. Poe's claim that the "Poetic Sentiment" can develop in landscape gardening and in interior decorating is also paralleled in *The Critique of Judgment*, where Kant categorizes landscape gardening as a kind of painting, just as Poe does.

Omans then discusses an interesting problem: there was no English translation of the *Judgment* in the 1840s. Assuming for the sake of argument that Poe did not know German, Omans surveys essays and reviews by English-speaking rhetoricians and writers as well as translations—concluding that Poe would have been able to pick up many Kantian ideas from the magazines of the time but not the precise three-faculty paradigm. Since all other writers in English followed the lead of Coleridgean *Imagination*, that left Poe as the sole Kantian in aesthetics in the English-speaking world! But Omans is still not satisfied, and he sets out systematically to track down every Kantian discussion in French, which, of course, Poe read with ease. Nowhere is there to be found a "single adequate source" in French or English of the Kantian model—nor could Poe have pieced it together in precisely Kant's way from the hundreds of books and articles available. How Poe did it is still a mystery.

A general study (indubitably "factual" on one level) of parallels and affinities is Elsa Nettels' "Poe and James on the Art of Fiction" (*PoeS* 13:4–8). This is an examination of a "number of points at which the critical principles of Poe and James coincide," rather than a source or influence study, as Nettels is careful to point out. The cumulative effect of the details of the specific parallels (even to phrasing) that she lucidly brings together in brief compass is impressive. She analyzes their mutual concern with an affective theory, with unity of form, with the revelant detail, with the difference in genres and the relation of length to unity of effect, with the predetermined quality of the whole, with the creative role of the artist as opposed to mere mimesis, with the conception of a "center of consciousness" in a narrative character, with the relation of reader "identification" to that consciousness for true "verisimilitude," with *donnée* and execution as first principles, and with the open-ended quality of the fantastic and improbable.

iii. Softcore: Formula Fiction, Genre, Psychocriticism, Textplay

A number of related studies reveal a spectrum of critics grappling with an appropriate critical methodology. Several attempt to deal with literary conventions and formulas as problems of genre, culture, and psychology, with special reference to detective fiction and the Gothic. In these one finds a curious mix of social and Marxist criticism, Freudian and Jungian psychoanalysis, and more-or-less structuralist and deconstructionist "play." The work on *Pym* illustrates a range from a peculiar kind of "source" study to "old" New Critical close reading for unity to a metaphoric species of historical semiotic criticism.

John Cawelti's wonderfully clear *Adventure, Mystery, and Romance: Formula Stories as Art and Popular Culture* (see ALS 1977, pp. 447–48) demonstrated how formula fiction, literary conventions, and cultural assumptions are intertwined and how artistic works make use of and go beyond formulas. The detective story has also recently received sophisticated treatment by Ian K. Ousby, Robert L. Caserio, and others (but see comment on David Grossvogel's *Mystery and Its Fictions* in ALS 1979, p. 45). Acknowledging his debt to Cawelti, Stephen Knight in *Form and Ideology in Crime Fiction* (Indiana) proposes to analyze his subject in a broad social context according to three methodological principles: (1) selection of central popular examples to be analyzed in detail as autonomous works; (2) identification of their "immanent social ideologies"; (3) discovery of ideologies immanent in form as well as content. This sounds promising, but for the Poe scholar the application to "Murders in the Rue Morgue," "The Mystery of Marie Rogêt," and "The Purloined Letter" does not reveal very much.

Prompted by the reference to "the rules of Hoyle" and by the games of draughts and whist in "Rue Morgue," LeRoy Lad Panek in "Poe and Long's Hoyle" (*SSF* 16[1979]:344–48) gives an account of the contents of George Long's *Hoyle's Games Improved* (1821), Poe's most likely source. Hoyle's influence extends beyond the introductory games section of the tale, Panek suggests, and colors the interpretation of the words "calculation" and "calculus" as they appear in all the detective tales. The stories are fictions about play in which the writer and his main character are players. A somewhat similar orientation is found in Mark M. Hennelly's treatment of "The Gold-Bug." In "LeGrand, Captain Kidder, and His Bogus Bug" (*SSF* 17:77–79) Hennelly sees the tale's two-part structure forming a "joking" artistic "parable." The narrator of the first part of the tale represents the uninformed and bewildered reader who is obsessed with the gold-bug to the exclusion of the mysterious but meaningful parchment; this narrator/reader gives way in the second part of the tale to the artist/hoaxer who is both the "rightful" narrator and a "mask" for Poe. As the narrator/reader of the first part learn(s) to grasp the secret of the cryptographic riddle, the tale becomes a parable of the aesthetic process. (Hennelly disarmingly observes that finding elements of aesthetic process in the ratiocinative tales has become a kind of "critical commonplace.")

Gamelike narrative strategy that subverts traditional narrative formula is the subject of Sandra Whipple Spanier's " 'Nests of Boxes': Form, Sense, and Style in Poe's 'The Imp of the Perverse' " (*SSF* 17: 307–16). The tale, she says, explores and embraces paradox in an "involuted" pattern in which dualities such as creation and destruction, art and life, cause and effect, style and sense, are contained in each other ad infinitum. The form of the tale, moving from "broad generality" to a "terminal point" and out again, resembles a "Yeatsian gyre" (doubtful). Art and life are contained within each other, for the narrator is continually "*doing* what he is discussing," thereby manipulating the reader into experiencing his discursive subject matter. The last lines of the tale are stylistically disturbing, she says, possibly illustrating that the Imp is at work, spoiling the "stasis and perfection of the conclusion." Despite the nice application of Poe's criticism of Bulwer's "atrociously involute" plots as "nests of boxes," I prefer the analysis of Eugene R. Kanjo (*PN* 2[1969]:41–44), who also makes quite clear the appropriateness of the concluding sentences.

Is "The Assignation" romantic formula fiction or not? Yes and no. Edward W. Pitcher in "Poe's 'The Assignation': A Reconsideration" (*PoeS* 13:1–4) identifies what he calls the Benton-Thompson thesis that the tale is a comic hoax and argues that it is more precisely a structure of opposed perspectives. "Poe meant to *sustain* the tension and consequent ambiguity and thereby leave the reader poised between optional readings of the tale, 'bewildered' along with the narrator but able to entertain, at once, the comic and the serious perspectives" (p. 1). Now to be precise here, the view that the tale is a comic hoax is the Richard P. Benton thesis. I merely follow his lead, reassembling his proofs—calling his essay on "The Assignation" as important to a reassessment of Poe's fiction as Darrel Abel's famous essay on "Usher," since the tale, prior to Benton's analysis, had generally been taken as a totally serious, highly romantic production. The Thompson part of the thesis is that there is a carefully maintained "romantic-ironic" design to the whole—a pattern of the serious and the comic that European, especially German, romantics knew as the "Arabesque." What Pitcher does, then, is to make more specific these tensions, especially those between the "mundane" (what he says Poe regards as the world of "appearances") and the "visionary" (for Poe, "realities"). In the tale, the worldly man of reason in whom the mystical is suppressed" (i.e., the narrator) is drawn together with the "over-reaching mystic/artist" (the Byronic stranger); "reason infects the mystic with a sense of the absurd; the mystic infects the rationalist with an intuition of higher bewildering truths" (p. 3). Although the claim that the mundane, "rational" narrator "infects" the Byronic stranger is not substantiated, Pitcher's conclusion about the symmetry of the tale is of interest: "as much as the man of the world may mock [where in the text?] the visionary's 'bewildered' sense of reality, so too the visionary feels that one 'must laugh' . . . about much of the world" (p. 1).

In "Poe's 'Ligeia' and the Pleasures of Terror" (*Gothic* 2:39–48) Terry Heller addresses large matters of Gothic and terror fiction in terms of reader-response to psychological and aesthetic "distance." He places his test case, "Ligeia," in critical perspective—succinctly surveying the controversies over how to read the tale and indeed how to read Poe—and then builds on and radically extends previous critical insights. He employs a three-level system. On what he calls the "literal" level of apparent supernaturalism (a debatable assumption of what is "literal" in the text) he finds "Ligeia" a powerful tale in which the degree of terror felt by the reader increases "in intensity as one approaches nearer to believing [the] fictional world a true picture of his own world" (p. 41). Disputing what he conceives to be my own contention that an "ironic" distance between the reader and narrator opens up (I would counter that what I really discuss is a "romantic-ironic" distance, a somewhat different matter; cf. Pitcher above), Heller suggests that when "the supernatural events begin to change into psychological symbols, the reader is more likely to abandon the supernatural world view than his closeness to the narrator. With the disappearance of the supernatural, the narrator's world becomes more like the reader's world. The distance between reader and narrator is reduced" (p. 42). The third level involves the indeterminancy of the whole text: Poe's narrative strategy opens up an ambiguous world of possibilities in which terror resides in "the ways in which the text mocks the reader's attempts to know it." The reader cannot "escape the terrifying world in which one must remain so long as one attends to the story." This world is "precisely the one in which the narrator finds himself, a world which will not yield to his attempts to know it" (p. 43). Heller's radical conclusion is that terror literature is an assault on the *reader's* integration of personality, inducing claustrophobia, paranoia, and schizophrenia. These are large claims to make for the effect on a generalized, hypothetical, implied reader. When Heller says that "to the degree that 'Ligeia' succeeds at threatening the reader with these psychoses, it must test the reader's ability to resist such states," I for one resist the extravagance of his claim for the power of "Ligeia." But if I substitute the nightmare world as rendered in Kafka (or Dostoevsky), then Heller's analysis of the dynamics of reader response to literary terror seems more acute.

David R. Saliba's *Psychology of Fear: The Nightmare Formula of Edgar Allan Poe* (Univ. Press) is the only booklength critical study devoted entirely to Poe this year. It is an ambitious attempt to combine an analytics of affective reader involvement with Jungian psychology, dream theory, and Gothic and formula fiction in 19th-century magazines in an effort to develop a thesis about Poe's "formula" for fear. Saliba defines "fear" as anxiety over alternations of "control" and "loss of control" felt by a dreamer, a character, a reader, and apparently an author. The "formula for fear" derives from Poe's own "actual dreams." The critic's authority for this curious "biographical" assurance is "circumstantial." Poe's tales have the feel of an "actual" nightmare; and nightmares are apparently variants of an archetype out of the Jungian unconscious. Moreover, the "essence of the gothic tradition" is also archetypal of the "collective unconscious." Saliba proceeds in two opposing ways: nightmare as defense mechanism for the author; and nightmare as strategy of deception of the reader. There are four aspects of the latter: isolating the reader; stunning his sensibility; victimizing his emotions; and "premature burial" of his reason. The reader is confused, "drawn in" by the seeming logic of a "fast-talking, frenzied narrator." Once the reader feels the slightest identification with the narrator, "the bond is complete." The logic here escapes me. Saliba should read Heller on reader identification and distance.

Saliba's specific Jungian analyses depend on tenuous verbal associations between his own metaphors and Jung's, rarely on Poe's. The argument does have random insights but needs thorough revision. A strength is Saliba's attempt (if finally unsuccessful) to assimilate major scholarship. His acquaintance with Poe scholarship and with scholarship on the gothic is quite apparent. Therefore, it is with some unhappiness that I turn to a much superior Jungian study in which the scholarship on Poe is slighted.

In *The Unsounded Centre* Martin Bickman juxtaposes three "paradigmatic" works—Poe's *Eureka*, Emerson's "Plato," Whitman's "Passage to India"—that embody the underlying schema of "unity-division-reintegration that M. H. Abrams and Northrop Frye see as central to Romantic thought." The conjunction is nice, but Bickman merely summarizes the disintegration-integration cycle of *Eureka*. In the chapter on Poe Bickman focuses on the symbolic "meeting and fusing of contraries, the *coincidentia oppositorum*," characteristically imaged as marriage or sexual union. By discussing only "To Helen," "The Assignation," "Morella," and "Ligeia," Bickman dodges the problems raised by the satires and comic pieces. His discussion of "Morella" (based on his previous essay noticed in *ALS 1975*, pp. 46–47) is the most fully developed; but I might mention here that Bickman's case is strengthened by his pointing to Morella's obsession with those very romantic thinkers who so influenced Jung—Schelling and Fichte. There is a similar pattern in "Ligeia." In a general way this parallels Saliba's treatment, but Bickman handles it with greater discrimination. In his handling of "The Assignation" he fails to confront the debate over problems of comedy, mockery, unreliable narrators, and dramatic irony. In effect, he ignores the extended text.

Nevertheless, the Jungian and mythic studies of Poe's fiction, especially of *Arthur Gordon Pym*, that have multiplied in the last ten years do centrally engage what still seems to be the major controversy in Poe criticism: how negative or affirmative is Poe's vision? Overall, the criticism on *Pym*, whatever the orientation, suggests that it presents a hauntingly indeterminate text that evokes *something* provocative about initiation ritual, maturation or regression, death and rebirth, the myth of eternal return, the integration-disintegration of the psyche—and also something about artistic process itself. Paul Rosenzweig's "The Search for Identity: The Enclosure Motif in *The Narrative of Arthur Gordon Pym*" (*ESQ* 26:111–26) comes at these matters from a Freudian angle. At first he deals deftly with evidence from the text; but he becomes increasingly arbitrary, truncating his argument, and forcing the text into a prescribed Freudian paradigm. Yet his is one of the more interesting pieces of the year. Rosenzweig inverts the basic structuring principle that most critics have seen— the journey motif—and suggests that it is secondary to the real structuring pattern, the enclosure motif, itself enclosing the journey motif. The story of Pym is that of "an incipient self, a thinly protected ego," in battle against not only the environment (an enclosure) but also against "those potential aspects of the self which the ego has not yet truly incorporated into its identity" (seemingly another kind of enclosure). Rosenzweig demonstrates the pervasiveness of food and drink in the text and shows how they are persistently associated with enclosures. But about the middle of the essay, he begins to indulge in rhetorical sleight-of-hand, slipping more and more references to the "womb," the "nourishment" of the "Mother figure," the "prenatal mother of primal consciousness," and the "umbilical connections" of the text; these are Rosenzweig's metaphors, not Poe's.

In a rather too exuberant article, "The Gothic at Absolute Zero: Poe's *The Narrative of Arthur Gordon Pym*" (*Extrapolation* 21:21– 30) Frederick S. Frank claims that Poe purposefully ignores "the boundaries of the Gothic genre and moves through layers of Gothic blackness to the "reunion" with the "white goddess," thus reducing "the destructive patterns of conventional gothicism to an absolute zero." "The Secret of Arthur Gordon Pym: The Text and the Source" (*SAF* 8:203–18) by Richard Kopley argues that the shrouded figure of the last scene is most probably the figurehead of a ship, just possibly the *Penguin*, the ship in the first portion of the book which hits the *Ariel* and rescues the two shipwrecked boys. Evidence? J. N. Reynolds' "Leaves from an Unpublished Journal" (1838), which has an account of shipwrecked mariners rescued by a ship, the *Penguin*.

There is space here for only general remarks about John T. Irwin's *American Hieroglyphics*—though Poe gets nearly 200 of the

350 pages. According to the preface, the book "deals with the notion of the writer's corpus as an inscribed shadow self, a hieroglyphic double. [It] begins by examining the impact of the decipherment of the Egyptian hieroglyphics on nineteenth-century American literature, and then, ranging back and forth over literary history, practical criticism of individual works, and speculative criticism, it relates the image of the hieroglyphics to the larger reciprocal questions of the origin and limits of symbolization and the symbolization of origins and ends. The only part of the book that may pose some difficulty for the reader is the series of speculative digressions in the section on Poe. In the process of providing background material for Poe's work, these digressions sometimes elaborate their specialized lines of inquiry at such length that Poe seems to fade into the background and vanish—an enactment of the kind of figure/ground reversal that is one of the themes of the Poe section. Yet this reversal inevitably reverses itself in turn, and the figure of Poe reemerges against a more complex background with, one hopes, even greater definition." I do not find, however, that Poe, or Poe's texts, so reemerge—though Irwin returns to *a* text of *Arthur Gordon Pym*, from the standpoint of which he offers a fascinating discussion of the roots of words that throws some light (and some shadow) on the subterranean encryptions at Tsalal. His book pretends to offer practical, applied criticism of texts, but his main concern is with the grand schema.

What does Irwin reveal about *Pym* as a structural text? Mainly that the Pym-Poe unity-distinction in the preface initiates doubling, calls attention to the "precariousness" of the art of writing, and recurs as extended doubling in Augustus and Parker, and especially in Peters, a "half-breed," who as Pym's "shadow self" represents the "irrational aspect of nature." Variants of such ideas are critical commonplaces in Poe scholarship. That the figure in the mist at the end is Pym's projection of self is more a consequence of Irwin's metaphoric language model than a derivation from the text.

Poe and *Pym* do not emerge from this study critically illuminated in a new way. What we get is a highblown, philosophically tenuous hypothesis about language and self. Yet the work is scholarly in its own way. Irwin has read a multitude of obscure works of the romantic era and before. And he has read Poe carefully. Acknowledgment of others' work is minimal. There is not a single reference to

Barthes or to Derrida. Not a single study or critic of Poe is recognized —not even studies by Lacan or Ricardou, which are directly pertinent to some of his linguistic speculations.

Almost nothing he has to say about Poe is new. Virtually every speculation, reduced to ordinary language, has been anticipated. There is an inscripted shadow text here: ours is not a cumulative and progressive discipline, and such a publication as *American Literary Scholarship* is pointless. The arrogance of it is stunning. Irwin projects his shadow on the mist; the rest of us are consigned to the scholarly vortextual abyss, deprived of our immortality, dissolved in the blank margins of the pages of his looming Self.

Purdue University

4. Melville

Hershel Parker

Since several items refused to fall into neat categories this year, I invite you to scan the whole chapter rather than thinking, for instance, that everything on *Typee* will be discussed in section *iv.*, "*Typee* through *White-Jacket.*"

i. Miscellaneous

There were several biographical tidbits. Haskell Springer in "The Scottish Connection" (*MSEx* 42:15–16) prints the letter Melville's father wrote to the Earl of Leven and Melville from Paris on 5 July 1818; it contains new details of Allan Melvill's visit to his titled kinsman. David K. Titus' corrective essay on "Herman Melville at the Albany Academy" (*MSEx* 42:1,4–10) shows, among much else, that Melville "never pursued a commercial course but rather pursued a standard course leading to classical studies." Donald Yannella prints a note from Melville dated 1 July 1852, apparently a response to an autograph collector (*MSEx* 44:13). A new addition to the accumulating recollections of old Melville hands is Wilson L. Heflin's charming account of "Researching in New Bedford, Circa 1947" (*MSEx* 42:1–4); also of note is Heflin's "More Researching in New Bedford" (*MSEx* 43:11–14). Joyce D. and Frederick J. Kennedy, who recently have done most to supplement Jay Leyda's researches, offer recollections and advice in their "In Pursuit of Manuscripts: True Yarns, or, Seek and Ye Shall Find" (*MSEx* 43:8–11). A new sample of their research (this time among manuscripts untouched by any other Melvillean besides Heflin) is "Some Naval Officers React to *White-Jacket*: An Untold Story" (*MSEx* 41:3–11), a hilarious account of how Samuel Francis Dupont (the Dupont of Washington's Dupont Circle) schemed over the best way to reply to that "undyed villain" Herman Melville, then finally let silence be the best response to his attacks on naval policies and personages. Nelson C. Smith adds to knowledge of "Melville's Reputation in the Colonies" (*MSEx* 42:13–14) with a reprinting of three reviews and a list of notices in the *Home News*, a London semimonthly intended for colonial readership. Stanton Garner in "Rosemarine: Melville's 'Pebbles' and Ben Jonson's *Masque of Blackness*" (*MSEx* 41:13–14) identifies a source of a line in the Melville poem. In "The Revival That Failed: Elizabeth Shaw Melville and the Stedmans: 1891–1894" (*WS* 7:75–84) Kathleen E. Kier adds a little (a very, very little) to what Merton M. Sealts, Jr., Amy Puett, and the Kennedys have told us; Kier unsportingly credits only the female Kennedy as author of a jointly-signed article.

A great boon for study of the growth of psychological and philosophical thought in America is *Endeavors in Psychology: Selections from the Personology of Henry A. Murray* (Harper & Row), edited by Edwin S. Shneidman; Melvilleans will welcome the republication in it of almost all Murray has ever published on Melville, enough to remind us that in our time great people have responded greatly to Melville, despite the trivia that clutters most of these annual chapters in *ALS*. A final item in this catchall section deserves pondering by anyone who is thinking of writing a critical article on Melville and anyone who might read such an article as a member of an editorial board: Robert Milder's thoughtful "Melville Criticism in the 1970s; or, Who's Afraid of Wellek and Warren" (*MSEx* 43:4–7).

ii. Melville and His Contemporaries: Emerson, Goethe, Hawthorne, and Thoreau

In "Melville and Emerson's Rainbow" (*ESQ* 26:53–78) Merton M. Sealts, Jr., has written one of the handful of classic scholarly essays on Melville, a meticulous, immensely judicious evaluation of Melville's knowledge of and ambivalent responses to Ralph Waldo Emerson. It is a corrective not only to recent pieces by Nina Baym (1979) and Philip D. Beidler (1978) but to many other studies which have exaggerated, underestimated, or misdated Melville's reading in Emerson and misconstrued his always complicated responses. The essay is informed by Sealts's thorough knowledge of the ancient and modern philosophers whose ideas Melville also knew and responded to. I cannot take space to quote Sealts's "tentative conclusions" (pp. 71–

72) but caution all readers for scholarly journals to reject any essay which does not show that the writer has worked through all of Sealts's arguments. Throughout his long demonstration Sealts labels plainly what is known, what is possible, what is probable. I hope that the users of this essay will show the same cautious restraint—will realize, for instance, that Sealts does not say that Melville lied to Duyckinck about having only glanced at something by Emerson in Putnam's bookstore before hearing him lecture, that Sealts is only giving his best guess when he suggests that Melville read some of Emerson's essays soon after hearing him lecture, and that Sealts does not champion the most recent identifications of characters in *The Confidence-Man* as portraits of real people (he says "if Helen Trimpi is right").

As if to give us almost too much of a good thing after years of half-baked influence studies, James McIntosh offers "Melville's Use and Abuse of Goethe: The Weaver-Gods in *Faust* and *Moby-Dick*" (*Amst* 25:158–73), a brilliant, judicious study of Melville's vacillations between "scornful hostility to Goethe" and grudging admiration of him. (McIntosh and Sealts both emphasize the ambivalence of Melville's attitudes toward thinkers who challenged him profoundly.) McIntosh's essay is now required reading for anyone interested in Goethe (and his translator Carlyle) as well as in Melville's philosophical development. I want also to point out that McIntosh's reading of the Goethe references in the 1 (?) June 1851 letter to Hawthorne demonstrates what rewards can come to the sensitive and patient critic.

Arlin Turner in *Nathaniel Hawthorne: A Biography* (Oxford) and James R. Mellow in *Nathaniel Hawthorne in His Times* (Houghton Mifflin) both retell the old and tantalizing story of the Melville-Hawthorne relationship. Turner's is a meagre version marred by odd lapses in Hawthorne scholarship as well as more predictable lapses in Melville scholarship. Turner asserts more than he proves—asserts, for instance, that Melville "felt he had been rebuffed in his display of affection" for Hawthorne and asserts that meeting Hawthorne caused Melville to plan his whaling story anew, "turning it into a symbolic narrative of man's warfare against evil." Of the 1 (?) June 1851 letter Turner says that Melville's mind seemed "to move at random"; yet the quotations Turner uses from the letter are not only inaccurate (as many others are) but are also scrambled, so that words from different paragraphs are joined and leapfrogged with other quotations. Turner's version of the story is simplistic and misleading. As Richard Brodhead says (*MSEx* 44:6–7), Turner "refuses even to ask" the most important questions about the relationship. Mellow's version is more scholarly, more intuitively sympathetic, more detailed, and more judicious. Sensitized by Edwin H. Miller's lurid notion that Melville made a homosexual pass at Hawthorne, Mellow stops dead in his tracks to give a four-page exegesis on the blurring of the distinction between love and friendship in "the upper reaches of transcendental thought." Neither of these versions, however, supersedes earlier accounts by such writers as Luther S. Mansfield, Randall Stewart, Leon Howard, Eleanor Melville Metcalf, and Sidney Moss (you may have missed his long essay in *Literary Monographs*; see *ALS 1975*, p. 65).

We've known all along that *Typee* must have inspired some passages in "Economy," and Joseph J. Moldenhauer in his edition of *The Maine Woods* described a manuscript which contains "a response to Melville's *Typee*." Now Robert Sattelmeyer in "Thoreau and Melville's *Typee*" (*AL* 52:462–68) transcribes those comments which Thoreau made in a notebook in the fall of 1846, the year he went to Walden. In his own commentary Sattelmeyer may strain slightly (as in interpreting a passage as "a swipe at Melville's tendency to embellish the grotesqueness of the natives" or in saying that Thoreau "may have grown skeptical of Melville" by 1848); it's usually better, when printing such a document for the first time, to let it speak for itself. *Typee* was of interest to Thoreau because, like any travel book, it described unfamiliar ways human beings can live; what's ultimately fascinating, of course, is the way Thoreau turned the tables in "Economy" and took on the role of traveler bemused by the odd behavior not of South Sea Islanders but of his Concord neighbors.

iii. Books or Chapters in Books—General

Charles J. Haberstroh, Jr.'s *Melville and Male Identity* (Assoc. Univ.), familiar from parts published in the 1970s, is a simplistic treatment of Melville's ambivalences "caused by the tension between his hopeless and introverted sense of himself as a lost boy, and his desire to

fulfill the extroverted traditions of male status, success, and assertiveness with which he grew up." Errors of fact and typos abound, and
fiction too often blurs with biography. Some passages are just too
lurid to bear thinking on; avoid page 62 on Elizabeth Melville and
"the destructive turmoils of sexuality." Bernard Rosenthal's *City of
Nature* (Del.) attempts to place various writings by Melville (notably *The Confidence-Man*) in relation to what he sees as a 19th-
century American paradox: "Nature in its most important and pervasive metaphorical use connoted the values of civilization and often
implied civilization itself. In its purest form nature took the shape
of urban America, and the journey to nature became the journey to
the city." In *The Development of American Romance* (Chicago)
Michael Davitt Bell focuses on the tension in Melville "between arbitrary authority and revolutionary impulse": beneath "the overtly
messianic revolutionary rhetoric of Melville and his characters lurks
the compulsion to deny the promptings of desperate but buried aggression." The topic has been treated before, notably in Hayford's
" 'Loomings' " in *Artful Thunder* (see *ALS 1975*, p. 75), which Bell
does not mention. Chicago ought to have screened out misspellings
of such names as Nicholas Canaday, Jr., Merrell R. Davis, Edwin
Fussell, Henry A. Pochmann, and John W. Shroeder. John T. Irwin's
American Hieroglyphics (Yale) comes with an intimidatingly wor-
shipful welcome by Robert Con Davis in our most prestigious journal (*AL* 52:656–59): a "huge study" with a "grand scope" demanding comparison with Feidelson's *Symbolism in American Literature*
"or even with F. O. Matthiessen's *American Renaissance*." Whoa,
whoa, there. Maybe, just maybe, this application of Jacques Lacan
and Jacques Derrida to the American Renaissance will mark "a fundamental shift in our understanding of the period." If it does, I'll bet
it will be with Poe alone. Melvilleans have known a little about the
importance of Egyptology, hieroglyphics, and doubling for quite
some time. To name only some obvious discussions, there is Sealts on
"I and My Chimney" (1941), Dorothee Metlitsky Finkelstein's 1961
book, *Melville's Orienda*, H. Bruce Franklin's *The Wake of the Gods*
(1963), Hayford's " 'Loomings' " essay (1975) and "Unnecessary
Duplicates" (1978), and Leon Howard's nod toward an influential
Hayford speech in his Minnesota Pamphlet (1961), as well as Harold
P. Simonson's paraphrasing of a Hayford hand-out on the prisoner

image in *The Closed Frontier* (Holt, 1970). Like Bell's book, Irwin's is not as fresh as it purports to be.

iv. *Typee* through *White-Jacket*

Gavan Daws in *A Dream of Islands: Voyages of Self-Discovery in the South Seas* (Norton) retells the stories of "five famous figures of the nineteenth century who found their fate" in the South Seas—John Williams, Herman Melville, Walter Murray Gibson, Robert Louis Stevenson, and Paul Gauguin. The Melville chapter (pp. 71–127) is frequently inexact (e.g., Malcolm Melville was "born not long after *Mardi* came out and did so badly") and at times seems a slick bit of popularizing, but at least it is vividly, vigorously written by someone with a thesis, albeit a borrowed one: "D. H. Lawrence was right about him: 'Melville hated the world: was born hating it.'"

T. Walter Herbert, Jr.'s *Marquesan Encounters: Melville and the Meaning of Civilization* (Harvard) is more ambitious and more ambiguous than Daws's book. Despite the subtitle, much of the book is not about Melville but various missionaries and naval men. Herbert claims to take an approach "now developing within anthropology that differs from structuralism in seeking to elucidate the meanings present in occasions of significant activity by considering their particularities of context and reference, as well as by scanning them for evidences of internally consistent general structures." What began, he says, "as a pursuit of historical sources for Melville's *Typee*," became "a sociodramatic analysis in which the essential metaphors and themes are seen to pervade action as well as writing." The chapter devoted to Melville (pp. 149–91) does not fulfill the expectations thus set up, for it consists largely of an old-fashioned examination of the narration as blending the perspective of a beachcomber with that of a "sophisticated gentleman-at-large." But just as Herbert's *"Moby-Dick" and Calvinism* (1977) valuably supplemented William H. Gilman's researches, this book supplements Charles Roberts Anderson's.

Janet Giltrow's "Speaking Out: Travel and Structure in Herman Melville's Early Narratives" (*AL* 52:18–32), is mainly about *Typee*. Like James Jubak's essay (see *ALS 1976*, p. 51), it is a welcome break from New Criticism. Giltrow's point, obvious enough, one would think, but one which needs the repetition it is now getting, is that modern critics go wrong in reading travel books like *Typee* "in the light of another prose form, the novel." As she says, *Typee, Omoo, Redburn,* and *White-Jacket* all "have a certain amorphousness for the modern reader who grasps their often slight fictions as generic signals leading him to expectations of novelistic form." Her useful treatment of the varying narrative attitudes in *Typee* as a natural part of shifting requirements in the travel genre should be compared with Herbert's analysis. David Charles Leonard's "Descartes, Melville, and the Mardian Vortex" (*SAB* 45:13–25) ought to have been combined with his very similar study last year (*AL* 51:105–09). This piece comes to the identically worded conclusion that "Melville's affinity with Cartesianism alienated him from the maincurrents of nineteenth century transcendental thought."

The long title of an article by Scott Giantvalley and Christina C. Stough, "'Precedents Are Against It': An Examination of *White-Jacket* as a Corrective for the 'Two *Moby-Dicks*' Theory" (*SAF* 8: 165–81) clarifies its purpose at the possible expense of its content. The article is about *White-Jacket,* not *Moby-Dick.* The authors' purpose is not mainly to discuss the order in which *White-Jacket* was composed, although they do show that in all reasonable likelihood it was composed in a sequence "generally reflected by the order in the published book." Rather, their purpose is to explore the chapter linkages in *White-Jacket* as a reminder and a challenge to those who speculate about the composition of *Moby-Dick.* Any hypothesizing about the composition of the later book, they caution, should take account "of the structural similarities it shares with *White-Jacket.*" Critics may find it hard to do justice to this modest and limited but potentially very useful article; it came out too late to be taken account of in the James Barbour–Harrison Hayford exchange too briefly reported in their "The Composition of *Moby-Dick*" (*MSEx* 43:2–4), a recapitulation of old arguments with teasing perspectives for future criticism.

v. *Moby-Dick*

The best comments on *Moby-Dick* this year are in the Sealts and McIntosh essays in section *i*; see also the last item in section *iv*. Viola

Sachs's "The Gnosis of Hawthorne and Melville: An Interpretation
of *The Scarlet Letter* and *Moby-Dick*" (*AQ* 32:123–43) is launched
with an editorial claimer or disclaimer: "*American Quarterly* is
pleased to publish this leading example of French work in American
Studies. We recognize its provocative and controversial character."
Sachs argues coolly that *Moby-Dick* "contains a consciously coded
message based on numerology, and on a whole set of correspondences
of words, images, evoked graphical signs and geometrical figures,
colors, letters, phonemes, and even punctuation marks, and typographical signs." It all makes me want to go home and have my
mother read me a story. Chapter 4 of Robert M. MacLean's *Narcissus and the Voyeur* (Mouton, 1979) is called "Locked Out: *Moby-
Dick* and the Flotsam of Narrative Continuity." Time warp again:
typical citations are the 1923 Chapman and Dodd *Mardi*, the 1966
Oxford *White-Jacket*, the 1957 Grove *Pierre*, the 1948 F. Barron Freeman *Billy Budd, Foretopman* and, best of all, Byron Gysin, "Cut me
up," in *Minutes to Go* (City Lights, 1968). MacLean's title is a pun,
for his concern is with the developing in *Moby-Dick* of a voyeurism
"which corresponds to Locke's inexpressible understanding, the eye
which cannot be inferred from the visual field, and of the concomitant limitations of empiricism." Judging from the references, Mac-
Lean thinks no one has ever written before about Melville and Locke.
Bert Bender in "The Allegory of the Whale's Head" (*Renascence* 32:
152–66) offers a simple religious interpretation of the chapters dealing with the whale's head. The "allegory" of these chapters has
"deep religious and epistemological significance" built upon biblical
prophecies, "each of which deals with man's limited ability to know,
and therefore, implicitly, his desperate need for humility and faith."
Larry J. Reynolds in "Kings and Commoners in *Moby-Dick*" (*SNNTS*
12:101–13) argues that a "democratic-elitist tension" is found in
Moby-Dick as well as in the rest of Melville's works. Indeed it is, but
good critics of Melville have been saying so for many years. Newton
Arvin's biography (1950) was grounded in the notion that with
Melville "one has to reckon with the psychology, the tormented
psychology, of the decayed patrician," a more felicitous formulation
than Reynolds' "déclassé patrician." Nor does Reynolds mention
the most complex recent discussion of the theme of physical and
metaphysical dignity and indignity, Hayford's " 'Loomings' " in *Art-*

ful Thunder (1975). Reynolds' point is reasonable, but it has been made before, and made better.

vi. The Stories and *The Confidence-Man*

There were minor pieces and one monumental essay. Charlotte Walker Mendez' "Scriveners Forlorn: Dickens's Nemo and Melville's Bartleby" (*DSN* 11:33–38) makes one long again for a full, responsible study of Melville and Dickens; the timing makes it unlikely that *Bleak House* could have had much if any impact on "Bartleby." Nancy Roundy's " '*That* is All I Know of Him . . .' Epistemology and Art in Melville's 'Bartleby' " (*EAS* 9:33–43) is thin and routine. Lewis H. Miller, Jr.'s " 'Bartleby' and the Dead Letter" (*SAF* 8:1–11) is another unneeded essay which justifies its existence by ignoring a body of similar criticism.

Merton M. Sealts, Jr.'s "The Chronology of Melville's Short Fiction, 1853–1856" (*HLB* 28:391–403) would be enough to crown any career, but see section *ii*, above. This is a breathtaking demonstration of what a learned scholar can do by patiently, meticulously putting pieces together. Using a little new information (letters or parts of letters unknown to Davis and Gilman, for instance) and a large portion of perspicacity, Sealts tells the story of when Melville wrote his stories, when he submitted them, and, of course, when they were published, a simple enough feat, you'd think, but not one that it ever occurred to writers of books on the stories to attempt. The judiciousness Sealts displays cannot be overestimated, nor can the potential usefulness of his sometimes stunning revelations to other serious scholars. There's a slight awkwardness in Sealts's extracting this from his forthcoming "Historical Note" to the Northwestern-Newberry *"The Piazza Tales" and Other Prose Pieces, 1839–1860*, for the "Agatha" story is referred to rather than explained, but I mention this problem only to assure you that the full "Historical Note" will surely stand as a masterpiece of its kind.

There was nothing exciting on *The Confidence-Man* this year. Nancy Roundy's routine "Melville's *The Confidence-Man*: Epistemology and Art" (*BSUF* 21:3–11) delivers less than it promises in seeing the narrator as "the ultimate Confidence-Man" who never provides the certainty he promises. Steven E. Kemper in *"The Con-*

fidence-Man: A Knavishly-Packed Deck" (*SAF* 8:23–35) points out examples of a technique by which the narrator on introducing characters first speculates "on their possible occupations, personalities, or histories," then proceeds "as if these surmises are absolute certainties," a technique by which, Kemper holds, "Melville undermines his own fiction and cons the reader as surely as the confidence man gulls the passengers." Kemper pays attention to the text.

vii. Billy Budd, Sailor

Harold Aspiz's "The 'Lurch of the Torpedo-Fish': Electrical Concepts in *Billy Budd*" (*ESQ* 26:127–36) draws on wide background reading in arguing that "the motif of electricity particularly animal and human electricity . . . permeates the incidents, themes, and language of *Billy Budd*." Terence J. Matheson's "A New Look at Melville's Claggart" (*SAF* 17:445–53) is indeed new, a partial defense of the much-abused master-at-arms; Claggart, like Billy and Vere, is something of a victim, sincerely believing the accusation he makes against Billy. In "*Billy Budd*: What Goes on Behind Closed Doors?" (*AI* 37:65–67) Larry Rubin surmises that what happened in the stateroom that night was a sexual intimacy between two consenting adults. Now we know.

University of Delaware

5. Whitman and Dickinson

Jerome Loving

The year of the 125th anniversary of the publication of the first *Leaves of Grass* and the sesquicentennial anniversary of Emily Dickinson's birth produced more on Whitman (both in terms of quality and quantity) than it did on Dickinson. Most notable are Justin Kaplan's life of Whitman and the long-awaited New York University variorum edition of his poetry. For Dickinson, the critical angle of vision is often feminist—so much so, in fact, that an admonition from a more traditional critic that we too often forget that the "Myth of Amherst" was both a poet *and* a woman had its own special shock value. Few Dickinson scholars have overlooked her gender in 1980. And in many cases the result has been extravagant speculation—criticism which exaggerates the possibilities of Gilbert and Gubar's *The Madwoman in the Attic* (*ALS*, *1979*, pp. 75–77). One investigation, however, stands above the rest for its originality and penetration: Margaret Homans' *Women Writers and Poetic Identity: Dorothy Wordsworth, Emily Brontë, and Emily Dickinson.*

i. Whitman

a. **Bibliography, Editing.** Besides William White's quarterly bibliography of the poet in the *WWR*, the only other secondary bibliographies are George Monteiro's "Addenda to the Bibliographies of Cather, Conrad, DeForest, Dreiser, Forster, Hardy, Hawthorne, London, Norris, Poe, Wharton, and Whitman" (*PBSA* 72:478–81), and Jeanette Boswell's *Walt Whitman and the Critics; A Checklist of Criticism, 1900–1978* (Scarecrow). In the case of the latter, it was judicious that the compiler chose "Checklist" instead of "Bibliography" to describe her work, for the volume is exactly that—a ten-

Preparation of this chapter was facilitated by the research assistance of Marcia Carr.—*J.L.*

tative survey of the material published in the years demarcated by the title. It may lack as many as 200 relevant items. A random check of the contents failed, for example, to show a study as recent as Ivan Marki's *The Trial of the Poet* (*ALS, 1976*, pp. 62–63). Other oversights are obvious as well as errors (such as the inclusion of Herbert Bergman's edition of Whitman's collected journalism for 1980—when in fact it has yet to appear), but the volume also suffers from a lack of criteria for selecting the materials. Boswell borrows from Gay Wilson Allen's bibliographies of Whitman and the Holloway-Saunders bibliography in the *CHAL*; this is not done consistently, however, and some of the items she lists from these works and elsewhere bear little relevance (or none) to Whitman. Boswell also lists as anonymous items authored by Horace Traubel, Richard Maurice Bucke, and others. Also missing from the Checklist are several important literary histories, histories of poetry (with valuable introductions concerning Whitman), and introductions to reprinted texts with a historical interest involving Whitman. It is doubtful that Boswell's contribution to the Whitman bibliography will do more for scholars than to serve as a handy but tentative guide to the wealth of secondary material.

This year sees the publication of the overdue variorum edition of *Leaves of Grass*, a work whose original target date was 1965. The wait has been worth it. In the meantime, the original editors, Sculley Bradley and Harold W. Blodgett, were joined by William White and Arthur Golden to complete what has been called "the most difficult, gigantic, and problem-haunted [editorial task] in the whole field of American letters." The result is *Walt Whitman*, Leaves of Grass: *A Textual Variorum of the Printed Poems* (NYU). As the title suggests, the three-volume set is not a variorum in the strict sense of presenting both variant readings of Whitman's poems and critical interpretations by various authorities. Nor is it—as was originally planned but now projected for part 2 of the variorum—an edition concerned with variant readings of the poems in manuscript and periodical publication. The present volume is confined to all of the poems ever printed in the successive editions of *Leaves of Grass* during the poet's lifetime. The copy-text is that of the final, authorized impression of the 1891–92 *Leaves*, but the poems are arranged in the order of their first appearance in Whitman's various editions. Footnotes—not endnotes—reconstruct all variant readings, as well as those of Whitman's two annexes. The volumes also include two appendices: "Old Age Echoes" (here with a significant clarification of matter treated in the 1965 *Comprehensive Reader's Edition*) and one presenting variant readings within editions of and annexes to the poetry. Finally, the work is handsomely improved by facsimiles of all the title and content pages. This is one scholarly tool no serious student of American literature can exclude from his library.

The variorum does not reflect, of course, the first English edition of *Leaves of Grass* (1868) because it was not an edition in the strict sense but a selection (and a *de facto* expurgation) made by William Michael Rossetti. In "John Camden Hotten and the First British Editions of Walt Whitman: 'A Nice Milky Cocoa-Nut'" (*Publishing Hist* 6[1979]:5–35) Morton D. Paley presents a solidly researched discussion of the facts surrounding this edition. Naturally, he is forced to cover familiar ground to provide an adequate context, but his endeavor is "newsworthy" in that it shifts the focus of investigation from Rossetti to John Camden Hotten, the first English publisher of *Leaves* and also a noted publisher (as well as collector) of pornography.

In another matter related to manuscripts and their use Richard F. Bauerle ("Whitman's Index to His Scrapbook: A 'Map' of His 'Language World,'" *WWR* 26:159–62,165–66) describes a scrapbook in the Ohio Wesleyan collection to speculate that the lists of words pasted in the front cover and end paper constitute a topic index for the scrapbook and a "synoptic view" of the poet's concerns throughout his first three editions. The poet's concern during the preparation of the "Death-Bed" edition extended even to the design of the cover according to William White, "Whitman Designs the 'Death-Bed Edition'" (*WWR* 26:125–26). R. D. Madison, however, thinks the poet went too far when he included "I'll Trace This Garden" in his complete works because he was merely recalling an Irish ballad ("Walt Whitman's 'Garden' Verses—Not Whitman's," *WWR* 26:29–31). If Whitman's Irish affinities were slight, his influence on Swedish Modernism is not—writes Carl D. Anderson, "Walt Whitman and Swedish Modernism" (*WWR* 26:83–91). Discussing translations of selections from Whitman's poetry in the magazine *Lynkvannen*, Anderson demonstrates that it is more Whitman the democrat (the one who contributed "toward the making of an America that in fact never came into existence") than Whitman the poet that is absorbed by the Swedish literati.

b. **Biography.** Grace and balance best describe the most important achievement in this area of concern: Justin Kaplan's *Walt Whitman: A Life* (Simon & Schuster). This biography will perhaps serve as the standard if not definitive life for many years to come. Highly readable without sacrificing factual reliability (in most cases), its narrative is a lucid demonstration of how inseparable Whitman's life was from the book which took half a lifetime to complete. This is not to say, however, that Kaplan's volume will replace Gay Wilson Allen's *The Solitary Singer* (1955), which in its time had other fish to fry. A century after the first *Leaves* had appeared, Allen set the record straight in a most comprehensive and satisfying biography. It was the job of the Whitman biographer writing in the 1950s to separate the myths from the facts, to sift through widely scattered manuscripts, letters, and diaries, to consolidate the best parts of the best biographies, and thus to produce a life that was at once definitive in its use of documentary evidence and compelling in its narrative. This was Allen's achievement, and Kaplan's a generation later was to update not so much the facts of the poet's life (though several of his interpretations are ingenious) as to update our impressions, to bring the reality of Whitman's life another twenty-five years into the future. In this Kaplan succeeds splendidly. Such an intimate portrait would have been injudicious at best in the 1950s. The question of Whitman's homosexuality, for example, is clearly accepted in Kaplan's biography. Allen chose "homoeroticism" to suggest that Whitman possessed homosexual tendencies. Kaplan prefers "homosexuality," but does not argue that Whitman was actively homosexual —nor does he seem to care. The tendency is enough, and even here it might not have shaped the poetry as much as many would argue. For Kaplan, the poet's homosexuality was secondary to his sense of sexuality in general, and this he considers a primary force in *Leaves of Grass*. Kaplan is most original and sagacious when he turns his attention to the obscure "foreground" of Whitman's book. Through an examination of the poet's early fiction, he uncovers a foreground darker and more profound than has been previously described. "Whitman's stories," he writes, "are basically fantasies about the erosion of relationship and about the terrors of growing up, separation from parents, death . . . and the obliteration of identity." This period in Whitman's career, then, as it is seen through the fiction projects the same gamut of themes found in *Leaves of Grass*—from the whistling in the dark of "Song of Myself" to the loss of "original energy" in "As I Ebb'd with the Ocean of Life." In making the connection, Kaplan skillfully interpolates the poetry into his narrative and so balances the man against his work.

In 1879 Whitman made a trip out west, and some of the details of his journey are given in Walter H. Eitner's "Walt Whitman's Companions Report His Western Trip" (*MarkhamR* 9:61–64). The article also contains a newspaper interview (not planted by the poet himself on this occasion) in which Whitman assesses the state of American letters. Another piece of biographical data is added by William White in "Whitman to [Charles W.] Eldridge: The Full Version" (*WWR* 26:79–80). Penned in the summer of 1889, the letter shows the poet in mourning over the death of his friend and champion, William Douglas O'Connor. Of less value is William T. Innes, "Walt Whitman's Optimism" (*WWR* 26:154–56), which is the printing of an essay (c. 1889) by one of Traubel's Camden friends, who with his father printed *The Conservator*. Like most of the screeds that filled Traubel's journal, however, this one regards Whitman as a prophet rather than as a poet.

c. **Criticism: General.**   One of the more noteworthy studies of the poet is Harold Aspiz' *Walt Whitman and the Body Beautiful* (Illinois). More than the sum of his articles on the subject over the years, the volume relates Whitman's writings to 19th-century pseudoscientific contexts "which help to clarify the implications, or 'meanings,' of his poetic treatment of such matters as physical beauty, sexuality, personal magnetism, or even the nature of poetry." The study is divided into three general units of several chapters each: the poet's ideas about physiology, the pseudomedical lore of the day, and his beliefs about the evolution of a gallery of eugenically superb prototypes in the New World. But the material under these headings is loosely organized, and one gets the clear impression that chapters or parts of chapters might be easily interchanged. Also, general information about Whitman is needlessly rehearsed, while other facts from more recently published sources are neglected. This is particularly true in the chapter on women in part 3 of the volume (the

least impressive unit). Yet the study is otherwise filled with useful
information about Whitman and the science of his day, and frequently
Aspiz succeeds admirably in showing us (especially in the chapter
entitled "The Body Electric") how the poet's knowledge of natural
science produced some of his most "dazzling" imagery.

The subjects of medical lore and women in Whitman's world are
also taken up, respectively, by Myrth Jimmie Killingsworth and Arthur Wrobel. Using as his point of departure "One Hour to Madness
and Joy" in "Whitman's Love-Spendings" (WWR 26:145–53), Killingsworth argues that the poet was rebelling against the 19th-
century notion that excessive sexual activity (more than once a
month) was unhealthy because the loss of one ounce of semen was
equal to the loss of 40 ounces of blood (a theory fostered by the
creator of the Graham Cracker). Killingsworth appears to be proving
the obvious as Leaves of Grass challenged Victorian sensibilities altogether. Furthermore, the poet—as Aspiz suggests—may have done
more than to simply patronize the pseudosciences of his times. (Certainly, phrenology, though he later became suspicious of its usefulness.) The following line from "Song of Myself" seems to indicate
Whitman's belief in at least part of Sylvester Graham's theory: "You
my rich blood! your milky stream pale strippings of my life!" In
"'Noble Motherhood': Whitman, Women, and the Ideal Democracy"
(AmerS 21:7–25) Wrobel mildly scolds the feminist critics for con-
demning Whitman's celebration of motherhood above women's rights.
Whitman, he points out, was merely responding to and echoing the
American ideal of his time that motherhood "offered moral salvation
and national and human salvation as well." His preference for the
home and family as the proper sphere for women, furthermore, is not
a contradiction of his insistence on the equality of the sexes in Leaves
of Grass but rather a reflection of his program of eugenics.

Focus on Whitman takes up the better part of The Transcendental
Constant in American Literature (NYU) by Roger Asselineau. For
the most recent French biographer of the poet, the transcendental
constant is simply "the ingrained idealism of American literature"
—transcendentalism in the most general sense of the term. The first
six chapters (on Whitman) as well as the others are versions of essays
Asselineau has published over the years. General in nature, the ones
on Whitman range from the poet's transcendentalism to his transcendental humor. The Whitman enthusiast might also consider reading

Asselineau's "A Complex Fate" (*JAmS* 14:67–81), which presents a brief account of how the French scholar learned about America (seeing all 50 states by Greyhound bus before the construction of the interstate highways hid the local color of the country) and eventually became one of the ablest interpreters of Whitman's life and work.

In another volume of essays, however, we have a hodgepodge of material both worthy and unworthy of publication. A special supplement to the *WWR, 1980: Leaves of Grass at 125* (Wayne), ed. William White, opens with Gay Wilson Allen's "Annus Mirabilis, 1955"—an interesting account of the difficulties the biographer of Whitman encountered at Macmillan over the production and distribution of *The Solitary Singer* (1955) once the publishing house had been sold to a conglomerate. Allen also provides a survey of other significant volumes and events in the centenary year of *Leaves of Grass*. In "The Katinka Mystery: or, Who Will Unknot 'Abbie Nott and the Other Knots'?" Roger Asselineau discusses a literary mystery that has teased him for the past 25 years: the authorship of an 1856 volume that quotes lines from the 1855 *Leaves*. He hazards three guesses, including one for Fanny Fern (Sara Parton), a popular writer of her day and an early admirer of Whitman's poetry. With the exception of Milton Hindus' speculation as to the motives behind Guillaume Apollinaire's 1913 hoax which described Whitman's funeral as a homosexual orgy ("Apollinaire's April Fool's Day Whitman Hoax"), the value of the remaining essays is dubious at best. Richard F. Giles's "Symonds' Annotations in the 1860 *Leaves of Grass*" is obscured by a hopelessly complicated system of editorial signs and symbols. William L. Moore in "L. of G.'s Purport: Evolution—The Cumulative" opens with a romanticized version of the poet's foreground and then (after finding parallels between the "Death-Bed" edition and snatches from the philosophy of Pierre Teilhard Chardin) crowns Whitman "Intuitional Evolutionist" of the universe. Slightly more reasonable is Richard Pascall in " 'What Is It Then Between Us?': 'Crossing Brooklyn Ferry' As Dramatic Meditation," which views the old "Sun-Down Poem" as the clearest example of Whitman's attempt to bridge the ultimate gap of personal communication. The personal-communication gap is narrowed a bit by Susan Hunter Walker (1864–1933) in "I Knew Walt Whitman," a previously unpublished reminiscence by the daughter of a Camden native who occasionally chatted with the poet in Mickle Street. Last is the editor's own contribution to this potpourri—" 'Some Late Occurences, Facts, in Boston': Unpublished Whitman Prose." William White, a prodigious editor of Whitman, has unfortunately rushed into print without consulting *all* of the facts in this instance. For what he presents are three relatively disparate documents concerning the Boston "suppression" of the Osgood edition of *Leaves of Grass*: (1) Whitman's (1882) notation concerning George Chainey's plan to send the "obscene" *Leaves* through the mail, (2) an otherwise undated 1882 clipping from the New York *Tribune* featuring an ambivalent defense of *Leaves of Grass* by a Philadelphia clergyman, and (3) a letter to a Philadelphia journalist in which Whitman fuels the fires of his defense locally. Had White bothered to discover the actual historical context for these documents (in volume 3 of Edwin Haviland Miller's edition of Whitman's letters [*ALS 1964*, p. 43] and Jerome Loving's *Walt Whitman's Champion* [*ALS 1977*, pp. 67–68]), he would have learned that the first document (as listed above) concerns a relatively isolated incident in Boston, that the second was copied by the *Tribune* from the Philadelphia *Press* of 15 July 1882, and that the third shows Whitman taking an active part in a defense largely orchestrated by William Douglas O'Connor.

The celebrant of the "uniform hieroglyphic" receives surprisingly little attention in John T. Irwin's *American Hieroglyphics*. Whitman's interest in Egyptology is rehearsed to argue vaguely that *Leaves of Grass* is a kind of hieroglyphic Bible with characters and images which suggest the poet's return "to a childlike simplicity of character, to those radically simple, written characters of the original language of natural signs through which the poet's character is expressed." The poet's use of language is also the subject of Eric R. Birdsall, "Translating the Hints: Whitman's Theory of Poetry" (*WWR* 26:113–23). After noting that Whitman preferred the aboriginal names, he cites "A Song of the Rolling Earth" as the poet's clearest statement about words and reality. Of course, the point is not new. Nor is the conclusion that Whitman—like the English romantics before him—told the Truth by indirection.

John B. Mason also focuses on the poet's lack of faith in the ability of words to clothe the spirit ("Whitman at the Edge of Silence," *WWR* 26:11–18). Though the poet resists the transcendental notion that "silence represents a perfect rapport with Nature," he comes to the edge of silence himself in the "Calamus" poems and accepts it because language is meaningless between perfect comrades. Mason's observations overlook the loneliness that pervades those poems, but less satisfying is his "Questions and Answers in Whitman's 'Confab'" (*AL* 51:493–506), which examines the poet's "dialogical" poems to show how the persona "manages to converse rather than to perform." Whenever the reader's response is an essential part of the argument, it appears, the essay becomes an exercise in "creative reading" in which the obvious is sometimes taken out of the context that best serves the poem as a whole. In this case, the "Listener up there" of "Song of Myself" is identified as the reader. A more likely candidate, however, is the deity or Over-Soul—to whom the poet pleads for "Outlines! . . . for my brothers and sisters." And yet Timothy J. Lockyer appears to recreate entirely new contexts in "The Mocking Voice: Whitman's Poems of Doubt" (*WWR* 26:101–12), which attempts to divide what it cannot define (i.e., "poems of doubt") into classifications of "rhetorical" and "felt" doubt. Even more wildly subjective—though cleverly written—is Karl Keller's "Walt Whitman Camping" (*WWR* 26:138–44), which also appeared last year in *Odyssey* (*ALS*, 1979, p. 64). In "'Time's Accumulations to Justify the Past': Whitman's Evolving Structure in 'Autumn Rivulets'" (*ESQ* 26:137–48) Paul A. Lizotte tries to justify Whitman's final arrangement of *Leaves* by seeing "Autumn Rivulets" as an apt transition between the sorrowful poems of *Drum-Taps* and the "great poems of passage." But since the poems in this cluster were written at various times during Whitman's career (one as early as 1850), the essay really investigates the poet's editorial ability and not the poems as they originally unfolded during his earlier and more vital years. Final intention in Whitman's case often obscures the best of Whitman. Finally, Robert J. Scholnick in "Individual Identity and Democratic Culture: The Problem of Whitman's *Democratic Vistas*," *SEASA* 79, *Proceedings* [Southeastern Amer. Studies Assn.] (Tampa, Fla.: American Studies Press, 1979), pp. 17–23, presents an excellent survey of the essays that were ultimately consolidated in the 1871 *Democratic Vistas*. Whitman's solution to the opposing forces in democracy lay not in any kind of "culture," which was European, but in his concept of "Personalism" —which encouraged the individual "Americano" to retain his "selfhood" while also finding strength from the "vital human solidarity, inherent in democracy."

d. Criticism: Individual Works.   The annual attempt to divine the structure of "Song of Myself" is written by Ann Cleary, "The Prism and Night Vision: Walt Whitman's Use of Color in 'Song of Myself'" (*WWR* 26:92–100). Wisely, she does not claim that her reading is "definitive" but rather states that her observations will aid us in appreciating the fact that the poet's use of color in the poem "enhances not so much the pictorial description of an exterior world as the interior processes of growth in spiritual or psychological perception." The poet's application of specific colors decreases to suggest both a temporal movement from day to night and the prismatic effect of refracted poetic vision. "Song of Myself" is also the subject of Patrick V. Rizzo, "Whitman and a Cosmic Connection" (*WWR* 26:67–69), where a line in section 31 is traced to an early notebook jotting on astronomy. More diffusely argued is Richard Collins, "Whitman's Transcendent Corpus: 'Crossing Brooklyn Ferry' to History" (*Calamus* 19:24–39). With this poem Whitman overcomes his solipsism and can believe in immortality. For Lawrence Kramer the key poem is "As I Ebb'd with the Ocean of Life," where the inevitable conflict between the Romantic imagination and the natural world are resolved ("Ocean and Vision: Imaginative Dilemma in Wordsworth, Whitman, and Stevens," *JEGP* 79: 210–30). The poet, Kramer insists, is not thwarted by the "peals of distant ironical laughter" from the Eternal Shore in his search for the "Real-Me." Rather, by falling hopefully at the feet of God, he achieves "a final flawed resurgence."

In Martin Bickman's *The Unsounded Centre: Jungian Studies in American Romanticism* (N.Car.), its companion poem, "Out of the Cradle Endlessly Rocking" is also viewed as ultimately optimistic. "The poet's backward glance . . . ," writes Bickman, "is not solely a regressive activity, for the hope is that this circuitous night-sea journey through the past will bring a future expansion of self." This book is a judiciously cautious application of Jungian psychology to major American writers of the 19th century. It is also an attempt to show how the works of this period illuminate the origins and nature of that psychology. The central figure of concern is Emerson, and through his double-consciousness principle (which is similar to Jung's concept of individuation) Bickman examines several of Whitman's poems. What the poet discovers in "Out of the Cradle Endlessly Rocking" when he hears the word "Death," for example, is what Emerson discovers in "Experience"—that he exists. The explications of other poems are generally illuminated and not obscured by Bickman's use of Jungian psychology. If the *Unsounded Centre* is unsound in any way, it is perhaps in the author's use of the 1881 versions of the poems he discusses, while conceding that the best of Whitman lies in the first three editions of *Leaves of Grass*.

Even the more reckless psychological interpretations of the last 20 years seem almost tame compared to the "frontier research" of the New Scholasticism. In "The Prophetic Intent of 'Passage to India'" (*WWR* 26:26–29) Jon-K. Adams finds a master-disciple relationship between the persona-prophet and his readers. Never mind that *prophecy* is confused with poetic *vision*, for these terms as well as much of the poem are reconstructed in Adams' mind. Applying the same sort of verbal gymnastics but with slightly more cogent results is Philip M. Withim in "Mythic Awareness and Literary Form: Verbal Ritual in Whitman's 'Bivouac on a Mountain Side'" in *The Binding of Proteus* (pp. 111–22). Withim discovers in this minor poem, generally regarded as an example of the poet's depiction of life arrested for a moment, a subtext—or pretext—which permits the reader to view it as a rehearsal of Whitman's life. And, of course, "through our responsive reading the poem [also] becomes a ritualistic repetition of our own." Finally, the best that can be said for the chapter on Whitman in *Destructive Poetics; Heidegger and Modern American Poetry* (Columbia), pp. 131–79, by Paul A. Bové is that it is an exercise in deconstruction with lucid intervals. In a reading of *Leaves of Grass*, Bové argues that Whitman did not reject the past but apprehended it indirectly in the fasion of Heidegger, i.e., "rhetorically and destructively." Passages he quotes from the 1855 Preface provide the soundest evidence for his claim. When he turns to the poetry itself to demonstrate how *Leaves of Grass* "represents the beginnings of the Modern and Postmodern attempt to deconstruct archetypes," however, Bové falls back completely upon the rhetoric of the New Scholasticism and is less effective. Ultimately, his method is more novel than his meaning. And at times his interpretations take him too far from the text and the facts of Whitman's life—so far at one point that he insists that "Out of the Cradle" was written upon the death of Whitman's brother. The poet had five, of course, and none succumbed before 1863, four years after the first publication of the poem.

e. Affinities and Influences. By far the most comprehensive undertaking in the category of "influence" studies is Betsy Erkkila's *Walt Whitman Among the French* (Princeton). Part of the thesis is that Whitman participated in a literary tradition "that was French rather than English in its roots." From it he found a model for his attempt "to liberate America from the deeply rooted Puritan sensibility and habits of mind that he associated with England." One might think this account of how *Leaves of Grass* came to life in 1855 a bit reductionist; for in the context of the poet's earlier journalism and politics, it is more than likely that he had no such program in mind —that it was not so much America he was trying to liberate but himself. Nevertheless, the chapter on "France in Whitman" is often original and quite perceptive in its demonstration of the influence of Volney, Rousseau, Michelet, Sand (here tempering Esther Shephard's thesis in *Walt Whitman's Pose* [1938]), Hugo, Baudelaire, and others. The rest of the book is devoted to showing Whitman's influence in turn on French writers. Erkkila's explications of such writers as Rimbaud, Laforgue, Gide, Apollinaire, and others are penetrating and vibrant, to be sure. Yet at the same time Whitman tends—necessarily—to fall into the background of the gallery of writers she surveys. It is indeed Whitman *among* the French.

If Whitman influenced the French, he also wanted it to appear as if he influenced—or at least overshadowed—such contemporary poets as Emerson, Longfellow, Whittier, and Poe. In "Whitman on Other Writers: Controlled 'Graciousness' in *Specimen Days*" (*ESQ* 26:79–87) Kenneth M. Price compares the earlier caustic remarks about American writers with those in *Specimen Days* (1882) to suggest that Whitman no longer felt the "anxiety of influence." With Emerson in the grave, he lost his fear that the Concordian's reputation would eclipse his own and so could pose in the later criticism as the poet who subsumes his fellows and hence explains his age. Price is probably correct in his theory about the poet's motives, but he unfortunately relies on an essay whose use of information is misleading. And while it is true that Whitman's change in attitude closely follows Emerson's death (indeed, as late as 1879, on his trip west, he was harshly critical of his fellow writers in newspaper interviews), to say that Whitman felt threatened by Emerson is to miss the point that transcendental self-reliance—rightly received—made discipleship impossible. It brought Whitman not to Emerson but to himself. That both men clearly understood this aspect of their literary relationship is affirmed in an 1859 journal entry by Emerson and an 1880 essay by Whitman. Whitman's later attitude toward Emerson is also examined in Fritz Oehlschlaeger, "Whitman on Thoreau and Emerson: A Correction and a Speculation" (*WWR* 26:156–58). Again the evidence (that Whitman thought Thoreau's reputation would eventually outshine Emerson's) is tenuous and—in this case—exaggerated. Emerson also figures in James S. Leonard, "The Achievement of Rondure in 'Passage to India'" (*WWR* 26:129–38), where the poet's use of Rondure (through which he links man to his source in God) is viewed as similar to Emerson's concept of spiritual growth in "Circles."

The "whole story" of the Emerson-Whitman relationship, of course, has yet to be told, but some of the evidence is reviewed in Justin Kaplan's "'Half Song-Thrush, Half Alligator'" (*AH* 31:62–67). Of greater interest and originality is Alan Trachtenberg's "Whitman's Romance of the Body: A Note on 'This Compost'" in *Medicine and Literature*, pp. 189–99. Although Trachtenberg errs in placing the Boston Common debate over the merits of "Children of Adam" in 1856 instead of 1860, he is otherwise faithful to the facts in his assessment of Whitman's difference from Emerson with regard to the body. Citing the "transparent eye-ball" passage in *Nature*, he states that Emerson ultimately obliterates the body. This is nothing new, of course, but Trachtenberg's achievement is in explaining Whitman's "new ground" for poetry. In "This Compost" he finds a process (also at work in "Song of Myself") "of revulsion from and return to the body analogous to medical immunization." The difference between Emerson and Whitman is in what is *left*—"the oneness of leaf and leavings." In other words, Emerson's eye disembodies, whereas Whitman's restores eye to body and body to eye. The sum of Trachtenberg's essay is to say that Emerson is the poet of spiritual amelioration, that Whitman is the poet of Body and Soul, but he is the first observer of Whitman—to my knowledge—to note the pun on such words as "compost," "leavings," and "composure."

Charles Keminitz finds "As I Ebb'd with the Ocean of Life" specifically influenced by Hegel's contention that spirit is a mediating force which produces from itself opposing forces of the universe ("A

Construction of Hegelian Spirit in Whitman's 'As I Ebb'd with the Ocean of Life,' " *WWR* 26:59–63). The argument is vague, however, and also diminished by the probability that Whitman did not become familiar with the Hegelian dialectic until the late 1860s—almost a decade after the initial publication of the poem. Whitman also read the Persian poet Jalal al-Din Rumi (1207–73) in the 1860s, and so Ghulam M. Fazey compares the two to produce a few rather unoriginal observations about Whitman's so-called mysticism ("Images of the Divine in Rumi and Whitman," *CLS* 17:33–43). In another parallel study of little consequence, "Multidimensional Reality in Whitman and Tillich" (*WWR* 26:22–26), Galen R. Hanson says that the poet and the theologian both emphasize doubt as an element of faith. A fourth parallel study is made in "Parallels to Shamanism in 'The Sleepers' " (*WWR* 26:43–52). Here George B. Hutchinson finds a correspondence between Whitman's vision in the 1855 poem and the shamanic consciousness of North American aborigines. In another, H. Keith Monroe ("Tocqueville, Whitman and the Poetry of Democracy," *WWR* 26:52–58) attempts—with limited success—to show the influence of *Democracy in America* (1840) on *Leaves of Grass*. Finally, Jacqueline O. Padgett in "The Poet in War: Walt Whitman and Wolfgang Borchert" (*Monatshefte* 72:149–61) discusses Borchert's poetic response to World War II at Whitman's expense. Although Padgett sees the probable influence of *Leaves of Grass* on the German writer's definition of the poet's role in war, she also echoes Thomas Wentworth Higginson's chastisement of Whitman for not participating directly in the Civil War. Since Borchert did fight in his war, the argument goes, his treatment of war is more censorious and hence realistic.

The source for Whitman's place names is investigated in two articles this year. Allan Walker Read traces the poet's preference for the original name in "Walt Whitman's Attraction to Indian Name Places" (*LOS* 7:189–204), and Michael R. Dressman suggests that many of Whitman's place names for *Leaves of Grass* came from Samuel Griswold Goodrich's *Comprehensive Geography* (1855) in "Goodrich's *Geography* and Whitman's Place Names" (*WWR* 26:64–67). More ambitious is David W. Hiscoe, "Whitman's Use of the Middle Ages" (*AL* 51:477–92), which attempts to show that a clearer understanding of the poet's familiarity with medieval history will "clarify the nature of the resolution [Whitman] expects from his reader." Unfortunately, the piece is somewhat arbitrary in the application of its materials and rendered almost unreadable through its excessive (and tedious) use of quotations.

Similarities between *Leaves of Grass* and the works of two novelists round out this area of work in Whitman. In "Filament Out of Itself: The Exploring Selves of Walt Whitman and James Joyce" (*WWR* 26:3–10) Frederick L. Rusch compares two stages of emotional development in the persona of "Song of Myself" with the characters of Stephen Dedalus and Leopold Bloom. Less useful but focused on a more probable matter of influence is Elizabeth Balkman House, "*The Awakening*: Kate Chopin's 'Endlessly Rocking' Cycle" (*BSUF* 20[1979]:53–58). In an attempt to see Whitman's poem as a key to understanding whether Edna Pontellier's suicide is a personal victory or a defeat at the hands of society, House misreads the poem. For example, she compares the protagonist's "awakening" to desire with the *boy's* awakening to his vocation as a poet. Whitman, of course, makes it clear that his protagonist is a "man, yet by these tears a little boy again"—singing a reminiscence. What this comparison misses is the realization by each protagonist that the state of euphoria brought on by infatuation or personal love cannot last. And that the mockingbirds of "Out of the Cradle" and the lovers that stroll the beach in *The Awakening*—both "minding no time"—are only temporarily out of the reach of the sea, whose message in both cases is *Death*.

ii. Dickinson

a. **Bibliography, Editing.** Willis J. Buckingham's "Emily Dickinson: Annual Bibliography for 1978" (*DicS* 37:31–40) consists of about 100 items. Most were published in 1978, and brief annotations are provided for entries not adequately described by title.

The big disappointment in editing this year was the failure of the Harvard Press to publish R. W. Franklin's facsimile edition of the Dickinson poems in manuscript (now projected for 1981). The work that Franklin began in *The Editing of Emily Dickinson* (*ALS, 1967*, p. 53) continues to appear in bits and pieces, however. In "The Houghton Library Dickinson Manuscript 157" (*HLB* 28:245–57) he examines two stanzas written on a single sheet (H 157) to challenge Martha Dickinson Bianchi's inclusion of the second stanza as the conclusion to "A still Volcano—Life" and to modify Thomas H. Johnson's use of both stanzas as the conclusion of "I tie my Hat—I crease my shawl" and his own 1967 speculation that the second stanza was intended as alternative lines in the conclusion of "A Pit—Heaven Over it." The source of the editorial confusion, Franklin theorizes, was Dickinson's practice of using a separate sheet for overflow. Franklin also makes suggestions for restoring the sequence of sheets in several other manuscripts in "The Dickinson Packet 14—and 20, 10 and 26" (*PBSA* 73[1979]:348–55). The epic journey of another manuscript is traced in Philip Cronenwett, " 'We Play at Paste': A Footnote on an Emily Dickinson Manuscript" (*RALS* 10:28–32). One of the poems originally sent to Thomas Wentworth Higginson, "We play at Paste—" travelled some 7,000 miles and changed hands three times before returning to Amherst and the Jones Library.

b. **Biography.**   Emily Dickinson is viewed from a feminist standpoint (at least at the outset) in a generally accurate profile by Jean Gould in the opening chapter of her *American Women Poets: Pioneers of Modern Poetry* (Dodd, Mead), pp. 1–27. Few would quarrel with the proposition that Dickinson was "the foremost of her sex among those who brought about the revolution that eventually resulted in modern American poetry"; and yet many might wince at also being told that Whitman in comparison "shouted" the same ideas, that "he was a speechmaker," or that he wrote *Leaves of Grass* in the early 1840s. We are also told that none of Dickinson's male mentors had the vision to see the real worth of her poetry—the implication being that gender was solely to blame for the poet's failure to publish no more than seven of her poems. But generally correct in its biographical details if not always judicious in their use, the essay is obviously not intended as a view that sharply departs from the traditional scenario. If any of its speculations are possibly new, it is Gould's theory that the poet's agoraphobic ways had their source in the influence of the eccentric aunt for whom she was named. More speculative and interesting is Barbara Ann Clarke Mossberg's "Reconstruction in the House of Art: Emily Dickinson's 'I never had a mother' " in *The Lost Tradition*, pp. 128–38. Through a thematic and psycholinguistic study of selected poems and letters (based, unfortunately, on the belief that Dickinson's literary style was "fully fashioned" by the time she was 15), Mossberg argues that the poet attempted to edit her mother out of her poems and her life as a means of avoiding the feminine "martyrdom" which threatened to keep her from a literary world where beards were required. Mossberg's most original observation, however, is that Dickinson was rebelling against her mother at an age when most of the poet's contemporaries were grandmothers. More is needed in this area of the biography, it appears.

In "'One Unbroken Company': Religion and Emily Dickinson" (*NEQ* 53:62–75) Joan Burbick studies the poet's letters to Abiah Root and Susan Gilbert to challenge the notion that Dickinson's rebellion from the Christianity taught at Mount Holyoke Academy followed either the "motif of the puritan or romantic journey." To the contrary, she was drawn to its atmosphere of familial love but ultimately could not join her compatriots in accepting Christ because she suspected that the deity was piqued by the fact "That we had rather not with Him/ But with each other play." In a less compelling use of the letters, Jonathan Morse takes issue with Richard B. Sewall's interpretation of Dickinson's letter of 6 November 1858, to the Hollands ("Dickinson's Letter J. 195: A Source," *DicS* 37:29–30). Not as clear as it might be, the essay argues that in the letter Dickinson was not manifesting that her poetry derived from a need to relieve the "palsy" but that it served "as an emotional power whose verbal form was an ambiguous camouflage of trepidation and ruthless self-assurance." Such self-reliance came later according to Sylvia Bailey Shurbutt, who traces the image of royalty to find four stages in the poet's emotional development ("A Developing Self As Revealed through the Royalty Imagery in the Poems and Letters of Emily Dickinson," *ATQ* 42[1979]:167–76).

c. **Criticism: General.** The most successful study of Dickinson's poetry this year draws its insights from a number of critical methodologies: psychoanalysis, structuralism, literary history, Biblical exegesis, and a feminist view of culture and society. In *Women Writers and Poetic Identity: Dorothy Wordsworth, Emily Brontë, and Emily Dickinson* (Princeton) Margaret Homans sees Dickinson as the only one of the three poets (selected as examples of various degrees of success) to overcome the inhibitions produced by the male tradition in literature. Dickinson did so, Homans argues lucidly, by identifying herself with Eve, who learned from Satan—so the Genesis story tells us—not to trust the language of God and Adam. For God spoke to

Adam, not to Eve, and hence such language is real to the male poet but "fictive" to the female bard. Though Homans might have strengthened her argument a bit by citing Emerson's definition of the poet as "Adam in the garden again," she nevertheless succeeds in demonstrating Dickinson's sense of linguistic dislocation. Emerson's language, as it came down from Adam (the original namer), was an imperfect emblem to Dickinson (as it was to Eve). Homans' achievement is to apply Emerson's caveat about the corruption of language to the dilemma of the female poet. "Right" may have at one time meant "straight," but before that it meant something else. In other words, Emerson's language is *learned*, the property of the ego. Dickinson, consequently, was forced beyond that language to the language of the id (because it precedes the ego in the sequence of thought). Her poetry, therefore, is often more oblique and pessimistic than Emerson's writings, for its quest is not Emerson's nature (or "Mother Nature") but actual *unnameable* nature. Along this line, John Reiss argues for a distinction between Emersonian self-reliance, which transcends nature or the Not-Me, and Dickinsonian self-reliance, in which nature remains a stranger: "For most who cite nature, nature reflects their own image. Those who can penetrate nature's reflection see the abyss" ("Emily Dickinson's Self-Reliance," *DicS* 38:25–33). For David B. Hopes as well the referents of Dickinson's metaphors are within rather than without. In this sense, it is suggested in "The Uses of Metaphor in Emily Dickinson's Poetry" (*DicS* 38:12–20) that the poet anticipated the Imagists.

Martin Bickman's analysis of Dickinson is more penetrating than his reading of Whitman in *The Unsounded Centre* (discussed above). Using at one point Ellen Greenberger's "Fantasies of Women Confronting Death," he makes some of his most original statements about Dickinson's theme of Love and Death. Here especially Jungian thought lends a new perspective and coherence to Dickinson, most immediately Jung's observation that the gut meaning of immortality is "simply a psychic activity that transcends the limits of consciousness." Joan Burbick in "Emily Dickinson and the Revenge of the Nerves" (*WS* 7:95–109) also examines the theme of Love and Death in conjunction with the phenomenon of neurosis common to 19th-century women, including Dickinson's mother. The poetry, Burbick maintains, is a cultural analysis of the pleasure/pain principle—as it ponders the need for both on the "death row" of life. In Joanne Feit

Diehl's "Dickinson and the American Self" (*ESQ* 26:1–9), Death is more important than Love to Dickinson, although the poet's focus upon Death is charged with a certain eroticism. Here, however, the feminist perspective may be leading the critic to false distinctions. Whereas the poet's male contemporaries (such as Emerson and Whitman) were concerned with dissolving the dualism of the Me and the Not-Me, Dickinson was compelled to explore that dualism. In other words, she—more than her male counterparts—experienced the tension between the Self and Death because of its antithetical male presence. Because of its male gender, Death was only a "half perceived" erotic presence. Yet one must ask how Dickinson's perception is radically different from, say, Whitman's in "Out of the Cradle Endlessly Rocking," where the protagonist begs for "some clew." Another concerned with the "gender" question is James L. Machor in "Emily Dickinson and the Feminine Rhetoric" (*ArQ* 36:131–46). A sociolinguistic study, it compares Dickinson's poetry with that of both her male and female contemporaries to conclude that Dickinson merely affects feminine timidity to achieve a more trenchant verse and at the same time creates a feminist rhetoric that transcends "limitations which the term implies."

Dickinson's poetry bridges the gap between mind and nature, according to Suzanne Juhasz in "'To Make a Prairie': Language and Form in Emily Dickinson's Poems About Mental Experience" (*BSUF* 21:12–25). Rambling in its argument, the essay fails to establish a clear difference between mind and matter. More to the point is David L. Green's "Emily Dickinson: The Spatial Drama of Centering" (*ELWIU* 7:191–200), which sees the poetry as using the image of the house as a poetic sanctuary where the opposing forces of belief and doubt are consolidated. Most useful is Green's observation about the company the poet kept in her solitude. Her relationship with others is probed in Greg Johnson, "'Broken Mathematics': Emily Dickinson's Concept of Ratio" (*CP* 13:21–26). Finally, Alan Helms examines the silence in the poetry that evolved from the poet's solitude. In "The Sense of Punctuation" (*YR* 69:177–96), an essay focusing on a number of American poets and their systems of silence, he notes that Dickinson's use of the dash implies a continuum of action beyond the actual descriptions in the poems. The essay is a useful one in Dickinson's case (though not so much in Whitman's)—and its lesson is effectively dramatized when Helms compares the version of

"After great pain" from the Johnson edition with one in which the
dashes have been removed.

d. **Criticism: Individual Works.** Perhaps more than any other
American poet, Emily Dickinson draws out the most exotic, bizarre,
and oblique interpretations from her critics. Theories about her work
as a whole are usually the safest and the soundest; for when the paradigms are applied to the poems individually, they frequently dissolve
into obscurity or blatant "misreadings." Marcella Taylor, for example,
indulges in creative reading when she detects the motifs of the Shaman experience in the poems written around 1862 ("Shaman Motifs in
the Poetry of Emily Dickinson," *DicS* 38:1–11). Greg Johnson, on the
other hand, is more precise in tracing the image of the pearl in the
poetry to suggest how it signifies the development and expression of
Dickinson's feminine identity ("'A Pearl of Great Price': The Identity of Emily Dickinson," *ESQ* 26:202–15). In expanding his thesis
through an analysis of "She rose to His Requirement—dropt," however, he overlooks the work of Gilbert and Gubar's *The Madwoman
in the Attic* (pp. 588–89) by saying that the "distinctly feminist perspective here has been missed by most of Dickinson's critics, who
have read the poem as a description of joyful marriage." In "Elegy
and Immortality: Emily Dickinson's 'Lay this Laurel on the One'"
(*ESQ* 26:10–15) Ronald A. Sudol thinks this 1877 poem marks an
important transition in Dickinson's attitude toward death as it is
revealed in the elegies. Thereafter, she shifts from affirming immortality to celebrating mortality.

The popular "I like to see it lap the miles" is linked to the theme
of progress in Hawthorne's "Celestial Railroad" and Thoreau's comments on the train in *Walden* by Patrick F. O'Connell, "Emily Dickinson's Train: Iron Horse or 'Rough Beast'?" (*AL* 52:469–74). The
poem, says O'Connell, is "a pointed commentary on the perennial
human capacity to create idols, and an ironic warning of impending
technological catastrophe." Although the poet seldom displayed an
extended interest in the external world around her, Curtis Dahl also
sees evidence of such awareness (initially, at least in "'To Fight
Aloud' and Tennyson's 'The Charge of the Light Brigade': Dickinson
on Tennyson" (*NEQ* 52[1979]:94–99). The poem, he suggests, is a
playful—and perhaps disapproving—reply to Tennyson's jingoism.
In her satire of the cavalry charge, she transforms the outward heroic

action into an image of the solitary soul's agonized struggle with it-self. And even "Success is counted sweetest" is more emotional than philosophical in the opinion of Brenda Murphy in "Emily Dickinson's Use of Definition by Antithesis" (*DicS* 38:21–24). The essay, how-ever, describes itself when calling the poem an intuitive rather than a rational understanding (of the concept of success).

For Seymour Gross and Frank Rashid, Dickinson anticipated the feminist revolution of the 1970s (as it is envisioned in Erica Jong's *Fear of Flying*). In "Emily Dickinson and the Erotic" (*DicS* 37:25–28), they see "A Bee His burnished Carriage" as a version, as it were, of one of Whitman's "native moments" in "Children of Adam." In other words, the bee is the male lover who assaults the female (the rose) without prior arrangement. Unlike the women of the Victorian Age in America, "the female figure exhibits no phallic fear of the male. . . ." Sexuality for Dickinson, then, is viewed from two different angles. Gross and Rashid examine the poet's attitudes about the male-female relationship to find a female for whom—like Jong's fe-male—the "purest thing" is the coupling with a total stranger. On the other hand, Diehl (see above, p. 85) finds a female who suffers anxiety over the half-perceived male presence. Diehl, of course, is concerned ultimately with the poet who confronts death, but a more quotidian Dickinson is found in "What Soft—Cherubic Creatures—" by Rochie Whittington Lawes in "Emily Dickinson and 'Dimity Convictions'" (*UMSE* 1[n.s.]:127–28). Because we too often forget that the poet was a woman in the pre-wash-and-wear age, we have overlooked the possibility that "dimity" in the poem refers to a fine, thin, corded fabric whose characteristics suggest that the convictions of the "Cherubic creatures" were undeviating, durable, shallow, and cool.

Two further explications do their work in the context of the poet's lifelong *angst*. Jennijoy LaBelle in "Savior! I've no one else to tell" (*Expl* 38:34–35) identifies the "imperial Heart" in line 7 of the poem as the same as that of the "Master" letters. LaBelle also assumes—without offering any new evidence—that the intended recipient of these bizarre letters was the Reverend Charles Wadsworth. But Dickinson was troubled by a number of issues according to David L. Green in "You've seen Balloons set—Haven't You?" (*DicS* 37:11–18). Not always clearly argued, the interpretation suggests that the "poem rises from [Dickinson's] depiction of the vivid splendor of popular balloon ascents to speak of her own troubled mind" as it circles about issues involving victory and defeat. "One of these," Green writes, "centers around [sic] her questioning the location of paradise."

e. **Affinities and Influences.** The "source" department in Dickinson studies is largely overshadowed by the "creative readings" that the Myth readily invites. Indeed, the material in this category amounts to three endeavors. Vincent J. Cleary in "Emily Dickinson's Classical Education" (*ELN* 28:119–29) surveys the evidence in the poet's schoolbooks, home books, and poetry to conclude that Dickinson was influenced by the classics "in more than a merely formal way." George Monteiro in "I reason Earth is Short" (*Expl* 38:23–25) finds a parallel between the poem and a passage entitled "The Significance of Life" in W. R. Greg's *Enigmas* (1873). Both use the refrain "what of that?" but the tone of Greg's piece is "affirmatively religious," whereas Dickinson's is "off-handedly ironic." Dickinson's sense of absence is also traced in Heather McClave's "Emily Dickinson: The Missing All" (*SHR* 14:1–12). She presents evidence from the letters and poems to suggest that Dickinson followed Emerson's advice in "Circles" and grew stronger from each loss in life: "To miss you, Sue, is power./ The stimulus of loss makes most Possession mean." Of course, there is no clear evidence that Dickinson read this Emerson essay. Assuming she did, however, McClave stops short of anything more than a superficial comparison. For "Circles," though early in the Emerson canon, reveals a strain of pessimism that Dickinson could not have missed. Inherent in the essay is its concept of the Unachieved: it is both the "inspirer and condemner of every success." In other words, as Dickinson suggests in "I like a look of Agony," the strength that Emerson hints at in his essay is essentially Dickinson's "homely Anguish strung."

Texas A&M University

6. Mark Twain

Louis J. Budd

The popular interest in Mark Twain rolls on like the national debt, though we have no comprehensive standard for measuring the flood of print and radio or TV programs that must hourly find something to palm off as content. It is impossible to determine who absorbs rather than merely endures what. For instance, what will the young readers of *Redbook* remember from "Who Wrote This Letter?" It plays a quick mystery-game with the charming message to a daughter that Papa composed on behalf of Santa Claus. The first clue is that the author is "usually pictured wearing a white suit." For the clientele of *Writer's Digest* Twain was interviewed through patched-up quotations. The serious point is that he is continually being reshaped in the public mind, seen as eager for more news about him. *TV Guide* thought it worthwhile to run a few paragraphs by Mark Harris about dramatizing "The Man That Corrupted Hadleyburg" and thus puff the screening of the production. Appropriately, Thomas A. Tenney's annual supplement to his *Reference Guide* (1977) now has a section on television. A happy result of such broad interest is that most writers who want to tap it assume a good level of knowledge out there and so do their homework. The section on Twain ("The Man in the White Suit") in Joseph Epstein's *Ambition: The Secret Passion* (Dutton) echoes the much-sung tune that he was "split down the middle," but it does use the recent arrangements of it.

A quantifiable kind of interest is coming from rare-book circles. In "Collecting Mark Twain: A Popular Author and His Market" (*BCM* 4,iv[1979]:1,6–9) J. W. Warnick reports that Twain ranks with Steinbeck and Faulkner as the hottest commodity and that prices for his books (like everything else, illogically) are rising faster than the rate of inflation. Alan Gribben's recent spate of scholarship has given the process extra lift. "Reconstructing Mark Twain's Library" (*ABBW* 66:755–73) sums up what his research means to dealers, less likely than ever to let a bargain slip past. For another kind of guidance, uncertain scholars can turn to Tenney's introduction for his "Fourth Annual Supplement" (*ALR* 13:161–224), which sounds a cogent warning against mistakes such as failing to use the most dependable texts but also lays out leads for anybody with more enthusiasm than focused ideas for doing original work. For all scholars Tenney continues to be indispensable as he unearths lost items and covers the latest year more thoroughly than anybody else, while his annotations show further precision because of his experience. Keeping up with Tenney will show that the road is always getting steeper, but it at least held a breathing space this year with Alan Gribben's two-part "Removing Mark Twain's Mask: A Decade of Criticism and Scholarship" (*ESQ* 26:100–108,149–71). He is objective without rancor and balanced without indecisiveness, and his mixture of evaluation and summary through quotation often lets readers judge for themselves. He likewise ends with suggestions for fresh research and criticism. A sharp beginner can become a quasi-expert and even get himself into Tenney's next supplement.

i. Primary Works

The Mark Twain Papers Edition steadily publishes more of its manuscript holdings so that scholars will eventually be spared the pleasant trouble of going to Berkeley. Edited by Robert Pack Browning, Michael B. Frank, and Lin Salamo, *Mark Twain's Notebooks & Journals, Volume III* (*1883–1891*) (Calif., 1979) continues a meticulous process: "Insofar as print can render the idiosyncrasies of inscription . . . this volume presents every entry that Clemens made . . . in its original, often unfinished form." This process has allowed time for serendipity and hunches and therefore some stunning deductions for which Twain himself would be grateful since he could not always recover the meaning of his scribbles. The sophisticated, cogent notes often comment on the related literary projects. Unfortunately, *N&J:3* may be less exciting, relative to the years it covers, than the first two volumes. In a review-essay on all three, Guy A. Cardwell (*ALR* 13:290–98) spells out the romantic expectation that a writer's notebooks will reveal the authentic, elusive "self." So far anyway, Cardwell concludes, "At best the author of the notebooks could not have been more than a hack writer for popular magazines and cheap publishers." It takes a true Romantic to hold that when creating fiction Twain's psyche emanated profundities and subtleties he could not even suggest elsewhere.

The Iowa/California Edition chose the path of virtue rather than sales with its three-legged *The Adventures of Tom Sawyer; Tom Sawyer Abroad; Tom Sawyer, Detective* (Calif.), edited by John C. Gerber, Paul Baender, and Terry Firkins. The last novel, a big handicap for any horse to carry, still awaits the discovery of any depths even if explication has fanned out beyond the major Twain books. As a deluxe feature, the omnibus volume prints both an uncluttered reading text and a genetic version of the "Boy's Manuscript" or ur-*Tom Sawyer*. As for introductions, the one to *Tom Sawyer Abroad* contributes most, partly because that novel has not been so thoroughly sifted as a try-your-luck diamond mine for tourists; some interesting parallels with both *A Connecticut Yankee* and the straight travel books are mapped. Also, it turns out, this edition can claim lengthy and vital restorations of the intended text.

John S. Tuckey has edited *Which Was the Dream?* and *Fables of Man* for the Mark Twain Papers. Now he has chosen the most saturnine pieces from those two fat tomes, to produce the general-audience selection (minus the textual editing documentation), *The Devil's Race Track, Mark Twain's Great Dark Writings: The Best from "Which Was the Dream?" and "Fables of Man"* (Calif.). His Introduction matches Bernard DeVoto in *Mark Twain at Work* (1942) for imaginative penetration. He achieves the impression that he is willing and also able to go either way, that is, to find pessimism or a rebounding vitality, depending on the piece discussed. In both veins his tone avoids the portentous, a relief if only because Twain used it too often in his old age. From the heart of his finest years as a writer comes Everett Emerson's "A Send-Off for Joe Goodman: Mark Twain's 'The Carson Fossil-Footprints'" (*RALS* 10:71–78). While very busy in 1884 he took the time to compose, evidently free of charge, a virtually overlooked and even suspect sketch for an ill-fated magazine being founded by an associate from his Nevada days. Though Emerson is careful not to claim too much for the sketch he authenticates, it is intriguing as a proof of how Twain could revert to the raucous spirit, localized burlesque, and pseudohoaxing vein of 1862–64.

ii. Biography

The most interesting new facts bearing on Twain's life come through
Raymond Martin Bell, *The Ancestry of Samuel Clemens, Grandfather
of Mark Twain* (mimeographed for the author), which manages to
track the male family line from Virginia to Pennsylvania to Massachusetts to 16th-century England. These progenitors were farmers,
not regicides or gentry, though the great scion's misstatements rose
from ignorance, not pretension. Twain (and William Faulkner)
would have enjoyed Bell's booklet, which will energize the biographers who believe greatly in heredity. A nearer look backward
comes through James M. Cox's too brief introduction for a reprinting
(New York: Chelsea House) of the three-volume set of A. B. Paine's
biography (1912). Unsurprisingly, Cox rejects the saccharine portrait
of Olivia Clemens, whom Paine did not meet and who deserved
much better, but he convincingly argues that Paine used well the
day-to-day intimacy with his future subject, learning to discount his
yarning and petty rages without undervaluing his unique virtues.
Cox concludes that Paine's work, whatever its faults, projected an
"impression" of a deeply vibrant personality and "remains the most
complete and authentic account yet written of Mark Twain as a
presence." In—one suspects—a commissioned essay, Robert H. Hirst's
"Mark Twain Becomes a Writer" (*WilsonQ* 4,iv:168–81) broadly
sketches a theory that in 1865–66 a dissatisfied reporter settled upon
humor as a vocation but consoled himself for such a low-status profession by resolving to "learn both how and what to preach" without
toppling into dullness and to perfect eventually "his discovery of how
to use a powerful wit to a high ethical purpose." It may be that we
have relaxed enough toward Victorian didacticism to reconsider
Hirst's thesis productively.

Otherwise, the most active biographical salient is the persisting
drive of the Southern Renaissance to draft Twain as a forebear. J. V.
Ridgely in his *Nineteenth-Century Southern Literature* (Kentucky)
reasonably finds criticism of Reconstruction society in *Life on the
Mississippi, Adventures of Huckleberry Finn,* and *Pudd'nhead Wilson* but decides that while Twain "could not go home again . . . that
home forever burned in his blood. It was 'the Southerner' in him
that gave him his most powerful themes." Louis D. Rubin, Jr., who
has made the point before, returns to it with more finesse in "Mark

Twain's South: Tom and Huck" (in *The American South*). More particularly he compares the "Old Times" essays and *Tom Sawyer* to elaborate the argument that only fiction could free up the memories of the violence, terror, pain, and injustice associated with Hannibal. Rubin also contends persuasively that Twain never portrayed himself as an adult southerner because he was ashamed of the social and racial attitudes he had held during the late 1850s. In a related interior analysis, Leland Krauth in "Mark Twain Fights Sam Clemens' Duel" (*MissQ* 33:141–53) compares three widely spaced accounts of the aborted attempt to play the "hot-blooded Southern gentleman" in 1864; sensitively, Krauth infers that Twain felt he had betrayed his heritage by skipping out but also that he resented the foolishness of the "manly role" which it prescribed. Otherwise, the stabs at biography look routine. If Jeffrey Steinbrink had used unpublished archives he might have gone further with "Mark Twain and Joe Twichell: Sublime Pedestrians" (*MTJ* 20,iii:1–6), might have come up with penetrating reasons—still needed—why the irreverent humorist kept up so cordial a friendship with a conventionally doctrinal preacher. Though Emmanuel Diel in "Mark Twain's Failure: Sexual Women Characters" (*SJS* 5,i(1979):47–59) does underline how frequently Twain picked 15 as the age when sexuality blossoms, he loses our confidence by classing *1601* as "pornography." Overall, Twain biography is still one of those "trouble spots" that looks hopelessly at odds, and I wonder if its conciliator is yet even in his or her cradle.

iii. General Interpretation

A historian, Wayne Mixon, in his *Southern Writers and the New South Movement, 1865–1913* (N.Car.) unexpectedly makes *The Gilded Age* his longest example of Twain's tension between nostalgia and anger concerning his native section. But Mixon sounds like those scholars who seize all handy territory when he argues that England, after it is shaped up by the Connecticut Yankee, "functions as an allegory of the New South." At least he adds support for those who perceive Twain as tied closely to current events. Likewise, Lawrence I. Berkove in "The Free Man of Color in *The Grandissimes* and Works by Harris and Mark Twain" (*SoQ* 18,iv:60–73) at least reminds us that literary friendships as well as the course of politics kept Twain sensitized to the "empty freedom" of the former slaves.

As thoroughly seasoned as he is learned, William M. Gibson carves out a far richer set of comparisons in *Theodore Roosevelt among the Humorists: W. D. Howells, Mark Twain, and Mr. Dooley* (Tenn.). Resisting the appeal of playing up Twainian invective, he demonstrates that his trio were shrewder than the public about the President and wiser than he about how its affairs were progressing. In "From Eden to the Dark Ages: Images of History in Mark Twain" (*CRevAS* 11:151–74) Nadia Khouri diagrams the sweep of Western culture on a much more abstract level yet confronts each of Twain's major books to emerge with the freshest commentary in several years on his social-political ideas. Her argument, very succinctly written, has to be left for tenacious readers. They may start off better if they know that she explores a dialectic between Twain's "cosmogony"—a myth of America as the Earthly Paradise—and his perceptions that events perversely denied it, forcing him to move outside of reality to preserve his model. More specifically, she explains for me how he "flattens . . . historical problems, even though their particular character is sensitively exhibited" and why he becomes a "naturalizer of myth and an allegorizer of immediate" society.

In Jeffrey L. Duncan's luminously graceful "The Empirical and the Ideal in Mark Twain" (*PMLA* 95:201–12) the flattening comes at Twain's expense through a series of generalizations ("humor is based in philosophical idealism," "by definition civilizations means a fallen state of affairs"). He concentrates on *Huckleberry Finn, A Connecticut Yankee,* and *The Mysterious Stranger* to assert that Twain finally embraced the "ideal of pure nothingness." Incidentally, Duncan drew a brickbat from Dorys C. Grover (*PMLA* 95:879–80) for arguing from the Paine-Duneka text, and he is also the example behind Tenney's protest against using a Dell edition for scholarly work. Less ambitiously and more inductively, Susan K. Harris in "'This Peace, This Deep Contentment': Images of Temporal Freedom in the Writings of Mark Twain" (*ELWIU* 7:201–12) starts from the "moments of repose" in both his life and his fiction. She finds them characterized by images of water and of space that marked a liberation from the historical present and by a lifelong movement toward a "disembodied mind, roaming" above reality, as in the Printshop version of *The Mysterious Stranger.* Limiting the horizon to literature, Joseph H. Harkey in "Mark Twain's Knights and Squires" (*MTJ* 20,iii:6–13) stretches the meanings of *Don Quixote* in order to account for too much of Twain, but all those intending to advance the subject along some precise tangent can now start from his footnotes. A seemingly narrow approach by Jesse Bier in "A Note on Twain and Hemingway" (*MQ* 21:261–65) builds up very meaningfully. By comparing the stylistics of passages from *Huckleberry Finn* and *The Sun Also Rises* he manages to indicate both how Twain's "self-effacement" into the "heard voice" was revolutionary and why he got that famous tribute in *The Green Hills of Africa*. A full-scale analysis might not take us much further, and more might even add up to less.

In Alan Gribben's *Mark Twain's Library: A Reconstruction* (Hall) generous detail produces a work with many applications that become evident when one tries to classify it as general study, bibliography, or archive for inner biography or for literary source-hunters. His two volumes result from years of patience as much as effort, organized as a dissertation in 1974 before further steps into print. He eventually refined his criteria and format into a highly useful and usable monument of research. Though it also covers the magazines Twain subscribed to or read, the plays he attended, and the songs he liked, its core is the books he owned (or just borrowed). Gribben establishes the history, contents, and present whereabouts of Twain's collection. This march of facts stops for mini-essays on the writers, often outside belles lettres, whom he pondered with unusual pleasure or rancor, visible in his marginalia. Gribben's project is so ambitious that he disclaims completeness, and more of Twain's books or particulars on his use of them will surely turn up. But Gribben's work will tell researchers whether their findings are new. Likewise, through unique interests or simply luck others will make further connections between Twain's library and his writings, but Gribben will have supplied the grid. Meanwhile, his two volumes will rekindle the debate about the quality of Twain's mind and will support a kinder verdict than the notebooks.

iv. Individual Works

Twain's writing from the 1860s is still relatively neglected though as more volumes of the early tales and sketches appear the activity will pick up. For literary analysis nobody ventured back further than Robert Regan's witty and excellent "*The Innocents Abroad*: A Rough-

hewn Monument" (in *American Bypaths,* pp. 187-211). Without
pretending to spring a surprise in arguing for the native distinctness
of Twain's first sustained book, he evolves an illuminating contrast
between the theme of male awareness or solidarity and the narrator's
drift into a personal feud with the Pilgrims. Intensifying some recent
approaches, in "Realistic Style and the Problem of Context in *The
Innocents Abroad* and *Roughing It*" (*AL* 52:33-49) Philip D. Beidler
examines Twain's aesthetic development as a self-contained process.
He takes the prefaces to the travel books as solemn, careful statements of artistic principle, for instance. Gradually he does expand his
key phrases to include attitudes toward experience, but his formalist
persuasions even encourage crediting the tacked-on Hawaii section
with a "kind of large scale 'contextual logic.'" He presumably would
reject Howard Mumford Jones's quick perception in "The Allure of
the West" (*HLB* 28:19-32) that *Roughing It* "contains virtually
every sort of literary genre in miniature." Starting instead from a
biographical base, Forrest G. Robinson in "'Seeing the Elephant':
Some Perspectives on Mark Twain's *Roughing It*" (*AmerS* 21,ii:43-
64) takes an overdue approach that would work better if he had
examined some of the unpublished letters. He compares Twain's
gritty realities of 1862-64 with the implied autobiography in the
western book and moves into questioning its currently accepted
counterpoint of greenhorn and benign old-timer. In effect he challenges Paine, who still rules the 1860s because Justin Kaplan chose to
start so late.

Joining Mixon's emphasis on *The Gilded Age,* Ralph E. Luker's
"The Lost World of Garry Wills" (*SAQ* 79:1-16) sees it as an influential dramatization of rage at the failure of the liberal tradition.
The river-days series is far more quickly rising in stature: as an integrated fiction rather than the warm-up for a travel book. Though
Leland Krauth in "The Proper Pilot: A New Look at 'Old Times on
the Mississippi'" (*WIRS* 2[1979]:52-69) tries that tack, his major
insight evaluates the cub as the readers of the *Atlantic Monthly* might
have done; undazzled by the humor he convincingly, indeed im-
pressively, elicits the adult Twain persona and his baggage of socio-
cultural values. With "The Two Pilots: Deism and Calvinism in Mark
Twain's *Old Times on the Mississippi*" (*ArAA* 5:87-98), Ronald J.
Gervais insists on a religiously based dichotomy between a loss of
innocence and a gain of manipulative power. In several ways the

larger pattern is familiar, while Gervais' narrowed terms may seem
more neat than accurate and may demand a darker conclusion than
the text itself. The readings of Twain's Hannibal novel are also getting gloomier, if possible. Cynthia Griffin Wolff in *"The Adventures
of Tom Sawyer*: A Nightmare Vision of American Boyhood" (*MR*
21:637–52) begins with the hero resentfully "adrift in a matriarchal
world," identifies Injun Joe as his "shadow self, a potential for ret-
rogression and destructiveness," and explores the cave as a "remnant
of man's prehistory." Unfortunately, Joe's death signals neither a release nor an exorcism but a harsh denial of Tom's healthy instincts
—leaving those of us who have warm memories of the novel feeling
jejune. We can thank John R. Byers, Jr., for a chance to escape to
neutral factuality. In "A Hannibal Summer: The Framework of *The
Adventures of Tom Sawyer*" (*SAF* 8:81–88) he charts the "slow but
steady progression of a very long" vacation. His article will not sink
into the deep and dank tarn of disposable scholarship.

Huckleberry Finn's annual consignment was heavy, proving that
the famous raft has buoyancy beyond natural law. Furthermore, it
drifts easily with sudden currents such as the interest in the concept
of Homo ludens or the play instinct, which also comes out gloomily
for most Twainians these days. Bruce Michelson's "Huck and the
Games of the World" (*ALR* 13:108–21) begins unimpeachably with
Twain's "lifelong obsession with play and games," then expands into
the proposition that the characters in *Huckleberry Finn* make "games
out of everything," such as the feud. This "wanton playfulness" results in a world where "selfishness, murder, and cruelty masquerade"
as "harmless practical joking." By the climax of the argument any
room for buffo comedy has been preempted, but the essay does close
with the beguiling judgment that it was the "perishability and betrayal" of the play spirit that saddened the novel's underlying tone.
In "From *Tom Sawyer* to *Huckleberry Finn*: Toward Godly Play"
(*SAF* 8:183–202) Michael Oriard lays down a wider definition of
Homo ludens. Then he raises standards until only Huck, especially
in the later novel, is the one "true player" for whom even reality "*is*
play." The peroration soars to the idea that such a commitment makes
him "the truly *religious* person" because God's "creation of life is
the model for all play." That leaves me gravely intimidated by Huck.
Again, it is a relief to consider Stanford W. Gregory, Jr., and Jerry
M. Lewis ("Huck Finn and the Game Model Gloss," *Qualitative*

Sociology 3:136–51) who—so far as the *ALS* audience cares—simply
testify to the fame of the novel by using it as a generally known and
transparent (hah!) text to exemplify the game metaphor for social
scientists.

Joining several recent commonplaces, Brook Thomas in "Language and Identity in the Adventures of Huckleberry Finn" (*MTJ*
20,iii:17–21) reasons (through words) that Twain meant to show
that all language ends in a "lie" and so the inherent misrepresentations drive Huck into taciturnity and flight. Thomas does not go on to
Twain's indictment elsewhere that some of the worst lying springs
from silence, insincere action, or even inaction. What will poor Huck
do if he learns to agree with that? On the religious front, more lively
of late, Raymond Benoit in "Again with Fair Creation: Holy Places
in American Literature" (*Prospects* 5:315–30) admits the raft into
the five classic passages where "momentarily the spiritual and the
material draw incarnationally together." Depth psychology is old
news except for the fact that Keith M. Opdahl's "You'll Be Sorry
When I'm Dead': Child-Adult Relations in *Huck Finn*" (*MFS* 25:
613–24) raises it to a bright prognosis. The "hidden anger" toward
his elders in Huck, who dreams subconsciously of "revenge" for their
inadequacies, is cleansed through respect for Jim. However, this
heartening analysis leaves Opdahl slightly perplexed about the final
chapters.

Sociopolitical approaches—my bias, I should admit—got their
share of attention. After laying out an abstract pattern that looks
more complicated than it is, Thomas Weaver and Merline A. Williams in "Mark Twain's Jim: Identity as an Index to Cultural Attitudes" (*ALR* 13:19–30) support the thesis that Jim has been interpreted through the stereotypes held by critics, who ordinarily share
the prejudices of their times. Objective whites are finally ready to
face the possibility that Jim, an experienced adult, is a "crafty, calculating student of human behavior" or, more immediately, manipulates Huck into helping him. To be sure, this reverse liberalism may
seem skewed in its turn when it is tested against Twain's black characters after Jim or even a later Jim. Michael Wilding's "The False
Freedoms of *Huckleberry Finn*," the first chapter of *Political Fictions* (Routledge), takes a still crowded path in emphasizing the
rejection of corrupt society as the guiding theme; his margin of
freshness, if any, lies in presenting Huck as beset from both sides

by falsely attractive choices, either "adult" respectability or Tom's make-believe. Wilding, a British critic, matches American expansiveness in acclaiming a "positive" flight toward the "possibility of creating a new society in the uncivilized frontier." By contrast Terence Martin, with "The Negative Character in American Fiction" (in *Toward a New American Literary History*, pp. 230–43) shines because he takes a reflective tone and reinforces Huck with three other eminent fictional heroes who "measure the world in which we live by the worlds in which they are unable to live." While this approach agrees with Wilding that Huck renounces society, it does not saddle Twain with paradisal dreams about a region where he had "seen the elephant."

As with *Tom Sawyer* it is a relief to confront the appeals to substantive fact. In "The Historical Ending of *Adventures of Huckleberry Finn*: How Nigger Jim Was Set Free" (*ALR* 13:280–83) L. Moffitt Cecil defends the Evasion sequence as a commentary on how slowly the nation was fulfilling its duty of making the ex-slave free in practice. Working entirely from within the text, Michael G. Miller's "Geography and Structure in *Huckleberry Finn*" (*SNNTS* 12: 192–209) maps the raft's journey. He finds an "astonishing accuracy concerning travel time, river distances, and landscape description"—but only through the feud (chapters 17–18), that is, where the manuscript stopped before Twain's revisit of 1882. Surprisingly, the rest of the novel blurred such details and changed from a "linear" to a "bipolar" pattern of repulsion between raft and shore, eventuating in Huck's flight west. I wish a pollster could tell us how many critics know that Henry Nash Smith, while certainly not recanting, has expressed uneasiness that the bipolar theory has become almost dogma.

Some critics should also notice that Smith's introduction to the Iowa/California Edition of *A Connecticut Yankee* (*ALS* 1979:83,91) does not insist on his earlier, much seconded view that the covert message attacks 19th-century technology. In "Hank Morgan as American Individualist" (*MTJ* 22,ii:19–21) Deborah Berger Turnbull carries the case against the Yankee so far as to need to grant him "some good qualities." Donald E. Winters, "The Utopianism of Survival: Bellamy's *Looking Backward* and Twain's *A Connecticut Yankee*" (*AmerS* 21,i:23–38), goes to social psychiatrist Robert Jay Lifton for a rationale before again judging that Hank's faith in technology causes a hardening cruelty toward humankind. A potentially more literary perspective is added by Darko Suvin in *Metamorphoses of Science Fiction: On the Poetics and History of a Literary Genre* (Yale, 1979). Lately the admirers of sci-fi have searched the academic canon for figures besides Poe, and Twain stands out as a likely prospect with *A Connecticut Yankee* as his most plausible exhibit. Though Suvin also maintains that Hank's authoritarian side takes over, he ends more convincingly not with a Victorian locked into nostalgia but with a refugee from both the 6th and the 19th centuries who casts himself adrift in time.

Partisans of *Pudd'nhead Wilson* will appreciate an offer (*ArmD* 13,i:8–11) to elevate it into the company of both good-guy Perry Mason and hard-nosed Raymond Chandler. Those sleuthing to establish its qualities of greatness push onward, foiled either by its profundity or the raggedness with which Twain sawed out the pieces of the puzzle. In "The Unmasking of Meaning: A Study of the Twins in *Pudd'nhead Wilson*" (*MissQ* 33:39–53) Murial B. Williams finds it "remarkable" for a coherence of theme and an "ironic design," in which the realization that the Italian strangers are "frauds" will unveil the "satiric mirror" of a morally distorted community. Jerry B. Hogan in "*Pudd'nhead Wilson*: Whose Tragedy Is It?" (*MTJ* 20,ii: 9–12) finds a yet broader ethical failure—the "region's, the culture's, the nation's." He might have commented on how well the original illustrations fit his view. Some of them are reproduced in the Norton Critical Edition by Sidney E. Berger, who provides a responsible text of a vexatious manuscript. (It will be interesting to see whether the Iowa/California Edition finishes with the same results.) Besides picking the secondary readings judiciously, he arranged for a new essay (pp. 370–81) by Barry Wood, "Narrative Action and Structural Symmetry in *Pudd'nhead Wilson*," which suggests that the opportunities for assuming Twain's success are "more plausible" than those based on a verdict of failure, promises to subordinate themes to "narrative movement." But Wood soon expands into discussing the "labyrinth" of a society that denies reality by "multiple layerings of fictions, deceptions, counterfeitings and imitations." Admittedly he works back to a "tightly controlled structure of burlesque and melodrama"; however, his best achievement is a mediation of previous readings that makes any unitary approach look rigid.

Personal Recollections of Joan of Arc is still mostly ignored by the explicators. Though that suits John Seelye, his Introduction for a

facsimile reprinting (Hartford, Conn.: Stowe-Day Foundation) does
not intend a coup de grace. Of course he slashes at its archaic sentimentality, but with his usual panache justified by scholarship he explores Twain's problems in managing his elderly I-narrator and persuasively contends that the final third, the trial section, comes off
best; though melodrama, it is conducted effectively. For *Following
the Equator* the year brought nothing except, belatedly, "Mark Twain
and Indian History" by Mohamed Elias in *Journal of Indian History*
(56[1978]:137–45). It gives a non-Western response to Twain's opinions about the British Raj and suggests a few parallels with his Missouri experiences that his visit may have aroused. A shakier groping
at sources, W. Gerald Marshall in "Mark Twain's 'The Man That Corrupted Hadleyburg' and the Myth of Baucis and Philemon" (*MTJ*
20,ii:4–7) settles for a "would have been easily accessible" standard
of evidence.

The very late writings have to ride mostly on past analysis for
another year anyway. In "Mark Twain's Absurd Universe and 'The
Great Dark'" (*SSF* 16[1979]:335–40) Mark Kosinski joins the recent
chorus that those writings deserve study for their aesthetic value aside
from any veiled autobiography. Specifically he suggests that the voyage in the illuminated drop of water should have been called "The
Great White Glare," thus emphasizing its inversion of color symbolism
as a device of its determinist though not nihilist speculations. With
"Deus Ludens: The Shaping of Mark Twain's Mysterious Stranger"
(*Novel* 14:44–56)—almost as hard to sum up as Khouri's essay—Bruce
Michelson repeats his plunge into the theme of play. He cogently
poses the question of what was Twain struggling to say that enmeshed him in three incomplete versions of a narrative. Tentatively,
Michelson answers that he was trying to combine "games, gods, literary necessities" and then works up to finding the highest degree of
success in the complex Printshop fantasy with its truly playful angel
a far more attractive model than the "limited, man-conceived, theistic
God." Therefore, a "vital, enduring, hopeful festivity and life have
been restored to Mark Twain's fiction. Through play the world we
cannot understand is celebrated in and by the very act of overwhelming the world we thought we knew." Unfortunately, Michelson
reaches this affirmation at the cost of denigrating the Philip Traum
text that has fascinated many even in a corrupted form.

Michelson's conclusion that Twain recovered his best manner is more appropriate these days than charges that he failed as an artist and therefore—presumably—should slump into oblivion. Halley's Comet is heading back to help his visibility; plans are afoot to mark the centenary of *Huckleberry Finn*; the 1981 fall season of PBS featured some Twain programs. Most important, the first three volumes of his letters will appear soon, and—aside from a few great books and sketches—they may prove his most attractive combination of spontaneity, liveliness of intellect, ethical seriousness, and force as a personality.

Duke University

7. Henry James

Robert L. Gale

The James boom may have lessened slightly, but it is still rolling along steadily. The *MLA Bibliography* for 1980 lists about 120 items on James, counting five books and several dissertations. It inevitably omits a few items. Critical work is evenly divided: about a score each on source, parallel, and influence studies, general critical pieces, items on individual novels, and essays on individual tales. The best critical work is exceptionally fine. The most impressive Jamesian devotees this year include Thaddio K. Babiiha, Annette Larson Benert, Leon Edel, James W. Gargano, Rosalie Hewitt, Richard A. Hocks, Susanne Kappeler, Donal O'Gorman, and Daniel J. Schneider. Works by James receiving the most attention are *The American, The Ambassadors,* "Daisy Miller," *The Portrait of a Lady,* and "The Turn of the Screw."

i. Letters, Autobiography, and Biography

Leon Edel's introduction to his edition of the third volume of selected letters—*Henry James Letters: 1883–1895* (Harvard)—is august. Edel points out that these letters show "the novelist's expanded relations with art and society in the old cities of Europe during the waning years of the nineteenth century." The letters tell us about James and his family and friends, money, France, Italy, the theater, his depression, and the start of "the breakdown in his egotism and his opening himself up to homoerotic love."

David L. Furth's *The Visionary Betrayed: Aesthetic Discontinuity in Henry James's* The American Scene (Harvard) is most valuable. Half scared, James revisited America in 1904 to gain new impressions for *the* travel book on the subject. But the flood of impressions caused him to retreat. The style of *The American Scene* is dense because James saw his subject as chaotic and himself as bewildered. Provinciality, which he once ridiculed, he now found felicitous. He deplored

America's unsuccessful attempts to build and buy an artistic past.
Failing in his effort to address the immigrant problem, James re-
treated from American modernity not only to ordered revision of his
fiction but also to ordered autobiography.

Adeline R. Tintner proves in "Henry James Writes His Own
Blurbs" (*ABBW* 19 May:3873–76) that James was so outraged by a
senseless blurb on his *Julia Bride* dustjacket that he prepared his own
blurbs for *The Finer Grain* and *The Outcry*.

Two publications on Alice James throw important light on her
brother Henry. They are Jean Strouse, *Alice James: A Biography*
(Houghton Mifflin), and *The Death and Letters of Alice James: Selected Correspondence* (Calif.), ed. and with a fine biographical essay
by Ruth Bernard Yeazell.

ii. Text, Bibliography

Edel has edited, with an introduction, *"The Europeans": A Facsimile
of the Manuscript* (Howard Fertig), uniquely reassembing four scattered sections of James's original manuscript.

"Henry James's *The American Scene*: Its Genesis and Its Reception, 1905–1977" (*JHR* 2:179–96) by Rosalie Hewitt is mainly a mag-
nificent annotated bibliography of the book. It offers data on editions,
bibliographies, contemporary reviews and comments, reviews of later
editions, and books, articles, and essays. In her introduction and discussion Hewitt makes two main points: early criticism both of James's
style in *The American Scene* and of its contents was perceptive; and
much of "the later commentary . . . has not superseded the earliest
criticism."

iii. Sources, Parallels, Influence

As has been the case for several years, some of the best work done on
James this year is in the realm of James and his sources, parallels be-
tween his work and that of others, and his influence on later authors.
Limitations of space prevent full treatment of such criticism here. I
move generally in chronological order with respect to the non-
Jamesian material.

Tintner in " 'The Papers': Henry James Rewrites *As You Like It*"
(*SSF* 17:165–70) contends that when James's Howard Bight and

Maud Blandy retire "from the world of Fleet Street to their own version of the pastoral," they resemble a latter-day Jacques and Rosalind. Tintner's valuable but badly printed "James' *King Lear: The Outcry and the Art Domain*" (*ABBW* 4 Feb:798–828 *passim*) describes James's awareness of the alarming "art drain" from about 1900 to 1910 out of England. James "saw the aristocratic 'guardians' of the nation's [art] treasure giving away their patrimony in the same irresponsible, 'lax' way in which Lear too had given away his kingdom." James in *The Outcry* "presented a situation in which his Lear [Lord Theign] also repudiates a good daughter [Grace] for a bad [Kitty]." James parallels *King Lear* in matters of tone, diction, imagery, and theme.

Lawrence Berkove in "Henry James and Sir Walter Scott: A 'Virtuous Attachment'?" (*SSL* 15:43–52) traces the origin of the phrase "virtuous attachment" to an 1815 review by Scott of Jane Austen's *Emma*, and then indicates parallels between *The Ambassadors* and the review by Scott, whom James admired. Michael Tilby in "Henry James and Mérimée: A Note of Caution" (*RomN* 21:165–68) corrects aspects of an essay on James and Prosper Mérimée by P. R. Grover (see *ALS 1969*, pp. 96–97). In "Taine, James, and Balzac: Toward an Aesthetic of Romantic Realism" (*HJR* 2:12–24) Sarah B. Daugherty images "[Hyppolyte] Taine . . . as [Honoré de] Balzac's elder son—a brother to the younger James," who endorsed Taine's praise of Balzac and used his "Balzac" (1858) as the main outside source of his 1875 essay and 1905 lecture on Balzac. Tintner in "Balzac's *La Comédie Humaine* in Henry James's *The American*" (*RLC* 54:101–04) suggests that when James wrote *The American* he heard specified echoes from several novels by Balzac.

Ronald Schleifer in "The Trap of the Imagination: The Gothic Tradition" (*Criticism* 22:297–319) sees Gothic fiction as "a response to [the] despair" which followed late 18th-century "rationalism and desacralization," and regards the contemporary *Dracula* as looking back to supernatural Gothicism and James's "The Turn of the Screw" as looking forward to modern Gothic, with its irony, laughter, and *nada*.

In "Emersonian Consciousness and *The Spoils of Poynton*" (*ESQ* 26:88–99) Carren O. Kasten sees Fleda Vetch as the culmination of James's efforts at creating characters capable of transcending the self. In her James "socialized [Ralph Waldo] Emerson's visionary eyeball self." Thaddeo K. Babiiha's *The James-Hawthorne Relation: Biblio-*

graphical Essays (Hall) summarizes secondary material of 1918–73 thus: James on Nathaniel Hawthorne; works on the general relationship of the two and their fiction; and James and *The Scarlet Letter*, *The House of the Seven Gables*, *The Blithedale Romance*, *The Marble Faun*, and Hawthorne's tales. (For temperate adverse criticism, see R. E. Long's review, *ALR* 13:303–06). Patrick O'Donnell's "Between Life and Art: Structures of Realism in the Fiction of Howells and James" (*EA* 33:142–55) distinguishes too neatly between the fiction of William Dean Howells and James, asserting on too little evidence that Howells' characters drift and his endings are unresolved compared to James's. Tintner attenuates strands of an alleged "web of Pater associations in 'The Author of Beltraffio'" in her essay "Another Germ for 'The Author of Beltraffio': On James, Pater, and Botticelli's Madonnas" (*Journal of Pre-Raphaelite Studies* 1,i:14–20). James makes Beatrice Ambient in his story as vicious toward her child as Walter Pater and James (after Pater) contend Sandro Botticelli's Madonnas appear to be toward the Infant Christ. In "The Stranger Case in *The Turn of the Screw* and *Heart of Darkness*" (*SSF* 16 [1979]:317–25) Hana Wirth-Nesher suggests that both works, unlike R. L. Stevenson's *The Strange Case of Dr. Jekyll and Mr. Hyde*, are modern and still intrigue us because they pose conflicts without resolving them, have "no revelatory endings," and say that evil cannot be contained, identified, and thus diminished. Tintner in "Some Notes for a Study of the Gissing Phase in Henry James's Fiction" (*GissingN*, 16,iii:1–15) shows that James read, wrote about, and met George Gissing. She identifies possible Gissing influences in a dozen of James's short stories, but is most intriguing when she suggests that James's *The Portrait of a Lady* inspired Gissing's *Isabel Clarendon*, which then influenced James's "The Bench of Desolation." It is Tintner's thesis in "Jamesian Structures in *The Age of Innocence* and Related Stories" (*TCL* 26:332–47) that Edith Wharton's novel reveals "a greater dependence in a technical sense on the work of James than we had thought from previous criticism." In addition, Tintner sniffs the Jamesian in Wharton's "quartet of novellas called *Old New York*."

M. E. Grenander's lively, beautifully printed essay "Henrietta Stackpole and Olive Harper: Emanations of the Great Democracy" (*BRH* 83:406–22) presents a real-life "female American foreign correspondent . . . writing from Europe in the 1870s" as James's major model for Henrietta Stackpole in *The Portrait of a Lady*. The model is Helen "Olive Harper" Burrell (1842–1915), whose appearance, personality, and career abroad closely resemble those of Henrietta. Heath Moon begins "James's 'A London Life' and the Campbell Divorce Scandal" (*ALR* 13:246–58) by correcting any reading of the 1888 story which places "Selina [Berrington] in a sympathetic light." Then Moon shows that James's disgust at the 1886 suit and countersuit of Lord Colin and Lady Campbell, noxiously reported in London and New York newspapers, finds indirect expression in his characterization of Selina's sister Laura Wing. Bernard Richards in "The Sources of Henry James's 'Mrs. Medwin'" (*N&Q* 27:226–30) proves that "Miss Balch" and "Lady G.," named by James in his *Notebooks* as inspiring his story, are Elizabeth and Lady Grantley (Katharine McVickar). Miss Balch, minor writer about Victorian society, could not help Lady Grantley, adulteress and then divorcée, to become socially more acceptable. So they correspond to Mamie Cutter and Mrs. Medwin in James's story. Then Richards more excitingly offers Robert Temple, James's cousin Minny Temple's brother, as a model for Scott Homer, Mamie's "ne'er-do-well half-brother who finally proves so irresistible and so invaluable" in James's tale.

Timothy P. Martin begins his essay "Henry James and Percy Lubbock: From Mimesis to Formalism" (*Novel* 14:20–29) by rebuking any number of reputable commentators for noting only the resemblances between James's criticism of fiction and Lubbock's without also observing the fundamental difference between James's view of the novel and Lubbock's. "James was ultimately a mimetic critic. . . . Lubbock, the formalist, discusses . . . the artistic integrity of the work of art." Martha Banta in her leisurely, abstruse essay "James and Stein on 'Being American' and 'Having France'" (*FAR* 3[1979]:63–84) considers the professional consequence of her subjects' expatriation. Neither James nor Gertrude Stein became French but both "gave themselves over to 'having' France." James knew the French language better than Stein. Both preferred cityscapes to landscapes. Neither was concerned with art as moralism. Banta concludes that "James and Stein differed in that, although Stein was entirely 'American' in her mind and 'French' in her human nature, James was a bit of both in each area." In "Mouths Biting Empty Air: Ezra Pound's Hugh Selwyn Mauberley and Henry James's Lambert Strether" (*RLC* 54:47–70) Anne-Marie Brumm tediously argues that James's Strether, hero of *The Ambassadors*, and Pound's Mauberley are both "fearful, hesitating, 'fumbler' type[s]," and are both passively imaginative, latently homosexual, pseudoartistic, and finally disillusioned. Brumm makes more sense contending that both writers adjure artists to devote themselves to the truth and to depict the horrors of an unfeeling, materialistic society.

Myfanwy Piper in "Writing for Britten" (pp. 8–21 in *The Operas of Benjamin Britten*, ed. David Herbert [Columbia, 1979]) has fascinating things to report about writing librettos for Britten's *The Turn of the Screw* (1954) and *Owen Wingrave* (1971). But she is outrageously incorrect when she says that "The Turn of the Screw" by James "is vague only in one thing: in what, if anything, actually happened between the children and the haunting pair." In "Truffaut's *La Chambre Verte*: Homage to Henry James" (*LFQ* 8:78–83) Tintner suggests that François Truffaut in his rendering of James's "The Altar of the Dead" "seems to have understood or at least to have projected James's intentions better than most literary critics." Tintner discusses immortality through consciousness-sharing and euhemerism in both tale and film.

iv. Criticism: General

The best critical study this year is unquestionably Susanne Kappeler's *Writing and Reading in Henry James* (Columbia). In his foreword to it, Tony Tanner rightly calls it decisive, constructive, brilliant, subtle, scrupulous, dazzling, trenchant, beautiful, admirable, informed, lucid, refreshing, and sophisticated. Rather than say too much more, I will say too little more. Opposing Vladimir Propp, Kappeler follows Clemens Lugowski and limns the modern reader of James as one thriving on ambiguity and narrative innovation, as one who, like a detective-fiction reader, traces and interprets clues creatively and endlessly. "The Aspern Papers" has both a folktale structure (cf. Alex Olrik) and a story beneath "the narrator's discourse." Next Kappeler analyzes relations—writer, critic, community; creativity, passion, mating—as shown in several of James's works (cf. Cesare Segre). Then Kappeler discusses the narrator of *The Sacred Fount* as artist, anthropologist, psychoanalyst, and critical interpreter. Trained and skilled, young Susanne Kappeler is already formidable.

Philip Sicker urges a bold theory in his *Love and the Quest for Identity in the Fiction of Henry James* (Princeton). Romantic love is James's main theme. "The quest for love" as expressed in James "is . . . a continual quest for identity in a universe that seems to deny both permanent, objective value and the integrity of the self." James's love for Minny Temple "was the 'primary relation' of his life," from which evolved his "early portrayal of love as an image worshiped in the mind." Weak on the minor early tales, Sicker more valuably discusses later, better fiction, and has good things to say about the unconscious of their heroines' minds and William James's profeminine studies in parapsychology. In my opinion, Sicker enlists fine *aperçus* in a losing cause: Love need not exclusively concern "tears and kisses or a quickening in the loins" (to quote him on James's negative position); but it ought to call tears, etc., into more frequent play than is evident on James's too courtly-love stage.

Charles Schug in *The Romantic Genesis of the Modern Novel* (Pittsburgh, 1979) theorizes that James among others illustrates the influence of romantic aesthetic concepts of form and structure, especially concerning discontinuity, nonnarrative movement, organicism, and the experiential rather than the photographic.

Robert L. Caserio's ultramodern, subtle *Plot, Story and the Novel from Dickens and Poe to the Modern Period* (Princeton, 1979) argues "that the most vital element in literature is not its self-containment, but its relation to historical human change—that literary structures are transformed in response to the human metamorphoses they represent." In part Caserio does so by reassessing James's major fiction from *The Awkward Age* forward.

The big purpose of Sam B. Girgus' slim book, *The Law of the Heart: Individualism and the Modern Self in American Literature* (Texas, 1979), is to apply modernist criticism to the writings and ideas of several "significant figures in our literature and culture." James among others "tend[s] to incorporate in . . . language and ideas the cultural dialogue between democratic as opposed to totalitarian versions of the individual self." A huge generalization supported by too little evidence.

Ellen Eve Frank's beautifully illustrated *Literary Architecture: Essays Toward a Tradition: Walter Pater, Gerard Manley Hopkins, Marcel Proust, Henry James* (Calif., 1979) is overwritten and reductively contends that the references in her subjects' works to architecture comprise their entire aesthetic philosophies. Frank sees James's prefaces as "literary architecture," his fictive points of view as windows, his fiction as a house with nicely designed, furnished, and decorated rooms. The authors discussed are all said to see architecture as spatial emblem of mind and as structure analogizing memory.

In his monograph *The International Fiction of Henry James* (Macmillan of India, 1979; Humanities Press, 1980), J. N. Sharma examines the evolution of James's theme of internationalism. James dramatized Americans in Europe instead of depicting flat American democracy. *The American* is too simply international. *The Portrait of a Lady* steps beyond, treats free will and wealth. *The Ambassadors* considers differing moral values. *The Wings of the Dove* and *The Golden Bowl* James elevates into "moral parables." Sharma vitiates his subject by discussing crucial noninternational aspects of these novels, and by discussing Edith Wharton, F. Scott Fitzgerald, and Ernest Hemingway as continuators of Jamesian supernational internationalism. More valuable than Sharma's book is P. T. Barry's short essay, "Physical Descriptions in the International Tales of Henry James" (*OL* 35:47–58), which crisply theorizes that James presents a pattern of thin, pallid American pilgrims to Europe who shrink from the amplitude of life symbolized by fully rounded Europeans. Barry finds persuasive evidence in six short stories of the 1870s. James favors Europe and deplores his countrymen's "instinctive moral and intellectual suspicion of it."

"Henry James and the Image of Franklin" (*SoR* 16:552–59) by Leo B. Levy counters the notion that James the high-brow differs from Benjamin Franklin the catchpenny opportunist. Barbara Wilkie Tedford shows in "The Attitudes of Henry James and Ivan Turgenev Toward the Russo-Turkish War" (*HJR* 1:257–61) that James was Turgenev's friend and disciple enough to publish a prose translation of his poem "Croquet at Windsor," in which Turgenev criticizes Queen Victoria's policy of condoning Turkish atrocities in Bulgaria. In "Who's Henry James? Further Lessons of the Master" (*HJR* 2:2–11) John Carlos Rowe comments on the androgynous aspects of tower and letter symbolism in *The Ivory Tower*, reasons that James contributes both to "modernist seriousness" and to post-Modern parody of the serious, and tries to relate James to the ultramodern theory and practice of Gerald Graff and Donald Barthelme. Mary M. Lay links the deaths of Morgan Moreen and Hyacinth Robinson in "The Real Beasts: Surrogate Brothers in James's 'The Pupil' and *The Princess Casamassima*" (*ALR* 13:73–84). Both fictional characters experience "the destruction of . . . the heart" because older surrogate brothers disappoint them brutally. Louise K. Barnett in "Displacement of Kin in the Fiction of Henry James" (*Criticism* 22:140–55) discusses James's "negative presentation of blood ties and his consequent creation of surrogate figures to assume the traditional obligations of kinship." Relatives fail their young; then surrogates do also; those in authority are regularly cruel, irresponsible, and senseless. Annette Larson Benert has published two long essays in which she applies Jungian principles to significant novels by James. "The Dark Source of Love: A Jungian Reading of Two Early James Novels" (*HSL* 12:99–123) begins with the statement that in James's novels the marriage bond "functions . . . as a key to the emotional development of individuals" who fail through lack of perception. Both James and Carl Gustav Jung see the psyche as androgynous, believe we approach reality subjectively, and regard sexual activity as personality-integrating. Benert applies Jung's theories of male Logos and female Eros to *Roderick Hudson* and *The Portrait of a Lady*. More enlightening is Benert's other essay, "Public Means and Private Ends: The Psychodynamics of Reform in James's Middle-Period Novels" (*SNNTS* 12:327–43). The political movements depicted in *The Bostonians* and *The Princess Casamassima* fail because of the failures of knowledge and of relationship. Knowledge relates to Logos; relationship, to Eros. James and Jung, says Benert, "associate the disintegration of modern society with the weakening or devaluation of the feminine principle." Benert offers a schema of political activities in *The Bostonians* and *The Princess Casamassima*; elements include "private mythology," homosexual linkage, and "masculine brutality." Benert is sharply clinical with Basil Ransom and Paul Muniment.

v. Criticism: Individual Novels

James W. Tuttleton begins his "Rereading *The American*: A Century Since" (*HJR* 1:139–53) by recording his preference for the unrevised version. Then he discusses James's reinforcing the international theme by the use of parallelism and symbolism. Tuttleton sees Christopher Newman neither as "a serious analogue to Christ" (does anyone?) nor as a lover who could hope to succeed in his "fairy-tale courtship." The Bellegardes and their friends wrongly take Newman to be "*the* American, the only American." James on revising "recov-

ered [his] affection for the romantic mode." David Wyatt begins his
Prodigal Sons, which explicates the metaphor of literary creations as
prodigal sons of authoritarian fathers, with a splendid reading of
The American. James saw his relationship to his books as resembling
that of parent to offspring. He admires the independence of any literary work; but, by his act of revision, he shows a desire for self-
assertive repossession. Compellingly described in J. P. Telotte's "Language and Perspective in James's *The American*" (*SAB* 44[1979]:
27-39) is Newman's nonsolipsistic voyage of discovery in the Old
World as an unsuccessful attempt to make his verbal representations
coincide with reality. The hero moves from a commercial to a touris-
tic perspective, fails to correlate words and causes, and turns in-
articulate.

As for *The Portrait of a Lady*, Alden R. Turner in "The Haunted
Portrait of a Lady" (*SNNTS* 12:228-38) traces the development in
Isabel Archer's painter-like creative consciousness of her picture of
her life. Isabel pierces the dead wall to which her marriage has
pushed her, moves through it to an awareness that her former naïve
states of mind have not corresponded to reality, and concludes that
she must no longer disjoin "her imagination and the reality of the
world" but instead "learn . . . the value of life within form." In
"Intimacy and Spectatorship in *The Portrait of a Lady*" (*HJR* 2:25-
35) Dennis L. O'Connor makes Isabel's fear of tumescent sexual
intimacy with Caspar Goodwood and her preference for spectatorship with dry, chilly Gilbert Osmond into a mode of behavior—"re-
nunciation that permits one to feel noble while ensuring narcissistic
regression." Carla L. Peterson in "Dialogue and Characterization in
The Portrait of a Lady" (*SAF* 8:13-22) digs under the humdrum
talk between Isabel and Gilbert during her first visit to his Florentine
villa, to unearth the truism that their "individual styles of speaking
indicate fundamental differences in personality." Peterson collects
examples of "personal and colloquial language," exclamations, sentence fragments, lexical borrowings, and "verbal *reprise*," and concludes that Gilbert wants to appear wise and plans to become dominant. Any doubters? In "Beyond the Victorians: *The Portrait of a
Lady*" (pp. 274-87 in *Reading the Victorian Novel: Detail into Form*,
ed. Ian Gregor [Barnes & Noble]) Stuart Hutchinson suggests that,
unlike heroines in earlier Victorian novels, Isabel "affront[s] a less
firmly established world" and wants "to be the artist of her own

life." Hence her story is "James's portrait of Isabel's portrait of herself." By chapter 42 Isabel no longer believes that her "world can offer fulfilment" and decides in a post-Victorian way to live instead in her consciousness. Edgar A. Dryden in "The Image in the Mirror: The Double Economy of James's *Portrait*" (*Genre* 13:31–49) reasons that for James the acts of writing and of reading "appear, paradoxically, to be mutually dependent but incompatible activities" which may be best elucidated through commercial metaphors. Dryden proves his thesis well by reference to James's preface to *The Portrait of a Lady*, less well by a discussion of characterization through imagery in the novel.

"Henry James: Revolutionary Involvement, The Princess, and the Hero" (*AI* 37:245–77) by M. D. Faber is almost interminably concerned with such psychoanalytical problems as "early separation and loss, the dynamics of the transference relation, the role of the maternal substitute in transitional crises, and the etiology of suicide" as they are dramatized in *The Princess Casamassima*. Faber tries to intertwine maternal figures, Hyacinth Robinson's " 'mixed' origin," and the revolution theme.

In "The Drama of Maisie's Vision" (*HJR* 2:36–48) M. A. Williams applies concepts of phenomenology, especially those of Edmund Husserl and Maurice Merleau-Ponty, to a tender reading of "Maisie's pain and bewilderment as she reaches out in vain to her self-absorbed companions." Williams admires the child for being able to learn from pain and confusion. But he disagrees with so many critics as to Maisie's sense, motivation, and actions that I cannot help feeling that the cause of all this critical nonconsensus must be James's happy ignorance of "natural attitude," "reduction," and "*epoché*" à la Husserl.

"James's *The Awkward Age*: A Reading and an Evaluation" (*HJR* 1:219–27) by Daniel J. Schneider is a major study. It assesses previous scholarship, then analyzes the alignment of the main characters as it elucidates the two themes of social "compromise which issues in failure" and "the constraint between the 'case' in England and that in France." Schneider shows that "Mrs. Brook . . . is the only person in the book who is unqualifiedly young and flexible. All the others, the divided Nanda included, show age and inflexibility." Neither tragic nor comic, the novel is a typical example of the Jamesian "ironic tragic-comedy." But it matters little, because James fails here to "establish . . . the importance of his central conflict"; nor does he sufficiently reveal "the motivations behind his characters' decisions." Amen! More modestly, Jean Frantz Blackall's "Literary Allusion as Imaginative Event in *The Awkward Age*" (*MFS* 26:179–97) provides an explication of the "fascinating sequence of muddled literary allusions" which Vanderbank delivers to Nanda in the last book of the novel. They are to Hugo's *Notre-Dame de Paris*, Goethe's *Faust*, and Zola's *Paris*, among works of lesser significance. Given an understanding of these writings, the reader may "discover . . . the complex inner and outer worlds of the novel . . . the author's own dividedness of mind," and even "the spiritual and imaginative experiences of James's central consciousness" here—that is, Van himself.

In "James's *The Sacred Fount*: The Phantasmagorical Made Evidential" (*HJR* 2:49–60) James W. Gargano scores the critics who expose the narrator of *The Sacred Fount* as demented, and praises those who instead call him intelligent, honorable, and clairvoyant. Gargano develops the arresting thesis that "the narrator's undertaking . . . should not be thought of in terms of strict realism but in terms of a phantasmagorical exploration of scenes and persons that change, fade, or dissolve into one another. The narrator's mind and intuitions [Gargano adds] confront the flux of a reality in which men and women exchange ages, personalities, and intellectual powers. In addition, the observer himself reverses *his* attitudes and roles: . . . he changes from pursuer to protector, from an amused and heady analyst to a gentle, defeated man who surrenders his inner vision because of external pressures." Bravo!

Virginia C. Fowler in "Milly Theale's Malady of Self" (*Novel* 14:57–74) suavely builds on the questionable thesis that in *The Wings of the Dove* Milly's malady may symbolize "an inner deficiency created by her situation as an American woman." Fowler links Milly Theale too closely to Minny Temple, who, in spite of James's notion that she had too intense a taste for life, died not of that taste but of tuberculosis. Fowler is safer when she argues that Milly seems to accept the identity others assign her. Fowler nicely analyzes the consequences of Milly's "death-in-life" self-presentation but neglects to relate the young woman to the deficient America allegedly thus symbolized.

More than a source study, "The Novel in *John Gabriel Borkman*:

Henry James's *The Ambassadors*" (*HJR* 1:211–18) by Quay Grigg begins by suggesting that the play which Maria Gostrey takes Lambert Strether to—depicting "the young man and the wicked older woman"—may be Henrik Ibsen's *John Gabriel Borkman*. Perhaps James not only took aspects of the mother-daughter relationship as well from Ibsen's play but also, indulging his persistent "mania to rewrite other people's works," relates Madame de Vionnet and Chad Newsome in a way "Ibsen did not do with Mrs. [Fanny] Wilton and Erhart [Borkman]" to maximize "the civilizing of Chad." Strether is also a bit like Ibsen's Ella Rentheim. Grigg wonders whether James's early reading of *John Gabriel Borkman* inspired *What Maisie Knew*, even while Ibsen's "leanness" and "scenic economy" shamed James's "anguished prolixity." In " 'To See Life Reflected': Seeing as Living in *The Ambassadors*" (*HJR* 1:204–10) William Cosgrove and Irene Mathees unconvincingly contend that in the last half of his adventures Strether "understands and enacts his new definition of 'living,' which is 'seeing.' "

In "*The Golden Bowl* and 'The Voice of Blood' " (*HJR* 1:154–63) Leo B. Levy works out the implications of the notion that the blood relationship between Adam Verver and his daughter Maggie "may contain all possible present and future relationships," that is, until this "close kinship tie . . . is interfered with." The consequence of interference—the two marriages—is dramatized in the epiphanic "scene in which father and daughter reconstitute their friendship." Better is "Gestural Pattern and Meaning in *The Golden Bowl*" (*TCL* 26:445–57), in which Marianne Torgovnick discusses "the tensions in the novel as conveyed by gesture . . . in the final scene." Torgovnick too brashly handles critics of this ambiguous novel who differ from her. Ralf Norrman in "End-Linking as an Intensity-Creating Device in the Dialogue of Henry James's *The Golden Bowl*" (*ES* 61:236–51) verbosely asserts that "repetition, in assorted forms, is one of the foremost characteristics of the prose of *The Golden Bowl*, including the dialogues." Norrman takes as model "a bipartition of the sentence [in dialogue] and the resulting four possible combinations, theme [beginning part] to theme, rheme [end part] to theme, rheme to rheme, and theme to rheme." He offers a few examples plus commentary, and concludes that James's end-linked dialogue "becomes a sort of dialectics of discovery . . . zig-zag[ging] towards the light."

vi. Criticism: Individual Tales

As one might expect, "Daisy Miller" and "The Turn of the Screw"
lead the other stories in popularity.

John E. Savarese in "Henry James's First Short Story: A Study in
Error" (SSF 17:431–35) neatly praises James for giving the murderer
in his first piece of fiction, "A Tragedy of Error," more depth than is
commonly realized. The man has dignity, a sense of fairness, some
notion of honor, and an ability to judge so-called respectability—all
of which is lost on the callous central female character.

W. R. Martin in "The Narrator's 'Retreat' in James's 'Four Meetings'" (SSF 17:497–99) notes that "the Countess's relation to Mr.
Mixter in Section IV is not very unlike [i.e., resembles] the narrator's
to Caroline [Spencer] in Section I." Martin adds that when the narrator suppresses an awareness of this resemblance, he retreats both
from Caroline and from "self-knowledge."

In a major study entitled "Daisy Miller, Backward into the Past:
A Centennial Essay" (HJR 1:164–78) Richard A. Hocks reminds our
furiously liberated feminist readers that "Daisy Miller" is more than
prophetic of late 20th-century freedom: it is still "intentionally ambivalent," a "true, critical dialectical inquiry." Is it so manifest that
Daisy is "the 'virtuous whore'"? Does she want what modern liberated American females have? Is she half in love with Winterbourne's "formal code"? Hocks examines "certain configurations . . .
in the critical literature" concerning the story. Daisy was always
popular, yes, but was never an early storm center as some critics now
believe. James's change in attitude toward his heroine parallels the
decline of literary realism after about 1900. Hocks relates James's
revisions in "Daisy Miller" to James's own reassessment of our cultural past as epitomized by American women in Europe, and balances
critical commentary on Winterbourne's role and Daisy's death. Hocks
treats the symbolic implications of the name "Daisy" and brilliantly
dissects "the operative irony" surrounding Winterbourne, who has,
like Billy Budd's Captain Vere and unlike both Daisy and Billy, a
necessary "reflecting consciousness." Related to part of Hocks's splendid essay but necessarily more restricted in scope is Louise K. Barnett's "Jamesian Feminism: Women in 'Daisy Miller'" (SSF 16
[1979]:281–87), the thesis of which is that, in spite of his lifelong
concern with the tension caused in women by societal restrictions,

"[o]nly in Daisy Miller does James portray a woman whose innocent devotion to her natural behavior causes her to flout society wilfully and persistently." By contrasting not only Daisy's wants and other women's possessions but also Daisy's and Winterbourne's freedoms, James indicts society. Still slighter is Carey H. Kirk's " 'Daisy Miller': The Reader's Choice" (*SSF* 17:275–83), which notes recent critical condemnation of Winterbourne, adds more (based on interpretations of Lord Byron allusions), but then defends Winterbourne by contending that Daisy may be viewed "as a girl on the make." The child is spoiled and uses Winterbourne "to compensate for . . . deprivations." Kirk asserts persuasively that James provokes his readers to weigh thematically layered evidence and decide whether Daisy is virtually a victim of murder or seeks to devour American men abroad. More exciting is Frankie Wilson's and Max Westbrook's "Daisy Miller and the Metaphysician" (*ALR* 13:270–79), which superbly sees James as the " 'metaphysician' " whom Mrs. Costello calls for while wondering whether the heroine's " 'being hopelessly vulgar is being "bad." ' " The critics see Daisy as willful, Lamia-like, and Undine-like, and Winterbourne as Calvinistic, tyrannical, perfidious, and self-ruinous.

Comments by Shlomith Rimmon on Jamesian ambiguity (see *ALS 1977*, pp. 105–06) have inspired critical essays on "The Figure in the Carpet." With a splendid essay entitled "A Marriage of Opposites: Henry James's 'The Figure in the Carpet' and the Problem of Ambiguity" (*ELH* 47:788–803) Rachel Salmon moves the study of ambiguous Jamesian texts not only beyond Christine Brooke-Rose's theory of "consistently binary readings on the story level" but, more importantly, also away from Rimmon's theory of nonmimetic " 'conjunction' of exclusive disjuncts (a·b)" to locate a "still point" in the figurative oscillation of textual analysis between opposite interpretations. For her example, Salmon chooses "The Figure in the Carpet" and labels Rimmon's explication of its diachronic states as "a serious misreading" and "a false view of James's poetic." Salmon then discusses paradox (a momentary transformation of ambiguity) in the tale as a legitimate "experience of simultaneity which abrogates . . . our ordinary framework of chronology." J. Hillis Miller's "The Figure in the Carpet" (*PoT* 1,iii:107–18) is partly exciting but also fruitlessly metaphysical in spots. It explicates the implications of the paradox of "figure" as employment of the configurating, flowerlike line to suggest completeness, continuity, and finite form in realistic fiction which is irreducibly plurisignificant. Miller's disagreeing with Rimmon prompted her response (see Shlomith Rimmon-Kenan, *PoT* 2,ib [1980–81]:185–88), which prompted Miller (*ibid.*:189–91). Enough?

And now for "The Turn of the Screw." Of the five essays on it discussed below, Donal O'Gorman's is significant, Anthony J. Mazzella's shaky, Edwin Fussell's pretentious, that of David A. Cook and Timothy J. Corrigan and that of E. C. Curtsinger thin to weak.

O'Gorman in "Henry James's Reading of *The Turn of the Screw*" (*HJR* 1:125–38,228–56) calls the story a "literary enigma," which James resolves through his view of both the governess and Evil. Inadequate criticism of his story between 1898 and 1908 (the time of his preface concerning it) made him defensively reject both main critical theories (ghost story vs. hallucination). He wrote it for Christmas-season publication because of the 28 December Childermas reversal of adult/child roles, akin to the Victorian master-servant class system. Irresponsibility in masters (including uncles) and servants forces children to seek freedom injuriously soon. James hints that we should regard Peter Quint and Miss Jessel as evil, persistent, interiorly active; they relate to folklore, history, and witchcraft. They may be "demon emissaries of Satan," and the governess may be a witness against the possessed, witch-like children; if so, the reader acts as judge. Next?—"the real master of Bly . . . [is] the Devil himself"! Much of James's language (perhaps including the name Bly [from Daniel Defoe's statement that "the Devil lies at Blye Bush"?]) hints to this effect. Perhaps the governess is possessed and hence is "an unwitting tool of Satan." James knew John L. Nevius' *Demon Possession and Allied Themes* (1894), passages from which as quoted by O'Gorman parallel James's text. O'Gorman stunningly connects Nevius' theory that 17th-century Salem contained devil-possessed judges of innocent "witches" with 19th-century Bly and its occupants.

Mazzella in "An Answer to the Mystery of *The Turn of the Screw*" (*SSF* 17:327–33) reports that the group gathers to hear the governess' tale during the Christmas season of 1894, the date James's *Guy Domville* was in rehearsal; theorizes that the frame narrator altered the manuscript given by the governess to Douglas; and wonders whether the homoeroticism of Quint and Miles may be "attributable to the relationship between Douglas and the narrator" (but must that narrator be male?). In "The Ontology of *The Turn of the Screw*" (*JML* 7:118–28) Fussell theorizes that the governess entrusted her "novel" to Douglas, who transcribed it and sent it to James; contrasts the governess' brief, energetic style and James's style; and suggests that her Harley Street employer is akin to James as her publisher. Cook and Corrigan in "Narrative Structure in *The Turn of the Screw*: A New Approach to Meaning" (*SSF* 17:55–66) apply aspects of Tzvetan Todorov's *The Fantastic* to the governess' narrative, which may be neither objective report nor evidence of "diseased consciousness" but instead "subtle fiction about the process of fiction." Curtsinger in "*The Turn of the Screw* as Writer's Parable" (*SNNTS* 12: 344–58) similarly reasons that the story "dramatizes the struggle of the writer's creative imagination with the forces of destruction," and thus becomes a parable about the tripartite writer—narrator, imagination, and their mediator. But meanwhile, back at the text. . . .

Six late stories attracted specialized attention. Robert E. Whelan, Jr., in "God, Henry James, and 'The Great Good Place'" (*RS* 47:212–20) beautifully identifies the landlord or abbot of George Dane's Good Place as God and Dane's "sacrifice of . . . egotism" as his price for peace, selflessness, awareness of the value of new elements of reality, and belief that appreciative consciousness is a sample of the hereafter. Kermit Vanderbilt's "'Complicated Music at Short Order' in 'Fordham Castle'" (*HJR* 2:61–66) takes its title from James's own image for the artistry of "Fordham Castle." James's treatment of the four intertwined characters parallels the fugue form. The three motifs of the story are vital being, social imagination, and giving. J. Peter Dyson in "Bartolozzi and Henry James's 'Mora Montravers'" (*HJR* 1:264–66) explicates a reference in the story to engravings by Francesco Bartolozzi. The Traffles value their Bartolozzis more than they do their niece Mora's painter friend Walter Puddick; but by the time of James's story, Bartolozzis were regarded as derivative, insipid, and trivial. Dyson in "Romantic Elements in Three Late Tales of Henry James: 'Mora Montravers,' 'The Velvet Glove,' and 'The Bench of Desolation'" (*ESC* 5[1979]:66–77) applies James's definition of "romance," from his preface to *The American*, to three tales written at about the time he was composing all of his prefaces. James the critic regards romance as having qualities uncontrolled by a sense of the way things really happen; James the artist finds it challenging and necessary to conceal "the fact that the material [in one's fiction] *is*

uncontrolled." In "'Crapy Cornelia': James's Self-Vindication?"
(*ArielE* 11,iv:57–68) W. R. Martin and Warren U. Ober gracefully
explicate a dance image in the late tale as presenting not only "the
nature of communication" between White-Mason and Cornelia Rasch
(the latter so unlike Mrs. Worthingham with her flat talk and frilly
dress surfaces) but also James's "meditated apology for his late style
and method, for the process by which he circles, surveys, and keeps
at a . . . distance from his topic and his reader"—so as to "seize on the
truth and display it" at the end.

University of Pittsburgh

8. Pound and Eliot

George Bornstein and
Stuart Y. McDougal

i. Pound

With eight new books for 1980, Pound studies have now produced 18 volumes in the past two years. Poundians may feel both pleasure and unease at that situation. Good work is always welcome, particularly for an author of such formidable difficulty. But interpretations, guides, and texts have appeared too rapidly for their authors and editors to profit from each other's labors. Such crowding has caused needless duplication of effort and has short-circuited normal testing and development of ideas. In that context the announcement of only three new books for 1981 at the time of writing may signal a needed period of consolidation. Study of *The Cantos*, which again claimed the bulk of the work this year, particularly needs more order. I would nominate Carroll F. Terrell's massive annotations and Michael Bernstein's thoughtful criticism as being in their different ways the most helpful early steps toward a future consensus.

a. **Text and Biography.** *Ezra Pound and the Visual Arts*, ed. Harriet Zinnes (New Directions) is the worst-edited of the recent annual volumes from New Directions. The book contains nearly all of Pound's extended remarks on the visual arts, divided into six sections —a long one of material from *The New Age* and shorter ones drawing in order on Vorticist pronouncements, miscellaneous publications, correspondence with John Quinn, published books, and uncollected manuscripts and papers. Much of the material is readily available elsewhere, but scholars will welcome the collection of fugitive essays

George Bornstein has contributed the section on Pound and Stuart Y. McDougal the section on Eliot.—*J.A.R.*

and gallery notes, the previously unpublished letters to Quinn, and the manuscripts from the Yale, Harvard, Cornell, and Chicago libraries. Unfortunately, poor editing reduces the value of the volume. A derivative and rambling introduction offers such naive assertions as "Through imagism he had revolutionized poetry." There are errors of citation; annotation is erratic and erroneous; identifications at times are gratuitous. In section 3 Zinnes abandons chronological arrangement to present materials alphabetically by magazine title; thus the reader moves from 1923 (*Dial*) to 1956 (*Edge*) to 1914 (*The Egoist*) according to the demands of the alphabet. And the index is spotty and unreliable. Disappointing, all around.

Six items add to our knowledge of Pound's texts and one to work about them. The most substantial, "Ezra Pound's Contributions to New Mexican Periodicals and His Relationship with Senator Bronson Cutting" (*Paideuma* 9:441–59) by E. P. Walkiewicz and Hugh Witemeyer, provides the context for Pound's 22 contributions to *Morada, Front,* and the Santa Fe *New Mexican* between 1929 and 1935. A solid piece of research, the article reminds us that the affiliation of Pound's economics to the populist tradition of the American West needs further study. James H. Thompson's "Ezra Pound: Letters to Elizabeth Winslow" (*Paideuma* 9:341–56) prints 17 letters of minor significance written to a North Carolina woman on the staff of the Reconstruction Finance Corporation who visited Pound at St. Elizabeths frequently during the '50s. More briefly, Don C. Gillespie's "John Becker's Correspondence with Ezra Pound: The Origins of a Musical Crusader" (*BRH* 83:163–71) includes extracts from Pound's eight letters to the American composer between 1927 and 1931; Philip Grover's "Manuscript Corrections in *Lustra*" (*Paideuma* 9:357–58) notes Pound's handwritten emendations to "Old Idea of Choan by Rosoriu" and "To-Em-Mei's 'The Unmoving Cloud'"; and Matthew Little presents "Corrections to Gallup's *Pound* and Some History of Pound's Essays on the Jefferson-Adams Letters" (*PBSA* 74:270–72). Perhaps the most unusual contribution, *The Music of the Troubadours,* vol. 1, ed. Peter Whigham (Ross-Erikson), prints Pound's English versions of Walter Morse Rummel's nine Troubadour songs *Hesternae Rosae* together with Provençal and French versions in their musical settings. Finally, Andrew Crosland completes his "Annotated Checklist of Criticism on Ezra

Pound, 1961–1965" with part 2 (*Paideuma* 9:361–78) and part 3 (*Paideuma* 9:521–48).

The best things in Peter Ackroyd's *Ezra Pound and His World* (Scribner's) are the plentiful photographs, many of them familiar but some more rarely reproduced. Otherwise, the text manages to tell Pound's story in lively but sometimes erroneous fashion (like locating Idaho in the American Midwest). Ackroyd's useful insistence on Pound's psychological preference for projection over introspection receives more profound if also more ponderous development in Daniel Pearlman's "Ezra Pound: America's Wandering Jew" (*Paideuma* 9:461–80), one of the most thoughtful explorations to date of Pound's anti-Semitism. Pearlman argues that a combination of rage against authority, and unconscious envy of it, led Pound to project his own inner divisions onto an archetypal Jewish caricature which he increasingly came to resemble. This probing reaction to material like that contained in Leonard W. Doob's recent edition of "*Ezra Pound Speaking*": *Radio Speeches of World War II* exemplifies the kind of honest confrontation of troublesome issues called for in the review of that volume two years ago in these pages.

Three other articles offer less help. The most interesting, Charles Tomlinson's "*Dove sta memoria*: In Italy" (*HudR* 33:13–34) weaves memories of Pound and of his works in and out of its retrospective fabric. An account which adds little new, Thomas Daniel Young's "The Little Houses Against the Great" (*SR* 88:320–30) analyzes the Bollingen Prize controversy as a vehicle for attacks on the New Critics and Southern Agrarians. Finally, in "The Night Pound Ate the Tulips: An Evening at the Ernes Rhys's" (*JML* 8:153–55) Kim Herzinger calls into question the dating and guest list of that amusing occasion.

b. **General Studies and Relation to Other Writers.** These two categories claimed less work than usual this year. For example, only two scholars significantly explored Pound's relation to earlier poets. William D. Paden, Jr., usefully but pedantically sketches "Pound's Use of Troubadour Manuscripts" (*CL* 32:402–12) on two occasions. Paden's article would have gained in grace had he incorporated new material from R. Murray Schafer's *Ezra Pound and Music* (1977) and Peter Makin's *Provence and Pound* (1978) into his text instead of relegating it to a disjointed postscript. Pound's attraction to Gavin Douglas' *Eneados* (1553) receives close scrutiny in Ronald E. Thomas' interesting "'Ere He His Goddis Brocht in Latio': On Pound's Appreciation of Gavin Douglas" (*Paideuma* 9:509–17). Emphasizing the discussions in "Notes on Elizabethan Classicists" and *ABC of Reading*, Thomas concludes that Pound admired Douglas' "precision or particularization," especially in descriptions of Venus, the sea, and the Golden Bough.

Work relating Pound to his own century is disappointing this year. The best of it, two chapters entitled "Ezra Pound, T. S. Eliot, and the European Horizon" and "*The Waste Land*: From *Ur* to *Echt*" in Harry Levin's *Memories of the Moderns* (New Directions) combine real learning with a scrupulous style but ultimately have little new to offer. Rather, they provide a gracious tour of well-known ground. In contrast to Levin's sophistication, Anne-Marie Brumm's rambling "Mouths Biting Empty Air: Ezra Pound's Hugh Selwyn Mauberley and Henry James's Lambert Strether" (*RLC* 14:47–70) abounds in oversimplications and may be safely skipped. William Bedford Clark's "Two of Will's Boys: The Political Humor of Ezra Pound and Woody Guthrie" (*SDR* 18,ii:54–60) does little besides marshal a few good one-liners from the newspaper columns "Ez Sez" and "Woody Sez." In "The Literary Revolutions of Hu Shih and Ezra Pound" (*Paideuma* 9:235–48) John J. Nolde establishes parallels but fails to prove "that Hu Shih was significantly influenced by Pound's ideas," since he cannot show that the two writers ever heard of one another.

Self-consciously free of the "intimidation" to criticize the master which it ascribes to Pound studies, William H. Pritchard's lively chapter on Pound in *Lives of the Modern Poets* (Oxford) succeeds better in the first of its twin aims of "introduction" and "revaluation."

Two substantial general articles deal primarily with prose. The "Neofism" in Stephen J. Adams' "Musical Neofism: Pound's Theory of Harmony in Context" (*Mosaic* 13:48–69) refers to George Antheil's abbreviation of Neo-Futurism. Adams uses Antheil to anchor a broad discussion of Pound as musical theorist in one of the few disciplined inquiries into that subject. At the other extreme of organization, David Matthew Rosen draws on the rarely discussed *Money Pamphlets* for "Art and Economics in Pound" (*Paideuma* 9:

481–97), which fulfills the assertion of its opening paragraph that "this paper has no thesis."

c. The Shorter Poems. Once dominant in Pound studies, work on the shorter poems has recently shrunk under the shade of *The Cantos.* This year saw a modest and welcome reemergence which may in time restore a balance between *Personae* and Pound's epic.

In the most thoughtful article, "Context, Contiguity, and Contact in Ezra Pound's *Personae*" (*ELH* 47:386–98), Max Nänny extends to the early poetry Roman Jakobson's distinction between metaphoric and metonymic modes of discourse, which Herbert Schneidau has recently applied to Pound's poetics. In Nänny's redaction, the metaphoric pole makes connections by internal similarities, while the metonymic pole does so by external contiguities in space and time. He convincingly demonstrates Pound's affinity for the metonymic pole, with its emphasis on presentational immediacy and contextual linkage. Although Nänny sometimes verges on merely using Pound to validate Jakobson's categories, he more often helps to define "Pound's often elusive *procedures* of contexture and deletion themselves." Future researchers would do well to divorce Jakobson's distinction from its scientific status as an explanation of aphasic disorders and instead consider it as a suggestive analogy for literary criticism.

In other broad articles, Bernard Duffey surveys "Ezra Pound and the Attainment of Imagism" (*Toward a New American Literary History*, pp. 181–94). Though mostly recounting well-known material, Duffey does establish the extent to which Imagist principles were present in Pound's criticism from an early date. Robert G. Eisenhauer's disorganized " 'Jeweler's Company': Topaz, Half-Light, and Bounding-Lines in *The Cantos*" (*Paideuma* 9:249–70) jumbles together "triangulations" on light, jewels, and a great many other subjects from both Pound and world literature. Peter Quatermain begins " 'Blocked. Make a Song out of That': Pound's 'E. P. Ode Pour L'Election de son Sepulchre' " (*KRev* 1,i:32–48) with a sketch of Thomas Bailey Aldrich and the milieu of ideality in turn-of-the-century American letters. Despite some good aperçus ("There are too many voices, working against each other, as the poem converses with itself"), the article reads more like an abstract of an interesting class paper than a work of advanced scholarship.

Three short notes merit notice. The best of them, Ian F. A. Bell's "Pound's SILET" (*Expl* 38:14–16), explicates that poem in terms of the tension between silence and expression. Bell traces Pound's line "It is enough that we once came together" back to Whitman's "It is enough for us that we are together." Bell's comments on the sieve image in "Instruments for Design: Mauberley's Sieve" (*ELN* 17:294–97) seem equally suggestive but less certain. Finally, W. G. Regier sees "The Allusive Fabric of " 'Apparuit' " (*Paideuma* 9:319–22) as pulling together late Victorian renderings of Dante and of Venus into a pattern of English Sapphics.

d. **The Cantos.** This year witnessed an explosion of scholarly work on *The Cantos*, with six entire books and 18 shorter pieces. Despite some variation, much of the work is of high quality. Several of the new studies aim at fundamental reorientations, but their very simultaneity prevents them from drawing upon each other and postpones anything like consolidation or consensus. The nature of Pound's epic makes commentary centrifugal enough anyway, not so much because critics intend marginality as because the text confers exceptional latitude in locating (or constructing) a center.

When joined by its second volume, Carroll F. Terrell's *A Companion to the Cantos of Ezra Pound* (Calif.) will supercede as well as largely incorporate the previous *Annotated Index to the Cantos* by Edwards and Vasse. Volume 1 covers the first 71 cantos. For each, Terrell—with the occasional assistance of other leading Poundians—provides a tripartite list of Sources, Background, and Exegeses, followed by a Glossary of allusions, foreign phrases, and other cruxes arranged according to order of appearance. Unlike the alphabetically-arranged *Index*, the *Companion* can thus function conveniently as a reader's guide through the contextual thicket of references. It would be ungenerous to bicker about minor points in such an encyclopaedic endeavor: Terrell has produced a vastly informative volume of major utility. I think that he is too modest in describing his audience as "new students" rather than "Pound scholars," and believe that all of us will want the *Companion* on our own shelves for handy reference as well as on reserve lists for our classes.

A lesser endeavor in the same genre, George Kearns's *Guide to Ezra Pound's Selected Cantos* (Rutgers) is keyed to the New Directions text of *Selected Cantos*. Kearns provides introductions to each of the independently published sections of the poem and then a brief essay on each canto followed by page-by-page annotation. The exegeses will help new readers grasp some essential patterns in the poem, though the discussion tends to assume an implicit unity rather than to confront the poem's lapses and discontinuities. The annotations are quite helpful, occasionally more so than in the more elaborate *Companion*. But the greater scope of Terrell's book means that Kearns's work will serve chiefly as a supplement for courses including *The Selected Cantos* as a text.

At the opposite extreme from patient, factual annotation stands the most theoretic new book on *The Cantos*, Michael André Bernstein's suggestive *The Tale of the Tribe: Ezra Pound and Modern Verse Epic* (Princeton). Bernstein has produced the best application yet of avant-garde French literary theory to Pound by the deplorably rare maneuver of using theory rather than being used by it. He sees the poem as attempting but not always sustaining a "precarious balance between the two codes: the historically analytic and explanatory elements (the 'prose tradition' of the great novels recaptured for verse) and the mythological, intuitive insights, the religious revelations of universal truths (traditionally the rightful domain of verse)." By taking the historical and mythological codes as conflicting rather than complementary, Bernstein generates some provocative accounts of culture, mind, time, language, and voice in *The Cantos*. He is weaker on literary history, particularly that of long 19th-century poems in English. Any critic who still thinks the English romantics believed simply "that Nature is at once man's comforter and source of his finest instincts" has neglected the last two decades of scholarship in that area, while the passing nods at Browning's *Sordello* show little insight into either that poem or its crucial relation to Pound's. The concluding chapters treat Williams' *Paterson* and Olson's *Maximus Poems* as successors to *The Cantos*. Bernstein comes off best when he focuses his considerable abilities on the texts before him, but less well when he succumbs to the universal theory-building so fashionable among some younger critics. As Pound paraphrased Aristotle in Canto 74, "philosophy is not for young men/ their *Katholou* can not be sufficiently derived from their *hekasta*/ their generalities cannot be born from a sufficient phalanx of particulars."

Wendy Flory's *Ezra Pound and The Cantos: A Record of Struggle*

(Yale) would have been stronger had there been opportunity to absorb Bernstein's sophisticated remarks on Pound's self-representation in the poem. In place of his generic distinction between "two narratives—the personal and lyric affirmations of a single voice with the 'objective,' communally guaranteed certitudes of traditional epic—in a new kind of text," she offers a simpler paradigm of "epic autobiography" informed by a personal struggle between subjectivity and objectivity which blurs the terms of Bernstein's discrimination. Flory sees a unified poem in which the poet struggles first against Usury and then against himself, with Pisa marking a pivotal stage. Her best remarks treat Pound's growing "emotional evasiveness" in both cultural and personal life until the shattering events at the end of the war. Flory also establishes surprisingly many allusions to Pound's women—Dorothy Pound, Bride Scratton, Olga Rudge, Sherri Martinelli, and Marcella Spann—though sometimes she goes too far. Lapses into "must have been," "surely," and "most likely" signal substitution of mere assertion for hard evidence, and few readers will agree that "Bride Scratton's eyes must have been green" simply to interpret "sky's clear/ night's sea/ green of the mountain pool" as alluding successively to Olga, Dorothy, and Bride. A similarly cavalier attitude toward documentation underlies the book's sparse acknowledgment of its debts to previous scholarship.

The adjective "sparse" cannot be applied to the 512 pages of Massimo Bacigalupo's sprawling *The Forméd Trace: The Later Poetry of Ezra Pound* (Columbia). By "later poetry" Bacigalupo means the cantos from Pisa onward, though it takes him 100 pages to arrive there. Throughout he shovels in an encylopaedic array of information and opinion which sometimes makes his book a scholarly analogue for the poem it studies, in both content and tone. He offers not a developing argument but a rambling meditation, sometimes rehearsing familiar information at needless length. Bacigalupo's specifically Italian perspective has the merit of taking Pound's fascist involvement seriously. But overstatements like consigning *The Cantos* to "those shops that sell swastikas and recordings of Mussolini's speeches" spoil a still-needed correction to more exculpatory accounts of Pound and have already inspired averse reaction (see reviews in *Paideuma* 9:385–91 and *TLS* 15 Aug. 1980, p. 917). Substanial shortening and rephrasing would have made *The Forméd Trace* a better book. Even so, future students of *The Cantos* will want to consult particularly the sections on *Rock-Drill* and *Thrones* (the concluding segment on *Drafts and Fragments* unexpectedly falters).

Anthony Woodward has aimed his agreeably brief *Ezra Pound and the Pisan Cantos* (Routledge) at "the educated reader" rather than "the specialist scholar." He offers few new specific insights but does usefully highlight the elegiac and contemplative side of the work, albeit at the expense of more didactic and active impulses. Woodward deals especially well with the first third of Canto 78 but slips up on the famous "eyes" passage from 81. General readers who may find the book helpful in opening up response to a great but difficult modern sequence should be wary of its distortions. Specialist scholars will note lapses like twice attributing the phrase "subject-rhyme" to Hugh Kenner (who used it) rather than to Ezra Pound (who coined it, in the famous letter to his father on 11 April 1927 about the "main scheme" of his epic). The remarks relating Pound to romanticism would have profited by knowledge of the several pertinent studies noted in *ALS* for 1977 and 1978.

As usual for the numerous essays and notes, I shall comment only on those of broad interest and otherwise simply list the cantos receiving individual attention. *Paideuma* again predominated in the latter category, with notes on Cantos 2, 3, 7, 74 (two items), 79, and 97, but *ELN* offered at least a distant challenge with notes on 4, 85, 89, and 113 (17:288–94). *AN&Q* (18:142–43) has a note on Canto 30, and *ESA* (23:103–16) a belletristic appreciation of Canto 81.

Two chapters in books claim attention not for freshly illuminating specific passages but for raising provocative contexts. "An Epic Is a Poem Containing History: Ezra Pound's Cantos," by James E. Miller, Jr., in *The American Quest for a Supreme Fiction* (Chicago, 1979, pp. 68–98) situates Pound's epic in relation to Whitman. Although Pound rightly identified Browning as his poetic father, Miller weaves enough of Pound's ambivalent responses to his "pig-headed" American ancestor together with suggestive poetic parallels to establish Whitman as at least an uncle of sorts. Kathleen Woodward meditates on *The Pisan Cantos* in *At Last*, pp. 69–98. Although Woodward's four ingredients of late style—a central image of a still point, a meditative interpenetration of mind and world, a wise old man as hero, and tradition and creativity as stays against chaos—ultimately yield a reductive summary of the Pisan sequence, her attempt to blend literary criticism with contemporary developmental psychology deserves praise. She opens an alternative both to traditional Freudian or Jungian approaches and to their recent Parisian metamorphoses. Michael Bernstein's "Identification and its Vicissitudes: The Narrative Structure of Ezra Pound's *Cantos*" may be more conveniently consulted as chapter 5 of his *The Tale of the Tribe*, discussed above.

Three articles from *Paideuma* vary in both quality and approach. In "A Primer for Some of Pound's Chinese Characters" (9:271–88) Randall Schroth conducts an introductory guided tour through the characters of 50 cantos. He interprets them from a Fenollosan point of view. John Steven Childs treats the Chinese characters from a French structuralist standpoint in "Larvatus Prodeo: Semiotic Aspects of the Ideogram in Pound's *Cantos*" (9:289–307). In contrast to the methodological ease of Michael Bernstein, Childs deploys concepts from Barthes and others more mechanically in a style that itself often reads like a translation from a foreign language ("the ideogram is the connective of the thematic musculature"). At the other extreme Ben Kimpel and T. C. Duncan Eaves employ little interpretive method in "American History in *Rock-Drill* and *Thrones*" (9:417–39) but do uncover so many new sources in Pound's reading that future students of the subject will be in their debt. Finally, E. P. Walkiewicz's "A Reading of Pound's Canto CXX" (*NMAL* 4,iv:item 28) elaborates James J. Wilhelm's suggestion that the phantom "Canto 120" makes a fitting close to the poem. Unfortunately, this alleged canto—originally part of the notes for 115 and inserted as 120 into the collected American edition in 1972—carries so little textual authority for separate status that even New Directions apparently plans to drop it as the conclusion to future editions.

ii. Eliot

While books on Pound appear at an almost unassimilable rate, Eliot scholarship seems to be in a period of consolidation. Pound scholarship has already begun to profit from recent theoretical developments in literary criticism, and the appearance of several fine essays on Eliot this year suggests that Eliot scholarship may at last be about to do the same.

a. **Texts and Biography.**   Although no textual work appeared this year, biographical studies continue to flourish. In *The American*

Quest for a Supreme Fiction: Whitman's Legacy in the Personal Epic (Chicago), James E. Miller, Jr. modifies his earlier biographical interpretation of *The Waste Land*. His focus now is on the "deep or original (or originating) structure of *The Waste Land*" which he classifies as " 'open' and 'confessional' in the Whitmanian-Lawrentian sense." Miller deemphasizes Eliot's relationship with Jean Verdenal, which had figured so prominently in his *T. S. Eliot's Personal Waste Land* (see *ALS 1977*, pp. 131–32), by stating that the "validity" of his reading "does not hang on identification of Phlebas the Phoenician in Eliot's life." Rather, Miller emphasizes how the editing of the poem effaced its "confessional" aspect, and he attributes this largely to Pound. However, the lines Miller examines in most detail, those which interpret the voice of the thunder, are lines which Eliot himself altered without Pound's assistance. Miller's biographical reading of the unedited manuscript is convincing, but he overemphasizes the work's relationship to Whitman and underestimates Eliot's own responsibility for obscuring the autobiographical origins of his poem.

Personal relations with other literary figures are the focus of several studies this year. Jeffrey Meyers chronicles Eliot's friendship with Wyndham Lewis from their first meeting in Pound's sitting room in 1915 to the death of Lewis in 1957 ("Wyndham Lewis and T. S. Eliot: A Friendship" [*VQR* 56:455–69]). Meyers attests to Eliot's great admiration for Lewis, which prompted Eliot's financial assistance and moral support, as well as to Lewis's envy of Eliot's position in English letters. In "Richard Aldington and T. S. Eliot" (*YER* 6,i [1979]:3–9), Michael B. Thompson summarizes remarks about Eliot from Aldington's fiction, essays, and autobiography. Thompson gives us an overview of their literary and social relations in London, and attributes the failure of their friendship to an "utterly fundamental opposition of vision, temperament, ambition, and procedure."

The best biographical study, George Mills Harper's "William Force Stead's Friendship with Yeats and Eliot" (*MR* 21:9–38) is a model of its kind. Harper recounts the story of a minor poet who went to England with the Foreign Service and remained to become a clergyman. Yeats included several of Stead's poems in *The Oxford Book of Modern Verse*, and Stead later asked Yeats for a letter of recommendation for an academic position. He made the same request of T. S. Eliot, whom he had baptised in 1927. Harper includes both letters as well as Eliot's annotations to an essay Stead published

toward the end of his life, "Some Personal Impressions on Mr. T. S.
Eliot." As Harper notes in his discussion, these annotations "cast
some light on Eliot's character as well as his friendship with Stead."

b. **General Studies and Relation to Other Writers.** William H.
Pritchard presents a very intelligent, clearly written introduction to
Eliot's work in his *Lives of the Modern Poets* (Oxford). Pritchard
suggests that Eliot's reputation will ultimately rest on "Prufrock,"
The Waste Land, Four Quartets, "and a few of his other poems," and
he devotes most of his chapter to a lucid discussion of these works
which will be of considerable interest to the student and general
reader. M. K. Naik has gathered together a collection of his own
essays on Eliot's work in *Mighty Voices: Studies in T. S. Eliot* (Humanities Press). This volume of "comparative studies, neglected
areas and unexplored approaches" includes "Intimations of Inferi-
ority: Prufrock and Walter Mitty," "Poems of the Evening and of the
Morning: 'Gerontion' and 'Sunday Morning,'" and the most successful in the volume, "Songs Terrestial and Celestial: The 'Four Quartets' and *The Bhagavad-Gita.*" These titles indicate the whimsical
wit which informs these essays and finds its perfect expression in
"T. S. Eliot Among the Cats: *Old Possum's Book of Practical Cats.*"
In general, however, these essays rehearse the commonplace. Surprises, such as the observation that "a typical American is said to
part his name—and his hair—in the middle" are often unintentionally
humorous.

In his survey of "The New American Romances" (*TCL* 26:269–
77) Paul Christensen postulates that *The Cantos, The Waste Land,
Paterson,* and *The Maximus Poems* "belong in the tradition of European verse romance." Although Christensen argues that "without a
generic identity, criticism of these great poems remains at cross-
purposes," he defines the genre so loosely that his argument dissolves
into unsatisfactory generalizations. Another far too general essay is
D. E. S. Maxwell's "Eliot, History and Contemporary Culture" (*ESC*
6:232–43). Maxwell distinguishes Eliot from Pound, Lawrence, and
especially Yeats as being "more professionally, more academically,
disposed towards the habits of abstract thought," and then identifies
a "new myth" in Eliot's poetry. This "new myth," Maxwell argues,
"emancipates the trappings of the present from their accidental properties . . . and re-animates history."

Anthony Suter examines "The Writer in the Mirror: Basil Bunting and T. S. Eliot: Parody and Parallel" (*Paideuma* 9:89–99). Suter gathers useful citations of early comments by Bunting on Eliot which suggest possibilities of interesting relationships between Bunting's work and Eliot's; however, neither the examples of parody nor the parallels cited by Suter are at all convincing. This is a topic which still needs to be explored. A figure who reacted very strongly to Eliot was William Carlos Williams, and John M. Slatin shows how Williams "conscripted" Marianne Moore "in his battle with Eliot" ("The War of the Roses: Williams, Eliot, Moore" [*WCWN* 6,i:1–10]). This topic, too, could be developed in greater detail. The same cannot be said about the possible relationship between May Sinclair and T. S. Eliot. May Sinclair was a British novelist of psychological fiction who wrote an early review of *Prufrock and Other Observations*. Rebeccah Kinnamon Neff suggests that "Sinclair's influence on Eliot's work was pervasive and positive" (" 'New Mysticism' in the Writings of May Sinclair and T. S. Eliot" [*TCL* 26:82–108]). Everywhere Neff looks in Eliot's later work there are traces of Sinclair's presence. At one point, Neff asserts that Eliot, like a character in one of Sinclair's stories, "probably frequently rebuked himself for not having spoken the word of love that might have saved his marriage." Far too little evidence is adduced to support these claims.

Three essays consider Eliot's impact on other writers. Claire Huffman examines "Montale, Eliot and the Poetic Object" (*IQ* 81:63–82). Huffman clearly demonstrates how Montale redefined Eliot's terms (and especially "objectivity") as a way of distancing himself from Eliot. In "*Winterset* and Some Early Eliot Poems" (*NDQ* 48, iii:26–37) Perry D. Luckett argues that Maxwell Anderson drew "heavily on Eliot's early poems in order to enrich and enlarge the significance of *Winterset* for his contemporaries." Letha Audhuy examines "*The Waste Land*: Myth and Symbolism in *The Great Gatsby*" (*EA* 33:41–54). Audhuy far exceeds earlier claims of influence by arguing that *The Waste Land* is the "informing myth" of *The Great Gatsby*. Parallels are sought everywhere (Nick, for example, is based on Tiresias!). Moreover, her reading of Eliot neglects all critical studies of the last 20 years. There is no excuse for such negligent work.

David Tomlinson asserts that Eliot was closer to the "world of contemporary art than we have been inclined to credit" ("T. S. Eliot and the Cubists" [*TCL* 26:64–81]). Tomlinson conjectures that Eliot's visit to the Picasso exhibition at the Leicester Galleries in London (January–February 1921) was "at least partly responsible for releasing the block on the 'Waste Land' material in [his] mind." Tomlinson argues that *The Waste Land* was "consciously constructed along the same basic intellectual principles" as cubism, but he neglects the question of Eliot's revisions. Although he presents a good overview of the artistic ferment of the period, his analysis of Eliot's poem is uninformed.

d. **Studies of Specific Works.** Readers continue to follow Prufrock's invocation, and this poem remains the most frequently discussed of Eliot's early work. In " 'Prufrock': An Absurdist View of the Poem" (*ESC* 6:430–43) Shyamal Bagchee attempts to "reclaim" the work "as a truly modern poem: as poetry that is as significant in our postmodernist times as it was in 1915." But as William Pritchard notes in his *Lives of the Modern Poets* (noticed above), uninitiated students react to "Prufrock" in precisely this way, and Bagchee's own contribution merely obscures the perennial appeal of the poem. His analysis of "the special feeling of the absurd [which] arises from Prufrock's, and our, apprehension that although the world is amoral and illogical, we are not yet prepared to accept it as such" lessens, rather than heightens, the contemporaneity of the poem. In "Prufrock's Magic Lantern and Plato's Cave" (*YER* 6,ii[1979]:19–21) Robert E. Finnegan suggests implausibly that the "magic lantern" evokes the myth of the cave in book 7 of *The Republic*. But the line expresses Prufrock's frustration with the problems of communication, and the image more likely evokes that modern cave, the darkened cinema. A more convincing identification is Francis E. Skipp's suggestion that Prufrock's peach "is an allusion to a poem by William Blake ['The Will and the Way' in Rosetti's 1891 edition] which affords both a dramatic analogy to Prufrock's dilemma and a contrasting resolution of it." In "Conflicts of Mind and Vision in 'Prufrock' and 'Gerontion' " (*YER* 6,i[1979]:10–15) David Spurr profitably considers the continuities between romanticism and these two poems. In both works, Spurr argues, "the protagonist's failure to organize experience according to intelligible structures . . . finally causes flight into the limitless world of imaginative vision."

Clayton C. Reeve examines "Mr. Eliot's Sunday Morning Service" and suggests a possible model for the strategy of using a painting, specifically a 15th-century Italian painting, to exemplify a Christian truth. His source is Hilda's sighting of a fresco in *The Marble Faun* ("A Possible Borrowing by Eliot from Nathaniel Hawthorne" [*YER* 6,i(1979):21–23]). Although this is an interesting parallel, there is insufficient evidence to establish it. Malcolm Pittock considers another perplexing quatrain poem in "Poet and Narrator in 'Sweeney Among the Nightingales'" (*EIC* 30:29–41). In a detailed examination of the narrative strategies, Pittock asserts that "the narrator has the role of omniscient author but [although] . . . he claims to know what is going on, he doesn't." In this case, Pittock's assertion about the narrator aptly mirrors his own predicament as reader of the poem. In "Portraits of Ladies" (*N&Q* 27:533–34) Eleanor Cook identifies the quotation "'false note'" as coming from chapter 10 of Henry James's *Portrait of a Lady*, and observes that "Eliot's lady and young man are characters or points of view that precisely reverse the characters or points of view of James's likeable pair [Henrietta Stackpole and Ralph Touchett]." Cook's identification illuminates our reading of Eliot's poem. Another elucidative source study is Patricia Clements' "Thomas Dekker and Eliot's 'Rhapsody on a Windy Night'" (*N&Q* 27:234–37). In Eliot's copy of René Taupin's *L'Influence du symbolisme français sur la poésie américaine, 1910–1920* Clements discovered the single word "Dekker" in Eliot's handwriting next to three lines from the "Rhapsody" cited by Taupin. Clements convincingly argues that this alludes to one of Dekker's *Prose Pamphlets*, "The Belman of London," where a nocturnal wanderer views the metropolis and provides Eliot with a model who can "unify impressions having no relation in narrative or logic."

In "*The Waste Land*: The Last Minstrel Show" (*JML* 8:23–38) Charles Sanders renders a potentially entertaining subject lifeless. Sanders suggests that "the American minstrel show and the British music-hall, decaying almost simultaneously, form, I believe, a 'familiar compound ghost' behind the many-textured arras of *The Waste Land*." Sanders belabors this point unconvincingly and pushes conjecture to its limits when he asserts that Tiresias is "both figuratively and *literally* Mr. Interlocutor" of minstrel shows. As the curtain falls we turn to another examination of Tiresias: "Tiresias and The Man from Somewhere" by Laurel Boone (*SAQ* 79:398–407). On the basis of the manuscripts Boone analyzes the relationship between *The*

Waste Land and *Our Mutual Friend,* and suggests that Eliot derived his "two most important symbols" (the river Thames and the dust) and the *"modus operandi"* of Tiresias from *Our Mutual Friend.* Boone overemphasizes the role of Tiresias and many of her examples seem rather forced. She does not add substantially to Hugh Kenner's earlier observations regarding this relationship.

A more innovative approach to the poem is taken by Margaret Dickie Uroff in "*The Waste Land*: Metatext" (*CentR* 24:148–66). Uroff argues that Eliot's poem should best be considered "like all revolutionary works, both a text and a metatext, a poem and a commentary on poetry." Uroff presents a provocative examination of the self-referential quality of the poem which "made possible a new understanding of language as a system that creates rather than imitates reality." In addition, the poem "contains Eliot's most trenchant criticism because in it . . . he is engaged . . . in questioning at every point the workings of his own imagination."

In "St. Magnus Visited" (*MR* 21:109–18) Elizabeth Huberman writes of her experience of visiting St. Magnus on Lower Thames Street, and of having been struck by the exterior grimness and blackness, which contrasted so markedly with the beauty of the church's interior. On rereading *The Waste Land,* she observed "the prominence of this motif of opposed spiritual states, dark and light, in the nine lines which conclude with the description of St. Magnus." Huberman's comments on the appearance of the church and its location (at the "very heart of London from the city's origins") are more helpful than her speculations on the meaning of the name for Eliot.

Mildred Meyer Boaz considers "Musical and Poetic Analogues in T. S. Eliot's *The Waste Land* and Igor Stravinsky's *The Rite of Spring* (*CentR* 24:218–31). Boaz points out that both works "have similar textual effects, created by the use of fragmentary motifs and structures, in the placement of rhythmic cells, in the diverse tone colors or voices, and in the sound patterns" as well as in their "mythic centers." The lack of specificity, however, weakens Boaz's argument, for most of these general parallels could be extended to countless other modernist works.

In "Eliot's Marianne: *The Waste Land* and its Poetry of Europe" (*RES* 31:41–53) Barbara Everett deftly demonstrates how "large questions of theme and form may proceed from the examination of a marginal gloss . . . as in the search for the identity of Eliot's and

Pound's Marianne." Everett convincingly identifies Marianne as the heroine of Mariveaux's *La Vie de Marianne*, and suggests that Pound was referring not specifically to the heroine but rather to Marivaux's idiosyncratic style which later critics called *marivaudage*. From here she conjectures suggestively about Eliot's balancing of opposing styles in the early drafts of the poem.

After more than a half century of criticism on *The Waste Land*, scholars continue to puzzle over the sources of this complex work. Matthew Little finds "A Source for 'The City Over the Mountains' in *The Waste Land*" (*ELN* 17:278–81) in Sir Ernest Shackleton's *South: The Story of Shackleton's Last Expedition 1914–1917*. Little suggests that Shackleton's work "may help to clarify the nature of the unreal in the fifth part of *The Waste Land*," especially Shackleton's descriptions of mirages which are "an image of something real" and unlike hallucinations and dreams, "can be seen by several people at once." Here verbal echos lead to a suggestive new reading of these lines. James Kissane uncovers another "altogether neglected source" for *The Waste Land* in C. F. G. Masterman's *The Condition of England* (1909) with its similar views of the urban landscape and its development of "the observer," a persona "who has penetrated unknown geographic regions and has returned to 'civilization' with his eyewitness testimony" ("Eliot's *Waste Land* and Masterman's Abyss: Social Exploration in the Urban Apocalypse" [*YER* 6,i(1979):24–28]). While there are unquestionably parallels here, so were there in many social and historical works of the time. Julia Bolton Holloway identifies the "Bradford millionaire" as Sir James Roberts, the wealthy Yorkshire investor who purchased the Haworth Parsonage in 1928 and donated it to his country ("Haworth and *The Waste Land* [*YER* 6,ii(1979):22–23]). Holloway bases her case on Roberts' contacts with Eliot in the Colonial and Foreign Department at Lloyds Bank after the war when he sought reparation payments for his investments in Russia. Even if such an identification could be established beyond a doubt, it adds little to our understanding of the poem. In "T. S. Eliot's Reading of George Chapman: One Model for *The Waste Land*" (*YER* 6,ii[1979]:26–28) Raymond B. Waddington argues that Eliot's reading of Chapman (and "specifically, in the end notes and glosses which accompany Chapman's first poem *Skia Nuktos*") gave him "a working paradigm of the process by which a poet's reading directly enters his verse, a paradigm which

The Waste Land follows." Yet, as the manuscript of *The Waste Land* demonstrates, this process is far too complex to be attributed to a single poet or work. Denise T. Askin also examines the "Notes" to *The Waste Land,* and adds a third association with "the hanged man" to the two suggested there by Eliot (*"The Waste Land's* Missing Hanged Man: A Source in *The Tempest"* [*ELN* 28:130–31]). Askin quotes Gonzalo's lines in *The Tempest* (I.i. 29–34) which are based on the proverb, "He that's born to be hanged need fear no drowning," and notes: "Because he *finds* the hanged man on board the ship, he ceases to fear death by water." This possibility is suggestive, but Askin weakens her case by her exaggerated opposition between *The Tempest* and *The Waste Land.*

The most significant study of Eliot for 1980 and one of the best essays in recent years is Daniel A. Harris' "Language, History, and Text in Eliot's 'Journey of the Magi'" (*PMLA* 95:838–56). As Harris acknowledges at the outset, "Journey of the Magi" is usually discounted as "an unassuming Christmas poem given only the most rudimentary of Biblical glosses" and he brilliantly demonstrates that the work "occupies a central position in [Eliot's] poetic development." Harris' sophisticated reading reveals the poem to be a highly experimental dramatic monologue which "generates a vision of historical process both more complex and more focussed than anything [Eliot] had previously attempted." This is precisely the sort of reconsideration of Eliot's work which needs to be done.

In "Eliot's *Four Quartets* and French Symbolism" (*English* 29: 1–37) Barbara Everett suggests that we view *Burnt Norton* as the culmination of a ten-year period of experimentation for Eliot, "characterized mainly by the fragmentary." *Burnt Norton* "emerges as the fruit of a long struggle . . . with French literary symbolism," a struggle which "forced into being that philosophical style which proves [the] unity" of the *Four Quartets.* While it is true that Eliot moves away from the fragmentary in *Four Quartets,* it is because he develops a form in *Burnt Norton* which he can duplicate in the other quartets. The symbolists certainly stand behind this sequence, but it is misleading to attribute a "philosophical style" to them alone.

Brian Hatton reconsiders the issue of the musicality of *Four Quartets* in "'Musical Form' in Poetry: *Four Quartets* and Beethoven" (*YER* 6,ii[1979]:3–14). Hatton argues against the "subjective and impressionistic" analyses of such critics as Herbert Howarth and

Harvey Gross, and asserts that "the logic of music lies in its harmonic and rhythmic relationships (not in its 'emotional effects'); the musicality of *Four Quartets* lies in its logical complexity, not the emotional response of its readers." Yet his own detailed study of the "so called variation form," presented in complex diagrams and classification, is itself a variation of a commonplace in criticism of *Four Quartets*. Stephen Spender compares *Four Quartets* to the *Duino Elegies* in "Rilke and Eliot" (*Rilke: The Alchemy of Alienation*, eds. Frank Baron, Ernst S. Dick, Warren R. Maurer [Kansas]). Spender argues that "in both poems the poetry realizes in its language the aims of symbolism and the aesthetic movement at the end of the last century, [and in both poems] this language of apparently pure poetry merges with meanings which are religious." Both works are illuminated by Spender's perceptive comparisons. Kathleen Woodward undertakes an examination of "endings" in *At Last*. Her chapter on "T. S. Eliot and the *Four Quartets*: The Still Point, Aging, and the Social Bond" (pp. 26–67) is at times hampered by the rather schematic parallels she draws between the four authors, but the general perspective in which she examines these poems yields interesting results. In "Eliot's *Burnt Norton*, II, 16–23" (*Expl* 38,iii:14–15), C. T. Thomas offers an "analogy from Hindu mythology" (one of the "best known manifestations of Siva") for these lines. But, as Barbara Everett remarks of this same passage in her article mentioned above (p. 15), "The concept of the still point is an ancient one, to be met in many cultures. To look for a single source for Eliot's use of the idea would be mistaken. . . ." Christopher Williams offers a second source for the opening lines of section 4 of *East Coker* ("*East Coker* and *The Lady of the Lake*" (*N&Q* 27:238). In addition to ll. 143–46 of Pope's *Essay on Man*, Williams proposes a passage from Sir Walter Scott (*The Lady of the Lake*, Canto I.vii.2). E. W. F. Tomlin recommends Sherwood Anderson's *Dark Laughter* as a possible source for those passages in *The Dry Salvages* which evoke the Mississippi ("T. S. Eliot, Wyndham Lewis and Sherwood Anderson" [*N&Q* 27:237–38]). Since Eliot was "not a great novel reader," Tomlin plausibly suggests that Eliot may have encountered the passages from Anderson's novel in Wyndham Lewis' *Paleface* (1929), where they are quoted at length. In "The Genesis of 'Little Gidding'" (*YER* 6,i[1979]:29–30) Barry Spurr recounts how Eliot suggested revisions for a liturgical drama (*Stalemate—The King at Little Gidding*) by George Every, a lay-brother of the Society of the Sacred Mission, an Anglican religious house where Eliot was a "familiar visitor." Two months after aiding Every, Eliot visited Little Gidding himself, a visit which, Spurr suggests, Eliot "commemorated" in the final poem of *Four Quartets*.

Eliot's plays continue to receive less attention than his poetry, attesting to the common judgment that they represent a falling off in quality. In "History Versus Mystery: The Test of Time in *Murder in the Cathedral*" (*ClioI* 10:47–56) Carol Billman examines the tension between "temporal history and unchanging transcendence" and praises the play for its "incorporation of puzzling ambiguities and [its] exploration of man's doubtful struggle to find his place in history and the cosmos." An essay which aims at providing assistance for actual productions of the play is William J. McGill's "Voices in the Cathedral: The Chorus in Eliot's *Murder in the Cathedral*" (*MD* 23:292–96). McGill presents a "reading of the choral odes which identifies the principal thematic and dramatic voices." Although his essay will not surprise scholars, it should assist amateur producers of the play. Lionel J. Pike explores the play's "debt to medieval liturgies" in "Liturgy and Time in Counterpoint: A View of T. S. Eliot's *Murder in the Cathedral*" (*MD* 23:277–91). Pike convincingly demonstrates that the play is "nearer to medieval liturgical drama than to modern theater," examines the play's elements of ritual and its liturgical background, and suggests that the play is "cast in the same shape as the Mass." Equally interesting is his analysis of those elements which "oppose the liturgical language with varying degrees of violence," and are timebound as opposed to the "eternal truths" of the liturgical language.

Two rather speculative source studies for the later dramas are Christopher Brown, "J. B. Priestley and *The Family Reunion*" (*YER* 6,i[1979]:16–20) and Mark Webb, "John Rhode and the Naming of Eliot's *Elder Statesman*" (*YER* 6,ii[1979]:15–18). Brown argues that Eliot's play is indebted to J. B. Priestley's drama, *Time and the Conways*, which had been produced in London in 1937. Although Priestley's play suggests a way of using the Eumenides as well as character types and human relationships which Eliot may have emulated, Brown admits to a "lack of corroborative evidence." Similarly, Webb suggests that Eliot chose the name for his elder Statesman from the title character of *The Claverton Mystery*, a detective novel published in 1933. Here too there are many parallels, but although Eliot was an avid reader of mysteries, we simply do not know if he read this one.

A more ambitious reconsideration of *The Family Reunion* is Michael T. Beehler's "Troping the Topic: Dis-Closing the Circle of *The Family Reunion*" (*Boundary* 8,iii:19–42). Beehler offers a "re-reading of *The Family Reunion* [that] seeks to partially extract the play from the circumscription of its title and to de-mystify that title's previously privileged metaphors." He identifies "the central *topos* of the play" as "a trope of the book, a figure upon which the entire play meditates. The book as house and the house as book." Beehler's analysis of the figurative language of the play is suggestive, but some of his interpretations become rather farfetched, as when he observes that the "hollow tree" by which Harry and Mary played as children "speaks of the linearity of the family tree and thus of the authority of the father. But here the tree is 'hollow,' the phallus empty or the father originally castrated of all authority."

No work appeared this year on Eliot's critical writings, but Brian Lee's *Theory and Personality: The Significance of T. S. Eliot's Criticism* (Athlone, 1979) slipped through last year's net. Lee offers a detailed reading of "Tradition and the Individual Talent" with "the same general attention that we give to a poem," in order to elucidate the relationship between "personality" and "impersonality": "Romantic confidence in the self," he notes, "had degenerated to a corrupt self-expression, which Eliot denoted by the word 'personality,' and against which he set his word 'impersonality.'" Unfortunately, Lee imposes rather severe restrictions on his study. Early in his book he speaks of the "need to adhere to non-specialist language, the language of which literature is made and in which its criticism is still largely written" and later he identifies "questions we are inhibited from asking by Eliot himself." But the language of criticism has become increasingly varied and although Lee may deplore this fact, he should at least recognize it. Lee's topic is an important one, but his methods are too shaped by Eliot's own dicta to do the topic justice. This remains a general failing of much criticism of Eliot's work.

University of Michigan

9. Faulkner

Karl F. Zender

The historian John Murrin once said that he could foresee the day when his colleagues in colonial history would have produced the equivalent of a scholarly book for every 40 or 50 adult males alive in New England in 1660. Reading my way through the year's work on Faulkner leads me to a similar conclusion about the future awaiting the residents of Yoknapatawpha County. Admittedly, measuring the year's 13 books and 100 or so articles and notes against Yoknapatawpha's 6,298 whites and 9,313 blacks suggests that Faulkner scholars have a way to go before reaching Murrin's ratio; but we should bear in mind that Murrin excludes women and children from his computation and does not limit himself to the output of a single year. All things considered, I think the colonial historians had better look to their laurels.

Unfortunately the quality of the year's work did not quite match its quantity. The year saw publication of the catalog of a significant Faulkner collection, of a valuable concordance to *The Sound and the Fury*, and of a useful trade edition of *Mayday*. It also saw the appearance of David Minter's insightful and comprehensive book on the relationship between Faulkner's life and his art. And too, several essays appeared that either made intelligent use of recent innovations in critical method or applied old methods to new topics. Here I have in mind Michael Millgate's two essays in *Fifty Years of Yoknapatawpha*, David Wyatt's chapter on Faulkner in *Prodigal Sons*, John M. Howell's essay on Faulkner and Eliot, Robert W. Hamblin's and Louis Daniel Brodsky's essay on "L'Après-Midi d'une Faune," and John T. Matthews' essay on *Absalom, Absalom!* With these exceptions noted, though, the rest of the year's work can be said merely to have marked time. The best among it enumerates old themes; the worst is vapid, boring, and unscholarly.

i. Bibliography, Editions, and Manuscripts

William Faulkner. The William B. Wisdom Collection: A Descriptive Catalogue (New Orleans: Tulane University Libraries) records the contents of a collection of Faulkneriana housed in the Howard-Tilton Memorial Library of Tulane University. Compiled by Thomas Bonner, Jr., and edited by Guillermo Náñez Falcón, the book contains a detailed introduction by Bonner, a warm and generous memoir of William Wisdom by Carvel Collins, and an essay assessing the significance of the collection by Cleanth Brooks. A perusal of the catalog confirms Brooks's judgment that the most important items in the collection are the manuscript books *Mayday* and *Helen: A Courtship* and five letters Faulkner wrote to Helen Baird in the 1920s. Of less importance, but worth noting, are two typescript versions of chapter 1 of *Absalom, Absalom!* and typescripts of seven published stories. The catalog is scrupulously edited and carefully cross-referenced to Linton Massey's *"Man Working"* and Joan St. C. Crane's and Anne E. H. Freudenberg's *Man Collecting*. With the exception of a tantalizing reference to an "added inscription" on one of Faulkner's presentation copies of *The Sound and the Fury*, the descriptive comments are full and informative.

A facsimile edition of the manuscript book *Mayday* was published by the University of Notre Dame Press in 1977. Accompanying the facsimile, but separately bound, was a provocative and informative essay by Carvel Collins entitled "Faulkner's *Mayday*." The same press has now published a trade edition of *Mayday* which incorporates Collins' essay as an introduction. The new edition does not purport to be an exact duplicate of the original book: page length is normalized, as are Faulkner's affected *u*'s, *v*'s, and reversed letters; the watercolors located throughout the manuscript book are grouped together; and only illustrative samples of Faulkner's hand-lettered pages are reproduced. Of necessity, then, the new edition cannot match the facsimile in conveying the intensity of Faulkner's early interest in books as artifacts. The trade edition is nonetheless most welcome, for, as Collins suggests, it makes widely accessible a work that affords valuable insight into the genesis of Faulkner's mature fiction.

Equally welcome is the republication of James B. Meriwether's and Michael Millgate's invaluable *Lion in the Garden: Interviews with William Faulkner, 1926–1962* (Nebraska). This book, a *vade mecum* for scholars interested in Faulkner's comments on his own fiction, has long been unavailable. Unfortunately a similar welcome cannot be extended to another republication, Max Putzel's "Faulkner's Trial Preface to *Sartoris*: An Eclectic Text" (*PBSA* 74:361–78). The preface Putzel reprints was first published by Joseph Blotner in "William Faulkner's Essay on the Composition of *Sartoris*" (*YULG* 47[1973]:121–24). Putzel's claim that Blotner's transcription is inaccurate may be valid, insofar as some readings of doubtful words and phrases are concerned. But Blotner's text is careful and consistent where Putzel's is careless and capricious. For example, Putzel is inconsistent in his treatment of elided words and phrases, and he changes punctuation and wording in ways that affect meaning. The result is a text that reflects neither Faulkner's final intention (insofar as it can be determined) nor his method of composition. The annual Faulkner number of *MissQ* provides us with two hitherto unpublished items by Faulkner. In "The Rejected Manuscript Opening of *Flags in the Dust*" (33:371–83) George F. Hayhoe reprints the first seven pages of the manuscript of *Flags in the Dust* housed at the University of Virginia. In his headnote Hayhoe argues cogently that the fragment is a rejected opening for the novel and not, as has been theorized, an incomplete draft of a short story. "The Uncut Text of Faulkner's Review of *Test Pilot*," ed. J. B. M. [James B. Meriwether] (33:385–89), reprints the final draft version of one of Faulkner's few book reviews. Readers interested in comparing Faulkner's draft with the heavily edited version that appeared in *American Mercury* may do so by consulting Meriwether's *Essays, Speeches, and Public Letters*. The annual Faulkner number of *MissQ* also continues to publish, under the capable editorship of Thomas L. McHaney, a review of the year's work on Faulkner somewhat similar to this one. Given the size and complexity of Faulkner studies at the present time, readers would probably be well advised to consult both.

In *The Ghosts of Rowan Oak: William Faulkner's Ghost Stories for Children* (Oxford, Miss.: Yoknapatawpha Press) Dean Faulkner Wells, Faulkner's niece, retells three of the ghost stories that Faulkner told to children on Halloween and on other festive occasions. The stories have a variety of affiliations with Faulkner's published fiction and should prove to be of interest to Faulkner scholars. In retelling them, Wells reveals herself to be a competent storyteller in her own right.

ii. Biography

The important event of the year in biography was the publication of David Minter's *William Faulkner: His Life and Work* (Johns Hopkins). Because of similarities in organization and intention, Minter's book invites comparison with Judith Bryant Wittenberg's *Faulkner: The Transfiguration of Biography* (see *ALS* 1979, pp. 137–38). I will therefore say at the outset that Minter's is the better book, outstripping its predecessor in the comprehensiveness of its research, in the soundness of its understanding of the ways in which life and art interrelate, and in the subtlety of its readings of Faulkner's fiction.

All this is not to say that Minter's book completely supersedes Wittenberg's, for if her study contained nothing but its insightful account of the relationship between Faulkner's impending marriage and his composition of *Sanctuary* it would remain necessary reading for Faulkner scholars. Nor is it to say that Minter's book is without defect. Though Minter's analyses of the fiction are often influenced by his belief that Faulkner suffered a painful early loss of a "sense of holistic unity with his family," he provides little biographical evidence in support of this view. Also, his application of Faulkner's biography to his fiction, though precise and convincing, is sometimes lacking in daring; the Faulkner he depicts, for example, seldom appears in his fiction in any guise other than that of a white male protagonist. A further reservation is that Minter only intermittently examines the inner dynamics of Faulkner's career. Though he explains major turning points in the career quite well, he more often devotes his energy to demonstrating the ways in which specific events and situations in Faulkner's life made their way into his fiction. This is arguably a proper orientation so long as the fiction being considered is that of Faulkner's major phase. But in the second half of Faulkner's career, the subject of biographical interest ceases to be how his experiences made their way into his novels and instead becomes how mounting public acclaim, relative imaginative impoverishment, and an intimidating awareness of his own former greatness conspired to alter the direction of his career. Minter's failure to focus his full attention on this topic diminishes the value of the last two chapters of his book, for it leaves him with little to do but summarize Blotner and explicate novels that compel neither his attention nor ours.

Despite these caveats, *William Faulkner: His Life and Work* is an important book, containing much that will be of worth to any serious student of Faulkner's fiction. Especially to be admired are Minter's analyses of the aesthetic changes Faulkner underwent when he abandoned poetry for prose, of the images of the artist Faulkner incorporates into the fiction between *Flags in the Dust* and *As I Lay Dying*, and of the various ways in which Faulkner's relationships with women influenced his art. Given the comprehensiveness, judiciousness, and general sanity of Minter's study, in fact, it may be safe to say that we are at a temporary point of closure in the history of Faulkner criticism. Although we can expect biographical studies of merit to continue to appear, any truly substantial advance in our understanding of the influence of Faulkner's life on his art beyond the point attained by Minter's book will probably have to await the revelation of new biographical data.

The remaining items in this section take a variety of forms: one is a transcription of a television script, four are anecdotal memoirs, another is a transcription of a classroom interview, and another is a psychobiographical study of the motif of revenge. *William Faulkner: A Life on Paper* (Miss.), adapted and edited by Ann Abadie, reprints A. I. Bezzerides' script of the film on Faulkner produced in 1979 by the Mississippi Center for Educational Television. In addition to the script and frame enlargements from the film, the volume contains a preface by Bezzerides and an introduction by Carvel Collins. Both the preface and the introduction suggest that an interesting history could be written of the difficulties involved in producing a program that would be acceptable to all the parties involved. For Collins the struggle was primarily between two critical factions and was evidently successfully resolved; for Bezzerides it had a different character and a different outcome, for he speaks darkly of friends, relatives, and professors "who deleted everything they thought to be offensive" in the script.

Bezzerides does not specify what was deleted from his script, but in reading through it one is struck by a number of noteworthy omissions. There is no mention, for example, of Estelle Faulkner's alcoholism or of the coolness that developed between Faulkner and Phil Stone in their later years. Meta Carpenter is mentioned only once, and then in passing. There is no mention of the family tensions caused by Faulkner's stand on racial matters. Despite these omissions, though, the script seems to be a sincere attempt to convey Faulkner's essential genius. The makers of the film are especially to be congratulated for having succeeded in obtaining Jill Faulkner Summers' involvement in the project. One only wishes that the script contained even more of her touching and insightful comments than it does.

The first of the four biographical memoirs to be discussed, Joan Williams' "Twenty Will Not Come Again" (*AtM* May:58–65), poignantly expresses her complex feelings toward Faulkner but does not materially alter the impression of their relationship that one gains from reading Blotner's biography. It is to be hoped that Williams brings to fruition the book-length memoir mentioned in the author's note to this essay, for we would benefit greatly from having a full account of her relationship with Faulkner.

In "Did You See Him Plain?" (*Fifty Years of Yoknapatawpha*, pp. 3–22) Joseph Blotner answers his title's question quite literally by providing a detailed account of Faulkner's physical appearance and mannerisms. This modest and engaging essay succeeds in the difficult task of giving those of us who never saw Faulkner a sense of what he was like in the flesh. The remaining two biographical memoirs are of less significance. Jim Faulkner's "Memories of Brother Will" (*SoR* 16:907–920) is a somewhat fictionalized account of two anecdotes involving Faulkner. Neither of the stories contains any new information about Faulkner. Carlos Baker's "Faulkner: An Orientation, 1940" (*FaSt* 1:9–13) is a pleasant but inconsequential account of a visit Baker made to Rowan Oak in 1940.

Perhaps the most puzzling item of the year is Harry Modean Campbell's "Faulkner in the Classroom—1947" (*Unappeased Imagination*, pp. 1–6). Though an editor's note says that the piece is a transcription of a classroom visit made by Faulkner and Phil Stone, its form suggests a more complex origin. Faulkner's comments, some of which duplicate comments to be found in his other published classroom interview from 1947, were clearly made in response to student questions. Stone's were not. His comments are responses to Faulkner's responses, and their rancorous tone suggests that they were not uttered in Faulkner's presence. This document is of little critical interest, but it provides a bleak testimonial to the nature of Stone's postwar relationship with his former protégé.

David Wyatt's "Faulkner and the Burdens of the Past" (*Prodigal Sons*, pp. 72–100) is an exciting, closely reasoned study of the motif of revenge in Faulkner's fiction between *Sartoris* and *The Unvanquished.* Though indebted, as Wyatt acknowledges, to John Irwin's *Doubling and Incest/Repetition and Revenge* (see *ALS 1975*, pp. 146–48), Wyatt's study departs from Irwin's by placing the motif of revenge in a biographical context and by emphasizing the ways in which Faulkner's use of the motif changed as his career advanced. After an ingenious and convincing analysis of the ways in which Faulkner used patterns of revenge and failed revenge from his family history in *Sartoris* and *Light in August*, Wyatt discusses the repudiation of revenge in *The Unvanquished.* Though he overreaches a bit in claiming to find a full resolution of Faulkner's interest in revenge in this rather slight work, he succeeds in enhancing its value and in explaining several of its puzzling features. I come away from this intelligent essay wishing that Wyatt would return to its subject and explore the complex shifts that the theme of revenge underwent in the second half of Faulkner's career.

iii. Criticism: General

a. **Books.** Although only one book of general criticism on Faulkner appeared during 1980, the year also saw the production of three collections of essays and five books in which one or more chapters are devoted to Faulkner. The one book of general criticism, Lyall H. Powers' *Faulkner's Yoknapatawpha Comedy* (Michigan), is disappointing. Uncritically accepting the now-outmoded saga theory, Powers argues that Faulkner's major fiction is a unified expression of the values espoused in the Nobel Prize Speech. Perhaps because he is almost exclusively concerned with the moral values expressed in the fiction, Powers shows little interest in recent developments in Faulkner criticism. This inattention to recent criticism is especially damaging in his discussions of the pattern he calls the "Second Chance." The pattern of a character repeatedly encountering the same decision is a real and important feature of Faulkner's fiction, and Powers is to be commended for pointing it out. Yet in discussing it he never refers to John Irwin's treatment of patterns of repetition in *Doubling and Incest/Repetition and Revenge*, or to any of the other recent interesting studies of the role of obsessive behavior in Faulkner's fiction. Had Powers sought to adjudicate between Irwin's psychoanalytic interpretation of repetition and his own ethical and religious interpretation of the "Second Chance," he might have achieved a real advance in our understanding of the Faulkner canon. As it is, his book, though well written, reads like a relic from a past age.

The three collections of essays on Faulkner that appeared during 1980 all combine studies of individual works with essays on more general subjects. I will discuss only the general essays here, reserving the essays on individual works for the appropriate categories below. *Fifty Years of Yoknapatawpha*, the sixth in the series of proceedings of the annual Faulkner conference at the University of Mississippi, maintains the high standards of the two preceding volumes. Handsomely produced and scrupulously proofread, the volume contains some general essays of real merit. Especially valuable are Michael Millgate's two essays, " 'A Cosmos of My Own': The Evolution of Yoknapatawpha" (pp. 23–43) and "Faulkner's First Trilogy: *Sartoris, Sanctuary,* and *Requiem for a Nun*" (pp. 90–109). The two essays together form a sustained meditation on the question of how we are to understand the simultaneous independence and interdependence of Faulkner's novels. Part of the strength of the essays lies in their record of Millgate's struggle "to resist the pull of the chronological, of the discoverable and demonstrable structure of the total career," in favor of a more challenging but ultimately more satisfying view of Yoknapatawpha as "a vast imaginative conception which Faulkner only fragmentarily realized on paper."

Also of interest in *Fifty Years of Yoknapatawpha* are the essays on general topics by Joseph Blotner, Thomas L. McHaney, Noel Polk, and James G. Watson. Blotner's "The Sources of Faulkner's Genius" (pp. 248–70) is a genial and comprehensive account of the elements in Faulkner's environment and personality that went together to form his ability as a writer. The very comprehensiveness of the account, though, tends to rob it of explanatory power: if everything formed Faulkner's genius, then perhaps nothing did.

McHaney's "Faulkner's Curious Tools" (pp. 179–201) is an engagingly written, though rather insistent, study of the unusual sorts of characters Faulkner uses to convey his moral meaning in his later fiction. Readers who do not agree—as I do not—with McHaney's claim that "the meanings we derive from the later fiction are not really different from those we derive from the earlier work" will find much to quarrel with in this essay. McHaney's high opinion of the moral philosophy of Faulkner's later fiction is shared by Noel Polk in "Faulkner and Respectability" (pp. 110–33) and " 'I Taken an Oath of Office Too': Faulkner and the Law" (pp. 159–78). In the first of these essays Polk uses *The Town* and the short story "Uncle Willy" as exempla for an argument that "respectability is not necessarily a bad thing" in Faulkner's fiction; in the second he attempts to discover a rather upbeat philosophy of the law in Faulkner's works (especially *Requiem for a Nun*). As with McHaney, my quarrel is not with the way Polk conducts his arguments but with the premise on which he founds them. Agreeing as I do with Lewis Simpson's contention that Faulkner's allegiance during the 1920s and 1930s was to the "obdurate self," the self in its resistance to society, I find it difficult to sympathize with the search for keys to his work in the moral and social pieties of the postwar fiction. James G. Watson's "Faulkner: The House of Fiction" (pp. 134–58) is a welcome instance of a critic finding something new to say by taking a close, careful look at a commonplace feature of Faulkner's fiction. Using Gaston Bachelard's poetics of space as a frame of reference, Watson makes a number of acute observations about Faulkner's depictions of houses in *The Sound and the Fury, Sanctuary*, and *As I Lay Dying*. I was surprised, though, that he did not mention the physical separation of the kitchen from the rest of the Old Frenchman's place in *Sanctuary*. This separation, a common feature of houses built when cooking was done over an open fire, figures in important ways in the early scenes of the novel.

Faulkner Studies: An Annual of Research, Criticism, and Reviews (Miami, Fla.: Published in cooperation with the Department of English, University of Miami), ed. Barnett Guttenberg, is the first of a new serial. Modeled on *Shakespeare Studies, Faulkner Studies* (*FaSt*) is a handsome volume combining essays by well-known and young critics with reviews, some quite lengthy, of all the important books on Faulkner published during the last few years. It remains to be seen, though, whether Faulkner scholarship, already blessed with the annual number of *MissQ* and the Faulkner and Yoknapatawpha series, can sustain yet another annual compendium of criticism.

Only two of the essays in *Faulkner Studies* are on general topics; both are of middling quality. In "Faulkner and Nature" (pp. 112–21), Ilse Dusoir Lind provides a mainly descriptive account of the many facets of Faulkner's use of physical nature in his fiction. Lind makes a good distinction between the willfully unrealistic images of nature in Faulkner's early poetry and fiction and the "hard images" of his mature work, but her essay is marred by a confusing use of the terms "imagistic" and "imagism" and by a general inattention to the previous work on her subject. No one is ever obliged to refer to any particular work of criticism, of course, but it is hard to see how Lind could write on nature in Faulkner's fiction without mentioning the seminal chapter entitled "Faulkner as Nature Poet" in Cleanth Brooks' *William Faulkner: The Yoknapatawpha Country*. The other essay, Joseph Reed's "Faulkner, Ford, Ives, and the Sense of the Canon" (pp. 136–52), is a quirky, stylistically self-indulgent attempt to draw parallels between three artists working in different media. The Ford of the title, incidentally, is John, not Ford Madox; Reed says that Ford's films are "as subtle an exploration" of the tension between individual and community "as Faulkner's novels are."

The contents of the third and final collection of essays, *Faulkner: The Unappeased Imagination* (Troy, N.Y.: Whitston Pub. Co.), ed. Glenn O. Carey, vary widely in quality, ranging from a low of two essays that scarcely merit review to a high of an essay by John M. Howell (noticed below) that is a substantial contribution to our understanding of the workings of Faulkner's imagination. The book itself is indifferently proofread and oddly styled. Though most of its essays focus on individual works, five of them—including a rather good one—are on general topics. Richard A. Milum's "Continuity and Change: The Horse, The Automobile, and the Airplane in Faulkner's Fiction" (pp. 157–74) is a sensible and well-written study of the ways Faulkner uses horses, cars, and planes to express the attitude of his characters toward a chivalric code of conduct. As might be expected, the essay is strongest when it deals with *Sartoris* and *Pylon*, works in which horses and planes have symbolic value.

An essay that holds promise for future achievement is Carolyn Porter's "Faulkner and His Reader" (pp. 231–58). Though Porter does not succeed in demonstrating the connections she posits between departures from fixed perspective in cubist painting and Faulkner's experiments with narrative technique, her temperate tone and alertness to the theoretical implications of her subject bode well for the future. Despite its title, P. P. Sharma's "Faulkner's South and the Other South" (pp. 123–37) discusses three Souths: the romanticized South of Thomas Nelson Page and the Fugitives, the decaying South of William Faulkner, and the routine-bound South of Eudora Welty. The interpretation of William Faulkner's fiction that is presented here is essentially that of George Marion O'Donnell. As her title suggests, Elizabeth D. Rankin's "Chasing Spotted Horses: The Quest for Human Dignity in Faulkner's Snopes Trilogy" (pp. 139–56) combines a study of the "Spotted Horses" episode in *The Hamlet* with observations on the Snopes trilogy as a whole. Rankin quotes but does heed Cleanth Brooks's warning against approaching the "Spotted Horses" episode with "any argument put too seriously or symbolism set forth too nakedly." Her very serious attempt to find "a metaphor for the human condition" in the episode distorts its tone and obscures the sources of its comic power. The final essay on a general topic in *Unappeased Imagination* is the editor's own "Faulkner and His Carpenter's Hammer" (pp. 259–69). This essay, reprinted from *ArQ*, was reviewed in *ALS* 1976.

The most significant of the four books containing chapters on Faulkner, Lewis P. Simpson's *The Brazen Face of History* (LSU), also reprints previously published material. One of its two chapters on Faulkner, "The Legend of the Artist" (pp. 181–208), first appeared in *Faulkner: Fifty Years After "The Marble Faun,"* ed. George H. Wolfe (see *ALS* 1976). The other, "A Fable of Civilization" (pp. 209–31), is a recasting of three previously published essays and reviews. Deriving from Simpson's longstanding interest in the effect on modern art of the dialectical interplay between myth and history, this essay provides an insightful interpretation of the place of *A Fable* in Faulkner's career. Simpson is also the author of an essay entitled "William Faulkner of Yoknapatawpha" in *The American South* (pp. 227–44). This volume, which derives from a project of the Voice of America Forum, contains introductory essays on a number of aspects of southern culture.

The other two books containing chapters on Faulkner are of limited value. The extended discussion of Faulkner in Richard H. King's *A Southern Renaissance* (Oxford) is schematic, aesthetically naive, and marred by errors of fact and judgment. Fonsiba in *Go Down, Moses* becomes Phonsiba, *The Sound and the Fury* is discussed as if it had been written before *Sartoris*, and *Go Down, Moses* is unequivocally acclaimed as Faulkner's greatest novel. Lucinda Hardwick MacKethan's *The Dream of Arcady* (LSU) suffers from narrowness of method. MacKethan appears to have derived her approach to pastoral literature almost entirely from Raymond Williams and William Empson. Her reliance on these authors' politicized way of reading pastoral has unfortunate effects in her chapter on Faulkner (pp. 153–80), for it leads her to a simplistic interpretation of the Quentin Compson and Shreve McCannon sections of *Absalom, Absalom!* and to a wholehearted endorsement of Ike McCaslin's repudiation of his heritage in *Go Down, Moses*.

b. **Articles.**   Only two articles of any consequence appeared on general topics during 1980. Ikuko Fujihira's "Beyond Closed Doors: Quentin Compson and Isaac McCaslin" (*WiF* 3,i:31–43) relies too heavily on ethical judgments in its discussion of Faulkner's heroes, but it contains a number of shrewd comments on the motif of passage through doorways. The journal in which this essay appears is now in its third year of existence. It publishes articles in both English and Japanese, and it has begun to publish articles by American scholars of note (see McHaney, "The Modernism of *Soldiers' Pay*," below). Susan Gallagher's "To Love and to Honor: Brothers and Sisters in Faulkner's Yoknapatawpha County" (*ELWIU* 7:213–24) begins with the startling assertion that "little critical attention has been paid to the frequent brother/sister pairings in the Yoknapatawpha chronicles." Gallagher then proceeds to quarrel with a large number of critics (though few recent ones) about particular points of interpretation.

iv. Criticism: Special Studies

a. **Ideas, Influences, Intellectual Background.**   Though not a year in which major influence studies appeared, 1980 did see the publication of some useful work, both on influences on Faulkner and on Faulkner's influence on others. As to influences on Faulkner, the best study is John M. Howell's "Faulkner, Prufrock, and Agamemnon: Horses, Hell, and High Water" (*Unappeased Imagination*, pp. 213–

29). In demonstrating how Faulkner absorbed and synthesized images from T. S. Eliot and other sources, Howell displays a wide-ranging knowledge of Faulkner's fiction and a sure instinct for how poetic association works. In "Faulkner and Eugene O'Neill" (*MissQ* 33:327–41) Judith Bryant Wittenberg makes a plausible case for the influence of *Mourning Becomes Electra* on *Absalom, Absalom!* Her claim that O'Neill may have influenced Faulkner in more general ways is, as she acknowledges, not amenable to definite proof. J. A. W. Bennett's "Faulkner and A. E. Housman" (*N&Q* 27:234) adds three items to Cleanth Brooks's list (in *William Faulkner: Toward Yoknapatawpha and Beyond*) of Faulkner's borrowings from Housman.

All three of the studies of Faulkner's influence on his contemporaries and successors are worth reading. The longest of the three, Harley D. Oberhelman's *The Presence of Faulkner in the Writings of García Márquez* (Texas Tech; Grad. Studies, No. 22), is a comprehensive and readable introduction to an important subject, but it is marred by insistently sociological readings and a shaky command of detail. Oberhelman speaks of a Faulkner character named "Gowin" and a story called "That is Fine" and praises Emily Grierson for resisting "the will of authority" by refusing to pay taxes. Shorter, but also of value, is Jan Nordby Gretlund's "The Wild Old Green Man of the Woods: Katherine Anne Porter's Faulkner" (*NMW* 12:67–79). Though lacking in critical and expository sophistication, this essay presents some interesting data on Porter's reactions to Faulkner. Also of interest is Thomas L. McHaney's "Watching for the Dixie Limited: Faulkner's Impact upon the Creative Writer" (*Fifty Years of Yoknapatawpha*, pp. 226–47). The thesis of this essay is that creative writers have always responded to Faulkner with a shock of recognition, even though reviewers and scholars have not.

For a variety of reasons the remaining items in this section (all studies of influence on Faulkner) are of little value. Victor Strandberg's "Faulkner's God: A Jamesian Perspective" (*FaSt* 1:122–35) is founded on the doubtful premise that Faulkner was primarily a religious writer. Strandberg's attempt to use William James's descriptive categories as a basis for classifying Faulkner's characters, results in some surprising assignments: Jack Houston is a "Sick Soul," whereas Januarius Jones, Cora Tull, and Narcissa Benbow are all "healthy minded" individuals. Margaret Church's "Two Views of Time: James Joyce and William Faulkner" (*UDR* 14,ii:65–69) is not long enough to give more than superficial treatment to its complex topic. The value of Church's study is also limited by her use of phrases like "the interpermeable flow of duration" and by her puzzling decision to compare Leopold Bloom and Joe Christmas as types of the Christian martyr. In "Quentin Durward and Quentin Compson: The Romantic Standard-Bearers of Scott and Faulkner" (*MSE* 7,iii:34–39) Carl E. Rollyson, Jr. provides no new insight into a shopworn pairing of characters. Masaji Onoe's "Some T. S. Eliot Echoes in Faulkner" (*WiF* 3,i:1–15) also suffers from the familiarity of its topic.

b. **Style and Structure.**   Surprisingly, no broadly based studies of either style or structure appeared during 1980. Structural analyses of individual works appeared by Davis, Komar, and Matthews. All three are discussed below.

c. **Race.**   Glancing back through *ALS* for the last few years, I note a steadily declining interest in the topic of race among Faulkner scholars. This decline continued in 1980, for with the exception of Richard Godden's essay (discussed below), no work on the topic appeared during the year.

v. Individual Works to 1929

Both Faulkner's early poetry and his first novel received a greater than usual amount of attention during 1980, some of it of very high quality. In "Faulkner's 'L'Apres-Midi D'Un Faune': The Evolution of a Poem" (*SB* 33:254–63) Robert W. Hamblin and Louis Daniel Brodsky provide us with a meticulous and carefully reasoned study of the compositional history of Faulkner's first published poem. Of special interest is their reproduction of the presumed first draft of the poem, which Faulkner wrote—without any strikeovers whatsoever and with a fine high disregard for pronoun reference—on the front cover of a copy of *The Saturday Evening Post*. Another valuable study of the early poetry is Martin Kreiswirth's "Faulkner's *The Marble Faun*: Dependence and Independence" (*ESC* 6:333–44). This oddly organized study combines an unexceptional analysis of the indebtedness of "L'Apres-Midi D'Un Faune" and "Naiads' Song" to Robert Nichols' "A Faun's Holiday" with a valuable study of the structure of *The Marble Faun*. Kreiswirth's provocative comments on Faulkner's use of dual perspectives in *The Marble Faun* suggest ways in which this apprentice work anticipates such mature novels as *The Sound and the Fury* and *Absalom, Absalom!*

The four studies of *Soldiers' Pay* that appeared during the year are headed by Margaret J. Yonce's "The Composition of *Soldiers' Pay*" (*MissQ* 33:291–326). This essay is a painstaking analysis of the typescript of *Soldiers' Pay* housed in the Berg Collection of the New York Public Library. Yonce's predilection for constructing improbable compositional sequences and then rejecting them makes her essay overly long and tedious to read, but the effort the essay demands is rewarded by the insight it affords into Faulkner's early compositional methods. Also of value is Thomas L. McHaney's "The Modernism of *Soldiers' Pay*" (*WiF* 3,i:16–30). Though this essay shows signs of having been written with the special needs of a Japanese audience in mind, it contains observations about the intellectual and artistic ambience of Faulkner's first novel that will be of value to American scholars as well.

The remaining two items on *Soldiers' Pay* are of less value. Duane J. MacMillan's " 'Carry on, Cadet': *Mores* and Morality in *Soldiers' Pay*" (*Unappeased Imagination*, pp. 39–57) argues that Faulkner's book rejects petty social conventions in favor of "deeper, vital, basic principles." In "A Source for the Title of *Soldiers' Pay*" (*NMAL* 5: Item 7) Jeffrey T. Folks suggests that the title of the novel stems from political debates over the issue of World War I veterans' bonuses. As Folks notes, the title came from an anonymous assistant at Liveright, not from Faulkner himself, so determining its source seems somewhat beside the point. The one item on *Mosquitoes* during the year (John Earl Bassett's "Faulkner's *Mosquitoes*: Toward a Self-Image of the Artist" [*SLJ* 12,ii:49–64]) also seems beside the point. Bassett does not find the novel to be either a major turning point in the author's career or of much intrinsic interest, so one wonders why he chose to write about it.

Marta Powell Harley's "Faulkner's *Sartoris* and the Legend of Rinaldo and Bayard" (*AN&Q* 18:92–93) finds a plausible source in Thomas Bulfinch's *Legends of Charlemagne* for Bayard Sartoris' first name and for the incident in which he rides an untamed horse. The other two items on *Sartoris* and *Flags in the Dust* are of little interest. In "Horace Benbow: Faulkner's Endymion" (*MissQ* 33:

363–70) Linda E. McDaniel attempts with little success to adduce specific parallels between Keats's *Endymion* and Faulkner's *Flags in the Dust*. Merle Wallace Keiser's "*Flags in the Dust* and *Sartoris*" (*Fifty Years of Yoknapatawpha*, pp. 44–70) combines an inconclusive review of the transformation of *Flags in the Dust* into *Sartoris* with a diffuse, moralistic interpretation of the novel as originally published.

The most important work to appear on *The Sound and the Fury* during 1980 is the two-volume "*The Sound and the Fury*": *A Concordance to the Novel* (Univ. Microfilms), ed. Noel Polk and Kenneth L. Privratsky. Textual editing for the work, the fifth in the series of Faulkner concordances, was done by Polk, with Privratsky providing technical and administrative assistance. The Introduction is by André Bleikasten. This concordance evinces the same high level of care in its production as the previous volumes in the series, but its usefulness is somewhat limited by its failure to gloss the Compson Appendix that Faulkner wrote in 1945. The editors' brief explanatory notes do not mention the Appendix, so I can only speculate as to Polk's reason for excluding it. Certainly one could argue that the Appendix should not have been glossed because it was not part of the novel as originally written. But this argument, though understandable from an aesthetic point of view, ignores both Faulkner's own view of the status of the Appendix and the practical benefits to be derived from including it. The second of these considerations is the more important one. As Bleikasten says in his Introduction, the Faulkner concordances will ultimately allow us "to trace the shifts that are most likely to have occurred in the course of [Faulkner's] literary production." Having this ability would be especially valuable in the case of the Compson Appendix, for it would allow us to determine in exactly what ways the Appendix does and does not stem from the same fictive vision as the novel of which it is ostensibly a part. This reservation to the side, the appearance of the *Sound and the Fury* concordance is most welcome, for it will permit critics to engage in detailed lexical analyses of Faulkner's most diversely textured novel.

The remaining eight items on *The Sound and the Fury* all fail to tell us much that is new or of value. The closest we come to an exception to this depressing conclusion is with James M. Mellard's *The Exploded Form*. This ambitious study of the fragmentation of the novel in the Modernist period is more valuable for its general observations than for its long chapter on *The Sound and the Fury*. Mellard's reminder that Faulkner was consciously exploding novelistic conventions in *The Sound and the Fury* is welcome, but his argument that the four sections of the novel comprise a deliberate return to four of the literary modes from which the novelistic genre originated fails to carry conviction. It is surely inaccurate, for example, to conclude from Benjy's inability to interpret events that his section entails a return to the narratorial anonymity of drama. Has there ever been a narrator of whose presence we are as constantly aware as we are of Benjy's? His very inability to interpret what he observes repeatedly reminds us of his hovering prosence.

Two other partial exceptions to the general mediocrity of the year's work on *The Sound and the Fury* are Margaret Simonton's "Faulkner's Influence on Robbe-Grillet: The Quentin Section of *The Sound and the Fury* and *La Jalousie*" (*IFR* 7:11–19) and May Cameron Brown's "The Language of Chaos: Quentin Compson in *The Sound and the Fury*" (*AL* 51:544–53). Simonton's essay is a convincing influence study, but it contains some factually inaccurate assertions, such as the claim that Quentin Compson loses his knife while attempting to lose his virginity with a girl from his neighborhood. Brown's essay is a well-written and sensible, but not very original, study of image patterns and patterns of association in the second section of *The Sound and the Fury*.

Beyond this point there are no exceptions whatsoever. Neither Mary Dell Fletcher's "Edenic Images in *The Sound and the Fury*" (*SCB* 40:142–44) nor Beth Burch's "Shades of Golden Fleece [*sic*]: Faulkner's Jason Once Again" (*NMW* 12:55–62) tells us anything new about Faulkner's use of mythic materials in *The Sound and the Fury*. Steve Carter's oddly titled "Caddy and Quentin: Anima and Animus Orbited Nice" (*HSL* 12:124–42) attempts with little success to apply Jungian concepts to the Caddie-Quentin relationship and makes no reference to any criticism published after 1967. Thom Seymour's "Faulkner's *The Sound and the Fury*" (*Expl* 39,i:24–25) is the second note to appear recently on the subject of Jason Compson's dislike for Babe Ruth and the New York Yankees. Seymour brings no new information to bear on the subject. Finally, Sanford Pinsker's "Squaring the Circle in *The Sound and the Fury*" (*Unappeased Imagination*, pp. 115–21) is a badly written, impressionistic study of the motif of circular motion in the novel. When Pinsker says "modern life merely exasperated the problem," he expresses my feelings exactly.

vi. Individual Works, 1930–39

With a few welcome exceptions, the work on the fiction of the 1930s is not of high quality. As I Lay Dying attracted a considerable amount of attention from critics interested in the novel's structure and the psychology of its characters, but much of the work is of indifferent worth. The best study of the novel to appear during the year, a long and thoughtful chapter in Fred Miller Robinson's The Comedy of Language (Mass.), departs from its ostensible subject of the kind of comedy "engendered by the contradictions between the nature of reality and the nature of language" to examine the conflict between the intractable reality of Addie's decaying body and her relatives' stubborn adherence to socially determined forms of behavior. This topic is not new, but the care and precision with which Robinson examines it allows him to make some fresh observations.

Two other studies of some worth are Melvin Backman's "Addie Bundren and William Faulkner" (Unappeased Imagination, pp. 7–23) and T. H. Adamowski's " 'Meet Mrs. Bundren': As I Lay Dying —Gentility, Tact, and Psychoanalysis" (UTQ 49:205–227). Backman's essay is an imaginative but incomplete study of the way in which tensions in Faulkner's life manifest themselves in As I Lay Dying. His valuable suggestion that the rejection of Darl at the end of the novel is Faulkner's way of "casting off . . . the poet for the sake of the family" would have benefited from being placed in the context of Faulkner's other fictional self-depictions of the early 1930s. As it is, Backman's too-exclusive identification of Faulkner with Darl leads him to view the end of the novel as an incoherent combination of a "conscious thrust . . . toward life and sanity" and an "unconscious thrust toward death and madness." In his essay Adamowski also examines the triumph of the family; he uses psychoanalytic critical techniques to show how Faulkner subtly foreshadows Anse Bundren's remarriage.

The remaining four studies of As I Lay Dying all fail for different reasons to illuminate the novel. I read Kathleen Komar's "A Structural Study of As I Lay Dying" (FaSt 1:48–57) with considerable anticipation, because it seemed to me that As I Lay Dying would respond particularly well to structuralist methods of interpretation. Unfortunately Komar's tendentious, woodenly written essay merely uses structuralist methods to conduct us to already known conclusions. Constance Pierce's "Being, Knowing, and Saying in the 'Addie' Section of Faulkner's *As I Lay Dying*" (*TCL* 26:294–305) is a relentless application of concepts drawn from Heidegger, Sartre, and Nietzsche to Addie's monologue. Given the level of abstraction at which Pierce pitches her argument, it is difficult to see why she needed to use a literary text as its occasion. The self-assurance with which she announces that "there is nothing to us but the fictions we create" makes me want to join Dr. Johnson in a little salutary rock kicking. Finally, Deborah Ayer Sitter's "Self and Object Representations in *As I Lay Dying*" (*HSL* 12:143–55) is a jargon-ridden attempt to apply Fairbairnian object relations theory to Faulkner's novel. At one point Sitter says "the libidinal ego, Darl as victim, is severely persecuted by the antilibidinal ego, Darl as persecutor, in alliance with the rejecting object, Addie at the deepest level." I think this means that Darl and Addie persecute Darl.

Sanctuary fared even worse than *As I Lay Dying* during 1980, for all three of the studies of this novel have significant flaws. In "'The Space Between': A Study of Faulkner's *Sanctuary*" (*TSLL* 22:22–47) George Toles has some illuminating things to say about the deceptively simple style of *Sanctuary*, but he obscures his insights by repeatedly blurring the distinction between speculation and fact. Especially disturbing is his attribution of a dubious psychosexual motive to Faulkner himself; Faulkner, he says, "can hardly restrain himself from prolonging [Temple's] 'exquisite torture.'" In "The Creative Evolution of *Sanctuary*" (*FaSt* 1:14–28) Elizabeth M. Kerr attempts to relate the changes that Faulkner made in the *Sanctuary* galleys to the evolution of his creative vision. This topic has real promise, but Kerr drifts away from it into a diffuse and repetitious reading of the published version of the novel. The final item on *Sanctuary*, Myles Hurd's "Faulkner's Horace Benbow: The Burden of Characterization and the Confusion of Meaning in *Sanctuary*" (*CLAJ* 23:416–30) is an example of a critic imposing expectations on a novel and then complaining because it fails to meet them. Almost the whole of Hurd's essay is given over to upbraiding Faulkner for the supposed incompatability of Horace Benbow's "Freudian storytelling role and his thematic responsibility to comment on evil."

Hurd's essay can serve as the occasion for a complaint of my own about the decline in the command of reference skills that appears to be taking place among Faulkner scholars. In the first two pages of his essay, Hurd has one footnote in which he names a text without naming an author, another in which he names an author without naming a text, and a third in which he misdates the second edition of Irving Howe's study of Faulkner by ten years. He is by no means the only offender of the year.

With the exception of Carole Anne Taylor's "*Light in August*: The Epistemology of Tragic Paradox" (*TSLL* 22:48–68), all five of the essays on *Light in August* confirm my low estimate of the quality of the year's work on the fiction of the 1930s. Taylor's fine essay is a difficult but rewarding study of "the tragic implications of epistemological crisis" in *Light in August*; she demonstrates that Gail Hightower, Byron Bunch, and Joe Christmas all face similar epistemological crises, but that only Christmas refuses to retreat from his. A special virtue of this essay is Taylor's ability to honor the contending demands of her literary subject matter and her philosophical terminology. A similar ability to honor contending demands is unfortunately absent from Paul J. Rosenzweig's "Faulkner's Motif of Food in *Light in August*" (*AI* 37:93–112). The narrowness and rigidity of Rosenzweig's application of Freudian theory to Faulkner's food imagery impoverishes his subject by robbing it of its specifically literary significance. The implication of Rosenzweig's argument is that Faulkner used images of food to depict the Freudian pattern of childhood development; a better view would be that he used both the images and the pattern to express his own unique vision of human experience. In "Call Me Nigger! Race and Speech in Faulkner's *Light in August*" (*JAmS* 14:235–48) Richard Godden suggests that the ambiguity of Joe Christmas' identity undermines the confidence the people of Jefferson have in their ability to use language to assign meanings. This is a suggestion worthy of consideration, but Godden unfortunately accompanies it with a number of bizarre readings. When Joe Christmas kills a sheep after learning about menstruation, Godden says that "presumably, he has cut out its womb in order to test the dirty talk." When Byron Bunch asks Gail Hightower to pretend that Joe Christmas has visited him in the evenings, Godden says that Bunch is asking Hightower to "confess to an extended homosexual liaison."

Virginia V. Hlavsa's "St. John and Frazer in *Light in August*:
Biblical Form and Mythic Function" (*BRH* 83:9–26) asserts the
existence of an incredible number of parallels between *Light in
August*, the St. John Gospel, and Frazer's *Golden Bough*. As is often
the case with studies of this sort, many of the so-called parallels derive their existence from the author's willingness to conflate literal
and metaphoric levels of meaning. They also evince Hlavsa's extraordinary willingness to identify almost anyone in the novel with almost
anyone in the St. John Gospel and the *Golden Bough*. Thus Lucas
Burch is at various times equated with Judas, Barabbas, Osiris, and
God the Father (because Lena follows his "word"); and Joe Christmas is said to parallel Christ, a lame man healed by Christ, and the
Golden Bough itself. The last item on *Light in August* can be briefly
treated. Stephen L. Tanner's "*Light in August*: The Varieties of Religious Fanaticism" (*ELWIU* 7:79–90) rehashes the familiar topic
named in its title. Tanner cites only one secondary work (a survey
of scholarship) published after 1963, so when he says that "a consensus of a sort" exists among critics as to "the relevant questions to
be asked" about *Light in August*, it should not surprise us that he
then proceeds to identify questions long since answered.

John T. Matthews' "The Marriage of Speaking and Hearing in
Absalom, Absalom!" (*ELH* 47:575–94) is a first-rate application of
deconstructionist literary theory to *Absalom, Absalom!* Using Derrida's critique of the metaphysics of presence as his point of departure, Matthews analyzes Rosa Coldfield's "economy of desire," showing how her language "celebrates a kind of love . . . that recoils from
full mutual possession and depends instead on the absence of its
object." This essay provides the first convincing explanation I have
seen of why Rosa emphasizes so strongly that she never saw Charles
Bon. It also contains a provocative analysis equating Thomas Sutpen's innocence to his ignorance about the nature of language.
Another essay that combines an openness to recent innovations in
literary theory with an interest in Rosa Coldfield is Robert Con
Davis' "The Symbolic Father in Yoknapatawpha County" (*JNT* 10:
39–55). Using a combination of Lacanian and structuralist approaches, Davis seeks to prove that Rosa Coldfield embodies the
"often inaccessible underside" of paternal authority. This essay,
though sometimes puzzling, is always stimulating; unfortunately it
contains a number of wrong or doubtful assertions, as when Davis

says that Charles Bon and Henry Sutpen "conspire to infuse black blood (Charles's) into Sutpen's heirs."

Five other essayists manage to find something of interest to say about *Absalom, Absalom!* John W. Hunt's "Keeping the Hoop Skirts Out: Historiography in Faulkner's *Absalom, Absalom!*" (*FaSt* 1:38–47) attempts to bring modern historiographical theory to bear on Faulkner's novel. Though somewhat diffuse and inconclusive, Hunt's essay provides us with an important context in which to view Faulkner's concern with truth, fiction, and historical method. *The David Myth* includes a chapter by Stephen M. Ross entitled "Faulkner's *Absalom, Absalom!* and the David Story: A Speculative Contemplation" (pp. 136–53). This essay lacks a strong central idea but includes a number of good observations, including a useful reminder that the David story should not be used merely to condemn Sutpen. Though John V. Hagopian spends too much time disputing with earlier critics in "Black Insight in *Absalom, Absalom!*" (*FaSt* 1:29–37), he also makes some insightful comments about how Quentin Compson comes to know of Charles Bon's black ancestry. I sympathize with Hagopian's claim that Quentin's knowledge comes to him through a flash of insight rather than through a factual revelation or a logical deduction, for it seems to me that Faulkner's careful balancing of determinate and indeterminate meanings would be undermined if this important question could be answered in the fashion of a detective story. The final two worthwhile items on *Absalom, Absalom!* require only brief mention. Terrence Doody's *Confession and Community in the Novel* (LSU) reprints in revised form an essay on the motif of confession that first appeared in *SNNTS* in 1974 (see *ALS 1975*, p. 161). Francis J. Bosha's "A Source for the Names Charles and Wash in *Absalom, Absalom!*" (*NMAL* 4:Item 13) notes that Faulkner's great-grandfather owned slaves named Charles and Wash.

The remaining three items on *Absalom, Absalom!* are of little value. Jerry A. Herndon's "Faulkner: Meteor, Earthquake, and Sword" (*Unappeased Imagination*, pp. 175–93) begins promisingly by challenging Cleanth Brooks's denial of a specifically southern meaning for Thomas Suten's rise and fall, but then inexplicably digresses into a rambling discussion of the New Madrid earthquake and the Leonid meteor shower. In her awkwardly titled "Faulkner's *Absalom, Absalom!* An Aesthetic Projection of the Religious Sense of Beauty" (*BSUF* 21,ii:34–41) Alma A. Ilacqua uses ideas loosely derived from Jonathan Edwards' writings to analyze Faulkner's novel. She assigns a number of Faulkner's characters to the categories of the elect and the damned, and she finds evidence of "Faulkner's basic optimism" in Jim Bond's presumed ability to reproduce. In "From Genesis to Revelation: The Grand Design of William Faulkner's *Absalom, Absalom!*" (*SAF* 8:219–28) Maxine Rose claims that *Absalom, Absalom!* has a structure coinciding with that of the Bible. Like Hlavsa's essay on *Light in August*, Rose's essay is characterized by an unrestrained use of analogical reasoning. Rose finds allusions to Goliath in the Haitian slave rebellion, to Adam's nakedness in Sutpen's nakedness, and to David's slingshot in the French architect's suspenders.

Another essay that relies far too heavily on loosely framed associations between ideas is Marjorie Pryse's "Miniaturizing Yoknapatawpha: *The Unvanquished* as Faulkner's Theory of Realism" (*MissQ* 33:343–54). Pryse identifies an interesting subject, but she claims far too much for it, finding in the idea of "scale" nothing less than "a theoretical model of Faulkner's narrative technique." Less ambitious but more valuable is John Pilkington's " 'Strange Times' in Yoknapatawpha" (*Fifty Years of Yoknapatawpha*, pp. 71–89). This well-written essay studies "Skirmish at Sartoris" in terms of its compositional history and its relation both to the rest of *The Unvanquished* and to the somewhat different accounts of John Sartoris' shooting of the carpetbaggers in *Sartoris* and *Light in August*. Pilkington's discussion of the three versions of the shooting is marred by a repeated concern with which of the accounts is more "reliable." Surely such concern is beside the point; all three accounts have the autonomy of art. Pilkington's essay should be read in conjunction with David Wyatt's psychobiographical study of the motif of revenge (see section *ii.*). In the last item on *The Unvanquished* to be discussed, "Faulkner's Verbena" (*MissQ* 33:355–62), Jane Isbell Haynes provides a great deal of information about verbena before concluding that Faulkner probably had a composite of two genuses in mind while writing "An Odor of Verbena." I now know why the verbena I once planted out here in California never had an odor above that of horses and courage.

Four items of varying quality appeared on *The Wild Palms* during 1980. The most informative of the four, Douglas Day's "Borges,

Faulkner, and *The Wild Palms*" (*VQR* 56:109–18), reflects on the significance of the translation of Faulkner's novel that Jorge Luis Borges apparently made in 1939. Day speculates that Borges' later reluctance to claim the translation as his own may have stemmed from his disenchantment with the aesthetic canons of psychological realism and with the novel as a form. In "Faulkner's Allusion to Virginia Woolf's *A Room of One's Own* in *The Wild Palms*" (*NMAL* 4: Item 10) James S. Hill uses the allusion he discovers as grounds for suggesting that Charlotte is a woman seeking to find herself in "a world dominated by males." In direct contrast to Hill's view, William Price Cushman in "Knowledge and Involvement in *The Wild Palms*" (*Unappeased Imagination*, pp. 25–38) claims that Charlotte fails to find meaning in life because she "refuses . . . commitment to family." This insistently moralistic essay arranges the three main characters of *The Wild Palms* on a scale ranging from rigidity and belief in the analytic powers of the mind at one end to flexibility and faith in the heart at the other. Given Cushman's romantic frame of reference, it is difficult to understand why he is so unsympathetic toward Charlotte. Similarly moralistic in tone is Dorothy H. Lee's "Denial of Time and the Failure of Moral Choice: Camus' *The Stranger*, Faulkner's *Old Man* [*sic*], Wright's *The Man Who Lived Underground*" (*CLAJ* 23:364–71). Lee magnifies the Tall Convict's "withdrawal from the continuum of time" into a "warning against the destructive abnegation of choice and responsibility."

vii. Individual Works, 1940–49

With the exception of Elizabeth D. Rankin's and Woodrow Stroble's essays *The Hamlet* received no attention during 1980. By contrast *Go Down, Moses* was the subject of several notes and articles, some of them of considerable interest. John M. Howell's "Hemingway, Faulkner, and 'The Bear'" (*AL* 52:115–26) notes a number of possible influences of *For Whom the Bell Tolls* on "The Bear." Howell is most convincing when discussing the influence of specific incidents, such as Pilar's comparison of the smell of fear to the smell of brass. Paul S. Stein's "Ike McCaslin: Traumatized in a Hawthornian Wilderness" (*SLJ* 12,ii:65–82) manages to find something new to say on the shopworn topic of Ike's relation to the wilderness. Stein argues forcefully and convincingly that the responsibility for Ike's severance from the world of the wilderness is partly his own; as he says, Ike plays an "extraordinarily active . . . role . . . in determining the rules, nature and significance of his own initiation."

J. Douglas Canfield's "Faulkner's Grecian Urn and Ike McCaslin's Empty Legacies" (*ArQ* 36:359–84) uses Cass Edmonds' allusion to the "Ode on a Grecian Urn" as a point of reference for a deconstructionist analysis of *Go Down, Moses*. This essay contains a number of unconvincing readings, such as Canfield's speculation that Eunice was L. Q. C. McCaslin's mistress prior to his trip to New Orleans to purchase her, and his interpretation of the word "host" in a discussion of guest-host relationships as a reference to the communion service. More alienating than these failures in reading, though, is the jaunty tone Canfield uses to proclaim the death of transcendent value. The trendiness and lack of true philosophic depth of this essay lends support to Hershel Parker's observation (in *ALS 1979*) that deconstructionist criticism is in the process of being "co-opted, institutionalized, and formularized." Both Margaret Church's "Faulkner and Frazer: The Bear" (*IFR* 7:126) and Barbara A. Saunders' " 'Sold My Benjamin': The Benjamin Reference in *Go Down, Moses*" (*NConL* 10:2–3) merit only brief mention. Church seems unaware that Frazer has been mined to exhaustion by previous commentators on *Go Down, Moses*; Saunders is unconvincing in her attempt to find parallels between the situations of Benjamin in the Bible and Butch Beauchamp in the last section of the novel. Finally I wish to note my own contribution to the year's work on *Go Down, Moses*. In "Reading in 'The Bear' " (*FaSt* 1:91–100) I examine Ike McCaslin's reading and rereading of the commissary ledgers in "The Bear" and discuss the changing significance that reading held for Faulkner during the middle and late phases of his career. Notice should also be taken here of James Seay's comments on "The Bear" in *The American South* (pp. 118–28).

Both studies of *Intruder in the Dust* that appeared during the year are by Patrick H. Samway, S.J. Unfortunately I must warn scholars against relying on the more ambitious of the two, *Faulkner's "Intruder in the Dust": A Critical Study of the Typescripts* (Troy, N.Y.: Whitston Pub. Co.). Though this book is clearly the product of a long and sincere interest, it fails to meet elementary standards of quality for scholarly work. It is marred by frequent errors in grammar and punctuation, by numerous typographical

errors, and by breakdowns in the production process (the pages of
the index and of Appendix C were intermingled in the copy I read).
The book's exposition is inchoate: Samway shifts topics of discussion
without warning in mid-paragraph and shows little sense of selection
in what he chooses to include in the book. The long opening chapter, which claims to be a study of the background and writing of the
novel, can more exactly be described as a summary biography of
Faulkner (based largely on Blotner) for the years 1940 to 1950. It
includes lengthy accounts of events of no consequence whatsoever
to the writing of *Intruder in the Dust* and reprints whole newspaper
interviews and letters, even though only a sentence or two of each
of them is germane to the point under discussion. The study of the
typescripts of the novel, which makes up the body of the book, is
useless. Approaching his subject with, as he says, "no specific methodology in mind," Samway is overwhelmed by it. After a confused
and self-contradictory attempt to adjudicate between his and James
B. Meriwether's differing counts of the number of draft pages of
Intruder in the Dust in the University of Virginia collection, Samway attempts to reconstruct the sequence in which Faulkner composed the novel. Failures in exposition make it difficult to determine
exactly what conclusions he has reached, but it is clear that his account of the order of composition is inaccurate, for it fails to dis-
criminate with any consistency between revisions typed on the verso
of Faulkner's typescript draft and the draft itself. With the exception
of Appendix C, which records the comments Albert Erskine made
on the setting copy of the novel, Samway's long appendices are also
of little value. The first, a description of each of the manuscript and
typescript pages, is often too cryptic to be of use, and the second is
merely a record of a Random House proofreader's corrections of type-
setter's errors. All this is a shame, because the body of draft material
with which Samway worked is full and coherent enough to permit
someone to write an accurate history of the novel's composition. As
it is, the topic has been preempted, but the work remains to be done.

Samway's other study, *"Intruder in the Dust*: A Re-evaluation"
(*Unappeased Imagination*, pp. 83–113), is an overly-long and wandering examination of the themes and structure of the novel. Despite
the essay's title, Samway neither identifies particular evaluations he
wishes us to reconsider nor presents a new one of his own. Much of

the essay is devoted to retelling the novel's story and describing its characters.

The only study of *Knight's Gambit* to appear during the year is Edmond L. Volpe's "Faulkner's 'Monk': The Detective Story and the Mystery of the Human Heart" (*FaSt* 1:86–90). In linking "Monk" to Faulkner's view of "the writer . . . as a kind of detective," Volpe says that Faulkner's narrations are "recreations of the processes of investigation . . . not merely reports of the author's completed investigation." This observation is certainly valid, but it can better be demonstrated when applied to works more substantial than "Monk."

viii. Individual Works, 1950–62

Two studies of the fiction of this period by Noel Polk appeared during 1980. In "The Nature of Sacrifice: *Requiem for a Nun* and *A Fable*" (*FaSt* 1:100–111) Polk examines the relationship between suffering and sacrifice in the novels named in his title and concludes that Faulkner rejects martyrdom in favor of the less dramatic kind of suffering exacted by selfless love. In "Nun out of Habit: Nancy Mannigoe, Gavin Stevens, and *Requiem for a Nun*" (*RANAM* 13: 64–75) Polk studies the confrontation between Mannigoe, Stevens, and Temple Drake in the third act of the novel and reaches a similar conclusion. A note at the beginning of this essay says that it summarizes arguments developed at greater length in an impending book-length study of the novel; it may be advisable to suspend judgment of the merits of Polk's views on *Requiem for a Nun* until the full arguments in their support can be examined.

The issue of *RANAM* in which "Nun out of Habit" appears contains five other essays on *Requiem for a Nun*, four in French (see "French Contributions," chapter 21) and one in English. The essay in English is "The Rebounding Images of Faulkner's *Sanctuary* and *Requiem for a Nun*" (pp. 90–111) by Patrick Samway.

The remaining work on the fiction of the 1950s is of little consequence. In "*Big Woods*: Faulkner's Elegy for Wilderness" (*SHR* 14:249–58) Glen M. Johnson argues that Faulkner's revision and rearrangement of previously published materials gives *Big Woods* "unity and a vision of its own." This may be so, but it is disconcerting to see Johnson analyzing unrevised passages as if they had been written with the structure of *Big Woods* in mind. Also bothersome is Johnson's implicit assumption that Faulkner's fiction improves as his moral attitudes become more overt. Another study that seeks to find unity and value where previous critics have failed to find much of either is Edwin Moses' "Comedy in *The Town*" (*Unappeased Imagination*, pp. 59–73). Moses claims that "the fundamental unifying principle of *The Town* . . . is the eternal collision between illusion and reality." This ubiquitous fictional subject can hardly serve as a unifying principle.

Woodrow Stroble's "Flem Snopes: A Crazed Mirror" (*Unappeased Imagination*, pp. 195–212) and Raymond J. Wilson III's "Imitative Flem Snopes and Faulkner's Causal Sequence in *The Town*" (*TCL* 26:432–44) both seek to rehabilitate Flem Snopes, but neither has much success. Stroble rightly takes to task those critics who find Linda Snopes Kohl's participation in her father's murder to be an act of "transcendent humanity," but he founds his defense of Flem on shaky ground when he discounts Ratliff's moral and narratorial authority in *The Hamlet* and claims that *The Town* and *The Mansion* are superior works. Wilson's defense of Flem is even less securely founded, for it is based on the incredible supposition that both Manfred de Spain and the elder Bayard Sartoris have engaged in large-scale embezzlement. Wilson doggedly follows out the implications of his belief, claiming at one point that Bayard begins riding in his grandson's car (in *Sartoris*) in the hope that he will die and thereby avoid exposure by the bank examiner. The only study of *A Fable* to appear during the year is the chapter in Lewis P. Simpson's book (see section *iii.a.*).

ix. The Stories

With the exception of James G. Watson's two essays, the work on Faulkner's fiction did not sustain the improvement in quality noted in *ALS 1978* and *ALS 1979*. Watson's "Short Story Fantasies and the Limits of Modernism" (*FaSt* 1:80–85) is a trenchant analysis of four early short stories containing strong elements of fantasy. Watson demonstrates that these stories anticipate Faulkner's mature treatments of "the theme of the subjectivity of reality" and shows that two of them ("Beyond" and "Carcassonne") embody an interest in artistic reflexivity from which Faulkner needed to free himself before he could become a mature story teller. This is a consistently stimulating brief essay.

Watson's other essay, "Faulkner's Short Stories and the Making of Yoknapatawpha County" (*Fifty Years of Yopnapatawpha*, pp. 202–25), combines a study of Faulkner's early indebtedness to Edwin Arlington Robinson and F. Scott Fitzgerald with an attempt to find structural unity in *These 13* and *Collected Stories*. Watson's demonstration of the indebtedness of "The Hill" to Robinson's poetry and of "Nympholepsy" to Fitzgerald's "Absolution" is new and valuable, but his search for unity in the short story collections fails to be convincing. Arthur F. Kinney's "Faulkner's Narrative Poetics and *Collected Stories*" (*FaSt* 1:58–79) also seeks to find unity in the *Collected Stories*. Kinney's overlong and overwritten essay asserts more than Watson's but achieves less. Many of the parallels between stories that Kinney adduces as evidence of structural unity are proof only of the continuity of Faulkner's fictional concerns. Others are factitious, as when Kinney claims significance for the placement of two stories involving amputation by noting that one is "the fourth episode from the end of *Collected Stories*" and the other is "the third from the beginning."

Edmond L. Volpe has published "'Barn Burning': A Definition of Evil" (*Unappeased Imagination*, pp. 75–82). Volpe rightly sees that the conflict in "Barn Burning" is not merely between "an aristocracy representing ethical order and a sharecropper . . . representing moral entropy," but the substitute he proposes—"ego blindness" versus "the individuality and rights of others"—invites a platitudinous reading of the story. The two studies of "A Rose for Emily" that appeared during the year may be briefly discussed. Jack Scherting's "Emily Grierson's Oedipus Complex: Motif, Motive, and Meaning in Faulkner's 'A Rose for Emily'" (*SSF* 17:397–405) contains a number of forced readings. Scherting calls Homer Barron a "common laborer," says that "the long sleep that outlasts love" refers to the time between Emily's father's death and hers, and suggests that the title of the story alludes to the Roman custom of holding secret meetings *sub rosa*. William B. Hunter, Jr.'s "A Chronology for Emily" (*NMAL* 4:Item 18) does not advance our understanding of the story's chronology beyond the point to which it was brought a number of years

ago by Paul D. McGlynn's "The Chronology of 'A Rose for Emily'"
(*SSF* 6[1969]:461–62) and Helen Nebeker's "Chronology Revised"
(*SSF* 8[1971]:471–73). Hunter does not refer to either of these
studies.

University of California, Davis

10. Fitzgerald and Hemingway

Scott Donaldson

It was a curious year for Fitzgerald and Hemingway scholarship. The only major work of significance—the well-edited *Correspondence of F. Scott Fitzgerald* and Brian Way's *F. Scott Fitzgerald and the Art of Social Fiction*—was done on Fitzgerald, though there were three books of uneven merit on Hemingway and film. (Each writer was also the subject of a special periodical number, Fitzgerald in *Twentieth Century Literature* and Hemingway in *College Literature*.) But quantitatively Hemingway research accounted for 85 citations in the *MLA* bibliography, the highest number in years, while Fitzgerald was the subject of but 35 items, the lowest total since 1972. The proportion represents a real change, since the ratio of Hemingway to Fitzgerald studies usually runs about three to two. Statistics often mislead, but there are other omens as well. The demise of the *Fitzgerald/Hemingway Annual* may have a more chilling effect on Fitzgerald scholarship than on that about Hemingway, especially since the newly formed Hemingway Society is upgrading *Hemingway Notes* into *The Hemingway Review* and supplementing it with a newsletter. Moreover, the availability of the Hemingway manuscripts at the Kennedy library in Boston promises to stimulate considerable research. *Dissertation Abstracts* for the year lists six dissertations on Hemingway, four on Hemingway and other writers, and nothing on Fitzgerald. This hardly proves that Fitzgerald's academic reputation is on the wane (*DAI* for the early months of 1981 noted two Fitzgerald dissertations) or that Hemingway's waxeth, or indeed that any posthumous struggle for preeminence is or should be going on. Still, a trend may be in the making.

i. Bibliographical Work and Texts

Matthew J. Bruccoli's welcome *Supplement to F. Scott Fitzgerald: A Descriptive Bibliography* (Pittsburgh) amplifies the 1972 edition.

The section on new books testifies to the past decade's boom in Fitz-gerald studies, much of it generated by Bruccoli himself. In addition, the supplement reprints some interesting material from auction cata-logues, and covers such new areas as recent publications of Fitzgerald stories and other writings and translations of his work (into 35 lan-guages!).

Linda C. Stanley's *The Foreign Critical Reputation of F. Scott Fitzgerald: An Analysis and Annotated Bibliography* (Greenwood) lists and meticulously annotates Fitzgerald scholarship abroad. Her incisive essays on his reputation in major countries reveal a basic pattern of silence or denigration until 1950, grudging acceptance for a decade or longer, and close critical scrutiny only since the late 1960s. Frank L. Ryan's thin pamphlet on *The Immediate Critical Re-ception of Ernest Hemingway* (Univ. Press) tends to insist upon what he calls the "sustained tension between Hemingway and the critics." At times his analysis illuminates such important reviews as Aiken's on *The Sun Also Rises*, Woolf's on *Men Without Women*, and Kazin's on *A Moveable Feast*. More often he merely paraphrases reviews which are available, wholly or in part, in Robert O. Stephens' *Ernest Hemingway: The Critical Reception* (1977). Incredibly, Ryan does not seem to distinguish between *in our time* and *In Our Time*.

Two articles look backward at Fitzgerald studies, two others look ahead at prospects for Hemingway research. Jackson R. Bryer's ex-tremely valuable "Four Decades of Fitzgerald Studies: The Best and the Brightest" (*TCL* 26:247–67) cites and provides brief comments on what he considers the best of the more than 50 books and 1,000 articles written since Fitzgerald's death. The article appropriately caps the fine work Bryer did for several years as reviewer of Fitz-gerald-Hemingway scholarship for this annual. As often in his *ALS* commentaries, Bryer here laments the lack of serious attention paid to Fitzgerald's fiction other than *The Great Gatsby* and, to a lesser degree, *Tender Is the Night*. Sergio Perosa's "Fitzgerald Studies in the 1970s" (*TCL* 26:222–46) is generous in its discussion of the bib-liographical, critical, and biographical books published in the last decade. Perosa well assesses the merits and deficiencies of two books which combine critical and biographical approaches: Stern's *The Golden Moment* and Latham's *Crazy Sunday*, but overvalues But-titta's not entirely reliable *The Good Gay Times* and Callahan's polemical *Illusions of a Nation*. Perosa strikes a chord in cautioning against future reinvocations of the doomed lovers' motif.

Michael S. Reynolds, who knows what's going on in the field, maintains in "Unexplored Territory: The Next Ten Years of Hemingway Studies" (*CollL* 7:189–201) that Hemingway scholars in the decade ahead must follow the path that leads through the Hemingway manuscript collection. "For the Hemingway scholar, the *PMLA* bibliography is no longer sufficient." Also needed is the computer (or the information it can store and rearrange) and a spirit of cooperation, so that researchers may avoid duplication of effort or pursue similar ends in collective endeavor. Reynolds proposes establishment of a sound text and completion of Hemingway's "literary biography" as major projects for the 1980s. Philip Young in his customarily witty "Hemingway Papers, Occasional Thoughts" (*CollL* 7: 310–18)—delivered, like Reynolds' paper, at the conference preceding the formal opening of the Hemingway room at the Kennedy library —issues a caveat against heedless proliferation of Hemingway scholarship and takes up two other unrelated matters: his probable error in placing "The End of Something" and "The Three-Day Blow" among the postwar tales in *The Nick Adams Stories* and the question of *why* Hemingway felt that Young's critical-biographical book might "put him out of business." Bruce Morton's "An Interview with Philip Young" (*HN* 6,i:2–13), combined with Gerald Locklin and Charles Stetler's "Response from Stetler-Locklin" (*HN* 6,i:13–15) and "Young Gets the Last Word" (*HN* 6,i:15)—all of which have to do with Young's defense of his famous book against attacks on it by Stetler and Locklin—thrashes up a fair amount of water to little purpose. Probably the most significant by-product is Young's statement that his remarks about the Hemingway code have been far too widely applied by readers and critics.

ii. Letters and Biography

The much-needed *Correspondence of F. Scott Fitzgerald*, ed. Matthew J. Bruccoli and Margaret M. Duggan with the assistance of Susan Walker (Random House), fills gaps left by Turnbull's original *Letters* and the volumes of letters to and from Perkins and Ober. Fitzgerald's misspellings are preserved, rendering his correspondence to the life and indicating that he didn't spell quite so badly as has generally been thought. To flesh out the book, the editors have added photos, drawings, book inscriptions, and above all letters to Fitzgerald from others, notable among them John Peale Bishop, Father Fay, Ring Lardner, and Zelda Fitzgerald herself, who wrote notes of unbelievable poignancy from the institutions that housed her before lapsing into overblown metaphor. Biographically, letters printed here for the first time illuminate Fitzgerald's affairs with Bert Barr and Beatrice Dance, document his dispute with Mama Sayre and Rosalind Smith over the care of Zelda, and reveal that at various times he considered divorcing Zelda and having his mother committed. In addition, his two long letters of criticism to Hemingway on *The Sun Also Rises* and *A Farewell to Arms* are usefully reprinted.

The only biographical publication on Fitzgerald is Joan Crane's "The True 'True Story of Appomattox': A Fitzgerald Fable Verified" (*ABC* 1,v:8–11), which retells in delightful detail the story of Fitzgerald's inventing a southernized version of Lee's surrender and inquires in conclusion if there might not be more than three copies of his mock-newspaper story in existence. By way of contrast, three articles presented at the Hemingway conference deal with his early life and career. E. R. Hagemann's fascinating and knowledgeable "'Dear Folks. . . . Dear Ezra': Hemingway's Early Years and Correspondence, 1917–1924" (*CollL* 7:202–12) is built around two recently unearthed sets of Hemingway correspondence: the remarkably boyish and enthusiastic letters he sent home from Italy in 1918, and the "gorgeously" profane thoughts on life and literature he exchanged with Pound between 1922 and 1924. Citing evidence from unpublished stories and story fragments, Zvonimir Radeljkovic's "Initial Europe: 1918 as a Shaping Element in Hemingway's *Weltanschauung*" (*CollL* 7:304–09) concludes, unsurprisingly, that Hemingway's overseas experience in Italy relieved him both of glamorous notions about war and of some of his Oak Park puritanism. Scott Donaldson's "Hemingway of *The Star*" (*CollL* 7:263–81) also draws on new evidence in an informative account of Hemingway's years with the *Toronto Daily Star* and *Star Weekly*, both in Europe and Canada. Another essay in this vein, Sarah R. Shaber's pedestrian "Hemingway's Literary Journalism: The Spanish Civil War Dispatches" (*JQ* 57:420–24,535), asserts that his "self-consciously lit-

erary" dispatches from Spain gave Hemingway a viable way of communicating his feelings about the war, but recommends that so
personal an approach should not often be followed in the profession.
Shaber is cavalier about accuracy in characterizing the *Toronto Star*
as "essentially a feature edition of the *Toronto Journal.*"

George Plimpton's "JFK and Hemingway" (*CollL* 7:181–88), an
address given at the ceremonial dinner to dedicate the Hemingway
collection at the Kennedy library, entertainingly tells how he
avoided a belligerent confrontation with Hemingway one evening
in Cuba and gracefully affirms the appropriateness of the wedding
of "art and government in the name of the best of both." George
Monteiro quotes from the letters of another American statesman in
"Justice Holmes on Hemingway" (*MarkhamR* 8[1978]:7–8) to demonstrate Holmes's wonderment that despite all the swearing and
drinking and sex in *The Sun Also Rises* he still liked the book. "Hemingway must be a clever writer for he interests me when I can't see
any reason for it," Holmes observed. Finally, Joan Crane's clever
"Hemingway and the Painter's Wife: A Romance" (*ABC* 1,v:4–6)
records Hemingway's fondness for the portrait of Andrea del Sarto's
wife that hangs in the Prado.

iii. Criticism

a. **Full-Length Studies.** The basic point of Brian Way's first-rate
F. Scott Fitzgerald and the Art of Social Fiction (St. Martin's) is
that Fitzgerald should be regarded as a social novelist in the tradition
of James and Wharton: one who reports "the observed manners of
the immediate social group" and focuses on those climactic moments
when a character's inner and social lives collide or blend together.
But Way does not force his thesis, and is at his best in close readings
of certain stories and in essays on *The Great Gatsby* and *Tender Is
the Night*. Widely literate in its range of reference and strongly
judgmental on the virtues and failings of Fitzgerald's fiction, this is
the best critical book on Fitzgerald in years. The one book on Hemingway's writing, P. G. Rama Rao's *Ernest Hemingway: A Study in
Narrative Technique* (New Delhi: S. Chand), consists of a largely
derivative and unenlightening overview. Marred by frequent typographical errors and dropped or transposed lines, this book finds
the "contrapuntal theme" running through his work to be "the human

drama versus the everlasting earth." Hemingway's rhetorical approach, however, is seen as shifting from irony, prior to *Green Hills of Africa*, to paradox thereafter.

Two books on motion pictures made from Hemingway's fiction deal at length with the aesthetic problem of transplantation, but Frank M. Laurence's *Hemingway and the Movies* (Miss., 1981[1]) does so with greater sophistication. Laurence writes with economy and humor, and shows depth of understanding about fiction and filmmaking alike. His book is also useful for its exploration of the part Hollywood played in creating and exploiting Hemingway's celebrity. Gene D. Phillips' *Hemingway and Film* (Ungar) discusses two films ignored by Laurence (*The Spanish Earth*, 1937, and the TV version of *My Old Man*, 1979) and tellingly fixes on the difficulty of making films from Hemingway's work: much of the impact comes from things unsaid, or, as Ben Hecht put it, "the son of a bitch writes on water." But Phillips' book lacks sufficient critical acumen and seems to take as gospel the word of directors interviewed. The screenplay of one of the best-known Hemingway films, the 1944 *To Have and Have Not*, also came out in 1980 in the Wisconsin/Warner Bros. screenplay series, with a 50-page introduction by Bruce F. Kawin describing the complicated process by which the episodic novel was transformed by writers Jules Furthman and William Faulkner to "yield virtually pure" Howard Hawks, a director Kawin compares to Conrad and Shakespeare.

b. **General Essays.**   In the context of a complaint that for "Americans, a writer's work is almost always secondary to his life," Gore Vidal's ill-spirited "Scott's Case" (*NYRB*, 1 May:12–20) concedes that Fitzgerald's personal story remains "a perennially fascinating Cautionary Tale" but generally depreciates the man and his writing and, in passing, that of Hemingway as well. Vidal thinks too much ink has been spilled about Fitzgerald, but spills some of his own on such issues as his sexuality and his dispute with Joe Mankiewicz about *Three Comrades* (Mankiewicz was right, Vidal thinks).

The best general essay is Richard Lehan's densely allusive "F. Scott Fitzgerald and Romantic Destiny" (*TCL* 26:137–56), which definitively places in perspective the issue of Spengler's influence on

1. Though published in January 1981, Laurence's book appeared only a short time after that of Phillips and hence both are reviewed here.

Fitzgerald. To demonstrate the probability that Fitzgerald was aware of *The Decline of the West* when writing *Gatsby*, Lehan locates nine separate review-articles in English on the philosopher's ideas published between 1922 and the summer of 1924. Such Spenglerian subcategories as the rise of the city, the growth of technology, the dominance of money-power, and the imminence of racial disharmony are reflected not only in *Gatsby* but in Fitzgerald's subsequent novels. Yet, Lehan warns, *Gatsby*, *Tender*, and *Tycoon* should not be considered novels of ideas, for Fitzgerald always began with the self, not with history. Spengler's *Decline* simply supplied "a convenient frame of historical reference" that coincided with his personal experience and convictions.

Peggy Maki Horodowich's revealing "Linguistics and Literary Style: Deriving F. Scott Fitzgerald's Linguistic Contours" (*Mid-America Linguistics Conf.*, pp. 461–72) analyzes clauses from all of Fitzgerald's novels but concentrates particularly on the differing patterns in *Gatsby* and *Tycoon*. *Gatsby* contains a high percentage of intransitive clauses which convey a sense of fluidity and mutability in passages of description. This sense of motion fades in *Tycoon*, where sentences also become shorter and the number of dependent clauses shrinks. Jerome Klinkowitz' well-written "*Gatsby* as Composition," chapter 4 in his *The Practice of Fiction in America: Writers from Hawthorne to the Present* (Iowa State), goes over the familiar ground of Fitzgerald's advance in artistry from *This Side of Paradise* to *Gatsby*. The trouble with the first novel, Klinkowitz states, is that it followed the straight historical line of Amory Blaine's experience and was uncontrolled by any firm narrative voice. *Gatsby*, however, was "composed"–the novel handles time and space like a jigsaw puzzle and is narrated by a conservative midwesterner "of no small complexity." David Fedo's brief "Women in the Fiction of F. Scott Fitzgerald" (*BSUF* 21,ii:26–33) traces the predatorial behavior of leading female characters in Fitzgerald's fiction and then decides, oddly, that they are "weak, frail creatures, unfit for the spell of their beauty."

A far more authoritative article on a similar subject, Linda W. Wagner's " 'Proud and Friendly and Gently': Women in Hemingway's Early Fiction" (*CollL* 7:239–47) is among several good general essays on Hemingway. Wagner regards Hemingway's portrayal of women as more skillful and more sympathetic in the 1920s than

thereafter, with *A Farewell to Arms* and the death of his father marking the change. Wagner's study of the manuscripts yields important
insights. It is useful to know, for example, that the opening two
chapters of *The Sun Also Rises* (cut before publication at Fitzgerald's
insistence) functioned to make Brett more sympathetic and to emphasize the strength of Jake's feeling for her, that the woman in
"Hills Like White Elephants" was originally named Hadley, and that
the changes in "Cat in the Rain" make George less likable. Though it
lacks this kind of documentation, Mona G. Rosenman's "Five Hemingway Women" (*CCR* 2,i[1977]:9–13) also helps to dispose of the
stereotypical view that Hemingway could not or would not depict
women sympathetically or in depth. Consideration of five short
stories leads Rosenman to assert that in fact his women "are not only
beautifully drawn but also tenderly treated" and generally superior
to the men around them. In her reading, even Margot Macomber's
behavior seems justified.

Bernard Oldsey's valuable "Hemingway's Beginnings and Endings" (*CollL* 7:213–38) sensitively examines the manuscripts of three
stories—"Indian Camp," "Big Two-Hearted River," and "The Short
Happy Life of Francis Macomber"—in support of his contention that
Hemingway was "a fine editor of his own fiction." David M. Wyatt's
wide-ranging and clever, if somewhat oracular, "The Hand of the
Master" (*VQR* 56:312–19) asserts that Hemingway at his best "resists the notion that anything can overtly be compared to anything
else," but that from 1940 on he self-consciously used metaphorical
language, particularly the metaphor of the hand, to communicate his
fading powers of creativity. Betty Moore's interesting "Ernest Hemingway and Spain: Growth of a 'Spanish' Prose Style" (*English
Studies* [Univ. of Valladolid] 9[1979]:227–53) divides Hemingway's
attempts to make his prose "Spanish" into two periods—1922–32
when he used various devices to portray (usually) the world of the
bullfight, and 1932 up to *For Whom the Bell Tolls* (1940), where he
combines those devices in an attempt "to solidify the reality of the
Spanish experience." In the novel Hemingway "was writing about a
country he felt much at home in," yet Moore notes certain inconsistencies and inaccuracies and suggests that by calling attention to
themselves Hemingway's stylistic Spanishisms "may obscure rather
than define the truth."

Sensible and dull, Wesley A. Kort's "Human Time in Hemingway's Fiction" (*MFS* 26:579–96) argues that overconcentration on placing Hemingway's fiction within the context of his life, overemphasis on character and tone, and a too-facile assumption of philosophical pessimism have militated against understanding of human time in his novels. The fiction is best understood, according to Kort, as granting "access to a human time which is primary, which is rhythmic, and which is productive of healing, wisdom, and peace." Time must have its stop, and Mark Scheel's unoriginal "Death and Dying: Hemingway's Predominant Theme" (*ESRS* 28,i[1979]:5–12) considers the probable causes—physical, psychological, and philosophical—of the preoccupation with death in Hemingway's writing. Philosophy is central to Phillip D. Adams' thoughtful "Husserl's Eidetic Object: An Approach to the Styles of Hemingway and the Cubists" (*Images and Innovations*, pp. 58–67), which relates Hemingway's fiction to the art and thought of his time by extending the phenomenological concept of "eidetic reduction," perceptible in the painting of Gris and Braque, to Hemingway's prose. In its concentration of nouns, the prose conveys an impression of hard reality, yet the actual diction is vague and imprecise, reflecting a "presumed factual world" which is "equally vague and imprecise."

c. **Essays on Specific Works: Fitzgerald.**   The usual cluster of commentary on *The Great Gatsby* falls largely into two categories—mythic readings and influence studies. In " 'Boats Against the Current': Morality and the Myth of Renewal in *The Great Gatsby*" (*TCL* 26:157–70), Jeffrey Steinbrink lucidly argues that Gatsby's failure stems from the force of his belief in the myth of rejuvenation, a belief which is necessarily false in an entropic universe. Jordan and Nick remark on life beginning all over again with a new season, but only Gatsby, "a victim of his past," believes that he can make this happen. Bruce Michelson's "The Myth of Gatsby" (*MFS* 26:563–77), another fine essay, contends that this "somewhat tawdry story" becomes a modern myth through the transforming power of Nick Carraway, who at the end is full of the capacity for wonder he has acquired from Gatsby, still mingled with his original "unaffected scorn." Michelson finds a likely source in the story of Phaeton, Ovid's skyborne mortal. The novel, he asserts, is "certainly more akin to

Ovid" than to Ben Franklin or Hopalong Cassidy or the Alger stories.
Its ancient provenance, in fact, is "precisely why it stays with us, not
only powerful, but invincibly new."

More recent mythic origins are cited in other essays. David D.
Anderson's "Midwestern Writers and the Myth of the Search" (*GaR*
34:131–43) makes an important point by placing the East-West
motifs in the novel within an "old, uniquely American, traditionally
Midwestern symbol, that of movement." The characters—mostly
midwesterners determined "to move, to seek, to pursue, and perhaps
ultimately to return"—typify a vast demographic movement away
from small middle-western towns to the cities, as also treated by
such writers as Sherwood Anderson, Floyd Dell, Louis Bromfield,
and Saul Bellow. Eric S. Lunde's "Return to Innocence? The Value
of Nick Carraway's Midwestern Perspective in F. Scott Fitzgerald's
The Great Gatsby" (*SSMLN* 10,ii:14–23) unpretentiously makes its
dual points that the novel is not so much a tale of East vs. West as
one of Eastern corruption seen from a midwestern perspective, and
that it is this perspective that enables Nick to keep his moral balance.
In an interesting note on this same theme, "Fitzgerald's *The Great
Gatsby* (*Expl* 38,iv:10–11), Leonard A. Podis characterizes Nick's
return to the Midwest as a "romantic" decision motivated by his assimilating a portion of Gatsby's romantic readiness.

Letha Audhuy's "*The Waste Land*: Myth and Symbols in *The
Great Gatsby*" (*EA* 33:41–54) goes further than other studies in asserting that Eliot's poem provides "the informing myth of the novel."
Parallels in setting, social criticism, characters, symbols, and morality are profusely cited to testify to what Audhuy calls a "coherent,
intricate network of significant details and what can only be specific
allusions" by which *The Waste Land* "permeates" *Gatsby*. This argument sometimes invests seemingly irrelevant details, such as the
persistent dunking of Miss Baedeker, with fresh meaning.

A number of articles and notes discover sources for *Gatsby* elsewhere. F. T. Flahiff's "*The Great Gatsby*: Scott Fitzgerald's Chau-
cerian Rag" (*Figures in a Ground*, pp. 87–98) effectively builds on
Nancy Y. Hoffman's 1971 essay to assert that *Gatsby* "is a sequel to
a source," Chaucer's *Troilus and Criseyde*. Robert Roulston's first-rate
"Traces of *Tono-Bungay* in *The Great Gatsby*" (*JNT* 10:68–76) convincingly demonstrates through similarities of structure, point of
view, plot and theme that Fitzgerald had not exorcised the influence

of H. G. Wells's novel—patent in *This Side of Paradise*—by the time he wrote *Gatsby*. Fitzgerald's growth, Roulston decides, "was often less a process of rejection and displacement than one of accretion." One of the novels which Fitzgerald assimilated en route to *Gatsby*, according to Marie J. Kilker's persuasive " 'Some Clews' to the Source of Doctor Eckleburg's Eyes and *The Great Gatsby*" (*PMLA* 5:44–48), was *Mumbo Jumbo* (1923) by American expatriate sculptor Harry Clews, Jr. Fitzgerald knew of *Mumbo Jumbo*: he called it an immoral book in a letter to Maxwell Perkins. And a large billboard featuring the "enormous head of 'Loyal Painless Thompson,' " purveyor of commercial laxatives, broods over the deplorably materialistic landscape of Clews's novel, much as the eyes of Eckleburg do over the valley of ashes.

Terence Doody makes original observations about Fitzgerald's use of the confession in *Confession and Community in the Novel* (LSU) in the course of comparing *Gatsby* to Dreiser's *American Tragedy*. Nick Carraway does not quite confess, he remarks, any more than Rudolph Miller does in "Absolution" or Fitzgerald himself in "The Crack-Up" essays, which betray an "utter lack of interest or trust in his audience." T. Jeff Evans' "F. Scott Fitzgerald and Henry James: The Raw Material of American Innocence" (*NMAL* 4:item 8) unconvincingly tries to locate connections between "Daisy Miller" and *Gatsby*. Chris Schroeder's somewhat overingenious note on "The Oculist, the Son and the Holy Owl Eyes" (*AN&Q* 18:89–90) claims that "a bastardized version of the Holy Trinity" exisits in the novel. Finally, Shyamal Bagchee discusses a case of Fitzgerald's influence on a contemporary author in "*The Great Gatsby* and John Fowles's *The Collector*" (*NConL* 10,iv:7–8). Fowles's first novel, Bagchee demonstrates, constitutes "a remarkably clever inversion or distortion" of *Gatsby*.

Two first-rate essays touch on neither myth nor provenance. Colin S. Cass's dense and enlightening " 'Pandered in Whispers': Narrative Reliability in *The Great Gatsby*" (*CollL* 7:113–24) deals with an old problem in a new way. According to Cass, Nick's apparent pandering should not disqualify him as a reliable narrator, since it was an inevitable by-product of Fitzgerald's desire to have him on the scene as witness as often as possible. The novel's coda in which the trees pander in whispers to Dutch sailors was not, he believes, intended to serve as a reminder of Nick's little tea. Robert E. Morsberger's well-researched "Trimalchio in West Egg: *The Great Gatsby Onstage*" (*Prospects* 5:489–506) takes up the neglected topic of Owen Davis' 1926 dramatization of *Gatsby* for the stage. According to Morsberger, this play was superior to the three films and one television production based on the novel.

Aside from *Gatsby*, Fitzgerald's novels received little attention. The only major article on *Tender Is the Night* was Ruth Prigozy's provocative "From Griffith's Girls to *Daddy's Girl*: The Masks of Innocence in *Tender Is the Night*" (*TCL* 26:189–221). Prigozy sees the daddy's girl theme in the novel as a metaphor for Fitzgerald's "most searching examination of American history," the metaphor itself deriving from popular culture and particularly from the films of D. W. Griffith, whose treatment of the father-daughter relationship she presents in detail. Lewis B. Horne's intelligent "The Gesture of Pity in 'Jude the Obscure' and 'Tender Is the Night' " (*ArielE* 11,ii: 53–62) compares the two protagonists, noting that by fading into obscurity both dramatize "the waning effectiveness of the altruistic impulse" and the shared pessimism of their creators.

In his speculative "Whistling 'Dixie' in Encino: *The Last Tycoon* and F. Scott Fitzgerald's Two Souths" (*SAQ* 79:355–63) Robert Roulston argues that Fitzgerald regarded southern California as a "bizarre" version of the old South in *The Last Tycoon* and might well have ended his novel with Stahr, like Jackson, leaving behind him "a heroic legend to sustain men in unheroic times." Scott Donaldson's "The Crisis of Fitzgerald's 'Crack-Up' " (*TCL* 26:171–88) describes reader reaction to the three confessional articles, outlines the circumstances of their composition, and attempts to isolate their somewhat covert message in the author's repudiation of himself as overly concerned with pleasing others.

There are four short pieces on the stories. Gail Moore Morrison's "Faulkner's Priests and Fitzgerald's 'Absolution' " (*MissQ* 32[1979]: 461–65) detects echoes of "Absolution" in Faulkner's "The Priest" (1925) and "Mistral" (1931). E. R. Hagemann's meticulous " 'Small Latine' in the Three Paintings of F. Scott Fitzgerald's 'Absolution' " (*NMAL* 4:item 7) discusses the Latin misquotations in the story and reminds Scribner's that it would be helpful to redirect the flight of the arrow in the nonsensical epigraph to part 5, where "Sagitta Volante in Dei." Donald J. Gervais' "The Snow of Twenty-Nine: *Babylon Revisited* as *ubi sunt* Lament" (*CollL* 7:47–52) connects this story to the lament exemplified in Villon's "Ballade of Dead Ladies." Both poem and story bid farewell to lost ladies, and Charlie Wales's "snow of twenty-nine" is reminiscent of the famous "snows of yester-year." Finally, John Gery's interesting "The Curious Grace of Benjamin Button" (*SSF* 17:495–97) maintains that the unusual power of this fable comes from Benjamin's ability to bewilder and conquer his social environment. The story thus represents the triumph of the "curious individual" and implies Fitzgerald's romantic admiration for those born "out of step" with their times.

d. **Essays on Specific Works: Hemingway.** Essays or notes of varying merit are devoted to all of Hemingway's novels save *To Have and Have Not* and *Across the River and Into the Trees.* The most substantial of these is Michael S. Reynolds' "False Dawn: *The Sun Also Rises* Manuscript" (*A Fair Day*, pp. 171–86). In a fascinating analysis of the holograph manuscript of the novel, Reynolds convincingly supports his contention that Hemingway originally intended to write about the corruption of bullfighter Cayetano Ordonez (or Niño de la Palma), whose name appears as a working title on the first page of the manuscript. Both in this case and in that of *Farewell,* he apparently worked out plot and structure as he went along. Another useful essay is Delbert E. Wylder's "The Two Faces of Brett: The Role of the New Woman in *The Sun Also Rises*" (*KPAB 1980,* pp. 27–33). Wylder challenges the interpretation of Brett as a bitch-goddess and maintains that her threatening and unconventional independence has prevented critics from recognizing that she is also a mother figure and an example of "the new woman," "the emancipated woman," "the Twentieth-century woman."

Patrick D. Morrow's 'The Bought Generation: Another Look at Money in *The Sun Also Rises*" (*Genre* 13:51–69), an extravagant reworking of a much-studied subject, concludes that the 142 direct references to financial matters in the novel (duly itemized in an appendix) signify the corruption of all the principals, Romero and Barnes included. Nothing changes at the end: "In Madrid, Jack still pays and Brett still buys." A still more doubtful assertion in Jesse Bier's confusing note on "Liquor and Caffeine in *The Sun Also Rises*" (*AN&Q* 18:142–44) is that Cohn may have been modeled on Fitzgerald.

Four good short pieces discuss *A Farewell to Arms.* The best is

Jim Steinke's "Harlotry and Love: A Friendship in *A Farewell to Arms*" (*Spectrum* [Univ. of California, Santa Barbara] 21,i–ii [1979]: 20–24), a sensitive close reading of the way the friendship between Frederic and Rinaldi is affected by his love affair with Catherine. William C. Slattery's "The Mountain, the Plain, and San Siro" (*PLL* 16:439–42) supports the validity of Carlos Baker's "mountain-plain" dichotomy in *Farewell* through perceptive examination of the "virtually untouched" chapter 20, with its description of an afternoon at San Siro when Frederic and Catherine become disgusted with the crooked horse-racing at the track on the Lombardy plain, while the blue mountains in the distance, associated with nature undefiled, serve to restore their spirits. William Gargan's " 'Death Once Dead': An Examination of an Alternative Title to Hemingway's *A Farewell to Arms*" (*NMAL* 4:item 26) persuasively and with admirable economy locates the source for "Death Once Dead," one of Hemingway's proposed titles for *Farewell*, in Shakespeare's Sonnet 146. Dale Edmonds in "*When* Does Frederic Henry Narrate *A Farewell to Arms*?" (*NMAL* 4:item 14) asserts on the basis of the way Frederic refers to Babe Ruth that he is narrating this "beautiful and deeply moving" love story in 1928, ten years after Catherine's death.

Of two fine articles on *For Whom the Bell Tolls*, Creath S. Thorne's "The Shape of Equivocation in Ernest Hemingway's *For Whom the Bell Tolls*" (*AL* 51:520–35) is the more important. Thorne asserts that though Hemingway aimed for narrative tragedy in this novel, he fell short of his achievement in *Farewell*. The later novel is flawed, Thorne believes, by its tendency toward abstraction of values and by the lack of clear significance in Robert Jordan's rather equivocal internal monologues. Though he minimizes the book's complexity in a drive for neat categorization, Thorne cogently presents the case that *For Whom*, like some Hemingway work, "finally . . . talk[s] itself to death." Paul R. Jackson's sensitive "*For Whom the Bell Tolls*: Patterns of Joking and Seriousness" (*HN* 6,i:15–24) traces the way in which the strong characters in the novel achieve an ideal of dignity leavened with humor. "I am so serious is why I can joke," as General Golz puts it. Jackson's is a useful study in a fertile field. Plenty of work remains to be done on Hemingway's humor.

O. P. Bhatnagar's "The Sixth Dimension in *The Woman and the Sea* and *The Old Man and the Sea*" (*OJES* 15[1979]:31–41) employs

what might be called spectral criticism to reach the conclusion that
Mary Ellen Chase's *The Woman and the Sea* (1934), like Hemingway's short novel, achieves the sixth dimension by concentrating not
on " 'the now' but 'the ever' of things." S. David Price's slight "Hemingway's *The Old Man and the Sea*" (*Expl* 38,iii:5) offers a fragment of evidence for the view that the novel presents an allegory of
the writing process. Far more significant is Richard B. Hovey's
thoughtful "*Islands in the Stream*: Death and the Artist" (*HSL* 12:
173–94), which sees this neglected novel as casting light on the compulsion of Hemingway characters to seek heroism in kill-or-be-killed
situations. Unlike alter ego Roger Davis, Thomas Hudson cannot be
liberated from depression by his art or the love of a good woman.
Instead he seeks release by risking death in combat, only to reflect
at the end that he should have stuck to his painting. The implicit
moral, according to Hovey, is that the "heroic code does not work."

Jacqueline Tavernier-Courbin's "The Mystery of the Ritz-Hotel
Papers" (*CollL* 7:289–303), an essay of remarkable scholarly thoroughness, sets out to answer two questions. Did Hemingway leave
two trunks containing manuscripts at the Ritz Hotel in Paris for 30
years? If so, did he then use those manuscripts as part or all of
A Moveable Feast? The answer to the first question is maybe:
Tavernier-Courbin can find no evidence for or against Hemingway's
claim (in correspondence) that he rediscovered the trunks. The answer to the second and more important question is, very probably,
no. "A study of the manuscripts reveals, with little chance of error,
that the book was written late in Hemingway's life."

In two separate essays E. R. Hagemann continues his exploration
of *In Our Time*. " 'Only Let the Story End as Soon as Possible':
Time-and-History in Ernest Hemingway's *In Our Time*" (*MFS* 26:
255–62) demonstrates in staccato prose that when taken chronologically the interchapters begin with death and end with death, with
death in the middle. "What Hemingway has done," Hagemann
writes, "is to reconstruct a [deadly] decade, 1914–1923." But if representing "time-and-history" was his ultimate purpose, why did he
jumble the chronology? "Word-Count and Statistical Survey of the
Chapters in Ernest Hemingway's *In Our Time*" (*LRN* 5:21–30)
reports on a computer study of word frequency and sentence length
in the interchapters. Walls and barriers appear frequently in this
sample of Hemingway diction.

Other studies of Hemingway's early stories include S. P. Jain's "'Up in Michigan': Hemingway in the Workshop" (*IJAS* 9,i[1979]: 80–83) and John R. Cooley's "Nick Adams and 'The Good Place'" (*SHR* 14:57–68). Jain seems on firm critical ground in regarding "Up in Michigan" as apprentice work, flawed by excessive repetition and apparently nonfunctional description. Cooley's significant essay focuses on the "calm and sacred" havens—pine forests midway between the inroads of the outside world and the darker side of nature —that Nick Adams finds both in "The Last Good Country" and "Big Two-Hearted River." Only in the latter story, upon his return from the war, does Nick come to value this hallowed ground properly.

Three separate notes concern themselves with the symbolic component of but one story. Mary Dell Fletcher's unpretentious "Hemingway's 'Hills Like White Elephants'" (*Expl* 38,iv:16–18) expands upon the often noted significance of the landscape on either side of the train station. Lewis E. Weeks, Jr's "Hemingway Hills: Symbolism in 'Hills Like White Elephants'" (*SSF* 17:75–77) makes the valid point that the symbolism of the hills contributes "more than any other single quality" to the story's impact, especially since they constitute a double-edged symbol, containing one set of meanings for the man, another for the woman. J. F. Kobler's "Hemingway's 'Hills Like White Elephants'" (*Expl* 38,iv:6–7) demonstrates that the bamboo curtain works the same way, serving as a "touchstone" for the conflicting emotions of the two principals. Kobler's useful note is marred by the unqualified declaration that Jig, the woman, means to carry her pregnacy through to birth. How is one to know?

Julie Hough's "Hemingway's 'The Sea Change': An Embracing of Reality" (*Ody* 2,ii[1978]:16–18) briefly examines the "intricate system of symbolism and contradiction" by which the various characters in this much neglected story come to understand and accept vice. Peter L. Hays takes up another often-overlooked story in "Self-Reflexive Laughter in 'A Day's Wait'" (*HN* 6,i:25). This note proposes that Hemingway may have been mocking his own insistence on stoicism in his portrait of a terrified boy silently anticipating the end. At the other end of the critical spectrum stands "The Short Happy Life of Francis Macomber," "the most written about" of any Hemingway story, according to William White. White supplies a "'Macomber' Bibliography" (*HN* 5,ii:35–38) of 101 items as an appendix to the issue of *Hemingway Notes* devoted to the story.

The most significant article in this issue is Paul R. Jackson's "Point of View, Distancing, and Hemingway's 'Short Happy Life' " (*HN* 5,ii:2–16). Jackson illuminatingly analyzes the effects achieved through a shifting point of view, one of them being to emphasize the isolation of Macomber at the beginning of the story and that of his wife toward the end. Like Jackson, Barbara Lounsberry takes a middle position on the issue of the white hunter's character in "The Education of Robert Wilson" (*HN* 5,ii:29–32). In his mixture of "courage, naivete, and small corruptions, [Wilson] is an ordinary human being" who, though frequently mistaken about the Macombers at the outset, goes through a process of education during the course of the safari. James M. Cahalan's "Hemingway's Last Word About the Ending of 'Macomber' " (*HN* 5,ii:33–34) reprints the author's 1959 observation that "the incidence of husbands shot accidentally by wives who are bitches and really work at it is very low." Calahan, like Lounsberry, notes a parallel between the courage of the lion on the first day and that of the rejuvenated Macomber on the second.

Five additional notes deal with "Macomber." In "That Hemingway Kind of Love: The Publicity Campaign for the Movie Version of 'The Short Happy Life of Francis Macomber' " (*HN* 5,ii:18–21) and "The Hemingway Radio Broadcasts: 'The Short Happy Life of Francis Macomber' " (*HN* 5,ii:22–25) Frank M. Laurence reports on popular adaptations of the story. Hollywood promotion sensationalized *The Macomber Affair*, a 1947 film whose title was undoubtedly chosen for its illicit connotations. The hour-long radio version of "Macomber" in 1948 did not, happily, vulgarize Hemingway's original. Eugene R. Kanjo's "A Fable for Hunters" (*HN* 5,ii:26–28) unpersuasively presents the story as a fable in which hunting, regarded as a basically immoral activity, serves as a "metaphor for the 20th century human condition." More useful are C. Harold Hurley's "Hemingway's 'The Short Happy Life of Francis Macomber' " (*Expl* 38,iii:9) and Joseph H. Harkey's "The Africans and Francis Macomber" (*SSF* 17:345–48), both of which depend upon sensitivity to language in arguing their case. Hurley maintains that when Wilson tells Macomber his sleep had been "topping," he is punning not only on his copulation with Margot but also on his sense of superiority to both Macombers. Harkey's revealing note suggests that the silent

Africans in the story are probably bemused by the phonetic similarity of Macomber's name to *mkubwa*, the Swahili word for leader
or master.

One article and one note are concerned with the Spanish Civil
War stories. Jay A. Gertzman's "Hemingway's Writer-Narrator in
'The Denunciation'" (*RS* 47[1979]:244–52) convincingly separates
the author of this story from its narrator, a writer who has not yet
managed to learn from his experiences. Kenneth G. Johnston's "Hemingway's 'Night Before Battle': Don Quixote, 1937" (*HN* 6,i:26–28)
argues on somewhat dubious grounds that place names in the story
allude to Cervantes and his famous knight-errant.

Nicholas Gerogiannis' interesting "Hemingway's Poetry: Angry
Notes of an Ambivalent Overman" (*CollL* 7:248–62) marshals an
impressive body of evidence to support the assertion that Hemingway's art and thought were strongly influenced by Nietzsche's *Thus
Spake Zarathustra* and that one of the Übermenschen he identified
with was the Italian writer-soldier-lover-hero Gabriele D'Annunzio.
A similar comparative approach informs a number of articles, best
among them Donald M. Murray's "Thoreau and Hemingway" (*TJQ*
11,iii–iv[1979]:13–33), a valuable discussion that finds the two writers akin in simplicity of style, admiration for the wild in nature, and
respect for individual integrity. George Monteiro's enlightening "Innocence and Experience: The Adolescent Child in the Works of
Mark Twain, Henry James and Ernest Hemingway" (*EAA* 1[1977]:
39–57) considers portraits of the child in romantic literature from
Huck Finn through Maisie Farange to Nick Adams. Huck also figures
in Jesse Bier's "A Note on Twain and Hemingway" (*MQ* 21[1979]:
261–65), a fine essay which locates evidence of the early Hemingway's debt to Twain in his prose style. "Straight back to Twain is the
chief way, especially before *For Whom the Bell Tolls*, that Hemingway went," Bier concludes. Not Maisie but Daisy is cited as a source
in Lois P. Rudnick's "Daisy Miller Revisited: Ernest Hemingway's
'A Canary for One'" (*MSE* 7,i[1978]:12–19), an unblinking assertion
that Hemingway's story is an "adaptation" of James's.

Ahmad K. Ardat addresses the question of artistic influences
closer at hand in his profitable linguistic study, "The Prose Style of
Selected Works by Ernest Hemingway, Sherwood Anderson, and
Gertrude Stein" (*Style* 14:1–21). The three "write more like one
another than they write differently," Ardat decides, yet there are sub-

stantial distinctions. Stein's style was the most distinctive, but even Hemingway and Anderson are "not so much alike that one might confuse a page of their prose."

Two separate contributions deal with connections between Hemingway and Faulkner. Bruce Morton's "The Irony and Significance of the Early Faulkner and Hemingway Poems Appearing in the *Double Dealer*" (*ZAA* 28:254–58) observes that both Faulkner's "Portrait" and Hemingway's "Ultimately," which appeared jointly in the June 1922 *Double Dealer*, presaged the young writers' future development. More significantly, John M. Howell notes striking similarities between *For Whom the Bell Tolls* and "The Bear" (1942: *Go Down, Moses*) in "Hemingway, Faulkner, and 'The Bear'" (*AL* 52:115–26). As Howell shows, both fictions use similar imagery, stress the "communal anonymity of brotherhood," and underline the tragedy of idealism and the ultimate isolation of their heroes by introducing a metaphysical debate.

e. Dissertations. In *Steinbeck and Hemingway: Dissertation Abtracts and Research Opportunities* (Scarecrow) editor Tetsumaro Hayashi reprints abstracts of 76 dissertations on Hemingway from 1950 to 1977 and notes nine others not acknowledged in *DAI*. Richard F. Peterson, in an accompanying article on research opportunities, notes that the dissertations have repeatedly worked over such topics as narrative technique and the figure of the hero and calls "for a slackening pace if not a temporary moratorium" on Hemingway dissertations that do not adopt new approaches. In their eclecticism and freshness of subject matter, most 1980 doctoral papers meet this standard. The topics are "The Inward Journey: Shape and Pattern in *Green Hills of Africa*," "Essays on the 'Functional' Minor Characters in Ernest Hemingway's Major Fiction," "Hemingway's Twentieth Century Medievalism," "Alcohol as Symbolic Buttress in Hemingway's Long Fiction," and—somewhat less originally—"Alienation and the Hemingway Hero" and "The Stoic Ideal in Hemingway's Fiction."

College of William and Mary

Part II

Part II

11. Literature to 1800

William J. Scheick

This was a mixed year for studies of Colonial and early National literature and culture, with special attention given to Jonathan Edwards and Charles Brockden Brown. Although on the whole scholarly activity consisted primarily of description, enumeration, documentation, editorial work, and bibliographic compilation, there were some surprises. The appearance of an excellent edition of Benjamin Tompson's poetry will have major impact on future studies of Puritan poetry. A similar impact on subsequent studies of Edwards will result from the publication this year of a new edition of his philosophical and scientific writings. The portraits of Thomas Hooker and Charles Chauncy were measurably embellished, and women's role in the American Revolution received prominent attention.

i. Puritan Poetry

The outstanding contribution this year to the study of Puritan verse is Peter White's *Benjamin Tompson, Colonial Bard: A Critical Edition* (Penn. State). White provides biographical information about William and Benjamin Tompson as well as a good essay on the achievement of Benjamin's poetry, especially the elegies. White's superb edition of poems heretofore neglected because of their general unavailability surely bodes well for the rise of Tompson's reputation as an artist in subsequent assessments of Puritan verse. Tompson's use of several Native American words is remarked, vis-à-vis Roger Williams' *A Key into the Languages of America*, in Wayne Franklin's "The Harangue of King Philip in *New-Englands Crisis*" (*AL* 51:536–40). Unwittingly Franklin repeats Edwin Fussell's observation of Tompson's approval of Williams (*NEQ* 26[1953]:494–511), a conclusion possibly vexed by a Tompson elegy (1666) emphasizing "Judicious Zeale."

In "The Development of the Puritan Funeral Sermon and Elegy: 1660–1750" (*EAL* 15:151–64) Emory Elliott argues that in the 18th-century funeral elegies, like funeral sermons, focus more on women than on men and that these poems do not exhibit sentimental elements, language, and imagery differently from elegies about men. Whereas the later elegies evince a modified structure which implies a decline of stress on a collective identity and an increase of emphasis on the deceased's individuality, the later funeral sermons became public performances revealing an increase in sentiment, a decrease in authorial familiarity with the deceased, and an emphasis upon the minister as the vital communal agent. Struggling valiantly to trace some patterns in a polymorphous poetic genre not readily codified, Elliott in effect invites others to take the elegy seriously as a cultural and artistic artifact.

The use of elegies as a form of personal expression informs Randall R. Mawer's " 'Farewell Dear Babe': Bradstreet's Elegy for Elizabeth" (*EAL* 15:29–41). In this poem, Mawer remarks, Bradstreet's ambiguity and irony engender a structure, rhythm, and imagery expressing the poet's inability to achieve the religious resignation the poem seems to describe. Ambiguity of another sort is mentioned in Ellen B. Brandt's "Anne Bradstreet: The Erotic Component in Puritan Poetry" (*WS* 7,i/ii:39–53), which unconvincingly asserts that Bradstreet experienced ambiguous (*sic*) feelings about her femininity and that her use of fire imagery corresponds to sexual excitement.

A biblically sanctioned language of correspondence defines the primary manner of expression in Taylor's verse, according to Parker H. Johnson's "Poetry and Praise in Edward Taylor's *Preparatory Meditations*" (*AL* 52:84–96). In the narrative voice of certain of Taylor's poems Johnson detects an assurance of salvation that transforms the theme of the depravity of human rhetoric to the promise of a transfigured rhetoric of heavenly praise. In "Christ the Glory of All Types: The Initial Sermon from Edward Taylor's 'Upon the Types of the Old Testament' " (*WMQ* 37:286–301) Charles W. Mignon transcribes the first of Taylor's 36 sermons on typology. Although Taylor is not mentioned in Margreta DeGrazia's "The Secularization of Language in the Seventeenth Century" (*JHI* 41:319–29), her discussion of the deverbalization of God's message and the dissociation of language from God as problems indicative of the plight of

17th-century poets and philosophers strikes me as an important contribution to our appreciation of the context for Taylor's poetic manner.

ii. Puritan Prose

Two Neo-Freudian interpretations of Puritan prose surfaced this year, one disappointingly reductive and the other fascinatingly insightful. In "Early American Puritanism: The Language of its Religion" (*AI* 37:278–333) Michael D. Reed reduces American Puritanism to doctrinal mechanisms developed to defend against the central Oedipal fantasy informing the concept of a covenant of grace. In *The Language of Puritan Feeling: An Exploration in Literature, Psychology, and Social History* (Rutgers) David Leverenz discloses the unconscious ambivalence of leading Puritan ministers concerning paternal authority, an ambivalence derived in part from a theological stress simultaneously on radical voluntarism and on complete submission, and resulting in nursing fantasies and obsessive literary styles. Leverenz makes good sense of how the dream of the perfect father and the fear of female contamination disrupting male identity underlie Puritan child-rearing practices and their condemnation of stage plays. He also provides an engaging analysis of the literary styles of Hooker, Cotton, and Shepard. Such a book inevitably raises for the reader a host of questions and reservations: e.g., doubts generated by the necessary (albeit candid) use of such words as *perhaps, possibly, probably*; queries arising from the absence of comparative English examples; uneasiness over a tendency toward exaggeration when applying psychoanalytic categories; and suspicions that the conclusions presented are more universally applicable than is suggested by Leverenz' emphasis on colonial Puritanism. But in my judgment his book is infused with an admirable courage, intelligence, and insight injecting special vitality into some old critical debates.

In contrast to this application of modern methods of literary and cultural investigation, other studies of Puritan prose this year made respectable use of more traditional modes of inquiry. Of these works the most notable is Mason I. Lowance, Jr.'s *The Language of Canaan: Metaphor and Symbol in New England from the Puritans to the Transcendentalists* (Harvard). Lowance traces how increasingly in Puritan society the tendency to discover providences throughout nature and history epistemologically rivaled the conservative tradition of typological exegesis; this development encouraged individuals to see their own rational processes as endowed with such powers of interpretation that they eventually relegated institutional authority to a secondary position. Especially good is Lowance's discussion of (1) how Cotton Mather began with Increase Mather's eschatological ideas and then transformed them into a historical allegory which made historical events at once prefigurative and spiritualized; (2) how Edwards extended the jeremiad tradition and reconciled the liberal (natural) and conservative (biblical) typological systems by treating types as reflections of a divine prophetic grand design pertaining to nature and to modern history; (3) how the biblical impulse behind the American sense of future promise not only defines the errand theme but also informs the colonists' use of language when expressing this theme. Worth debating is Lowance's conclusion that Taylor so manages the process of his own salvation in his meditations that he recapitulates prophetic biblical types in a way combining the historical fulfillment of these types and the external personal prophecy to which they belong. The use of typology to emphasize the spiritual significance of a personal experience is likewise the subject of "'Streams of Scriptural Comfort': Mary Rowlandson's Typological Use of the Bible" (*EAL* 15:252–59), in which David Downing indicates that Rowlandson interpreted her captivity by Native Americans as typical of Satan's victimization of the individual soul as well as of the collective Puritan experience in the New World.

Viewing Puritan sermons collectively and comparing their performance, form, and function to folk narratives, Phyllis M. Jones's "Puritan Progress: The Story of the Soul's Salvation in the Early New England Sermons" (*EAL* 15:14–28) makes several noteworthy observations about fragmentation as a manner inviting completion through audience participation. Closing the gap between audience and minister, George Selement reveals that the most prolific authors of published sermons held positions in well-established churches and that their printed works were most often routinely prepared sermons. In "Publication and the Puritan Minister" (*WMQ* 37:219–41) Selement concludes that most ministers eschewed publication: "a full 66 percent of the practicing clergymen in New England never published anything, an additional 11 percent of them wrote only a single publication, and a mere 5 percent published ten or more tracts during their lives." One minister in particular is emphasized in "Rhetoric

and History in Early New England: The Puritan Errand Reassessed"
(*Toward a New American Literary History*, pp. 54–68), in which
Sacvan Bercovitch focuses on Samuel Danforth's work to reinforce
several ideas developed in *The American Jeremiad* (1978).

The man who counseled Danforth concerning a controversy over
silential voting in the admission of church members to the Lord's
Supper has become the subject of a recent debate. In a review of an
edition of Cotton Mather's *Paterna* (*EAL* 15:80–86) Kenneth Silver-
man has appended "A Note on the Date of Cotton Mather's Visitation
by an Angel," in which he suggests 1692 to 1697 as the time range
for the event. In reply David Levin's "When Did Cotton Mather See
the Angel?" (*EAL* 15:271–75) insists on 1685 as the date. Experiences of another sort concern Parker H. Johnson, whose "Humiliation Followed by Deliverance: Metaphor and Plot in Cotton Mather's
Magnalia" (*EAL* 15:237–46) convincingly shows that in his narratives of shipwreck and Indian captivity Mather's basic metaphor of
distillation followed by reconstitution underscores a plot structure
of humiliation followed by salvation. The epic tendencies of the
Magnalia are contrasted to those of *The Columbiad* in Walter Sutton's "Apocalyptic History and the American Epic: Cotton Mather
and Joel Barlow" (*Toward a New American Literary History*, pp.
69–83). Whereas Barlow asserts an optimistic progressivism and an
active use of enlightened will, Sutton explains, Mather evinces a fear
of Puritan failure and a submission of will.

Mather's grandfather receives attention in Francis J. Bremer's
" 'In Defense of Regicide': John Cotton on the Execution of Charles
I" (*WMQ* 37:103–24), which prints a thanksgiving sermon referring
to Puritan millennial expectations in the execution of the English
King. In " 'Clearing the Medium': A Reevaluation of the Puritan
Plain Style in Light of John Cotton's *A Practicall Commentary Upon
the First Epistle General of John*" (*WMQ* 37:577–91) Jesper Rosenmeier remarks how Cotton's understanding of the Trinity (consisting of essence, image, and power) influenced his attitude toward
personal and verbal matters. Rosenmeier argues well for the correspondence between Cotton's view of prophetic words in a plain style
(imparting a vision of joyous friendship) and the Puritan anticipation of a regenerated Christian fellowship in the New Jerusalem.
His argument could have been strengthened had he referred to other
studies of the Puritan understanding of the function of the Logos in

the Trinity and the Puritan attention given to the relation between language and the will.

Cotton's fellow émigré and sometime opponent is the subject of *The Writings of Thomas Hooker: Spiritual Adventure in Two Worlds* (Wis.), a long and careful study by Sargent Bush, Jr. Especially noteworthy is Bush's designation of differences between Hooker's, Cotton's, and Shepard's typology; of similarities between Hooker's work and Bunyan's *Pilgrim's Progress*; and of the affinities between Hooker's manner and both Platonic idealism and Baconian empiricism. Equally valuable is Bush's detection of how the central elements of epic inform Hooker's writings, especially how typological exegesis provides a sermonic story with a narrative frame and how spatial imagery describes internal reality. In his portrait of Hooker as an incipient dramatist—using character sketches, allegorical scene painting and dialogue—Bush presents the fullest appreciation to date of this minister's work. Bush rarely stumbles (e.g., referring to the experience of regeneration when his sources mean the *process* of regeneration, p. 123) and hardly misses opportunities for insight (e.g., including a mere passing reference to Solomon Stoddard); and so his book achieves its purpose well.

Another minister, who thought Hooker's position on preparation for grace to be somewhat extreme, surfaces in James Egan's "Nathaniel Ward and the Marprelate Tradition" (*EAL* 15:59–71). Egan usefully remarks the stratagems apparently learned from Martin Marprelate, a Renaissance British satirical pamphleteer, but neglects important distinctive differences resulting specifically from the urgent colonial concerns informing Ward's work (see *NEQ* 47[1974]: 87–96). Not early New England satire in almanacs but the tension between the new science and Puritan theology, particularly the implication of an infinite universe, provides the topic of Rose Lockwood's informed "The Scientific Revolution in Seventeenth-Century New England" (*NEQ* 53:76–95). Less cogent because it lacks a thesis and eschews in-depth scholarship is Steven E. Kagle's *American Diary Literature: 1620–1799* (TUSAS 342), which might best be regarded as an annotated bibliography of representative diaries (though women are underrepresented) pertaining to spiritual development, travel, war, courtship, and life in general.

Three Latin prose works are edited by Leo M. Kaiser: "The

Question of Lamb" (*HLB* 28:16–18), printing a 1697 *quaestio* probably representative of Harvard student oratory in the late 17th century; "Leverett on Holyoke: *Ornamentum, Emolumentum*" (*HLB* 28:182–84), presenting an example of Leverett's flawless Latin; and "*Feriis Festisque Diebus*: The Salutatory Oration of Elisha Cooke, Jr., 7 July 1697" (*HLB* 28:380–90), exhibiting a long *oratio*. And imagery of survival and sanctuary is identified in Hollis L. Cote's "The Figurative Language of Recall in Sarah Kemble Knight's *Journal*" (*CEA* 43,i:32–35).

iii. The South

Awareness of itself as a displaced society occurred earlier in the South than in the North, an awareness literarily expressed as early as Robert Beverly's *The History and Present State of Virginia*. So contends Lewis P. Simpson, who in "The Southern Literary Vocation" (*Toward a New American Literary History*, pp. 19–35) also concludes that Jefferson confronted the burden by balancing it with the conviction that the Revolutionary War was an act of mind triumphing over accidents of history. Before Jefferson the literary pattern of colonial Virginia authors, explains Richard Beale Davis in "The Literary Climate of Jamestown Under the Virginia Company, 1607–1624" (*Toward a New American Literary History*, pp. 36–53), falls into three segments: the period of John Smith (1607–12); the years of significant and varied amateurs (1613–19); and the age of resident university-educated writers of letters, pamphlets, and reports of Company affairs.

Concerning drama in the South a century later, Jared A. Brown's "The Theater in the South During the American Revolution" (*SoQ* 18:44–59) documents that despite congressional resolutions prohibiting the performance of plays, British and American officers did participate in theatrical productions.

Concerning poetry in the South, Carl Dolmetsch, Cameron Nickels, and John O'Neill exchange letters (*EAL* 15:276–79) over the possible attribution of "Upon a Fart" to William Byrd of Westover. And in "Richard Lewis's 'Food for Criticks' As Aesthetic Statement" (*EAL* 15:205–16) C. R. Kropf argues that a poem by Byrd's Maryland neighbor constitutes a metaphorical declaration of neoclassical aesthetics that uses the American landscape to indicate the proper relation between art and nature. An edition of the poem is also printed.

iv. Edwards and the Great Awakening

This year Jonathan Edwards received a significant amount of attention ranging from Andrew Hudgins' excellent poem "Awaiting Winter Visitors: Jonathan Edwards, 1749" (*New Yorker* 24 Mar.:46) to the sixth volume in The Works of Jonathan Edwards, entitled *Scientific and Philosophical Writings* (Yale). Editor Wallace E. Anderson revises the dates heretofore mistakenly attributed to most of Edwards' early writings and makes several other revisions: "The Soul" was not necessarily written by Edwards but possibly by a member of the Edwards household; no basis exists for believing that as a child Edwards felt a keen interest in nature; evidence that as a student Edwards read Locke remains inconclusive; Newtonic influence upon Edwards' early writings was minimal; Edwards substantially disagrees with Locke. If these observations signal areas of discussion now requiring reinvestigation, nonetheless Anderson's edition elicits some reservations. For instance, one can only worry about a procedure whereby "most of the problems of wording, word order, and organization of the text . . . can be handled by silent editing"; and one can only wonder how David Wilson's study of the correspondence between Edwards' account of spiders and similar contemporary documents can be dismissed with a single negative assertion in a footnote, or how Edwards' approach to the physical world can be called modern when even in his late works he spoke of the stars as *reflectors* of light. Anderson's volume offers evidence that Edwards was less forward looking than some critics have claimed. That he was a man of his day is a conclusion also reached by Philip F. Gura in "Seasonable Thoughts: Reading Edwards" (*NEQ* 53:388–94), a review-essay covering all six volumes in the Yale series.

This conclusion is also thematically insisted upon in *Critical Essays on Jonathan Edwards*, ed. William J. Scheick (G. K. Hall), an anthology divided into four sections: biography (factual and interpretative), thought (theological, philosophical and historical), lineage (influences on Edwards and Edwardsean influences), and literary criticism (language and structure). The last section reprints essays by Edwin Cady, Daniel B. Shea and Wilson H. Kimnach, and includes a new essay, Wayne Lesser's "Jonathan Edwards: Textuality and the Language of Man." Lesser thoughtfully reveals how Edwards' language in the "Personal Narrative" conveys the gap between speaking self and desired transcendent self, between the self's fallen inaccessible past and possibly redeemed present, which at every immediate moment of self-awareness is displaced into pastness—a dilemma making self-reflection and its vehicular language indicative of humanity's fallen condition.

Clues to Edwards' identity, in a multiple sense of the word, are provided by four essays. In " 'For Their Spiritual Good': The Northampton, Massachusetts, Prayer Bids of the 1730s and 1740s" (*WMQ* 37:261–85) Stephen J. Stein publishes parishioner requests usually arising from distress, slips of paper expressing popular religious views of the Northampton people; Edwards sewed many of these slips into booklets so he could use the blank sides for his own writing. Clues of another sort surface in "Jonathan Edwards, Solomon Stoddard, and the Preparationist Model of Conversion" (*HTR* 72[1979]:267–83) in which David Laurence contends that Edwards' rejection of open communion resulted from his revaluation of the step-by-step conversion process; in lieu of this model of how belief occurs, Edwards stressed the believer's possession of a concept of what comprises spiritual knowledge. (This conclusion may relate to the promising subject of William J. Wainwright's "Jonathan Edwards and the Language of God" [*JAAR* 48:519–30], a copy of which I was unable to obtain.) In a second essay, "Jonathan Edwards, John Locke, and the Canon of Experience" (*EAL* 15:107–23), Laurence lucidly analyzes Edwards' major difference from Locke and concludes that Edwards insisted on a God-given "new sense" in saints that generates a simple idea (spiritual knowledge) when this special cognitive capacity encounters Scripture; although this simple idea is public, it is not universally available because the "new sense" responsible for it is not present in everyone.

Locke also appears in Terrence Erdt's *Jonathan Edwards: Art and the Sense of the Heart* (Mass.), which argues that Edwards altered Lockean psychology by modifying its concept of ideas of reflection so as to grant the sense of the heart (will) the status of an actual idea. Too much of Erdt's well-written monograph rehearses what is already well known about Puritan faculty psychology, Edwards' view of nature, and his use of figures of speech as a unifying principle in his sermons. The claim that "the novelty of Edwards' aesthetic rested in the dramatic intensity he wrought" by avoiding diverse similes in a manner making his imagery "display harmony and consistency rather than startling, conspicuous ingenuity" is certainly vexed by Erdt's necessary admission that "Edwards does introduce other images that do not directly pertain to . . . the dominant motif" (pp. 74–75). Because of missed opportunities Erdt sometimes belabors points: e.g., failing to recognize that Edwards' interface of the will and music (p. 57) derives from traditions designating the will as the ear of the soul and overlooking how Edwards' attribution of the sense of the heart as the source of spiritual knowledge does not violate the concepts of faculty psychology (pp. 13–15) because it has as its precedent prelapsarian Adam's possession of *scientia* (as in Locke's system) and *sapientia* (as in Calvin's system) and because the latter intuitive faculty is somewhat restored by grace in the saint's will. Useful, however, is Erdt's clarification of Edwards' attitude toward the imagination and art; and particularly important is Erdt's insistence upon the primacy of Calvin's notion of *sensus suavitatis* in Edwards' thought.

So much this year for influences on Edwards; the other side of the issue, Edwardsean influence, also received attention. Outstanding is "Jonathan Edwards: The First Two Hundred Years" (*JAmS* 14:181–97) in which Daniel B. Shea admits that no formula can describe adequately the multifarious response to Edwards at home and abroad during the 18th and 19th centuries. He also remarks exaggerated claims for Edwards, the hindrances to literary studies of Edwards' work, and several likely directions for future scholarship. "In the Wake of Mr. Edwards's 'Most Awakening' Sermon at Enfield" (*EAL* 15:217–21) by Alexander Medlicott, Jr. reports Reverend Stephen Williams' initially enthusiastic and eventually skeptical response to Edwards and the Great Awakening. That during the 1730s revival in Northampton, Edwards and Charles Chauncy held essentially sympathetic views is one of the clarifying surprises to be found in Edward M. Griffin's *Old Brick: Charles Chauncy of Boston, 1705–1787* (Minn.), a work making equally evident the differences between the two men on the subject of the affections during the 1740s. Griffin's life-and-times study performs a worthy service by filling in certain previously blank spaces in our understanding of Chauncy's role during the Great Awakening.

A Chauncy ally and correspondent was charitable to millenarians who interpreted the event of 19 May 1780 as a sign of the imminent end of the world, though personally he remained skeptical and maintained that a scientific explanation would be forthcoming. So concludes "Ezra Stiles and the Dark Day" (*YULG* 54:163–67) by Cora E. Lutz, who also reports Stiles's puzzlement over another phenomenon in "Ezra Stiles and the Challenge of the Dighton 'Writing Rock' " (*YULG* 55:14–21).

Not natural phenomena but the phenomenon of society and its interaction with the attainment of spiritual meaning is discussed in Carol Edkins' "Quest for Community: Spiritual Autobiographies of Eighteenth-Century Quaker and Puritan Women in America" (*Women's Autobiography*, pp. 39–52). Edkins notes that the colonial woman celebrates the fulfillment of her spiritual search through a sense of community expressed in the words of written spiritual autobiography; whereas Puritan women are restricted to the inner realm, Quaker women include external as well as internal realms so that their works manifest a latitude not found in the Puritan documents. Responses to a document by a leading American Quaker are reported by Jean A. Perkins in "The European Reception of John Woolman's Journal" (*QH* 69:91–101).

v. Franklin, Jefferson, and the Revolutionary Period

In contrast to the models provided by Augustine, Dante, and Bunyan, Franklin's *Autobiography* presents no true society to which the narrator can belong; this condition necessitates the creation of a prospective reasonable community based on the narrator's persuasion of others to imitate his example. So argues William C. Spengemann (*The Forms of Autobiography* pp. 51–61), who concludes that Franklin's work is not modern because instead of exhibiting a form appropriate to faith in individuality, the *Autobiography* evinces a manner wherein the lesson of individuality assumes the role traditionally taken in the genre by revealed eternal truth. A more eccentric comparison appears in Toshio Watanabe's "Benjamin Franklin and the Younger Generation of Japan" (*ASInt* 18,ii:35–49), which relates the autobiographies of Franklin and Fano Yukichi Fukuzawa.

That Franklin's use of details and statistics in an account narrated by a rascal reflects the influence of Daniel Defoe and Jonathan Swift on "The Sale of the Hessians" is reported by Walter Blair in "Franklin's Massacre of the Hessians" (*Toward a New American Literary History*, pp. 84–90). Dorothy Medlin's "Benjamin Franklin's Bagatelles for Madame Helvétius: Some Biographical and Stylistic Considerations" (*EAL* 15:42–58) exposes the Franklin-Helvétius romance to be an unsubstantiated 19th-century legend. A wide-ranging sample of humor by and about Franklin appears in *Ben Franklin Laughing: Anecdotes from Original Sources by and about Ben Franklin*, ed. P. M. Zall (Calif.). The introduction is derivative and there are no annotations, but the book is well edited and designed, with a table of contents by topics, a chronological index, an index of reporters and repositories, and an index of subjects.

Humor certainly does not characterize the ongoing controversy over Garry Wills's study of Jefferson (see *ALS 1978*, p. 191). This year in "Garry Wills and the New Debate over the Declaration of Independence" (*VQR* 56:244–61) Ralph E. Luker urges that we identify *Inventing America* as a distributist's reading of Jefferson, a reading highlighting the agrarian and communitarian features of Jefferson's thought. Luker contends that just as Wills's overstatement of the influence of the Scottish Enlightenment reflects an implicit political viewpoint, so too have other interpretations of Jefferson's thought disguised various political persuasions. French influence is similarly discounted in Lawrence S. Kaplan's "Reflections on Jefferson as a Francophile" (*SAQ* 79:38–50), a position vexed, I suspect, by E. Brooks Holifield's findings in *The Gentlemen Theologians* (*ALS 1979*, p. 188).

Still another possible influence on Jefferson's thought emerges in Robert A. Ferguson's " 'Mysterious Obligation': Jefferson's *Notes on the State of Virginia*" (*AL* 52:381–406), which contends that in response to a sense of chaos in his own life and in the New World Jefferson turned not to philosophy or to natural laws, but to 18th-century legal concepts for a structural pattern in the *Notes*. Except for the issue of slavery, which resists rational structuring in the *Notes* because it exists outside the legal framework of the book, everything else in the work contributes to an architectonic fusing Jefferson's need for artistic organization and his view of America as developmental. A linguistic approach to the same problem appears in Floyd Ogburn, Jr.'s "Structure and Meaning in Thomas Jefferson's *Notes on the State of Virginia*" (*EAL* 15:141–50). In the *Notes* Ogburn observes, the section on the Blue Ridge and the Natural Bridge are foregrounded to draw attention to themselves, attention accentuated by an aberrant collocation of nouns and verbs; the remainder of the book merely provides evidence for the thesis of the foregrounded passages, viz. that humanity should discover nature objectively and subjectively, for nature can exert a benign influence on society.

The two-sidedness of Jefferson's letters receives attention in "Jefferson's Public and Private Religion" (*SAQ* 79:286–301) in which William B. Huntley discloses that Jefferson reveals his private face in his epistolary language whenever he focuses on personal experience of the holy, creation of community through ritual, enactment of common law in daily life, and spiritual freedom through discipline. Letters by Jefferson's colleague John Adams are discussed by Leo M. Kaiser in "Solution of a Minor Mystery" (*PMHS* 91[1979]:212–13) and "*Nerone Neronior* in John Adams" (*ELN* 28:108–09), both of which identify Adams' use of Latin quotations. And Helen Saltzberg Saltman's "John Adams's Earliest Essays: The Humphrey Ploughjogger Letters" (*WMQ* 37:125–35) describes the content of six of Adams' earliest works criticizing Boston society and its political rhetoric.

Adams, deeply shocked by accusations about Jefferson's alleged affair with Sally Hemings, pronounced that such indiscretions were "a natural and almost unavoidable consequence of that foul contagion in the human character—Negro slavery." Slavery was in fact an important issue during the Revolutionary period, as F. Nwakueze Okoye demonstrates in "Chattel Slavery as the Nightmare of the American Revolutionaries" (*WMQ* 37:3–28); allusions, similes, and metaphors in the writings of colonial pamphleteers suggest one impetus for the Revolutionary War was resentment over the resemblance between slavery in America and the status of the colonies with Britain. The ways in which the Revolution nurtured social and ideological conditions encouraging blacks to resist collectively and to create a new sense of community are detailed in Jeffrey J. Crow's "Slave Rebelliousness and Social Conflict in North Carolina, 1775–1802" (*WMQ* 37:79–102).

A work by a slave, the first Afro-American poet, appears in Mukhtar Ali Isani's " 'On the Death of General Wooster': An Unpublished Poem by Phillis Wheatley" (*MP* 78:306–09). In "Phillis Wheatley: An Eighteenth-Century Black American Poet Revisited" (*CLAJ* 23:391–98) Albertha Sistrunk claims that a proper assessment of Wheatley's verse will derive its standard of evaluation only from her social and intellectual milieu. Context is indeed the central issue in John C. Shields's "Phillis Wheatley and Mather Byles" (*CLAJ* 23: 377–90), a highly speculative essay on Byles' possible influence on Wheatley. Context similarly figures in Shields's "Phillis Wheatley's Use of Classicism" (*AL* 52:97–111), an attempt to discern the originality of Wheatley's adaptations of the epyllion. Similarly to Wheatley, others were familiar with the Horation ode, as Leo M. Kaiser remarks in "Robert Proud, Horace, and the Revolution" (*CB* 56:76–77), which presents a Quaker Loyalist's translation and adaptation (in 1779) of a poem by Horace.

Sundry poems of the Revolutionary period are the concern of three other articles: Jeffrey Walker's "Benjamin Church's Commonplace Book of Verse: Exemplum for a Political Satirist" (*EAL* 15: 222–36) offers samples of Church's undergraduate verse adumbrating his more mature satiric work; Lewis Leary's "The 'Friends' of James Allen, or, How Partial Truth Is No Truth at All" (*EAL* 15: 165–71) traces the publishing history of an epic poem on the Battle of Bunker Hill; and Carla Mulford Micklus' "John Leacock's *A New Song, On the Repeal of the Stamp-Act*" (*EAL* 15:188–93) presents an edition of an early patriot broadside ballad published in Philadelphia. Broadsides and other works are mentioned in *The Press and the American Revolution*, ed. Bernard Bailyn and John B. Hench (Worcester, Mass., Amer. Antiquarian Soc.), a collection of essays on the place of journalism during the Revolutionary years.

vi. The Early National Period

Modern Chivalry is concerned with language as well as law, specifically how language is instrumental to social discourse and individual freedom. This is the thesis of "The Language of Rogues and

Fools in Brackenridge's *Modern Chivalry*" (*SNNTS* 12:289–300) in which William W. Hoffa also explains how through rogues and fools —including minor and major characters as well as the narrator—Brackenridge expresses his view of the need for common sense and for social consensus if the essential instability of the meanings of words is to be remedied. Brackenridge's language is likewise the subject of Barry K. Grant's "Literary Style as Political Metaphor in *Modern Chivalry*" (*CRevAS* 11:1–11). Grant suggests that Brackenridge's darkening perception of the problem of defining and maintaining a code of ethics in the potentially devaluing milieu of a democratic society is mirrored in the fate of the two chief characters as well as in the colloquial and classical extremities of the style of *Modern Chivalry*. The classical sources of the Latin quotations in *Modern Chivalry* are identified in Leo M. Kaiser's "An Aspect of Hugh Henry Brackenridge's Classicism" (*EAL* 15:260–70).

A man who in his youth collaborated with Brackenridge is the subject of "Later Freneau Poems in the New Brunswick *Fredonian*" (*EAL* 15:72–79) in which Judith R. Hiltner describes several poems in the Freneau manner and other verse Freneau apparently contributed but did not write. Attribution of authorship is similarly the concern of E. W. Pitcher's "Fiction in *The Boston Magazine* (1783–1786): A Checklist with Notes on Sources" (*WMQ* 37:473–83), "Anthologized Short Fiction in Eighteenth-Century America: The Example of *The American Bee*" (*EAL* 15:247–51), and "Some Sources for the Fiction of the *Massachusetts Magazine* (1789–96)" (*PBSA* 74:383–86), all of which trace much of the fiction to British sources. British influence is also noted by P. M. Zall, whose "The Old Age of American Jestbooks" (*EAL* 15:3–13) briefly discerns the tradition behind late 18th-century jestbooks and remarks the old-fashioned tendency to generalize persons and places as a characteristic distinguishing American from English humor.

vii. Brown and Contemporaries

Scholars interested in Brown's writings will be thankful for Patricia L. Parker's *Charles Brockden Brown: A Reference Guide* (G. K. Hall), a very useful bibliography inclusive in its coverage and careful in its abstracts. Scholars will be equally grateful for a reliable edition of *Arthur Mervyn* (Kent State), which includes a textual essay by S. W. Reid and a historical essay by Norman S. Grabo. Grabo reviews critical reactions to *Arthur Mervyn* and also speculates that Brown considered the second part (though less artistically satisfying than the first part) of his romance as an opportunity to resolve certain incompletions, to make clearer his didactic intentions, and to capitalize on the success of the preceding part.

Our estimation of Brown's characters ought to depend on the kinds of curiosity they evince, explains Robert Micklus in "Charles Brockden Brown's Curiosity Shop" (*EAL* 15:172–87); for Brown values curiosity when it is governed by reason and is selflessly directed toward the needs of others. Micklus, in my judgment, reduces Brown's irony too much and too readily posits a clear ethical standard in Brown's romances. Like Micklus, Stephen R. Yarbrough perceives a hopeful note in one of Brown's works. In "The Tragedy of Isolation: Fictional Technique and Environmentalism in *Wieland*" (*SAF* 8:98–105) Yarbrough uses William Godwin's environmental philosophy to read the house-burning incident in the romance as a symbol of how Clara's recovery of mental health results from a change in her surroundings. But, one must wonder, does Clara regain mental health? Another tangle in Brown's manner is discussed in Bill Christophersen's "Charles Brockden Brown's *Ormond*: The Secret Witness as Ironic Motif" (*MLS* 10,ii:37–41), a copy of which I was unable to obtain. Puzzling over "Jessika," a proposed Brown novel existing only in outline, Charles E. Bennett speculates on "Charles Brockden Brown and the International Novel" (*SNNTS* 12: 62–64).

Yarbrough (above) rightly instructs us to be attentive to the context of Brown's writings, and so is Michael Davitt Bell in "Sentiments and Words: Charles Brockden Brown" (*Development of American Romance*, pp. 41–61), a revision of an earlier essay under a different title (see *ALS* 1974, p. 186) that contends: Brown's manner of characterization, particularly when it equates villains and artists, derives from a self-conscious authorial management of conventional fears about the motives and effects of fiction; this manner results in Brown's deliberate exposure of the deceitful conservative theory of romance, the theory that reality and imagination are reconcilable. Social milieu also figures in Robert A. Ferguson's "Literature and Vocation in the Early Republic: The Example of Charles Brockden Brown" (*MP* 78:139–52), which I was unable to see; and it figures in Robert S. Levine's "Villainy and the Fear of Conspiracy in Charles Brockden Brown's *Ormond*" (*EAL* 15:124–40), which reminds us (without reference to previous commentary on the subject) of the conspiratorial anxieties of the 1790s and particularly of Brown's response to the Illuminati. Levine concludes that Brown's romance conveys a broad allegory of a naive America under assault by rootless refugees from abroad.

In a related discussion in "Explaining the Revolution: Ideology and Ethics in Mercy Otis Warren's Historical Theory" (*WMQ* 37: 200–18) Lester H. Cohen points to how Warren pits British avarice against American virtue in order to fuse ideology and ethics through historical interpretation; this effort was especially acute during the 1780s and 1790s when Warren was most sensitive to the potentially unhealthy effects of the Revolution. On Warren's contemporary, Susanna Rowson, Kenneth Dauber in "American Culture as Genre" (*Criticism* 22:101–15) explains that "*Charlotte Temple* is not yet an American novel because it refuses to take in the obligations of the rhetorical revolution it comes so close to initiating. It goes so far along the rhetorical path as to ask the reader for his assent of its truth. But it refuses to admit that assent would produce truth."

Rowson, Warren, Brown (*Ormond* warns women to maintain independence or risk falling into prostitution!), Eliza Foster Cushing, and Judith Sargent Murray appear in Linda K. Kerber's *Women of the Republic: Intellect and Ideology in Revolutionary America* (N.Car.). A solid contribution one would expect from the author of *Federalists in Dissent*, Kerber's study explores the emergent myth of "the Republican Mother" during the early National period when a public ideology of individual responsibility and virtue gave rise to the political activity of middle-class women. Even then, however, the terms of this new freedom polarized toward domesticity, the role of women in the home, where they were to educate their husbands and sons to be patriotic, benevolent, self-restrained and responsibly independent. Particularly noteworthy is Kerber's discussion of women's personal petitions, their use of satire to camouflage women's wish to engage political matters directly, and their authorship of broadsides revising the passivity of feminine patriotism. Unfortunately Kerber makes one sizable error, an especially bad one because her study is so reliable elsewhere that future scholars may unwittingly perpetuate it. In the Hannah Griffitts papers Kerber found some poems which she attributes to Griffitts. Without seeing the manuscripts I cannot judge whether any of them exhibit the sort of emendation which might imply Griffitts' authorship of two of the three works Kerber says are hers, but the ballad concerning Franklin (p. 73), dated November 1776, is not Griffitts'. It is a poem published in 1776, entitled "Inscription for a Curious Chamber-Stove," and written by Jonathan Odell, a Loyalist. Griffitts apparently copied this poem from a newspaper or some similar source, even as her contemporaries transcribed such items in commonplace books. The problem here is embarrassing and serious, for now on Kerber's normally reliable authority a new name has been added to the list of colonial women authors, when in fact Griffitts might not have authored any of the verse appearing in her manuscripts.

Support for the thesis of Kerber's otherwise praiseworthy book comes implicitly from Barbara G. Lacy, whose "Women in the Era of the American Revolution: The Case of Norwich, Connecticut" (*NEQ* 53:527–43) reports that at the end of the 18th century (and in contrast to the prewar years) fewer women were married, their families were smaller, their divorces and land holdings increased, and most importantly their interaction with other women (informally and in organizations) and their self-awareness as women grew.

The careers and works of two male contemporaries of Warren and Rowson are reviewed by Benjamin Franklin V: "Theodore Dwight and the Problem of Attributing Authorship" (*CHSB* 43 [1978]:120–28) and "Joseph Dennie, the *Farmer's Museum,* and the Promotion of Early American Literature" (*HNH* 33[1978]:296–307). And Leo M. Kaiser annotates "Latin Quotations of John Quincy Adams" (*CB* 57:20–21).

viii. Miscellaneous Studies

In "Lodge's *A Margarite of America*: A Dystopian Vision of the New World" (*SSF* 17:407–14) Josephine A. Roberts reports on an early (1596) account of the new world as a place of evil. A judicious sampling of 13 previously published critical essays, ranging from John Smith to Charles Brockden Brown, appears in *Early American Literature: A Collection of Critical Essays,* ed. Michael T. Gilmore (Prentice-Hall), whose Introduction reiterates the importance of the "court-country" debate during the formation of republican ideals and of millennialism in Puritan thought.

In "Puritanism in American Thought and Society: 1865–1910" (*NEQ* 53:508–26) Jan C. Dawson indicates how Puritan ideology was diluted until it became an unexamined attitude about being a responsible American citizen. An attitude unexamined by the Puritans themselves is remarked in James P. Walsh's "Holy Time and Sacred Space in Puritan New England" (*AQ* 32:79–95): that for the Puritans no day or place was holier than another, yet they considered Sundays and their own settlements as special to God. Still another attitude, the affinity between alchemy and Puritanism, is documented in Robert M. Schuler's "Some Spiritual Alchemies of Seventeenth-Century England" (*JHI* 41:293–318), the discussion of which can be readily applied to such New England Puritans as Edward Taylor.

Finally, in *Boston Printers, Publishers and Booksellers: 1640–1800* (G. K. Hall) Benjamin Franklin V compiles information on everyone known to have appeared in a Boston imprint up to 1800; a well-produced volume with illustrations and signatures, this book is a handy and readable reference work replete with choice tidbits of interesting information. And in "Women Poets in Pre-Revolutionary America, 1650–1775: A Checklist" (*BB* 37:72–79) Pattie Cowell provides a useful guide to primary sources.

University of Texas at Austin

12. 19th-Century Literature

Kermit Vanderbilt

The election-year campaign for a new supply-side economics has been accompanied and parodied by a virtual marketing glut of scholarship to be absorbed by the heavily taxed compiler of this chapter. Despite critical pruning, few departments have been trimmed. Seldom are books of such little worth that one can totally ignore them, and the year has produced a shower of monographs, multiple biographies, special studies, editions, and bibliographies, not to mention an unusual output of articles and notes. Chelsea publishers have reissued volumes in the old AML series, introduced by modern scholars: Warner's *Irving* (Philip McFarland), Cheney's *Alcott* (Ann Douglas), Bigelow's *Bryant* (John Hollander), Morse's *Holmes* (Earl Harbert), and Hale's *Lowell* (Lewis Simpson). Penguin has announced a new American Library of classics in paperback, edited by John Seelye, with introductions by a new generation of experts. These will be noticed in this chapter as they appear in the years ahead. For senior scholars, the notable and poignant event of the year is the publication of the late R. P. Blackmur's uncompleted study of Henry Adams, plausibly edited these 15 years later by Veronica Makowsky.

i. General Studies

One annual category where business did shrink is the survey of a nonregional subject through many decades. In his limited space Gary Scharnhorst only begins to compile "Images of the Millerites in American Literature" (*AQ* 32:19–36) from the 1840s to Robert Coover's *Origin of the Brunists* (1966). But he suggestively stakes out the territory. Whittier and Garrison resented the Millerites' directing attention away from contemporary reforms and onto eschatological mysteries. Longfellow and Holmes derided, but were rather unfamiliar with, the sect. Cooper saw in them further evidence of mob influence in America. After the war they were treated more considerately in Eggleston, Freeman, and others.

William J. Scheick's *The Half-Blood: A Cultural Symbol in 19th-Century American Fiction* (Kentucky, 1979) arrived too late for a notice last year. Especially important for readers of this chapter are Scheick's discussions of ambivalence toward the mixed-blood Indian in Irving and Parkman, the southern dread of miscegenation in Simms and Bird, the attempted integration of a white-red American prototype in William Snelling and John Neal, and the "half-blood in spirit," from Cooper to Harte. In the brief final chapter of this strenuously compressed survey Scheick opens some tantalizing vistas for others to pursue: how literary attitudes toward the mixed-blood Indian were influenced by romantic ideas, literary conventions, and the comforting decline of the red race after the Civil War (as opposed to the menacing proliferation of mulattoes). Out of this mixture writers created little of distinguished art but instead a figure who was "an instructive cultural symbol" embodying the tensions of American mind and blood in "an unsettled land uniting a civilized East and a primitive West."

The most far-reaching general study is *The Fantasy Tradition in American Literature: From Irving to Le Guin* (Indiana). Brian Attebery defines "fantasy" and illustrates it in the 19th-century pioneers of Americanized ballads, tales, legends, and romances, a legacy that has enlarged into a sophisticated tradition in the present century. His structure of the series of events or "functions" experienced by the hero of classic fantasy and fairy tale is supplied by Vladimir Propp's *Morphology of the Folk Tale* (1928). In America, the early democratic hero usually entered a more limited realm of fairyland than in Old World folk tradition. Whittier and, in lesser degree, Lowell felt that the supernatural was best contained within institutions like the church or a "pseudoscientific society." In their native ballads Harte and Mary Hallock Foote avoided the wondrous impossibilities of fairyland. But Irving, preëminently in "Rip Van Winkle," went to Old World sources and preserved most of the elements described by Propp. Irving, however, was unable to create a fantasy world in the nation outside his Catskills. Drake's "Culprit Fay," for all its popular acceptance, lacked a human protagonist "to put things in scale." On the frontier the Bunyan tales achieved "tentative fantasy." Attebery brings a number of other minor authors refreshingly to life, forgotten practitioners of fantasy like Paulding, Lydia M. Child, Julian Hawthorne, Stockton, Pyle, Cranch, and Eggleston. At the close of his 19th-century chapters he concludes that no "full-length work of satisfying and unmistakably American fantasy" had appeared, though the essential makings were scattered in various writings and an appetite had been stimulated. The scene was now set for a writer with "sheer storytelling, magic-making power." In 1900 L. Frank Baum created the land of Oz and with it our first "coherent American fantasy world."

ii. Irving, Cooper, and Their Contemporaries

Aside from Attebery's study, writing on Irving this year was minimal. No further volumes of the *Complete Works* appeared. Four articles deserve brief mention, all in the category of sources and resources. Henry J. Richards, like Attebery, uses Propp, this time to demonstrate that Manuel Gutiérrez Nájera honestly disavowed any borrowings from Irving ("On the Plot Structure of 'Rip Van Winkele' and 'Rip Rip'" [*RomN* 21:138–44]). Michael Clark in "A Source for Irving's 'The Young Italian'" (*AL* 52:111–14) presents biographical evidence and story parallels to make his case that Irving "closely modeled" his tale after Washington Allston's *Monaldi*. More ambitious is Mary W. Bowden's "Cocklofts and Slam-Whangers: The Historical Sources of Washington Irving's *Salmagundi*" (*NYH* 61: 133–60). She links satirical figures to real-life counterparts in the exhilarating, faction-ridden New York political life of 1807. Finally Richard D. Rust has published fragments of two notebooks of 1825 and 1826, unknown to Pierre Irving and Stanley T. Williams, which Irving had planned to expand into an American Sketch Book. Rust speculates why Irving never completed what promised to be superior essays with a cosmopolitan perspective on such topics as American character, manners, liberty, rural life, duelling, and American literature. All was not lost, for the five-volume *Life of Washington* may have begun here in an 1825 fragment, and Irving developed others in *A Tour on the Prairies, Astoria,* and articles for the *Knicker-bocker.* See "Washington Irving's 'American Essays'" (*RALS* 10: 3–27).

Although printing of the Irving complete edition slowed this year, the first two volumes of the Cooper Edition (*The Writings of James Fenimore Cooper* [SUNY]) made a triumphant appearance. *The Pioneers*, with historical introduction and explanatory notes by James F. Beard and text established by Lance Schachterle and Kenneth M. Andersen, is graced with illustrations from *The Port Folio* and the French edition of the novel, plus one painting by Thomas Cole. Beard's introduction, as one would expect, is richly explanatory and authoritative. The copy-text is primarily derived from the original 1823 edition. Cooper realized his carelessness and revised the novel on five more occasions. These revisions show Cooper to be a serious-minded craftsman, which is not to say that Mark Twain's examples to the contrary will now be forgotten. The other volume in this new edition is *Gleanings in Europe: Switzerland* (1832), the first of Cooper's five European epistolary travel narratives derived from his journals, 1826 to 1833. The new text is embellished with maps of his itinerary in the summer of 1828, together with many contemporary engravings of Swiss scenery by the prolific W. H. Bartlett, the plates keyed to Cooper's descriptive passages. An appendix offers a guide to parallel passages in the 1828 journal and the 1836 text. Kenneth W. Staggs and James P. Elliott have established the text, while James Beard has again provided a historical introduction and explanatory notes, this times in the company of—and here readers must rub their eyes—Robert E. Spiller. In the late 1920s Spiller was in Europe tracing Cooper's routes and residences and hoping to see one day a definitive edition of the travel books. More than half a century later, this energetic scholar, the unretired elder statesman of our profession, is now a participant in that edition.

A second annual symposium on Cooper was held at Oneonta last summer (1979), and the conference papers, once again, have been edited by coordinator George A. Test: *James Fenimore Cooper: His Country and His Art* (Oneonta: SUNY College). In the first paper Leslie Fiedler attributes the continuing importance of this flawed novelist to the dream of a redemptive "inter-ethnic male bonding" that extends from *The Deerslayer* to the Vietnam war-movie *The Deer Hunter* ("James Fenimore Cooper: The Problem of the Good Bad Writer"). The essay is mainly recommended to anyone who has not read Fiedler's *Love and Death in the American Novel*. H. Daniel Peck also features *The Deerslayer* as Cooper's most mythic novel. Here, unlike *The Pioneers*, Bumppo dominates a setting felt as pure space, the magic lake Glimmerglass, "in an environment uncontaminated by history" ("Place into Space: from *The Pioneers* to *The Deerslayer*"). The three other papers, by contrast, are more deliberately historical. James A. Pickering carefully assembles from his documents the convincing evidence that the setting, characters, and episodes in *The Pioneers* are indeed related to historic Cooperstown, Cooper's disclaimers notwithstanding ("Cooper's Otsego Heritage: The Sources of *The Pioneers*"). William A. Starna discusses the Indians of Cooper's time and before—the Delawares' Uncas and Chingachgook, the Huron Magua, and more broadly the linguistic populations, social organization, and lifeways of northeast Indians. He concludes that in the 18th century of Cooper's Leatherstocking tales the Hurons no longer existed, the Delawares were variously scattering, but that "in terms of history and demographic accuracy, Cooper is closest to the mark in his rendering of the Iroquois" ("Cooper's Indians: A Critique"). William P. Kelly's "History, Language, and the Leatherstocking Tales" explains how Cooper, with and without the aid of Scott and the Scottish Common Sense School, achieves a "historiographic language" in fictional terms. This is an important article despite the ponderous academic style.

An article on Cooper early and another on Cooper late complete the year's scholarship. *The Last of the Mohicans* has suffered unjustly a decline in popularity and significance, Robert Milder believes, for it is a "carefully patterned" novel in which the physical actions, uninterrupted by Cooper's usual narrative intrusions, comprise a richly "synthesized" version of a "new world fall." Cooper's white and red races both despoil the new world. Can the paradise be regained? Cooper finally denies the full redemptive force of Cora's Christian idealism and mixed blood and leaves us with the merely workable civilized marriage of Heyward and Alice ("*The Last of the Mohicans* and the New World Fall" [*AL* 52:407–29]). Cooper's last novel is given a sharp reassessment in Barbara A. Bardes and Suzanne Gossett, "Cooper and the 'Cup and Saucer' Law: A New Reading of *The Ways of the Hour*" (*AQ* 32:499–518). Cooper's dread over women's new property rights in New York of the 1840s is implicit here in his rendering mad the heroine who becomes the independent manager of her affairs. In his earlier fiction Cooper viewed property as an important ingredient of the happy ending, insuring perpetuation of families, estates, and a gentry class in democratic America. But the economic freedom of women, encouraged especially in the Married Women's Property Act of 1848, threatened Cooper's social order.

Work on Simms revived this year, and with the new *Reference Guide* by Keen Butterworth and James E. Kibler (Hall), more reinterpretations should be arriving. Kibler's introduction describes Simms's lifetime and posthumous reception and the annotated bibliography covers the critical commentaries from 1825 to the past year. Among the treatments of Simms that have since appeared, Mary A. Wimsatt, "Realism and Romance in Simms's Midcentury Fiction" (*SLJ* 12,ii:29–48), treats four works of the 1850s to show that, contrary to Parrington's influential case for realism in the fiction, Simms's "fundamental bent . . . was toward romance." Corinne Dale essentially agrees, at least in the instance of *Woodcraft*, "a domestic romance" in which Lt. Porgy should be viewed as a postwar "champion of social morality" who establishes "domestic harmony both in the wilderness and on his plantation" ("William Gilmore Simms's Porgy as Domestic Hero" [*SLJ* 13,i:55–71]). Dickson D. Bruce in *Violence and Culture in the Antebellum South* (Texas) looks at violence and civilized restraint in Simms and the Southwest humorists and discovers a "conflict between the virtuous and sinful passions that formed the basis of all Simms' novels."

Two articles of biographical interest are Miriam J. Schillingsburg, "The Southron as American: William Gilmore Simms" (*SAR* 80:409–25) and William M. Moss, "Vindicator of Southern Intellect and Institutions: The *Southern Quarterly Review*" (*SLJ* 13,i:72–108). Schillingsburg shows Simms the Unionist of 1832 having become the sectionalist editor of the *Southern Quarterly Review* in 1849 and the embittered "Southron" when his conciliatory Northern lecture tour in 1856 was aborted after a hostile reception in Buffalo. Moss writes a lucid capsule-history of the *Review* (1842–80) that includes Simms's tenure as editor from 1849 to 1854.

Bryant finally receives some critical attention again as Robert A. Ferguson disturbs a stereotype of the placidly sentimental nature poet. The best verses were written by the frustrated lawyer-poet of New England in whom "vocational tensions" merged with romantic esthetics to charge his nature poems with pain and joy, change and escape. Ferguson places "Thanatopsis" within these and other contexts and injects those deadly familiar lines with new vitality—a fine blending of biographical insight and critical explication ("William Cullen Bryant: The Creative Context of the Poet," *NEQ* 53:431–63).

Sylvester Judd's *Margaret* (1845) deserves more attention from scholars than the swift, obligatory skimming in graduate school. Francis B. Dedmond has a sensible, extended chapter on that novel in his monograph on Judd (*TUSAS* 365). He duly conducts us, also, through the other works but only to conclude that Judd is "thought of today—when he is thought of at all—as a man of one book. . . . And perhaps rightly." David O. Tomlinson's "John Pendleton Kennedy: An Essay in Bibliography" (*RALS* 9[1979]:140–70) is a helpful discussion of primary and critical items that clears the way for upcoming studies. Gerard M. Sweeney's reading of the incest taboo in Robert Montgomery Bird, on the other hand, confuses more than it clarifies. Roland Forrester's judgment, as Sweeney interprets it, is dulled by the "emotional chaos created by a consanguineous romantic alliance" with first cousin Edith. Possibly so in some measure, but his wounds and captivity may be equally strong reasons for his impaired judgment. Furthermore, not only Roland but also Ralph Stackpole is intensely dedicated to the welfare of his "anngelliferous madam." So, too, is Nathan. Roland's inflexible devotion may be only one more instance of Bird's satirizing the Cooperesque sentimental adoration of womanhood, a subject on which Sweeney comments intelligently. But his case for incest in "A Strong Family Likeness: The Love Plot of *Nick of the Woods*" (*MarkhamR* 9:49–52) is quite dubious.

The long shadow of Cooper, especially from *The Last of the Mohicans*, may also account for another literary "counterattack," according to Todd G. Willy, "Antipode to Cooper: Rhetoric and Reality in William Joseph Snelling's 'The Bois Brulé'" (*SAF* 8:69–79). A worthy addendum to William Scheick's discussion in *The Half-Blood*, this essay contrasts Cooper's frontier to Snelling's uppermidwest Fort Douglas, a foul-smelling sanctuary of malnourishment rampant with mixed breeds, dogs, fleas, and more. In Willy's opinion, Snelling also fashions a half-breed hero superior to Cooper's "white savage" Hawkeye. Joining Willy in frontier country is John Seelye, who wins this year's Groucho Marx award for most puns in one title: "A Well-Wrought Crockett: Or, How the Fakelorists Passed Through the Credibility Gap and Discovered Kentucky" (in *Toward a New American Literary History*, pp. 91–110). Seelye traces the entry of sailor Ben Harding into the Kentucky of the fictionalized post-Alamo Crockett, and shows that this pop-literary fare in the Nashville almanacs was fakelore created by literary imaginations in New England. Seelye sends up a nice speculation: Crockett's sidekick Ben Harding may have influenced Cooper's creation of Charles Cap, the old-salt companion of Pathfinder. Both pairs unite western wilderness with eastern maritime America.

iii. Popular Writers of Mid-Century

The Fireside Poets, excepting Holmes, stirred some polite interest during the year. *Critical Essays on John Greenleaf Whittier* (Hall) was edited by Jayne K. Kribbs with an extended introduction that locates four periods of the poet's critical fortunes and concludes that our central question is not how great Whittier is, but "How minor is he?" The critical essays are, almost without exception, by eminent oldsters. Perhaps this volume will help to increase Whittier's appeal to younger scholars. Meanwhile one of them, Lewis H. Miller, has given us a good reading of "The Supernaturalism of *Snow-Bound*" in *NEQ* 53:291–307. Miller illustrates how Whittier broke through his usually plain style to create the pressures of rhythm, tone, and syntax of a "poet-magus" who conjures with the bleak landscape in an alien, snow-bound universe and tries to bind the tempest "so that the storm, and the threatening disorder it embodies 'shall do no hurt.' "

Longfellow's poetry received at least nodding attention once again, but not even then for its own sake. Robert T. Cargo's "Baudelaire, Longfellow, and 'A Psalm of Life' " (*RLC* 54:196–201) theorizes that Longfellow's poem probably entered Baudelaire's sonnet, "Le Guignon," by way of a French translation in *Magasin pittoresque* (1848), whereupon Baudelaire sought out a copy of *Voices of the Night*. In the other article, " 'The Wind's Will': Another View of Frost and Longfellow" (*CLQ* 16:177–81), Jane D. Eberwein uses Longfellow's example of will only to show that a far more interesting treatment can be found in Frost, where human will often opposes nature's wind-will, wrestles with self-discipline and inner submission, and attains momentary reconciliation in the poetic act.

Two adventurous scholars have livened the study of Lowell this year. Brian Attebery relates the mood and outlook of the speaker in "The Cathedral" to Lowell's student, Henry Adams, another " 'born disciple of an elder time' " who was both enlightened and saddened by the past grandeur at Chartres. Attebery continues the line of influence to the cultural and religious tensions in T. S. Eliot. The development is plausible enough, though Edward Fitzgerald rather than Adams would seem the primary source of "Gerontion." C. David Heymann situates Lowell in his family dynasty in one of the daring multiple biographies of this or any year, *American Aristocracy: The Lives and Times of James Russell, Amy and Robert Lowell* (Dodd, Mead). After a sketch of the earliest American Lowells, those monied cultural aristocrats who scorned the aspirants to new wealth, Heymann develops his portrait of Lowell the man, poet, critic, and ambassador. The result is a deft, though unoriginal, first panel of the Lowell triptych. We appreciate once more the undisciplined brilliance, diversity, and facility of the poet, together with the lack of focus in the increasingly reactionary life and thought of "a sort of liberal reformer with conservative goals."

The same considerable research and difficult adjustments of tone and perspective have been undertaken by Madelon Bedell in her group portrait of another diversely talented family, *The Alcotts: Biography of a Family* (Potter). She was fortunate to have interviewed in Switzerland just before her death the daughter of May Alcott (Louisa's sister who painted). After eight years of sifting the extensive family records, Bedell limits the present book mainly to the parents, Bronson the eccentric visionary and reformer—Lowell's "angel with clipped wings"—and his formidable, devoted wife Abby. Bedell is not easily critical of the erratic Bronson, who seems always to have had an irresponsible little-boy charm for the women nearest him, including his daughters who will be featured in a second volume. While we await that book, other work goes on. Jean F. Yellin in "From *Success* to *Experience*: Louisa May Alcott's *Work*" (*MR* 21:527–39) weighs the strengths and commitments of the female protagonist in Louisa's feminist novel of 1873. Yellin judges the work a failure chiefly because it carries a preindustrial view of woman's rights into the postwar world populated by a new proletariat of immigrant working-class women whom Alcott and her heroine do not really know. The sentimental-novel genre is also ill adapted to serious social criticism. Yellin reminds us that Alcott's was a strenuous and varied life that ranged well beyond the world of her little women.

So, too, does Alma J. Payne. Education, reform, suffrage, theatre, travel, and anonymous or pseudonymous Gothic thrillers—these are among the interests in her nearly 300 primary works which Payne lists in a new *Reference Guide* (Hall), along with annotated secondary items from 1854 to 1979.

Harriet Beecher Stowe still commands center stage among woman novelists at mid-century and the studies this year add to her stature. Elizabeth Ammons has edited *Critical Essays on Harriet Beecher Stowe* (Hall), the first collection on Stowe. It is helpfully arranged into four groups: the antislavery books, the Byron furore, regional and social fiction, and reminiscences. E. Bruce Kirkham not only repeats some of his introduction to last year's edition in "The Writing of Harriet Beecher Stowe's *The Pearl of Orr's Island*" (*CLQ* 16:158–65) but also adds some refinements to the story of that novel's rather frenzied composition and publication. Scholarly underpinning to recent interpretations of religious and feminine qualities in *Uncle Tom's Cabin* is provided in Gayle Kimball's "Harriet Beecher Stowe's Revision of New England Theology" (*Jour. of Presbyterian Hist.* 58:64–81). Stowe disliked male theological dryness and Calvinist severity and advanced in her novels the "redeeming power of women" through self-sacrificing love. Her theological "formula" emphasized heaven over hell, preexisting goodness within human depravity, retribution that encourages virtue, and free will within a benign determinism. She also believed in the grace of a large family. On this last subject Mary Kelley has more to say in "At War with Herself: Harriet Beecher Stowe as Woman in Conflict within the Home" (in her edition of *Woman's Being, Woman's Place: Female Identity and Vocation in American History* [Hall 1979], pp. 201–19). Stowe's popular-sentimental message was that woman had the superior moral strength as mother and wife to redeem the erring husband and manage a joyous family in a purified domestic heaven. But this family, idealized in literature, was not so easily discovered in real-life households, including that of the Calvin Stowes. Harriet married the childless widower who wanted children as well as a goodly amount of sex for its own sake. She raised seven children, had at least two miscarriages, and knew her health was deteriorating even as she wrote her energy-draining novels to meet family expenses. Calvin was her dependent after he resigned from teaching, son Charley was an indigent preacher, and Fred was institutionalized for alcoholism.

Mary H. Grant follows Mary Kelley in the same collection with "Domestic Experience and Feminist Theory: The Case of Julia Ward Howe." Howe also raised a large family and glorified domesticity while enduring a difficult marriage, in her case to a domineering rather than dependent husband. Samuel Gridley ("Chev") Howe dictated the household arrangements, vetoed the visits of Julia's family, thwarted her public career, found her need for kisses unseemly (while he enjoyed a prolonged affair), and incited quarrels that left her debilitated, depressed, and hysterical. On the other hand, as an undomesticated bride she was a conspicuously inept housekeeper and she (like Stowe) welcomed abstinence to achieve birth control. In the last 30 years as a widow, Howe repeatedly celebrated family life, probably, as Grant argues, for several reasons: images of hearth and home made her a more reassuring and credible feminine reformist; the home is woman's effective political "power base"; and children, properly civilized, become the hope of a better society.

William S. Osborne claims that his *Lydia Maria Child* (TUSAS 380) is the first study to stress the more strictly literary career of this admirable champion of reform causes. Child, in fact, conveniently kept the workaday world of reform agitation at a distance when she courted the muse. To the chapter-length essays on her four novels Osborne supplies further analysis of the literary ephemera, only to conclude that Child's appeal to the modern reader lies elsewhere than in the fiction he has explicated. Gary Scharnhorst denies at once in *Horatio Alger, Jr.* (TUSAS 363) that his writer's fiction has any "merit" or that his life is "particularly interesting or representative." Alger is simply an important part of our mass-cultural tradition, especially after the surge of popularity that followed his death in 1899. Scharnhorst aims to describe the life accurately and relate it to Alger's morality of success. Among his valuable conclusions is that Alger was far more critical of Gilded Age business practices—strike-busting, combinations, stock manipulation—than readers have been aware.

Child receives two sentences and Alger just over four pages in Herbert F. Smith's *The Popular American Novel 1865–1920* (TUSAS 372). Smith tries not only to assemble dozens of popular writers coherently and comment in some intelligible manner on each of them but also to supply occasional links with the major authors of the time. The book is a useful shortcut for the busy scholar and it will be a delightful source book for the more leisurely who enjoy playing quiz games of literary trivia. (Who was W. Fraser Rae? Name the author of *A Leap in the Dark*.) A companion volume is Madeleine B. Stern's edition of *Publishers for Mass Entertainment in Nineteenth Century America* (Hall). A team of researchers, some of them experts in the field, have written brief publisher histories of 45 houses that thrived in an era of advancing technology and marketing before the international copyright law of 1891 and the Panic of 1893. An author-title index conveniently locates the books and their publishers. Allied to this volume and the dime-novel publishers that it records is Norman D. Smith's crisp and lucid "Mexican Stereotypes on Fictional Battlefields: Or Dime Novel Romances of the Mexican War" (*JPC* 13:526–40). Smith goes mainly to the Ned Buntline series to extract five Mexican stereotypes that heated up the xenophobia attending the Mexican War and corroborated Anglo-Saxon Manifest Destiny. The types include the *hidalgo*, a high-born Spaniard in disgraceful straits who mortgages his estate and daughter; the Spanish Venus, his exotic daughter or sister whose charms entrap the white hero (and vicariously titillate the Victorian readers); the dishonest Catholic *padre*; the *bandido*, either ineffectually vicious or suavely deceptive; and the inevitably lazy, servile *peon*.

The literary Lincoln resurfaced this year in "All the Living and the Dead: Lincoln's Imagery" (*AL* 52:351–80) wherein James Hurt subtly reveals Lincoln's developing selfhood in his literary style. The early, undefined personality was expressed in water imagery. Filial rebellion came in the Springfield years, accompanied by guilt, depression, ambition, abstract love, reason, and the long view of historical process. After 20 difficult years Lincoln achieved a fairly integrated personality, and the process is reflected in his domestic-patriotic imagery that depicts the heroic Founding Fathers, acceptable filial revolt, loyalty, duty, and union. The "Farewell to Springfield" speech (1861) marks the beginning of the late style, as Lincoln's ambition is reconciled with feminine emotion and filiopiety, accompanied by images of fatherhood (domestic and national), divine being, time and space. Hurt then shows how all of this and more come together in the Gettysburg Address.

Finally, the alert student of the movies who has spotted the name J. H. Ingraham among the author credits of Cecil B. De Mille's *The*

Ten Commandments can make his acquaintance in Robert W. Weatherby's monograph (TUSAS 361), a book that will be useful to literary historians as well. Besides his three ministerial novels (*The Pillar of Fire; or Israel in Bondage*, 1859, was De Mille's source), Ingraham wrote nonstop on virtually every nameable subject. In one five-year siege he produced 80 novels. He accidentally shot himself in 1860. But there was a son, Prentiss, also a novelist. Twayne Publishers take notice!

iv. Local Color and Literary Regionalism

The year will be remembered for the eruption of Mt. St. Helens in the Pacific Northwest and secondary explosions of books and articles touching nearly every other definable region. The only manageable way to describe the fallout is from area to area. New England's Jewett and Freeman inspired seven pieces that test my notion last year that analyses of women writers may be shifting from feminist concerns in the fiction to a larger social reality and problems of literary craft. This year's returns are ambiguous. Ann Romines, "In *Deephaven*: Skirmishes near the Swamp" (*CLQ* 16:205–19), looks at the ceremonial New England of the early Jewett—the yarn-spinning of old salts, watching the lighthouse sunsets, and attending household teas and prayers, church services, and funerals. These rituals add up to "an education in the stringencies, complications, and constant demands, as well as satisfactions, of being human *anywhere*," but the education escapes Kate and Helen. Later, it will be mastered by the "awakened" nameless narrator of *Pointed Firs*. Another interpretation beyond feminism is Malinda Snow's "'That One Talent': The Vocation as Theme in Sarah Orne Jewett's *A Country Doctor*" (*CLQ* 16:138–47). This novel concerns talents and calling (the tradition of Milton's sonnet) and incidentally depicts a role-reversal in which a man plays the potential spoiler of the woman's career. Snow regards the novel as artistically a relative failure lacking the economy, directness, and simple design of Jewett's more sucessful shorter fiction. This interest in craft also dominates Joseph R. McElrath's "The Artistry of Mary E. Wilkins Freeman's 'The Revolt'" (*SSF* 17:255–61). For her magazine audience Freeman designed a series of crises, climaxes, and resolutions, together with an "artful use of anticlimax as a deliberate narrative device." Her short-story technique here, says McElrath, is "literary gimmickry at its best."

Other writers on Jewett and Freeman kept watch on feminist themes. "Pure and Passionate: Female Friendship in Sarah Orne Jewett's 'Martha's Lady'" (SSF 17:21–29) by Glenda Hobbs traces the mutual blooming and flourishing of two women through a transcendental friendship similar to, though more emotional than, Thoreau's description in A Week. Despite a 40-year separation after one marries, the women continue to experience both "caring and autonomy" in this ideal friendship. Josephine Donovan's "A Woman's Vision of Transcendence: A New Interpretation of the Works of Sarah Orne Jewett" (MR 21:365–81) also underscores companionship of women, along with a purposeful career and "matriarchal Christianity," as important to Jewett if women are to transcend the emotional and social starvation of atrophied community in New England. In her monograph for the Modern Literature Series (Ungar) Donovan slightly elaborates Jewett's characteristic themes and techniques, but the effort is mainly defeated by a cramped series-format. Sarah W. Sherman also treats the regional transcendence of woman in "The Great Goddess in New England: Mary Wilkins Freeman's 'Christmas Jenny'" (SSF 17:157–64). Described in the same terms as the Christmas evergreen she grows and the animals she tends, the androgynous Jenny, far fram "love-cracked" by an early jilting, is a St. Francis, a Santa Claus, an "incarnation of archaic woman," a "Virgin Mary radically redefined," and consummately Mircea Eliade's Great Goddess of world religions.

Criticism of southern writers flourished in 1980, particularly on the work of Cable, for The Grandissimes enjoyed centennial celebration and reinterpretation in a special number of the Southern Quarterly (18,iv:1–73). The issue is appropriately dedicated to the memory of Arlin Turner. It is ably edited and introduced by Thomas J. Richardson, who also sums up the critical history and adds to it an incisive plot paraphrase centering on the white Honoré Grandissime as spokesman for Cable's ambivalent view of the South in 1880. Donald A. Ringe then explains "Narrative Voice in Cable's The Grandissimes" as a third-person strategy that is chatty and intimate at first to engage and enlighten the reader. But it becomes darker and more objective after the central episode with Bras-Coupé, and Cable's historical meaning, too, grows more serious and dramatic.

Alfred Bendixen in "Cable's *The Grandissimes*: A Literary Pioneer Confronts the Southern Tradition" praises Cable's characterization and imaginative plotting as the means of internalizing the conflicts between pride and love, innocence and experience, justice and racism, democracy and aristocracy, old and new, American and Europe, and North and South. The next selection is a photo-essay of "*The Grandissimes* and the French Quarter" by W. Kenneth Holditch and Drayton Hamilton. They claim that the Quarter is well enough preserved today to suggest Cable's 1880 or even 1803 of the novel. Very little historical charm, however, looks out from these sharp black-and-white daylight photographs. William B. Clark discusses a further aspect of tone in "Humor in Cable's *The Grandissimes*." The comic muse presides in several guises: in the "witty authorial tone," in the tough-minded comic side of the death-haunted Dr. Keene and the acerbic Clemence, and in Old Southwest dark humor involving subjects of horror or moments of grim absurdity. Do the two marriages at the end brighten the historical scene, past and present, including the fate of the free man of color? Lawrence I. Berkove thinks not: "the realistic conclusion of the novel is tragic, wrapped in the utter defeat of the f.m.c., and pessimistic, boding ill for the freedmen of the post-Reconstruction South." He suspects, too, that Cable's novel influenced the portrayal of Harris' Free Joe and Mark Twain's Jim ("The Free Man of Color in *The Grandissimes* and Works by Harris and Mark Twain"). Last, Joseph J. Egan suggests a pair of doubles, beyond the two Honorés, in "Lions Rampant: Agricola Fusilier and Bras-Coupé as Antithetical Doubles in *The Grandissimes*." Their black-white polarities aside, both characters are proud, regal, leonine, prejudiced, foolishly patriotic, and grotesquely religious. At death, both invoke their respective homelands ("Africa," "Louisiana").

Perhaps with the centennial of Cable's first novel now observed, his 14 other novels and plentiful short fiction will attract some critics. Two more publications this year, however, herald no such movement. Robert O. Stevens in "Cable's *The Grandissimes* and the Comedy of Manners" (*AL* 51:507–19) claims that this novel is quite strictly about Creole society and "not the clash between Creole and American civilizations," and he then demonstrates that Cable's plot fits the comedy-of-manners formula of Northrop Frye. Arlin Turner, before his death, assembled *Critical Essays on George W. Cable* (Hall), a task for which he was eminently fit. The modern essays he selects are top-heavy with readings of *The Grandissimes*, leaving the impression (which Turner does not discourage) that the bulk of Cable's other fiction does not merit very serious reconsideration.

There are two surveys of southern writing, the more extensive being J. V. Ridgely's *Nineteenth-Century Southern Literature* (Kentucky) in the "New Perspectives on the South" series edited by Charles P. Roland. Given the enormity of the subject to be treated in just over 100 pages, Ridgely has little opportunity for "new perspectives," but he does write a well-conceived introduction to the growth of a southern mentality and its best literary expression during the crucial phases of a troubled history a century ago. An even more difficult assignment is C. Hugh Holman's ten-page essay, "Another Look at Nineteenth-Century Southern Fiction" (*SHR* 14:235-45). In effect he writes a tribute to Ellen Glasgow. After rehashing the influence of Scott, the critical legacy of Simms, and the postwar apologists of the Old South, he gets down to the business of praising Glasgow for her new brand of critical realism that scrutinized the region for a first time with an incisive mixture of irony, intelligence, and love. Disregarded by Holman and Ridgely but resurrected by L. Moody Simms is one "Margaret Junkin Preston: Southern Poet" (*SoSt* 19:94–100), who wrote six volumes of verse and corresponded with Browning, Tennyson, Longfellow, and others.

In a class by itself is Michael Orlard's "Shifty in a New Country: Games in Southwest Humor" (*SLJ* 12,ii:1–28). That Southwest humor mirrors a fluid social order on the frontier is not news, but Orlard stresses the all-pervasive role of the competitive game in the social activities and literary forms. Games on the frontier encouraged survival, order, and personal and social identity, though they had less productive cultural ends among the con-men, speculators, and rogues, the Simon Suggses and Sut Luvingoods.

The Midwest literary journal or newsletter today does not always reach tightly budgeted libraries elsewhere, but Peter Benson's "No 'Murmured Thanks': Women and Johnson Brigham's *Midland Monthly*" (*AmerS* 21:57–71) turned up as a welcome example of original regional scholarship. Founded in Des Moines, Iowa, in 1894, Brigham's magazine was surprisingly hospitable to women, both as literary contributors and citizens. On the other hand, Brigham duly tempered the progressive with the timid, reform with convention, and realism with sentimentality. A second workmanlike study is *Prairie Voices: A Literary History of Chicago from the Frontier to 1893* (Nashville: Townsend) by Kenny J. Williams. He carries the Chicago story up to Fuller's shattering vision of urban life in *The Cliff-Dwellers.* Williams clearly delineates the important stages along the way: the chauvinistic Western journalism of the 1840s and 1850s, the rebirth of a Chicago ethos after the fire of 1871, the beginnings of the *Dial* (1880) and genteel-versus-realistic polemics of the 1880s, and the prominent rise of the postwar novel. Three helpful appendices list Chicago journals and newspapers, novels, and publishers of fiction.

A broader perspective on western regionalism is found in the January special issue of "The American Literary West" in *Jour. of the West,* edited by the well-informed Richard W. Etulain. His opening essay, "Western American Literature: The Colonial Period" (19,i:6–8), reminds us that most of the writing to 1865 was on the West as seen by narrators, critics, or romanticists from the outside: Lewis and Clark, Pike, Long, Cooper, Irving, Garrard, George Rupton (English), and the area's first poetizer, Whitman. Patrick D. Morrow continues the history as San Francisco, unburdened by the postwar disruptions farther east, became a cultural center that nourished the local color parables of Harte and parodies of Mark Twain ("Parody and Parable in Early Western Local Color Writing" [19,i: 9–16]). Sanford E. Marovitz then describes the final decades of the century when the Western novel was seldom realistic or purely indigenous. The leading writers were usally bent on giving their Eastern audience a West "as it was, as it was not, and as it might be." His carefully reasoned discussion is titled "Bridging the Continent with Romantic Western Realism" (19,i:17–28).

In his article just mentioned Patrick Morrow briefly treats Bret Harte's first book, *Outcroppings* (1865), an anthology of pretentious California verse. Morrow has more to say about this venture in "Bret Harte and the Perils of Pop Poetry" (*JPC* 13:476–82). After vitriolic critics lambasted the book ("hogwash and purp stuff ladled out from the slop bucket") Harte took the offensive in *The Californian* with satirical counterattacks and mocking advice on how to write a Western classical-epic. The experience, at least for a time, sharpened the wits of "the tough-minded, demanding, logical satirist and critic." The reviews of *Outcroppings* lead off Linda D. Barnett's *Bret Harte:*

A Reference Guide (Hall), an annotated bibliography of some 2,350 secondary works from 1865 to 1977, revised from her earlier listing in *ALR* (see *ALS 1972*, pp. 191–92). To her entries under "Tennessee's Partner" can be added two readings in the current year. In "For Better or for Worse, Tennessee and His Partner: A New Approach to Bret Harte" (*ArQ* 36:211–16) Linda Burton reads the motivation of the two men before, during, and after the partner's marriage as convincingly homosexual. Both sought their heterosexuality with the same woman, but the Partner remains the long-term indulgent wife of the wayward Tennessee, even sharing his name. William F. Conner will have none of this or any sentimental interpretation. Like Charles E. May (*SDR* 15[1977]:109–17), Conner discovers a sardonic Harte at work here. "Tennessee's deadpan partner is complex, clever, and hard-boiled," writes Conner in "The Euchring of Tennessee: A Reexamination of Bret Harte's 'Tennessee's Partner'" (*SSF* 17:113–20). After Tennessee's return from the wife-stealing, the Partner awaits his moments of revenge and gains it at the trial by irritating the judge and jurors, thereby insuring Tennessee's conviction. When Tennessee exclaims, " 'Euchred, old man!' " he is acknowledging the Partner's victory.

Harte's strongest competition in supplying the East and Europe with romantic images of the West came from Joaquin Miller, now favored with a compact and informative pamphlet by Benjamin S. Lawson in the Western Writers Series (Boise State). Miller's triumphant decade was the 1870s, when he adapted England's Byron to versifyings of the West and then brought the West to England. There for a time, as Lawson vividly sketches him, Miller in sombrero, flowing locks, riding boots, and bearskin serape strode among the English literary notables. In 1876 one captivated English critic hailed Miller as America's "most remarkable narrative poet." One cavil with Lawson is that he does not quote enough of Miller to establish the poetic voice that charmed so many non-Westerners. Miller is also among the trio in Ray C. Longtin's edition, *Three Writers of the Far West: A Reference Guide* (Hall). With him are Charles Warren Stoddard, who welcomed Miller to San Francisco in 1871, and George Sterling, who moved there in 1891, made his pilgrimages to the Miller home in Oakland, and learned from a master the rudiments of posing and role-playing. Longtin's bibliographies will become a valuable research guide to all three writers.

v. Henry Adams

R. P. Blackmur's long-awaited book on Adams, uncompleted at his death in 1965, has now appeared in an edited version, *Henry Adams* (Harcourt), by Veronica A. Makowsky, with a foreword by Denis Donoghue. In 1936 Blackmur planned his book not as a chronological biography but a multifaceted portrait of Adams. In the late 1940s he outlined a new book in two parts: (1) from the Harvard years to the later 1890s, and (2) the final two decades. The manuscript for part 1, half-completed and fragmentary, is deposited at Princeton. Part 2 comprises the bulk of Makowsky's edition, based almost completely on "The Virgin and the Dynamo," Blackmur's 11-chapter analysis of Adams' symbolic vision and artistic unity in the *Education* and *Mont-Saint Michel and Chartres*. (Blackmur did not finish chapter 11.) Makowsky also includes an elegiac account of Adams' last six years, "King Richard's Prison Song," which Blackmur wrote in 1938. Inescapably, one encounters Adams here through a double- or triple-tiered perspective as the biographer's distinctively convoluted and frequently eloquent prose calls attention to R. P. Blackmur, who is discovering his own correlative of rational and imaginative experience in the distinctive style and double vision (12th century upon 19th century) of Henry Adams.

Two other books on Adams are not so strenuous, nor so distinguished and edifying. William Dusinberre's *Henry Adams: The Myth of Failure* (Virginia) dramatically reverses Blackmur's verdict on the imaginative success of the two late works and pronounces the *History of the United States* Adams' intellectual and literary masterpiece, worthy to be compared with his masters Macaulay and Gibbon. *Chartres* and *Education*, for all Adams' bold theorizing, do not constitute the "Major Phase" but instead betray an aging mind "not strong enough to project a series of illuminating theories supported with valuable subsidiary detail." They suffer, as well, from "failures of tone." Dusinberre merely states these weaknesses; but he explores the strengths of the *History*. In the chapter, "History as Art," he assigns Adams high marks for his transitions, syntax, iteration, and, of course, indirection and irony. After this plodding analysis one returns to Blackmur with gratitude even for his idiosyncratic difficulties. The third book, *Henry Adams and the American Experiment* (Little, Brown Library of American Biography) by David R. Contosta, is an introduction for history students, giving a biographical account of Adams' conservative pessimism over the democratic experiment. There is no substantial literary or character analysis of Adams.

A pair of valuable articles also enriched this season on Adams. The images of polarity in the late work have never been explained more subtly than by James M. Cox, "Learning through Ignorance: *The Education of Henry Adams*" (*SR* 88:198–227). The masculine *Education* and feminine *Chartres* are like twin poles of Faraday's horseshoe magnet, and Adams' historical imagination becomes a "dynamic intrusion cutting across the lines of force to generate its own continuous narrative current." More important than Marian's death is the earlier one of Adams' sister, she of the mind that feels, and that event generates energy across the 20-year hiatus into the second half of the *Education* to the Adams mind that reasons a synthesis of the Dynamo and Virgin. B. L. Reid agrees (in "The View from the Side," *SR* 88:228–57) that the later chapters of the *Education* embody a triumph of intellectual energy, and it is expressed in a style of elegiac, autumnal brilliance. By consensus in 1980, the later period still remains Adams' Major Phase.

vi. Realism and the Age of Howells

Howells biography and criticism this year were evenly divided and once again abundant. Of first importance are the *Selected Letters*, vol. 3, 1882–91 (Twayne), ed. Robert C. Leitz, Richard H. Ballinger, and Christoph K. Lohmann. These are the momentous years of Howells' literary career when he was writing almost without interruption his best novels and some others only just less distinguished; had begun his realism polemics in the "Editor's Study" of *Harper's*; and became immersed in Tolstoy, the Haymarket Affair, socialistic reform, and pre-Freudian parental agonies over the decline of daughter Winnie. The record of these years is preserved in a voluminous correspondence which scholars in the past have ferreted from manuscript collections throughout the country. Hereafter, a bonanza of these letters, with immensely helpful annotations, will be no further distant than arm's reach.

To supplement this harvest of Howells matter, George Monteiro and Brenda Murphy have added the largely unpublished *John Hay-*

Howells Letters (Twayne)—42 by Howells and 71 from Hay. The introduction and notes fully chronicle the personal and literary relationship, and an appendix includes Howells' reviews and essays on this literary friend who was, in Theodore Roosevelt's view, "the best letter-writer of his age." Howells was not so close to that President (Hay was his secretary of state), but there was a significant literary friendship that William M. Gibson describes in chapter 2 of *Theodore Roosevelt Among the Humorists* (Tenn.). After Howells reviewed Roosevelt's early work, they began a friendly correspondence in 1890, though Roosevelt cared little for realism, Tolstoy, or socialism. Relations were less cordial during TR's misguided (in Howells' view) turn-of-century jingoist imperialism and campaign for large families; but Howells' comments in *Harper's* were temperate and good-naturedly ironic. He later thought Roosevelt a good Progressive.

In these later years (1902–11) Howells spent extended summer vacations in Kittery Point, Maine. His house has now been declared a memorial dwelling and donated to Harvard. In a dedication ceremony last year David J. Nordloh described Howells' writing, his guests (including Henry James in June, 1905), and the quiet, joyous seasons in this most permanent of all residences in his nomadic life. Daniel Aaron then spoke on Howells' ambivalent responses to Harvard and its Cambridge notables. The two speeches, "W. D. Howells at Kittery Point" and "Howells and Harvard," are printed in *HLB* 28:431–37, 438–42. In the same journal is the history of an earlier Howells residence, "Redtop and the Belmont Years of W. D. Howells and His Family" (28:33–57) by Ginette de B. Merrill, present owner and restorer of the house which is now a National Historical Landmark. From the Howells correspondence, sketches of plans, and revisions of design and color scheme for the house, she writes a pleasant domestic history of the Howellses in Belmont Village from 1878 to 1882.

Criticism on Howells' work, early to late, leads off with a sustained and frightening critique of "Two Recent Volumes of A Selected Edition of W. D. Howells" (*MP* 78:59–72) by Watson Branch. The two volumes are *A Modern Instance* and *The Minister's Charge*, though Branch has done his more devastating homework on the first. He points to editorial decisions and errors, large and small, that lead to a copy-text of questionable value. Patrick O'Donnell compares *A*

Modern Instance and *The Rise of Silas Lapham* with *The Princess Casamassima* and *The Ambassadors* in "Between Life and Art: Structures of Realism in the Fiction of Howells and James" (*EA* 33: 142–55). The familiar thesis is unconvincing: Howells creates unresolved drift in a slice of life but James achieves completed form because his characters, being more sensitive and intelligent, make ultimate choices amid life's perplexing ambiguities. One can as well argue, however, that American life receives pattern and definition in *A Modern Instance* at least equal to Hyacinth Robinson's London life, while Howells' characters make "choices" as problematical as James's that lead to endings similarly dark and closed. Or again, Silas Lapham fashions a final choice and retreat with as much moral ardor as Strether to resolve an even more painful dilemma. Lapham's moral decision is also the subject of Patrick Dooley's intelligently conceived "Nineteenth Century Business Ethics and *The Rise of Silas Lapham* (*AmerS* 21:79–93). Why did the early reviews overlook the drama of business ethics in Howells' novel? Dooley replies that popular moral textbooks like Francis Wayland's *The Elements of Moral Science* (1835) stressed practical and legal, not moral, business solutions. Lapham's partner Rogers is moral in Wayland's sense: the businessman had no obligation to volunteer information on his product, but only to avoid lying about it. (The moral issues of Howells' love plot, being noncommercial and personal, were more obvious to his readers.) Lapham does not seek technical or legal release from his crisis by declaring bankruptcy, and such business integrity—closer to moral philosopher James H. Fairchild's more recent *The Science of Obligation* (1869)—was yet unfamiliar in the 1880s.

Ranging among several novels, including *Lapham* and especially *The Minister's Charge*, Elsa Nettels shapes some important insights on a neglected topic, Howells' colloquial style, in "William Dean Howells and the American Language" (*NEQ* 53:308–28). Dialect and the vernacular advance characterization as well as the ideal of complicity in *The Minister's Charge*, for class and language divisions defeat the true community of man. To groom Lemuel as a mediating hero, Howells spares him really countrified speech, so that he becomes rapidly polished in the company of Sewell and the Coreys. At the same time he remains admirably faithful and sympathetic to the ungrammatical Statira. Nicolaus Mills, "Class and Crowd in

American Fiction" (*CentR* 24:192–217), pauses long enough at the strike action in *A Hazard of New Fortunes* to recognize it as the forerunner of lower-class crowd scenes in modern literature from *Sister Carrie* to *Invisible Man*. Mills overstates, however, the sympathy Howells felt for the working classes.

"*The World of Chance*: Howells' Hawthornian Self-Parody" (*AL* 52:279–93) is a sophisticated article by Scott A. Dennis, probably the best critical reading this year. Among Dennis' conclusions are, first, that this novel portrays Howells' "cynical view of life in general and literary success in particular, and it does so with a large irony that often approaches self-parody." Second, in this last of the "economic novels" (a mistaken old label Dennis might have done without) Howells had brought certain aesthetic and social questions begun in *Hazard* forward into an ironic and self-parodying "psychodrama" with many dead endings, and the survival of his art now demanded some crucial new direction.

Perhaps not a new direction but an intensified concern is apparent in Howells' later treatment of psychological trauma, tragedy, death, religion, and the supernatural. James R. Payne examines a neglected book of 1902 and connects it to Howells' previous work in "Psychological and Supernatural Themes in Howells's *The Flight of Pony Baker*" (*MarkhamR* 9:52–55). Three chapters on Howells' nine-year-old hero had appeared in *Youth's Companion*, but this novel, as Payne deftly interprets it, is adult fare. Nightmares, storms, floods, supernatural visitations, and "startling imagery of tragic potentialities of life" add up to a Howellsian psychological ordeal from which his characters sometimes do not recover. This time, however, the character's severe trials benefit his moral growth. The next year, in *Questionable Shapes*, came the story "His Apparition," another of Howells' darker fictions. Natural merges with supernatural and psychological with spiritual in a tale of fear, vanity, cupidity, and also purposive moral responsibility and self-awareness. So the story is interpreted by Charles Feigenoff, who then observes that few readers today will identify themselves with Howells' hero, an erstwhile skeptic who happily discovers that "spiritual reality is at the core of experience" and that "some orderly force governs the universe" ("'His Apparition': The Howells No One Believes In" [*ALR* 13:85–89]). In a second article Feigenoff modestly advances previous interpretations of "Sexuality in *The Leatherwood God*" (*SNNTS* 12:

183–91) by offering a well-documented explanation of the continuous sexual disruptions in the frontier hamlet, among men and women alike, caused by Howells' magnetic revivalist, the Gantry-like Dylks.

Bernard F. Engel has recently carved out an undisputed territorial right to Howells' poetry, including "William Dean Howells and the Verse Drama" (*ELWIU* 7:67–78). From 1874 to 1909 Howells wrote five verse plays. Engel examines Howells' alterations in the translated *Yorick's Love*, compares *Priscilla* to Longfellow's poem, points to resemblances with Robinson and Frost in the late *The Mother and the Father*, but concludes that there is not much here to conclude about.

In "Howells and the Battle of Words over 'Genius'" (*ALR* 13: 101–07) Lannom Smith rehearses the debate Howells waged with Stedman, Hearn, Bierce, and others over romantic spontaneity and inborn creativity versus realistic hard work, close observation, and patient craft. In these polemics, Howells owned a valuable ally in Hjalmar Hjorth Boyeson, a well-rounded man of letters who deserves book-length consideration and has lately received it in Robert S. Frederickson's monograph (TUSAS 350). Author of *Mammon of Unrighteousness* (1891), a novel of power, social insight, and characters we remember and care about, Boyeson is also important to Frederickson as a sensitive observer who was able to envision order and progress in a world where Henry Adams found chaos and entropy. This book is flawed critically, however, by a plethora of casually employed isms, most irritatingly a self-explanatory use of "Realism."

Three lesser contemporaries of Howells are studied in Dan Vogel's *Emma Lazarus*, David Kirby's *Grace King*, and Clara C. Mackenzie's *Sarah Barnwell Elliott* (TUSAS 353, 357, and 359). Useful and comfortably patterned as the monographs in this series have become, they suggest missed opportunities for illuminating our cultural history, always the special contribution of minor figures. Rather than treat these three women singly at book length, their many forgettable works paraphrased in chapter after tedious chapter, the three scholars might have co-authored a single study that ignored their writers' most painful subliterary lapses and highlighted, instead, the lines of cultural connection and contrast in their backgrounds, careers, and literary relationships.

Charles Dudley Warner, who figured in the careers of King,

Elliott, and more obliquely Lazarus, has his own productive, civilized life gracefully defined in an article by Eugene E. Leach, "Charles Dudley Warner's 'Little Journey in the World'" (*NEQ* 53: 329–44). Despite his friendship with Howells, Mark Twain, and Stowe, and his social criticism in *The Gilded Age* and *Little Journey*, Warner was less the reform-minded citizen than a "champion of respectable leisure." As Hartford's sentimental escapist from New York's gilded-age Sodom, he "measured the world against the standards of sensibility and bonhomie maintained at Nook Farm." Through the postwar decades, he was the "leading ladies' man of American literature," a successor to Irving whose biography Warner contributed to his own American Men of Letters series.

Edward Bellamy's critical utopian vision is newly defined by Donald E. Winters, "The Utopianism of Survival: Bellamy's *Looking Backward* and Twain's *A Connecticut Yankee*" (*AmerS* 21:23–38). While Bellamy is "more positive and concrete," both writers portray in their respective heroes a psychology of survival and self-renewal after holocaust that suggests the "'survivor's ethos'" of Robert J. Lifton's recent *The Life of the Self*. Two of Bellamy's unfamiliar earlier novels are examined for their parallels with Hawthorne in Robert E. Hogan's "*Dr. Heidenhoff's Process* and *Miss Ludington's Sister*: Edward Bellamy's Romances of Immortality" (*SAF* 8:51–68). In a rather loosely organized discussion he makes some revealing comparisons with *The House of the Seven Gables* and especially *Septimius Felton*—a convincing demonstration that large areas of discovery await the scholar with imagination enough to explore the many neglected works in our literary past.

vii. Fin-de-Siècle America: Stephen Crane and the 1890s

The year's new book on Crane is by James Nagel, *Stephen Crane and Literary Impressionism* (Penn. State). Following a critical introduction to clear the decks, Nagel gives his version of Crane's impressionistic method in narration, dramatized epistemology, characters, images, and plot structure. At the least he helpfully sets forth the arguments over impressionism, as well as realism, naturalism, and symbolism in Crane. But arguments they will no doubt remain. Indeed, Edwin Cady has revised his 1962 monograph on Crane (TUSAS 23) and reaffirms that these isms in Crane are forever moot, for Crane was "forever a Seeker, an apprentice to himself." (See Joseph Kwiat's similar conclusion last year, *ALS 1979*, p. 217.) Cady was prompted to revise and update his book in the light of newer studies and the printing of the 1893 text of *Maggie*. In that novel he now views the ending rather than Maggie's death in chapter 17 as the true climax which "confirms *Maggie* as a book about moral ecology, the real meaning of the slums, the effect of the puddle on its flower." The ending teaches those who "see falsely how to use their eyes aright."

A number of the new articles on Crane hold minor revelations intelligently argued. Joseph L. Candela summarizes part of his 1978 dissertation (Chicago) in "The Domestic Orientation of American Novels, 1893–1913" (*ALR* 13:1–18), placing *Maggie* at the beginning of a spate of novels that fed a public fear that family life was being destroyed in the American city's filth, fun, sin, alcoholism, dangerous jobs, and infant mortality. Joseph Kwiat sees the ordeal of Crane's experience in *Maggie*, before and after publication, to be pivotal in his journalistic shift from reporter to opinionated freelancer of feature articles. Newspaper work gave him not only literary opportunity and subject matter but also a growing honesty and self-assurance ("Stephen Crane, Literary Reporter: Commonplace Experience and Artistic Transcendence" [*JML* 7:129–38]). Bernard Weinstein also discovers growth in Crane's art and urban perceptions. In *"George's Mother* and the Bowery of Experience" (*MarkhamR* 9:45–49) he reads in these later Bowery impressions not the hyperbole, melodrama, and obtrusive animal imagery of *Maggie* but new psychological subtlety and a more complex understanding of the environment as it impinges on human lives.

Robert G. Deamer in "Remarks on the Western Stance of Stephen Crane" (*WAL* 15:123–41) reiterates, with slightly more evidence, his earlier claim that critics overstate parody, satire, and irony in the western stories (see *ALS 1972*, p. 202). Crane was a youth who read Westerns, owned a gun at Lafayette, travelled the West, and in England wore cowboy breeches, brandished a gun before his guests, and decorated his den with western blanket and spurs. He was a faithful admirer of that region's self-reliance, courage, and generosity. In fictions like "Yellow Sky" his protagonist seriously undergoes a true testing because Crane "envisioned his ideal self as a Jack Potter." Crane's West is also scrutinized in Sue L. Kimball,

"Circles and Squares: The Designs of Stephen Crane's 'The Blue Hotel'" (*SSF* 17:425–30). This is a "close reading" of incidentals that one encounters rather infrequently now, though Robert C. Basye conducts a similar inquiry in "Color Imagery in Stephen Crane's Poetry" (*ALR* 13:122–31). He does suggest important and possibly valid conclusions about reality and illusion in Crane's color symbolism. Unfortunately, Crane employs certain colors so seldom that the inductive researcher is given over to desperate speculation.

Among several additions and corrections in Crane bibliography, one item contains the nearest we have this year to a controversy, and it involves the veteran of many skirmishes, Robert W. Stallman. Stanley Wertheim visited the Columbia University Libraries and returned with "H. G. Wells to Cora Crane: Some Letters and Corrections" (*RALS* 9:207–12). Wells's correspondence proves that he was in fact solicitous of Crane's health in the final weeks, visited him at Dover as Crane was en route to the Black Forest (and wished to see him again at Dover but Cora thought Crane too weak), and hoped to see him in Germany during the summer. After Crane's death in early June 1900, he lay in state at a Baker Street mortuary, but Wells declined to come, writing Cora that he wished to preserve unmarred the image of the living Crane rather than view "something that was no longer him." Wertheim notices that Stallman misdated this comment to the previous month, so that Wells seemed callously unwilling to see the *living*, ailing Crane ("something that was no longer him") at Dover. Stallman then used more of this same letter in its proper, posthumous context, though with further errors of fact and inference.

Frank Norris has been fortunate in his recent younger critics, we realize in Don Graham's *Critical Essays on Frank Norris* (Hall). His older ones—Pizer, French, Walcutt, and Dillingham—are not so bad, either. Of the recent scholarship, Glen Love's fresh reading of Norris' "Western Metropolitans" (cited in *ALS 1976*, pp. 223–24) is one of several valuable essays reprinted here, and the ink is hardly dry on two new essays Graham secured for this collection, Joseph R. McElrath's "Frank Norris's *The Octopus*: The Christian Ethic as Pragmatic Response" and Robert A. Morace's "The Writer and His Middle Class Audience: Frank Norris A Case in Point." McElrath reads *The Octopus* as a moral standoff, Behrman and the ranchers both culpable, and the answers from sympathetic individual characters either facile or impotent in the present impasse. The "problem of inhumaneness in the economic order," Norris suggests, will remain a problem indeterminately. Morace in his 1976 dissertation (So. Calif.) studied Norris' association with the San Francisco *Wave* (1896–98). For this upper-middle-class audience, and similar readers in his subsequent journalism, Norris accommodated his point of view and tone to their social and intellectual expectations. Morace enlarges on this respectability in "Frank Norris and the Magazine Experience" (*MarkhamR* 9:64–67), where he disagrees with Joseph Kwiat for pairing Norris' magazine career with Crane's (see *ALS 1976*, p. 220). Unlike Crane, Norris did not admire or engage in the "revolt" of the little magazines. What he did publish in them was the tame potboiler or romances like *Moran* and *Blix*.

A varied trio of essays complete the roundup on Norris. Fritz H. Oehlschlaeger reports "An Additional Source for Frank Norris's *A Man's Woman*" (*ALR* 13:93–96), namely the English translation of Fridtjof Nansen's *Fram Over Polhavet*. Norris borrowed details from that Polar expedition (1893–96) for Ward Bennett's table of sea water temperatures, the rationed amounts of butter and "aleuronate" bread, and more generally, for the ideal size of an arctic ship and crew. William Freedman is not the first to discuss "Oral Passivity and Oral Sadism in Norris's *McTeague*" (*L&P* 30:52–61), but his examples and analyses, using Freud and Fromm, are so abundant that little more need be said on this subject for a while. The third essay is Debra B. Munn's lucid and tidy "The Revision of Frank Norris's *Blix*" (*RALS* 10:47–55). During serialization of *Blix* (March to August, 1899) Norris sold the book to Doubleday and McClure and with one of the editors he sanitized the language as well as details, such as sexual odors and hints of undergarments. He also vivified setting and character in revisions that show his progress toward the more fully realized art of *The Octopus* and *The Pit*.

Fears of a permanently slumping interest in Hamlin Garland have been allayed. David W. Hiscoe eschews, so to speak, the oral Freudianism we might anticipate in "Feeding and Consuming in Garland's *Main-Travelled Roads*" (*WAL* 15:13–15) and, instead, relates the persistent imagery of eating to Garland's conflict between controlled moral choice and Darwinian rapacity. The agents of business speculation, abetted by government, are the consuming "voracious destroyers of humanity and humaneness" in Garland, while the farmers are the feeding "nurturer of these qualities." In later years farther west, Garland was even more depressed by the rampant exploitation of America's resources. His Rocky Mountain novels feature a new westerner, the forest ranger, as a transitional hero mediating between conservation and greed. This phase is summed up in Daniel F. Littlefield and Lonnie E. Underhill, "The Emerging New West in Hamlin Garland's Fiction, 1910–1916" (*MarkhamR* 9:35–40) and will receive fully illuminating context in Glen A. Love's book on the new western hero in Garland and others soon to be published. Roger E. Carp's "Hamlin Garland and the Cult of True Womanhood" in *Women, Women Writers, and the West*, ed. L. L. Lee and Merrill Lewis (Whitston, 1979), is a superior essay on Garland's uncertain views of women. He grew up worshipping the "true" woman, "pure, pious, submissive and domestic." In the early fiction, influenced by Howells, Zola, and Ibsen, he vacillated "between radical and traditional conceptions of femininity." But after 1900 in his romances, diaries, and autobiographies, the True Woman, not the New Woman, returned as the only ideal.

We pass from Garland's women to Kate Chopin's men, but the familiar sexist attitudes remain. "The Masculine Dilemma in Kate Chopin's *The Awakening*" by Anne-Lise Strømness Paulsen (*SoSt* 18[1979]:381–424), though in need of severe editorial pruning, is a systematic look at how the six men in Edna's life respond to her and to their own male sex. Only the sixth, Dr. Mandelet, "a man of wisdom and insight," sees into the dilemmas and the conventions which have produced them, but he cannot help either the independent-minded Edna or her bemused husband. An essay by Eleanor B. Wymard returns the focus to Edna: "Kate Chopin: Her Existential Imagination" (*SoSt* 19:373–84). The predictable array of existential authorities are put on parade and the jargon abounds ("psychic space," "authentic," "actualizing her own life") but Wymard makes her case that Chopin, though surrounded by naturalists, was writing a novel about Edna's serious individual choice.

Joseph Candela in "The Domestic Orientation of American Novels," cited earlier on Howells, is not so certain that Chopin intended Edna's family-shattering liberation to be a responsible act of choice. Biological determinants are implied, including even hereditary alcoholism. To the degree that free choice operates, Chopin suggests, the individual must impose limits on private freedom or disastrously undermine the family, the self, and society. Jerome Klinkowitz sides emphatically with Candela. A previously unpublished chapter in his *The Practice of Fiction in America* (Iowa State), titled "Kate Chopin's Awakening to Naturalism," stresses the formative power in Edna's development that Chopin imputes to heredity and an awakening new environment. These forces release Edna's animalism and cause the deterioration of her social relationships—a typically naturalistic portrayal of the instinct-dominated character swept along to her doom.

Chopin's literary echoings and sources are suggested in two essays. Parallels between Edna and Emma Bovary are drawn by Lawrence Thornton, "*The Awakening*: A Political Romance" (*AL* 52:50–66), but he regards the differences as more crucial. Unlike Flaubert, Chopin "treats questions about romanticism, narcissism, and woman's independence" in a manner "essentially political." Edna comes to realize her "insurmountable social dilemma," but Emma lapses into male-oriented "sentimental fatuities." Thornton also alludes to parallels with *The Doll's House* and *Tristan and Isolde*, a neat coincidence with Susan Wolstenholme, "Kate Chopin's Sources for 'Mrs. Mobry's Reason'" (*AL* 51:540–43), who contends that Ibsen's *Ghosts* and Wagner's *Ring* cycle must have influenced Chopin's story treating the sins of the parents visited on the offspring.

These few essays show that the Chopin harvest continues to decline since the five or six years of vigorous activity that began with Per Seyerstad's critical biography and two-volume edition of the *Complete Works* in 1969. Perhaps Seyerstad has supplied new adrenalin with his *A Kate Chopin Miscellany*, ed. with Chopin scholar Emily Toth (Oslo: Universitetsforlaget and Natchitoches, La.: Northwestern State Univ., 1979). The collection includes unpublished short fiction, poems, diaries, letters by and to the author, and some unavailable secondary matter. The esthetic and practical Chopin even composed and published one number, the "Lilia Polka," for the piano in 1888 (repr. on pp. 365–67). A primary and annotated secondary bibliography add to the scholarly value of the book.

Henry B. Fuller had his first major brush with the woman question at age eighteen, when he wrote letters to the *Chicago Tribune* in 1875 warning young men to be wary of a marriage trap with the currently prodigal young women. When the *Tribune* received angry responses, Fuller replied that these damsels might, of course, be reformed if given the experience of dating intellectual males. Kenneth Scambray, working on the biography, discovered these letters which the homosexual Fuller signed "Harry B. Free." See "He Caught It for This: Four Letters by Henry Blake Fuller" (*ALR* 13:266–69). Twenty years later, with the city's triumphant Columbian Exposition only a recent memory, Fuller was still the needling aesthete, with more of Chicago society now his target. G. Thomas Couser in "Art in Chicago: Fuller's *With the Procession*" (*ALR* 13:31–40) believes that the characters in "his best Chicago novel" variously express or exhibit Fuller's despairing sense that the arts in Chicago were not appreciated for their own sake, and even the patrons were philistines for whom art is one more means of conspicuous consumption.

Any reports of Ignatius Donnelly's demise are exaggerated. Reed T. Ueda makes him more our contemporary than ever before in "Economic and Technological Evil in the Modern Apocalypse: Donnelly's *Caesar's Column* & *The Golden Bottle*" (*JPC* 14:1–9). With help from Norman O. Brown, who has noted the excremental vision in many critiques of capitalism, Ueda goes on to uncover the "obsessive images of Satan, sorcery, and the demonic power of money" with which Donnelly "pointed to the psychopathological basis of economic aggression" in America's degenerate plutocracy. The essay is a convincing demonstration of the Judaeo-Christian apocalyptic imagery in Donnelly's nightmares of capitalist perversion, money-gratification, and self-destruction—recommended reading that will pique some appetites for more of Donnelly. For these readers David D. Anderson has served up a new Twayne monograph (*TUSAS* 362), but he is far less provocative than Ueda. The book also falls notably short of the fine study by Martin Ridge, on whom Anderson relies for biographical narration as he surveys the works to discover the unifying concepts among Donnelly's ambiguities and wild inconsistencies.

A much gentler outlook on urban civilization than Donnelly's is described in Richard Tuerk's "The Short Stories of Jacob A. Riis" (*ALR* 13:259–65). Riis's aesthetic sounded like a critical realist's, the writer to study and thereby improve the lot of the other half, especially New York's immigrant workers. But in practice Riis's settings and characters lack the grime, bestiality, and degradation of Crane's Bowery world (and also the artistic power). Optimism, goodness, sharing, and free will emerge in Riis's fictional slums which bring out the best as well as worst in ghetto dwellers.

Ambrose Bierce is back in a substantial essay by John R. Brazil, "Behind the Bitterness: Ambrose Bierce in Text and Context" (*ALR* 13:225–37). Brazil directs us to the radical contradictions of art and politics in the early romanticism, through the crucial horrors of the Civil War, and on to Bierce's quarrel with the esthetics of Harte and Howells. But his own "rigid esthetic" (Kevin Starr's phrase)— designed to protect him, as Brazil says, "from the vagaries and mind-threatening confusion of a modern society that would not conform to his Victorian assumptions and presumptive frontier values"— failed as an instrument of control and defense against historical or personal despair.

Two other tartly critical spirits at the turn of the century whose voices have been too often silent—Moody and Dunne—return in separate essays by George Arms and William Gibson, who bring to their subjects an expected scholarly thoroughness and humanity. Moody is chief of three participants in Arms's "The Poet as Theme Reader: William Vaughn Moody, to a Student, and Louisa May Alcott" (in *Toward a New Literary History*). At Harvard in 1894–95, Moody was grading papers in his English 22, Advanced Composition, when he read an unusually interesting theme by a 30-year-old student who described her meeting with Alcott some ten years before. Moody's corrections tell something of the instructor's diligence and the poet's sensitiveness to language. But the interest does not stop there. Arms went on to recover three letters that Alcott, then in ailing health, wrote to Moody's student when she was a troubled younger woman. The gesture to lend counsel and comfort was typical of Alcott: personal, kind, and distinctly Victorian.

Gibson's Dunne also shares the spotlight with another celebrity in "Theodore Roosevelt and Finley Peter Dunne, 'Mr. Dooley': 'He was my most cherished source of copy,' " the last and best chapter in *Theodore Roosevelt Among the Humorists* (Tenn.). Dunne was invited to the White House after Mr. Dooley had burlesqued rough-rider "Tiddy Rosenfelt" in *Harper's*. Many visits and letters followed, Dunne alternately admiring, fascinated by, and disapproving of the exuberant, many-sided TR. The outlet for his disapproval came in the usually genial satire of Mr. Dooley: the Irish jibes at "Tiddy's" English "lie-ance," his weak stand on immigrant and black rights, his imperialism in the Philippines, and the tight-rope politics with big business and organized labor. Gibson not only writes enjoyably on Dunne's penetrating humor but helps us appreciate the complex President. A public show-off, happy political warrior, man of letters, and much more, Roosevelt was also the generously human leader who enjoyed, rather than resented, his satirical critics.

San Diego State University

13. Fiction: 1900 to the 1930s

David Stouck

During the seven years that I have been writing this chapter there has been increasing critical attention paid to the women writers from this period. The reputations of Wharton, Cather, and Stein as significant American authors have not only been secured but also advanced to the front rank. In 1980 there was an important new biography of Dos Passos, but most of the other books were on women writers—Wharton, Cather, Stein, Glasgow, and such minor figures as Gene Stratton Porter and Mary Hallock Foote. The old imbalance of a male-dominated literary tradition is quickly being redressed.

i. John Dos Passos

Although the bulk of criticism in 1980 was on Cather, the most significant new work was on Dos Passos. Townsend Ludington's *John Dos Passos: A Twentieth Century Odyssey* (Dutton) is a definitive biography of one of America's most complex writers and as well a meticulous portrait of the era in which he lived and moved. This is the first biography authorized by the Dos Passos estate and its author was assisted by Dos Passos' widow, Elizabeth. For Ludington the key to Dos Passos is his acute sense of being illegitimate and an outsider in every phase of life. Ludington sees his artistic life as a quest to establish a place for himself in the world. One of Ludington's central concerns is to explore Dos Passos' political shift from the radical left to the far right. He was unalterably disillusioned, Ludington contends, by his experience in the Spanish Civil War, where he felt he had been betrayed by the Communists. He came to believe in Jeffersonian democracy as the only answer for America. Ludington sees Dos Passos as isolated and embattled, yet the portrait is balanced. In its details the biography shows that "he was less a social loner than he often cast himself or than he seemed to be to others," and that "he was also less the political activist than his writings made him appear or than many of his readers assumed." Ludington locates the lasting value of Dos Passos' works in their function as a "panorama—personal yet wide-ranging—of the state of his nation during the twentieth century."

There is also a new Dos Passos bibliography. John Rohrkemper's *John Dos Passos: A Reference Guide* (Hall) provides scholars with a comprehensive bibliography of writings about Dos Passos. An introduction gives an overview of Dos Passos' critical fortunes and suggests that there is a Dos Passos renaissance beginning. New critical evaluations of his work will be important, writes Rohrkemper, because they will be uninfluenced by the author's contentious personality.

One of the pleasures in preparing this essay over the years has been reading from time to time the special numbers devoted to an author in *Modern Fiction Studies*. This journal consistently publishes well-written essays of high intellectual quality and the 1980 issue on Dos Passos (26,iii) is no exception. Curiously there were no essays on *Manhattan Transfer* but there were on Dos Passos' other major work, the *U.S.A.* trilogy. In "*U.S.A.*: Chronicle and Performance" (pp. 398–415) Charles Marz suggests that the central tension in the trilogy lies in the conflict between the destructive chaos of public voices, manifest in the Newsreel sections, and the private voice of the Camera Eye sections struggling to survive. But in such a world, survival, says Marz, demands submission to the public voice and dehumanizing public values and so the narrator experiences the world as a nightmare and speaks in an ironic voice that struggles to resist conformity without retreating into solipsism. In "The Camera Eye in *U.S.A.*: The Sexual Center" (pp. 417–30) Donald Pizer describes the Camera Eye sequence throughout the trilogy as "a kind of development novel in which Dos Passos presents the reader with a valuable and suggestive account of his maturation as an artist." Central to that maturation, says Pizer, is the artist's quest for a fully masculine literary identity which, in association with his father's immigrant status, he locates in a partisanship for the working class and a denunciation of America's corrupted democratic ideal.

One of the best essays attempts to describe Dos Passos' use of history. In "The Treatment of Time in *The Big Money*: An Examination of Ideology and Literary Form" (pp. 447–67) Barbara Foley argues that Dos Passos' fiction is so thoroughly immersed in the actual truth of historical documents that it is closer to the nonfiction novel such as Mailer's *Armies of the Night* than to the naturalist tradition. Dos Passos, Foley adds, was never really a Marxist because he viewed history as a mechanical, impersonal force beyond individual human agency. Considering the trilogy as a whole, Robert P. Weeks in "The Novel as Poem: Whitman's Legacy to Dos Passos" (pp. 431–46) identifies certain Whitmanesque poetic devices such as parallelism, catalogs, and extended parentheses as integral to Dos Passos' narrative technique. This essay should be read in conjunction with one by Lois Hughson (see *ALS 1973*, p. 238).

Two more essays relate Dos Passos to other writers. In "John Dos Passos: *Three Soldiers* and Thoreau" (pp. 470–81) Owen W. Gilman relates John Andrew's desertion from the army to a Thoreauvian tradition of rebellion according to individual conscience and as a result sees Dos Passos' novel as more affirmative than the majority of disillusioned war fictions. In "The Boyg: A Note on Dos Passos and Ibsen" (*Arcadia* 15:44–48) Hartwig Isernhagen explains that the Boyg, an amorphous and detrimental being in Ibsen's *Peer Gynt*, is used by Dos Passos as "a metaphor or symbol for a whole complex of sociopsychological problems" that immobilize and hasten the decay of civilization.

Two further essays in the *Modern Fictions Studies* special number consider the life and work of the older Dos Passos. Robert C. Rosen in "Dos Passos' Other Trilogy" (pp. 483–502) examines the *District of Columbia* novels and finds them lacking in any unified thematic purpose, but says they are valuable nonetheless for illuminating the evolution of a major American political novelist. Dos Passos' move to the right politically is the subject of Macel D. Ezell's "John Dos Passos: Conservative Republican" (pp. 503–17). This issue of *MFS* also includes a selected checklist of Dos Passos criticism compiled by John Rohrkemper (pp. 525–38). Finally, there appeared elsewhere another essay on Dos Passos' use of history. In "Dos Passos's World War: Narrative Technique and History" (*SNNTS* 12:46–61) Lois Hughson contends that Dos Passos ultimately abandoned biography or individual consciousness as the center of meaning in his fiction and looked to history and the collective community of readers as the repository of wisdom.

ii. Edith Wharton

Some of the best essays on Edith Wharton to appear in the 1970s are now part of a book, *Edith Wharton's Argument with America* (Georgia) by Elizabeth Ammons. In this fine study Ammons shows that Wharton's imagination in her early fiction was obsessed by the isolation and powerlessness of women, that she repeatedly wrote about women enmeshed in lives they detest, and wrote with a tendency to misandry. In *The House of Mirth*, says Ammons, Wharton reveals the political and economic obstacles that prevent women enjoying freedom in a patriarchal society. Wharton's vision of the dependency of women was in stark contrast, Ammons points out, to the prevailing notion of the New Woman from the Progressive Era. Romantic love and marriage as forms of bondage are the deep, tragic themes of *Ethan Frome* and *The Reef* according to Ammons, who examines these novels in terms of fairy-tale fantasies in which women are trapped and mutilated. In the satirical novel, *The Custom of the Country*, says Ammons, Wharton portrayed marriage wholly in ruthless mercantile terms, making a joke of romantic love. The concern for women's freedom also informs *Summer* and *The Age of Innocence*, writes Ammons, but in Wharton's later novels there is a reactionary endorsement of motherhood as woman's highest mission in life. Ammons concludes her study with a chapter on Wharton's interest in a spiritual matriarchy manifested in her last two novels. Ammons' book expands on the biographical and psychological studies by R. W. B. Lewis and Cynthia Griffin Wolff (see *ALS 1975*, pp. 273–74, and *ALS 1977*, pp. 250–52) to reveal the sociopolitical content of Wharton's fiction. These insights are always drawn from the texts, and thus happily extend our appreciation of Wharton's art as well as her significance in American cultural history. Wharton is well served by feminist criticism and Ammons' work is the very best of its kind.

Edith Wharton is also the subject of some interesting comparative studies. In "American Dreams and American Cities in Three Post–World War I Novels" (*SAQ* 79:274–85) Sidney H. Bremer looks at *The Age of Innocence* beside *The Great Gatsby* and *Miss Lonely-*

hearts and shows how postwar skepticism functions in all three novels to tarnish the old ideals, especially the New-World vision of a democratic community. Postwar pessimism in these novels, writes Bremer, is reflected in a crisis of dreams and dreaming. In *"The Whirlpool* and *The House of Mirth"* (*GissingN* 16,iv:12–16) C. S. Collinson lists the striking similarities of events in the Gissing and Wharton novels but shows how fundamentally different the heroines of the novels are. Dreiser and Wharton are brought together in "Lily Bart and Carrie Meeber: Cultural Sisters" (*ALR* 13:238–45) wherein Alan Price shows how despite class differences Carrie and Lily suffer similar fates as decorative objects in an acquisitive, male-dominated society.

Alan Price has published another essay on Wharton. In "The Composition of Edith Wharton's *The Age of Innocence*" (*YULG* 55:22–30) Price, consulting a notebook that covered the years 1918–23, finds that Wharton originally centered the action of *The Age of Innocence* upon Ellen Olenska and reworked her story in outline several times before the novel as we have it emerged. Accordingly Price cautions against Wharton's statement in *A Backward Glance* that she knew from the first exactly what would happen to each one of her characters, that their fate is settled beyond rescue. The same novel figures significantly in "Jamesian Structures in *The Age of Innocence* and Related Stories" (*TCL* 26:332–47) where Adeline R. Tintner examines scenes, characters, images, and phrases from James's fiction which are echoed in Wharton's fiction about "Old New York."

And there were two essays which looked carefully at Wharton's short fiction. In "A New Look at the Oldest Profession in Wharton's *New Year's Day*" (*SSF* 17:121–26) Judith P. Saunders gives a good reading of the Wharton story in which the heroine enters prostitution in order to make her husband's dying easier and the reader's moral expectations are turned upside down. In "Darwin, Wharton and 'The Descent of Man': Blueprints of American Society" (*SSF* 17:31–38) Mary Sue Schriber writes that Wharton's story demonstrates that divisions of labor based on sexual differences place men in a wider world physically and intellectually and women into a narrow domesticity, and that Wharton felt this was a very real threat to the quality of American life. Schriber's "Edith Wharton and the French Critics, 1906–1937" (*ALR* 13:61–68) is a review of early French criticism of Wharton's fiction and is followed by a checklist (*ALR* 13:69–72) which includes 40 items.

iii. Willa Cather

There were several items on Cather of a biographical nature, two of which assumed book form. *Only One Point of the Compass: Willa Cather in the Northeast* (Danbury, Conn.: Archer Editions Press) by Marion Marsh Brown and Ruth Crone is a fictionalized biography about Cather's summers spent on Grand Manan Island. The book is without documentation and so of little scholarly value, but specialists will be intrigued nonetheless to find printed here three letters to Cather from her close friend Isabelle McClung, the only such letters known to have survived. *Chrysalis: Willa Cather in Pittsburgh* (Pittsburgh: Hist. Soc. of Western Penn.) by Kathleen D. Byrne and Richard C. Snyder does not contain significant new information to change our view of Cather's career. But it does amplify in carefully documented detail our knowledge about the ten years that Cather lived and worked in Pittsburgh, first as a newspaperwoman and then as a high-school teacher. Much of the information the authors have gathered concerns Cather's friends in Pittsburgh—the Seibels, composer Ethelbert Nevin, May Willard, Ethel Litchfield, and Isabelle McClung. The book is intended as a factual record but the authors state their conclusions on certain biographical questions being raised today. For example, they assert that although Cather was very fond of Nevin she never rivaled his wife for his affections. Similarly they argue that although there is some evidence of family discord when Cather moved into the McClung house, her relationship with Isabelle was never more than a close friendship.

The most original and informative of the biographical items is Patricia Lee Yongue's two-part essay, "Willa Cather's Aristocrats" (*SHR* 14:43–56;111–25), which tells us something about her friendship with the eccentric and wealthy Englishman, the Honourable Stephen Tennant. Yongue uses this biographical information to illuminate an aristocratic ideal present in Cather's fiction which she says is a quest "for a way of life that possesses the grace, beauty, and utter civility of art itself." That ideal is most closely pursued, says Yongue, in *My Mortal Enemy* and *A Lost Lady.* In "The Friendship of Willa Cather and Dorothy Canfield" (*Vermont Hist.* 48:

144–54) Joseph P. Lovering describes the contents of the Cather letters at the University of Vermont but has no new biographical information to contribute.

Bibliographers will be interested in Joan St. C. Crane's "Willa Cather's Corrections in the Text of *Death Comes for the Archbishop, 1927 to 1945*" (*PBSA* 74:117–31). Crane's article illustrates Cather's meticulous concern for accuracy in all matters from spelling to botanical and mechanical detail, but reassures the reader of the Vintage paperback, which does not include all of Cather's corrections, that the classic story remains intact. In a similar vein Robin Hayeck and James Woodress in "Willa Cather's Cuts and Revisions in *The Song of the Lark*" (*MFS* 25:651–58) establish that for the library edition Houghton Mifflin brought out in 1937 Cather deleted roughly 5 percent of the words in the 1915 edition, not 10 percent as biographers have wrongly estimated. These critics specify such eliminations as dated political and social references, excessive descriptive detail, and stylistically inflated passages. The novel, they agree, is not changed in any basic way, but the collation tables give a rare glimpse of the artist at work.

One of the most interesting interpretive articles to appear recently is Kathleen L. Nichols' Freudian reading of *A Lost Lady*. In "The Celibate Male in *A Lost Lady*: The Unreliable Center of Consciousness" (*RFI* 4,i[1978]:13–23) Nichols argues that Niel Herbert views Marian Forrester as a surrogate mother figure and accordingly is dismayed and embittered by the revelation of her sexual nature. Nichols demonstrates that oedipal conflict is central to the literary allusions in the novel, particularly those from Shakespeare's *Hamlet* and "Sonnet 94." Cather's literary debts are explored further in two articles on *The Professor's House*. Meredith R. Machen's "Carlyle's Presence in *The Professor's House* (*WAL* 14:273–86) suggests structural and thematic parallels between *Sartor Resartus* and Cather's novel. Especially interesting are the structural similarities of the two works wherein an autobiographical middle section breaks into a third person narrative about two professors. Alice Bell Salo's "*The Professor's House* and *Le Mannequin d'Osier*: A Note on Willa Cather's Narrative Technique" (*SAF* 8:229–31) outlines the connection between the Cather and Anatole France novels but leaves the subject to be more fully explored.

There were three thoughtful essays by veteran Cather scholars,

two of which focus on later, less often read works. In " 'Lucy's Case':
An Interpretation of *Lucy Gayheart*" (*MarkhamR* 9:26–29) John J.
Murphy views the heroine of the novel, like the protagonist in
"Paul's Case," turning to art as an escape from the confines of reality.
It is also a novel, observes Murphy, about the process whereby people become symbols and legends. In "Willa Cather as Psalmist"
(*NDEJ* 13:1–15) Richard Giannone shows how Psalm 23 provides
a fitting correlative for the story of Mrs. Harris' pilgrimage in *Obscure Destinies*. And finally in "Willa Cather and the Sense of History" (*Women, Women Writers, and the West*, pp. 161–71) Bernice
Slote observes that Cather was concerned with the truth of feeling
and belief rather than literal fact, so that her historical novels are
only loosely accurate. Further, says Slote, she did not write about
cowboys and Indians in the West but about settlement and the
process of acculturation, and in a vision of the cycles of history ultimately revealed the Old World and the New World to be one.

iv. Theodore Dreiser

Central to Yoshinobu Hakutani's *Young Dreiser, A Critical Study*
(Fairleigh Dickinson) is the conviction that Dreiser was not influenced in any conscious way by naturalism as a literary movement.
Hakutani's concern is to show how instead it was the experiences of
Dreiser's youth—the crises in his family life, his work as a news-
paperman, and his career as an editor and freelance magazine writer
—that inspired the ideas and situations central to his early fictions.
This book leans heavily on Dreiser's voluminous autobiographical
writings, especially *Dawn* and *A Book About Myself*, in order to re-
count the author's early years. Hakutani believes Dreiser's chief interest lay not in determinism or mechanistic theories of man, but in
living individuals and their endless aspirations. This study focuses
on the early stories and *Sister Carrie*.

Almost all the recent articles on Dreiser are similarly concerned
with *Sister Carrie*. In "*Sister Carrie* and the Tolstoyan Artist" (*RS*
47[1979]:1–16) Stephen C. Brennan tries to show that when writing
his first novel Dreiser was influenced by reading Tolstoy's theories in
What To Do? on the social responsibility of the artist and by his
aesthetic ideas in *What is Art?* Carrie, says Brennan, is endowed
with the ability to express what others feel (Tolstoy's term was "in-

fection"), but because of her society's false materialistic values her potential to be a great artist is perverted. Looking at the influence of economic theories on Dreiser, Walter Benn Michaels in "*Sister Carrie's* Popular Economy" (*CritI* 7:373–90) argues that Dreiser's novel is not anticapitalist but structured by an economy in which excess is seen to generate the power of capitalism and nurture the arts.

Three of the *Sister Carrie* articles deal in some way with the perennial question of the heroine's integrity and maturity. In "The Two Faces of Sister Carrie: The Characterization of Dreiser's First Heroine" (*ArielE* 11,iv:71–86) Terence J. Matheson demonstrates from the text of the novel that Carrie is presented as both a naive, sympathetic young girl and a cunning, ambitious egotist whose every movement is determined by self-interest. The reason for this dual portrait, says Matheson, is that Dreiser wants us to forgive Carrie's sexual behavior (as he forgave his sister Emma's) but also wants to portray her rise to theatrical success realistically. Contributing to the debate as to whether Carrie matures in the novel, Lawrence E. Hussman, Jr. in "A Measure of Sister Carrie's Growth" (*DrN* 11,i: 13–23) examines the relationship between Carrie and Ames and concludes that there is no evidence of Carrie's maturation, for as a Dreiser heroine she has not discovered that giving is more important than taking in life. Ronald James Butler's "Movement in Dreiser's *Sister Carrie*" (*DrN* 11,i:1–12) is an excellent examination of motion as a metaphor for unlimited personal development in Dreiser's novel. Butler also points out that spatial movement creates for the characters a negative condition of living without a stable moral center.

There were also some miscellaneous items of interest. Thomas P. Riggio's "The Dreisers in Sullivan: A Biographical Revision" (*DrN* 10,ii[1979]:1–12) provides evidence for believing Dreiser's account of his father's life and misfortunes in Sullivan, Indiana. Because of its melodramatic character and its attractive picture of the author's rise from poverty, the veracity of this part of Dreiser's autobiographical record has been questioned by historians and biographers; but Riggio has found that newspaper files and church and school records authenticate Dreiser's story. Joseph P. Griffin in "'When the Old Century was New': An Early Dreiser Parody" (*SSF* 17:285–89) examines one of Dreiser's short stories and identifies it as a parody of popular works of historical romance, much in the same way that

Sister Carrie is a parody of the working-girl novel and Horatio Alger story. Joseph L. Candela, Jr.'s "The Domestic Orientation of American Novels, 1893–1913" (*ALR* 13:1–18) looks at several writers in this period, including Upton Sinclair and Edith Wharton, but the most interesting part of the essay in my opinion treats Dreiser's *Sister Carrie*. Candela suggests that the rocking chair is really a ghostly reminder of the domestic world that Carrie has rejected and that she is unhappy because success does not include home and children. Finally, in "Dreiser's Views on Art and Fiction" (*ALR* 12[1979]: 338–42) R. N. Mookerjee points out that Dreiser wrote very few pieces on the art of fiction because he believed theoretical issues had little to do with the creation of works of art. His one persistent statement, writes Mookerjee, was that the artist "tell the truth" and that the artist be given freedom to express himself without fear and restraint.

v. Gertrude Stein

S. C. Neuman's monograph, *Gertrude Stein: Autobiography and the Problem of Narration* (ELS 18[1979]) wrestles in an illuminating way with the problems of autobiography as a literary genre and specifically with Stein's innovations to the genre. Neuman argues that the element of misrepresentation that is present in every autobiography is consciously used by Stein in order to create an impersonal self. Stein was concerned, writes Neuman, to write narrative that would exist without time or a sense of identity. She took autobiography, the most temporal and personal mode of writing, and "shifted the thrust of the genre away from involvement in the past and the creation of self as artifact towards a consciousness, on the part of both writer and reader, of knowing and writing as ongoing process."

Two recent articles deal with Stein's treatment of sex in her writings. In "Guardians and Witnesses: Narrative Technique in Gertrude Stein's *Useful Knowledge*" (*JNT* 10:115–27) Elizabeth Fifer defines Stein's collection of short pieces as a philosophical inquiry into our sexual and imaginative lives. The collection, says Fifer, has no constant narrator but rather uses the method of philosophical inquiry and "leading questions" to dramatize all sides of the argument, including a disapproving general audience. "To help her say many things in many voices, Stein creates distinct metaphorical fields," writes Fifer, including an analogy between the nuclear family and homosexual marriage and an analogy between the body and geography. This same critic in "Is Flesh Advisable? The Interior Theater of Gertrude Stein" (*Signs* 4[1979]:472–83) examines some of Stein's other erotic works such as "Pink Melon Joy," "Not a Hole," and "Lifting Belly" and explores the witty code she invented in order to describe the details of her sexual and domestic life.

There were a couple of miscellaneous items on Stein of some interest. Anna Gibb's essay, "Hélène Cixous and Gertrude Stein: New Directions in Feminist Criticism" (*Meanjin* 38[1979]:281–93) focuses on Stein's *Ida* as a fiction by a woman which represents characteristically not an escape from life, as in male fictions, but an opening up to life's infinite possibilities. More traditionally, Keith Waldorp in "Gertrude Stein's Tears" (*Novel* 12[1979]:236–46) analyzes briefly the development of Stein's style between 1906 and 1914, focusing on the syntax of the inner speech in her portraits. There is now a one volume selection of *The Yale Gertrude Stein* (Yale) which puts an emphasis on Stein's poetry. Richard Kostelanetz's introduction is drawn largely from an essay he published in the *Hollins Critic* (see *ALS 1975*, p. 279).

vi. Ellen Glasgow

The essence of Julius Rowan Raper's new book, *From the Sunken Garden: The Fiction of Ellen Glasgow, 1916–1945* (LSU), is contained in a previously published discussion of Glasgow's short fiction (see *ALS 1977*, pp. 264–65). Raper sees Glasgow after 1916 turning away from surface realism toward the invisible hemisphere of the human mind. To explore human psychology, however, she did not turn to Freud, says Raper, but used the old techniques of literature, particularly that of *phantasies*, the foils or doubles through which characters are confronted with and explore the dark secrets of their own psyches. This was her means, says Raper, of handling "large powers and emotions that seem to come from outside the characters and take authority over their lives." Thus for example in *Barren Ground* the actions of the secondary characters and the changes in the landscape reflect the inner drama of Dorinda Oakley's spiritual and psychological development. The exception to this pattern of psychological projections, says Raper, is *The Sheltered*

Life, which is a study of the malignity of evasive idealism rather than psychological growth. *Phantasies* there have been perverted into lifeless social ideals and Eva Birdsong becomes their tragic victim. Raper's thesis is both clear and responsive to the texts; his book alters significantly our view of Glasgow's themes and techniques.

Veteran Glasgow scholar C. Hugh Holman has contributed an essay titled "The Tragedy of Self-Entrapment: Ellen Glasgow's *The Romance of a Plain Man*" (pp. 154–63) to *Toward a New American Literary History.* Holman defends Glasgow's 18th novel from the charge of sentimentality by showing that the dilemma of the characters is tied to the dialectic of southern history, that when Ben Starr, self-made man of the poor, refuses the railway presidency in order to devote himself to his wife Sally, he ultimately espouses old southern values over the new. There is an extended essay, *The Social Situation of Women in the Novels of Ellen Glasgow* (Exposition [1978]) by Elizabeth Gallup Myer, who is concerned to show that Glasgow's "gallery of ladies, who depend upon the . . . attention of gentlemen, and of middle-class women who can fend for themselves furnishes a true history of emancipation of women in the U. S." This is a sketchy survey of Glasgow's women, adding little to our understanding of either Glasgow's fiction or American social history. *The Ellen Glasgow Newsletter* continues to publish reviews, letters, and notes of interest. For example, Annie Woodbridge's "Two Virginia Utopias: Mary Johnston's Sweet Rocket, Ellen Glasgow's Hunter's Fare" (*EGN* 13:13–14) compares a romantic and a realistic novel from Virginia and finds a similar vision of selflessness at the moral center of both writers' fictions.

Insightful discussions of Glasgow also appear in chapters of books and in essays with broad thematic purposes. In "The New South and the Old Problems: Ellen Glasgow" (*The Literature of Memory* [Johns Hopkins, 1977], pp. 27–40) Richard Gray discusses Glasgow's vision of a new agrarian society based on "the plain man of character" which gives way in her later fiction to a celebration of the old patrimony. Perry D. Westbrook in "Ellen Glasgow and William Faulkner: Vestigial Calvinism and Naturalism Combined" (Percy D. Westbrook, *Free Will and Determinism in American Literature* [Fairleigh Dickinson, 1979], pp. 161–77) writes that "Calvinistic predestination, scientific determinism, and . . . transcendentalism . . . are brought together in *Barren Ground* with a plausibility seldom equaled in American literature." And in "Images of Women: A Female Perspective" (*CollL* 6[1979]:41–56) Audrey T. Rogers discusses Glasgow's women as survivors conforming to "a single vision: the test of endurance."

vii. Anderson, London, Lewis

These three writers all received relatively little attention in 1980. Most of the essays on Sherwood Anderson were psychological readings of his fiction, focusing on the ambiguous quests of his immature male protagonists. In "Sherwood Anderson's *Many Marriages*: A Model of the Most Perilous Journey" (*MidAmerica* 7:96–107) Mia Klein sees the 37-year-old protagonist in Anderson's novel as a "child" who undertakes the ritual journey to "adulthood" but who fashions his lover into a mother figure and learns nothing from his experience. Klein sees the pathology of the novel stronger than its art. In "A Triumph of the Ego in Anderson's 'The Egg'" (*SSF* 17:180–83) David R. Mesher argues that Anderson's story is not really about the father but the son who, as narrator, projects his own sense of defeat onto his subject. In "Sherwood Anderson's *Death in the Woods*: Towards a New Realism" (*MidAmerica* 7:73–95) Mary Anne Ferguson examines Anderson's 1933 volume of stories and describes a psychological progression taking place as the stories unfold. Women and death are archetypally conjoined in the famous opening story, "Death in the Woods," but by the end of the collection they are no longer synonymous and the young male figures in the stories are able to enjoy women and living in spite of man's mortal condition. The final piece, "Brother Death," says Ferguson, "is a story not about writing a story but about living a life." The only other essay of note is Sister Martha Curry's "Sherwood Anderson and James Joyce" (*AL* 52:236–49), which demonstrates the unlikelihood that Anderson read *Dubliners* before writing *Winesburg, Ohio*. Curry concedes nonetheless the remarkable similarity of the two books, a similarity grounded in their revelations of modern man as essentially lonely and frustrated. Ray Lewis White's "Of Time and *Winesburg, Ohio*: An Experiment in Chronology" (*MFS* 25:658–66) strikes this reviewer as a pointless endeavor to establish a precise fictional time scheme for Anderson's stories.

Although there were three dissertations completed on Jack London in 1980, only a handful of short articles were published and most of those appeared in the *Jack London Newsletter*. Two focus on London's futuristic fiction. In "The Apocalyptic Structure of Jack London's *The Iron Heel*" (*JLN* 13:1–11) D. Seed places London's novel in the tradition of apocalyptic literature, with its picture of rapidly increasing contemporary crisis, social decadence, and the beginnings of revolution. Gordon Blackman, Jr.'s "Jack London: Visionary Realist" (*JLN* 13:82–95) is the first part of a lengthy study of London as a science-fiction writer.

In "California and After: Jack London's Quest for the West" (*JLN* 13:41–54) Jacqueline Tavernier-Courbin identifies the West or the frontier in London's fiction as the Yukon and the Pacific ocean where epic adventures take place and California, the author's home, as a pastoral retreat. In "The Many Facets of Jack London's Humor" (*Thalia* 2,iii[1979]:3–9) this same critic looks at examples of different kinds of humor in London's fiction which range from irony and parody to black humor and a rollicking sense of the absurd. This article, by its own admission, is too brief to explore the topic in depth but makes an interesting beginning.

There were some miscellaneous items that would be of interest to London specialists. The *Pacific Historian* devotes part of its Summer 1980 issue to places and events associated with London. For London collectors there is *Jack London First Editions: A Chronological Reference Guide* by James E. Sisson III and Robert W. Martens (Oakland: Star Rover [1979]). Another collector's item is *Jack London's Scorn of Women: World Premiere Booklet*, ed. Marlan Bielke (Amador City, Ca.: Quintessence Publ. [1979]), which contains information about London's obscure 1906 play and about his abortive career as a playwright.

Three articles on Sinclair Lewis focus primarily on *Main Street*. In "Rebellion as Tradition: Sinclair Lewis's *Main Street*" (*SDR* 18, ii:44–53) John E. Hart argues that Carol's struggle against the philistinism of the small town is not a futile, negative act but a way of defining her values and acquiring the courage of her beliefs. In "The Wilderness Convention in *Main Street, Babbitt* and *Arrowsmith*" (*Gypsy Scholar* 6[1979]:74–92) Dennis Allen reveals that at least three of Lewis' novels have at their core "some version of one of the major conventions of the American novel: the flight of two men into the wilderness." And in a comparative essay titled "They

Are Such Things as Dreams Are Made On: A Study of Carol Ken-
nicott and Emma Bovary" (*McNR* 26:35–39) George O. Norris, III
briefly considers the American and French heroines in terms of pro-
vincial philistinism and romantic escape.

Sinclair Lewis: A Reference Guide (Hall) by Robert E. and
Esther Fleming is the first comprehensive annotated bibliography
of writings about Lewis. It covers the years between 1914 and 1978
and includes all the major reviews as well as articles and books about
Lewis' work. Especially significant here, given Lewis' international
popularity, is the inclusion of significant foreign criticism as well.
The Flemings' introduction draws attention to the resurgence of interest in Lewis in the 1960s led by Mark Schorer; the number of
entries for the 1970s, however, suggests a diminishing interest once
again.

viii. Women and Women Writers

Lee Ann Johnson's *Mary Hallock Foote* (TUSAS 369) is an excellent
study of the popular 19th-century illustrator and fiction writer, whose
best work was done late in life, well into the 20th century. In a comprehensive and highly sophisticated fashion, Johnson has woven together biography and criticism so the reader can see how Foote's
fiction grew out of the experiences of her life—her New England
Quaker background, her intimate, lifelong friendship with Helena
Gilder, her marriage to engineer Arthur Foote and their hard life as
pioneers in the Far West. Johnson relates the themes of marriage by
default and feminine sacrifice to the difficult years Foote endured in
various bleak western towns. Her fiction, writes Johnson, is largely
peopled with heroines who lack control over their destiny and who
often escape untenable emotional situations through death. Foote's
weakness as a writer, says Johnson, was her fondness for romance.
Her best fiction, Johnson judges, is her late work where realistic details of setting are more than colorful backdrop and have some
bearing on the story being told. Foote cannot be claimed as an important writer, Johnson concludes, but her firsthand chronicles of the
West secure her a place in the history of American letters.

In style Bertrand F. Richards' *Gene Stratton Porter* (TUSAS 364)
is a plodding and repetitive book, but at the same time it is a very
informative account of one of the most commercially successful

women writers of this period. Richards readily concedes that Porter's romantic and frequently sentimental novels hold little interest for today's reader, but he argues that her nature books with their vivid portrayal of her native Indiana and their realistic depiction of birds and outdor life are of enduring value. He believes she should occupy an important place in any history of popular American culture.

There were two articles of interest on Ruth Suckow, the fiction writer from Iowa. In an introductory styled essay titled "Iowans in the Arts: Ruth Suckow in the Twenties" (*The Annals of Iowa* 45: 259–87) Margaret Matlack Kiesel discusses how Suckow eventually rediscovered her German roots and how she asserted in the essay "Iowa" that the bedrock of her state's culture was not to be found in conventional, New England stamped society, but in the hard-working, stubborn individualistic farm people who worked the soil. In "The Art of Ruth Suckow's 'A Start in Life'" (*WAL* 15:177–86) Fritz Oehlschlaeger describes the Suckow story of a hired girl being initiated into a life of poverty and subservience as a critique of American society where "the labor of one person is owned by another." He shows how the carefully selected details in the story reflect ironically on the American dream and praises Suckow for revealing the meanness and repression that occur when economic relations between people supplant human ones.

ix. Proletarian Writers

The most intriguing book from this period is Will Wyatt's *The Secret of the Sierra Madre: The Man Who Was B. Traven* (Doubleday), which appears to solve at last the riddle of Traven's identity. Wyatt, a documentary filmmaker for BBC Television, was able to verify from 1924 police photographs in London that Traven was Ret Marut, the German anarchist and actor. Wyatt discovered further from a letter to the U.S. State Department that Marut was an alias for one Otto Feige, the illegitimate son of a mill hand and a potter living in Polish Prussia. Wyatt presents his account in the manner of a detective story, but his evidence for Traven's identity as Feige, which includes photographs and the recollections of a surviving brother and sister, seems sterling. He relates Traven's pathological secrecy and contempt for public identity to his illegitimate origins. It is now for scholars to determine whether Traven, who was not born or ever lived in the U.S., should be regarded as an American novelist! Wyatt's book completely upstages Jonah Raskin's *My Search for B. Traven* (Methuen). Through Traven's widow, Rosa Elena Lujan, Raskin apparently had access to the author's papers, including letters and diaries, and met a number of his friends and acquaintances. But evidence of Traven's origins and identity eluded him. Although Raskin's descriptions of Traven's widow and home are entertaining, this is a self-indulgent personal narrative, undocumented, and of no value as scholarship. While there was much research and speculation into Traven's life, there was only one item which dealt with his writings. In "Maker Versus Profit-Maker: B. Traven's 'Assembly Line'" (*SSF* 17:9–14) Donald Gutierrez examines Traven's story about an Indian basket-maker being swindled by a New York businessman and argues that the interest of the story rests not simply in an opposition of communal and capitalist societies but in the revelation of universal human greed. Gutierrez focuses on the figure of the woman basket-buyer who tries to exploit her fellow villager and argues that Traven's final concern is with the artist as victim.

There was only one substantial essay on Upton Sinclair in 1980. In "The Socialist and Socialite Heroes of Upton Sinclair" (*Toward a New American Literary History*, pp. 164–80) L. S. Dembo argues that in *The Jungle* Sinclair's socialist ideas are authentically developed because it is shown that for Jurgis in the workers' inferno there is no other savior except socialism. Sinclair fails to implement a social vision in books like *King Coal* and *Oil!*, says Dembo, because his heroes are upper-class idealists who have only sentimental notions about class relations.

x. Mencken, Van Vechten, Rølvaag, and Others

Mencken's 1980 centennial was marked by several short essays on his life and by a volume edited by John Dorsey titled *On Mencken* (Knopf). The latter combines essays about Mencken with selections from Mencken's work. The essays do not represent new scholarship but rather the seasoned opinions of veteran Mencken enthusiasts. Pieces by William Manchester and Alfred A. Knopf are personal memoirs. Other contributors to the volume discuss the aspects of Mencken they are most familiar with. Thus, Charles A. Fecher writes a summary essay on Mencken's thought drawn from his 1978 book on that subject and Carl Bode discusses the Mencken letters he edited and published in 1977. Alistair Cooke, who edited *The Vintage Mencken*, has contributed one of the most interesting essays. In "Mencken and the English Language" (pp. 84–113) he points out that although Mencken was concerned in *The American Language* to describe American English as a new dialect, his own style "is hardly different in any particular of vocabulary, syntax, or cadence from that of the prevailing English models." Cooke believes Mencken is overrated as a thinker but underrated as a humorist. He describes the technique of that humor as combining "an affected naivete with the pose of a conscientious reporter of absurd events." With samples of Mencken's writing included, *On Mencken* is a good volume to introduce the general reader to Mencken in his second century.

In "The Novels of Carl Van Vechten and the Spirit of the Age" (*Towards a New American Literary History*, pp. 211–29) Donald Pizer points out that if one wants to glimpse something of sophisticated American tastes and interests in the '20s, Van Vechten's fiction is an entertaining source. He goes on to evaluate Van Vechten's seven novels, singling out for attention *The Tattooed Countess* as a version of "the revolt from the village" fiction, *The Blind Bow-Boy* as a parody of the American *Bildungsroman*, and bestowing high praise on *Parties*, Van Vechten's portrayal of contemporary New York life which Pizer likens in its impressionistic method to atonal music and surrealistic art. Abraham Cahan is another minor writer from this period whose work is still occasionally discussed by critics. David Engel's "The Discrepancies of the Modern: Reevaluating Abraham Cahan's *The Rise of David Levinsky*" (*SAJL* 5,ii[1978]: 68–91) is a substantial discussion of Cahan's writing showing how thematically his fiction belongs to the phenomenon of modernism with its values of change and innovation. Engel relates David Levinsky's inability to unify the two parts of his life, European and American, to the historical discontinuities of modernism.

There were five items of interest on the Norwegian immigrant author whose work has increasingly drawn critical attention over the last few years. In "Values in Rølvaag's Trilogy" (*Big Sioux Pioneers*, ed. Arthur R. Huseboe, Sioux Falls, S.D.: Augustana College Press, pp. 79–88) Lloyd Hustvedt measures the major characters in Ole Rølvaag's fiction against the ideals of godliness, self-reliance, ambition, and spirituality that the author himself listed in an address at St. Olaf College. The implication of Rølvaag's trilogy, writes Hustveldt, is that it takes several generations before continuity can be established between old and new world values and that much is lost between. Similarly, Kristoffer Paulson in "What Was Lost: Ole Rølvaag's *The Boat of Longing*" (*MELUS* 7,i:51–60) looks at one of Rølvaag's less well-known works and finds its chief theme to be the invisibility or loss of identity of the immigrant within American society. In "Madness and Personification in *Giants in the Earth*" (*Women, Women Writers, and the West*, pp. 111–17) Sylvia Grider argues that Beret becomes demonically possessed by the adverse spirit of the plains. And in a rambling essay titled "Rølvaag, the Ash Lad, and New and Old World Values" (*Big Sioux Pioneers*) Curtis Ruud relates *Giants in the Earth* to Norwegian folklore. He shows how Per Hansa embodies the characteristics of the Ash Lad—ingenuity, ambition, and naturalness—but in his sacrificial act of love for Hans Olsa affirms Christian goals which are higher than the Ash Lad's quest to win "the princess and half the kingdom."

Finally, one is a little surprised by the appearance of a volume like Richard C. Harris' *William Sydney Porter (O. Henry): A Reference Guide* (Hall). It seems to indicate the intention of the G. K. Hall bibliography series to be as comprehensive in coverage as possible. This book follows the by now well-established format for reference guides to writings about an author. Harris extends Paul S. Clarkson's 1938 bibliography by including some newspaper articles previously unidentified or identified incorrectly. As in the Sinclair Lewis bibliography, one notes for the last decade a decrease in the number of entries for the once very popuar short-story writer.

Simon Fraser University

14. Fiction: The 1930s to the 1950s

Jack Salzman

i. "Art for Humanity's Sake"—Proletarians and Others

A number of volumes were published in 1980 which add considerably to our understanding of the temperament of the 1930s if not directly to the literature of the period. Victor Navasky's *Naming Names* (Viking) and Larry Ceplair's and Steven Englund's *The Inquisition in Hollywood: Politics in the Film Community, 1930–1960* (Anchor Press/Doubleday) are concerned with the Hollywood blacklist and as such have numerous references to such writers as Ring Lardner, Jr., John Howard Lawson, Albert Maltz, and Dalton Trumbo. Karin Becker Ohrn offers an admirable study of *Dorothea Lange and the Documentary Tradition* (LSU), in which Lange's work for the Farm Security Administration is carefully examined, and Joe Klein offers a most readable life of *Woody Guthrie* (Knopf). But Edmund Wilson's *The Thirties* (Farrar) is surprisingly mundane and uninformative.

More specifically related to some of the writers of the period is Lawrence H. Schwartz's *Marxism and Culture: The CPUSA and Aesthetics in the 1930s* (Kennikat) which, however, is too superficial to be of much value. The study apparently began as a doctoral dissertation and reads as if it still is one. That, of course, cannot be said of Malcolm Cowley's *The Dream of the Golden Mountains: Remembering the 1930s* (Viking), a volume of mostly previously published pieces. As always, the essays are marked by Cowley's fine prose; but all too often they also are marked by a glossy shallowness which is equally characteristic of Cowley's work.

Cowley, I should point out, is quoted with considerable regard by Joel D. Wingard, who argues in " 'Folded in a Single Party': Agrarians and Proletarians" (*SoR* 16:776–81) that although their differences were "real and diverse in the 1930s," now, after nearly 50 years, "the Agrarians and the Proletarians seem to have been not so much opposing as complementary groups." Wingard not very convincingly offers such modern literary and cultural figures as Wendell Berry, Martin Luther King, Jr., and Woody Guthrie as proof of the underlying unity in the Agrarian and Proletarian movements. Much more convincing and thorough, I think, is Amy Godine's "Notes Toward a Reappraisal of Depression Literature" (*Prospects* 5:197–239), which deals with three literary types—the explicitly political novel of the Communists and their sympathizers, the nonpolitical novels of the "Bottom Dogs" writers, and the literature of the documentary—to show the shape and the outcome of the struggle that takes place in these works between creative imagination and the felt facts of experience.

In addition to these general considerations two writers received individual attention. Douglas Wixson looks at "Literature from the Crucible of Experience: Jack Conroy in Ohio, 1927–30" (*MMisc* 8: 44–60) and concludes that "Conroy carried on the ark [sic] of proletarian literature long after many of its followers became disillusioned or changed sides." Neala J. Y. Schleung offers a valuable study of "Meridel Le Sueur: Toward a New Regionalism" (*BI* 33: 22–41). Little has been written about Le Sueur, and Schleung not only tries to show that "seldom has the prairie been infused with deeper sensitivity and greater passion than through the eyes and heart of this poet-feminist-philosopher," but she concludes her piece with a useful "Selected Bibliography" of Le Sueur's work. Also of considerable value are reprints of two works by relatively forgotten writers: Evelyn Scott's 1937 book of childhood recollections, *Background in Tennessee* (Tenn.), and John Fante's 1939 novel, *Ask the Dusk* (Black Sparrow). It is good to once again have both books available in attractive editions.

a. **James Agee.**   Agee continues to attract considerable critical attention, much of which is devoted to *Let Us Now Praise Famous Men.* Of these essays, Carol Shloss's "The Privilege of Perception" (*VQR* 56:596–611) and James C. Curtis' and Sheila Grannen's "Let Us Now Appraise Famous Photographs: Walker Evans and Documentary Photography" (*Winterthur Portfolio* 15:1–23) are primarily concerned with Walker Evans. But in "James Agee and the Furious Angel" (*CRevAS* 11:313–45) Michael Klug discusses *Famous Men* as the work in which Agee's personal conflict between "art and ordinary life" is at the center, while in "The Sound of Jubilation: Toward an Explication of Agee's Musical Form" (*SoQ* 18,ii:18–31) Ruthann K. Johansen argues that in *Famous Men* Agee turned "conventional treatment of the poor and the oppressed upside down"; "ultimately, he has called forth the anti-authoritative individual consciousness and invited it to create new forms with which to live." Richard H. King in his first-rate *A Southern Renaissance: The Cultural Awakening of the American South 1930–1955* (Oxford, pp. 204–31) first notes that although Agee's major writings are generally set in the South he has "rarely been considered a major figure in the Southern Renaissance," then goes on to point out that *A Death in the Family* is a minor masterpiece—"one of the few works by an American writer (and certainly a Southern one) which depicts family life as more than a chamber of horrors"—and *Famous Men*, "the work which will define Agee's status and which stands as a landmark in Southern writing of the 1930s and 1940s." And, perhaps most interesting of all, David Wyatt in his chapter on *Family* in *Prodigal Sons* (pp. 101–12)—the only essay this year devoted exclusively to Agee's novel—observes that the work is "haunted by the problem of inexpressibility," that the "writing of the novel constitutes a troubled passing of silence into voice," and that the act of writing the novel itself constitutes Agee's most ambitious generation of voice. The story, Wyatt notes, "is not only about surviving one's creator; the act of telling it embodies Agee's will to assume a creator's role."

In "Heartbreak at the Blue Hotel: James Agee's Scenario of Stephen Crane's Story" (*MQ* 21:423–34) James R. Fultz examines Agee's film script of Crane's "The Blue Hotel" and concludes that the script not only shows "the novelist's eye for detail," but "In his obvious sympathy for a reckless innocent who is rejected by a closed and cruel community, Agee creates a more fully human and tragic Swede than Crane's." Scott Newton in "David McDowell on James Agee" (*WHR* 34:117–30) devotes his attention not to any of Agee's works but to the relationship between Agee and the man who edited *A Death in the Family*. It is a most disappointing piece. There is little value at this point in being told that McDowell considers *The Morning Watch* to be the "most superficially autobiographical work Agee ever wrote," or that *Family* is not as autobiographical as everyone assumes it to be, or that "Agee had the best ear and best eye of any writer I've known. I never expect to see the likes of him again." This does tell us something about McDowell but little about Agee.

b. Jesse Stuart.   Certainly the most important contribution to Stuart scholarship this year once again comes from J. R. LeMaster, whose *Jesse Stuart: Kentucky's Chronicler-Poet* (Memphis) is one of the most important works yet written about Stuart. Because the study's focus is on Stuart's poetry, a detailed consideration of the volume is outside the purview of this chapter, but because Stuart scholarship on the whole is so sparse and LeMaster's study tells us so much about Jesse Stuart, it must be mentioned here. So, too, should LeMaster's "Jesse Stuart's Humanism" (*BLRev* 1,i[1979]:4–13), which proposes "that we view Stuart as a modernist in his rejection of contemporary values, as a humanist in his effort to create a habitable world, and as a symbolist in technique. . . ."

As has been the case in the past, *JLN* offers several pieces on Stuart. Most valuable is Hensley C. Woodridge's "Jesse and Jane Stuart: A Bibliography, 3rd ed.: Supplement 3, Supplement 4" (13: 73–74,103–04). In addition, Nancy Patrick writes about "Jesse Stuart's Water Symbolism in 'Rain on Tanyard Hollow' and 'The Storm'" (13:72) and "A Delineation of Folklore Elements in Jesse Stuart's *Tales from the Plum Grove Hills*" (13:66–71), while Mickie Griffin suggests in "Jesse Stuart's Life Force" (13:97–102) that Stuart's "unique creative genius" has "contributed largely to his own well-being in the midst of many challenges." Only one other work appeared on Stuart this year: in "Jesse Stuart and the Other Writers" (*American Bypaths*, pp. 79–108) Frank H. Leavell explores the influence of older writers upon Stuart and then attempts to relate his acquaintances with contemporary writers. The material used by Leavell was gathered from Stuart's own writings, his scrapbooks, and interviews, and as Leavell notes, while the study does not pretend to be a complete catalogue of Stuart's references to other writers—especially the Fugitives—it is a start.

c. John Steinbeck.   Work on Steinbeck this year has been most uneven. The only book-length study published, Paul McCarthy's *John Steinbeck* (Ungar), is a not very inspired introduction to its subject. McCarthy writes about the importance of California to Steinbeck, about "The Steinbeck Territory," "Conflicts and Searches in the 1930s," and "Postwar Allegory, Realism, and Romance." There are eight chapters in all, a chronology, and bibliography. But there is little if anything that is not well-known to the Steinbeck scholar. This is a book for the student who has not studied or thought very much about Steinbeck.

A book for the Steinbeck collector, on the other hand, is Maxine Knox and Mary Rodriguez's *Steinbeck's Street: Cannery Row* (San Rafael, Calif.: Presidio Press), a volume which includes several interesting photographs and a text that moves from "Before Cannery Row Began" to "The Way to Save Sardines." Intended not for the collector but "graduate faculty and students," Tetsumaro Hayashi's *Steinbeck and Hemingway: Dissertation Abstracts and Research Opportunities* (Scarecrow) anthologizes all of the available English-language abstracts of doctoral dissertations on Steinbeck and Hemingway. The volume also includes two essays by Richard F. Patterson which assess earlier dissertations and suggest research possibilities.

Hayashi also has compiled a volume devoted to *Steinbeck's Travel Literature: Essays in Criticism*, Steinbeck Monograph Series 10 (Muncie, Ind.: Steinbeck Soc. of America). All of the essays were previously published, but it is convenient to have them collected in one issue. In addition to the two volumes just discussed, Hayashi once again has been responsible for the issue of *StQ*. As has been the case in the past, the essays are as uneven as they are wide-ranging. The essays in *StQ* (13,i–ii) include Richard C. Bedford's consideration of "Steinbeck's Uses of the Oriental" (pp. 5–19), Richard R. Mawer's "Takashi Kato, 'Good American': The Central Episode in Steinbeck's *The Pastures of Heaven*" (pp. 23–31), Jerry W. Wilson's "*In Dubious Battle*: Engagement in Collectivity" (pp. 31–42), as well as Hayashi's "Why Is Steinbeck's Literature Widely Read?" (pp. 20–23). The essays in *StQ* (13,iii–iv) are even more diverse, covering such areas as the John Steinbeck Room at the Southampton College Library by Robert Louis Gerbereux (pp. 69–71), Barry W. Sarchett's reevaluation of *In Dubious Battle* (pp. 87–97), and Edward E. Waldron's comparative analysis of *The Pearl* and *The Old Man and the Sea* (pp. 98–106).

Although there are two essays in *StQ* devoted to *In Dubious Battle*, neither is at all comparable to the really fine essay by Jackson J.

Benson and Anne Loftis in *AL* (52:194–223), "John Steinbeck and
Farm Labor Unionization: The Background of *In Dubious Battle*."
Benson and Loftis explore the degree to which Steinbeck's novel is
historically accurate, and convincingly demonstrate that not only
the "strike and location of the strike in *In Dubious Battle* were com-
posites, so too were the novel's main characters." Steinbeck, they
contend, eliminated nearly everything positive about the strikes he
used as his models. It would therefore be a mistake to think of the
novel as being "true to life"; moreover, as a kind of historical record
the novel "does a disservice to those who led the strikes with courage
and compassion." It is an intriguing article, one that makes a most
important contribution to Steinbeck scholarship.

The same may be said for Vivian C. Sobchack's "*The Grapes of
Wrath* (1940): Thematic Emphasis Through Visual Style" (*AQ* 31
[1979]:596–615), by far the best comparative piece we have on
Steinbeck's novel and John Ford's cinematic adaptation. Sobchack
notes that, although Steinbeck and Ford share some common bonds,
"their sympathies and interests are dramatically divergent"—thus,
"where the novel *moves out* both structurally and imagistically from
the Joads to continually emphasize the land, biological presence,
and the crush of thousands of migrants on the move, the film's movement visually *closes in* on the Joads, at times to such a degree that
they have only a minimal connection with either the land or the rest
of society." Ford's film, Sobchack concludes, evidences his interest
in the Joads as a family unit, while Steinbeck "emphasizes them in
the novel as a family of Man." Doug Emory also deals with the two
versions of *Grapes* but his consideration of "Point of View and Narrative Voice in *The Grapes of Wrath*: Steinbeck and Ford" (*Narrative Strategies*, pp. 129–35)—in which he contends that Steinbeck's
novel contains two distinct points of view—pales greatly in value and
interest next to Sobchack's essay.

Nor do Louis Owens' "*The Wayward Bus*: A Triumph of Nature"
(*SJS* 6,i:45–53) and Edward J. Piacentino's "Patterns of Animal
Imagery in Steinbeck's 'Flight'" (*SSF* 17:437–43) add significantly
to our understanding of Steinbeck. Owens argues that *The Wayward
Bus* is the most positive statement in all of Steinbeck's fiction, and
Piacentino attempts to demonstrate that there are a significant number of animal references in "Flight" which seem to function either
"to define features of Pepe Torres' character or to accent some of
the physical challenges he experiences during his flight for survival

and the resulting psychological traumas of this ordeal." But if neither of these two pieces will greatly alter our way of thinking about Steinbeck, the essays by Benson and Loftis and by Sobchack should, and to that extent this has been a good year for Steinbeck studies.

d. **Farrell and Halper.** Scholarship on James T. Farrell continues to be sparse. In "James T. Farrell: A Memoir" (*SSMLN* 9,iii[1979]: 5–7) David D. Anderson tells of his meetings with Farrell but we learn little that is new about Farrell from the account. More valuable is the piece about Farrell in Paris by Farrell's biographer, Edgar Branch, which appears in *American Writers in Paris, 1920–1939* (Gale, pp. 128–31). And an eloquent tribute is offered Farrell by Ann Douglas in "James T. Farrell, the Artist Militant" (*Dissent* 27,ii: 214–16) in which Douglas first stresses that "if there is anything that James Farrell was not, it was a one book author," and concludes by noting that with Farrell's death "we have lost our finest literary perspective on the meaning of assimilation and ambition in American life, and a writer uniquely and admirably free from that most malignant form of cultural life: audience dependency."

The two other essays devoted to Farrell this year (that by Stephen Moore in *SAQ* and that by Robert James Butler in *Thought*) are well intentioned but fail to add to our understanding.

Little criticism exists about the works of Albert Halper. As John E. Hart writes in the first full-length study we have, *Albert Halper* (TUSAS 352), consideration of Halper's writings has hardly gone beyond mention of *Union Square* or *The Foundry*. So Hart's volume is most welcome. There is more here about Halper's work and life than has ever appeared before. The short stories and novels are given more than adequate consideration and there is a valuable bibliography of Halper's work. Hart does make the 1930s seem less complex than they were, but in so doing he does little harm to the volume's real value. *Albert Halper* is an intelligent and well-written (much more so than most volumes in this series) introduction to a writer "who has not so much been misinterpreted as neglected and forgotten."

ii. Social Iconoclasts—Salinger and Rosenfeld

Although seven essays on Salinger's work appeared in 1980, Salinger scholarship continues to disappoint. Of the four essays devoted to

Catcher in the Rye, one is a favorable consideration of Heinrich Böll's translation and adaptation of Salinger's novel (Walter E. Riedel, "Some German Ripples of Holden Caulfield's 'Goddam Autobiography': On Translating and Adapting J. D. Salinger's *The Catcher in the Rye*" (*CRCL* 7:196–205) and one—Aleksandar Flaker's "Salinger's Model in East European Prose" in *Fiction and Drama in Eastern and Southeastern Europe* (UCLA Slavic Studies 1; Columbus: Slavica), pp. 151–60—deals with Salinger's influence on "jeans-prose" in the works of Central and East European authors. A note by John S. Martin in *NMAL* (4:item 29) is devoted to "Copperfield and Caulfield: Dickens in the Rye," in which several oblique parallels between *Catcher* and *David Copperfield* are pointed out. Finally, there is Lawrence Jay Dessner's "The Salinger Story, Or, Have It Your Own Way" (*Seasoned Authors*, pp. 91–97), a piece which argues that Holden is "immaturity's best defense, a non-stop assault on maturity" and the novel itself "an insult to our ideas of civilization, to our ideal land in which ladies and gentlemen try to grow up, try to find and save their dignity." Sadly, Dessner seems *not* to be writing with pen in cheek.

The three other essays to appear in 1980 are devoted to Salinger's short stories. Roger Lewis in "Textual Variants in J. D. Salinger's *Nine Stories*" (*RALS* 10:79–83) lists the variants between the magazine printing and the printed book. The variants are of little substance. In "The Admiral and Her Sailor in Salinger's 'Down at the Dinghy'" (*SSF* 17:174–78) James Bryan deals with one of the *Nine Stories*, which he sees as having been written in counterpoint to another of the *Nine*, "Uncle Wiggly in Connecticut," for "it treats a mother-child relationship that is as winning as the Eloise-Ramona Wengler situation is pathetic." Eberhard Alsen devotes his attention to a later story in "'Raise High the Roofbeam, Carpenters' and the Amateur Reader" (*SSF* 17:39–47), which he contends "stands out in Salinger's later fiction because its form does not pose any problems that require a specialist's knowledge of narrative technique and because the core of its meaning can be understood without the help of outside information from other Seymour stories and from Eastern philosophy." Perhaps, but Alsen's reading of the story leaves too many questions unanswered; in his desire to convince the reader that "Carpenters" can be understood by the "amateur reader" Alsen has ignored some of the more complex issues raised by the story.

Since his death in 1956 Isaac Rosenfeld has attracted little scholarly attention. The publication of excerpts from his journals, therefore, is especially noteworthy. The material published in *PR* ("From Isaac Rosenfeld's Journals" [47:9–28]) and *Salmagundi* ("The Journals of Isaac Rosenfeld" [47–48:30–47]) are of equal interest. Mark Shechner, who has selected the material, states that in publishing the excerpts it was not his intention to explain Rosenfeld or to justify his life or even to shed new light on his writing; according to Shechner, "what I take to be of value here is the image of a life carried out with all the passion, awareness, and integrity a man could muster." Still, I suspect the real value of these excerpts will be to remind us once again both of Rosenfeld's enormous talent and of the fact that his critical neglect is our failure and our loss.

iii. Expatriates and Emigrés

a. **Henry Miller.** The two most significant additions to Miller scholarship in the year of his death came from Miller himself. Capra Press has issued *The World of Lawrence: A Passionate Appreciation,* ed. Evelyn J. Hinz and John J. Teunissen; and Black Sparrow has brought out the slimmer *Notes on "Aaron's Rod" and Other Notes from the Paris Notebook,* ed. Seamus Cooney. *The World of Lawrence* had its origin in 1932, when Miller was asked by Obelisk Press to prepare a brief volume on Lawrence, while *Notes* had its starting point in Miller's wish to refute the view of Lawrence offered by John Middleton Murray's critical biography, *Son of Woman* (1931). Both books, though somewhat chaotic, are of exceptional interest, and both are models of book production.

The most substantial assessment of Miller to appear in 1980 is to be found in Warner Berthoff's *A Literature Without Qualities: American Writing Since 1945* (Calif.). In a section entitled "Old Masters: Henry Miller and Wallace Stevens" (pp. 106–51) Berthoff considers the writing of "two notably independent figures who were in their creative prime in the years leading into the 1945–1975 era and who . . . more and more seem to have anticipated with particular clarity its central imaginative characters." Berthoff insists that Miller is something more than a one-book author, "but what he mainly counts for in literary history is fully displayed in his first and most recognized book, *Tropic of Cancer.*" And in a "Coda" to the entire volume, Berthoff offers "A Note on the Influence of *Tropic of Cancer*," a book which Berthoff argues has had "a clear and not dishonorable place in the fluctuations of expressed moral and cultural attitude in our century, and conceivably of political attitude as well."

The two other pieces to appear on Miller are much less substantial. In *USP* (11,iv:2–8) Lawrence J. Shifreen contends in "Henry Miller's Literary Legacy" that "Miller achieved the distinction of creating a new genre that lacks the pretention of the novel and looks to real events for its form, content, subject, and meaning." And in "Bald Bad Trapped in Miller's Fiction" (*LGJ* 6,ii:8–9) Tom Wood offers a brief and rambling look at Wambly Bald, the prototype of Van Norden in *Tropic of Cancer*.

b. **Anaïs Nin.** This year's contributions to Nin scholarship have been disappointing. The most substantial addition by far is the 7th and final volume of *The Diary of Anaïs Nin* (Harcourt), which covers the period from 1966 to 1974. The earlier volumes are the subject of Lynn Z. Bloom's and Orlee Holder's "Anaïs Nin's *Diary* in Context" in *Women's Autobiography* (pp. 206–20). According to Bloom and Holder, Nin's *Diary* illustrates "the structural discontinuity and pervasive thematic concerns which seem to typify women's autobiography in particular." What most distinguishes Nin's *Diary*, they conclude, is that without imposing any artificial structure on the material, Nin still "compels the reader to perceive her life and career as unified, cohesive, and of one fabric."

The remainder of this year's work on Nin is to be found in *USP*. In addition to the usual biographical and bibliographical notes, there are articles which range from Suzette Henke's "Anaïs Nin: A Freudian Perspective" (11,i:6–13) to Kathleen Chase's "Anaïs Nin and Music: Jazz" (11,i:15–22). But by far the most valuable material in this year's *USP* are the three supplements compiled by Richard R. Centing to Rose Marie Cutting's *Anaïs Nin: A Reference Guide*: "Writings About Anaïs Nin" (First Supplement, 11,ii:1–13; Second Supplement, 11,iii:9–24; Third Supplement, 11,iv:14–23). Centing's annotations are lucid and judicious, and his supplements should prove to be as invaluable to the Nin scholar as is Cutting's *Guide*.

c. **Vladimir Nabokov.** Scholarship on Nabokov continues to proliferate. To begin with, there is the somewhat oversized volume,

Vladimir Nabokov: Lectures on Literature (Harcourt), a collection of lectures Nabokov delivered at Wellesley and Cornell on such writers as Austen, Flaubert, Kafka, and Joyce. The importance of these lectures is self-evident, and the volume is enhanced by John Updike's Introduction. All that detracts from the volume is Fredson Bowers' ponderous explanation of the editorial method he employed in preparing the text. The lectures themselves are sometimes cantankerous, at times are somewhat obvious, but they are never less than thoughtful and elegant. This is not always true of the essays in *Vladimir Nabokov—His Life, His Work, His World: A Tribute* (London: Weidenfeld & Nicholson, 1979), ed. Peter Quinnell. The ten selections are very uneven in quality: there is a fine piece by Hannah Green, "Mister Nabokov," but there also is an uninteresting "The Last Interview" by Robert Robinson. A bibliography of Nabokov's major works and several previously unpublished photographs are included.

For the rest, *Lolita* continues to attract the most attention. Nomi Tamir-Ghez deals with "Rhetorical Manipulation in Nabokov's *Lolita*" (in *The Structural Analysis of Narrative Texts*, ed. Andrej Kodjak et al. Columbus: Slavica Publishers, pp. 172–95); Frederick W. Shilstone in "The Courtly Misogynist: Humbert Humbert in *Lolita*" (*StHum* 8,i:5–10) contends that the courtly misogynist, "the poet who both reveres and despises the women to whom he addresses his songs . . . finds a modern voice in Humbert Humbert's account of his love for Lolita"; Adams Gillon comments on the similarities between Nabokov and Conrad in "Conrad's *Victory* and Nabokov's *Lolita*: Imitations of Imitations" (*Conradiana* 12:51–71); while David Madden suggests in "We Poets: Humbert and Keats" (*NConL* 10,iii:5–6) that Humbert "deliberately attempts to live out in his own art the life the poet did." William Anderson notes that despite all the studies done on *Lolita* "there has been no substantial examination of *Lolita* as a novel built around the central themes of time and memory," and so he offers just such a consideration in "Time and Memory in Nabokov's *Lolita*" (*CentR* 24:360–83). And Phillip F. O'Connor writes about "*Lolita*: A Modern Classic in Spite of Its Readers" (in *Seasoned Authors*, pp. 139–43), a piece which he intends to be "informative and stimulating" but in fact is neither.

Of the other works by Nabokov to gain critical attention in 1980, two essays focus on "Signs and Symbols." In "The Importance of

Reader Response in Nabokov's 'Signs and Symbols'" (*ELWIU* 7: 255–60) Paul J. Rosenzweig contends that the story "demonstrates how the very conventions of the fictional world impose a distorting order on our perceptions that is so insidious we normally fail to notice its subverting influence," and in "Nabokov's Signs of Reference, Symbols of Design" (*CollL* 7:104–12) Geoffrey Green argues that "from a language of referential design, in 'Signs and Symbols,' it is but a brief and exultant interval to the buoyant and incandescent imaginative construction of *Bend Sinister*, and from there to the serpentine form and circuitous structural pattern of Vladimir Nabokov's finest novels—*Pnin, Lolita, Pale Fire, Ada.*"

Pnin is discussed by Joseph L. Schneider in his comparative consideration of "The Immigrant Experience in *Pnin* and *Mr. Sammler's Planet* (*On Poets and Poetry*, pp. 31–48). Schneider concludes that although both novels share an almost uncanny awareness of the historical problems of the immigrant in America, "Because Nabokov is himself an immigrant, something Bellow is not, he transmits an even more vivid picture of an immigrant's problems than does Bellow whose protagonist has an Englishman's orientation toward America." And *The Gift*, the last novel Nabokov wrote in Russian, is the subject of Michael H. Begnal's "Fiction, Biography, History: Nabokov's *The Gift*" (*JNT* 10:138–43) in which Begnal suggests that in *The Gift* "Nabokov has left a tightly wrought vision of an emigré past and an emigré present, and this gift may be the most impressive one of all."

More general considerations are to be found in Virgil Nemoianu's "Wrestling with Time: Some Tendencies in Nabokov's and Eliade's Later Works" (*Southeastern Europe* [Ariz. State Univ.] 7,i:74–90), a convoluted essay which finally manages to suggest that both Nabokov and Eliade are trying to "re-establish a new type of multidimensionality in which Time will no longer appear as an exclusive factor in human existence," and in Janet K. Gezari's and W. K. Wimsatt's "Vladimir Nabokov: More Chess Problems and the Novel" (*YFS* 58[1979]:102–16), which contends that "the lines of connection between Nabokov's novels and his chess problems are substantial and revealing."

Finally, attention must be called to the existence of the *Vladimir Nabokov Research Newsletter*, which first appeared in 1978 and is published by the Vladimir Nabokov Society with the expressed intention of reporting and stimulating Nabokov scholarship as well as creating a link between Nabokov scholars both in the United States and abroad. *VNRN* contains news items, notations of work in progress, abstracts of papers read, articles and books published, completed theses and dissertations, annotations, bibliographical information, and notes and queries pertinent to Nabokov research interests. Five numbers have been published to date, and *VNRN* clearly has lived up to its stated editorial expectations. The most valuable contribution it has to make to Nabokov scholarship no doubt is bibliographical—not only the revision, completion, and updating it has undertaken of Andrew Field's *Nabokov: A Bibliography* and the checklist of Nabokov scholarship, but also such matters as Stephen J. Parker's listing by container number of the Nabokov papers in the Library of Congress (*VNRN* 3[1979]:16–23;4:20–34). At the same time the publication of abstracts and the news items should prove to be of continuing interest to Nabokov scholars. In short, *VNRN* seems to be an indispensable tool for anyone seriously interested in the works of Nabokov.

iv. The Southerners

In addition to the work on individual southern authors, 1980 saw the publication of two interesting essays on *I'll Take My Stand*, William C. Havard's "The Politics of *I'll Take My Stand*" (*SoR* 16:757–75) and Lucinda H. Mackethan's "*I'll Take My Stand*: The Relevance of the Agrarian Vision" (*VQR* 56:577–95). Even more noteworthy is the publication of *The American South: Portrait of a Culture* (LSU), ed. Louis D. Rubin, Jr., a collection of 21 original essays and two transcribed "conversations" by numerous scholars and critics which deal with the South as "A Changing Culture" and "Literary Images of the South," including George Core's "The Dominion of the Fugitives and Agrarians" (pp. 289–303). And best of all is Richard H. King's *A Southern Renaissance* (see the section on Agee), a richly suggestive study of the way "an exhausted tradition gave way to the possibility of a revitalized Southern present and future."

a. Robert Penn Warren, Allen Tate, and Caroline Gordon. This

has been a particularly productive year for Warren studies. His meditation on Jefferson Davis and southern history, *Jefferson Davis Gets His Citizenship Back*, was published by the University Press of Kentucky, and Floyd C. Watkins and John T. Hiers edited *Robert Penn Warren Talking: Interviews, 1950–1978* (Random House), a first-rate collection of 18 interviews in which Warren participated. Louis D. Rubin, Jr. includes "The South: Distance and Change. A Conversation with Robert Penn Warren, William Styron, and Louis D. Rubin, Jr." in *The American South* (pp. 304–22); an interview with Warren serves as an "Appendix" to Marshall Walker's *Robert Penn Warren: A Vision Earned* (Harper, 1979); and David Farrell offers an account of a 1977 visit with Warren in "Reminiscences: A Conversation with Robert Penn Warren" (*SoR* 16:782–98).

Richard Gray has edited *Robert Penn Warren: A Collection of Critical Essays* for Prentice-Hall's Twentieth Century Views Series. The essays, save for Gray's Introduction, have been previously published, but it is helpful to have such pieces as James H. Justus' "On the Politics of the Self-Created: *At Heaven's Gate*" (pp. 40–50), Arthur Mizener's "Robert Penn Warren: *All the King's Men*" (pp. 51–66), and Leonard Casper's "Trial by Wilderness: Warren's Exemplum" (pp. 97–104) in one volume. Gray also provides an adequate "Chronology of Important Dates," but his selected bibliography is somewhat too selective to be of much help.

In *Prodigal Sons*, David Wyatt devotes a chapter to "Robert Penn Warren: The Critic as Artist" (pp. 113–28) in which he argues that in his work Warren is stationed "on the border between two modes of imagination, between the artist who works from experience and the critic who works toward meaning." His characters tend to be placed out of themselves, "the bemused or obsessive spectators of their own wayward acts." Wyatt then devotes considerable attention to *A Place to Come To*, a work which explores the psychology of exile and return and is Warren's most ambitious attempt "to study 'the relationship of the concept of Love to that of Time.' "

A Place to Come To attracted the attention of three other critics this year. In "Robert Penn Warren the Novelist, Now (and Then)" (*SLJ* 12,ii:83–96) Allen Shepherd addresses himself to the way in which *A Place to Come To* both recalls its nine predecessors, even recapitulates them, at the same time that it "surely enters new territory, Warren doing things in this new novel that he has never done before." Leonard Casper in "Circle with a Center Outside: Robert Penn Warren's *A Place to Come To*" (*SWR* 65:399–410), suggests that Warren "risks a structure so open, so full of drift and irresolve" to better convey a sense of alienation and frustration. The real purpose of Warren in this novel, Casper writes, "is not to miniaturize history but—in a way more skeptical than Whitman's—to justify the world without exemption and each man's portion in that spacious whole." Diane S. Bonds in "Vision and Being in *A Place to Come To*" (*SoR* 16:816–28) sees the distinctive nature of *A Place to Come To* to be in the "stress that it lays on the relationship between vision and being (or selfhood)." What we finally come to recognize is that the analogy the novel establishes between imaginative vision and fullness of being "defines *A Place to Come To* as a meditation on life as art."

All the King's Men, of course, continued to attract critical attention. Richard H. King devotes a section of *A Southern Renaissance* to "From Politics to Psychology: Warren's *All the King's Men*" (pp. 231–41). King sees Warren's weakness as a novelist to be his "proclivity to preach at his characters and at his readers, and to philosophize," a weakness which can be seen in his best-known novel: "*All the King's Men* begins with the wider political world and ends by withdrawing from it into the rhetorical resolution of a private quest. Consciousness defeats action; the private vision, the public involvement; the ironic son, the strong fathers." The two remaining pieces to be mentioned are notes: Glen M. Johnson argues in "The Pastness of *All the King's Men*" (*AL* 51:553–57) that Warren's sense of cultural responsibility is embodied in his book's rhetorical structure, which opens out to include a reader's wider historical experience, and thus to enlist that reader as a participant in history on both levels, fictional and factual." And in "Jack Burden's 'Kingdom by the Sea'" (*NConL* 10,i:4–5) Kent Ljungquist suggests that Jack Burden's allusions to Poe's "Annabel Lee" are meant to underscore Burden's adolescent idealism.

Warren's "Blackberry Winter," written shortly after he completed *All the King's Men*, received the attention of two critics this year. In "Warren's 'Blackberry Winter': A Reading" (*UMSE* 1:97–105) James E. Rocks points out that "Blackberry Winter" and *All the King's Men* share similar themes, characters, techniques, and treat-

ment of time, while Albert E. Wilhelm offers a note on "Images of
Initiation in Robert Penn Warren's 'Blackberry Winter'" (*SSF* 17:
343–45). *God's Own Time*, an unpublished Warren novel, is the subject of Allen Shepherd's "The Craft of Salvage: Robert Penn Warren's
God's Own Time and Three Stories" (*KRev* 2,i:11–19). Shepherd
sees Warren's attempt to salvage three stories from his discarded
journeyman novel as "an early stage of what was subsequently to
become Warren's customary artistic practice—of reconceiving, that is,
imagining anew, essential issues, often in a succession of genres."

Finally, there is Alexander Mulyarchik's "Responding to the Call
of the Times: For the 75th Birthday of Robert Penn Warren" (*SovL*
vii:157–60), a well-intentioned but irrelevant tribute which leads to
the almost requisite conclusion that Warren's best works "have in-
variably contained no small measure of criticism of the social establishment which stands in the way of a free and happy life for the
common people of America."

After all this it is a little distressing to be reminded of the scant
attention given to Allen Tate. This year only two essays about *The
Fathers* appeared: Thomas Hubert's "Myth and Ritual in Allen Tate's
The Fathers" (*Interpretations* 12:5–13), which makes no attempt to
"strike out on an entirely new course" but which considers "myth and
ritual and their relation to theme and character in more detail than
has been done before in studies of Tate's novels," and Daniel B.
Ahlport's "Tate's *The Fathers* and the Problem of Tradition" (*SoSt*
19:355–64), which considers *The Fathers* to be not only one of the
best novels about the South but also "seems to be Tate's clearest and
most complete statement on the conflict between tradition and modernism."

Caroline Gordon usually attracts even less attention than Tate
but this year has been an exception. In addition to the substantial
"Life at Benfolly 1930–1931: Letters of Caroline Gordon to a Northern Friend, Sally Wood," ed. Donald E. Stanford (*SoR* 16:229–336),
two important essays on Gordon's craft were published. John Alvis
examines "The Miltonic Argument in Caroline Gordon's *The Glory
of Hera*" (*SoR* 16:560–73), a novel that is also at the center of Bainard
Cowan's "The Serpent's Coils: How to Read Caroline Gordon's Later
Fiction" (*SoR* 16:281–98), which concludes that Gordon's readers must take *The Glory of Hera* "as a kind of guide to her entire
writing."

b. **Carson McCullers.** Two substantial additions were made to Mc-Cullers scholarship this year. In *Carson McCullers* (TUSAS 354) Margaret McDowell offers what may now be the most comprehensive, if not the most gracefully written study we have of McCullers' work. In addition to a chronology and selected bibliography, Mc-Dowell devotes a chapter to McCullers' development as a writer and her theory of fiction, to each of the novels, one to *The Member of the Wedding* (which, together with *The Ballad of the Sad Café*, she considers to be McCullers' best work), and another to the short stories, poems, and a second play. The study concludes with a chapter entitled "Perspectives," in which McDowell sums up what she has argued throughout the volume: "In the few years in which she created her first four novels, her first play, and her best short stories, McCullers built a diverse world and filled it with people possessing great energy and forcefulness." But, despite the fact that McCullers' achievement is "substantial and undeniable," we still must wonder "what might have been had she lived long enough to consolidate her powers and to mature even more richly her artistry and her insight into human nature." Readers, however, need no longer wonder where to go for a good critical introduction to McCullers' work: McDowell's study will do very well. So will the bibliography edited by Adrian M. Shapiro, Jackson R. Bryer, and Kathleen Field, *Carson McCullers: A Descriptive Listing and Annotated Bibliography of Criticism* (Garland), "the first attempt to present a full and scholarly bibliography of writings by and about Carson McCullers." Part 1, prepared by Adrian Shapiro, is a descriptive listing of McCullers' works, including various printings and editions of her works in English. Part 2 is an annotated bibliography of writings about McCullers. This section is of lesser value than Part 1 because it contains much of the same information as one finds in Robert F. Kiernan's *Katherine Anne Porter and Carson McCullers: A Reference Guide* (1976). Still, for those who want a bibliography devoted exclusively to McCullers this is the volume to have.

Five articles also appeared on McCullers this year, the most substantial of which are Mary Roberts' consideration of "Imperfect Androgyny and Imperfect Love in the Works of Carson McCullers" (*HSL* 12:73–98) and Louise Westling's "Carson McCullers's Tomboys" (*SHR* 14:339–50), a look at Mick Kelly and Frankie Adams, in whom "McCullers dramatizes the crisis of identity which faces ambitious girls as they leave childhood and stumble into an understanding of what the world expects them to become." Of somewhat lesser significance are the three remaining works to be mentioned here: Marzenna Rączkowska's study of "The Patterns of Love in Carson McCuller's Fiction" (*SAP* 12:169–76), Nancy B. Rich's "Carson McCullers and Human Rights" (in *A Fair Day*, pp. 205–12), and Amberys R. Whittle's "McCullers' 'The Twelve Mortal Men' and *The Ballad of the Sad Café*" (*AN&Q* 18:158–59).

c. **Katherine Anne Porter and Eudora Welty.** George Bixby has compiled "Katherine Anne Porter: A Bibliographical Checklist" for *ABC* (1,vi:19–33). Section A contains primary publications and Section B contains secondary appearances. The checklist includes more publishing information than the standard checklist, "offering bibliographical information sufficient for accurate identification of the first edition of every title listed." As such, however, the compilation will be of more value to the collector than the student of Porter, who may find the checklist a little too cumbersome.

In "Xochitl: Katherine Anne Porter's Changing Goddess" (*AL* 52:183–93) Thomas F. Walsh sees the 1921 sketch, "The Children of Xochitl," as Porter's first literary expression "of her yearning for happiness" whose lost promise deepens her sense of terror in "Hacienda." Together the works "form a paradigm for her later works in which characters attempt to recover from their sense of betrayal when their dreams of Eden are shattered." David R. Mayer offers an explication of "The Jilting of Granny Weatherall" (*Expl* 38,iv:33–34) —"Granny Weatherall is both the jilted and the jilter"—and Jan Nordby Gretlund in "The Wild Old Green Man of the Woods: Katherine Anne Porter's Faulkner" (*NMW* 12:67–79) spends several pages to do little more than verify the soundness of Robert Penn Warren's comment in his Introduction to *Katherine Anne Porter: A Collection of Critical Essays* (Prentice-Hall, 1979) that there are numerous similarities between the theme and ideas of Faulkner and Porter.

This has been another good year for Welty scholarship. Preeminent, by all accounts, is the publication of *The Collected Stories of Eudora Welty* (Harcourt), which gathers all the stories previously published in *A Curtain of Green, The Wide Net, The Golden Apples,* and *The Bride of the Innisfallen,* as well as two stories previously uncollected. The collection more than bears out Welty's statement in her preface that "It is the act of a writer's imagination that I set most high." It is this imagination which Michael Kreyling explores in his first-rate study, *Eudora Welty's Achievement of Order* (LSU). Kreyling is intent upon showing that Welty's fiction offers much more than "quaint characters and picturesque settings." The South is there, to be sure, but Welty's is a vision of an artist "who must be considered with her peers—Woolf, Bowen, and Forster, among others—who have never been called regional." Kreyling argues with considerable skill that "Welty is always directing the eye to the essence behind the curtain of appearance." In her fiction "Life is included not only in the subject matter but also in the means of discovering it." Kreyling's *Achievement of Order* discovers more of Welty, it seems to me, than we find in almost any other volume. It now stands as the best study we have on Welty's art.

In addition to *The Collected Stories*, Welty's own voice is heard most directly in Jan Nordby Gretlund's "An Interview with Eudora Welty" (*SHR* 14:193–208), a compilation of two conversations Gretlund had with Welty; as well as in the more chatty "Growing Up in the Deep South: A Conversation with Eudora Welty, Shelby Foote, and Louis D. Rubin, Jr." (*The American South*, pp. 59–85).

The essays published this year cover a wide range of Welty's fiction. The most interesting piece, I think, is Peggy Prenshaw's "Persephone in Eudora Welty's 'Livvie'" (*SSF* 17:149–55), which examines Welty's fusing of "a realistic story set in the Mississippi countryside not only with the well-known episode involving Persephone, but with the motif of death and regeneration drawn from the related myths of Demeter and Dionysus, specifically, from the Eleusinian Mysteries." The other essays are devoted to "Eudora Welty's *The Robber Bridegroom* as American Romance" (*MHLS* 3: 101–15) which, Jennifer Randisi suggests, combines elements of myth, legend, folktale, and regional mythology" more successfully than any other narrative; "Eudora Welty's *The Ponder Heart*: The Judgment of Art" (*SoSt* 19:261–73), a novel, according to Rachel V. Weiner, which like *Delta Wedding* is about "the rite of indulgence"; and "Aunt Studney's Sack" (*SoR* 16:591–96), in which Carol A. Moore examines the theme in *Delta Wedding* "of innocence submitted to experience, to a vision of the breadth of life in its infinite possibilities, both good and evil."

Four brief pieces also should be noted: Robert G. Walker points out "Another Medusa Allusion in Welty's 'Petrified Man'" (*NConL* 9,ii:10); Wayne D. McGinnis addresses himself to "Welty's 'Death of a Traveling Salesman' and William Blake Once Again" (*NMW* 11[1979]:52–54); while Mary Ann Dazey offers an explication of "Phoenix Jackson and the Nice Lady: A Note on Eudora Welty's 'A Worn Path'" (*AN&Q* 17[1979],92–93); and Marilynn Keys writes about "'A Worn Path': The Way of Dispossession" (*SSF* 16[1979]: 354–56).

Attention must again be called to the two numbers of the always valuable *EuWN*, which include short bibliographical notes, source studies, checklists of writings by and about Welty, and news about Welty and Welty scholars. *EuWN* continues to be a model of its kind.

d. **Thomas Wolfe.** Wolfe scholarship was even less impressive this year than last year. In addition to William Domnarski's "Thomas Wolfe's Success as Short Novelist: Theme and Structure in *A Portrait of Bascom Hawke*" (*SLJ* 13,i:32–41), which argues that Wolfe's short novel is a much more tightly structured work than his long novels, and Timothy Dow Adams' "The Ebb and Flow of Time and Place in 'The Lost Boy'" (*SoSt* 19:400–08), which considers Wolfe's long story as a "classic example" of the southern use of time, Wolfe scholarship for the main is to be found in the pages of *TWN*. There, along with the usual sections devoted to news and notes, bibliography, questions and answers, and Thomas Wolfe society news, are brief pieces devoted to "Thomas Wolfe: Jack Kerouac's Alter Ego" by James Henry (4,i:24–26), "Wolfe and *Sophie's Choice*" by Monte Lowe Faltacosh (4,i:39–41), and "Wolfe's Final Days: The Correspondence of Elizabeth Nowell and Annie Laurie Crawford" by Elizabeth Evans (4,ii:1–14).

The one work to attract considerable attention has been John Halberstadt's "The Making of Thomas Wolfe's Posthumous Novels" (*YR* 70:79–94). Halberstadt's contention is that *The Web and the Rock, You Can't Go Home Again,* and *The Hills Beyond* were so drastically shaped by Edward Aswell at Harper's from more than one million words of finished and unfinished chapters that it is impossible to "distinguish the voice of Wolfe from the voice of Edward Aswell, the vision of Wolfe from the editorial administration of Aswell." All we can be certain of, Halberstadt states, is that the words of Wolfe's three posthumous works were written by Wolfe, but "the *books* were made by Aswell." Whatever the significance of Halberstadt's argument, it has (at least for the moment) been lost in a heated debate over the propriety of Halberstadt's publishing the article at all, since in doing so he violated an agreement with the Houghton Library at Harvard and the lawyer who is executor of the Thomas Wolfe estate. There are, to be sure, a number of important ethical issues which have been raised and no doubt will continue to be debated for some time. But there is little evidence that any of the interest in Halberstadt's article will lead to a greater interest in Wolfe himself, who ironically seems to be the forgotten person in all the furor.

v. Humanists, Critics, and Others

Some critical attention finally has been given to S. J. Perelman. In "Jumping on Hollywood's Bones, or How S. J. Perelman and Woody Allen Found It at the Movies" (*MQ* 21:371–83) Sanford Pinsker offers a breezy but interesting view of two of our finest humorists and their response to Hollywood. The typical Perelman creation, Pinsker points out, "is an irritated innocent, a man of rarified taste and extravagant metaphor who sets his particular 'No!' in thunder against our culture's expectation and its junk."

Two eminent men-of-letters were the subject of full-length volumes this year. Richard Hauer Costa in *Edmund Wilson: Our Neighbor from Talcottvile* offers a most readable memoir of Wilson's final years (1962–72) in upstate New York. It is an informal, not at all scholarly, view, and if we don't learn quite as much about Wilson's literary attitudes as we might wish there is much here about his interest in films, his struggle with the Internal Revenue Service, and his dispute with the MLA. It is a most interesting, at times touching, glimpse of the formidable Wilson who, as Costa notes in his preface, frequently was off-guard during this period, applying himself as fully as possible "to the effort of self-reformulation to which he was devoting himself in old age." For just this reason it is a volume of very real value, as is the reissue of Wilson's only novel *Memoir of Hecate County* (Boston: David R. Godine). The David Godine reissue not only is most attractively done but it also contains a fine Afterword by John Updike.

Much more formal than Costa's memoir is John D. Margolis'
Joseph Wood Krutch: A Writer's Life (Tenn.). This is the first book-
length study of Krutch and it is an excellent one. Margolis notes that
Krutch's career as a whole "offers a moving account of a man's quest
for values and for a style of life which would be more temperamen-
tally congenial, more authentically his own, than those which brought
him his earliest literary fame." His study of Krutch "seeks to describe
the distinctive shape of that career, and the place of Krutch's various
literary activities in the larger pattern of that quest." *A Writer's Life*
succeeds admirably in doing just that.

Mabel Dodge Luhan attracted the attention of two critics this
year: Robert A. Rosenstone offered "Mabel Dodge: Evenings in New
York" (*Affairs of the Mind*, pp. 131–51) and in "Journey to the Edge
of History: Narrative Form in Mabel Dodge Luhan's *Intimate Memories*" (*Biography* 3:240–52) Jane Nelson concerns herself with Luhan's autobiography, which she finds to be "remarkably unified and
often powerful in effect, a success that can be attributed above all to
Luhan's development of a narrative form that would convey her
vision of the Southwest."

vi. Popular Fiction

a. **Best Sellers.** Several important works devoted to popular writers
appeared this year, the best of which is Frank MacShane's *The Life
of John O'Hara* (Dutton). MacShane sees O'Hara as "a writer about
people far more than a chronicler of society." There was a turbulence
and violence in his work, MacShane argues, just as there was in
O'Hara himself. And the best works—30 or 40 short stories and
novellas unsurpassed in American literature "for their artistic deli-
cacy and a psychological acuteness," *Appointment in Samarra, From
the Terrace,* and *The Lockwood Concern*—"make O'Hara one of the
half-dozen most important writers of his time." If MacShane overstates the case for O'Hara, which he does, he at least does so in a
volume that is always as readable as it is informative. I suspect it
will be a while before we have another study of O'Hara to equal
that of MacShane's. What we will have, however, is the fine work
Vincent D. Balitas continues to bring to the *John O'Hara Journal.*
This year, in addition to the regular issue of *JOHJ,* which contains
pieces by Charles Mann on "John O'Hara: Pennsylvania Novelist"

(2,ii:1–13), Sheldon Grebstein's "John O'Hara: The Mystery of Character" (2,ii:14–21), and Rex Roberts' "On *Ten North Frederick*" (2,ii:69–87), Balitas has brought out a Special Issue of *JOHJ* (3,i/ii) to mark O'Hara's death and what would have been his 75th birthday. The memorial volume is just more than 200 pages long and contains fiction, poetry, criticism, and comments by such writers and critics as Robert Creeley, Robert Penn Warren, Arthur Miller, and John Barth.

Several works devoted to Thornton Wilder also appeared this year but none does for him what MacShane's *Life* does for O'Hara. Most disappointing is the slim volume by Amos Niven Wilder on his brother, *Thornton Wilder and His Public* (Philadelphia: Fortress). Amos Wilder offers some comments about his older brother's education and formative influences, and writes in greater detail of the reception of Wilder's plays and novels in Germany, but there is little here that will be of much consequence to the Wilder scholar. More valuable is Mary Ellen Williams' monograph, *A Vast Landscape: Time in the Novels of Thornton Wilder* (Idaho State, 1979), which argues that the themes relating to the individual in Wilder's novels "result from Wilder's recognition of a cosmic, eternal order." The individual may be essentially isolated, but the very fact that he is part of this cosmic whole "embues him and his life with an eternal importance." Williams may be right when she contends that Wilder's concept of time "is basic to a complete understanding of both the form and the content of the novels," but as the earlier studies by Malcolm Goldstein and Linda Simon make clear, there is more to Wilder's art than time alone. Unfortunately, neither of the other two pieces still to be considered here add to an understanding of that art. W. Craig Turner does state in "Thornton Wilder: Neglected Novelist" (*American Bypaths*, pp. 213–30) that the novels of Wilder deserve serious critical attention but he does not give it that attention and Frazer Drew's "For 'Faithful Subscriber': Some Thornton Wilder Inscriptions" (*ABC* 1,iii:23–27) is a slight piece about Wilder's letters and book inscriptions to Drew.

Margaret Mitchell's *Gone with the Wind* is the focus of three essays, two of which are of little significance: Darden Asbury Pyron argues in " 'Gone with the Wind': Southern History and National Popular Culture" (*Studies in Popular Culture* 3:12–14) that there is a "yawning gap between Mitchell's intentions and the popular and even high culture impressions of her work" which help define "a dominant set of national culture values" and in "Margaret Mitchell: *Gone with the Wind* and *War and Peace*" (*SoSt* 19:243–60) Harold K. Schefski offers "several concrete parallels in genre, theme, character, and style" between the two novels which the reader is asked to take seriously. An essay we *must* take seriously is Blanche Gelfant's richly suggestive "*Gone with the Wind* and the Impossibilities of Fiction" (*SLJ* 13,i:3–31), which contends that *GWTW* is "a novel that revolves around secrets," and "unites child and adult into one reader, and then by the divisions in its form and its characters, divides and at the same time doubles the reader's response, doubles his pleasure."

Erskine Caldwell also attracted the attention of three critics this year. In "Georgia Boys: The Redclay Satyrs of Erskine Caldwell and Harry Crews" (*VQR* 56:612–26) John Seelye ponders "the Beverly Hiltonizing of the American South" and notes that although the best of Caldwell's work "is derived from (or at least chronologically follows) Faulkner's early work," it was "Caldwell's genius to popularize Faulkner's formulaics of rural violence and degeneracy . . . by instilling a dimension of social consciousness while adding also a quasi-pornographic element of explicit sex." Robert D. Jacobs devotes himself to "*Tobacco Road*: Lowlife and the Comic Tradition" (*The American South*, pp. 206–26) and points out that the enormous popularity of *Tobacco Road* made the name Jeeter Lester synonymous with the southern redneck, which was unfortunate "because Caldwell's purpose was not to disparage the poor white but to account for his degeneracy on economic grounds and to drive the lesson home through comic exaggeration." Early Caldwell is the focus of Guy Owen's "The Apprenticeship of Erskine Caldwell: An Examination of *The Bastard* and *Poor Fool*" (*A Fair Day*, pp. 197–204), which notes that Caldwell's first two novellas show Caldwell "developing the themes and techniques that led to his major fiction of the 1930s."

Truman Capote's *Other Voices, Other Rooms* is the subject of studies by Robert C. Davis ("*Other Voices, Other Rooms* and the Ocularity of American Fiction" [*DeltaES* 11:1–14]) and Nancy Blake ("*Other Voices, Other Rooms*: Southern Gothic or Medieval Quest?" [*DeltaES* 11:31–47]), while James Gould Cozzens, Marjorie Rawlings, John Marquand, and Edna Ferber each received the attention of a single critic. James McNally discusses "[Robert]

Browning Traits in Cozzens' *Morning Noon and Night*" (*SBHC* 8, i:20–31); John Cech writes about "Marjorie Kinnan Rawlings' *The Secret River*: A Fairy Tale, a Place, a Life" (*SoSt* 19:29–38); "John Marquand: The Reluctant Prophet" (*NER* 2:614–24) is the subject of George Green's essay, while Ellen Serlen Uffen writes about "Edna Ferber and the 'Theatricalization' of American Mythology" (*MMisc* 8:82–93).

Finally, attention must be called to Gabriel Miller's *Screening the Novel: Rediscovered American Fiction in Film* (Ungar) and Paul A. Doyle's *Pearl S. Buck* (TUSAS 85). Miller's book is an examination of eight neglected American novels and the films made from them. Among the eight novels-into-films discussed by Miller three are of particular interest to readers of this section: James M. Cain's *The Postman Always Rings Twice* (pp. 46–63), Horace McCoy's *They Shoot Horses, Don't They?* (pp. 64–83), and Daniel Fuchs's *Low Company* (pp. 143–66). Doyle's study is a revised edition of his Twayne volume originally completed in 1963. In the new edition Doyle has analyzed the principal novels of Buck's last decade, has brought the bibliography up to date, and has noted post-1963 research. But not *everything* has been brought up to date. For example, Doyle writes in his Preface that Buck's reputation has suffered for two shameful reasons: she was a woman writer and her work deals with Chinese and Asiatic material. There is not much evidence to support the latter contention, and as for the claim that Buck's reputation suffered unjustly because she was a woman, here is Doyle on Buck's short fiction: "Pearl Buck's short fiction is comprised mainly of what used to be called women's magazine stories. The tales are smooth and readable, but usually sentimental, improbable, and simplistic in approach." Shameful, indeed?

b. **Western Fiction.** In *The Novels of the American West* (Nebraska) John R. Milton, who is concerned with distinguishing between the serious literary Western novelist and the popular formulaic western, devotes chapters to "Vardis Fisher: The Struggle of Rationalism" (pp. 117–59) and "Walter Van Tilburg Clark: The Western Attitude" (pp. 195–229), two of the writers whose novels he believes "rank with the best novels of any other region in the United States." Among the writers whom Milton believes transcend the formula western but fall short "of the high seriousness and literary quality

of the best of the Western novelists" is Tom Lea, the subject of a
1979 interview with Patrick Bennett, "Wells of Sight and Sound"
(*SWR* 65:113-27).

Milton also is represented by two essays—including "The Primitive World of Vardis Fisher: The Idaho Novels" (pp. 125-35)—in
William T. Pilkington's *Critical Essays on the Western American
Novel* (Hall). The volume is divided into two main sections: general
criticism and critical essays on individual novelists. In addition to
Vardis Fisher, essays on A. B. Guthrie, Louis L'Amour, Walter Van
Tilburg Clark, and Frederick Manfred are included in the second
section. The essays have been previously published, but it is well
worth having them together in one volume. A bibliography, however,
would have made the collection both more useful and more valuable.
The absence of a bibliography also detracts from *Women, Women
Writers, and the West* (Whitston, 1979), ed. L. L. Lee and Merrill
Lewis. The collection includes studies by Helen Stauffer of "Mari
Sandoz and Western Biography" (pp. 55-69), Barbara Meldrum's
"Conrad Richter's Southwestern Ladies" (pp. 119-29), and M. Lou
Rodenberger's "Folk Narrative in Caroline Gordon's Frontier Fic-
tion" (pp. 197-208). If the essays in this volume are less thorough
than those in the study by Milton and the collection by Pilkington,
they are nevertheless of considerable interest and give focus to a
subject that has been neglected for much too long.

A monograph by Charles L. Crow devoted to *Janet Lewis* has
been included in the Boise State University Western Writers Series
(No. 41). Crow offers a sketch of Lewis' life and brief considerations
of her novels and short stories. Although it might be argued that
Lewis is hardly a Western writer at all, and although neither Lewis'
life nor her work is considered with any serious critical attention,
this monograph will at least serve to introduce some readers to a
writer who may have "a circle of enthusiastic admirers" but still
remains little known.

c. **Detective Fiction.**   Raymond Chandler and Dashiell Hammett
continue to attract serious critical attention. This year Chandler has
been the focus of three substantial essays. David Smith addresses
himself to "The Public Eye of Raymond Chandler" (*JAmS* 14:423-
41) whose literary intentions—after the Depression finally took him
away "from his belle-lettrist origins in England and his anonymous

businessman's life in the 1920s"—were focused "on a popular form whose origins made it, for him, a perfect vehicle to diagnose the mean streets *and* the grandiose homes of his place and his time." An equally fine essay is offered by Peter J. Rabinowitz, who explores "Rats Behind the Wainscoting: Politics, Convention, and Chandler's *The Big Sleep*" (*TSLL* 22:224–45) and concludes that Chandler is a political writer because "his novels challenge, in a dynamic and forceful way, the hidden political assumptions of other novels which have been widely read and extremely influential." So at the end of *The Big Sleep* we feel dissatisfied. Instead of calming us Chandler purposely irritates us, disrupts our peace; he "forces us to disapprove of the world we live in and demands that we reexamine our political outlook." Somewhat less interesting than the essays by Smith and Rabinowitz is the chapter devoted to Chandler, " '. . . a hard-boiled gentleman'—Raymond Chandler" (pp. 135–67), by Stephen Knight in his study of *Form and Ideology in Crime Fiction* (Indiana), which concentrates on *Farewell My Lovely* to show that "the collective world is innately oppressive" and it is only in private acts which show private morality that positive value is to be found.

Although Knight chose not to discuss the works of Dashiell Hammett in any detail—even though he acknowledged that Hammett "remains an interesting figure, not the least because each novel is different from the others"—Hammett's work is discussed at length by Peter Wolfe in *Beams Falling: The Art of Dashiell Hammett* (Popular). After a chapter about "The Detective Nobody Knows" —"Dashiell Hammett is nothing at all if he isn't mysterious"—Wolfe devotes a chapter to "The Mind and Heart of the Short Stories," then gives five chapters to the novels—of which *The Maltese Falcon* and *The Glass Key* are most highly regarded. Despite moments of enlightenment, Wolfe's study ultimately disappoints. The writing often is cumbersome and, finally, little is added to our understanding of the art of Hammett. Perhaps, as Wolfe writes, "Hammett's primitivism survives chiefly as stylistic flourish," and it may be that fiction writing was "more of a denial than a fulfillment for Dashiell Hammett," but if so something more than such simple statements is demanded, and that something more all too often is missing from Wolfe's study. It is also missing from the two other pieces to appear on Hammett this year, both much less ambitious than Wolfe's *Falling Beams*. W. V. Reeves offers a note on "The Mutation of *The Maltese*

Falcon" (*AN&Q* 18[1979]:21–24) and in "Stirring Things Up:
Dashiell Hammett's Continental Op" (*JAmS* 14:442–55) John S.
Whitley concentrates on features in Hammett's novels which seem
to break sharply with previous conventions of the detective story.
Whitley concludes that although Hammett's detectives rely on their
own strength and invention to maintain their security, their strength
resides not in a stable personality "but in the ability to change like
a chameleon to meet the needs of a fluctuating world, to hold to the
security of the present moment, and their invention is always power-
fully destructive in human terms."

Two other works remain to be mentioned here. David Skene
Melvin and Ann Skene Melvin have compiled *Crime, Detective, Es-
pionage, Mystery, and Thriller Fiction and Film: A Comprehensive
Bibliography of Critical Writing Through 1979* (Greenwood). The
volume *is* comprehensive, but it is not exhaustive; no attempt was
made, for example, to index *The Armchair Detective*. But the volume
is comprehensive enough (more than 1,600 items are listed), and
despite the omissions and the sheer ugliness of its physical appearance it is a work of considerable value. And although it may not be
as valuable a tool, Steven R. Carter's "Karma and Spiritual Responsibility in James Jones' *A Touch of Danger*" (*ArmD* 13:230–36) is an
unexpected and rewarding discussion of Jones's detective novel,
which "not only adheres to the conventional patterns of hard-boiled
detective fiction but also remains true to the basic pattern of his
philosophy, including those which relate to his views on individual
responsibility and Karmic relationships."

d. Science Fiction. Isaac Asimov continues to outdo himself. *In
Memory Yet Green*, the first volume of his autobiography, was more
than 700 pages of vainglorious tedium; now, in *In Joy Still Felt: The
Autobiography of Isaac Asimov, 1954–1978* (Doubleday) he has
given us the same dull prose but there are almost 100 more pages
of it. I hasten to note, however, that in "I, Asimov" (*Extrapolation*
21:309–27) James Gunn makes it clear that he finds the "triumph"
of Asimov's autobiographical writings to be that he makes "it all so
readable." Gunn then goes on to the task at hand, "to tell the Asimov
story more selectively and send the still curious on to fuller accounts
elsewhere, to bring the details of the life into focus in illuminating
the work, and to explain the work in terms of a thesis that may be

too close to Asimov for him to perceive." Gunn does just this, and his "I, Asimov" is a much less painful way to learn about Asimov than reading the *Autobiography*. And to learn about the fiction there are two substantial essays for the Asimov fan to turn to this year. In "The Frankenstein Complex and Asimov's Robots" (*Mosaic* 13, iii–iv:83–94) Gorman Beauchamp takes exception to the generally held view of Asimov's robots and argues that in *I, Robot* and several of his other robot stories Asimov "actually reinforces the Frankenstein complex—by offering scenarios of man's fate at the hands of his technological creations more frightening, because more subtle, than those of Mary Shelley and Capek." A more conventional view of Asimov is offered by Patricia S. Warrick in *The Cybernetic Imagination in Science Fiction* (MIT). In her chapter devoted to "Science Fiction Images of Computers and Robots" (pp. 53–79) Warrick acknowledges Asimov's position as "the father of robot stories in SF," notes that "the quality of his fiction is consistently high," and then writes that "Asimov is optimistic about the relationship of man and intelligent machines." He has labeled the fear of mechanical intelligence the "Frankenstein complex" and Asimov himself neither has this fear "nor does he approve of those who do."

Scholarship on Ray Bradbury also continues to flourish. In addition to the publication of *The Stories of Ray Bradbury* (Knopf), which contains 100 stories (six of which were not previously published in a book), this year was marked by two substantial additions to Bradbury scholarship. Martin Harry Greenberg and Joseph D. Olander have edited *Ray Bradbury* (Ungar) for their Writers of the 21st Century Series. This volume, which is as excellent as the previous ones in the series, deals with such diverse topics as the frontier myth in Bradbury, the thematic structure of *The Martian Chronicles*, Bradbury's attitude toward science and technology, religion in Bradbury's science fantasies, and *Fahrenheit 451* as symbolic dystopia. A bibliography of primary and secondary material compiled by Marshall B. Tymn adds to the usefulness of this exceptionally fine collection. Also of some interest but less valuable is Wayne L. Johnson's *Ray Bradbury* (Ungar), which concentrates on the major themes in Bradbury's fiction. Much of Bradbury's work Johnson sees as belonging to the tradition of such fantasists as Derleth and Lovecraft, while some works call to mind Sinclair Lewis and Mark Twain. It is a book about a dreamer, Johnson writes: "Ray Bradbury is a writer with a particular skill at committing his dreams to paper and, in so doing, making them live for others." The problem with the volume is that it too often fails to get beyond this level of superficiality. It is, in the not very best sense of the term, a popular study which finally deals too generally with too much material.

The three essays to appear on Bradbury this year all are of some interest. In the special issue of *Mosaic* devoted to "Other Worlds: Fantasy and Science Fiction Since 1939," William F. Touponce discusses "The Existential Fabulous: A Reading of Ray Bradbury's 'The Golden Apples of the Sun'" (13,iii–iv:203–18), a story which contains a theme still central to Bradbury's imagination: "The romance of space exploration and mankind's quest for identity with the cosmos." Noël M. Valis writes about "*The Martian Chronicles* and Jorge Luis Borges" (*Extrapolation* 20[1979]:50–59) and notes that for both Bradbury and Borges reality is not what one expects it to be, for in the work of both writers "things are not what they seem to be." And in "The Fiction of Ray Bradbury: Universal Themes in Midwestern Settings" (*MMisc* 8:94–101), Thomas P. Linkfield addresses himself to those works which have nothing to do with either space or science fiction but with those works in which Bradbury has blended "images of the Midwest with universal themes concerning ordinary people and their adjustment to life."

Philip K. Dick is represented this year by three essays, two of which are included in *Bridges to Science Fiction*, eds. George E. Slosser, George R. Guffey, and Mark Rose (So. Ill.). The volume consists of ten essays, all of which were written specifically for the Eaton Conference on Science Fiction and Fantasy Literature (1979). In "Visionary States and the Search for Transcendence in Science Fiction" (pp. 64–77) Robert Hunt discusses the handling of religious revelation in the fiction of Dick (as well as that of Ian Watson and Robert Silverberg) and Carl D. Malmgren examines "Philip Dick's *The Man in the High Castle* and the Nature of Science Fictional Worlds" (pp. 120–30). *The Man in the High Castle* is also one of the works discussed by Patricia S. Warrick in her section on "Philip K. Dick's Robots" (pp. 206–30) in *The Cybernetic Imagination in Science Fiction*. Dick, together with Isaac Asimov, is seen as one of two American giants whose imagination creates "more abundant and brilliant models of life in an electronic future than any others."

Only one work appeared on Lovecraft this year, but it is a substantial volume, *H. P. Lovecraft: Four Decades of Criticism* (Ohio), ed. S. T. Joshi. More than 20 essays are here reprinted, covering such areas as "The Lovecraft Mythos," "Literary Influences," "Philosophical, Psychological and Historical Analyses," and "Lovecraft's Poetry." An appendix devoted to "The Collected Works of H. P. Lovecraft" and "Supplementary Readings" also is included. Not all of the essays are first-rate but enough are to make this a valuable collection for the student of Lovecraft's fiction. Of equal if not even greater value for the Heinlein enthusiast is H. Bruce Franklin's *Robert A. Heinlein: America as Science Fiction* (Oxford), a volume in The Science-Fiction Writers Series. Franklin is one of those critics with whom one may frequently disagree but from whom one almost always learns. So it is with the book on Heinlein. As Franklin sees him, Heinlein not only is "our most popular author of science fiction, easily the most controversial, and perhaps the most influential"; he also "embodies the contradictions that have been developing in our society ever since the Depression flowed into the Second World War." To understand the phenomenon of Robert Heinlein, therefore, "is finally to understand the culture that is the matrix for ourselves." In an attempt to understand that phenomenon, Franklin deals with all of Heinlein's tales and novels, including the 1980 novel, *The Number of the Beast* (Fawcett), and the result is not only the best work yet published about Heinlein; it also is one of the finest books we have on any writer of science fiction as well as being an important addition to American cultural studies.

Heinlein receives frequent mention in Lester del Rey's *The World of Science Fiction, 1926–1976: The History of a Subculture* (Garland), but these comments seldom tell us anything about Heinlein's fiction. What del Rey has attempted is a "guide to the major forces in the subculture of science fiction, to help the reader understand, the history of the field and related developments that have shaped the literature." I don't think he has succeeded very well. The book is marred by the superficiality of its observations and the blandness of its prose. One example will have to suffice: "I've known a fair number of [science fiction] fans who do not seem to have had any serious social problems or maladjustments," dey Rey writes in a section on "The Active Fan." "A few have even been active in sports and outdoor affairs." So it goes.

Hofstra University

15. Fiction: The 1950s to the Present

Jerome Klinkowitz

A stubborn polarity of tradition versus innovation dominates work on contemporary fiction. Once a neutral topic and convenient handle for the discussion of all American literature, the recent controversies over postmodernism, anti-Aristotelian aesthetics, deconstructionist literary theory, and general cultural change have at once elevated the debate over fiction to major status in the history of ideas while at the same time opening the gates to partisan squabbling about just what the contemporary American novel should be. Both the best and the worst scholarship are affected by it; in the spirit of Richard Kostelanetz' seminal *The End of Intelligent Writing* (1974), the most helpful work of 1980 has been that which acknowledges the deep political and philosophical divisions within the contemporary period and uses them to gauge the larger importance of fiction living Americans have produced.

i. General Studies

The year's most comprehensively important study is James M. Mellard's *The Exploded Form: The Modernist Novel in America* (Illinois), which takes a conservative approach to recent fiction and the arguments about it. There is no post-Modern novel, Mellard insists —just a three-part history of development, exploitation, and exhaustion of the modernist aesthetic from William Faulkner's *The Sound and the Fury* (the naive) through Joseph Heller's *Catch-22* (modernism's critical phase) to Richard Brautigan's *Trout Fishing in America* (the sophisticated stage which in Thomas Kuhn's *The Structure of Scientific Revolutions* signals a movement's completion). The key to Mellard's argument is its grounding in the myth criticism of Northrop Frye. Mellard grants that there is an increasing challenge to tradition in the works of Faulkner, Heller, and Brautigan, but believes this very challenge reaffirms the essentially realistic substructure of fiction. "When a reader is himself forced . . . to close hermeneutical gaps created by an epistemological indeterminacy," Mellard insists, "he must turn to other, more familiar determinants. In general this means he returns to the archetypal, ontological modes, the narrative *mythoi*, that he knows implicitly from his experience of reading fiction." Geoffrey Hartman contests this view; in *Criticism in the Wilderness* (Hopkins) he reminds us of the essentially materialist impulse in Frye's work: "What Frye calls 'approximation' is surely 'accommodation': the work of the critic or commentator rather than of the poet, whose mind is by no means as unified as Frye pretends." Mellard's virtue is that he admits his preferred style of fiction must be grounded in the real—whether that be consciousness, self, language, myth, or history. He is not ready to let fiction be about itself —and given such limitation, he has demonstrated that on the level of content contemporary fiction has not eclipsed its modernist limits.

Has the level of form in American fiction risen above the "crude 'message hunting' approach to literature" which Gerald Graff in *Poetic Statement and Critical Dogma* (2nd ed., Chicago) says typifies our worst scholarship? Apparently not, since Graff characterizes William H. Gass's work by its insistence that words mean themselves and not their referents but then argues that the case for nonmimetic fiction is prima facie impossible. "Has Gass actually succeeded in carrying out his purpose?" Graff inquires. "One does not need to read far in this novella [*Willie Masters' Lonesome Wife*] to see that it offers a number of assertions about the world in the very process of justifying its avoidance of assertions," an example on Graff's part of the same reductiveness Hartman notes in Frye (and by extension in Mellard's use of archetypes to explain fiction which resists such grounding).

Sanford Pinsker's briskly written *Between Two Worlds: The American Novel in the 1960s* (Whitston) also favors message over form, censuring John Barth and Kurt Vonnegut for their lack of solid statement while preferring "the darkly serious fiction of Joyce Carol Oates and Isaac Bashevis Singer." His Arnoldian title describes an essentially cautious thesis: that modernism may have waned but that postmodernism is as yet undefinable (if it may be perceived at all). In lieu of guessing at a new aesthetic for fiction which resists modernist standards Pinsker gives what he admits is a "zig-zagging account of the postmodernist's sense of backdrop." Hence his emphasis is on material concerns, none of them having much vitalistic promise: the thematic exhaustion of black humor, the diminishing intellectual challenge of Jewish-American fiction, and the gothic visions of Oates and Singer.

Resolute in his intention not to be a prophet, Pinsker paints a depressing picture of the contemporary novel, an ambivalent and uncertain position dictated by his own method. Judging abstract work by mimetic standards hardly seems a satisfying way to proceed, but legions of critics do it nevertheless—a disgraceful situation for scholars who had had over a decade to absorb the pioneering and redirective work of Robert Scholes, Ihab Hassan, Philip Stevick, and others. David Madden's *A Primer of the Novel* (Scarecrow) is particularly biased against formal innovation; in a discussion of Steve Katz, Madden argues that there is no difference between Katz's use of graphic devices and those of Laurence Sterne's in *Tristram Shandy*, forgetting that for all his play with technique Sterne never dropped the pose of telling a story, which Katz and his colleagues often do and which makes the rules for judging such fiction as different as the art critic's must be when moving from Rembrandt to Pollock.

Some scholars condemn the post-Modern for not being modern; others such as Alfred Kazin (in "American Writing Now," *NewRep* 18 Oct.:27–30) despair in the face of its complexity and willingness to consider what traditionalist writers ignore. In a convincing answer ("Hope for American Writing," *NewRep* 22 Nov.:3) Thomas LeClair lists the writers who "do imagine, contra Kazin, the 'important technological storm on our mental life'; this is exactly the achievement of much recent fiction," including that of Joseph McElroy, Don De-Lillo, William Gaddis, Stanley Elkin, and Robert Coover—writers Kazin has overlooked in favor of the more easily deplorable *Good as Gold* by Joseph Heller and Tom Wolfe's *The Right Stuff*.

"What is ominous about our literary state is that so much is accepted as ad hoc, temporary, spasmodic—and so has to be 'sensational' in order to show some effect," Kazin complains. Recognizing the provisionality of content, however, clears the air for intelligent discussion of thematically troublesome works, as Robert Detweiler and Glenn Meeter manage in their superb introduction to *Faith and Fiction: The Modern Short Story* (Eerdmans, 1979). Content, here

viewed with utmost seriousness for its religious message, is not simply reductive. Instead, realistic fiction uses the mode of what the editors call "Canaan" (mimetic credibility to enhance a notion of free
will) while antirealistic work ("Rome") seeks "to create meaning
rather than to discover it." Although as respective critic and fictionist Detweiler and Meeter are as realistically inclined as scholar Sanford Pinsker and novelist David Madden, their fair distinction lets
us appreciate innovators such as Richard Brautigan and Donald
Barthelme for what their own new terms contrive, rather than consigning them to an outer darkness of factual chaos and moral decay.
A similarly open-minded view of realistic content within formally
experimental work (notably in the fiction of Stanley Elkin, Harold
Brodkey, and Jonathan Baumbach) distinguishes Bill Buford and
Pete de Bolla's "Introduction" to the "New American Writing" issue
of the reorganized British journal Granta (No. 1, n.s. [1979]:3–10);
in a subsequent number (No. 3, n.s.:7–16) Buford expands his argument on "Magic Realism" to comparative proportions.

As the debate over "the death of the novel" characterized scholarship of the late 1960s, a corresponding fuss over "moral fiction" began to brew in the late '70s and has now boiled over into books,
special issues of journals, and even popular magazines. Fiction International No. 12 is devoted to the points raised by John Gardner's
On Moral Fiction (1978); "A Writers' Forum on Moral Fiction" contains noteworthy postmodernist challenges by Jerry Bumpus (pp.
8–9), Raymond Federman (pp. 10–11), and Harold Jaffe (pp. 11–
15) plus one revealing defense (by Gordon Weaver, pp. 22–23)
which places Gardner's book in the tradition of Wayne Booth's The
Rhetoric of Fiction (1961) and Gerald Graff's Literature Against
Itself (1979). In the same issue is Peter Bailey's "Moral Fiction and
Metafiction" (pp. 221–31) arguing that Gardner reveals too sympathetic an understanding of innovative fiction to be its Aristotelian
enemy (as Weaver suggests). Instead, Gardner's comments on Donald Barthelme, Robert Coover, and John Barth indicate his shared
belief that "the aesthetic structures of the mind are, if not the real
foe with which we must contend, then at least significantly determi-
nistic elements in our actions and behavior to make their understanding crucial to our comprehension of ourselves and of our circumstances"—this latter rubric being the moral essence of metafiction.

Some '60s opinions were recanted as the 1980s began, most prominently by Leslie Fiedler and John Barth, whose respective "Cross the Border, Close the Gap" and "The Literature of Exhaustion" essays helped introduce (via *Playboy* and *The Atlantic*) innovative fiction to a larger audience. In "The Death and Rebirths of the Novel" (*Salmagundi* 51–52:143–52) Fiedler confesses that he was wrong to suggest the art novel and more popular forms of fiction would eventually merge; instead, the former (from "surfiction" in general to Barth's *Letters* in particular) has died entirely while pop forms such as fantasy and science fiction flourish because they "live on in the collective memory of us all." It is not their virtuosity, elegance of structure, or subtlety of thought which win them the readership forfeited by the inaccessible experimentalists. Rather it is "something quite other: their mythic resonance, their archetypal appeal." Naive fantasy does well, and science fiction does best of all "because a generation of rebels largely male and at least covertly misogynist needed some form of masculine protest literature to call their own." To his credit John Barth stays off the SF bandwagon in his own formal retraction, "The Literature of Replenishment" (*AtM* Jan.: 65–71); he simply admits that the 19th century is no longer worth rebelling against and that modernism itself deserves a second chance. "A worthy program for postmodernist fiction," he suggests, "is the synthesis or transcension of these anti-theses, which may be summed up as premodernist and modernist modes of writing." His new models are the Magic Realism of Italo Calvino's *Cosmicomics* and Gabriel García Márquez' *One Hundred Years of Solitude*, with passing reference to his own latest novel *Letters*. "One foot in fantasy, one in objective reality" is the standard Barth admires, which is none too distant from Leslie Fiedler's latest prophecy for fiction (Fiedler's essay in turn describes *Letters* as "the beginning of a return to tradition").

Does a valid postmodernism in fiction exist at all? Those who ignore the question are easy targets. In "The Effacement of Contemporary American Literature" (*CE* 42:382–89) Jerome Klinkowitz demonstrates what a conservative academia's denial does to a developing sense of literary tradition, while Robert R. Fox extends the argument to include the publishing industry, marketing practices, and reviewing media in his aptly titled "The Survival of Contemporary Literature" (*Ohio Lib. Assn. Bull.* 50,iv:1–5). Nor has the creative writing business escaped the anti-innovative backlash: Gene

Lyons' "The Famous Breadloaf Writers' School (*Harper's* Feb.: 75–80) reports that "These days, the bias of the staff, in keeping with the participation of John Gardner, is Aristotelian."

Getting down to the hard work of determining just how the cultural and aesthetic transformations within postmodernism have influenced contemporary American fiction (among other disciplines) is the concern of a symposium organized by Ihab Hassan and occupying half of *BuR* (25,ii:115–93). Hassan himself (in "The Question of Postmodernism," pp. 117–26) constructs a 60-item table of contrasts, in which modernism's characteristic Hierarchy of values is played against postmodernism's Anarchy, its Readerly fiction against the Writerly, its Transcendence against Immanence. "We have created in our minds a model of postmodernism, a particular typology of culture and imagination," Hassan suggests, "and have proceeded to 'rediscover' the affinities of various authors and different moments within that model." The cultural shift is not so sharply historical as idiosyncratically personal. "We have, that is, reinvented our ancestors—and always shall. Consequently, 'older' authors can be postmodern . . . while 'younger' authors need not be—Styron, Updike, Gardner." Wallace Martin's "Postmodernism: Ultima Thule or Seim Anew?" (pp. 142–54) addresses the confusing literary history to which Hassan alludes. " 'Post-modern' was adopted by Irving Howe and Harry Levin (1959, 1960) to designate the literature that had appeared after World War II," Martin notes. In their view (which we have seen Kazin and Pinsker maintain) "it was inferior to the literature of the preceding period" and led to their facile disparagement of fiction which chose to innovate in directions different from Bellow's or Malamud's. The mainstream Howe and Levin celebrated had in fact "returned to 'premodern' techniques, and so when a remarkable development in literary history did occur it was entirely off the establishment's scale. "The innovative fiction that appeared unexpectedly in the late 1960s (Barthelme, Coover, Brautigan, Gass, Pynchon), the belated awareness that some contemporary poetry was not confessional, and the flood of startling translations from South American and European literature made postmodernism appear in an entirely new light." Martin notes that "During the two decades after World War II, music and painting, the harbingers of cultural change in the twentieth century, had no noticeable influence on developments in American literature." Now suddenly they did, and "The original definition of postmodernism was displaced by a new one in which technical, conceptual, and ontological manipulation loomed large."

The balance of Hassan's symposium corrects the all-too-common misreadings of contemporary fiction by scholars who have neglected this sense of literary history and closed their eyes to the theoretical developments which have been an important part of it. Matei Calinescu's "Ways of Looking at Fiction" (pp. 155–70) indicates how William H. Gass's worlds of words in fiction have just as real (if not more real) an existence as words in the works of philosophers, yet in a nonjudgmental way which preserves their essential fictionality. Charles Russell's "The Context of the Concept" (pp. 181–93) further argues for the substansiveness of metafictional discourse as displayed by a "focus on the 'language' of art and on cultural codes of signification" in the works of Gass, Barth, Pynchon, Coover, and Federman. What have they learned? That "Hermetic art necessarily tended toward tautology" and that for fiction to succeed they must "continually turn back from their referential possibilities toward the linguistic domain in order to force the audience to observe and critique the processes of creation, questioning, and eventual deconstruction of the literary text."

Complementing and extending his symposium's work is Hassan's excellent full-length study of how Indeterminacy and Immanence characterize the post-Modern "backdrop" for fiction (the essentials of which Pinsker and others avoid) in *The Right Promethean Fire: Imagination, Science, and Cultural Change* (Illinois). In a special issue of *Sub-Stance* (27) on "Current Trends in American Fiction" Charles Russell addresses himself to specific postmodern influences on fiction ("Individual Voice in the Collective Discourse," pp. 29–39). "A new aesthetic and social configuration" has replaced avantgardist alienation with a new posture of "textual immediacy" traceable through the works of Burroughs, Pynchon, Sukenick, Kosinski, and Federman. David Porush's "Technology and Postmodernism: Cybernetic Fiction" (pp. 92–100) studies these authors plus Barth, Barthelme, and Coover to show how a "Fourth Discontinuity" between man and machine has now been bridged just as the previous gaps between man and the natural universe (Copernicus), animals (Darwin), and the unconscious (Freud).

Certain studies have hinged their arguments on the bad blood between modernists and postmodernists. John Griffiths' *Three Tomorrows: American, British, and Soviet Science Fiction* (Barnes and Noble) explains why SF has won so many popular and academic converts; its ideal reader "prefers not to gaze endlessly into his own emotional entrails in the way demanded of the modern psychological novel. He is still prepared to be excited, rather than awestruck and overwhelmed, by the infinite variety of the universe." SF of course demands a suspension-of-disbelief in exchange for an internally realistic story—in short, a premodernist style of reading. James Guetti's *Word-Music: The Aesthetic Aspect of Narrative Fiction* (Rutgers) argues that we cling to realism even when antirealistic elements are present in the text because of "our hold upon our own imaginative autonomy. Though at rare times we are content to relinquish, momentarily, imaginative authority, much more often we demand that our imaginations continue dominant. And for that purpose, whatever fiction we are reading must continue realistic, as basis and material for the process and product." Guetti blames a wrong-headed "inseparableness of seeing and knowing" for most misreadings of fiction and also for the basic timidity of some otherwise adventurous authors. John Barth and Thomas Pynchon, the token antirealists approved of by scholars otherwise hostile to the avant-garde, are not innovators at all: "My feeling that Pynchon may be the finest realist of our time springs not only from his dominantly visual narrative processes but also from his dedication to plausibility, which is also his dedication to mystery: he is committed to the grid of knowing-not knowing and is fascinated with that sort of power" which he pursues on the level of discourse rather than fiction. As for Barth, "a story's realistic drive, its manner of resisting our intelligence, may escalate from a narrator's mere uncommittedness and invisibility to his obtrusive and declared elusiveness and to an imaginative resistance in the fiction that becomes absolutely the nonproductive subject of the story itself"—in other words, the regressive parodies of Barth's *The Floating Opera* and Pynchon's *V.*

That Barth and Pynchon are indeed closet Aristotelians, offering not truly self-reflexive metafictions but rather imitations of imitations of actions, is the thesis of Christine Brooke-Rose's "Where Do We Go From Here?" (*Granta* 3, n.s.: 161–88). "Parodic dramatization is one long stylization of realism," Brooke-Rose suggests; "over-interpretation is not, *as technique,* sufficiently opposed to 'in-

terpretation' to stop the discourse from tipping over into imitation."
Parody expands but stylization itself reduces, and the fictions of
Ronald Sukenick, Robert Coover, Donald Barthelme, and William H.
Gass proceed in this latter less-imitative direction (where at least
the effect is unreal). Answering her title's question, Brooke-Rose
anticipates "a fantastic realism" much as Leslie Fiedler, John Barth,
and Bill Buford have prophesied, each from his own bases of judgment and preference. What seems clear is that no fiction or criticism
of it can hope to succeed by rejecting or ignoring the philosophical
givens of our time; such work would be escapist, which is not what
Brooke-Rose has in mind.

Two general studies which accept the post-Modern world-view
are Steven G. Kellman's *The Self-Begetting Novel* (Columbia) and
Richard Kostelanetz' introductory material for his *Text-Sound Texts*
(Morrow). Although Kellman agrees with Brooke-Rose that self-
reflexive fiction reaches its parodistic limits with Donald Barthelme,
he corrects misapprehensions about the novels of Raymond Federman, Ronald Sukenick, Steve Katz, Ishmael Reed, John Irving, and
Gilbert Sorrentino by showing how "America's coming of age" has
transpired in harmony with both Continental developments and certain elements within the native tradition (including Henry James's
and Henry Adams' use of the artist, Hawthorne's and Melville's
artistic presence in their own works, and Sherwood Anderson's
Proustian employment of George Willard in *Winesburg, Ohio*). Fiction need not cohere in terms of message alone for a statement about
American life and values to be made, Kellman shows; metafictional
processes can do the same thing. Surveying the fiction of Walter
Abish, William S. Burroughs, and others, Richard Kostelanetz offers
the term "text-sound" as typifying "language whose principal means
of coherence is sound, rather than syntax or semantics—where the
sounds made by comprehensible words create their own coherence
apart from denotative meanings." Attending to such new forms of
coherence means breaking loose from the "tyrannical hold" visual
ways of determining meaning have exercised over our imaginations,
as James Guetti argues in *Word-Music*. But if American scholarship
is to do something better than "plod along at the level on which plot
and characters are rehearsed and admired for their 'reality'" (as
William H. Pritchard puts it in his notes to *Word-Music*) the examples of Kellman, Kostelanetz, and Guetti must be followed.

Kostelanetz' own *Metamorphosis in the Arts: A Critical History of the 1960s* (Brooklyn: Assembling Press) explains how inference, word-imagery, environment, mixed-means, and the machine contribute to a new aesthetic. Jerome Klinkowitz' *The American 1960s: Imaginative Acts in a Decade of Change* (Iowa State) relies on more popularly social elements to describe the same transformation, including fictional qualities in the works of John F. Kennedy and Richard Nixon, politics in Ken Kesey's *One Flew Over the Cuckoo's Nest* and Joseph Heller's *Catch-22*, the new American image crafted by Kurt Vonnegut and Donald Barthelme, Richard Brautigan's disarming use of personality, the nonfiction novels of James Kunen, Dotson Rader, and Hunter S. Thompson, and parallel changes in rock music and mainstream art. A chapter on Vietnam's transforming effect on American fiction reaches the same conclusion as Gordon O. Taylor's "American Personal Narrative of the War in Vietnam" (*AL* 52:294–308): for fictionists and journalists alike, in Taylor's words, "Their efforts have come to constitute a process of ongoing inquiry as to the appropriate terms of literary treatment." New forms of writing had to be developed because the experience of Vietnam outstripped or defied so many previous conventions.

A revised and expanded edition of Klinkowitz' *Literary Disruptions* (Illinois) traces the cautious movement toward moral statement in the later-1970s work of Kurt Vonnegut, Donald Barthelme, Jerzy Kosinski, Ronald Sukenick, Raymond Federman, and Gilbert Sorrentino, and finds a new lyricism and metafictional use of language in work by Steve Katz, Clarence Major, and Michael Stephens. *The Practice of Fiction in America* (Iowa State) is Klinkowitz' attempt to trace an experimental impulse through all major developments from Hawthorne to the present, including a new consciousness of America's changing culture in John Updike, a generic ambivalence of structure (between drama and fiction) in the works of Vonnegut, and an extra-verbal experimentation with collage by Barthelme. An epilogue, "Avant-Garde and After" (reprinted in *Sub-Stance* 27: 125–38), describes the structural sophistications of Walter Abish and Sorrentino, the recent successes of Sukenick and Major in deconceptualizing fictive language, and the retreat from violently disruptive fiction in favor of a more comically accessible style of "experimental realism" in the novels of Tom Robbins, William Kotzwinkle, Rob Swigart, and Gerald Rosen.

Two comprehensive projects deserve special notice for their fairness and insight. *American Novelists Since World War II, Second Series*, ed. James E. Kibler, Jr. (Gale) is more than a reference book. Like its first series companion edited by Jeffrey Helterman and Richard Layman in 1978, Kibler's book is distinguished by several major essays on newly emergent writers which, like Larry McCaffery's seminal piece on Robert Coover from the 1978 volume, are original and substantial contributions to scholarship. The contributors in this Dictionary of Literary Biography series are doing a better job on new authors than many of their colleagues in academic journals and university press lists which are sometimes more committed to inane redundancies than genuinely new work. Among the best in Kibler's book are detailed factual and analytical essays on Frederick Busch (by Donald J. Grenier), William Eastlake (Mary Ellen Brooks), John Hersey (Sam B. Girgus), John Irving (Hugh M. Ruppersburg), David Madden (Thomas E. Dasher), Peter Matthiessen (John K. Cobbs), Cormac McCarthy (Dianne L. Cox), and Larry Woiwode (Michael E. Connaughton). Finally, Jill Krementz' *The Writer's Image* (Godine) is presented without a word, yet her framing of subjects and especially her juxtaposition of photographs tells a remarkable story about writing in our time, from Saul Bellow's measured glance through Gore Vidal's haughtily formal pose to Donald Barthelme's capture as an elfish woodsman prowling in his very real garden.

ii. Saul Bellow

The single major book and most appealingly valuable piece of scholarship on Bellow this year is Mark Harris' *Saul Bellow: Drumlin Woodchuck* (Georgia). Harris proceeds by indirection, pretending to tell the story of a book that never was, his authorized Bellow biography which the subject persistently thwarted. Explaining this very absence, however—like looking aside to see the tail of a comet —reveals more about Bellow's life and work than many conventional studies. Balancing between the intellectual and social worlds of Chicago's Hyde Park, fighting to maintain one's creative work in an atmosphere of deadening scholarship, yet drawing the spirit of one's art from those same elements: these are the essentials of Bellow's story which Harris lives vicariously as a rejected Boswell. Like hunt-

ing with a movie camera instead of an elephant gun, Harris captures
his subject in a uniquely animistic way.

Compared to Harris' bright and lively insightfulness, much of the
year's scholarship on Bellow is pale and languid. The few good essays (by virtue of their original statement on this much-studied
author) consider Bellow's struggles with dying literary conventions
and his successes with philosophical themes. In "Saul Bellow and the
'Lost Cause' of Character" (*Novel* 13:264–83) H. Porter Abbott
chooses *Dangling Man, Herzog*, "Looking for Mr. Green," and "Mos-
by's Memoirs" as examples of how character can be transformed
from a convention into the subject itself, and of how such "theorizing"
can avoid the rigidity which not only kills fiction but becomes an
"intellectual fascism." Zvonimir Radeljković's "Bellow's Search for
Meaning" (*Yugoslav Perspectives*, pp. 181–84) establishes this intellectual role for fiction by associating Bellow's motives in *Herzog*
with Cervantes' ("the shadowy region of human individuality, on
Adam's fall and Don Quixote's redemption"). One of Bellow's first
booklength commentators was Keith M. Opdahl, who in " 'Strange
Things, Savage Things': Saul Bellow's Hidden Theme" (*IowaR* 10,
iv[1979]:1–15) explains that the notion of sensuality is "the central
tale to which Bellow returns" and so provides "a remarkably coherent
explanation of the evolution" of his fiction. Sex is something "Bellow's women impose upon the men" and "the supreme lover is
death." A detail-packed but critically limited book by Joseph F.
McCadden, *The Flight From Women in the Fiction of Saul Bellow*
(Univ. Press), simplifies this argument down to the "bitch-goddess"
level.

Three briefer studies make further useful points about Bellow's philosophical thematics. Sanford Pinsker's "Saul Bellow, Søren
Kierkegaard and the Question of Boredom" (*CentR* 24:118–25) says
Bellow's comedy strives for an effect of "disorientation" to counter
"boredom," a mode of ironic balance learned from the Danish
philosopher. Judie Newman's "Saul Bellow: *Humboldt's Gift*, the
Comedy of History" (*DUJ* 72[1979]:79–87) challenges previous
critics' emphasis on Bellow's transcendently imposed order by showing his novelistic preference for "disorder" is a way of demonstrating
the "chaos and contingency of history." Gerald Duchovnay's "The
Urgency of Survival" (*CEA* 43,i:20–24) sees this same practice ex-

tended in *To Jerusalem and Back* as a way of giving "a glimpse of truth" without the distracting business of imposing solutions.

Source-studies of Bellow, as they should for any major author, continue to be productive. Among the best are Sanford Pinsker's "*Rameau's Nephew* and Saul Bellow's *Dangling Man*" (*NMAL* 4: Item 22) which shows there's as much of Diderot involved as Dostoevsky, Allan Chavkin's "Ivan Karamazov's Rebellion and Bellow's *The Victim*" (*PLL* 16:316–20) which argues that the "tickets to the future" ending owes more to *The Brothers Karamazov* than to Dostoevsky's *The Eternal Husband* (as previously assumed), and P. Shiv Kumar's "*Yahudim* and *Ostjude*: Social Stratification in Mr. Sammler's Planet" (*LHY* 21,ii:53–67), which shows how the greater cultural difference of the latter Yiddish sect "becomes the ordering principle" of Bellow's seventh novel.

iii. Isaac Bashevis Singer, Bernard Malamud, Philip Roth, and other Jewish Americans

Edward Alexander's *Isaac Bashevis Singer* (TWAS 582) ascribes the Nobel Laureate's vision to several influences, including the "New Yiddish" he writes in ("a Jewish dialect of English in the way that 'Old' Yiddish was a Jewish dialect of Middle high German") and the "willingness to believe in the mystical and the supernatural" he acquired in his father's court. Singer explores these concerns in a talk with Stephen H. Garrin, "Isaac Bashevis Singer in Texas: Public Queries and a Private Interview" (*TSLL* 22:91–98), and more familiar ground is covered in Richard Burgin's "A Conversation with Isaac Bashevis Singer" (*ChiR* 31,iv:53–60), including Singer's reminiscences about his first view of America and the changes he has witnessed since, plus asides on the staying power of Dostoevsky over Kafka. Burgin's accompanying article, "The Sly Modernism of Isaac Singer" (pp. 61–67), winds up describing the man as a premodernist, since his "conservative techniques" of strong characterization and plotting derive from an interest in social structure and are employed, Burgin insists, "to return literature to life." Joseph Sherman sees Singer as a much more contemporary author, one who avoids easy emotions so that the artistic may work its effect and who shuns the doctrinaire in favor of the richly problematic, all as shown by "Yentl the Yeshiva Boy" ("Isaac Bashevis Singer: Art versus Propaganda," (*ESA* 23:117–26).

Sheldon J. Hershinow's *Bernard Malamud* (Ungar) is a curiously limited study. On the one hand it credits Malamud's Jewish humor as a way of calling into question "the political and philosophical status quo," yet on the other praises his apparently easy exercise of "a unified moral vision based upon the values of humanism, which have been central to Western civilization since the ancient Greeks." In "The Schizoid Implied Authors of Two Jewish-American Novels" (*MELUS* 7,i:21–39) Marilyn Nelson Waniek argues against reductively ethnic interpretations which ignore such countervailing tendencies. "The duality of cultures . . . produces a duality of personality" which helps create a unique voice "for all the characters" (Jewish and Gentile) in Malamud's *The Assistant* and for the narrator's conflicting concerns in Philip Roth's *Portnoy's Complaint.* "When we . . . embrace the paradox of being one and many," Waniek counsels, "we will understand that these novels should be differently evaluated."

Readers still have more to learn from Malamud and Roth, and scholars need to readjust their views as each author's canon grows in length and complexity. Malamud's *The Tenants* and *Dubin's Lives* have confused some of his earlier admirers, who suspect his fascination with the artist is a sign of decadence; not so, argues Irving Malin in "Portrait of the Artist in Slapstick: Malamud's *Pictures of Fidelman*" (*LitR* 24:121–38), since this mid-career novel summarizes Malamud's treatment of the isolation of artistic creation versus the richer participation in life and establishes its centrality to all his novels. "The Jewbird," an odd little metafictional story collected in *Idiots First,* is analyzed by J. Gerald Kennedy as a "literary exorcism" which "effects a psychological release and completes the demystification (or detoxication) of the prior text" ("Parody as Exorcism: 'The Raven' and 'The Jewbird,'" *Genre* 13: 161–69). For all his own recent metafictional adventures Philip Roth is shown to be a realist, since his *The Ghost Writer* stacks the deck against fantasy, says Judith Yaross Lee in "Flights of Fancy" (*ChiR* 31,iv:46–52); in "The Novelist as Narcissus: Philip Roth's *My Life as a Man*" (*Descant* 24,i–ii:61–76) Ben Siegel counters that Roth's use of self eclipses simple realism in all his work since *Portnoy's Complaint.*

Holocaust literature has produced a growing and increasingly so-phisticated body of scholarship. Sidra DeKoven Ezrahi's *By Words Alone: The Holocaust in Literature* (Chicago) makes the case against conventionally aesthetic judgments, since the experience itself defies all standards of reason; so too have old forms proven inadequate to express this experience, and therefore "the new journalism" or "non-fiction novel" has been employed by the most successful Holocaust writers because it is a new form which "suggests a faith in memory over imagination and a loyalty to one's dead over the creations of one's mind." Real atrocities foreclose the conventions of art, Simone de Beauvoir believed: "I longed for all such lying beauty to be ut-terly destroyed." *A Double Dying: Reflections on Holocaust Litera-ture* (Indiana) is Alvin H. Rosenfeld's very apt title for the Holo-caust's two crises: the destruction of human lives but also of the language needed to express and protest that sacrifice. "How does what happens to human form, the form of man, seriously affect artis-tic form?" One postmodernist solution has been an aesthetics of silence, but "To submit to the finality of silence is to confirm, how-ever unwillingly, the triumphant nihilism of Nazism." Like Ezrahi, Rosenfeld traces in all genres of Holocaust writing a movement toward "assertiveness," a reaction "against the effacement of memory" and in favor of a reinforcement of "the idea and integrity of history" —these are the standards by which the literature must be judged. A collapse of such standards would be William Styron's novel *Sophie's Choice*, for its attempt "to universalize Auschwitz as a murderous thrust against 'mankind'" has the effect of "removing the Holocaust from its place within Jewish and Christian history and placing it within a generalized history of evil, for which no one in particular need be held accountable" and over which the "lying beauty" dis-paraged by Simone de Beauvoir can shed its voluptuous tears. The best known Holocaust writer in this country, Elie Wiesel, earns his place in Rosenfeld's aesthetic by virtue of his continuously inter-rogative and exclamatory modes—such is the thesis behind Ted L. Estess' fine critical biography *Elie Wiesel* (Ungar).

iv. Norman Mailer

Whether to take Norman Mailer as an intellectual spokesman or as an experimental fictionist is a debate created by two excellent books, Robert J. Begiebing's *Acts of Regeneration: Allegory and Archetype in the Works of Norman Mailer* (Missouri) and Jennifer Bailey's *Norman Mailer: Quick-Change Artist* (Barnes and Noble). Each scholar seizes upon Mailer's pronouncement in *Advertisements for Myself* that he wished to create "a revolution in the consciousness of our time" (the words Begiebing quotes) in order "to reshape reality in some small way with the 'fiction' as a guide" (Bailey's choice from the same source). Begiebing uses Jungian archetypes to establish an allegorical mode which supposedly motivates Mailer's quest through the various genres in search of "heroic consciousness." Rejecting *The Naked and the Dead* as "derivative naturalism" which suffers from "a mechanical use of narrative levels and symbols," Begiebing prefers to begin his analysis with *Barbary Shore* and proceed through *The Executioner's Song*, charting Mailer's "life-long obsession with the discovery of the deepest self." Jennifer Bailey is more interested with Mailer as a writer than as a thinker. For her, he is an "essentially innovatory" fictionist who "has attempted to transgress and transform the boundaries between literary genres" not in order to change consciousness but to transform reality itself. Hence for Bailey *The Naked and the Dead* is an important first step in exploring "the discrepancy that seems to exist between the individual and the world," and his use of the nonfiction novel is a much more important development than Begiebing would admit, since he sees Mailer committed to "the literature of ideas" and little else. A more nakedly biographical study by Andrew Gordon, *An American Dreamer: A Psychoanalytic Study of the Fiction of Norman Mailer* (Fairleigh Dickinson), gives support to Bailey, since Gordon's analysis shows how Mailer tends to be a romantic artist who wishes "to convert his own private fantasies into matters of public concern." Taking personal journalism as a cover for the making of "dream books" necessarily leads to cross-genre fertilization. Using Freud (plus Erik Erikson and Wilhelm Reich) instead of Jung gives Gordon a decided advantage over Begiebing when it comes to squaring accounts with Mailer's own self-publicized image.

The *Executioner's Song* dominated periodical criticism in 1980. In "Mailer: Settling for Less" (*Commentary* Feb.:65–67) Pearl K. Bell complains that Mailer has "no novelist's eye" for the Gary Gilmore materials and therefore cannot successfully wed the stuff of fact and imagination. Carl E. Rollyson's "Biography in a New Key"

(*ChiR* 31,iv:31–38) corrects this misapprehension by explaining that Mailer's typical flamboyancy of voice, his trademark in earlier non-fiction novels, would not be appropriate for *The Executioner's Song* where the announced intent of characterizing "innate evil" demands a spare and even artistically silent prose. John W. Aldridge's "An Interview with Norman Mailer" (*PR* 47:174–82) confirms Rollyson's belief with some excellent comments from Mailer on precisely why he avoided an *In Cold Blood*-style of fictionalization. Many readers, however, may not get beyond Mailer's quick answer to Aldridge's first question about motivation: "You know, when I was young, I used to meditate about literature, now I think about money. I never dare consider a book any longer just because it appeals to me."

v. Flannery O'Connor, Walker Percy, and the South

Criticism on O'Connor and Percy may be having a Greshman's Law effect on literary scholarship of the American South: the most useful work on each of them having been done several years ago, mediocre and repetitious criticism is smothering their reputations in banality and allowing precious little room for either genuinely new interpretations or for much consideration at all of other Southern writers.

One culprit is Robert Coles's *Flannery O'Connor's South* (LSU). Much like Barbara McKenzie's *Flannery O'Connor's Georgia* (Georgia), it memorializes other scholars' mind's-eye portraits of O'Connor's places, attitudes, and themes. The difference is McKenzie's book is largely given over to photographs—valid enshrinements of O'Connor's world—whereas Coles's labors on for 166 pages to tell us what we already know and to further hector us about such "human dramas." Reducing O'Connor's richly textured prose to a series of quaintly social messages is the last thing other scholars and readers need, and the volume's numerous factual misreadings and questionable interpretations (detailed by Joel Conarroe, *AL* 53:138–140) are a positive misservice. In a much stronger study, *Flannery O'Connor's Dark Comedies* (LSU), Carol Shloss explains in effect why Coles and others must spend so much time belaboring the obvious in O'Connor's themes. O'Connor wished to establish "a private topology of biblical analogs" among her contemporary characters; but because, as she said, "My audience are the people who think God is dead," she could not be satisfied with inference alone and so added a thick level of rhetoric to heighten her stories' meanings. "Interpretation is a constructive process," Shloss reminds us, but adds that "a reader constructs according to identifiable qualities of language." When those qualities are located in narrative voice, dramatization, and other formal techniques, O'Connor's work inspires rewarding reading. But to this reviewer O'Connor's rhetoric, especially when needlessly heightened, prompts the worst kind of sentimental handwringing and patronizing explanations.

"Flannery O'Connor's stories shock her readers by their violence and horror, but . . .": it seems this sentence appears in every formula-O'Connor essay written in the past 20 years; only in the pioneering work of Ihab Hassan's *Radical Innocence* (1961) was it an original and insightful statement. Horton Davies' "Anagogical Signals in Flannery O'Connor's Fiction" (*Thought* 55:428–38) agrees with Shloss to the extent that a readership familiar with traditions of the Catholic Church would be more receptive to her "inference" and less in need of her "rhetoric"; "theological pointers" are Davies' characterization of what Shloss calls rhetorical devices. In "The Moral Meaning of Flannery O'Connor" (*ModA* 24:274–83) Henry McDonald claims that "while O'Connor effectively transcended sectarianism, she at the same time made few if any concessions to the secularist mentality of those whom she mainly wrote for." Diane Tolomeo's "Home to her True Country: The Final Trilogy of Flannery O'Connor" (*SSF* 17: 335–41) takes the standard line on O'Connor's use of violence (that her stories ended with a shock in order to startle an unbelieving audience) and shows how her last three stories ("Revelation," "Parker's Back," and "Judgement Day") locate the predictable moment of violence earlier so that "the remainder of the story can then be concerned with the implications such as awareness holds for the character." J. O. Tate's "Flannery O'Connor's Counterplot" (*SoR* 16: 869–78) is one of many all-too-familiar apologies for O'Connor's "dark energies"; she is no more of the Devil's party than was Milton, Tate argues, because she only uses sinful material as "counterplot" to her "celebration of [the world's] beauty and vitality." Paul W. Nisly disagrees, saying *Wise Blood* and other characteristic works show how when O'Connor's characters sense their isolation from others they simply turn inward and thus reaffirm that isolation ("The Prison of the Self: Isolation in Flannery O'Connor's Fiction," *SSF* 17:49–54).

The publication of Walker Percy's *The Message in the Bottle* has set off a debate over the pertinence of his linguistic theory to his fiction. James Walter argues against it, claiming that "a neglect of the artistic integrity of his novels" comes from "efforts to read them primarily as illustrations of concepts more schematically presented in the essays." The symbolism which emerges from the novels themselves involves "three basic myths that vie for dominance in contemporary culture": humanism, Christian salvation, and secular comforts ("Spinning and Spieling: A Trick and a Kick in Walker Percy's *The Moviegoer,*" *SoR* 16:574–90). On the other side is J. P. Telotte, whose "A Symbolic Structure for Walker Percy's Fiction" (*MFS* 26:227–40) claims scholarship must move beyond simple existentialist explication of Percy's thought to its true roots in the philosophy of Charles Sanders Peirce. The novelist is a prophet, correcting secular notions of reality; since man understands his world through a symbolic medium, the "naming act," fictional descriptions of reality can be the best way to keep our culture in touch with its own creative impulses (*Love in the Ruins,* where the protagonist speaks correctively rather than confessionally, is the key).

The speculations of Telotte and others fill a special issue of *SoQ* 18,iii:1–166, which is reprinted (excepting Randolph Bates's review of Percy scholarship [pp. 158–164], which the book's Introduction confusingly refers to as present) as *Walker Percy: Art and Ethics,* ed. Jac Tharpe (Miss.). Unlike Panthea Reid Broughton's comprehensive collection *The Art of Walker Percy* (1979), Tharpe's gathering of original pieces is restricted to *The Message in the Bottle* and *Lancelot,* hence favoring the discursive side of this major novelist and thinker; but together with Broughton's book it constitutes a rich and satisfactorily complete harvest of Percy material. Telotte continues his advocacy of Percy's linguistic theory as a key to his fiction in "Charles Peirce and Walker Percy: From Semiotic to Narrative" (65–79); man's failure to be "uniquely human" is the job of the theoretician to point out and the novelist to solve: "Through his linguistic model, Percy holds out the hope that proper communication can help reverse this modern tendency [the ignoring of interrelationship] and better enable man to deal with his natural condition as 'exile and wanderer.'" Other essays debate Percy's humanism versus evidence of his fundamentalist Christian opposition to it as a secular distraction. Robert Brinkmeyer, Jr.'s "Percy's Bludgeon: Message and Narrative Strategy" (pp. 80–90) cites *Lancelot* as an argument in favor of "the old via dolorosa" and against "the rosy way of scientific humanists." Susan S. Kissel's "Voices in the Wilderness" (pp. 91–98) presents the even more frightening spectre in Percy's work of humanistic love being rejected in preference to Christian militancy ("the sword"). The more salutary influences of Heidegger and other existentialist sources are explored respectively by Charles P. Bigger and Lewis A. Lawson in "Walker Percy and the Resonance of the Word" (pp. 53–54) and "Moviegoing and *The Moviegoer*" (pp. 26–42). Other essays by John Edward Hardy, Michael Pearson, Corinne Dale, Jerome C. Christensen, and Cecil L. Eubanks (not to mention the painstakingly complete primary and secondary bibliography by the indefatigable Joe Weixlmann and Daniel H. Gann) all make their valuable points; the collection as a whole is essential.

Less innovative but helpful as a general introduction (if readers still need one) is Joe Holley's "Walker Percy and the Novel of Ultimate Concern" (*SWR* 65:225–33), which outlines the "radical disquiet" experienced by each of Percy's narrators, the inadequacy of "conventional religious, social, and scientific pieties" to answer their needs, the bland unawareness of their doltish mates (a bit of misogyny here of which Percy may not be guilty), and a final condemnation of "abstraction" as a sure way to lose one's individuality. Martin Luschei's *The Sovereign Wayfarer* (1972) says all this better, but as with O'Connor criticism American literary scholarship seems fated to decades of repetition when it comes to weighty moral fictionists. Two less repetitive essays are Lewis A. Lawson's "Walker Percy's Silent Character" (*MissQ* 33:123–40) which complements Dale's piece in Tharpe's collection with a carefully-outlined pattern of meetings in *Lancelot* ("an implicit structure" imbedded in the more obvious chronological one) between Lancelot and Percy and Thomas Young's "A New Breed: Walker Percy's Critics" (*MissQ* 33:489–98), a review-essay which makes the interesting point that Percy denies his Southern roots in order to avoid an easy optimism which his own childhood traumas obviate.

Two general and two single-author studies round out the year's work on Southern literature. In "Violence, Passion, and Sexual Racism: The Plantation Novel in the 1970s" (*SoQ* 18,ii:60–72) Christopher D. Geist establishes a "plantation formula" for historical novels of the South in recent years; not surprisingly, "The appeal of this fiction is its complex mixture of folk beliefs about blacks and the psychological fantasies and insecurities of whites," but Geist's structural charts lend added credibility to the argument that "The popularity of these novels indicates a continuing fascination with and fear of black sexuality on the part of white readers." Louis D. Rubin, Jr.'s "The Boll Weevil, the Iron Horse, and the End of the Line: Thoughts on the South" (in his *The American South: Portrait of a Culture* (LSU, pp. 346–71) is a personal reminiscence which touches the works of both Walker Percy and his uncle, William Alexander Percy; the lesson is that despite all fond memories "there never was any such generation of earlier heroes who were exempt from human straits and contingency," and that to imagine so is "actually a romantic escape from the compromised actuality of human life in time." Shelby Foote and Reynolds Price are the only two contemporary Southerners not swept away by the flood of O'Connor and Percy scholarship. Robert L. Phillips' "Shelby Foote's Bristol in 'Child by Fever'" (*SoQ* 19:172–83) discusses time as history, while Michael Kreyling's "Motion and Rest in the Novels of Reynolds Price" (*SoR* 16:853–68) looks back on Price's earlier work but focuses on the use of St. Augustine's *Confessions* within the dialogue structure of *The Surface of Earth* to establish Price's multilevel complexity (which "equips his novels to speak on the multiple levels on which his listeners need narrative").

vi. Older Realists: Truman Capote, Gore Vidal, Mary McCarthy, Paul Goodman, William Goyen, and Lionel Trilling

Helen S. Garson's *Truman Capote* (Ungar) is a disappointingly pedestrian account; her approach to Capote's career is more biographical than critical, and for the novels and stories she offers more synopsis than analysis. Robert J. Stanton's superbly comprehensive *Truman Capote: A Reference Guide* (Hall) provides the materials for a much better study; attention to Capote by a group of French academics centered on the brilliant young French scholar Régis Durand (in a special issue of *DeltaES*, No. 11) suggests that major work on his full career may not be far off. In "Capote's 'Miriam' and the Literature of the Double" (*IFR* 7:53–54) Michael J. Larsen uses this very early story to establish that Capote set off to be more than just a fantasist, and that his use of the Dopplegänger creates the impression of objective reality (as opposed to its usual gothic embodiments). Capote's "third stage"—the nonfiction novel—is given excellent treatment in John Hellmann's "Death and Design in *In Cold Blood*: Capote's 'Nonfiction Novel' as Allegory" (*BSUF* 21,ii:65–78). Capote's "goal of timelessness and perception of symbolic significance" pushes journalism beyond conventional fiction itself into "fabulation" (Robert Scholes's term for narrative which exploits the joy of its own manner of telling). "By constructing an allegory which is journalistic in subject matter and realistic in formal method," Hellmann explains, "Capote presents a fabulist vision which has both the credibility of promised fact and the authority of apparent objectivity." *Apparent* is the key word, for the patterns of allegory Capote abstracts from our culture lead to a deliberate blankness, thus creating "an allegory of possible meanings, not meaning."

Gore Vidal seems fated to be shelved as a simple satirist. Charles Berryman's "Satire in Gore Vidal's *Kalki*" (*Crit* 22,ii:88–96) makes a convincing argument for reducing this recent work to a simple satiric complaint against the superstitious elements of religion. Vidal seals the case in *Views From a Window*, 20 years of commentary "selected, arranged and introduced" by Robert J. Stanton and co-edited by the two (Lyle Stuart). Mixed in with Vidal's views on fiction and current events are revealing little nuggets from other aspects of his public life, such as his confessed upstaging of comedienne Louise Lasser on the set of "Mary Hartman, Mary Hartman"; with every breath, it seems, Vidal is a satirist at heart.

More promising is the scholarship on Mary McCarthy, and though only one fully original piece appeared this year, we are fortunate to have Irvin Stock's fine American Writer's Series pamphlet (Minn.) reprinted and expanded with a helpful analysis of *Birds of America* in Stock's *Fiction as Wisdom*. McCarthy is not the "heartless satirist" other critics perceive her to be; the "norms of decency" she suggests are just as positive as in her model Charles Dickens. *Birds of America* confirms this by showing how nature itself is less egalitarian than "the realm of minute particulars" and that all relationships within it cannot be treated alike. In "Nature as Birthright and Birthloss: Mary McCarthy and Colette" (*PCL* 5[1979]:42–54) Gayle Whittier compares the authors' childhood memoirs as they "reflect our post-Romantic sense of nature as the source of the sought self"; Colette "affirms the source" while McCarthy "rejects nature almost altogether" (hers is "a self to be outlived, not a childhood to be recreated").

Paul Goodman and William Goyen are the subjects of Twayne studies by Kingsley Widmer (TUSAS 358) and Robert Phillips (TUSAS 329) respectively. Although Goyen's fiction is given full and responsible treatment, Goodman's stature as an intellectual partisan leads Widmer to dismiss his novels (with some unfairness) as "so bad as to cast doubt on all his writing and thinking"; they are best seen "as the products of hobbyism," an approach which leads Widmer to consider themes only as they pale before the stronger statements of *Growing Up Absurd* and techniques only as they compare poorly with the superior efforts of Bernard Malamud. Goyen himself speaks nostalgically about San Antonio and the genesis of *House of Breath* with John Igo in "Learning to See Simply: An Interview with William Goyen" (*SWR* 65:267–84); since his purge by the New University Conference in the late-'60s and his death in 1972, Goodman languishes for want of such appreciation. Lionel Trilling flourishes in William M. Chace's study of that name (Stanford), though his short fiction (with its treatment of death as the great leveller) is seen as secondary to literary essays on the same topic while *The Middle of the Journey*'s roman à clef politics submerge that same theme.

vii. The Mannerists: John Updike and John Cheever

Updike scholarship is unique, profiting from year after year of first-class studies of a seemingly inexhaustible canon; 1980 was no exception, producing two excellent books which together explore both sides of this writer's intellectually pregnant art.

Suzanne Henning Uphaus does not let the introductory format of the "Modern Literature Monographs" inhibit her critical sense; *John Updike* (Ungar) not only covers the basics of Updike's work but is one of the most critically insightful books on his novelistic art. A "remarkable mastery of language" is common to all of Updike's writings, she observes (as have many others), but from this premise she explores his "profound sympathy for his characters that

his narrative voice conveys" and the revelation that "Metaphorical
language is, after all, an assertion that a reality exists beyond the
literal." Uphaus' readings are uniformly insightful, focusing on technique to make Updike's thematic messages all the more convincing.
George Hunt's *John Updike and the Three Great Secret Things: Sex,
Religion, and Art* (Eerdmans) is a similarly complete study from
the perspective of theme; each interest describes one element in the
succeeding thirds of Updike's career, and coupled with studies of
Søren Kierkegaard and Karl Barth the three establish "a religious
conviction that buttresses [Updike's] convictions about Art."

Uphaus and Hunt feel compelled by space limitations to spend
little time on Updike's short stories. Donald J. Greiner's forthcoming
study, *The Other John Updike*, will fill this gap, but in the meantime
Jerome Klinkowitz shows how *Olinger Stories* and *Too Far To Go:
The Maples Stories* reveal Updike's artistic self-consciousness at
work ("John Updike's America," *North American Review*, 265,iii:
68–71). Robert J. Nadon's "Updike's *Olinger Stories*: In the Middle
Landscape Tradition" (*PCL* 5[1979],62–68) makes a similar argument based on Crèvecoeur's geographical theory of American literary
response. Klinkowitz' chapter on Updike in *The Practice of Fiction*
(pp. 85–97) looks at the novels and senses a shift to postmodernism
as evidenced by a change in preference from the theologies of Karl
Barth to Paul Tillich (Hunt would disagree). Robert Detweiler en-
dorses the claims for a postmodernist Updike in "Updike's Sermons"
(*AAus* 5[1979]:11–26), citing Updike's interpolations of sermons
within fictions as evidence "that the boundary between fiction and
nonfiction is blurring increasingly" and (contra Hunt) that "If we
can no longer believe with the heart, we can still believe with the
imagination and thereby create models of originary [*sic*] and future
wholeness and integration." Detweiler's "Updike's *A Month of Sundays* and the Language of the Unconscious" (*Jour. of the Amer.
Academy of Religion* 47[1979]:609–25; also *Stürzl Festschrift*, 76–
100) marshalls support from Jacques Lacan and Jacques Derrida to
indicate that Updike is willing and anxious to explore themes embracing "language and the unconscious, self and other, the Imaginary
and the Symbolic, and the penis and the phallus." Detweiler returns
to Updike's Barthian metaphysics to show that "the inability to say
what we mean need not be the end of meaningful utterance."

Religious and in one instance political thought remain central to even the simplest essays on Updike. Ronald Wesley Hoag's "The Centaur: What Cures George Caldwell" (*SAF* 8:88–98) answers: "Vera Hummel . . . Caldwell must recover one paramount form of touching if he is to heal his mind/body split and become a whole man." On the other hand, womanly pleasures are a distracting foil to the male protagonist's "peculiar emotional malaise," says Dee Birch Cameron in "The Unitarian Wife and the One-Eyed Man: Updike's *Marry Me* and 'Sunday Teasing'" (*BSUF* 21,ii:54–64). In "Catharism and John Updike's *Rabbit, Run* (*Renascence* 32:229–39) Robert E. Hogan traces Rabbit's perfectionism to a 12th-century heretical sect discussed in Updike's acknowledged source, Dénis de Rougemont's *Love in the Western World*. Finally, Irving Leonard Markovitz faults Updike's "sense of self-indulgence and self-absorption" for perpetuating fallacies about African politics in *The Coup* ("John Updike's Africa," *CJAS* 14:536–45).

In an interview with Jo Brans ("Stories to Comprehend Life," *SWR* 65:337–45) John Cheever discussed his life and influences (notably E. E. Cummings) and praises John Gardner's *On Moral Fiction* for its commitment to "life." Robert A. Morace's "The Religious Experience and the 'Mystery of Imprisonment' in John Cheever's *Falconer*" (*Cithara* 20,i:44–53) is a major reading inspired by John Gardner's praise; Cheever's "depth of moral vision" enables the spiritual rebirth of his protagonist from various sorts of real and metaphorical confinement. Morace argues further that "salvation and freedom are not static conditions; rather they must be put to some appropriate use, and this is what the remainder of the book considers." Susan Gilbert's "Children of the Seventies: The American Family in Recent Fiction" (*Soundings* 63:199–213) uses *Falconer* as the mean for a discussion of a recent thematic variation (also evidenced in John Irving's *The World According to Garp*, Joan Didion's *A Book of Common Prayer*, and Wallace Stegner's *The Spectator Bird*) that "in a few much noted and noteworthy books of the last years of the seventies the cries of parents were drowning out those of their offspring." The nuclear family has failed, children have deserted their parents' world, Americans have no sense of past or of present community—these are the mannerist novel's new themes. Two interesting pieces by James O'Hara on vintage Cheever are " 'Independence Day at St. Botolph's: The Wapshot Saga Begins" (*MSE* 7,iii: 20–25) which finds in this story's themes and narrative details the experimental beginnings of Cheever's first major work, and "Cheever's *The Wapshot Chronicle*: A Narrative of Exploration" (*Crit* 22,ii:20–30) where the male's needs for escaping the female are examined.

viii. Newer Realists: Joyce Carol Oates, William Styron, E. L. Doctorow, John Gardner and Others

In *Joyce Carol Oates* (Ungar) Ellen G. Friedman clarifies what keeps the realists and the innovators in contemporary American fiction apart. "Along with the fabulators, Oates recognizes the fabulous quality in American life, but in her writing she makes an extraordinary peace with the reality of this life." Oates's motivation to do so, Friedman claims, comes from her emphasis on family ties among her characters' lives and because "the individual is always viewed in the perspective of the larger world—most often, in the perspective of culture and history." Such "self-conscious exploration of the American experience" carries an implicit thesis which Friedman sees as a paradigm "of American history. As America loosed its bonds from England, Oates's protagonists find themselves by a variety of routes free from the strictures of family, place, and history. Yet when they attempt to follow the imperatives of the self, they inevitably confront chaos, madness, or death." Under such conditions many of her characters are defeated, and some critics (notably Larry McCaffery and Mas'ud Zavarzadeh) would argue this stacking-of-the-deck makes for an escapist literature which ignores the transformed conditions of post-Modern life; but without challenging this argument (the newest contrary study Friedman quotes is Raymond M. Olderman's *Beyond the Waste Land* from 1972) Friedman is free to study Oates on the latter's own terms, and within this limited view presents an excellent picture of the realist at work. Joan D. Winslow's "The Stranger Within: Two Stories by Oates and Hawthorne" (*SSF* 17:263–68) and Eileen T. Bender's "Between the Categories: Recent Short Fiction by Joyce Carol Oates" (*SSF* 17:415–23) respectively discuss "Where Are You Going, Where Have You Been" as an exercise in shocking readers out of their simple categorizing of evil (so that they might recognize it in themselves) and the collections *The Hungry Ghosts* and *The Poisoned Kiss* as fragmented novels which explore the "predicament of the artist" caught between categories of the voiceless and the articulate, the traditional and the "new."

Some earlier critics of William Styron, says James L. W. West III, have been "hampered or led astray by biographical myths about him," and so constructs from reliable sources a helpful "William Styron: A Biographical Account" (*MissQ* 34:3–14). Meanwhile, Styron is given pages in *SAB* (45,ii:1–6) to spin his own account of early rejection (for the best, he claims) in "Almost a Rhodes Scholar: A Personal Reminiscence." Still more biography figures in "William Styron and the Spell of the South" (*MissQ* 34:25–36) in which Valarie Meliotes Arms traces "the dominant influence" of Styron's father and the essential "Southerness" of the young man's education. In "Styron's False Start: The Discarded Opening for *Set This House on Fire*" (*MissQ* 34:37–50) Arthur D. Casciato examines a false start among Styron's papers at the Library of Congress and finds "clues to Styron's conception of the 'square' narrator" (a "transformative" ocean journey, later dropped, did the trick). The year's best piece is John L. Cobbs's "Baring the Unbearable: William Styron and the Problem of Pain" (*MissQ* 34:15–24), which isolates "physical suffering" as Styron's "primary metaphor for the nature of man's empty and agonizing relationship with the universe," a central concern which "illuminates the internal integrity of his canon." Far less satisfactory is Robert Boyars' "The Weightless Characters of William Styron" (*Granta* No. 2, n.s.:158–66), a mushy critique of *Sophie's Choice* which condemns Styron for not giving his creations "free will." Some similar critiques of *The Confessions of Nat Turner* are answered by William J. McGill, whose "William Styron's Nat Turner and Religion" (*SAQ* 79:75–81) examines just what happens within the "religious dimension" of Turner's sermon (which is "reasonably consistent with what we can know of the real man").

The work of E. L. Doctorow has exerted a great staying power among scholars, far beyond the momentary dazzle of *Ragtime*. That the promotion of Doctorow's fourth novel was an exceptional affair is documented by Kathy Piehl in "E. L. Doctorow and Random House: The *Ragtime* Rhythms of Cash" (*JPC* 13:404–11), but Doctorow's own intentions are found to be meritorious in Barbara Cooper's "The

Artist as Historian in the Novels of E. L. Doctorow" (*ESRS* 29,ii:5–44). All along Doctorow has tried to bridge the distance between post-Cartesian novelistic philosophy and the reading habits of "working class people." Internal evidence shows that "Each of Doctorow's artist-figures . . . illustrates the problems of the writer. Each is an historian attempting to write about reality which each sees in a different way" as "The problems of the Cartesian universe take definite shape in Doctorow's four novels." History as either theme or technique occupies the more particular studies as well. Marjorie Gelus and Ruth Crowley trace the deep affinities of mode, theme, and philosophy in *Ragtime's* distant source, Henrich von Kleist's *Michael Kolhaas* ("Kleis [*sic*] and Ragtime: Doctorow's Novel, Its German Source and Its Reviewers," *JPC* 14:20–26). In *Welcome to Hard Times* Doctorow "looks at historical processes through the consciousness of an observer-recorder, and suggests that such processes tend to create the future in the image of the past, producing an inevitable cycling of history," says Marilyn Arnold ("History as Fate in E. L. Doctorow's Tale of a Western Town," *SDR* 18,i:53–63), while Peggy A. Knapp agrees the *The Book of Daniel* dramatizes "the pressures of the past on the present, the deaths of the fathers on the lives of sons", the thesis of her "Hamlet and Daniel (and Freud and Marx)" (*MR* 21:487–501). A long socioeconomic debate on the determining nature of money precedes David S. Gross's "Tales of Obscene Power: Money, Culture, and the Historical Fictions of E. L. Doctorow" (*Genre* 13,i; also *Money Talks*, pp. 71–92); Gross's conclusion is that "Doctorow uses irony to debunk the mystifications which support the illusions which keep us from facing the truths of the money complex." Cushing Strout uses an outdated view of fiction and history (C. Vann Woodward's versus Hayden White's) to deny Doctorow's innovative talents in *Ragtime* ("Historicizing Fiction and Fictionalizing History: The Case of E. L. Doctorow," *Prospects* 5:423–37). *The Book of Daniel* is superior, Strout claims, because of its "veracious" use of the imagination to deck out the historical past in charmingly humanistic clothes; *Ragtime*, however, is "voracious" as in the "black humor" experiments of John Barth, which Strout sees as mere "cleverness" incapable of being taken "seriously."

James Dickey's single novel *Deliverance* has not sustained scholarship at all. Chet Taylor's "A Look Into the Heart of Darkness: A View of *Deliverance* (*James Dickey, Splintered Sunlight: Interview, Essays, and Bibliography*, ed. Patricia De La Fuente, et al., Edinburg, Texas: Pan American Univ., 1979, pp. 59–64) presents a Freudian reading of "the organized pattern of guilt that holds society together" and its steady disintegration in Dickey's novel, while Ronald T. Curran cites the influence of biology and culture on Ed Gentry's behavior ("Biology and Culture: Hollywood and the Deliverance of Dickey's Weekend Backwoodsmen," *SoQ* 18,iv:81–90); most revealing is each critic's reliance upon film to make his point, as *Deliverance* yields itself up so easily to superficial readings. Worthy of more attention is "James Dickey: An Interview" which prefaces the Pan American collection (pp. 6–23), where Dickey decries James T. Farrell's "flatness and lack of interest," Faulkner's baggy misuse of language, and the need for style to shape vision—cautions which too many Dickey scholars have not heeded.

Nearly all John Gardner scholarship this year cues itself off the arguments of Gardner's own critical argument, *On Moral Fiction*. Leonard C. Butts sees nature as a standard of judgment in "Locking and Unlocking: Nature as Moral Center in John Gardner's *October Light*" (*Crit* 22,ii:47–60). In "New Fiction, Popular Fiction, and the Middle/Moral Way" (*FInt* 12:232–46) Robert A. Morace is more specific. He quotes Gardner: "Art leads, it doesn't follow. Art doesn't imitate life, art makes people do things." From this position Morace analyzes the innovative-novel-within-a-novel of *October Light* showing how it points out, "in comic fashion, the serious and harmful consequences for individuals and for society of fiction that is not morally responsible." With some daring Morace then cites Gardner's published appreciation of creators who do practice moral responsibility: Norman Rockwell and Walt Disney (Gardner's nastiest critics might make the same claim tongue-in-cheek). Richard C. Harris looks back to an earlier novel in "Ecclesiastical Wisdom and *Nickel Mountain*" (*TCL* 26:424–31) to find a less ridiculous moral model: Ecclesiastes, which as "Old Testament wisdom literature" examines the same "tragic sense of life" Gardner wishes to explore. Gardner is best served by John M. Howell's *John Gardner: A Bibliographical Profile* (So. Ill.), a masterful piece of work which not only scrupulously gathers all pertinent primary and secondary material but also frames this achievement within a lengthy "Chronology" sorting out several critical and textual problems.

There was a smattering of brief essays on other figures, all of whom deserve more extended treatment. William H. Gass's reconsideration of friend and colleague "Stanley Elkin's *The Franchiser*" (*NewRep* 28 June:29–32) praises this novel's insightful realism (how people are defined by menial jobs) but also its stylistic genius ("Elkin composes a song from the clutter of the country"). Gass argues that "Elkin is a visionary writer; he is a Brueghel or he is a Bosch," whose art succeeds by "the unerring instinct of the verbal eye." The career of a similarly comic stylist is surveyed by T. Jeff Evans in "Peter DeVries: A Retrospective" (*AHumor* 7,ii:13–16), with an emphasis on biographical influences and the "comic investigation of our cultural experience" in DeVries' recent *Consenting Adults*. In "The Apprentice Fiction of Peter DeVries" (*Crit* 21,iii:28–42) Evans takes the "battle of the sexes" featured in DeVries's first three novels and shows how it establishes both comic structure and vision of conflicts within the self. Don DeLillo is another realist whose vision is expressed *through* (rather than "by") language; Norman Bryson's "City of Dis: The Fiction of Don DeLillo" (*Granta* 2, n.s.:145–57) is the best introduction available, since it locates an "intricate, fluctuating *address* of speaker to speaker" in the "essentially acoustic" languages of *End Zone* (football), *Ratner's Star* (science), *Players*, and *Running Dogs* (each the language of the metropolis). How the Vietnam experience tests conventional notions of reality is studied in Arthur M. Saltzman's "The Betrayal of the Imagination: Paul Brodeur's *The Stunt Man* and Tim O'Brien's *Going after Cacciato*" (*Crit* 22,i:32–38); Thomas Berger's experiment with the American experience at large is reviewed in Michael Cleary's "Finding the Center of the Earth: Satire, History, and Myth in *Little Big Man*" (*WAL* 15:195–211). Frank W. Shelton discovers a less visionary and more autobiographical scheme in "Harry Crews: Man's Search for Perfection" (*SLJ* 12,ii:97–113), adding up to a thematic complaint against the "encroachment of modernism on the traditional Southern ways of life." A similar devotion to fiction which makes an "affirmation of human values" clouds John Gerlach's introduction to a much richer fictionist, Ann Beattie ("Through 'The Octascope': A View of Ann Beattie," *SSF* 17:489–94).

ix. Early Innovators: Paul Bowles, William S. Burroughs, Jack Kerouac, and John Rechy

Paul Bowles has had a rich and varied career, beginning with a surrealistic style of fiction which yielded to the "fantastically real" material of his African years; recent work shows him returning to surrealism as he explores abnormal states of mind, all clearly detailed by H. C. Ricks in "Another Country" (*ChiR* 31,iv:83–88). Two studies of William S. Burroughs also focus on his content, one pertinently (Michael B. Goodman, "The Customs' Censorship of William Burroughs' *Naked Lunch*," (*Crit* 22,i:92–104) and the other not (Donald Palumbo, "William Burroughs' Quartet of Science Fiction Novels as Dystopian Social Satire," *Extrapolation* 20[1979]:321–29), a misinterpretation of content which tries to justify Burroughs' *Naked Lunch* and its three sequels by the same misplaced analysis the custom officials used to condemn it. Much better is Anthony Channell Hilfer's "Mariner and Wedding Guest in William Burroughs' *Naked Lunch*" (*Criticism* 22:252–65) which examines Burroughs' treatment of the reader who is "either being seduced into complicity . . . or being warned against such seductions or both at once."

After years of neglect or of patronizing treatment at best, scholars have begun considering Jack Kerouac as a valid contributor to the American tradition defined so well by *Moby-Dick, Adventures of Huckleberry Finn,* and *The Great Gatsby.* Positive comparisons to these novels run through the newer essays collected in Scott Donaldson's critical edition of *On the Road* (Viking, 1979), especially the two original pieces by Örm Øverland ("West and Back Again," pp. 451–64) and Timothy A. Hunt ("*On the Road*: An Adventurous American Education," pp. 465–84). Øverland's is the more conservative piece, picturing Kerouac as drawn to home as "the final refuge"; *On the Road* shows just as much "resignation to life rather than acceptance" as the more domesticated *The Town and the City.* Hunt sees less need to make Kerouac sell out thematically to an earlier generation's standards; as for technique, *On the Road* "exhibits the control and distance typically associated with fiction [as opposed to autobiography]." Putting part 1 in perspective "suggests that *On the Road* is a more ambitious book thematically than its reputation indicates," since the novel is actually structured around Sal and not the more promiscuously attractive Dean.

Sadly, John Rechy scholarship still pussyfoots around with his sexually challenging themes and with his innovative approach to expressing them. Two of the three studies in a special section of *Minority Voices* (3,i[1979]) are hampered by the same prudish need to reaffirm "straight" values which precluded intelligent work on Kerouac for so long. Charles M. Tatum's "The Sexual Underworld of John Rechy" (pp. 47–52) rightly charts the progress of his first five novels in which "the myths of maternal, homosexual, and divine love have fallen one by one"; however, Tatum feels compelled to say of Rechy's sexual protagonist (without any supporting analysis) that "This life produces in him a slow decay of the soul, a decay more final than the physical decay of waning youth." "Odysseys in John Rechy's *City of Night*: The Epistemological Journey" (pp. 53–62) finds Carlos Zamora struggling to convince readers that "far from being principally a salacious book about homosexual life, it is an important achievement as a *Bildungsroman*." Only Juan D. Bruce-Novoa seems willing to take Rechy on his own revolutionary terms; indeed, "In Search of an Honest Outlaw: John Rechy" (pp. 37–45) calls him "an outlaw among sexual outlaws" because of his unwillingness to compromise his "Rechian dialectic" (which combines the Appolonian with the Dionysian) as he proceeds from his first novel through *The Sexual Outlaw*.

x. Innovative Fiction

a. **Ken Kesey and Joseph Heller.** The first wave of mainstream innovators has now become "as mythic as you can get," as the young Englishman Dick Madelin explains on his way to meet Ken Kesey and view the famous Pranksters' Bus now in mothballs with so many other legends which are these days "Down on the Farm with Ken Kesey" (*London Magazine* 20,v–vi:105–09). That Randall Patrick McMurphy sports "borrowed characteristics from western heroes" is reaffirmed by Mark Busby in "Eugene Manlove Rhodes: Ken Kesey Passed by Here" (*WAL* 15:83–92); Rhodes's *Pasó Por Aquí*, described as "one of the finest western stories ever written," is Kesey's model. In *The American 1960s* (Iowa State) Jerome Klinkowitz finds that Kesey's *One Flew Over the Cuckoo's Nest* and Heller's *Catch-22* anticipate the coming decade's disruptive and transformative politics.

All but one of the individual essays on Joseph Heller similarly incline themselves toward epic and myth. Yossarian is not described as an Assyrian for paltry reasons, argues Peter L. Hays in "Yossarian and Gilgamesh" (*NMAL* 4:Item 9); Susan Resneck Parr looks back to the Bible in "Everything Green Looked Black: *Catch-22* as an Inverted Eden" (*NMAL* 4:Item 27), as does Marcus K. Billson in "The Un-Minderbinding of Yossarian: Genesis Inverted in *Catch-22*" (*ArQ* 36:315–29), for when Yossarian resists the tempter Milo he "dismantles the old myth" of Adam's fall—Heller's new Adam shuns "the destructiveness of discourse" and so rejects the "mind bender." Albert E. Wilhelm's "Two Responses to Death in Heller's *Catch-22* (*IllQ* 42,iii:45–48) discusses "simple-minded pleasures" versus fortitude in a "time of stress." Terry Heller's "Notes on Technique in Black Humor" (*Thalia* 2,iii[1979]:15–21) finds the play with readers to be a bit more complex, as they are "suspended . . . between two extremes of response," the moral simplistics of each being self-cancelling.

b. **John Barth.** Whether in praise or damnation, mythologizing John Barth as an avatar of "the literature of exhaustion" has obscured what actually happens in his fictive innovations. Because it corrects these early attempts to eulogize Barth and offers in their place such clearheaded analyses of his art, Douglas Robinson's *John Barth's* Giles-Goat Boy: A Study (*Jyväskyla Studies in the Arts* 15, University of Jyväskyla, Finland) ranks as the most important contribution to scholarship since David Morrell's *John Barth: An Introduction* (1976). Though centered on Barth's massive fourth novel, Robinson's study makes frequent reference to the full career stretching through *Letters* (its regeneration of epistolary techniques is a road back to tradition after metafictional diversions). Barth's energy comes from his productively paradoxical tension between storytelling (celebrated in an "exuberance of metaphor") and a subtly undermining irony, just as his gingerly use of metafiction (there's no commitment to it as in Coover or Gass) calls metaphysics into question without cancelling it. Style, setting, story, and theme are each in turn rejuvenated by this tension. Robinson's brilliance is his ability to see how Barth eclipses the literature of silence which has swallowed up so many other fictionists: "one writes about truth as if it were truth, but constantly reminds the reader that it is fiction."

A study less cognizant of post-Modern considerations is Elaine B. Safer's "The Allusive Mode and Black Humor in Barth's *Giles Goat-Boy* and Pynchon's *Gravity's Rainbow*" (*Renascence* 32:89–104), which tells us that Barth and Pynchon yearn for "a commonly accepted set of values—such as existed in great Renaissance works like the King James Bible and the epic—and utilize this nostalgia and its contradiction in a fragmented universe to create the absurd" as Albert Camus defined it. A more culturally legitimate study (along the lines of Robinson's) is Richard Alan Schwartz' "Some Formal Devices in John Barth's Early Novels" (*NConL* 10,iii:6–8), which locates "important associations between opposites" in the structural and thematic resolutions to Barth's first two novels. An interesting sexual study is Cynthia Davis' "Heroes, Earth Mothers and Muses: Gender Identity in Barth's Fiction" (*CentR* 24:309–21), which finds a similar tension: women are reality symbols for Barth, but he prefers the "male side" in each mythic configuration (whether the romantic triangle or competition among males).

The stories of *Lost in the Funhouse* continue to inspire excellent analysis. Heide Ziegler ("John Barth's 'Echo': The Story in Love With its Author" [*IFR* 7:90–93]) says that, although his self-reflection was destructive in his first two novels and turned creative in subsequent work, "not until *Lost in the Funhouse* does Barth become aware of the exemplary nature of the process of his own irony and begin to reflect upon it." Exhausting the process of one's search for identity is what Sonja Bašić finds in the volume, "a story rendered both from the outside and from the inside . . . both about Life creating a Book and a Book creating Life" (*Yugoslav Perspectives*, pp. 185–205). The "innocence" of all this is discovered by Laura Rice-Sayre in "The Lost Construction of Barth's Funhouse" (*SSF* 17:463–73).

The 1979 publication of Barth's novel *Letters* has prompted a similar flow of essays, each appreciative of his first publication in seven years and reflective of his renewal of tradition. The best piece is by Larry McCaffery; his "Barth's *Letters* and the Literature of Replenishment" (*ChiR* 31,iv:75–82) associates Barth's achievement with Latin American Magic Realism as a return of fiction to life, and also finds its "reenactment" view of history suits Barth's authorial reenactment of artistic patterns. A more specific study of Barth's "external patterning" in this novel may be found in Gary Thompson's "Barth's Letters and Hawkes' Passion" (*MQR* 19:270–78), while Barth himself directs all questions on his earlier works into a discussion of his new novel in Heide Ziegler's important "Interview with John Barth" (*Granta* 2, n.s.:169–77). Of the two essays on *Letters* in *FInt* No. 12, John Domini's "*Letters* and Ethics: The Moral Fiction of John Barth" (pp. 246–57) claims the most, insisting that the novel "manages to recapitulate all American history, rising in the end to a drama of the conflict between those who make events happen and those who stand back to see their effect." Brian Stonehill's "A Trestle of *Letters*" (pp. 259–68) argues more modestly that Barth is simply trying to build bridges between "'postmodern' sophistication and the 'old-fashioned' springs of narrative" and "between the word as exploratory tool and the word as reflexive toy."

c. Thomas Pynchon. The very first reviews of Thomas Pynchon nearly two decades ago told readers of his encyclopedic use of science, technology, psychology, history, and religion. In *Pynchon's Fictions: Thomas Pynchon and the Literature of Information* (Ohio) John O. Stark simply catalogues Pynchon's information on these subjects (plus "film" and "literature" as evident in his later work) with no thought for their technical or thematic contributions to his art. Much more pertinent is David Cowart's work in *Thomas Pynchon: The Art of Allusion* (So. Ill.), the freshest view of Pynchon in years and (with William Plater's *The Grim Phoenix* [1978], which explains the use of science) one of the two truly essential books on this extremely demanding novelist. By shifting his inquiry from the philosophic implications of contemporary science to the imaginative, Cowart shows how "uncertainty has its positive aspect. It is somehow reassuring to be confronted afresh with evidence of mystery. Pynchon has it both ways, celebrating the promise of the unknown without blinking the horrors of the Void." By looking at Pynchon's use of art and music Cowart establishes that "the worlds of unplumbed reality hold infinite promise," open to the speculative talents of man which previous critics have slighted in his work.

Amazingly there were no essay-length studies of *V.* beyond Mark Siegel's introductory "Pynchon's Anti-Quests" (*PNotes* 3:5–9) which finds in all three novels an inverted pattern reflecting "the anguish caused by the contemporary sense of fragmentation of experience and values, the confusion and futility of attempting to understand the connections of past-to-present-to-future by traditional means." Pynchon's second novel gets two passes: Stephen D. Cox in "Berkeley, Blake, and the Apocalypse of Pynchon's *The Crying of Lot 49*" (*ELWIU* 7:91–99) who finds 18th-century roots for Oedipa's anxious empiricism; and William Nelson in "The Humor and Humanizing of Outrage" (*Thalia* 2,i–ii[1979]:31–34), who uses Garbiel García Márquez' Magic Realism as an analog for Pynchon's nonmimetic distancing (a stance which "involves a refusal to lapse into self-pity or dramatic posturing in the face of physical and spiritual disaster").

Pynchon's "big novel" continues to attract proportionate attention. An essential roadmap is "An Index to *Gravity's Rainbow*" prepared by Khachig Tölöyan and Clay Leighton (booklet published by *PNotes*), which lists references to proper names, acronyms, and capitalized nouns. A knowledge of Jung is also helpful, since the "apparently disparate items reveal their fundamental oneness by signals obvious only to an uninformed initiate," argues N. F. George in "The *Chymische Hochzeit* of Thomas Pynchon" (*PNotes* 4:5–22). Familiarity with "the deep intellectual disturbances which the seventeenth-century 'scientific revolution' set off in the Romantic world" and "the Romantic radicals' traumatic recognition of gravitation as a demonic force" is also pertinent, as Joel D. Black explains in "Probing a Post-Romantic Paleontology: Thomas Pynchon's *Gravity's Rainbow*" (*Boundary* 8,ii:229–54). Not surprisingly all this "encyclopedic detail" forces Pynchon's readers to "systemize this work to make any sense of it," explains Linda A. Westervelt ("A Place Dependent on Ourselves: The Reader as System-Builder in *Gravity's Rainbow*" [*TSLL* 22:69–90]). Lawrence Kappel studies the landscape of European culture to show how Pynchon creates a spy novel as his protagonist moves toward "monstrous self-knowledge, and finally oblivion" ("Psychic Geography in *Gravity's Rainbow*," *ConL* 21:225–51). The two best essays on this novel, however, are those which face Pynchon's challenge squarely. Douglas Fowler ("Pynchon's Magic World," *SAQ* 79:51–60) brushes off suggestions that the author is a bottom-line humanist and insists his impulses are "largely gothic" as he creates "a magic world more interesting than ours." Richard Pearce explains this crucial difference in cultural terms, a departure from Whitman's "barbaric nature" (the direction of which poets could divine) in favor of something radically different: "As Pynchon approaches *Gravity's Rainbow* he realizes all the implications of the 'original energy' that early writers could either not accept or not reflect in a literary form. He finally evolves a novel of motion rather than movement—a novel which abrogates direction, which focuses on the field of forces that governs contemporary life" ("Thomas Pynchon and the Novel of Motion," *MR* 21:177–95).

d. John Hawkes, Jerzy Kosinski, and Susan Sontag. Hawkes's celebrated trilogy—*The Blood Oranges*; *Death, Sleep and the Traveler*; and *Travesty*—continues to get most critical interest. C. J. Allen's "Desire, Design, and Debris: The Submerged Narrative of John Hawkes' Recent Trilogy" (*MFS* 25:579–92) suggests that "the power of the conscious mind is gradually undermined by unconscious needs and fears." William F. Van Wert relates this movement to the development from children's fears to adults' fantasies ("Narration in John Hawkes' *Trilogy*," *LitR* 24:21–39), while Charles Baxter claims there is symbolic violence against the reader in the final novel ("In the Suicide Seat: Reading John Hawkes's *Travesty*," *GaR* 34:871–85); Baxter notes how Hawkes "asserts his own authority by inventing games the reader must learn," particularly lessons on "the imagination's amoral powers." A similar reader-oriented study touching Hawkes's *The Lime Twig* (Terry Heller's "Notes on Technique in Black Humor" cited for Joseph Heller above) shows how Hawkes "provides signals that the [terrifying] event could be humorous to others knowing less than the reader or even to the reader if the situation were just slightly different." Paul J. Emmett's "*The Cannibal* to *The Passion Artist*: Hawkes's Journey Toward the Depths of the Unconscious" (*ChiR* 32,i:135–52) examines the distortions of the psychologically real as they appear in surface reality; Hawkes's movement through twelve books of fiction has been from an initial irrealism through realism and now back to irrealism again.

The person of Jerzy Kosinski remains as fascinating as his fiction. In his somewhat sensationalized biography *The Roman Polanski Story* (Grove) Thomas Kiernan discusses Kosinski's reputation as a student in Poland, his friendship with the controversial director (dating from 1950, not 1956 as Kiernan misrecords), and the role *The Painted Bird* played in Polanski's expatriate experience. This first novel continues to interest scholars, from Wayne D. McGinnis' "Transcendence and Primitive Sympathy in Kosinski's *The Painted Bird*"

(*StHum* 8,i:22–27), which identifies polar opposites within the novel through Terry Heller's essay (op. cit.) which admires Kosinski's use of traditional tales "to create comic expectations" which he then shatters with unexpected horror. *Steps* and *Being There* interest Earl B. Brown, Jr. ("Kosinski's Modern Proposal: The Problem of Satire in the Mid-Twentieth Century," *Crit* 22,ii:83–87), who argues that their respective attempts to find order in an illogical manner and to blithely ignore the conventional "steps" in life demonstrate that "Without shared assumptions, without absolute standards of right and wrong, satire cannot exist" except "as horror." Paul R. Lilly, Jr. is more optimistic: his "Jerzy Kosinski: Words in Search of Victims" (*Crit* 22,ii:69–82) finds in all seven of Kosinski's novels to date a "relationship between victim and oppressor" which is "conceived in terms of conflicting languages" and therefore resolvable through "the creation of a counterlanguage from another language, and the transformation of the self from vulnerability to strength, from victim to oppressor, by means of an act of language."

Two studies by Daniel J. Cahill and a third by Jerome Klinkowitz view the full canon in terms of Kosinski's professed aim to write a five-book cycle (from *The Painted Bird* through *Cockpit*) centered on the struggles between collective culture and the individual, followed by a full synthesis in *Blind Date* and the beginning of a second, more artistically personal stage in *Passion Play*. Cahill's "Kosinski and His Critics" (*NAR* 265,i:66–68) describes how his novels since *Steps* make him less an experimentalist and more a writer in "the tradition of classic European modernism, a tradition in which ideas are as important as physical sensation"; in *Passion Play* "Kosinski is answering his critics through the alter-ego character of Fabian" (who like Kosinski writes "manuals of safety in a high-risk game"). Cahill's historically and analytically comprehensive "Jerzy Kosinski: A Play on Passion" (*ChiR* 32,i:118–34) is the most useful single piece yet published on this complex and sometimes confusing author; all seven novels plus occasional essays and interviews are interpreted for their development of Kosinski's "grand theme—man in collision with society." His intention is "to expose the vanity of humanistic mythology, leaving only the strength or weakness of a determined self." Having followed the self's progress through the early novels, Cahill sees the more recent work as "a second stage" centered on "the development of a highly potent mind and soul

which is not capable any more of self-definition but is still capable
of individualizing the definitions proposed or given by a large collective society." This direction leads to the "most inward" and "wis-
est" of all protagonists, the person who is "all insight and instinct"
—qualities which Cahill believes Kosinski has established as his own.
In the "Postface: 1980" to his revised *Literary Disruptions* Jerome
Klinkowitz claims an even greater change in Kosinski's "ideology"
which now favors autobiographical candor and more blatantly discursive statement. *Blind Date* becomes "an *auto-bibliography*, the
furthest extreme from Kosinski's careful self-detachment from the
subjects of *The Painted Bird.*"

The publication of Susan Sontag's collected stories in *I, Etcetera*
(1978) should have produced much good retrospective scholarship.
The best is Benjamin Taylor's "A Centered Voice: Susan Sontag's
Short Fiction" (*GaR* 34:907–16), which spends much time on postmodernist philosophy and her own literary aesthetics to conclude
that if she has written her short fiction "out of the nothing (and not
the Montaignian everything) of the self, she has done so in the hard
teeth of a paradox: reduced to nullity, the self is still something;
wizened into impotence, it yet retains the genius for a new beginning; given up to disintegration, it persists withal as our strength to
conceive a personal future, to make choices, to be ready." Cary Nelson fears that this aesthetic leads instead to a "profound silence"
and an alienation from the text ("Soliciting Self-Knowledge: The
Rhetoric of Susan Sontag's Criticism," *CritI* 6:707–26). In her interview with Monika Beyer in *Polish Perspectives* 23,ix:42–46, "A Life
Style is not a Life," Sontag virtually despairs of great fiction coming
from the current American experience (looking instead to Eastern
Europe and Latin America) but understands that, to survive, the
novel "can either be the most vulgar entertainment competing with
television or it must become art, and consequently have a limited
audience."

e. Donald Barthelme, Robert Coover, and William H. Gass. That
Donald Barthelme's metafictional themes parallel his personal ones,
especially in his first collection *Come Back, Dr. Caligari*, is clear from
Larry McCaffery's detailed analysis in "Donald Barthelme and the
Metafictional Muse" (*Sub-Stance* 27:75–88). In *After the Wake*
(Clarendon) Christopher Butler finds that "experimental writing has

often been most effective when it has incorporated popular content";
he praises *Snow White* for its "particularly satirical relationship with
contemporary society, without losing in any way its fantastic qualities." Three studies by Jerome Klinkowitz show how Barthelme has
become the successor to John O'Hara and John Updike as a *New
Yorker*-style imagist (*The American 1960s*); how his story "Por-
cupines at the University" uses ready-made items from our culture
which in collage-fashion refer to themselves even as they create a
new reality (*The Practice of Fiction in America*); and how in *The
Dead Father* and *Great Days* the narrative voice effaces itself in
favor of linguistic play (*Literary Disruptions*, revised ed.). Régis
Durand agrees with this last point in "On Conversing: In/On Writing" (*Sub-Stance* 27:47–51), reminding socially and morally inclined
critics (such as Robert A. Morace) that "In Barthelme, although
there are enough loose fragments or remnants of codes to keep a
semiotician on his toes, the dynamics of the stories lie elsewhere":
not in the phatic nor in the affective function but rather in "pure
transaction"—in "the existence of speech itself, the conditions and the
circumstances in which it can survive the invasions of 'dreck,' the
tedium of repetition, the hazards of pure violence."

Coover scholarship has split in two directions: those who see him
committed to exposing the fictionalization of history (Richard Martin commenting on *The Public Burning* in "Clio Bemused," *Sub-
Stance* 27:13–24) and others who seem in taking conventions from
other media (here silent film) to reshape his fictional text (Charla
Gabert discussing *Charlie in the House of Rue* in "The Metamorphosis of Charlie," *ChiR* 32,ii:60–64). William H. Gass inspires contradictory responses within individual critics. Don Guttenplan cannot
decide if his words are referential to the outside world or to themselves ("The Wor(l)ds of William Gass," *Granta* 1, n.s.[1979]:147–
60), while Charles Caramello suspects that Gass's allegiance to the
"book, word, and authority" creates an ambivalence in terms of the
writerly oppositions established by Jacques Derrida and Roland
Barthes ("Fleshing Out *Willie Masters' Lonesome Wife*," *Sub-Stance*
27:56–69).

f. Kurt Vonnegut, John Irving, and Tom Robbins. Kurt Vonnegut's
use of science plus the figure of Vonnegut himself dominate the
year's scholarship, each to good effect. Charlie Reilly's excellent "Two

Conversations with Kurt Vonnegut" (*CollL* 7:1–29) finds the author candid and articulate about a number of subjects concerning him as he worked on *Slapstick* and *Jailbird*. In "Kurt Vonnegut on Censorship and Moral Values" (*MFS* 26:631–35) Richard Ziegfeld performs a valuable service by sorting through publishers' files and transcripts of interviews to establish Vonnegut's attitudes toward the banning of his own books and the larger implications of such acts (Vonnegut's thoughtfully argued letter to the Drake, N. D. school board is reprinted in full).

In *The Cybernetic Imagination in Science Fiction* (MIT) Patricia S. Warrick ranks *Player Piano* as among the first and "the best dystopian fiction picturing a cybernetic future" because of Vonnegut's "authenticity" (its action is set but a short distance forward in time and draws realistic details from Vonnegut's work at General Electric). Robert L. Nadeau has similar praise in "Physics and Metaphysics in the Novels of Kurt Vonnegut, Jr." (*Mosaic* 13,ii:37–47). Like Warrick he finds Vonnegut less of a "science fiction" writer than a "metaphysician" who draws ideas from physics as a way of articulating the human condition. Ellen Cronan Rose agrees; her "It's All a Joke: Science Fiction in Kurt Vonnegut's *The Sirens of Titan*" (*L&P* 29[1979]:160–68) reminds us that the novel's "science fiction components are . . . wildly implausible" and that by "not making jokes *about* science fiction, but *with* it" Vonnegut achieves the displacement characteristic of Freud's "tendentious jokes." *Slapstick* shows Vonnegut being less tendentious, Jerome Klinkowitz suggests in *Literary Disruptions*; only with *Jailbird* does he perfect a structure for his newly assumed moral spokesmanship. In *The Practice of Fiction* Klinkowitz further argues that a change in genre from fiction to drama caused Vonnegut's vision of social change to take a 180-degree turn; his redefinitions of what constitutes the social good are detailed in Klinkowitz' *The American 1960s*. Peter C. Mayer argues that Vonnegut's sense of structure in *Slaughterhouse-Five* is essentially "filmic" and that his writing "displays techniques which can be considered as "photographic" to the point of inspiring its own cinematic adaptation ("Film, Ontology, and the Structure of a Novel," *LFQ* 8:204–08); Mayer should know, however, that the character Billy Pilgrim and the autobiographical voice which speaks as Kurt Vonnegut are not the same figure, especially since the latter's role was dropped from the film.

Vonnegut's successors are the highly-praised John Irving (his former student from the Iowa Writers Workshop) and the widely-popular Tom Robbins (who together with Rob Swigart, William Kotzwinkle, and Gerald Rosen writes what Jerome Klinkowitz in *The Practice of Fiction* approvingly calls "Bubble Gum Fiction"). In the year's most brilliant essay on contemporary fiction Terrence Des Pres explains just how Irving's four novels to date confront the "sinister energy" of post-Modern life; by forgoing the escapist "aid of tragic resolution" they create a "mode of compassion" which makes "human communion" possible ("Against the Under Toad," *London Magazine* 20,iv:49–56; reprinted in part as the Introduction to *3 by Irving* [Random House]). Mark Siegel suspects Zen wisdom is behind Tom Robbins' infectiously comic fiction (*Tom Robbins*, WWS 42); he reaches even farther to claim that by virtue of Robbins' "romantic vision . . . pioneering spirit . . . climactic showdowns . . . [and] conflicts between unambiguously good and bad guys" he is a Western novelist. Siegel is on safer ground when he claims "Robbins shows that the outdated vision of . . . mechanistic physics is responsible for our dysfunctional, reactionary metaphysics"—a point other critics have made about Kurt Vonnegut.

g. Raymond Federman, Ronald Sukenick, Clarence Major, Gilbert Sorrentino, Walter Abish, and Kenneth Gangemi. Federman, Sukenick, and Major are a common triumvirate in the avant-garde of innovative fiction: comments on their collectively enriching recent work fill the pages of Jerome Klinkowitz' *Literary Disruptions* and *The Practice of Fiction* while his *The American 1960s* and Christine Brooke-Rose's "Where Do We Go From Here?" (*Granta* 3, n.s.:161–88) debate the centrality of Sukenick's aesthetics to their common program. The best study of them yet, however, is Peter Quartermain's "Trusting the Reader" (*ChiR* 32,ii:65–74), an essential inquiry into how fiction can be written given the axioms that "life and fiction are no longer distinguishable from one another" and that "writing should be a thrust into reality rather than a retreat into literature." Major avoids the exposition to which so much illusionistic fiction is given over—instead, his statements alert the reader to his artifice. Sukenick "avoids the problem altogether by writing prose which is largely internal speech." He therefore moves into silence, whereas "Federman's voice comes from it and struggles toward articulation" as he tries to speak the unspeakable. Quartermain's absolutely essential conclusion is that "Major and Sukenick and Federman use pre-existent narrative as something to refer to, not as structure, and they are thus freed into the writing itself as a source of structure."

Implications behind such fiction are explored by Federman himself and by Charles Caramello in complementary essays on "The Self in Fiction" featured in *Descant* (24,i–ii), "From Past Self to Present Self" (pp. 51–53) and "Authorial Self, Textual Self" (pp. 54–56). How moral instruction figures in the same aesthetic is discussed by Caramello in his major study of Kenneth Gangemi, "On the Guideless Guidebooks of Postmodernism: Reading *The Volcanoes from Puebla* in Context" (*Sun & Moon* 9–10:59–99). The interesting structural accommodation made by Gilbert Sorrentino in *Mulligan Stew* is examined by Jerome Klinkowitz in *Literary Disruptions* ("the 'living novel' is expanded to allow the full range of writing techniques—narrative, notebooks, source material, author's letters, character's complaints. . . . Every element of the book being made is an invitation for Sorrentino to display all the excitement his pen can command") and by Douglas Messerli in "Experimental and Traditional Forms in Contemporary Literature" (*Sun & Moon* 9–10:3–25), who shows how "Sorrentino directly enters into the fiction through the play of words. His fiction does not present a life as lived, but a life as it is being lived in linguistic presentism." Arthur M. Saltzman praises the novel's comprehensiveness ("Wordy Tombs," *ChiR* 31,iv: 95–99): "for Sorrentino these inventories represent not only the sheer weight of cultural and pseudo-cultural 'dreck' in the world, but also Sorrentino's capacity for reinvigorating language by placing it in unusual and surprising forms."

Contemporary fiction which responds fully to its age, rather than seeking an easy escapism in superannuated paradigms from the past, uses language in a self-apparent manner central to the philosophical debates of our era but foreign to the methodology of too many Americanists who find it easier to synopsize plot and gossip about characters. In last year's *ALS* Jonathan Morse suggested that "Americanist scholars as a group have some theoretical homework to do." Two who have done their work are Tony Tanner and Alain Arias-Misson, though their proximity to European centers of theory gives them an edge. Their respective studies of Walter Abish ("Present Imperfect: A Note on the Work of Walter Abish," *Granta* 1, n.s.

[1979]:65–72; "The Puzzle of Walter Abish: *In the Future Perfect*," *Sub-Stance* 27:115–24) find in his fiction what Tanner calls an essentially American outlook: "that by opening up new possibilities (and disrupting old clusterings) in the language system" which Abish sees as determining behavior "the writer by the same token is opening up new possibilities in our life networks. It is a brave hope—though sometimes, I think, a fond one." Arias-Misson draws on the thought of Michel Foucault and Jacques Derrida to show how Abish works within the "unreadable text" of our culture; writing is an "impenetrable membrane" between the reader and event which only the most careful technique can pierce—mindless mimesis only alienates us all the more from the "voided metaphysical assumptions" of our culture.

xi. Sub-Genres

a. The New Journalism.   Of the six significant studies which consider the nonfiction novel, five are polarized on theoretical grounds: those who accept the aesthetic changes involved in the postmodernist transformation praise this subgenre, while those who don't condemn it. Only Ronald Weber in *The Literature of Fact: Literary Nonfiction in American Writing* (Ohio) finds a way to praise it from conventional standards. "The art of narrative, in fact, is the same," he quotes from Robert Louis Stevenson, "whether it is applied to the selection and illustration of a real series of events or of an imaginary series." Weber therefore denies that there is anything "radically innovative" in the work of Tom Wolfe, Norman Mailer, Gay Talese, and others; instead, he accepts Tom Wolfe's thesis that in the 1960s innovative fictionists abandoned their Dickensian duty to report realistically on the world they lived in and left journalists to assume the job, who in the process could pick up the discarded conventions of plot, character, development-by-dialogue, symbolic inference, and the like.

John Hersey ("The Legend on the License," *YR* 70:1–25) and Ivo Vidan ("The Capitulation of Literature? The Scope of the 'Nonfiction Novel,'" *Yugoslav Perspectives*, pp. 157–80) are much less optimistic. The practitioners of the New Journalism have done nothing to save the standards with which Weber and Wolfe have entrusted them. "The writer of fiction must invent," Hersey acknowledges, but then cautions: "The journalist must not invent." The "legend" on artistic license reads "THIS WAS MADE UP," a standard which Hersey finds incompatible with the messages Truman Capote, Norman Mailer, and Wolfe himself need to convey—he is particularly hard on *In Cold Blood, The Executioner's Song,* and *The Right Stuff.* Vidan takes on just *In Cold Blood,* but incorporates novelistic thought back to Zola in order to protest Capote's capitulation to Alain Robbe-Grillet's axiom that "The world is neither meaningful, nor is it absurd. It just simply *is.*" John Hellmann's *BSUF* essay on *In Cold Blood* (cited in *vi.* above) answers Vidan by explaining how Capote expresses "a unique tension between the impervious mystery of fact and the human need to meaning" (Vidan, Hersey, and Weber assume the latter must always prevail). Hellmann's equally convincing "The New Journalism and Viet Nam: Memory as Structure in Michael Herr's *Dispatches*" (*SAQ* 79:141–51) reaches the same conclusion as Gordon O. Taylor's more general study in *AL* (discussed near the end of *i.* above): the New Journalism helps the author avoid the falsifying conventions of both fiction and fact by letting him construct his book "not as a direct report on the Viet Nam war, but rather as an exploration of his *memory* of the war" for which the self-reflexive techniques of innovative fiction are appropriate.

b. **Science Fiction.** Limitation of space precludes comment on all but the most general trends within the crushingly immense amount of work published on SF this year. Worthy of attention by all scholars is *Bridges to Science Fiction* (So. Ill.), papers from the Eaton Conference edited by George E. Slusser et al. Harry Levin's "Science and Fiction" (pp. 3–21) locates the subgenre in history, while Thomas A. Hanzo's "The Past of Science Fiction" (pp. 131–46) considers how "As material of the future, the past is rediscovered, repeated in a new key, and given new emotional valuation." In *Three Tomorrows: American, British, and Soviet Science Fiction* (Barnes and Noble) John Griffiths is considerably less sanguine, fearing "We are entering another Dark Age and the prospects of a renaissant dawn are small. If the despairing SF writers of the West and the silent and conforming ones of the East are right in their image of what the future holds then there will be no tomorrow. Tomorrow has been cancelled." Patricia S. Warrick's *The Cybernetic Imagination in Science Fiction* (MIT) shows how one writer, Philip K. Dick, shares

Griffiths' pessimism; his use of robots is less optimistic because Dick has his doubts about the benefits of wartime technology.

Two essays which accept the new postmodernism more cheerfully are Teresa L. Ebert's "The Convergence of Postmodern Innovative Fiction and Science Fiction: An Encounter with Samuel R. Delany's Technotopia" (*PoT* 1,iv:91–104) and "Science Fiction to Superfiction" (*Granta* 2, n.s.:86–102). The latter piece argues that SF writers have traditionally enjoyed the freedom to innovate which their mainstream colleagues won only in the last two decades; Ebert's study links *Dhalgren's* rejection of an easy mimesis of constructed meaning with similar works by Donald Barthelme, Steve Katz, and Ronald Sukenick.

The two figures getting the most attention this year are Ray Bradbury and Ursula Le Guin. Wayne L. Johnson's *Ray Bradbury* (Ungar) sees the author as a genuine product of American popular culture in his fascination with Hollywood and stage theatrics, especially those relating to magic. The impact of science is given thematic attention in the essays commissioned by Joseph D. Olander and Martin Harry Greenburg for their *Ray Bradbury* (Taplinger). The strongest SF study is Brian Attebery's *The Fantasy Tradition in American Literature* (Indiana), which locates Bradbury in the "Wizard of Oz" tradition while placing Le Guin within a "native tradition" of American fantasy dating back to Washington Irving and developing through T. S. Eliot and Theodore Roethke. The best individual essays on Le Guin survey her broader influences and fill a special issue of *Extrapolation* (21,iii). Also worth noting is M. Teresa Tavormina's "Physics as Metaphor: The General Temporal Theory in *The Dispossessed*" (*Mosaic* 13,iii–iv:51–62). *Science-Fiction Studies* 7,i is given in part to essays which explore "Science Fiction in Women—Science Fiction by Women" in which the predictable mythologies are made to work both ways.

c. Feminist Fiction. Whether by their own preference or by critical fiat, certain writers who direct their fiction to womanly concerns continue to be grouped together, not always to their advantage. Evelyn Gross Avery's "Tradition and Independence in Jewish Feminist Novels" (*MELUS* 7,iv:49–55) places Ann Roiphe's *Long Division*, Erica Jong's *Fear of Flying*, and Susan Fromberg Schaeffer's *Falling* within a tradition which makes only the last book look good.

Joyce R. Ladenson takes what should be a limitation (a "pronounced didacticism") and makes it a literary virtue in "Marge Piercy's Revolutionary Feminism" (*SSMLN* 10,ii:24–31).

A tendency to thematisize such fiction instead of examining its art does little to help us understand the writers involved. The concern need not be feminine, as message-hunting is just as detrimental to Marilyn J. Smith's thematic study of "The Role of the South in the Novels of Gail Godwin" (*Crit* 21,iii:103–10), which says the South is a retreat from the "harsh realities" of the North. In a more insightful approach in " 'Beauty and the Beast' in Gail Godwin's *Glass People*" (*Crit* 21,iii:94–102) Karen C. Gaston shows how the psychological structure of the fairy tale contributes to the novel's structure.

Joan Didion is one writer who survives such subgenre treatment. Her mastery of writing is given full due in Mark Royden Winchell's *Joan Didion* (TUSAS 370), which singles out her "prismatic" vision and uncommon ear for speech. How Didion's characters relate structurally to the past is examined in two helpful studies, Thomas Mallon's "The Limits of History in the Novels of Joan Didion" (*Crit* 21, iii:43–52) and C. Barry Chabot's "Joan Didion's *Play It As It Lays* and the Vacuity of the 'Here and Now' " (*Crit* 21,iii:53–60).

The most helpful approach to the subject of women in literature, both as authors and as characters, is provided by Grace Stewart in *A New Mythos: The Novel of the Artist as Heroine, 1877–1977* (Toronto: Eden Press). Basically an application of the *Künstlerroman* typology to novels written by women about artist-heroine figures, Stewart's book shows just how old myths are encountered and new ones are formed as women novelists struggle to write within and against the tradition of patriarchal mythology. Isolation, entrapment, flight, and rebirth are the images Stewart finds repeated in such contemporary novels as *Fear of Flying*, *The Bell Jar*, and *Surfacing*.

d. **Mysteries and Crime Thrillers.** "Stories, myth, books, rituals are not so much an answer about the world," says Stephen Knight in *Form and Ideology in Crime Fiction* (Indiana), "but a set of questions shaped to provide a consoling result for the anxieties of those who share in the cultural activity." This bit of literary wisdom borrowed from Roland Barthes creates one of the most insightful studies we've had of this oft-maligned subgenre. The one contemporary

American Knight surveys is Evan Hunter, whose Ed McBain novels reflect the postwar transformation of detective into policeman, "acting with institutional support" within the "protective romance of technology." The result is an "end of ideology" as troublesome complexities are handled with a reassuringly empirical, pragmatic, and objective approach. "Fourth generation" detective writers—the 1970s crop typified by Robert B. Parker, Roger L. Simon, and Andrew Bergman—are given booklength treatment in David Geherin's *Sons of Sam Spade: The Private Eye Novel in the 70s* (Ungar). In their hands a long-building trend has become dominant: the private detective is now "a tough guy with a poet's sensitivity, a hero with a healthy dose of humanity," and these new vulnerabilities expand the subgenre for younger detective writers. Why one author gave up on SF and chose detective fiction for its superior ability to cope with the future is explained by Joe Sanders in "Science Fiction and Detective Fiction: The Case of John D. McDonald" (*SFS* 7,ii:157–63); finding a literary genre for the works of Joseph Wambaugh is David K. Jeffrey's concern in "Wambaugh's Police Stories" (*MQ* 21: 470–83).

e. **Native American, Chicano, and Western Fiction.** Studies of Native American fiction have praised its use of tradition and sorrowed over the heartbreaks its themes sometimes convey; the danger is that each can become an automatic response. Per Seyersted's *Leslie Marmon Silko* (*WWS* 45) avoids such simplifications while still determining how her use of oral storytelling traditions and "her transformation of local material into general significance" have made for literary success. William W. Thackeray combines literary analysis with an anthropological approach to find the underlying mystical structure used by James Welch ("'Crying for Pity' in *Winter in the Blood*," *MELUS* 7,i:61–78). The most deeply searching essay, however, encompasses the work of all three popular Native American authors—Welch, Silko, and N. Scott Momaday—in its study of "a preoccupation with the process of alienation." Paula Gunn Allen's "A Stranger in My Own Life: Alienation in American Indian Prose and Poetry" (*MELUS* 7,ii:3–19) makes the familiar point that "The ancient thrust toward unification with the people is not lost in modern American Indian literature," but moves on the peculiar nature of that quest today: "The protagonist or speaker does not create actual unity with the people as a result of this stance because the people are turned into a dream of faraway times and conditions. What is articulated is a world that might have been or that might be, but not one that is."

The backgrounds and concerns of 14 leading figures are explored by [Juan D.] Bruce-Novoa in his *Chicano Authors: Inquiry by Interview* (Texas); how this literature developed from politics through cultural expression into a full-fledged aesthetics is treated in the various discussions and in Bruce-Novoa's excellently detailed and organized introduction. Carol Mitchell's "Rudolfo Anaya's *Bless Me, Ultima*: Folk Culture in Literature" (*Crit* 22,i:55–64) is one study which would have benefited from Bruce-Novoa's book, for Mitchell spends almost all her time laboring through plot summary and character relationships to establish what Anaya's talk with Bruce-Novoa makes obvious: that there is a definable Chicano culture out of which serious fiction can arise. A more sophisticated inquiry into the works of Tomas Rivera and Rolando Hinojosa is made by Carlota Cárdenas de Dwyer in "Cultural Regionalism and Chicano Literature" (*WAL* 15:187–94), where "the constant presence of the Chicano migrant farmworkers' way of life and culture" contributes to and in some cases assumes the role of narrative voice.

John R. Milton's monumental *The Novel of the American West* (Nebraska), while an essential contribution to the field at large, is hampered by two peculiarly contemporary limitations. For one, Milton pays little attention to Western writers who have come to prominence during the past 30 years; Larry McMurtry, for example, is dismissed because he pays little attention to the West as a whole, which becomes the volume's second limiting factor—by his own definition Milton makes it impossible for a fictionist to be in the West and in the contemporary world at the same time, nor does he have any affection for the "popular Western" so loved by Americans at large. A much smaller but ultimately more helpful study for contemporary concerns is William Bloodworth's "Literary Extensions of the Formula Western" (*WAL* 14:287–96) which finds room for McMurtry, E. L. Doctorow, Thomas Berger and others by showing the "common mythic aspects" of the traditional Western novel they retain as essential to their art. Two other essays make important contributions to our understanding of key Western elements. In "Ritual Patterns in Western Film and Fiction" (*Narrative Strategies*, pp. 105–

14) Robert T. Self takes the Western formula and considers "the ritualistic aspects of its structure, the relation of that structure to social communication, and the relation in that communication between ambiguity and artistic quality." Mark Busby takes some of these same elements and shows how in one case they have been misapplied; his "Damn the Saddle on the Wall: Anti-Myth in Larry McMurtry's *Horseman, Pass By*" (*New Mex. Humanities Rev.* 3,i:5–10) combines passages from the novel and statements from *In a Narrow Grave* to suggest that "Rather than a saddened nostalgia for a past way of life, much of *Horseman, Pass By* indicates a goodbye-good riddance attitude."

University of Northern Iowa

16. Poetry: 1900 to the 1940s

Richard Crowder

Despite the addition of William Carlos Williams to this chapter fewer dissertations were recorded in DAI for 1980 than for any of the preceding three years. In 1977 our poets were the subject of 29 theses, either alone or with other writers. In 1978 the number jumped to 31, in 1979 to an astounding 39. This year we have 25 to report, including seven on Williams. Stevens was considered in five dissertations, H. D., Hart Crane, and Moore in two each, and Frost, Louise Bogan, MacLeish, Elinor Wylie, Jeffers, and an obscure Bohemian Harry Kemp in one each. This is in contrast to last year, when Frost was treated in ten studies, Stevens in eight. Of the 121 dissertations recorded for 1977–80 Stevens was the subject of 35, Frost of 19, Crane of 12. Next follow Moore with six and Tate with four. These five poets are wide-ranging in their appeal: their differences are marked in subject matter, themes, techniques, tone, diction. Add Williams now and we have a feast to suit a wide variety of consumers. My contention still is that, interesting and challenging though these poets are, there are others that need to come under the closer scrutiny of our graduate students, Robinson and Aiken among them.

Publications featuring brief notes underscored the interest trend of the dissertations. NMAL 4 and 5 contained one item each on Stevens, Williams, Cummings, Frost, and Sandburg. Expl 38 and 39, on the other hand, gave us two items on Frost and five on Stevens. AN&Q 18 presented one each on Ransom and Williams. PBSA 74 published an item on Stevens and one on Fletcher (bibliography). Finally, NConL 10 had one item on Masters and six on Frost. Clearly Frost and Stevens are the leaders here in the area of making small points.

William H. Pritchard's Lives of the Modern Poets (Oxford) examines anew biographical details concerning nine poets. Hardy, Yeats, Pound, and Eliot are not included in our chapter. Reprinted

from earlier publications are "The Grip of Frost" (*ALS 1976*, p. 323),
"Edwin Arlington Robinson: The Prince of Heartachers" (*ALS 1979*,
p. 319), and "Poet of the Academy" (on Stevens) (*ALS 1979*, p.
330). Previously unpublished essays concerning Hart Crane and
William Carlos Williams will be discussed later.

i. Women Poets

Earl Rovit in "Our Lady-Poets of the Twenties" (*SoR* 16:65–84)
discusses the female quandary about marriage in the work of Sara
Teasdale and Elinor Wylie. His opinion is that "current evaluation
has condescended egregiously to" Laura Riding, Genevieve Tag-
gard, Leonie Adams, and a half dozen more frequently anthologized
poets like Marianne Moore and H. D. They were actually "a remarkable group of women," but their barriers, concealments, and
evasions created a defensive posture that may explain their feeling
of obligation to go to intellectual extremes: consider Amy Lowell
and Keats, Wylie and Shelley, Teasdale and Sappho, Moore and
"her magpie museum of natural history" and her translation of Fon-
taine, and Millay and Baudelaire. The list does not end there. As
these women ascended the hill of achievement, they were struck
with "terrible loneliness" and the possibility of failure at the last.
No matter what they did in actuality in their poems they gave marriage the cold shoulder, but paradoxically they were also repelled by
the notion of independence. Rovit makes a dangerously sweeping
claim that they were conventional, shallow, cautious, with narrow
range. (I would say he is especially wrong about Moore and H. D.)
He says, however, that they set out to sing, and we must admit that
here they were successful.

   The first issue of the *Edna St. Vincent Millay Newsletter* (Newport, R.I.) featured a report of a San Antonio College celebration
of the poet's birthday and excerpts from Norma Millay's "Log and
Digressions," written during her first winter on the Pacific coast.
There has been nothing of a scholarly nature so far. In *MMN* 3,ii
(Fall 1979, copyright 1980) Patricia C. Willis and Clive Driver (editors) describe in "Comment" (pp. 2–4) the "long sifting process"
in the archive of the Rosenbach Museum and Library (Philadelphia)
necessary for finding "sources of inspiration" for Moore's poems.
Thorough acquaintance with the poems naturally often permits dis-

covery of sources in unexpected archival encounters. Willis, in "Marianne Moore on Ezra Pound, 1909–1915" (pp. 5–8), traces the growth of Moore's interest in the eccentric expatriate culminating in a poem which she sent to *The Little Review*. It was never published, and Pound probably was not even ever aware of it. " 'To a Snail': A Lesson in Compression" (pp. 11–15) by Bonnie Costello uses early drafts of the poem to point out increased emphasis on the image as a means of clarification and compacting. It is obvious that Moore knew well William Cowper's "A Snail." The editors also present evidence that Moore was a conscious collaborator with photographers and other artists, choosing her costumes with care, "intent upon contributing her own image to the visual record." "In Her Own Image: Photographers, Painters and Sculptors View Marianne Moore" (pp. 20–24) is a descriptive analysis of an exhibit at the Rosenbach Museum and Library in early 1980.

Kenneth Hopkins draws our attention to a little-known poet in "Gamel Woolsey: A Poet from Aiken, South Carolina" (*SCR* 12,ii: 31–43). Hopkins stresses Woolsey's links with the Powys family, especially her sexual encounters with Llewellyn Powys, whose wife, Alyse Gregory, consented to the liaison. Her various loves were hopelessly entangled, marked by several abortions. After a stormy parting from Llewellyn she "married Gerald Brenen though she was not divorced from her legal husband, Reginald Hunter." *Middle Earth* appeared in 1931, her only book of poems to be published in her lifetime (1899–1968). Recently other small collections have been published: *Twenty-Eight Sonnets* (1977), *The Last Leaf Falls* (1978), *Middle Earth* (reissued in 1979), and *The Search for Demeter* (1980). Hopkins believes Woolsey "to be one of the significant poets of her generation, because she writes of the stuff of human life as felt and suffered and enjoyed *from within*."

Three New England poets, descendants of Percy Lowle, who emigrated from England in 1639, are the subject of C. David Hermann's *American Aristocracy: The Lives and Times of James Russell, Amy, and Robert Lowell* (Dodd, Mead). Though there is little new biographical or critical matter concerning Amy, it is good to review her devotion to imagism, her aggressive defense of literary figures and movements, her fascination with Keats, her generosity, all against the background of membership in the Brahmin clan of Lowell.

Ruth Limmer has arranged selections from Louise Bogan's writings in roughly chronological order to give us an account of the poet's life. The records collected in *Journey Around My Room: The Autobiography of Louise Bogan, A Mosaic* (Viking) are from various pieces of writing composed over a span of 40 years, with frequent gaps. The editor has done what she could "to suggest the flow of experience," not an easy task in the absence of any real account of events. In introductory remarks Limmer gives some details that Bogan ignores: her first marriage; her jobs at Brentano's, the New York Public Library, Columbia University; her early critical reviews. The editor warns the reader that this book is made from her choices, not the poet's. A chronology at the beginning lists all of Bogan's books and introductions and provides dates for early poems. It cannot indicate all the places Bogan lived but does name the principal milestones in her life: e.g., the Helen Haire Levenson Prize from *Poetry*, her appointment as Consultant in Poetry to the Library of Congress, sojourns at the MacDowell Colony, her election to the American Academy of Arts and Letters. Following the main body of the book is a noting of the sources of the passages used in the compilation.

Disappointment, incompleteness, and sexual repression inform the poems of Mina Loy, for the development of whose female selfhood Whitman and the Futurist painters were probably the most important influences. This is the finding of Virginia M. Kouidis in *Mina Loy: American Modernist Poet* (LSU). Her earlier poems develop the prevailing metaphysics and introduce her experiments in technique and structure. The Futurist device of the collage creates complexity through fragments juxtaposed without logic. She uses no punctuation and invents typographical deviations. Kouidis studies the poems in the light of Loy's modernist vision and her relationship to a problematic universe. The chapter called "Radium of the Word" gives attention to the poet's experiments with language especially in the later work. "Polarities of Vision" explains the emblematic figures of the artist and the bum—essential intuition as against "timid or failed vision." British-born, Loy did not become a naturalized American citizen until 1946. Kouidis, however, develops three links that join the poet to the American modernists: her awareness in 1910 of the inadequacy of English poetry, her verbalism ("logopoeia"), and her use of modern European painting (in the manner of Moore,

Stevens, and Williams). This book is a well-presented case for a highly talented artist till now virtually unknown or ignored by the critics. Kouidis' "Rediscovering Our Sources: The Poetry of Mina Loy" (*Boundary 2* 8,iii:167–88) says much of what is to be found in her book in slightly different language. The author quotes the same poems and makes similar comments. Both book and article, for example, use Constantin Brancusi's brass sculpture as an object of comparison with Loy's poetry (shaped and polished). Elsewhere both book and article tell us that, "having been unjustly punished by her parents, Ova flees to the garden where she has an 'illumination.'" If one reads the book, it is probably unnecessary to read the article, interesting though it is in itself. The book has more to say, naturally.

H. D. and Richard Aldington first met D. H. Lawrence in 1914 through Amy Lowell. "Rico and Julia: The Hilda Doolittle–D. H. Lawrence Affair Reconsidered" (*JML* 8:51–76) by Peter E. Firchow conjectures that Lawrence and H. D. were unable to maintain a "close" relationship and suggests that a comparative study of H. D.'s *Bid Me to Live*, Lawrence's *Aaron's Rod* and Aldington's *Death of a Hero* would emphasize the fact that for H. D. and Lawrence (but not for Aldington) copulation was an act of worship, not simply a momentary pleasure. In a rather precious analogy the author says that possibly H. D. was to Lawrence what Mary Magdalene was to Jesus—one who loved him but not his whole body.

Two articles are based on H. D.'s interest in the Helen legends. L. M. Freiburt follows the changes in Helen (all women?) as she moves from ideal to real through role of creator and prophet to realization and acceptance of selfhood. H. D. uses the method of myth to stop time so that Helen can at last "stabilize and strengthen her identity as the creator of her own future." By process of kaleidoscoping and fusing, H. D. pictures how precarious has been the evolution of woman in our culture. Freiburt's article is entitled "From Semblance to Selfhood: The Evolution of Woman in H. D.'s Neo-Epic *Helen in Egypt*" (*ArQ* 36:165–75). Charlotte Mandel opines in "Garbo/Helen: The Self-Projection of Beauty by H. D." (*WS* 7,i: 127–35) that the poet's fascination with the early Garbo films transmogrified the screen star into a goddess, the equivalent of Beauty-Goodness to be found in the early poem "Helen" and the later *Helen in Egypt*. Herself extraordinarily beautiful, H. D. accepted with solemn responsibility accolades proclaiming her a Greek nobly fair "revisiting earth" and "drew from herself the projections of her poetic vision."

ii. The Harvard Connection

John Dos Passos' one volume of verse (*A Pushcart at the Curb*, 1922) has created little critical attention. John Rohrkemper's *John Dos Passos: A Reference Guide* (Hall) itemizes five reviews, four in 1922 and one in 1923. The bibliography is more concerned (and properly) with the author's prose. Townsend Ludington, however, in his richly detailed biography *John Dos Passos: A Twentieth Century Odyssey* (Dutton) uses the poems to punctuate the narrative effectively beginning with "From Simonides" and "Salvation Army" written in Dos Passos' senior year at Harvard through some 15 years to the prose poem "The Body of an American" ("one of his finest") with which he concludes *1919*. Ludington relates the poems to the life from 1915 to 1931, after which the writer seems not to have published any more verse. The volume is illustrated with a portfolio of photographs and with sketches drawn from time to time by this multitalented novelist, poet, and essayist. There are copious notes and a thorough index, which guides the reader directly to the scattered discussion of the poems as related to the writer's life story.

George Arms has opened a new page in the biography of William Vaughn Moody in his contribution to *Towards a New American Literary History*. His essay, "The Poet as Theme Reader: William Vaughn Moody, a Student, and Louisa May Alcott" (pp. 140–53), begins with a 100-word comment of Moody's on a theme by one Florence Phillips at Harvard-Radcliffe. Arms remarks on Moody's reading and annotating the student themes of Gertrude Stein and a Wilhelm Segerbloom, but regrets the loss of Phillips' later themes with comments by Moody. (Phillips had had correspondence with Alcott.) Bruce Morton has published "Addenda and Corrigenda to *John Gould Fletcher: A Bibliography*" (*PBSA* 74:404–08), bringing us up to date with items found since his book went to press (see *ALS 1979*, pp. 322–23).

The Conrad Aiken Issue of *SLitI* (13:ii) consists of 142 pages of analytical chronology, criticism, extensive explication, examination of concepts both philosophical and psychological, and a descriptive essay of the Aiken collection at the Huntington Library. Nearly all of the eight critical essays have interesting things to say about the poetry. Helen Hagenbuechle writes of "Epistemology and Musical Form." Joseph Killorin, whose edition of Aiken letters was reviewed in *ALS 1978* (pp. 326–27), discusses the autobiographical elements in the poetry. Harry Marten and E. P. Bollier study the influence of Aiken's forebears. Mary Martin Rountree looks at the heroes of the novels and pronounces them to be portraits of a confessed failure. Douglas Robillard considers Melville's influence and Ted R. Spivey that of Freud and Jung. Catherine K. Harris encapsulates critical opinion through the years. This is a fascinating collection of studies in what appear to be the long-delayed rediscovery and elevation of the most shamefully neglected poet of the 20th century.

Two articles on Aiken's "Silent Snow, Secret Snow" explicate the snow as symbol. Robert Kloss's "The Secret of Aiken's Snow" (*HSL* 12:29–38) supports the idea that the snow is masturbation. Laura A. Slap in "Conrad Aiken's 'Silent Snow, Secret Snow': Defenses against the Primal Scream" (*AI* 37:1–11) interprets the snow as a wall against rage and other conscious subjective aspects of the emotions.

Louis J. Budd focuses on a letter to Jay B. Hubbell from A. Gayle Waldrop in "E. A. Robinson Unbends for Academe" (*CLQ* 16:248–51) detailing a visit to Robinson by Waldrop (a graduate student in journalism) and Albert Shipp Pegues (a professor of English). Robinson was cordial toward these academic men and later toward Hubbell in an exchange of notes. The year was 1922. Relationships with professors having heretofore been severely limited, the poet found the experience "both pleasant and gratifying."

The following four papers were delivered at a Robinson seminar during the annual meeting of MLA in Chicago December 1977. The occasion marked the 50th anniversary of the publication of *Tristram*. Wallace L. Anderson is editing the complete letters of the poet to be published by Harvard. In "The Letters of E. A. Robinson: A Sampler" (*CLQ* 16:51–62) he begins by quoting and discussing the first extant letter (8 January 1882) and the last (25 March 1935). Then he reviews and comments on various other letters over the years, relating them to Robinson's poetry and his personal traits. Scott Donaldson is planning a biography of Robinson after the publication of the letters. His contribution to the seminar was "Robinson and

Music" (*CLQ* 16:63–72). He explains that the poet tried his hand
at composing music, his taste ranging from the symphonies of Brahms
to the light operas of Gilbert and Sullivan. He was in fact quite
knowledgeable about music. Donaldson considers "Captain Craig"
and *The Man Who Died Twice* as well as shorter works in their relation to music and finally draws a lengthy analogy between *Tristram*
and musical form.

Richard Crowder's "Robinson's *Tristram* and the American Reviewers" (*CLQ* 16:123–32) gives an account of 39 reviews published
in 1927 from May to December. (There are 86 such reviews on
record.) During these seven months the reviewers made note of
Robinson's omissions from the received Tristram legend and referred
to other authors including Wagner, the Victorians, the early tale-
tellers like Chrétien de Troyes, and other writers from Homer to
Walter de la Mare and John Erskine. The poem's characters most
frequently mentioned were Tristram, the two Isolts, Morgan, and
Mark. Analysis of theme varied as did that of tone. The role of time
received consideration as well as the possibly excessive emphasis
on cerebration (though some critics did not find that element altogether bad). Mostly the reviewers praised the total design but had
differing opinions on the quality of the diction. The overall judgment
of the 1927 critics, however, was that *Tristram* was among the best
of the world's narrative poems.

Nancy Carol Joyner, whose *Edwin Arlington Robinson: A Reference Guide* was reviewed in *ALS 1978* (p. 328), was chairman of
the MLA seminar. Her paper was titled "What Ever Happened to
Tristram?" (*CLQ* 16:118–22). She follows the history of the criticism
of the poem after 1927, including, among several topics, comparison
with the work of other poets and with Robinson's own two other
Arthurian works, textual analyses, characterizations, and autobiographical elements. She suggests future studies that would be profitable: the language, the image patterns (particularly beasts), narrative point of view, and the poet's attitude toward religion.

In an ingenious examination of aesthetic principles the arts can
have in common ("Picture into Poem: The Genesis of Cummings' 'i
am a little church'" in *ConL* 21:315–30) Rushworth Kidder argues
that E. E. Cummings composed his poem having in mind a photograph of the church of Saint Germain-de-Charonne at the edge of
Paris. On the other hand, Kidder insists that Cummings' paintings

of landscapes and churches were not so influential in this poem as were his self-portraits, for the poem is autobiographical and analytical of the speaker. Kidder finds also that the syntactic parallelism and the feminine endings of the poem relate it to the photograph. Kidder's continuing interest in Cummings as both poet and graphic artist is an important route to follow.

Cummings has become a favorite of the linguists. Eleanor Cotton's "Linguistic Design in a Poem by Cummings" (*Style* 14:274–86) dissects the poem "if everything" with relation to rhetoric, semantics, syntax, and phonology. For example, the three speakers, "the reasoning adult, the impertinent youth, and the playful child," differ in logic, semantics, and syntax. Always, however, linguistic design is achieved through coupling, "the co-occurrence of equivalent forms in equivalent positions." The joining force here is not logic but love. " 'he danced his did': an Analysis" by Richard D. Cureton (*JL* 16:245–62) surveys the controversy over this well-known line, which has been the subject of many pages of discussion as to "its linguistic status and aesthetic success." Cureton takes the clause through the strategies of structural description: major-minor categories, conversion of affixed forms, case and agreement affixes, normal order, transfer rules, iconic deviance, and productive ambiguity. He decides that the syntactic deviation of this phrase infuses into the poem a "remarkable 'extraloquial' potential." This article is a meticulous analysis bringing together the disciplines of linguistics and aesthetics.

Dreams in the Mirror: A Biography of E. E. Cummings (Liveright) is the title of Richard S. Kennedy's new book, on the whole an agreeably readable account of the poet's life, packed with detail. Chapter 5 on Cummings' curriculum at Harvard and chapter 6 on his college experiments with verse, his friends, and his rebellion have been published in *HLB* (reviewed in *ALS 1976*, pp. 330–31, and *ALS 1977*, p. 348). Possibly the most important new contribution is the story of Cummings' daughter Nancy, whom he first met only after she was an adult and a married woman. Cummings is revealed as a poor parent, self-centered, sometimes cantankerous. Kennedy insists on offering proof that Cummings was a major poet, an opinion the reader can worry over if he wants to. The book closes with a chronological list of the works of Cummings, a three-page bibliographical essay, a 23-page section of notes more or less copious, and an adequate index. This is no doubt the best Cummings biography we will have for many years. Southern Illinois Univ. Press has reissued in welcome paperback (Arcturus) Norman Friedman's 1964 *e.e. cummings: The Growth of a Writer* (see *ALS 1964*, pp. 186–87).

In a review-essay entitled "Satyr and Transcendentalist" (*Parnassus* 8,ii:42–50) on Kennedy's biography Guy Davenport traces many of Cummings' eccentricities to his Greek major at Harvard. He suggests also the mutual influence between Cummings and Don Marquis (*archy and mehitabel*) as well as the poet's devotion to George Herriman's Krazy Kat cartoons. In addition he was magnetized by Pound's gallery of Provençal, Italian, Greek, and Chinese lyricists, Apollinaire and Mallarmé, satiric poets from Archilochos to Villon, and folk writers from Aesop to Joel Chandler Harris. At bottom Davenport sees Cummings' strongest poems as exercises of a gift for mimicry, practiced with malicious humor. His genius at its best lies "in exact observation commented on with wit." He is least satisfactory in "his gaily sentimental verse, in which he is the Gene Kelly of poetry." "He was not a wise person, but had the wisdom of his folly, a bravado of spirit, and his own special way of knowing and talking about the world; and these are better than wisdom, to a poet, in any choice."

The leading Unitarians of Cummings' day rejected a religious interpretation of the biblical Canticles. It may be said that the poet rebelled against even the traditional Unitarian view. In "Biblical Sexuality as Literary Convention: The Song of Songs in E. E. Cummings' 'Orientale'" (*PLL* 16:184–200) Noam Flinker reports that in the first of the six poems of "Orientale" he finds Cummings deviating from the Canticles in moving toward death rather than the sexual fulfillment implied in the biblical version. Flinker's further analysis points out not only the poet's debt to this poem in the Bible but the extent of his departure from it.

David V. Forrest's " E. E. Cummings and the Thoughts That Lie Too Deep for Tears" (*Psychiatry* 43:13–42) is a remarkably sane study of the poet, covering all periods of his productive life. The author discusses such topics as "mature" and "neurotic" defenses and, on the other hand, "immature" and "narcissistic" defenses, which he considers of deeper significance. He expands on many areas of interest to psychiatrists (and potentially to all of us) including denial, embracing entropy, impulsive action, orgasm, merging, mad-

ness, heterostasis, muteness, and silence. Along the way he calls upon
many poems to bear witness to the validity of his views. It is good for
us to see "our" poems from another angle. In spite of the psychiatric
vocabulary this is an absorbing study.

iii. Illinois, California, the Fugitives

Robert Narveson in "*Spoon River Anthology*: An Introduction" (*Mid-
America* 7:52–72) sees Masters' chief work as a "record of a particular moment in history" as well as "an intensely personal book."
The poet is demanding genuine dignity for his commonplace villag-
ers. As others have noted, there is progression in the book toward a
climactic aura of calm that contrasts with the earlier agitation.
Throughout the volume are descriptive passages suggesting a benign
nature (summer and fall) contrasted with the emotional tumult of
humanity. Many of the speakers, however, feel the healing power
of nature. Narveson also reports discovery of a typescript of a poem
later revised and included in the *Anthology*. "Masters's 'Griffy the
Cooper': Two Versions" (*MMisc* 8:39–43) contrasts the early piece,
called "The Tub," with the *Anthology* version, showing how Masters
changed the original to make it more appropriate to the rural setting
of his book. All in all Narveson finds "Griffy the Cooper" more satisfying than "The Tub."

Critics have not paid much notice to "the personal mysticism,
the systematic imagery, and the almost obsessive recurrence of subjective motifs" in Masters' best-known book. In "The Sources of the
Spoon: Edgar Lee Masters and the *Spoon River Anthology*" (*CentR*
24:403–31) James Hurt reviews details of Masters' life—his illnesses,
his relations with his family, his views of women—and argues that
the writing of the book was cathartic. The group of epitaphs of the
Pantier family, for example, is descriptive of the poet's own family,
the conflicts and the gossip. Unifying images occur throughout the
book, but mainly in the last third—fire, light, and sun; earth and
clay; stars and music. Hurt views the *Anthology* as "a spiritual autobiography—personal and subjective."

To his considerable list of Masters studies Herb Russell has added
"Edgar Lee Masters: A Selected Guide to Secondary Materials,
1914–1950" (*BB* 37:80–89). The longest section lists reviews and
criticism. The other less imposing sections cover biography and bib-

liography; and interviews and conversations. This compilation witnesses to the scarcity of in-depth biographical and critical investigation. Russell has included some entries about the poet's later life that
will be useful to an eventual biographer.

Using Sandburg as one of several examples Laurence Goldstein's
"The Automobile and American Poetry" (*MQR* 19:619–38) describes
how American poets tried to bridge the growing gap between their
craft and the early 20th century. Carl Sandburg pictured Henry
Ford and Thomas A. Edison as "the truest native geniuses." The
author explicates Sandburg's "Portrait of a Motorcar" as well as a
passage from *The People, Yes* about a Cherokee and his purchase of
a glittering white hearse. Goldstein has also contributed an article
on "The American Poet at the Movies: A Life and Times" (*CentR*
24:432–52). After reviewing Vachel Lindsay's fascination with film,
the author examines the poem "Mae Marsh, Motion Picture Actress."
He shows how Lindsay was in awe of the likes of Marsh, Blanche
Sweet, and Mary Pickford as bringers of light and dispensers of
beauty. He also writes of the influence of the movies on several
younger poets.

The *Robinson Jeffers Newsletter* 56 gives the text of Una Jeffers'
letters to Hazel Pinkerton, 1912–20, lists "Judith Anderson Letters
and Memorabilia, Tor House, Carmel," and continues to catalogue
"Jeffers Scholarly Materials," this installment subtitled "Small and
Minor Holdings" and edited by Robb Kafka and Michael Mooney,
who purport to expand and correct entries in *American Literary
Manuscripts* (1977). Una's letters to Pinkham, 1921–25, appear in
RJN 57, which also contains (pp. 26–35) an essay by Arnold T.
Schwab on "The Robinson Connection: New Jeffers Letters," a fully
annotated account of Jeffers' slender relationship with E. A. Robinson, who wrote Jeffers two very brief notes. Published here for the
first time in explanatory context are the letters of Jeffers to Craven
Longstreth Betts, an aspiring but comparatively ungifted verse-
writing friend of Robinson's. Sixteen years older than Robinson,
Betts befriended the poet in time of need and later expressed gratitude for the privilege of close friendship with "a great poet." Jeffers'
letters often mention Robinson.

Jeffers was not a native Californian, as Roy Meador reminds us
in "The Pittsburg Years of Robinson Jeffers" (*Western Penn. Hist.
Mag.* 63:17–30). Meador tells the story of Jeffers' first 16 years in-

cluding the effect of his father's being a theologian. A lonely child, he was forcefully led by his father into a thorough education. He often explored the woods near his home, not just for diversion but as a learning process. His knowledge of botany, forestry, astronomy, and other sciences put down its roots in this Pennsylvania environment.

In reviewing *The Collected Poems of Yvor Winters* Thomas Parkinson advises taking the poet literally ("The Untranslatable Poetry of Yvor Winters" [*GaR* 34:671–77]). He finds much of merit in the poems ("hard work, integrity, accomplishment") and says that disregarding them is risky for critics, scholars, and general readers. Grosvenor Powell's *Language as Being in the Poetry of Yvor Winters* (LSU) is divided into eight chapters, six of which have been published previously in journals. Chapter 2, "Poetic Convention and Norms of Feeling," and chapter 6, "Metamorphosis of an Obsession," add fresh support to the structuring of this book, divided into two parts: chapters 1–4, "Philosophical and Formal Background," and chapters 5–8, "A Chronological Analysis of the Poetry." These chapters succeed, not because they perhaps unnecessarily explicate Winters' generally accessible poems, but because they set out the issues and ideas that dominated his thinking in both criticism and poetry. Powell argues that Winters' metaphysical, social, and cultural attitudes are even now "overwhelmingly pertinent." While Winters was still in the English department at Stanford in 1965, Powell defended his dissertation on "Romantic Mysticism and the Poetry of Wallace Stevens," on which he draws heavily in this present treatise.

Little attention has been paid recently to George Sterling beyond the scattered publication of a few of his letters. Now comes Thomas Benediktsson's *George Sterling* (TUSAS 337), a development of the author's 1974 dissertation, noted in *ALS 1975*, p. 363. The first two (biographical) chapters summarize his life from his birth in Sag Harbor, Long Island, in 1869 to his 1926 suicide in San Francisco. The examination of his work in the remaining four chapters treats the poet's decadent verse, the influence of Ambrose Bierce, his tilt toward 19th-century values, his pessimism (admired by Robinson Jeffers), and his despair.

Taking its place in a useful series (e.g., Rohrkemper's *John Dos Passos*, above) is Ray C. Longtin's *Three Writers of the Far West: A Reference Guide* (Hall), the subjects being Joaquin Miller, Charles

W. Stoddard, and George Sterling. Longtin's introduction to the Sterling section presents briefly the facts of the poet's life and shows how recent scholars have begun paying him more attention as a traditional figure. His poetry may be neglected, but his value as symbol remains. Sterling wrote 25 books. The items about Sterling begin with a review of his first book in 1903 and extend through a 1979 article by John Brazil in *MarkhamR*. The peak of his critical reputation appears to have been in 1926 (21 items) and 1927 (54 items). In no other year did he receive more than 13 notices. An addendum lists ten further references to writings about Sterling including two from 1978. The index follows the customary practical and thorough pattern of the series.

Lucinda H. MacKethan in *"I'll Take My Stand*: The Relevance of the Agrarian Vision" (*VQR* 56:577–95) considers the land of the South, its history, and its patterns of life and concludes that the manifesto defined "many compelling concerns of modern man in general and modern Southern writers in particular." Also examining this same book, *"I'll Take My Stand*: Fifty Years Later" edited by Thomas Daniel Young (*MissQ* 33:420–60) is a collection of four papers presented by the Society for the Study of Southern Literature at the San Francisco MLA in December 1979. They are by Young, Martha E. Cook, Mary Ann Wimsatt, and M. Thomas Inge and are followed by an appendix quoting opinion of current critical authorities. In these essays we are reminded that the Agrarian authors of the book in question were poets and novelists (i.e., stylists) and that their theme was of permanent value—the return to an environment unhampered by the waste and filth of modern urban industrialization.

Young and John Hindle have edited "Allen Tate and John Peale Bishop: An Exchange of Letters, 1931" (*SoR* 16:879–906). The entire correspondence extended from 1929 to 1944. These 1931 letters were written as Bishop took up his literary career again after some years. Bishop in France and Tate in Tennessee show mutual trust and honesty in their criticism of each other's work.

Brief tributes to two of the Fugitives show the love and respect which their colleagues continue to feel for them. Anthony Hecht in "John Crowe Ransom" (*ASch* 49:379–83) vividly recalls Ransom as teacher at Kenyon in the mid-40s. Sometimes disagreeing with his mentor, Hecht nevertheless learned from him "a posture of the mind and spirit, a humanity and courtesy, a manly considerateness." He also absorbed the importance of paying "keen attention to poetic detail." "Remembering Allen Tate" (*GaR* 34:7–10) was Malcolm Cowley's tribute delivered before the American Academy of Arts and Letters. Written in Cowley's graceful style, it says little new except for a few personal recollections. The flavor of Tate's life, says Cowley, was a "mixture of cosmopolitanism and localism."

iv. Cape Cod, New York, and New Jersey

An odd emphasis this year is placed on a deservedly forgotten Provincetown writer, Harry Kemp (1883–1960). He was the subject of a dissertation at Connecticut, "Harry Kemp: The Last Bohemian," and of an article by Marshall Brooks, "Harry Kemp: Lest We Forget" (*EON* 4,i/ii:15–17). According to Brooks, Kemp had a knack for knowing, abusing, and boring the right people at the right time (including O'Neill). In contrast to their Bohemian author his poems were "defiantly traditional," often in imitation of Keats, Shelley, and Byron. Kemp led a wildly unconventional life, surviving on handouts of acquaintances. E. E. Cummings wrote a poem about him, living his life out in Cape Cod shacks and never ceasing his skirt-chasing. He died at age 77, having remained elusive his entire life, always determined to be "the greatest living poet in the world." In spite of his numerous publications of poems, plays, novels, and biographies, he remained a mystery and a nuisance. No one can ever know "the real Harry Kemp story."

Roger Asselineau has introduced a little-known writer of our period in "A Neglected Transcendentalist Poet of the Twentieth Century: Walter Lowenfels (1897–1976)," the last essay in *The Transcendentalist Constant in American Literature* (NYU). Lowenfels was a New Yorker, the son of eastern European immigrants who entered his father's prosperous butter business from which he separated himself on two occasions, the first to live in Paris and write some books of poetry, the second to remain in New York and become a Communist. After abstaining for several years he returned at age 54 to the writing of poetry and came under Whitman's influence. He felt that every poem ought to suggest "the infinite context surrounding the least object." He was like Whitman in his use of the language of science, though he lacked Whitman's power. Asselineau thinks he deserves serious consideration in the canon of 20th-century American poetry.

Pritchard's essay on Hart Crane in *Lives of the Modern Poets* (pp. 235–62) is called "Hart Crane: A Fine Messed-up Life," a phrase used by Samuel Loveman, a friend of the poet's. In writing for "the intelligent unspecialist," as he calls his wife, Pritchard not only richly outlines the telling details of the poet's life within the limits of less than 30 pages, but also looks to the poems to clarify that life and to the life to understand the poems. He makes especial use of "Voyages" not only as autobiography but as a case study of Crane's "uncanny ability to end poems in absolutely conclusive ways." He expresses impatience with critics who worry about the lack of unity in *The Bridge*, but agrees with the critic who sees the changing moods as reflections of life's own blessings and nightmares. He does not agree that "The Broken Tower" is wholly admirable; for him obscurities remain. He thinks of Crane's suicide as "his last improvisation." Probably the best testimony favoring the poet is that he had such friends as Robert Lowell, Allen Tate, Malcolm Cowley, and Yvor Winters.

Carol Shloss draws some thoughtful conclusions from her careful perusal of John Unterrecker's and Philip Horton's biographies of Crane. In spite of impressive documentation Unterrecker was aware of missing papers and faulty memories. Nevertheless, he felt it necessary to use legend to flesh out his story, admitting that his book would eventually be superseded. Horton's earlier work had been based on even less sufficient evidence. Both writers attempted to explain events by linking Crane "to his sociocultural present." Shloss illustrates how Unterrecker's accumulation of facts changed Horton's story and interpretation. One difference is that, whereas Horton's biography is colored by determinism, Unterrecker's allows his subject a degree of self-direction. (See Carol Shloss, "The Lives of Hart Crane," *Biography* 3:132–46.)

Mary Ann Caws has made another venture into the area of comparative literature frequented by Crane scholars. Her article is titled "On One Crossing-Over: Valery's Sea into Hart Crane's Scene" in *The Analysis of Literary Texts: Current Trends in Methodology*, edited by Randolph D. Pope (Ypsilanti, Mich.: Bilingual Press), pp. 100–06. Exercising yet more psychoanalytic effort at getting at the heart of Crane's meaning, John T. Irwin has contributed "Figuration of the Writer's Death: Freud and Hart Crane" to *The Literary Freud: Mechanisms of Defense and the Poetic Will,* edited by Joseph H. Smith (Yale), pp. 217–60.

Warren Herendeen and Donald G. Parker have edited "Windblown Flames: Letters of Hart Crane to Wilbur Underwood" (*SoR* 16:337–76). These frank, informal letters develop for the reader various aspects of the writer's life: his sexual problems, his relation to his parents, his friendship with Harry Candee of Akron, his general growing consciousness of the power of literature and art, and his ability to "sell" poetry and literature in general. The editors' introduction explains that Underwood was a Washington poet (born 29 May 1876) with whom Crane had only a brief personal contact but developed a life-long genuine friendship. In Washington Underwood introduced Crane to interesting people, took him to plays, discussed poetry, books, and life, and became a total confidant for the young poet. The editors maintain that Underwood was "a far more significant and potent influence on Crane than Samuel Greenberg." They feel that Underwood was especially effective in helping Crane move on toward the writing of *The Bridge.* They quote enough of his poetry to show that he had an authentic gift, though his later poems, still good, are more resigned and muted than his early work. By the way, Ph.D. candidates looking for a fresh subject would do well to search out Wilbur Underwood.

Helge Norman Nilsen's *Hart Crane's Divided Vision: An Analysis of "The Bridge"* (Columbia) is a revision of the author's doctoral dissertation at the University of Bergen, Norway. After summarizing the commentaries of earlier critics of *The Bridge* (Allen Tate, Yvor Winters, F. O. Matthiessen, Babette Deutsch, and numerous others) and analyzing particularly the influence on the poet of Whitman and Waldo Frank, Nilsen proceeds to close-read the nine sections of the work (ending with the "undeniable splendor" of "Atlantis"), following Crane's path as he pursues his vision of his native country. The author finds the significant theme of the work to be "the destiny of America itself," developed through "heraldic images" creating "a truly American mystique," in which the poet wanted to but never quite could believe. (His was both faith and doubt.) He was constantly challenged to identify with every aspect of life, from lovemaking to sophisticated technology, in order to see America whole.

He created a bridge of love (equivalent to mystic America), all-embracing and tolerant. Though admiring *The Bridge* as a whole, Nilsen is not blind to its flaws: strain, obscurity, artificiality, melodrama, thinness. She thinks it is superb, however, in insisting "on the religious function of the manifestations of American life."

Likewise, Roger Ramsey looks on *The Bridge* as a religious lyric, expressing "ritualized ecstasy." Following Longinus, Ramsey finds no important symbols in the poem, which is intended for participants, not spectators. In it the god dies and the god is I (and thus the reader is drawn into participation). Ramsey points out ecstatic passages where poet, reader, and poem experience intense identification. Because the poem has no simile, only metaphor, it requires close sharing. Not trying to impose myth, vision, or pattern on the work, the reader must be openly responsive to the ecstatic moments. Ramsey's currently fashionable approach to the poem is explained in "A Poetics for *The Bridge*" (*TCL* 26:278–93). Norman D. Hinton and Lise Rodgers in "Hart Crane's 'The Moth That God Made Blind' " (*PLL* 16:287–94) examine thoroughly and extensively an early poem generally given short shrift by the critics. The authors see it not as stumbling juvenilia but as "a worthy first step" towards the eventual composition of *The Bridge*.

Again we turn to Pritchard's *Lives of the Modern Poets*. His essay "William Carlos Williams: In the American Grain" (pp. 263–94), as in the other sections of this book, gives us the essential facts of the subject's life, stressing here the American quality of his whole-hearted devotion to what he was doing at a given time, whether delivering a baby or composing a poem. Pritchard discusses many of the poems, arriving at the view that (as he says particularly of the late "Asphodel, That Greeny Flower") one should expect to read all Williams' poems "with a mixture of respect, affection, boredom, and exasperation," understanding all the while that their imperfections are necessary contributions to their "peculiar power."

John M. Slatin testifies to Williams' debt to Marianne Moore for ammunition in his battle with T. S. Eliot over tradition. "The War of the Roses: Williams, Eliot, Moore" (*WCWR* 6,ii:1–10) calls particular attention to Moore's "Roses Only" and Williams' seventh poem in *Spring and All*: "The rose is obsolete." Linda M. W. Wagner is of the opinion that *Spring and All* is the most important of the poet's aesthetic statements. Wagner's last article in her *American Modern:*

Essays in Fiction and Poetry (Kennikat) is entitled "Coda: Damn It, Bill: They Still Haven't Listened!" (pp. 244–52). She says that the book, written in a mood of joy and enthusiasm without restraint, zeroes in on the use of American language in tandem with American subjects, the poet's insistence on form as meaning, and his dependence on the object, tangible and concrete. Detesting the shoddy, Williams was honest and genuinely compassionate. Never satisfied, he kept experimenting with technique, theme, and genre. Always he found himself returning to the principles he so happily explained in *Spring and All*.

Section A of Michael André Bernstein's *The Tale of the Tribe: Ezra Pound and the Modern Verse Epic* (Princeton) focuses on Pound's *Cantos*; section C examines Charles Olson's *Maximus Poems*. It is section B, devoted to *Paterson* (chaps. 7–9, pp. 189–224), that is pertinent here. In discussing Olson in section C, Bernstein says incidentally that "*Paterson* avoids much of the shrillness [found in *The Cantos* and *The Maximus Poems*] by including numerous different, and even conflicting, voices within its own argument. The poem's emotional openness enables Williams to dispense with the hortatory tone more consistently than Pound or Olson." Yet the price of this accomplishment is "a distinct blurring of *Paterson*'s capacity to sustain specific politico-ethical judgments and a partial surrender of its authority as a source of instruction for the tribe" (pp. 231–32). The three chapters devoted to *Paterson* declare in sum that Williams' work, like any modern verse epic, "must itself always be both provisional and collective," serving only as a model, "the groundwork for the next attempt."

The paradox of Williams' poetry and of all modern poetry is "that both presence and absence are inseparable aspects of undifferentiated experience." This is the discovery of James S. Hans, whose "Presence and Absence in Modern Poetry" (*Criticism* 22: 320–40) points out, for example, that in the image of fire there is "both presence and absence, gentleness and violence, life and death." Williams' early work was "a poetry of innocent presence" followed by "the violence of absence" and then by the concession that the darkness of absence is always near "the light of presence." The article also explores similar themes in Eliot's poetry. Both men lived with "a movement of hope and clearing modulated by man's fortitude."

Enid Rhodes Peschel is editor of a volume of essays entitled

Medicine and Literature (New York: Neale Watson). She has included an article by Marie Borroff called "William Carlos Williams: The Diagnostic Eye" (pp. 56–65) in which the author points out that Williams' poems tell us little about his daily experience as physician (with perhaps a dozen exceptions). "Spring and All" is an example of the way this poet-doctor's imagination works. Not a pictorial poem, it is nevertheless full of energy and activity, one of a number of poems in which Williams "trained his diagnostic eye" on the mystery of the quotidian.

Margaret Glynne Lloyd's *William Carlos Williams' "Paterson": A Critical Reappraisal* (Fairleigh Dickinson) is based on the author's dissertation at the University of Leeds, England. It looks closely at the poem in three contexts: the "aesthetic ambivalence" of its century, its place in Williams' total work, and its contribution to the epic tradition. Lloyd deals with the literary context, with the city as metaphor ("man in himself is a city"), with technical concerns (extended experimental patterns, themes, and structures), and with relationships with the great poets from Homer to Eliot. Though the author admits that there is room for a great deal more Williams criticism, she has nevertheless published a sound book, using not only Williams' printed texts but many worksheets and unpublished *Paterson* manuscripts to enrich her exegesis. The index is twofold: names of persons mentioned and quoted in her text and a list of Williams' works examined or alluded to.

Joseph N. Riddel in "Keep Your Pecker Up—*Paterson Five* and the Question of Metapoetry" (*Glyph* 8:203–23) sees Williams' work as a poem about poetry, based on the thesis that the art of the poem violently invading life is made up of words, not the original "story" but a story of the real thing. Art, says the poet, is a memory system. Dr. Paterson is looking specifically at the medieval tapestries in the Cloisters. Williams makes constant use of doubles such as "the Derridan pun on the border as a *band*, as a *bander* or erection." Riddel's interestingly complex essay defines the poet's hope "in his submission to a play of language which undoes all myths of a last (res)erection." "Paterson,/keep your pecker up/whatever the detail!" Also referring to *Paterson*, David Frail's " 'The Regular Fourth of July Stuff': William Carlos Williams' Colonial Figures as Poets" (*WCWR* 6,ii:1–14) first explicates references to Cotton Mather in *In the American Grain* and then proposes that the Williams opera

The First President is in fact "an allegory of the American Poet," for its "libretto and its introduction form part of the matrix of the poetics of *Paterson*." That is, the character of Washington suggested revolutionary poetics to Williams.

Williams is the modern poet most complexly influenced by the visual arts. "For the same reason that Williams descends into industrial Paterson, Duchamp descends into a world of mechanized and unfulfilled love: both see in the descent the promise of subsequent ascent." Williams remade visual art into poetry, found that his poetic vision was indeed based in the visual, which actually dominated his later poetry. These are the findings of Henry M. Sayre, recorded in "Ready-mades and Other Measures: The Poetics of Marcel Duchamp and William Carlos Williams" (*JML* 8:3–22). Sayre asserts that Williams was the equal of Duchamp in every way in aesthetic theory and artistic invention. Both men influenced the next generation immeasurably. This is a very useful article in opening up the ongoing problem of the relation of literature to the other arts.

Peter Schmidt draws on his 1980 Virginia dissertation ("Williams and the Visual Arts, 1915–1945") in "Some Versions of Modernist Pastoral: Williams and the Precisionists" (*ConL* 21:383–406). Many of the poet's lyrics "share the Precisionist's idealized, Arcadian vision of modern industry" as well as a revision of still life and landscape. The photographic rather than painterly images of Charles Sheeler and Georgia O'Keeffe are typical. They seek to present objects as "equivalents" for human emotion (similar to Eliot's objective correlative). Also they try to produce a radically American art, uninfluenced by Paris. Schmidt's article analyzes several Williams poems, among them "Spring and All" and "Burning the Christmas Greens," to illustrate that the poems renewed literary tradition as they related to the Precisionists' concepts.

William Carlos Williams: The Critical Heritage, edited by Charles Doyle, is the first book about one of our poets in the proposed extensive Critical Heritage Series under the general editorship of B. C. Southern (Routledge). It is a gathering of letter excerpts and reviews covering Williams' entire career from 1909 to 1963. All the contributions have appeared before in a far-ranging number of books and periodicals. The editor's 47-page introduction is a chronological presentation of the trends in criticism, including Pound's interest in Williams, the decades of the 1920s and 1930s, the poet's "Redeeming

(Lang) wedge," and his position from 1951 to 1963 as "'The Grand Old Man' of Letters." The bibliography after the critical selections lists primary materials, sources, reviews, and comments other than those reprinted in this anthology, books about Williams (totally or chiefly), and books with considerable material on Williams. An appendix provides a selected list of the printings of Williams' works: title, place of publication, date, quantity, and price. The four-part index directs the reader to Williams' writings, his characteristics and aspects of his work and career, persons connected with the poet and/ or the criticism, and the newspapers, periodicals, anthologies, and small publishers related in some way to the criticism. Doyle's workmanlike job ought to be a great time-saver for scholars further interested in Williams. We can hope for other collections in this important Critical Heritage Series to be concerned with our poets.

v. Frost

Robert F. Fleissner questions whether Frost quotes Shakespeare's "Put out the light" because Lanier did, as critics have suggested, and reminds us that other familiar poets used the line and could have influenced the New Englander. "Frost and Lanier: An Immediate Literary Source of 'Once by the Pacific'" (*PLL* 16:320–25) asserts that in any event Frost's borrowing from *Othello* is more effective than that of any of the 19th-century poets he had read. In "'The Wind's Will': Another view of Frost and Longfellow" (*CLQ* 16:177–81) Jane Donahue Eberwein states that Frost's emphasis on will (and willfulness) is stronger than Longfellow's. *A Boy's Will* points up the issues central to his early "struggle for an integrated personality," plays on the conflict between his will and the wind's, and shows that Frost had "a distinctive sense of poetic values." Frost here employs, as did Longfellow in his old Lapland melody, "the minstrel ideal of poetry," from which he was to depart almost totally in later poems.

As an example of Frost's conscious effort at being "so subtle at this game as to seem to the casual person altogether obvious," William S. Waddell's "Aphorism in Robert Frost's 'The Tuft of Flowers': the Sound of Certainty" (*CP* 13,i:41–44) follows the change of heart in the poet from the opening maxim (how all men are alone) to its contrasting statement at the end: "Men work together." "The Dra-

matic Monologue in Robert Frost's 'The Pauper Witch of Grafton'"
(*BSUF* 21,ii:48–52) by Christine A. Briggs focuses on the "self-
revelation of the speaker." The leitmotif is erotic fulfillment, the
witch taking pleasure in sensuality and libidinous inventiveness. The
plot is Browning-like as is the "internal revelation." The witch, both
as young woman and now of an age, registers disappointment at the
refusal of the public to recognize "her libidinous impulse." The
speaker is forced to face "decline and deterioration" mostly through
her rich memories, and the confrontation brings her to the brink of
despair, for she can no longer keep up the vision of a young woman.
This poem develops a familiar Frostian contradiction between remembered or imagined experience and the limited experience of
reality.

In "The Symbolic Vistas of Frost and Stevens" (*CollL* 7:146–52)
William E. McMahon observes that both poets compose their scenes
consciously to carry the metaphysical import central to a given poem
(as in allegory). They differ in some respects, however. Frost's vistas, though reductive, are nonetheless "synecdoches of cosmic design." In this connection McMahon looks at such poems as "Stopping
by Woods on a Snowy Evening," "Two Look at Two," and "A Considerable Speck." On the other hand Stevens' vistas are large and
richly complicated. For this reason they may give Stevens an advantage over Frost with the critics. McMahon supports his point by
analyzing "Connoisseur of Chaos," "The Sense of the Sleight-of-
Hand Man," "Sunday Morning," and "An Ordinary Evening in New
Haven." The author concludes that to get at the heart of symbolic
vistas the critic must know as much as possible "about the history of
art forms and thought forms and of the writer and all other writers."
(Contrast the opinion of the New Critics, who looked solely at the
design of the poem itself.)

Frost always felt himself in competition with Wordsworth. So
opines Sydney Lea in "From Sublime to Rigamarole: Relations of
Frost to Wordsworth" (*SIR* 19:83–108). Frost thought of Wordsworth as a disenchanted poet who discarded romanticism in "Ode
to Duty." Frost consciously "dropped below" his English predecessor. For example, the nature of "Closed for Good" contradicts what
Wordsworth expresses in "Tintern Abbey," in which the poet's load
is lightened, whereas Frost is wary of such a release. If Wordsworth's
"Lines Written in Early Spring" declares a hope of renewal, Frost's

"Spring Pools" does not go beyond the natural harmony of the present. Other poems from each writer show similar points of comparison and contrast. Lea uses "Michael" and "Directive" as guide poems to contrast the Wordsworthian "boisterous brook" with Frost's quiet water "too lofty and original to rage" (liveliness as against tranquillity). This is a challenging article suggesting many good ideas for further exploration.

Darrel Abel explicates Frost's attitude further. The poet, he says, does not consider the world as either chaotic or cosmic, but something in between "which gives human intelligence work to do." In "Robert Frost's 'Second-Highest Heaven'" (CLQ 16:78–90) he cites Pascal, Leibnitz, Emerson, Whitman, Melville, and Tillich, then reminds his reader that Frost finds only indifference in the universe and turns to defining man as existential entity with his "own desert places." The author relates Frost to Bergson and William James in his exercise of intelligent will on otherwise formless material. For the poet the " 'second-highest heaven' is a world of indetermination confined by necessity." What matters is "knowing what to do with things." One can borrow a "piece of reality" for his own temporary use, but it continues nevertheless playing its part in the larger reality. This essay takes its rightful place beside the other recent, thoughtful Frost studies Abel has been giving us (ALS 1978, pp. 340–41, and ALS 1979, pp. 333–34).

Linda Ray Pratt considers "The Most of It," "For Once, Then, Something," "On Looking by Chance at the Constellations," and "Design" as marked (not necessarily marred) by "a riddle of logical contradictions, excesses, or voices." In these four poems the poet does not explore the implications of the positions he assumes, nor does he take a definite stance. Pratt draws an interesting contrast between the basically unafraid attitude of Dickinson and Stevens on the one hand and Frost on the other as he customarily runs for cover at the threat of revelation. "Design" and "Desert Places" are among those rare Frost works that appear to play no games. There is evidence that Frost tried (not always successfully) "to conceal the fear, stall criticism, pretend to wisdom, and outdistance the enemy." The author concedes that Frost's habit of shielding himself from vulnerability and pain, though it weakens the art, makes the poetry compelling. Her article is titled "Robert Frost and the Limits of Thought" (ArQ 36:240–60).

David M. Wyatt defines this shielding habit, at least in part, as a taming of the subject "by giving it room to move while being sure to rein it in before the poem can become a runaway." "Frost and the Grammar of Action" (*SoR* 16:86–99) shows that the poet has recourse to "the whole range of strategies for forwarding, retarding, or in any other way shaping the motion of a poem invented and sanctioned by tradition." Typically, a Frost poem images physical action, if only gestures. Wyatt illustrates his point with several well-known poems. For Frost "man's ideal location can best be derived from the patterns which underlie, like a grammar, his actual and continual motion": reaching up, stooping down, descent, ascent, meeting and passing, and so on. Wisely the author warns the reader not to stop at diagramming but to permit the poem to touch him.

Sheldon W. Liebman's study of Frost's statements on both poetry and prose in "Robert Frost: On the Dialectics of Poetry" (*AL* 52: 264–78) yields the proposition that the poet saw his work and that of others as bringing some kind of order out of a necessary chaos ("beyond culture and below consciousness"). Because logic comes after the act of "discovering" a poem, a poet is not making his sounds but catching them. Form is mood, not just shape. Language must always be new and unprecedented. In metaphor a word is reestablished in a fresh, definite, particular place. Further, as many critics are reminding us today, a poem requires involvement by the reader, not simply observation. As Frost sees it, "the best poetry is a communion of minds and souls," for spirits with a mutual awareness, an understanding of self as the reader comes to see and understand others.

Andrew J. Angyal points out that Frost omitted certain poems from his published collections in order to establish himself as a poet of rural America. His critics accuse him of being indifferent to the human situation, but Angyal proves the opposite in discussing such early efforts as "The Mill City," "The Parlor Joke," and "When the Speed Comes" in "Literary Politics and the Shaping of the Frost Poetic Canon" (*SCR* 12,ii:47–55). These "labor poems" reflect the poet's early experiences in Lawrence, Massachusetts, and must be acknowledged before the complete "canon" can be consummated. One may speculate that Frost, in omitting them, was trying to avoid being classed with proletarian sympathizers like Sandburg. From Åbo Akademi (Finland) comes Roger D. Sell's *Robert Frost: Four*

Studies, somewhat loosely related essays dealing with the making of some poems, the use of children as "point of view," two of the poet's unpublished plays, and certain "social-cultural distinctions" drawn by the poet from time to time.

In addition to the expected chronology and various bibliographies (well annotated, by the way), James L. Potter's *The Robert Frost Handbook* (Penn. State) discusses the subject's life, his "poetic stance," and the "literary contexts and techniques." The first section neatly divides itself into the early period (to 1912), the emergence (to 1930), and the final years of both adulation and deep problems (to his death in 1963). The second section examines the poet's "deceptions" and tensions, the hopes and fears, and the middle road of resolution (what Linda Ray Pratt calls "the limits of thought" expressed in David M. Wyatt's "grammar of motion"). The third section covers Frost's heritage (with special attention to Wordsworth, Emerson, and Thoreau) and his techniques, including structure, music, and metaphor. There is a fully adequate index. The book is especially useful to the neophyte.

vi. Stevens

Several studies this year consider Wallace Stevens in conjunction with other poets. *At Last, the Real Distinguished Thing: The Late Poems of Eliot, Pound, Stevens, and Williams* by Kathleen Woodward (Ohio State) takes as its title the deathbed words of Henry James. Woodward here continues her concern and fascination with the phenomenon of old age. (In 1978 she was coeditor of and contributor to *Aging and the Elderly,* a collection of essays.) This recent work deals at length with Eliot's *Four Quartets,* Pound's *Pisan Cantos,* Stevens' *The Rock,* and Williams' *Paterson V,* showing that each poet in his own way was designing the closure of his life with composure, imagination, and wisdom. (Eliot was only 54 when he completed the *Four Quartets,* but they were his last book of poetry. Pound lived 24 more years after the *Pisan Cantos,* but Woodward feels the work crowned his career.)

The central image for all four poets is "the still point," the meditative center. "The American Adam has grown up and more importantly has grown old with grace and dignity." Woodward has deliberately limited her examination to these four men, among the

"greatest Modern American poets of the twentieth century." She
suggests that other scholars might pursue this theme elsewhere.
Nevertheless, as a kind of coda, it would have been interesting to
see what her conclusions would have been about Moore's *Tell Me,
Tell Me*, Aiken's *Thee: A Poem*, Cummings' *73 Poems*, Sandburg's
Honey and Salt, Robinson's *King Jasper*, and Jeffers' *The Beginning
and the End*. Some enterprising researcher might indeed find such
analysis an attractive study. Woodward's book sets a pattern both
thoughtful and stimulating.

"The Fictive and the Real: Myth and Form in the Poetry of Wallace Stevens and William Carlos Williams" is the title of an essay by
Ronald L. Dotterer in *The Binding of Proteus: Perspectives on Myth
and the Literary Process* edited by Marjorie W. McCune, Tucker
Orbison, and Philip M. Withim (Bucknell). Papers in this volume
were presented in programs on myth and literature sponsored by
Bucknell and Susquehanna Universities. Dotterer's article is included in the third section of the book, "Mythic Thought as Process,"
along with essays on knighthood in terms of quest, 12th- and 13th-
century French poetry, Eliade and Lévi-Strauss, Baudelaire, and the
late work of Rilke. Dotterer studies both Williams and Stevens as
writers of influential long poems "giving order to life," i.e., *Paterson*
and *Notes Toward a Supreme Fiction*. In tracing the growth of these
works the author notes the contrast between "*Paterson's* open, ac-
cumulative form" and "the measured regularity of thirty strophes of
tercets" in the Stevens work. Though differing from one another in
detail, tone, and shape each poem is "the voice of the poet speaking
of the moment of making as well as the creation itself, that point at
which the making of myths may yet begin." Taken in the context
of the accompanying essays in this book Dotterer's paper ought to
deepen our appreciation of the accomplishment of Williams and
Stevens.

Helen Vendler's *Part of Nature, Part of Us: Modern American
Poets* (Harvard) contains chapters on Moore and Stevens and part
of a chapter devoted to Cummings. Vendler is a first-rate reviewer
of poetry. This book consists of a good many of her interesting comments in newspapers and periodicals, some of which have been
mentioned in *ALS* (e.g., *ALS 1979*, p. 325). Except for the writers
here named and Pound and Eliot all the other poets under discussion
were born after 1900 (our cut-off date). An essay called "Stevens

and Keats's 'To Autumn' " (pp. 20–40) discloses that Keats's ode was a life-long influence on Stevens: "the central problems of the ode became central to Stevens' poetry as well." Vendler's entire volume is a typical product of her always fertile mind, well worth any reader's time. It won the National Book Critics Circle Award for 1980.

Freud calls the blending of the psyche with all being an "oceanic feeling." For Lawrence Kramer the "oceanic dilemma" arises out of the tension between the romantic imagination and the natural world resisting transformation by that imagination, especially when the sublime is involved, the sublime being vast, terrifying, or mysterious. In "Ocean and Vision: Imaginative Dilemma in Wordsworth, Whitman, and Stevens" (*JEGP* 79:210–30) Kramer says that to comprehend the sublime the mind must empty itself, thus nullifying its own presence. The oceanic dilemma is "the mind's refusal to submit to an external sublimity." Kramer draws illustrations from the three poets of the title as well as others. Except for Byron, who "proposes a triumphant recovery" from the struggle between the imagination and the sublime, the poets are left with the irony that the mind in replenishing itself is actually maimed. If this situation is troubling, nevertheless, "the Romantic imagination is at its most majestic in the midst of its most evasive self-celebrations and helplessly candid self-judgments." In a brief treatment of Stevens in this context (pp. 224–26) Kramer suggests that the poet confronts his dilemma with a cavalier attitude, illustrated in "Variations on a Summer Day," "The Idea of Order at Key West," and "Sea Surface Full of Clouds."

Paul Saagpakk's "The Apollonian Impulse: Aleksis Rannit and Wallace Stevens" (*MR* 21:157–73) is a study of how the rage for order in both the Estonian Rannit and the American Stevens is always battling against Dionysian forces by seeking sublimity through the moral order of the aesthetic (the base of Kramer's article). Among other techniques Saagpakk examines the poets' common use of certain images, such as mirror, flame, light, diamond, bird. The two writers part company in tone and attitude: whereas Rannit is gravely dramatic, Stevens tends toward a light irony (what Kramer would term cavalier). Both writers began as neoimpressionists but became ascetic though still gentle.

In another comparative study David L. Lavery pits a science-fiction novel against a Stevens poem. " 'The Genius of the Sea': Wallace Stevens' 'The Idea of Order at Key West,' Stanislaw Lem's *Solaris*, and the Earth as a Muse" (*Extrapolation* 21:101–05) finds that the sea gets revenge against the solipsism of the Stevens' poem. Rather than "transcendent analogue," poetry for Lem is "an immanent homologue of the particulars of reality." Lavery calls on Loren Eiseley, Teilhard de Chardin, Claude Lévi-Strauss, and Rainer Maria Rilke to support his view that all poets are dependent on the earth; "nature speaks through them as ventriloquists."

"The Public Monument and Public Poetry: Stevens, Berryman, and Lowell" by Michael North (*ConL* 21:267–85) avers that *Owl's Clover* is almost a battleground in itself "as the poet yearns for the monumental," though his material prevents that achievement. An analysis of the details of this long poem arrives at how Stevens moves more and more toward community. "The desire for public significance" here is in conflict with the poet's faithfulness to symbolism. As a result the poem ends in a standstill. North's article also discusses John Berryman's "Boston Common" and Robert Lowell's "For the Union Dead."

By reinterpreting "Carnet de Voyage" Wallace Martin points to the necessity of revision of certain biographical assumptions in reading Stevens' early poems. "The Figure of the Virile Poet as Youth: 'Carnet de Voyage' and Stevens' Journals" (*WSJour* 4:58–67) proposes reading the poet's entries "as a literary document requiring detailed explication." Martin finds "Carnet de Voyage" more complex in theme than most of the *Harmonium* poems. For him the ontology of this early work is of a piece with the middle and late poetry. It can, with the reread journals, bring us a "new conception of [Stevens'] literary development from 1898 to 1914." Edward Guereschi in "Wallace Stevens' Testimonial Poem: 'The Man with the Blue Guitar'" (*UDR* 14,ii:55–64) thinks of the speaker in this series as "a seer without moonshine" making an effort to move beyond the poet's egocentricism and to draw on the latent expressive power of society itself. Stevens here has stepped down into the world, mingling his "aesthetic perception with social facts" and addressing "the masses whose need for self-expression must be his own." In so doing he must look at himself afresh. Guereschi concludes that from 1937 on Stevens was ready to recapitulate and refine his major themes: "The irreducible world, the uses of poetry as a focus of order against disorder, the constant search for balance between opposites." This article offers a definite scheme for a profitable study of the poems of Stevens' last years.

Tenebrism, "the tension of light next to darkness," is the subject of T. D. Webb's "Wallace Stevens: A Notion of Chiaroscuro" (*BSUF* 21,i:34–39). The author sees "Domination of Black," "Anecdote of the Jar," and "The Idea of Order at Key West" as "almost a set," progressing philosophically as they interpret Stevens' feeling for "imagination within reality." Originally read at the Northeast Student Conference at Yale in 1978, Lea Hamaoui's "Sound as Image in Stevens' 'Not Ideas About the Thing, But the Thing Itself'" (*CLS* 17:251–59) reminds us that the "thing itself" is a "scrawny cry." The author explicates various poems to show that feeling and perception of reality are embodied in the idea of sound. The present poem gradually evolves from mind to reality, "the matter outside" (the cry), but a parallel movement leads it from reality back to mind. The result is the growth "of awareness attempting to expand into and absorb a thereby expanded universe."

Paul A. Bové in *Destructive Poetics: Heidegger and Modern American Poetry* (Columbia) begins by showing that Whitman rediscovers and revitalizes tradition and in *Leaves of Grass* goes back to things themselves unsatisfied with the traditional language that "re-presents" them. Bové then proceeds to illustrate the fallacies of the New Criticism. He analyzes how Stevens breaks up the forms and responses of the past to prove that all poetic statement is basically fiction (chapter 5: "Fiction, Risk, and Reconstruction: The Poetry of Wallace Stevens," pp. 181–215). The author says that Stevens works from the theory that language is based on "nothingness." Bové draws amply on the language and thinking of Søren Kierkegaard, Martin Heidegger, Roy Harvey Pearce, and Joseph N. Riddel. He questions in varying degrees the methods and indeed the results of the critical views of the chief writers about Stevens, including Helen Vendler and Harold Bloom. He takes a long look at "The Snow Man" and "The Comedian as the Letter C" and relies on Jacques Derrida and Roland Barthes to help him establish a "centerless vision" for Stevens, who he maintains believes only in "the fictional nature of even the most humanly valuable and sympathetic attitudes." Eleanor Cook maintains that Stevens makes a careful distinction between decreation and destruction. She uses especially two

poems of "Notes toward a Supreme Fiction" in "The Decreations of
Wallace Stevens" (*WSJour* 4:46–57), the first as a poem of genesis
and the second as a poem of revelation. Phoebus dies, rots away into
the uncreated (not into nothingness), then partly reappears in the
ephebe, beginning again.

Chapter 3 of *Word-Music: The Aesthetic Aspect of Narrative
Fiction* by James L. Guetti (Rutgers), called "Noncognitive Images:
Wallace Stevens" (pp. 33–53), claims that the poet's figures are not
characterized by knowledge, perception, or notion. Beginning with
metaphysical problems, the poems do not provide answers. What
initially appears to be argumentative, even realistic, is transformed
into musical images, seemingly putting aside the understanding.
Guetti looks at several poems and decides that intelligence in a
Stevens work is as a matrix on and within which ride images "beyond our powers to know." The author uses poems to show how
"unknowable" images operate and relates the poet's technique of
repetition to the processes in narrative fiction and in all imaginative
perception (especially the aural and the visual). Denis Donoghue's
"Two Notes on Stevens" (*WSJour* 4:40–45) records how the author
used to see Stevens' *Collected Poems* as wishing to become an "interior object," a romantic idea. He has now come to feel that pleasure
and desire are important—to enjoy each poem in its mood rather
than hook it on to a larger doctrine derived from the book as a whole.
He departs from Georges Poulet's *La conscience critique* in admon-
ishing the reader to accept from poem to poem "sequence, change,
and process."

Allen Chavkin seeks to reconcile the poet's imagism (pre-
Harmonium and later) with "his non-transcendental romanticism."
"Wallace Stevens: The Romantic Imagist" (*BSUF* 21,i:40–47) grants
that in later poems Stevens was less interested in images than in
ideas, but he was cautious of didacticism in spite of his ongoing
tendency to use it. He wanted to communicate his ideas, to express
himself in his own way. He was influenced by the critics of the 1930s
who blamed him for not assuming social and political attitudes (see
Guereschi on "The Man with the Blue Guitar" above). For these
reasons he was always somewhat didactic, though in the long run he
was "a precise romantic, a romantic imagist."

The names of Stevens' poems "are proverbs or word games or
quibbles" designed to draw the reader's attention. So says Mary Britt

in "Notes Toward Supreme Poetry: A Study of Wallace Stevens' Titles" (*TSL* 25:110–19). They have identity apart from the poems they head, originating in "random thought, observations, things over- heard or read from newspapers, even sidewalk graffiti." The poet accumulated hundreds of such possible titles, most of them unused. They show Stevens to have been the supreme virtuoso: pedagogue, linguist, comedian, philosopher. They point to a mind struggling to comprehend reality. This article is ingenious and illuminating.

In "A Dithering of Presences: Style and Language in Stevens' Essays" (*ConL* 21:100–17) Lisa M. Steinman reminds us that Stevens had no systematically formulated poetics. He even made apparently contradictory statements, but his essays show his method of develop- ing "a style which includes insistence upon itself and upon poetry as an act of using language." For him language is process, stressed by analogy, difference, ornamentation, or excess, which suggest "figu- ration." Supported by tone and style these concepts are part and parcel of both the essays and the poems.

Following up his *Stevens' Poetry of Thought* (see *ALS* 1966, pp. 211–12), Frank Doggett has now given us *Wallace Stevens: The Making of the Poem* (Johns Hopkins), in which at the beginning he brings together and analyzes the poet's own statements (found in his journals, letters, and poems) concerning the two sources of poetry—the conscious level of intelligence and the unconscious level, i.e., the "meditating sleep," irrational, involuntary. The contribution of these two origins dominates Doggett's book with emphasis on the necessity for "integration." Stevens' own analysis of various poems is useful to the author in explaining the theory about poetry making. As the book proceeds, he considers such problems as the possible (a continuation of the given), the prodigality of imagery, characters, and situations, the function of the sea, the influence of critics on the poet's creative process, style and the poem itself as inseparable. Dog- gett writes well and helps considerably in clarifying Stevens' method, theory, and purpose. The explication of many poems supports the findings.

Finally, Doggett has collaborated with Robert Buttell in compil- ing *Wallace Stevens: A Celebration* (Princeton). The editors have collected several early versions of poems, unpublished endings, note- book entries, and letters as well as biographical essays. With a few typographical differences from the version in her *Part of Nature* (see above), Helen Vendler's study of Stevens in relation to Keats's "To Autumn" is here. Isabel G. McCaffrey takes a long look at "Le Monocle de Mon Oncle." There are essays on sounds in Stevens (both nonsense and music) as well as sturdy articles by Frank Kermode (the Hölderlin-Heidegger connection), J. Hillis Miller (the importance of a poem's resisting intelligence), Roy Harvey Pearce (decreation and recreation through the poetic act), and Joseph N. Riddel (geneses as "poetic and abyssal"). If the book superficially appears like a patchwork, it achieves unity in its overall function—to throw more light on the work of a singularly astounding poet.

Purdue University

17. Poetry: The 1940s to the Present

Lee Bartlett

In an attempt to deflate the balloon of self-importance some literary critics (from textual scholars to theorists) have blown up for themselves, George Steiner employs an apt simile: historically, the critic is like a very small pilot fish, usually rather drably colored, clearing the way for a much larger, splendidly arrayed fish, and that larger fish is the great artist. Moving into the '80s, we students of recent American poetry should perhaps adapt Steiner's simile to our particular situation; through the past three decades, the myriad pilot fish have been clearing the way not only for great poets (we are too close to recognize them fully yet), but also for that large dappled fish of the poetry which has come after Pound, Eliot, Williams, Stein, Jeffers, and Stevens itself. After reading through the 40-odd books and over 100 essays published in our area of concern in 1980, I find it clear that the serious readers of recent American verse continue either explicitly or implicitly to attempt to discover the nature of their vast charge—the pied body of postmodernism. Who are the inheritors of the tradition, the *line*? "Open" poets? The formalists? The Black Mountaineers, the Beats, the Confessionals, the New York crowd? Do these labels have any meaning at all, or are all contemporary poets finally neo-Romantics? In short, who, to shift the metaphor from the aquarium to the street corner, has all the marbles?

i. General

An important work which appeared too late to be included in last year's chapter was James E. Miller, Jr.'s *The American Quest for a Supreme Fiction: Whitman's Legacy in the Personal Epic* (Chicago), a first-rate study of the American long poem, with an opening chapter on Robert Lowell and John Berryman, followed by separate chapters of Charles Olson's *Maximus Poems* ("Projective Verse" appears to be Olson's "preparation for launching his *Maximus Poems* and surely serves the same function as Whitman's 1855 Preface"), Berryman's *Dream Songs* (Berryman shifted "poetic allegiances" to Whitman in mid-career), and Allen Ginsberg's *Fall of America* (Ginsberg is "the heir" of the Pound-Williams-Olson line "of revolutionary theory and practice, but he interestingly sensed that he could take from the primal source itself: Whitman"). Miller sees Whitman as "the pivotal figure for the American epic form," though a figure who has never been given his due, thanks primarily to the myth (nourished by the modernists) that American poetry in this century has its source in France and England. In the first few pages of his book Miller argues that the epic impulse has its origins in America "deep in the national psyche," in the American poet's search for a supreme fiction in Stevens' sense; he then outlines the twin geometries of his program: (1) that "every American poet must come to terms with [Whitman's] presence and is influenced as deeply in rejecting as in accepting him" (which, for example, accounted for the shift in sensibility in both Lowell and Berryman in the mid-'50s), and (2) that the lineage of the American poet is "from Whitman to Pound and from Pound to Eliot and Williams, and thus to the latest moderns of whatever school." These notions certainly are not novel, but what follows is a sensitive attempt to sort out the ways in which Whitman's presence has informed several important poets of our time. A useful expansion of (and often corrective to) Pearce's chapter on the American long poem in *The Continuity of American Poetry*, Miller's book is one no student of American writing or culture can afford to overlook.

This year's more general book-length discussions of modern American poetry are limited to five volumes of previously published essays and reviews by Jerome Mazzaro, Helen Vendler, Jonathan Holden, Linda W. Wagner, and Harry Levin, and the reprinting of an enlarged edition of a collection by Richard Howard; of these books, Mazzaro's comes the closest to being a developed study. In *Postmodern American Poetry* (Illinois), he collects his essays on Jarrell, Roethke, Ignatow, Berryman, Plath, and Bishop. Mazzaro notes that his discussion is "not an attempt to define or detail a movement in contemporary letters," but an attempt at isolating recurrent patterns in the work of certain poets who are post-Modern primarily because of their refusal to accept the Eliotic proposal that poetry is an escape from personality. In his first chapter (previously unpublished), "The Genesis of Postmodernism: W. H. Auden," Mazzaro carefully charts Auden's critical reputation through the '30s and '40s, taking the poet's interest in Freud, Marx, and Darwin as the fount of his post- (or anti-) modernism. American poets' acceptance of Freud is, for Mazzaro, clearly manifested in a poetry of "emotive language, overtly sexual matter, and special typographies to represent surface and latent content as well as associative leaps." Specifically for Auden, "the bidirectional thrusts of Freud (past) and Marx (future)" finally merge in a belief in a notion of linear history provided by Christianity. In the chapters that follow (all reviewed in earlier volumes of *ALS*), Mazzaro describes how the six poets above take their cues from Auden on these matters, and shows how unlike the modernists these post-Modern poets accept "the fall from unity" precipitated by language in their willingness to use language for self-definition.

While Helen Vendler's *Part of Nature, Part of Us: Modern American Poets* (Harvard) finally might not be the most important book published this year on recent American poetry, it was certainly the most noticed. The book was roundly praised in the major reviews and journals, and it won the National Book Critics Circle Award for Criticism. Vendler probably is not, as the *New Republic* blurb to her book states, "the best poetry reviewer in America," though she is very good; this collection of essays and reviews written over ten years deals with 32 poets, from Eliot to James Tate, and on the whole the pieces are gracefully written, the judgments sound. Because the book received so much press (and because most of the essays were reviewed in previous volumes of *ALS*) there is really no reason to speak at length about it here, other than to especially recommend Vendler's pieces on Robert Lowell, Frank O'Hara, James Merrill, Adrienne Rich, and Dave Smith.

In *The Rhetoric of the Contemporary Lyric* (Indiana) Jonathan Holden collects seven essays (four of which are previously published and reviewed in earlier *ALS* volumes) which, "while conceived independently of each other . . . prompted by what appeared at the time to be a single discrete issue," emerged as finally centering on a single question—"rhetoric" in the contemporary lyric. Throughout his essays, Holden prefers to use the term rhetoric in its original sense, not so much as referring to style but rather persuasion, examining such issues as "who is speaking to whom, through what mask, and for what ostensible purpose." Touching on work by Hugo, Strand, Bly, Snyder, Stafford, and Creeley (with entire chapters devoted to Stephen Dunn and John Ashbery), Holden ventures such observations as the first-person stance of a poem is not a stylistic question but rather "a convention that requires a style," and the emphasis on metaphor in contemporary American poetry "is a natural outgrowth of the recession of music in favor of closure as the dominant convention." Holden argues (though not fully convincingly) that of all contemporary poets, Stephen Dunn "exhibits the greatest sensitivity to poetry as rhetoric and demonstrates the greatest rhetorical inventiveness," as opposed to the "beautiful but detached postmodernist games that a poet such as Ashbery plays." In his final chapter he responds to an attack by Marjorie Perloff on Hugo's "In Your Young Dream," refuting her notion that Hugo's poem is premodernist, "instant Wordsworth."

In Harry Levin's *Memories of the Moderns* (New Directions) one of our finest critics brings together 20 previously published essays which are a mix of memoir and criticism. The book includes Levin's defense of Conrad Aiken, a memoir of Delmore Schwartz, and a review of Randall Jarrell's *Faust*; there is also a wonderful opening letter to James Laughlin which discusses the crucial role of New Directions in the history of the modern. Linda W. Wagner's "exploratory and commendatory" occasional essays and reviews on more recent American poetry are collected in *American Modern: Essays in Fiction and Poetry* (Kennikat). Considering Wagner's very prolific critical output, I am surprised at the generally high quality of the 18 pieces on poets (Ignatow, Stafford, Olson, Berryman, Plath, Levertov, and others) which are reprinted here; while a few of the reviews are rather slight, some of the longer essays are certainly as enlightening as Vendler's. Finally, Richard Howard has published an enlarged edition of his 1969 *Alone With America: Essays on the Art of Poetry in the United States Since 1950* (Atheneum). The first edition was stylistically quirky, almost hermetic at times, and this enlarged edition is no less so; still, it remains a useful book on 41 contemporary poets from A. R. Ammons to James Wright primarily because of its inclusiveness. Howard has added essays to many of the original chapters, bringing the text more current.

Charles Altieri continues to work out his theories of American post-Modern poetry in his lively "From Experience to Discourse: American Poetry and Poetics in the Seventies" (*ConL* 21:191–224) positing "a general opposition between a poetics of immediate experience and a poetics acknowledging its status as discourse in the hope that this distinction can clarify the work of many younger poets only now developing mature voices." The first group (Stanley Plumly, William Matthews, Robert Hass, and others) "is largely a transform of the quiet dramatic mode of Wright and Stafford," while the second group (Albert Goldbarth, Richard Shelton, Norman Dubie, and David St. John) "engages in various transformations of more surreal uses of the deep image" à la Bly and Merwin. Altieri goes on to explain that these transformations are the product of a kind of "pressure," a Bloomean "anxiety," both historical and social. His comments on Hass (who uses "negation to transcend itself") and Simic (whose "poetry occupies an imaginative space between the dramatic naturalism of Hass and the radically discontinuous surface we find in the most experimental younger poets") are useful; unfortunately, his acrimonious remarks on Bly and Kinnell are not. His complaint that Bly's "diffuse emotion is not tempered by sharp recognitions or verbal wit" certainly misses the point, as for Bly those qualities are exactly what mitigate against true poetic statement; his opinion that "Kinnell ultimately has no significant ideas" in *The Book of Nightmares* (for "what do trees know or bones think") is neither less contentious nor more astute. Altieri is a penetrating and often stunning critic, and his occasional blind spots and partisanship are all the more unfortunate for that.

At its inception, the term "romance" was applied to vernacular French literature, to differentiate it from the Latin; in "The New American Romances" (*TCL* 26:269–77), however, Paul Christensen uses romance in a looser sense in an attempt to set *The Cantos*, "The Waste Land," *Paterson*, and *The Maximus Poems* in what he sees as their proper context—the "tradition of the European verse romance." He argues that while these poems are often read as epics (as in Miller's study), they are not epics for "the epic is the expression of an age that has achieved a philosophy, which a poet articulates with eloquent certainty." The romance, however, "is the chief expression of an age that has exhausted its philosophy and seeks a new one." Rather than celebrations of culture, the new American romances (like their medieval counterparts) reject the status quo:

The Cantos rejects modern economics, "The Waste Land" rejects Arnold's version of a literary tradition, *Paterson* rejects industrialism, *The Maximus Poems* rejects "mass society." Yet, while all these poems are interrelated, they are "fundamentally opposed to each other in their ideological visions," as they all are quests "for new bearings after the shock of deep social transformation."

A special *APR* supplement, "Considering Poetry" (9,vi), prints four papers on contemporary American verse. In "The Power of Reflection" (pp. 18–21) Ira Sadoff discusses the "reemergence of the meditative poem," seeing its roots in the "deep-image school" and the growing interest in Rilke. Robert Miklitsch (*"Ut Pictura Poesis,"* [pp. 21–25]) focuses on "reduction" (minimalism) in contemporary painting and poetry as a reaction to modernism. Theodore Weiss's "An American Poet's Dilemma" (pp. 25–29) centers on the questions of language and place. Finally, Michael Ryan's "On the Nature of Poetry" (pp. 29–32) discusses the problems of rhythm, form, and the mythic in poetry.

Certainly all serious poets attend to form, and paradoxically enough it is probably those poets whose work seems the least "formal" who most worry over questions of form. In the Fall 1979 issue of *Epoch* (29,i) Robert Schultz has a "Preface to a Symposium on the Line in Contemporary Poetry" (pp. 90–93). The next issue (29,ii; Winter 1980) is devoted to "A Symposium on the Theory and Practice of the Line in Contemporary Poetry." There is an introduction by Rory Holscher and Robert Schultz (pp. 162–70), followed by statements by 29 English and American poets (pp. 171–224), including Philip Booth, William Dickey, Robert Kelly, Allen Ginsberg, Josephine Miles, and Robert Pinsky. Tom Henighan ("Shamans, Tribes, and the Sorcerer's Apprentices: Notes on the Discovery of the Primitive in Modern Poetry," *The Dalhousie Review* 59:605–20) also concerns himself with poetics, arguing that while it is, on the whole, a minor trend, "the search for the primitive, the desire to take on the role of the tribal shaman, and even to use his language, is one of the permanent fascinations of the modern poet." He sees the historical source of our modern ideas of the poet as shaman in romanticism; however, where the primitive shaman "is accepted and sanctioned by the culture he operates in," the modern poet "is driven more and more into a position of isolation." The chief contemporary "shaman poet," according to Henighan, is Gary Snyder, while one of the chief "academic explorations" of the phenomenon takes place at the Jack Kerouac School of Disembodied Poetics at Naropa.

The JK School gets less positive treatment in Ishmael Reed's spirited "American Poetry Looking for a Center" (*San Francisco Review of Books*, Nov.–Dec., pp. 18–19). Reed concerns himself with the continuing "Naropa Wars," attending to *Time Magazine's* 1977 quotation by Anne Waldman that "Naropa is fast becoming the center of American poetics." Reed's three-part "diary and commentary" gives his own impressions of Naropa, along with observations by other poets—from Victor Cruz's assessment that at Naropa "they write Disco poetry" to Bob Callahan's notion that Naropa is "part of a 200-year old American tradition, 'the dude ranch' . . . merely the Saint Mark's Project gone west."

Finally, this year there are three new anthologies and three new reference books of note. Robert Bly's *News of the Universe* (Sierra Club) anthologizes 150 poems from many periods and cultures, interspersed with Bly's essays on the evolution of "poems of two-fold consciousness" (seen most recently in the work of Kinnell, Snyder, James Wright, and others). *Surrealism & Its Popular Accomplices*, ed. Franklin Rosemont (City Lights) contains many original articles by Philip Lamantia, Rosemont, and others on the ongoing Surrealist program, as well as translations, poems, "archival material," and reviews. Alan F. Pater has edited the first volume in a new series, an *Anthology of Magazine Verse and Yearbook of American Poetry* (Monitor Book Company), with an introduction by William H. Pritchard; the fat and expensive ($25) book collects "a selection of 1979's finest poetry from magazines in the United States and Canada," as well as a bibliography of books of and about poetry published in 1979 and a list of poetry prize winners for that year. While this secondary material is useful, the quality of the poetry included ranges from quite good to doggerel, with poems which have appeared in *Poetry*, APR, and the quarterlies appearing alongside verse from *The Christian Century*, *Unity*, and *Insight*.

The most important of the reference works is, of course, the third edition of *Contemporary Poets* (St. Martin's), ed. James Vinson, with an introduction by Marjorie Perloff. The current volume contains biographies, bibliographies, and comments for 840 contemporary poets, including an appendix of 22 poets who have died since 1950, and 70 new entries. The book continues to set the standard for its type. John Somer and Barbara Eck Cooper's *American & British Literature, 1945–1975: An Annotated Bibliography of Contemporary Scholarship* (Kansas) attempts to survey "the general trends in contemporary criticism," and contains a separate section on book-length studies of contemporary poetry and poetics. While the volume is highly selective (our section lists 171 items), the annotation of individual entries makes it a useful quick-reference. Sander W. Zulauf and Edward M. Cifelli's eighth *Index of American Periodical Verse: 1978* (Scarecrow) continues their series started in 1971; the book locates poems published in almost 200 magazines in 1978, listed by author.[1]

ii. John Berryman, Robert Lowell, Theodore Roethke, Stanley Kunitz, Elizabeth Bishop, Richard Wilbur, Muriel Rukeyser, Howard Nemerov, John Ciardi, Paul Goodman, Louis Simpson

Critics continue to be drawn to these "middle generation" poets, with, as might be expected, Berryman, Lowell, and Roethke receiving the most sustained attention.

1. Several fairly important items published in 1978 and not mentioned previously in *ALS* should be noticed here. *Towards a New American Poetics: Essays & Interviews* (Black Sparrow Press), edited by Ekbert Faas, contains short essays on Olson, Snyder, Creeley, Bly, and Ginsberg, and interviews with Duncan and the others (excluding, of course, Olson). While the essays really add nothing new to our understanding of the poets, they are solid introductions; the interviews, however, especially Duncan's and Creeley's, must be considered major statements. The two-volume *Talking Poetics From Naropa Institute: Annals of the Jack Kerouac School of Disembodied Poetics* (Shambhala), edited by Anne Waldman and Marilyn Webb, contains the transcripts of 18 "lectures" given by poets (Duncan, DiPrima, Ted Berrigan, Dorn, McClure, Padgett, Coolidge, MacLow, Brownstein, Whalen, Rothenberg, Waldman, Algarin, MacAdams, Sanders, and Ginsberg) and others at Naropa since 1974. The quality of these papers varies, but the collection cannot be overlooked as it deals with many issues vital to an understanding of contemporary poetics. Charles Olson's *Muthologus: The Collected Lectures & Interviews* (Four Seasons), edited by George Butterick, appeared in two volumes (the second in 1979), drawing together a record of "the public voice of Charles Olson as transcribed from the surviving tapes"; *Muthologus* collects 13 seminal Olson pieces, and Butterick's notes are quite good. The second volume of Cid Corman's *At Their Word: Essays on the Arts of Language* (Black Sparrow Press) brings together 15 essays and reviews centering on poetry, some of which are previously unpublished. *Off the Wall: Interviews with Philip Whalen* (Four Seasons), edited by Donald Allen, collects interviews with the poet by Anne Waldman, Aram Saroyan, Yves LePellec, Lee Bartlett, Barry Gifford, and Larry Lee.

John Haffenden is John Berryman's official biographer, and while we await the *Life*, he has given us *John Berryman: A Critical Commentary* (NYU). Haffenden divides his book into two parts: the first offers essays on the work of Berryman's "maturity" (*Homage, Dream Songs, Love & Fame*), with close examinations of "the genesis of the poems" based on working drafts and notes, while the second ("Notes and Commentary") gives a gloss of many difficult or obscure references in *Dream Songs* and *Delusions, Etc.* Though Haffenden's thesis certainly is not news to Berryman's readers ("the soul under stress, under observation, is Berryman's, and the poet is everywhere in his work"; Berryman's poetry emerges as "the mythopoeic recomposition of his own experience"), he has given us a book rich in first-class source material, one which stands well beside Joel Conarroe's 1977 *Introduction*. Jack V. Barbera is also interested in source material in his note to "Berryman's 'Dream Song 110'" (*Expl* 38,iii: 29–31), wherein he points out that the poem is based on the accidental drowning of Berryman's brother's son in New York in 1944.

In "The Public Monument and Public Poetry: Stevens, Berryman, and Lowell" (*ConL* 21:267–85) Michael North argues that in Stevens' *Owl's Clover*, Berryman's "Boston Common," and Robert Lowell's "For the Union Dead," the poets' "attempt to reconcile the personal and the monumental tells a great deal about the problems and possibilities of public poetry in this century." North feels that all three of these poets "reject the method of abstraction" which made earlier, generalized public poetry possible. He finds both Berryman's and Lowell's irony giving us a "real world which is tangible and accessible to the public, but impossibly barren."

Agenda (18,iii) devotes a special issue, edited by William Bedford, to Robert Lowell this year. The journal opens with Lowell's "Mills of the Kavanaughs" which, interestingly enough, had appeared in England previously only in an appendix to a critical book. An "Elegy" (pp. 21–22) by Seamus Heany follows, then the reprinting of Heany's now well-known memorial address given in London on the death of Lowell in 1977, a death that "shook the frame of poetry." In "Lowell and Hölderlin: A Note and a Suggestion" (pp. 30–33), John Bayley discusses Lowell's poem "Unwanted," arguing that while on the surface these two poets seem to have little in common, in fact they are linked by the *angst* of their vocations; in Lowell's later poems, he approximates "the sense of loss which Hölderlin records," which in turn becomes a celebration. M. L. Rosenthal's "Our Neurotic Angel: Robert Lowell (1917–77)" (pp. 34–45) assesses Lowell's career, concluding that if he had not died he would "very likely have become our first poet to be a Nobel laureate." Rosenthal focuses primarily on *Life Studies*, which he feels remains Lowell's most powerful book, bridging the "aristocratically oriented sensibility that still held sway earlier this century and the mystique of the anti-poetic," an achievement the poet was never able to equal. In "The Reshaping of 'Waking Early Sunday Morning'" (pp. 47–62), Alan Williamson reprints a few of Lowell's worksheets for "Waking Early," in an extended discussion of the 41 drafts of the poem; according to Williamson, these drafts seem to indicate that Lowell "associated his own more formal high style with political engagement," and that his "best public writing" was "linked to his 'confessional' writing by an analogy . . . between his own experience of madness" and social irrationality. J. P. Ward's "'But Lowell He Did Not Touch'" (pp. 63–74) sees the poet's primary "mode of cognition" as "historical-hermeneutic," while Neil Corcoran's "Lowell *Retiarius*: Towards *The Dolphin*" (pp. 75–85) reads that collection as "notoriously closest to the most potentially embarrassing circumstances of Lowell's private life," presenting itself as the poet's "most obviously constructed, sustained, and integrated poetic form." In "Reading Through Robert Lowell's Enigmas" (pp. 86–93), the poet Richard Tillinghast briefly explicates four of Lowell's poems, concluding that while Lowell is aware of his "complex relation to his masters," his poems are not about poetry itself but are born of a "deep reflection on human life." Wyatt Prunty's "Allegory to Causality" (pp. 94–103) makes an extended analysis of two published versions of "The Mills of the Kavanaughs," arguing that the latter of which "represents the major shift in Lowell's poetic thinking" in its "removal of a Catholic framework" in favor of "an empirical and causal mode of thought." The final essay is Marjorie Perloff's "'Fearlessly Holding Back Nothing'" (104–14), a discussion of Lowell's last poems, which in *Day By Day* emerge as "*self-centered* in the best sense of the word" as the poet "renounces, one by one, the roles he played in his earlier work" through a "process of de-mythologizing." This special issue concludes with two poems for Lowell by Donald Davie and Peter Dale.

J. Barton Rollins traces the influence of Richard Eberhart, Allen

Tate, and others on the young Robert Lowell in "Robert Lowell's Apprenticeship and Early Poems" (*AL* 52:67–83). Eberhart commented that even in Lowell's earliest verse he was obsessed with the "heavy" and the "essentially religious," and Rollins feels that both poets share a major concern with "conflict and tension," Eberhart's example leading Lowell to a poetry possessing "the qualities of I. A. Richards' poetry of inclusion and synthesis." Rollins discusses the poems Lowell included in his manuscript for the "Katherine Irene Memorial Poetry Prize, May 1938," while a student at Kenyon College, and early poems published in the Kenyon College magazine *Hika*. He finds this early work rather predictable, but discovers in "*Sublime Feriam Sidera Vertice*" "the first of Lowell's works to incorporate the apocalyptic, religious violence" of his first volumes.

Two views of *Life Studies* are presented by Raffel Burton (pp. 293–325) and Richard J. Fein (pp. 326–38) in *The Literary Review* (vol. 23). Focusing primarily on Lowell's prosody in *Life Studies*, Burton feels that the book signals a "renewed and deepening failure of nerve." While part three of the volume contains four poems of "unqualified success," and while some individual passages of other poems take Lowell further than his earlier work, Burton argues, the final section of the book signals the poet's backing away from greatness in his "anecdotal skimming off of potentially stunning material." Richard Fein disagrees with Burton's assessment, seeing in *Life Studies* a group of fully realized poems which "casually yet intensively" reflect upon each other. He directs most of his discussion towards "Skunk Hour," which he senses is the climax of a collection "which captures so deftly and so sympathetically, so wryly and so casually, the physical facts of people's lives. The comic and stubborn furniture of the soul resides in this poetry."

Finally, Philip Cooper's note on "The Quaker Graveyard in Nantucket" (*Expl* 38,iv:43) argues that Lowell's use of "westward" in the poem is not an error in geography, but an "imaginative slurring of geographical coordinates into emotive ones," Martha George Meek's note on "The Mills of the Kavanaughs" (*Expl* 38,ii:46–47) discusses the mythological allusions in Anne Kavanaugh's dream, and K. J. Dover's "Translation: The Speakable and the Unspeakable" (*EIC* 30,1:1–8) mentions Lowell's work as a translator.

Of the five articles which appeared on Roethke this year Don Bogan's "From *Open House* to the Greenhouse: Theodore Roethke's

Poetic Breakthrough" (*ELH* 47:399–418) is probably the most ambitious. To notice that between Roethke's first volume, *Open House*,
in 1941, and his second, *The Lost Son*, in 1948, the poet "immersed
himself in new work of a significantly different order" has become
a commonplace in Roethke criticism. Yet in his careful examination
of the development of three Roethke poems (the early "Genesis,"
"On the Road to Woodlawn" from the mid-'30s, and "Cuttings" from
the mid-'40s) as preserved in the unpublished drafts in Roethke's
Papers at the University of Washington, Bogan gives us a clearer
understanding of just how this deepening of sensibility took place.
In "The Explorer's Rose: Theodore Roethke's Mystical Symbol" (*CP*
13:4–49) Susan R. Bowers attempts to solve the critical controversy
over "North American Sequence" (is the poem an effort to transcend
nature or to reintegrate with it?) by focusing on the symbol of the
rose. Roses have appeared earlier in Roethke's work, Bowers suggests, but prior to this poem never a "wild rose." Thus, in "NAS"
Roethke moves "outside the confines of the greenhouse to the wild,
open edge of his own life and country," as the poem suggests "neither
transcendence over nor re-integration with *things*, but re-integration
with *relations*." In two *Explicator* notes Charles Sanders discusses
Roethke's "The Swan" (38,iii:27–28) and "The Sensualists" (38,4:
9–10). For Sanders, the poet's identification of the act of love with
poetry in "The Swan" makes the poem an "epitome of the mature
Roethkean mode," while the "ghostly figure" in "The Sensualists"
heralds both the renewal of a father's love and "the Muse's poetic
inspiration." Lastly, nowhere is the ludicrous lag-time between acceptance and publication of an article so apparent as in the appearance this year of Jay Parini's "Theodore Roethke: The Poetics of
Expression" in *Forum* (21:5–11); this essay was published *last year*
as a chapter in Parini's fine *Theodore Roethke: An American Romantic*.

Marie Henault feels that the poetry of Stanley Kunitz has been
undervalued by critics, and has tried to remedy the situation by
writing the first book-length study of Kunitz's poetry, prose, and
translations, *Stanley Kunitz* (TUSAS 351). Reading Kunitz's verse
through 1974, Henault sees the work in the main as "lyrical, personal, emotional, and intense," yet not "confessional"; rather, Kunitz
turns his "own life into fable," finding therein "mythic parallels."
Though students of Kunitz's writing will obviously find Henault's

handbook useful in their studies, perhaps a more graceful and perceptive evaluation of the poet appears in Gregory Orr's extended review of Kunitz's collected poems (*APR* 9,iv:36–41). Orr argues that "a primary source of Kunitz's art is personal trauma, specifically the mysterious and violent death of his father"; his "primary experience is loss or absence," and the poet's major theme emerges as the quest of the son for the father, which is finally a search for Kunitz's own identity. Kunitz comes closest to fulfilling his "ambitions of tragic stance and intensity," Orr concludes, in his later work, where poems move from the impersonal to the "unadorned personal source."

Students of Kunitz's poetry will also want to look at *Antaeus* (37), which includes a "Feature on the Poetry of Stanley Kunitz," five essays on the poet by five younger poets. In "The Difficult Journey" (pp. 101–14) Louise Glück notes that "in Kunitz, the narrative has seemed lyric too, in that his tales—mythic, parabolic—drive toward a single, complex epiphany," and follows with an extended discussion of "The Lincoln Relics." Robert Hass ("What Furies," pp. 115–28) argues that while there is some similarity between Kunitz and Wallace Stevens, Stevens was a "meditative poet," while Kunitz "has practiced the dramatic lyric all his life." David Ignatow's short appreciation, "A Figure of Change and Freedom" (pp. 129–32), sees Kunitz's *The Testing Tree* as a seminal volume, marking the poet's break with closed forms. In "The Healing Imagination" (pp. 133–38), Gregory Orr again touches on Kunitz's relationship with his father, while Michael Ryan discusses the early poems in "Isolation and Apocalypse" (pp. 139–48), noting that Kunitz's later development "can be seen as a layering, an adding to the core of essential character" present in his early poems.

Candace W. MacMahon's *Elizabeth Bishop: A Bibliography, 1927–1979* (Virginia), the first bibliography of Bishop's work, is an impressive work of scholarship. MacMahon's volume is fully descriptive; in addition, it includes photographs of the title pages and passages of Bishop's letters relating to the publication of her books. Ruth Quebe discusses Elizabeth Bishop's "imagery of detachment" in "Water, Windows, and Birds: Image–Theme Patterns in Elizabeth Bishop's *Questions of Travel*" (*MPS* 10:68–82). According to Quebe, Bishop's major themes in *Questions* are the permanence of human potential, the "puzzles of epistemology," and the "temporary resolutions of the imagination." These themes correspond to recurrent

images—"of transformation, of frames, and of suspension"—which
revolve around water, colors, and birds. These images, Quebe feels,
seldom "grow into delicate symbols," but rather indicate a certain
interdependence of theme and imagery itself. This short essay is
valuable not only for its concise readings of some individual poems,
but also for its attempt to disprove the oft-made assertion that
Bishop's poems are not organically related. In a note (*Expl* 38,iv:
28–29), Charles Sanders analyzes the structure of Bishop's two-part
poem "Roosters," seeing the second section growing "almost systematically out of the first."

Randall Jarrell set the tone for subsequent criticism of Richard
Wilbur when he wrote of the poet that he was "*attractive* and *appealing* and *engaging*," but finally a master craftsman out of touch
with life, whose "manners and manner" never failed him. In "Encounters with Experience: The Poems of Richard Wilbur" (*NER*
2:594–613) Ejner J. Jensen attempts to correct this view of the poet
as "gentleman," arguing that Wilbur's detractors mistake his style
for his vision, and that in fact the poet is "aware of the darker elements of human experience." In his reading of poems like "For Dudley," "On the Marginal Way," and "In the Field," Jensen finds an
intense struggle sourced in a powerful engagement with the world,
while in the strongest earlier work ("Marginalia," "Beasts," and "The
Undead") he detects a serious and haunting sense of evil, one certainly the equal of Frost's. Jensen's essay was convincing enough to
send me back to Wilbur's poetry with renewed interest. Marcia B.
Dinneen provides "Richard Wilbur: A Bibliography of Secondary
Sources" (*BB* 37:16–22), a useful checklist.

In *The Poetic Vision of Muriel Rukeyser* (LSU) Louise Kertesz
traces the evolution of Rukeyser's poetry from her first volume
(*Theory of Flight*, a book which won the 1935 Yale Younger Poets
Prize, and one which Kertesz feels "succeeds where *The Bridge*
fails") through *The Gates* (1976), placing the poet squarely in the
Whitman tradition. Kertesz's work suffers a bit from her too obvious
loyalty to her subject, though this is also its strength as her volume
becomes not only the first book-length explication of Rukeyser's
writing, but also a spirited defense of a relatively neglected (thanks
to her efforts to do battle with the New Critics 40 years ago) American poet of power, range, and sensitivity.

Besides the Twayne volume on Kunitz discussed earlier, three other Twayne studies of interest to students of recent American poetry appeared this year: Edward Krickel's *John Ciardi* (TUSAS 367), Ross Labrie's *Howard Nemerov* (TUSAS 356), and Kingsley Widmer's *Paul Goodman* (TUSAS 358). The first two books trace the development of Ciardi and Nemerov chronologically, offering along the way useful biographical information and generally sensible readings of the poets' work (the chapters on Ciardi's translations and Nemerov's later poetry are particularly useful). Widmer's book departs from the usual Twayne format in that its author sets out to be controversial. He sees Paul Goodman as primarily a "libertarian social critic," arguing that his poetry and his fiction are the result of "literary hobbyism," and are in general "literally incompetent—marked by trite and mangled language, bumblingly inconsistent manners and tones, garbled syntax and forms." Though Widmer's conclusion that Goodman's poems "monument the failure" of his poetasting does ring true, one feels a need for a more extended discussion of Goodman's literary work than Widmer offers here.

William H. Robertson's *Louis Simpson: A Reference Guide* (Hall) will be welcomed by Simpson's readers. Robertson includes a chronology of important dates, a complete checklist of writings by the poet, and an extended, annotated checklist of criticism and reviews.

Finally, in "Louis Coxe: Misplaced Poet" (*HC* 14,2:1–17), Robert McGovern feels Coxe's work has been neglected due to a "combination of history, both political and poetical, and the cultural development in our country" (i.e., Coxe has written often of the Second World War, his work is "agonizing and brutal," he is more or less a regionalist, his prosody tends toward the traditional); here he attempts an overview of the poet's "quiet" achievement.

iii. Charles Olson, Robert Creeley, Edward Dorn, Robert Duncan

Although last year it seemed as if Charles Olson criticism had gone into a holding pattern (with only two items reviewed in *ALS*), 1980 saw much activity, including the publication of the first two volumes of a major letter collection, a book-length study of *Maximus* (and a chapter in another), and three articles of note. In 1950 Olson wrote to Henry A. Murray that he and Robert Creeley had begun "perhaps the most important correspondence" of his life, an exchange which would continue until his death 20 years later. Approximately 1,000 letters and cards survive, and George Butterick and Black Sparrow Press have undertaken the considerable task of publishing them entire in a number of volumes to be released at the rate of one or two a year until complete. The first two volumes of *Charles Olson & Robert Creeley: The Complete Correspondence*, edited by Butterick, takes us, amazingly enough, only through six months of 1950. While the letters often are difficult to follow given both Olson's and Creeley's propensity for a Poundian quirkiness of syntax and abbreviation, there is much important material here, including drafts of previously unpublished poems by both men. In addition, Butterick has provided his usual accurate and detailed notes.

With *Charles Olson's Maximus* (Illinois), Don Byrd joins the ranks of Sherman Paul, Paul Christensen, and Robert von Hallberg, that second generation of Olson scholars who are interpretive rather than editorial. Byrd begins his discussion by setting the context, attempting to clarify Olson's relationship to the modernists by declaring that while the poet was of course heavily influenced by Pound and Williams, through his strategy "to deny the sham clarity of the Apollonian intelligence . . . in the *Maximus* the fire is space, and it is space as a source of energy that replaces for Olson" the modernist tradition. He devotes a chapter to the poet's poetics, arguing that while Olson "was not primarily an innovator," his synthesis of space, fact, and stance "opens a poetic space larger and more useful than any to be found" in modernist poetics. Following are three chapters which give a close reading of *Maximus*, a poem whose drama, Byrd argues, emerges as "the *agon* between love and death." While the book does not have the range of Sherman Paul's *Olson's Push*, and while Byrd's style is sometimes a little too self-consciously hermetic, this is the first full-length critical work devoted to Olson's long poem, and Byrd is a discriminating reader.

In his penetrating *Tale of the Tribe: Ezra Pound and the Modern Verse Epic* (Princeton) Michael Andre Bernstein confines his final 40 pages to a discussion of *The Maximus Poems*. He does not attempt a full reading of Olson's long poem, but rather tries to explain Olson's contribution to the modern verse epic. Like Byrd, Bernstein feels that for Olson both Pound and Williams represented "formidable *peres-ennemis*" whose influence he "could neither wholly outgrow nor painlessly absorb." While all three poets hoped to regain for

poetry the "entire domain of public, ideological utterances," Olson
sought to transcend Pound's finally subjective stance in *The Cantos*
and Williams' "sentimental humanism" in *Paterson.*

William V. Spanos attempts to show both how Olson achieves a
"new and significant voice in the American poetic 'tradition'" and
why he is properly a post-Modern poet in "Charles Olson and Negative Capability: A Phenomenological Interpretation" (*ConL* 21,i:38–
80). Spanos focuses on Olson's interpretation of "negative capability"
as a "destruction of the ontotheological tradition"; for Olson, the core
of the post-Modern is "to dis-cover the primordial meaning of the
logos," to recapture "the relationship between the speech act" and
the "fundamentally existential/phenomenological character of the
being of *Dasein*." While Spanos' argument is in general rewarding,
I feel that this essay suffers from its reliance on currently fashionable deconstructivist jargon. Though James F. Knapp's "The Un-
divided World of Pleistocene Eden: Charles Olson's *Maximus*"
(*Cithara* 19,ii:55–65) is overshadowed by Byrd's study, it still manages to raise a few interesting issues. Set against a Platonic language
wherein myth is replaced by a "limited, abstracting discourse,"
Knapp proposes, Olson offers a "world like the Mayan" in *Maximus*,
"concrete detail of the poet's voice and his world, arrayed like glyphs,"
in an attempt to make the world "whole again."[2]

In his "Archeologist of Morning: Charles Olson, Edward Dorn
and Historical Method" (*ELH* 47:158–79) Michael Davidson argues
that Dorn's "radical interpretation and use of Olson's method is
fundamental to understanding the possibilities for history in post-
Modern poetry." Davidson opens with a clear and intriguing discussion of the ways in which critics tend to see (he feels, in a sense,
wrongly) the post-Modern poetic "gesture" as emphasis on the poem's
"temporality," then demonstrates how in fact both Olson and Dorn
(in, at least, *Maximus* and *Slinger*) "indicate a sustained interest in
history and the means of its dissemination through art."

Edward Dorn's own *Views* and *Interviews* (Four Seasons Foundation) are collected in two volumes, edited by Donald Allen. The
first contains 17 essays, reviews, and notes, and an interview con-

2. While it is not strictly speaking a work of scholarship, students of Olson
will want to notice *Olson's Gloucester* (LSU), a collection of photographs of
Olson's *polis* by Lynn Swigart, with a foreword by George Butterick and an
interview with Swigart conducted by Sherman Paul.

ducted by Tom Clark; "What I See in *The Maximus Poems*" is reprinted, along with two short pieces on Creeley. The second book reprints six interviews with Dorn conducted between 1961 and 1978, including two extensive interviews by Barry Alpert and Stephen Fredman. As almost all of this prose has been until now fairly fugitive, Dorn's readers will appreciate Allen's efforts.

Any discussion of the work of Robert Duncan seems eventually to become an analysis of his poetics, as the three substantial essays on the poet published this year suggest. In "A Materialist Critique of Robert Duncan's Grand Collage" (*Boundary* 8:21–43) Peter Michaelson argues that Duncan's "comprehensive" poetics—his positing of a "dialectical communion" between art and religion—poses perhaps one of the profoundest challenges to scientific materialism, as Duncan seeks to "infuse us with a devotional rather than a critical spirit." Dennis Cooley attempts an overview of "The Poetics of Robert Duncan" (*Boundary* 8:45–73), mapping both Duncan's sense of the poet as receiver rather than shaper and Duncan's sense of the importance of a "compressed ideographic or associational logic" over the "logic of grammar"; his work exists in "the continuous present." Finally, Nathaniel Mackey's "The World-Poem in Microcosm" (*ELH* 47:595–618) suggests that Duncan's self-described stance as a derivative poet "is belied by the strikingly contentious character of his relationships to the poets, both present and past, from whom his work is derived." Mackey continues with a close reading of "The Continent" which, he feels, attempts to include "both the fable- or myth-world" of Duncan's earlier rhetorical poetry and "a here-and-now colloquialness of Williams," in addition to an undercurrent of "apocalyptic portent."

iv. Kenneth Rexroth, Allen Ginsberg, Gary Snyder, William Everson, Lew Welch, Josephine Miles

In his introduction to a 400-page *festschrift* for Kenneth Rexroth, *For Rexroth* (*The Ark*, 14), Geoffrey Gardner points out that "one of the great paradoxes of Rexroth's enormously paradoxical career is that his widest reputation is for being the promoter of some vaguely defined avant garde of which he is also a member." This is both true and unfortunate: true because Rexroth has done much to aid younger writers through the years (he was the presiding figure over at least two important "movements" in contemporary verse—the first San Francisco Renaissance of the '40s, which brought attention to writers like Robert Duncan, William Everson, and Philip Lamantia, and the later Beat Generation, which proved a breakthrough for Allen Ginsberg, Gary Snyder, and others); unfortunate because Rexroth's efforts in this area, and his incredible polemical skill which he put at the service of those writers and causes he believed in, have tended to overshadow (and he is not unlike Pound in this regard) his real achievement as a poet. Here, in an excerpt from a letter, James Wright says that Rexroth "is a great love poet during the most loveless of times," and indeed over the past 60 years Rexroth has written some of the most moving and most influential American verse of our century. *For Rexroth* celebrates this achievement with 19 essays, memoirs, and notes on Rexroth and his work by William Everson, John Haines, David Meltzer, W. S. Merwin, and others, and a garland of poems and stories dedicated to him.

This year saw four Allen Ginsberg items of note. The first is Michelle P. Kraus's *Allen Ginsberg: An Annotated Bibliography, 1969–1977* (Scarecrow), a book students of Ginsberg's work will use with some pleasure. Kraus attempts to update Dowden's 1971 bibliography, and in the process gives us an extremely thorough (and, it seems, accurate) 300-page accounting of books, periodical appearances, interviews, nonprint materials, reviews, and criticism through 1977. Unfortunately, she has followed Dowden's lead in that again the entries are listed alphabetically rather than chronologically, a deplorable bibliographic practice. Still, among contemporary poets Ginsberg is one of the most prolific and most written about, and his publishing career has been at best labyrinthine; Kraus had access to the poet's own library and his files, and she has given us a muchneeded map through Ginsberg's more recent work.

In "Allen Ginsberg's Paul Cezanne and the Pater Omnipotens Aeterna Deus" (*ConL* 21:435–49) Paul Portuges returns to a concern of his book-length study of Ginsberg's visionary experience. Portuges explains that Ginsberg discovered Cezanne through Meyer Shapiro, and after some study of Cezanne's work began to associate "the strange feelings" he got from the painter with his own Blake visions. In paintings like "The Black Clock" Cezanne "fulfilled Ginsberg's mystical needs," and "Howl" emerged as an "homage to art but also in specific terms an homage to Cezanne's methods." *Composed on*

the Tongue (Grey Fox), edited by Donald Allen, collects a few of
Ginsberg's better magazine interviews, including the first English
translation of Yves LePellec's *Etretiens* interview, "The New Consciousness," and *Improvised Poetics*. Ginsberg's own *Straight Heart's
Delight* (Gay Sunshine Press), cowritten with Peter Orlovsky, collects many of the poet's letters to Orlovsky.

   In "Gary Snyder's Descent to Turtle Island: Searching for Fossil
Love" (*WAL* 15:103–21) L. Edwin Folsom proposes that while in
the past American poets looked "west and and to the future," now
they are obsessed with a "poetics of archeology" and thus now
"move *down* and toward the past." Folsom feels that earlier poets
have sought to "get in touch with the virgin soil again" (Crane in
The Bridge, Williams in the "Descent" chapter of *In the American
Grain*, Roethke in "North American Sequence"), but of them all
Snyder has been, with *Turtle Island*, the most successful, entering
"his book as a genesis-point far before any other American poet."
Snyder is finally, for Folsom, the "fulfillment of Columbus' dream;
he merges the East and West by bringing his Oriental insight to bear
on the wilderness beneath present-day America." Anthony Hunt gives
a fairly close reading, focusing on Buddhist imagery, in " 'Bubbs
Creek Haircut': Gary Snyder's 'Great Departure' in *Mountains and
Rivers Without End*" (*WAL* 15:163–75). He argues that while
"Bubbs Creek Haircut" may not finally be the starting point of Snyder's in-progress long poem, it has served as an opening strategy for
the poet; the poem, Hunt feels, "commemorates the ritual setting-
out of an initiate upon the traditional Buddhist path of detachment"
followed by Gautama Buddha. Many of Snyder's interviews and
talks have been drawn together by William Scott McLean in *The
Real Work* (New Directions); a collection of "exploratory dialogues,"
this is an important adjunct to Snyder's *Earth House Hold* and
The Old Ways.

   William Everson was the subject of one article this year, David
Carpenter's "William Everson: Peacemaker with Himself" (*CP* 13:
19–34). Carpenter, like other critics, sees Everson as a Dionysian
poet, though his reliance on Monroe K. Spears' *Dionysus and the City*
(1970) merely muddies the issue; while Spears makes reference to
Dionysus as a *mythic image* and thus opens the possibility for defining the archetype, he places the Dionysian impulse squarely with
the modernists—the very tradition Everson has set himself directly

against throughout his career. Still, as a brief introduction to the range of Everson's poetry, Carpenter's piece may be of some value to those new to the poet's work.

In his continuing effort to bring to print all of Lew Welch's previously uncollected and unpublished work, Donald Allen has edited *I Remain: The Letters of Lew Welch & The Correspondence of His Friends* (Grey Fox) in two volumes. While one would like to have more editorial help with the text (most references are unglossed), the books include some first-rate letters from Welch to close friends like Gary Snyder, Philip Whalen, and Allen himself, with many replies.

In "Dickinson With a Difference: The Poetry of Josephine Miles" (*HC* 17,3:1–10) Julia Randall explains that while most of Miles' poetry "clearly belongs, by intention, to the School of Whitman," it often also captures "the very accent . . . the best and brightest" of Emily Dickinson. Still, Randall finds Miles' poetry finally "pedestrian," perhaps because of its "lack of presumption" which in turn allows dull and trivial passages.

v. Sylvia Plath, Anne Sexton, Denise Levertov, Susan Griffin, Adrienne Rich, Michele Murray

After some years of almost furious scholarly activity on many of these poets, 1980 saw a sudden calmness in the critical waters. Sylvia Plath received the most attention, with a first-rate book-length study, mention in another, three essays, and a note; otherwise, however, Anne Sexton and Denise Levertov attracted only one essay each, while Susan Griffin and Adrienne Rich were discussed in a single comparative study.

Mary Lynn Broe's *Protean Poetic: The Poetry of Sylvia Plath* (Missouri) is a self-proclaimed "remedial" reading of Plath's poetry, an attempt to demythologize the "Pyrrhic goddess of suicide who defied the last societal taboo." Broe proceeds knowledgeably through discussions of the poet's early poems and stories (many of which are uncollected), *The Colossus* (wherein Plath fails to synthesize perfection of form with imaginative vision), the transitional *Crossing the Water* (the poet's "technical, thematic, and imaginative coming of age"), and the late *Ariel* and *Winter Trees* (powerful and mature poems describing the "mobility, not choice, between the poles of passivity and theatrical display"). She is aware of both the complex editorial and the tangled bibliographical problems Plath's work presents, and the body of Plath scholarship which precedes her. Her readings of individual poems are sensitive and informative, her conclusions sensible. In short, students of Plath will find much of value in Broe's well-written work.

Ekbert Faas's *Ted Hughes: The Unaccommodated Universe* (Black Sparrow) reprints two of Hughes's short essays on Plath, and in an interview with Faas, Hughes discusses briefly his life with the poet. In "Sylvia Plath: Troubled Bones" (*NER* 2:447–65) Heather McClave argues that while Plath's "estrangement" seems to place her with the transcendentalists, in fact where their sense of separation is merely a "delimited phase within a cycle of substantial unity," hers is "annihilating absence." McClave believes that Plath has interest in "things" only as "correlatives for private responses." Compared to the "power" that Whitman, Dickinson, Stevens, and Eliot demonstrate in their sense of centrality, Plath's sense of center is "desperate and constrictive: without her small pivot, it would seem, the world falls apart." Like Broe, Greg Johnson feels too much stress has been placed by critics on Plath's life, and in his discussion, "A Passage to 'Ariel'" (*SwR* 65,i:1–11), he suggests that while the "evolution of self" is the major theme in Plath's work, her poetry's final achievement resides not in its "'cries from the heart'" but in its control, intelligence, and accessibility; additionally, Johnson finds a "remarkable coherence" throughout Plath's work. In "The Self in the World: The Social Context of Sylvia Plath's Late Poems" (*Women's Studies* 7:171–83) Pamela J. Annas attempts a brief Marxist reading of some poems from *Ariel*, concluding that the poet's "shocking images" are "the end result of an underlying depersonalization, an abdication of people to their artifacts." Finally, Thomas Mallon suggests in his note, "Sylvia Plath's 'Insomniac' and the British Museum" (*NMAL*, 4:item 25), that the poem was influenced by both the architecture of the British Museum and by Virginia Woolf's descriptions of it.

"Anne Sexton's *Love Poems*: The Genre and the Differences" (*MPS* 10,1:58–68) by William H. Shurr proposes that *Love Poems* is not a more or less random collection of love lyrics, but rather the record of a four-year love affair in its four stages of evolution: preparation, sexual awakening, celebration, and "bitter aftermath."

In "Inside and Outside in the Poetry of Denise Levertov" (*CritQ* 22,i:57–69) Dianna Surman touches on Levertov's relationship to the objectivists, Williams, and Olson, arguing that she moves from an early romanticism to a point where, like Williams, "there is no *depth*, no measurable distance between what is said and what is meant" in her poetry.

Dianne Middlebrook briefly discusses the work of Susan Griffin and Adrienne Rich in "Making Visible the Common World: Walt Whitman and Feminist Poetry" (*KenR* 2,iv:14–27). Like Whitman in "Song of Myself," she contends, Griffin and Rich, in *Women in Nature* and *Dream of a Common Language*, seek not the "universal," but rather a "common world that has never attained the publicity bestowed by art." These two feminist poets adopt much of Whitman's language and stance, along with many of his techniques, to delineate a world of women speaking to women. Middlebrook's essay has an interesting thesis, though it needs much fuller treatment with a closer and more extended reading of Griffin and Rich than Middlebrook gives here.

In "The Poetry of Michele Murray" (*Women's Studies* 7:195–203) Thomazine Shanahan doesn't really discuss Murray's work at all, but rather gives us a brief biographical sketch of the poet who died of cancer at the age of 40; she takes the opportunity to observe that Murray probably didn't realize her poetic vocation fully because of the demands of motherhood.

vi. John Ashbery, A. R. Ammons, James Dickey, Richard Hugo, James Merrill, W. S. Merwin, Donald Justice

David Lehman's *Beyond Amazement: New Essays on John Ashbery* (Cornell) offers ten previously unpublished essays on Ashbery's work. While Lehman's introduction is slightly strained in its effort to "rescue" Ashbery from his critics—and in its effort to convince us that Ashbery's poetry "could be said to open up a path of entry to whole areas of consciousness and feeling that could otherwise not be reached"—the collection provides some good perspectives on a difficult poet. In "The Prophetic Ashbery" Donald Case argues that the poet's work is not hermetic, but "most ruthlessly available to the present." Marjorie Perloff (" 'Fragments of a Buried Life': John Ashbery's Dream Songs") sees much of Ashbery's work as truly dream-like—as opposed to Berryman's "Dream Songs" which are "filtered through the rationalizing consciousness." John Koethke finds "The Metaphysical Subject of John Ashbery's Poetry" to be not "primarily a psychological one" but "a unitary consciousness from which his voice originates, positioned outside the temporal flux of thought and experience his poetry manages to monitor and record." In "The Shield of a Greeting" Lehman argues that "with his ironies and cultivated eccentricities," Ashbery becomes "a redemptive and affirmative poet." Keith Cohn ("Ashbery's Dismantling of Bourgeois Discourse") sees much of the poet's work as "a frontal attack on such props of bourgeois discourse as continuity, utility, and closure." Fred Monamarco, Charles Berger, and David Rigsbee contribute new readings of *The Tennis Court Oath, The Double Dream of Spring,* and "These Lacustine Cities" respectively, while in "The Brushstroke's Integrity" Leslie Wolf discusses Ashbery's relationship to modern painting. Finally, Lawrence Kramer ("'Syringa': John Ashbery and Elliott Carter") outlines the poet's attempts to "broaden the boundaries of temporality."

In his interesting "The Reader is the Medium: Ashbery and Ammons Ensphered" (*ConL* 21:588–610) John W. Erwin reads *Self-Portrait in a Convex Mirror* and *Sphere* (both published in 1974) as effective invitations to "readers to collaborate in reexamining clichés of perception and expression" which demonstrate "limitations in the self-elected spokesmen for the common reader who challenge them." For Erwin, in these poems both poets are clearly followers of Stevens—Ashbery developing Stevens' darker Mallarméan elements, Ammons emulating Stevens' Whitmanesque transcendence—as each attempts to reconcile conflicting views of the poem as "impersonal process" and "collaborative action."

James Dickey: Splintered Sunlight, a pamphlet edited by Patricia De La Fuentes, (Edinburg, Texas: Pan American University, 1979), contains an interview with the poet by Will Davis, an "Updated Checklist of Scholarship, 1975–1978" by Donald E. Fritz and De La Fuentes, and five short essays: Jan Seale's "Narrative Technique in James Dickey's 'May Day Sermon,' " James M. Haule's " 'The Thing Itself is in that': Closure in the Poetry of James Dickey," Violette Metz's "The Blessed Beasts and Children: An Examination of Imagery in James Dickey's Poems *1957–1967*," Izora Skinner's "A Fun Poem by James Dickey" (*Tuckey the Hunter*), and "A Look into the Heart of Darkness: A Vision of *Deliverance*" by Chet Taylor. While regular readers of Dickey's work will find nothing really new here, the bibliography is useful; the pamphlet itself serves as a concise, student introduction to some aspects of the poet.

Ross Bennett's " 'The Firebombing': A Reappraisal" (*AL* 52:430–48), however, is an important essay on an "important major poem of our age." In clear and convincing language Bennett suggests that "central to a proper understanding" of "The Firebombing" is "appreciation of Dickey's manipulation of multiple narrative perspectives." Bennett counters Robert Bly's well-known criticism of the poem by arguing that there is not only *one* "persona" in the poem (who finally "is just as much a tragic victim as the dead"), but in certain passages "dual protagonists in an interior drama." In her brief "James Dickey's 'Pursuit From Under' " (*CP* 13,i:27–31) Ruth Evelyn Quebe reads Dickey's poem in terms of the "danger and the creative potential of exploration" typified by "the downed dead."

Robert Peters offers another of his usual lively commentaries in "The Phenomenon of James Dickey, Currently" (*WHR* 34:159–66). For Peters, "an avid Dickey fan," the writer "is a much decorated ace among American poets" deserving of a place in "that Poetry-Pilot Hall-of-Fame." His discussion focuses on poems in *Strength of Fields*, which he finds "maddeningly self-indulgent" and "ennervated"; Peters seems in general to feel that Dickey is probably written out, living now on the strength of his early reputation.

Michael Allen's concise but astute " 'Only the eternal nothing of Space': Richard Hugo's West" (*WAL* 15:25–35) examines Hugo's view of the American West in *The Lady in Kicking Horse Reservoir* and *What Thou Lovest Well, Remains American*. Allen takes as the central problem in these two books Hugo's attempt to discover a sense of community in the West; he finds that Hugo's "poetry has moved from those images remaining from Old West myth—the hardened hero, isolated town, harsh wind—to images from the lives of people who live in something other than the saloon or open range."

Two useful essays on James Merrill appeared this year. In "James Merrill: 'Revealing by Obscuring' " (*ConL* 21:549–71) Robert von Hallberg demonstrates that Merrill attempts to set himself against "confessional poets" in his earlier work with an "ironic wrenching" of convention—a "calculated reticence" toward clarity—which emerges as "thematic secrecy," "periphrasis," "archness," and "camp";

he is a "coterie poet by rhetorical choice." Judith Moffett's extended
"'I Have Received From Whom I Do Not Know/These Letters,
Show Me, Light, If They Make Sense'" (*Shenandoah* 31,ii:35–74)
is an entertaining "precis, a summary with critical asides" of Merrill's
complex "Gothic opera," *Scripts From the Pageant.*

Linda Tregen and Gary Storhoff discuss "Order and Energy in
Merwin's *The Drunk in the Furnace*" (*CP* 13:47–52), concluding that
while the volume portrays a series of directionless and alienated
lives, the title poem offers an alternative to the mundane with its
"hostility to the orderly and harmonious."

In his appreciative "The Principle of Apprenticeship: Donald
Justice's Poetry" (*MPS* 10,i:44–58) Thomas Swiss examines the poet's
Selected Poems. Swiss argues that Justice's central theme is loss, his
action and language consciously contrived, and his aesthetic finally
the "discovery of what is necessary."

vii. Mark Strand, James Tate, John Peck, and Others

Strand: A Profile (Grilled Flower Press, 1979), edited by Frank
Graziano, is an attractive volume collecting a few poems and trans-
lations by Mark Strand, an interesting interview with the poet by
Graziano, two short essays ("Writing as Erasure: the Poetry of Mark
Strand" by Octavio Armand, "The Genuine Remains" by David
Brooks), and a select bibliography.

James Crenner's "Introducing Night and Wind" (*SenR* 10,ii/11,i:
73–80) is occasioned by the publication of James Tate's *Riven Dog-
geries,* but attempts an "approach" to Tate rather than simply a review. Crenner's argument that Tate is seen more fruitfully as a
"Dadaist" (after Duchamp) than as a "surrealist" (a term, he feels,
which has become rather catch-all, and in any event is not really
"sympathetic" to Tate's spirit) is convincing. Tate himself discusses
his own unease at being described as a surrealist in his first published interview (*Durak* 2:23–38).

Joan Hutton Landis' well developed "'Shipwreck, Autochthony
and Nostos'" (*Salmagundi* 47–48:159–200) is also concerned with
establishing an "approach," here to the poetry of John Peck. Landis
finds Peck "a formalist *par excellence*," for whom "doubleness of the
word and of the world" is endlessly fascinating. Landis gives a close
reading of Peck's first book, *SHAGBARK,* concluding that "Cider

and Vesalius" is his "most ambitious, most splendid, and in some ways most mysterious poem."

"Lucian Stryk stands with Gary Snyder as the two most distinguished American Zen poets," Dennis Lynch states in "The Poetry of Lucian Stryk" (*APR* 9,5:44–46). Lynch sees Stryk's first three books as false starts—"lifeless, ornamental, derivative." Then Stryk discovered Zen, experienced Satori, and from *The Pit and Other Poems*, his first Zen-influenced volume, his work has achieved "a stark dignity and a subtle and graceful profundity" through its simplicity of diction. These matters are discussed further in an interesting interview conducted by Stryk, "Conversations with Zenists" (*APR* 9,ii: 44–47).

Leverett T. Smith, Jr. attempts an overview of "The Poetry of Joel Oppenheimer" (*StAR* 5:127–40), finding *The Women Poems* (1975) to be "the culmination of a three-fold development" in Oppenheimer's work—from the psychological through the cultural to the mythic.

In *CP*'s "Western Issue" (vol. 13) Mark Sanders briefly discusses "Measurements of Compatibility in Contemporary Nebraska Poetry: The Verse of William Kloeforn, Ted Kooser, and Don Welch" (pp. 65–72), seeing these three poets as primary influences on a current poetry renaissance in Nebraska. In the same issue Carol Bangs ("The Voice Over Our Shoulders: The Poetry of Vern Rutsala," 75–84) examines a few themes and strategies of a much-neglected, anti-transcendentalist, "underground voice of Northwest Poetry."

Robert Miklitsch's "Praise: The Poetry of Robert Hass" (*HC* 17,i: 1–13) sees the flaws of Hass' first book, *Field Guide*, absent from his second, *Praise*, which "marks the emergence of a major American poet." In the earlier volume Miklitsch senses Hass presented "two aesthetics" set against themselves—poetry as "description" and poetry as "moral or political statement." In *Praise*, however, these two aesthetics are reconciled into a "more complex understanding of the relationship between, in Saussure's terms, the signifier and the signified." Hank Lazer also concerns himself with the problem of relationship in his reading of Hass' *Praise*, "In Opposition to True Friendship" (*Black Warrior Review* 6,ii:112–27). Hass, Lazer feels, is a poet "in search of an absolute," but a poet "sure that no such absolute exists." Therefore, throughout his poems pure praise is always balanced by a critical sense.

Jack Hicks' "A Wendell Berry Checklist" (*BB* 37:127–31) lists both primary and secondary sources for a writer who commands increasingly more of our attention.

In "Listening to Blue: The Poetry of Dave Smith" (*Ontario Rev.* 13:73–80) John Ditsky briefly discusses Smith's earlier work, then focuses on the poet's newest volume, *Goshawk, Antelope*. Ditsky finds the influence of both James Dickey and Robert Penn Warren in Smith's poetry, though he does not see Smith as in any way derivative; at the center of the younger poet's best work is an "affirmation of the mystery of things."

Smith conducted a major interview with James Wright not long before Wright's death; it appears this year in *APR* (9,iii:19–30), as does Karla Hammond's interview with Audre Lorde (9,ii:18–21). Finally, the ongoing Michigan series "Poets on Poetry" continues to offer us valuable collections in the recent *Pot Shots at Poetry* (Robert Francis), *Open Between Us* (David Ignatow), *Don't Ask* (Philip Levine), and *A Company of Poets* (Louis Simpson).

The University of New Mexico
Albuquerque

18. Drama

Winifred Frazer

i. From the Beginning

With Broadway being called "the great red way," the expense of putting on anything but sure hits being prohibitive, theatre has moved to the various regions of the country in the preceding decades, and the trend promises to continue in the '80s. There continues to be, nevertheless, scholarly interest in the colonial theatre through the 19th century with emphasis on individual performers and trends in types of performance and in the dramas themselves whether in New York or on the road.

At least one "first" emerges each year: Leo M. Kaiser's "*Elektra* Revisited: The First American Translation of a Greek Tragedy" (*CF* 33[1979]:35–56) includes a moving translation of Sophocles' great tragedy, edited from the manuscript in the Historical Society of Pennsylvania left by Robert Proud, a Quaker schoolmaster who came to America in 1759 to teach in the Friends' Academy of Philadelphia and who is best known for *The History of Pennsylvania* (1797–98). Two essays deal with pre- or post-Revolutionary censorship of the stage. David D. Mays in "On the Authenticity of the 'Moral Dialogues' Playbill" (*ThS* 20:1–14) produces overwhelming evidence, both internal and external, that the handbill supposedly distributed by David Douglass in Newport, R.I., 10 June 1761, justifying his production of *Othello* on the grounds of its moral benefits is subject to serious question. Kurt L. Garrett, on the other hand, describes in "Dennis Ryan's Temple of Apollo" (*ThS* 21:73–78) a genuine attempt to avoid censorship which failed. Billing his play and pantomine as a concert, reading, and dance did not fool the sheriff, who closed The Temple of Apollo after three nights. Ryan, in spite of his failure, had shown the way for Hallam and others to return plays and players to the northern United States.

In another article, "The Flexible Loyalties of American Actors

in the Eighteenth Century" (*TJ* 32:223–34) Garrett points out how
acting companies skirted the line between loyalty to America and to
Britain according to public sentiment where they were playing. Companies such as that of Lewis Hallam Jr., which before the war were
careful not to appear traitorous to either side, became full-fledged
nationalists after the war with "Vivat Respublica" replacing "Vivant
Rex et Regina" on their banners. Billy J. Harbin in "The Role of Mrs.
Hallam in the Hodgkinson-Hallam Controversy: 1794–1797" (*TJ*
32:213–22) puts blame for the problems of the Old American Company, not on John Hodgkinson, as Dunlap in his *History* had, but
on the alcoholism of Mrs. Hallam, providing detailed evidence of her
frequent inability to perform and her acrimonious abuse of Hodgkinson and his actress wife. Besides interest in individuals and companies is a growing curiosity about the physical buildings which
housed the players. James S. Moy has used drawings and playbills
to illustrate his "The Greenwich Street Theatre 1797–1799" (*ThS*
20:15–26). The first theatre to give competition to the well-known
John Street Theatre, the one on Greenwich was also the first mul-
tiple-use theatre in New York, built to house Ricketts' Circus and
spectacular pantomimes as well as dramas such as *The School for
Scandal* on the stage which had a proscenium and scenic wings.

In 19th-century dramatic criticism such terms as "pantomime,"
"variety," "vaudeville," and "burlesque," among others, become
somewhat slippery, perhaps due to the nature of a changing theatre
scene and culture which cannot be completely categorized or defined. Each year there are some critics who try, among them Robert
C. Allen, who in "B. F. Keith and the Origins of American Vaudeville" (*ThS* 21:105–15), discerns at least two paths—the variety concert saloon made respectable and the dime museum made less
plebian—which led to the emergence of vaudeville and Keith's success with the continuous performance format in New York beginning
in 1894. In two articles Laurence Senelick traces figures and movements during the second half of the 19th century. "George L. Fox
and American Pantomime" (NCTR 7:1–25) describes one of the
great entertainers on the American stage, whose clown portrayals
included Jackadaw Jaculation and Humpty Dumpty and who created
numerous other characters and pantomimic dramas on the New York
stage between 1850 and 1875, elevating pantomime from an after-
piece for more serious theatre to a full evening's performance and

from imitation of British clowns to an American art. "Variety into Vaudeville, the Process Observed in Two Manuscript Gagbooks" (*ThS* 19[1978]:1–15) explains from evidence in hand how variety star J. C. Murphy, playing one-night stands of gag-jokes, songs, and dances between 1873 and 1893, using ethnic jokes, jokes about corpses and interments, and off-color limericks, was replaced in the 1890s by the Four Cohans, who made a point of clean family skits and songs and soothing entertainments—perhaps no real gain over the elemental Murphy, who played for audiences troubled by economic crashes and panics, who saw life in less sugary terms than did those at the end of the century.

Something of American cultures of the 19th century emerges in several books and articles which detail the stories of individual performers or types of popular theatre. W. Porter Ware and Thaddeus C. Lockard Jr. in *P. T. Barnum Presents Jenny Lind: The American Tour of the Swedish Nightingale* (LSU) carefully document the travels of Jenny Lind and the hardships of the road in the 1850s, along with stories of her admiring audiences and Barnum's management. Another hearty performer is revealed in Alan Wood's "Mademoiselle Rhea: An American Bernhardt" (*ThS* 21:129–44). Hortense Rhea, a French actress who spoke English, partly capitalizing on the publicity given Bernhardt, played in numerous American cities (although not New York) for 17 years between 1881 and 1898 in romantic plays to admiring audiences, providing far more regular and dependable fare than Bernhardt, whom she otherwise resembled in many ways. Besides such serious drama the American public, like Mark Twain, didn't mind making fun of pretension. In "Burlesques of Shakespeare: The Democratic American's 'Light Artillery'" (*ThS* 21:49–62) Claudia D. Johnson explains that, sensing Shakespeare's aristocratic leanings and resenting some of the British companies of actors, American audiences, while admiring the bard, heartily enjoyed a variety of takeoffs which between the 1840s and 1880s included *The Macbeth Travestie, Hamlet the Dainty, Desdemonum*, and *Julius Sneezer*, some of which also included satire of American politicians.

Pointing out a neglected area of study, Roger Allan Hall in "Frontier Drama Classification" (*NCTR* 7:27–38) categorizes certain dramas about the frontier or frontier figures from among the many thousands produced from 1851 to 1900 according to star vehicles, major authors, reenactment of events, melodramas, and others, urging further study of an influential form of theatre before and during the 19th century. Following his own advice, Hall examines one series of dramas about a famous frontiersman. In "Frontier Dramatizations: The James Gang" (*ThS* 21:117–28) he remarks that less than a year after the death of Jesse James in 1882 three different companies were presenting his story on the New York stage with actual events made melodramatic and interspersed with songs and animal acts—aesthetically deficient but emotionally very appealing to large audiences, perhaps mostly because of the dramatization of events that shaped Amercian history and because of the romance of the James gang. Hardly a frontier drama but just as popular is one described by Myron Matlaw in "English and American Dramatizations of *Le Comte de Monte Cristo*" (*NCTR* 7:39–53). The version of the play in which James O'Neill starred between 1883 and 1912 was by French actor, Charles Fechter, but since it did not appear in print until 1941 and then with many errors, and since there were three Fechter scripts, Matlaw documents variations in these and in other versions which are extant.

The extent to which Americans responded to serious productions of one Shakespearean play is carefully documented by John Ripley in *Julius Caesar on Stage in England and America* (Cambridge). Extended descriptions of the acting, costumes, sets, and directing of the productions of *Julius Caesar* in America between 1770 and 1870 are followed by lengthier analyses of the long runs of the play in the Booth-Barrett-Davenport era of 1871 to 1891 when the play "enjoyed a degree of popular favour unmatched in its history." Booth became identified with the role of Brutus, and Barrett with Cassius, for tremendous popular success until Barrett's death in 1891, after which Booth never played Brutus. There were few productions between Mansfield's in 1902 and Orson Welles's Mercury Theatre production in 1937, and even fewer since, Welles's success seeming to discourage rather than encourage successors. Another type of theatre traced from colonial times to the present is described in Richard Kislan's *The Musical: A Look at the American Musical Theater* (Prentice-Hall). Divided into three sections—Forms of Musical Theater, The Mature Musical, and Elements of the Musical Theater—the book describes the history of the form on the American stage from colonial times to Sondheim today, and attempts Aristotle-style to classify the elements which make up any musical. Like the *Poetics*, it is both theoretical and practical, so that one learns into which genres various productions fit as well as how they are put together. Besides there are dozens of photographs of actors and choric staging—an addition which Aristotle lacked.

ii. 20th Century

Several items deal with the theatre of the '30s. *Free, Adult, Uncensored: The Living History of the Federal Theatre Project* (Washington, D.C.: New Republic Books, 1978), ed. John O'Connor and Lorraine Brown with foreword by John Houseman, is the result of the unearthing of a huge number of manuscripts and records in a hangar-warehouse, now housed at George Mason University. The present volume, a mere excerpt of the material now available for scholars, includes a history of each of the performances of the Federal Theatre during its existence between 1935 and 1939 accompanied by more than 200 photographs. One wonders what American theatre might have become in the following four decades if the "experiment" had been allowed to continue. Another volume, John Willett's *The Theatre of Erwin Piscator* (New York: Holmes and Meier, 1979), documents the work of a great director best known in America for his work with the Dramatic Workshop in New York, where he lived between 1939 and 1951. Piscator's *Das politische Theater* (Berlin, 1929) had already influenced the Federal Theatre's *Living Newspaper* productions (see *ALS 1979*, pp. 373–74). In this biographical account Willett documents the influence of Piscator on the theatrical world in Berlin, Moscow, Paris, Zurich, and New York through nearly half a century.

Another biographical history of a great figure on the American scene is Cindy Adams' *Lee Strasberg: the Imperfect Genius of the Actors Studio* (Doubleday), the story of a director and teacher, who at almost 80 was still teaching actors in two studios in New York and Los Angeles, theoretically through Stanislavskian methods, but often through concentration on the needs of individual students. From the evidence supplied through photographs and the testimony of numerous American actors, one might conclude that hardly any prominent figure on the stage today has been unaffected by the influence of this great director-teacher-trainer from the time of the founding of the Actors Studio and Group Theatre until the present. Orson Welles, another influential figure of the '30s and since, is the subject of John S. O'Connor's "But Was It 'Shakespeare'?: Welles's *Macbeth* and *Julius Caesar*" (*TJ* 32:337–48). In 1936 Welles's Negro-cast *Macbeth* in Harlem, although extremely popular, was considered untrue to the bard, partly because of the untraditional reading of the lines and the fact that black actors were not taken seriously. His *Julius Caesar*, on the other hand, produced at the Mercury Theatre in 1937 in fascist costume with connotations of Hitler's Nuremberg, was considered a faithful interpretation. While questioning the judgment of the times, O'Connor urges open-mindedness and freedom from preconceptions in assessing the validity of any Shakespearean productions in any era.

Two volumes deal with figures, the first preceding the '30s, the second, the decade following. Morris U. Burns's *The Dramatic Criticism of Alexander Woollcott* (Scarecrow) contains in a useful appendix all of Woollcott's dramatic criticism between 1915 and 1928 listed alphabetically by the play reviewed, and in the body of the book his opinions on various playwrights, actors, and theatrical issues grouped under appropriate subheadings. James K. Lyon's *Bertolt Brecht in America* (Princeton) is a thoroughly researched work on Brecht's life in New York and Hollywood between 1941 and 1947, including his relationship with various collaborators, his uncompromising character and cinematic view of America, and ending with his testimony before HUAC in Washington.

iii. Lillian Hellman, Maxwell Anderson

Among important mid-century playwrights, Lillian Hellman each year figures in several items, partly perhaps because of her late autobiographical volumes. The same cannot usually be said of Maxwell Anderson, who this year, however, was featured in an issue of the *North Dakota Quarterly* in a number of useful critical essays. The difficulty of making a film based on an autobiographical account of Hellman, a living author, is described by Marsha McCreadie in "'Julia': Memory in *Pentimento* and on Film" (*LFQ* 7:260–69). In spite of problems the story is well filmed, partly because of the dialogue already supplied by the narrator and because the film concentrates on an objective, visual portrayal rather than on the narra-

tor's psychological state of mind. The question of the relationship
of the visual to the literary continues to haunt the filmmaker, who
on the one hand may be accused of being too static and on the other
too talky. As the novel becomes influenced by film and the film by
written fiction, film and literary criticism cross lines with ever-
increasing theoretical and practical considerations.

Another indication of Hellman's importance is that two bibliographical volumes have appeared this year: Mark W. Estrin's *Lillian
Hellman: Plays, Films, Memoirs: A Reference Guide* (Hall) and
Mary Marguerite Riordan's *Lillian Hellman: A Bibliography, 1926–
1978* (Scarecrow). The first consists of a year-by-year listing between
1934 and 1979 of writings about Hellman's life and work with an
introduction describing Hellman's work itself. The annotations on all
items are extensive enough to make scholars able to judge the content
and slant of each. The second consists of a lengthy chronology of
Hellman's life and a chronological listing by genre of her own works
with brief annotations, followed by a listing of pieces about Hellman's life and about her works by genre. Although the alphabetical
listing "About the Plays" seems out of order, this volume supplements
Estrin's more full and annotated coverage of critical writing about
Hellman by its chronologies and its listing of special Hellman Collections in several libraries. Along with Steven H. Bills's *Lillian
Hellman: An Annotated Bibliography* (Garland) described in *ALS
1979*, p. 375, these two volumes should supply scholars with all their
needs in reference to Lillian Hellman.

Maxwell Anderson's dramatic theory, artistry, themes, and sources
furnish subjects for the contributors to the issue in his honor, the
least of which might be J. F. S. Smeall's "Additions to the Maxwell
Anderson Bibliography" (*NDQ* 48,iii:60–63) were it not for the fact
that 15 of the 23 early texts not formerly noted are poems in the
student publications of the University of North Dakota, 1910–11,
which may be a source of some pride to the *Quarterly* which issues
from the college where Anderson got his start. In "*Lost in the Stars*
and *Cry, the Beloved Country*: A Thematic Comparison" (*NDQ* 48,
iii:53–59) Susan Wanless Smock describes how Anderson, long interested in better race relations and having worked for the cause
of brotherhood for years, was highly moved when he read Paton's
story and immediately asked to dramatize it. Smock's summary of
Anderson's changes—all in the interest of providing a more hopeful

conclusion than Paton's—includes changes in the relationships within
and between the black and white families, in the performance of
Absalom's crime itself, and in the reconciliation of the two fathers
at the end—all acceptable changes in a dramatization for an American audience. In another essay on technique, "*Night Over Taos*:
Maxwell Anderson's Sources and Artistry" (*NDQ* 48,iii:12–25), Lena
Cowen Orlin explains Anderson's use, as a source for his play, of a
series of historical articles by Harvey Fergusson entitled "Rio
Grande" which appeared in the *American Mercury* during May
through October 1931, the year before the Group Theatre production
of 1932. Mainly dramatizing the final losing battle of the Spanish
overlords to the invading American army, Anderson, in accord with
his theory of tragedy, creates a hero who, having come to a self-
recognition of his situation, dies heroically. The plot of the play is
based on Racine's tragedy, *Mithridates*, which it resembles in characters, scenes, and action. Anderson himself, using a source for historical background and one for plot, created the defeated hero,
Montoya.

Using still another play to illustrate Anderson's use of source
material, Perry D. Luckett in "*Winterset* and Some Early Eliot
Poems" (*NDQ* 48,iii:26–37) most convincingly shows that besides
enriching his play through Shakespearean and Hebrew mythology
and language, Anderson uses close parallels from "Gerontion," *The
Waste Land*, and "The Hollow Men" to give the tone of the meaningless universe and the critique of myth of modernist poet Eliot. In
a more simplistic essay, "Maxwell Anderson's Changing Attitude
Toward War" (*NDQ* 48,iii:5–11), Arthur T. Tees summarizes Anderson's attitudes from his antiwar stance in 1917 through *What
Price Glory?* (1924), when such a stance was much more acceptable,
through *Valley Forge* (1934), which sanctioned the Revolutionary
War, and *High Tor* (1937) and *Masque of Kings* (1937), which were
pacifistic, to *Key Largo* (1939), which was activist, along with *Candle
in the Wind* (1941) and *The Eve of St. Mark* (1942), after which,
although not propagandistically so, his attitude was never as pacifistic as during World War I. Yet another play serves Jeffrey D.
Mason's purpose, in "Maxwell Anderson's Dramatic Theory and *Key
Largo*" (*NDQ* 48,iii:38–52), of bringing Anderson's use of verse to
bear on his theory of drama. Mason contends that critics who write
about Anderson's *theory* concentrate on structure and purpose; those

who write about the *plays* concentrate on verse. He analyzes the theory and how the verse metaphorically complements the character, structure, and meaning of one play, thereby bridging a gap, while also pointing out the difficulty which Anderson experienced in making realistic characters speak in verse.

iv. Eugene O'Neill

Included in O'Neill studies this year is one book, which unfortunately cannot be said to add hitherto unexplored vistas to work on America's greatest playwright. Claiming that critics have shown interest in dramatic theory to the exclusion of the language in contemporary drama, Jean Chothia in *Forging a Language: A Study of the Plays of Eugene O'Neill* (Cambridge) proposes to use the O'Neill canon to illustrate how the imaginative use of realistic language has contributed to O'Neill's great plays. It is true that O'Neill is a prize subject for such a study because of the often reiterated criticism that his plays are better than the language in which they are couched. It is well that O'Neill figures in the subtitle of the book, however, because, far from arriving at a theory for analysis of dramatic language in general, Chothia covers what many of O'Neill's critics have touched on in concluding that his best plays are those in which his language seems to ring true to everyday speech, while having an evocative content beyond that of common prose.

Albert Wertheim in "Gaspard the Miser in O'Neill's *Long Day's Journey Into Night* (*AN&Q* 18[1979]:39–42) points out the many connotations in a literary reference in O'Neill's most admired play. Tyrone, referred to seven times by his sons as Old Gaspard, the miser in *The Bells of Corneville*, a part he "could play with no makeup," is thereby mocked not only for his penuriousness but for his playing in melodrama instead of Shakespeare, with ironic intimations" that the fake ghosts of the comic opera in reality haunt the Tyrones.

Although America's greatest playwright probably never met the greatest southern novelist, who lived through approximately the same time span, Judith B. Wittenberg in "Faulkner and Eugene O'Neill" (*MissQ* 33:327–41) sums up considerable biographical and literary evidence that Faulkner knew a number of O'Neill's plays from reading and from seeing them staged. Although she overstresses minor ways in which Faulkner made use of O'Neill's plays in his fiction, she does make an extended case for the influence of *Mourning Becomes Electra* upon *Absalom, Absalom!*, which if true is of considerable interest to O'Neill's admirers. In "Taoism and O'Neill's *Marco Millions*" (*CompD* 14:251–62) James A. Robinson tries to elevate *Marco Millions* by reviewing the extent to which the Taoist way rather than Hindu or Buddhist is exemplified in Kukanchin, Kublai Khan, and especially in his advisor Chu Yin.

In a lengthy, arcane essay, "Aeschylus and O'Neill: A Phenomenological View" (*CompD* 14:159–87), John Chioles posits, if I understand him, that O'Neill interprets modern life in his *Electra* trilogy as it fits the state and as the theatre "is the state," just as Aeschylus did for the "sociopolitical" life of Greece, both playwrights—and Artaud for good measure—being phenomenological in placing man at the center of his world. O'Neill's *Electra* trilogy reveals the rift at the core of real life which makes him "a far greater dramatic genius than the critics would allow." Michael Hinden, while making no claim for his genius in "Desire and Forgiveness: O'Neill's Diptych" (*CompD* 14:240–50), does show a change in the playwright's attitude and technique between an early and late play. Citing many similarities between *Desire Under the Elms* and *A Moon for the Misbegotten*, Hinden illustrates the autobiographical nature of both and the therapy O'Neill achieved through his softened attitude in the latter toward his mother, father, and Jamie. Although "sun's a rizin" at the end of both, *Moon* is a mellow play and more artistic with its touch of Jamie's metatheatrical remark about the sunrise, "Act-Four Stuff."

The Eugene O'Neill Newsletter, completing its fourth year, carries, besides reports of O'Neill productions on stage and screen throughout the country, reviews of books and articles on the playwright, and newsnotes and an ever-increasing number of scholarly articles. In the January issue (3,iii) Joseph Jurich in "Jack London and *The Hairy Ape*" (pp. 6–8) compares the disillusionment of Yank and of the hero of *Martin Eden*, both of whom die in complete hopelessness of finding love or success socially or individually. In the same issue are three pieces describing and illustrating the production at Dartmouth's Hopkins Center of *The Hairy Ape*, not one of O'Neill's frequently produced plays. Frederick Wilkins reviews it, "*The Hairy Ape* Goes to Dartmouth" (pp. 9–10); Michael E. Rutenberg in "Bob Smith Ain't So Dumb" (pp. 11–15) explains the problem of making Yank sympathetic by showing his mind at work; and Bernard Vyzga in "Designing O'Neill's *The Hairy Ape*" (pp. 15–17) illustrates the sets which depict the background for Yank's process toward suicide. In a critical article on another early play, *"The Emperor Jones*: O'Neill, Nietzsche, and the American Past" (pp. 2–4) Michael Hinden provides convincing evidence that Brutus Jones represents not the black man but all Americans, forgetting in their greed for possessions and power that the country was envisioned to liberate the Dionysian spirit of man instead of which it has enslaved his spirit and tragically brought about his destruction.

In the next, a double issue (*EON* 4,i–ii), Hinden again treats an early play. In "The Transitional Nature of *All God's Chillun Got Wings*" (pp. 3–5) he posits that Jim might be called "the son of Emperor Jones," struggling at the center of society rather than on an island, surrounded by a picture of his father in outlandish lodge regalia like an Emperor and by an African mask conceived in a true religious spirit, torn between the desire to succeed in a white world and the old collective unity between the tribe and nature. And, through its depiction of the psychological relationship between man and woman the play looks forward to character studies in O'Neill's later plays. In *"The Emperor Jones*: A Jungian View of the Origin of Fear in the Black Race" (pp. 6–9) Patrick J. Nolan sees Brutus Jones, not as Hinden suggests as representing all Americans, but more traditionally as the black man undermined by the materialistic goals of the whites, so that fear induced by the loss of his old God and the psychological destruction of the new, brings about, as Jung postulated, his personal and racial downfall.

In the year's last *Newsletter* (*EON* 4,iii) in a third contribution on *Jones*, "The Ship Scene in *The Emperor Jones*" (pp. 3–5), R. Viswanathan points out that the imaginary ship in scene six, instead of being a slave ship, appears to be a generalized Jungian symbol of Jones's regression to his roots, water being the element which represents the human psyche in search of the self. LeRoy Robinson in "John Howard Lawson's *Souls*: A Harbinger of *Strange Interlude*" (pp. 12–13) suggests that Lawson's technique in *Souls* (1915), which is to have each of several characters reminisce in soliloquies called "interludes," is a crude presage of the more polished work of O'Neill. A lively parody of *Strange Interlude* by Scotch novelist Eric Linklater, who saw the play in 1931, is reproduced (pp. 14–15) as an example of the satire which O'Neill's technique of having characters soliloquize while others stand motionless created among some theatre-goers. Besides a lengthy review of *Desire Under the Elms* at the Guthrie in Minneapolis and a listing of films about O'Neill and of his plays, the last issue of *EON* includes Winifred Frazer's review of O'Neill's *Poems: 1912–1944* (pp. 5–9), a volume which includes most of O'Neill's known poems, edited by Donald Gallup from manuscripts mainly in the Beinecke Library at Yale. Although none of the newly printed poems enhance O'Neill's reputation as a poet, it is interesting biographically to have the dated and annotated poems gathered together under one cover and to note that poetry is a genre which the playwright attempted through many years.

v. Arthur Miller, Tennessee Williams, Edward Albee

This year more interest lies in Miller on Broadway or in interviews concerning theatrical and social matters than in critical articles on his important plays. A revised edition by Leonard Moss of *Arthur Miller* (TUSAS 115) includes an extensive interview with Miller and an added chapter on *The Price* and *The Creation of the World*. In this updating of the 1967 edition Moss makes a very fair analytical appraisal of how Miller's last plays fit the thesis of his life's work concerning the struggle of the individual to fit into his society. One article which is concerned with Miller's earlier work is Einer Haugen's "Ibsen as Fellow Traveller: Arthur Miller's Adaptation of *An Enemy of the People*" (*SS* 51[1979]:343–53). Although Haugen approves of Miller's adapting Ibsen's play for the American audience of 1950, he regrets that it was needlessly diminished from the original. In Ibsen's view Stockman is strong because he is fighting for the truth; in Miller's he is strong because he stands alone—a truism which avoids the irony of the original.

Three interviews, besides that in the Twayne volume, include one with Studs Terkel (*Sat.Rev.*, Sept. 24–27) in which the information is elicited that it was reading Terkel's *Hard Times* that led Miller to write *The American Clock*, which is described in the same publication (pp. 22–23) as the autobiographical account of the depression which Miller hopes will restore his reputation on Broadway. In "Melvyn Bragg in Conversation with Arthur Miller" (*The Lis-*

tener 104:645–47) at the time of the opening on Broadway of *The American Clock*, Miller reminisces about the depression, which made people ashamed of their failure; about the book he read, *The Brothers Karamazov*, which "simply burned my brains"; and about Americans who have made a lifetime investment in some false idea which they don't recognize until too late to change. V. Rajakrishnan in "After Commitment: An Interview with Arthur Miller" (*TJ* 32:196–204) discusses with Miller his later plays and their trend away from social causes to personal dilemmas—for example the tendency in people "to obliterate the murderousness of their own wishes," after which, having returned to a state of false innocence, they murder again. Miller also discusses the absurd and existential playwrights and the difference between the realistic attic full of furniture in *The Price* and Ionesco or Beckett's parodistic sets.

Arthur Miller and Inge Morath have produced a beautifully illustrated account of their journey to China in 1978. In *Chinese Encounters* (Farrar, 1979) Miller has written the commentary for their travels and the description for Morath's many fine photographs, as a Westerner finally allowed into China tries to understand the politics and the culture. A useful volume, *Arthur Miller: A Reference Guide* (Hall, 1979) by John H. Ferris, includes "Writings about Arthur Miller, 1944–1977" with items all annotated and listed chronologically. Purporting to include all books, pamphlets, dissertations, reviews, and articles about the playwright, it includes a list of Miller's own major works and is well indexed to serve the scholar doing research on Miller's life or works.

In the case of Tennessee Williams, as with Miller, there is more interest in present plays and in his life story in interviews than in scholarly investigation of his best plays. Williams participates even more frequently than Miller in recorded conversations, as John J. McKenna points out in a summary of "Interviews with Williams" (*TWNew* 2,ii:26–28). Noting the many repetitions of questions, McKenna praises the wit and candor with which Williams responds, making each a different experience. Besides extensive reviews of productions of Williams' plays throughout the country and summaries of papers delivered at theatre meetings, the *Tennessee Williams Newsletter* carries items on teaching and directing of his plays, including in the Fall issue (2,ii:47–52) especially stimulating suggestions by Professor J. H. Clay of Brandeis on imaginative student participation in creating the setting for *The Glass Menagerie.* In the same issue Esther M. Jackson in "Tennessee Williams' *Out Cry*: Studies in Dramatic Form at the University of Wisconsin, Madison" (pp. 6–12) describes in depth a research seminar which, while concentrating on the form of the play, included a study of Williams' related poetry and fiction and resulted in staged readings and an experimental production in preparation for a full-scale production in the succeeding semester. In the same section William Prosser in "Loneliness, Apparitions, and the Saving Grace of the Imagination" (pp. 13–15) describes the premiere of *Will Mr. Merriwether Return from Memphis?* at the Tennessee Williams Fine Arts Center in Key West. Two widows, who allay their loneliness through apparitions, leave the audience uncertain as to whom—including Mr. Merriwether —is real, who illusory. Albert E. Kalson sees J. B. Priestley's *Dangerous Corner* as "A Source for *Cat on a Hot Tin Roof*" (pp. 21–22) but Betty in the play being "a greedy little cat on the tiles" seems quite different from a cat dancing around because of heat underfoot.

The Spring *Newsletter* carries two bibliographies—Charles Carpenter's "Studies of Tennessee Williams' Drama: A Selective International Bibliography: 1966–1978" (2,i:11–23) and "Tennessee Williams in the Seventies: A Checklist" (2,i:24–29) by Thomas P. Adler, Judith Hersh Clark, and Lyle Taylor, which lists by genre the work of Williams, including interviews, during the past decade.

Jac Tharpe has reduced his 900-page collection of essays about Williams (see *ALS 1977,* p. 396) to *Tennessee Williams: Thirteen Essays* (Miss.), including in the main those that deal with the body of Williams' work as a whole. Peter Buckley, on the other hand, in "Tennessee Williams' New Lady" (*Horizon* Apr.: 66–71) shows that the character of Zelda in *Clothes for a Summer Hotel* has similarities to Williams' other heroines in spite of being the only one admittedly based on a real person, the play's weakness being due to the characterization of Scott as a tiresome complainant. In a slight article, "Meaning by Analogy in *Suddenly Last Summer*" (*NMAL* 4,iv:Item 24), Neal B. Houston explains that three key analogies—God as voracious devourer, Sebastian as God, and Sebastian as the devoured —reinforce the message of God as a malevolent Being who determines the fate of vulnerable man.

Edward Albee, though not so frequently as the older playwrights, is the subject of an interview by Peter Adam, "Edward Albee: A Playwright vs. the Theatre" (*Listener* 103:70–71). In this interview for the BBC Albee deplores the lack of interest in theatre in America, mentioning that in February of 1980 he could not see any of some 15 great playwrights anywhere in New York, as well as pressures to make playwrights simplify their work in order to reach a large audience. As a playwright Albee expects to provide questions for which the audience must find the answers. That not everyone has yet found the answers to one of his plays is evident in two different interpretations. Mary Castiglie Anderson in "Staging the Unconscious: Edward Albee's *Tiny Alice*" (*Renascence* 33:178–92) claims that the characters of Alice, Butler, and Lawyer, being but aspects of Julian's mind, grow and develop according to what he learns from the trial he is undergoing, his death scene with its heartbeats being perhaps a scene of birth into his self-possession. Kristin Morrison on the other hand in "Pinter, Albee and 'The Maiden in the Shark Pond'" (*AI* 35[1978]:259–74) believes that hostility towards women, basic to *Tiny Alice* and to *No Man's Land*, nevertheless encourages sexual fantasies. Julian dies in the embrace of Miss Alice, the shark in the water, in a violent act of orgasmic death, while Hirsch ends statically in the frozen embrace of the "shark in the harbour" or no man's land and no woman's either.

Paul Sawyer in "Some Observations on the Character of George in *Who's Afraid of Virginia Woolf?*" (*CEA* 42,iv:15–19) wants more answers than Albee provides. Sawyer concludes that since we know nothing of George's research or teaching or what his parenticide has to do with his being a bog in the history department, his characterization is "incomplete and therefore unsatisfactory." James A. Robinson in "O'Neill and Albee" (*WVUPP* 25:38–45) may have found more answers than are warranted. In a comparison of the upbringing, professional success, and dramaturgy of the two playwrights, Robinson strains to show similarities and influences of the older on the younger. As far as similar themes go, can *The Hairy Ape* and *The Zoo Story* be said to be on "identical subjects," that of "urban alienation"? As far as lives go, is having a drug-addicted mother the same as being adopted? Although Miller, Williams, and Albee have failed to have dramatic successes in late years, they continue to elicit a lot of public interest as well as scholarly examination of their work.

vi. Contemporary

Several books, each with its own slant, contribute ideas on the American theatre scene. Samuel J. Bernstein's *The Strands Entwined: A New Direction in American Drama* (Northeastern) consists of an examination of five recent American plays, a review of the criticism of each, a discussion of the play, and an explanation of how the strands of Ibsenite realism and European absurdism are combined in each. His optimistic conclusion about the future of this hybrid child, however, seems unwarranted by the evidence.

Nelvin Vos in *The Great Pendulum of Becoming: Images in Modern Drama* (Eerdmans), an impressionistic, unindexed volume, reaches even more optimistic conclusions. Commenting on such American playwrights as O'Neill, Miller, Williams, and Albee, Vos expresses the hope that the chaotic modern theatre, with its images of bestiality, impotency, and death, which reflects the culture, is now waiting (as in *Godot*) at the still point of the pendulum for relief from restless nightmares.

Robert Brustein in *Critical Moments: Reflecting on Theatre and Society* (Random House) is less certain where the American theatre is going. Consisting of essays published during the "whey-faced decade" of the seventies, "an epoch of fits and starts," Brustein comments on funding for the arts, on recent books, and on the changing state of the theatre in an uncertain America, to which state Brustein, for more than a decade dean of the Yale Drama School, testifies in moving to Harvard. A fourth volume on the modern theatre is Robert N. Wilson's *The Writer as Social Seer* (N.Car., 1979). Using as two examples, *Death of a Salesman* and *Long Day's Journey Into Night* to illustrate his thesis, Wilson shows how the playwrights prophetically portray the social scene—which in the first case causes the destruction of the individual whom modern economic life drives to suicide, and in the second destroys any sense of selfhood among the family members caught in a web of love and hate.

Some dozen contemporary theatrical figures are the subjects of articles and books. Jerrold A. Phillips in "Descent into the Abyss: The Plays of David Rabe" (*WVUPP* 25:108–17) makes a good case of proving that Rabe, rather than treating of topical social problems, exposes the existential void at the heart of human experience. Pavlo (*The Basic Training of Pavlo Hummel*) finds that the only meaningful thing, his life, is ripped away; David and finally Ozzie (*Sticks and Bones*) see all meanings crumble; Chrissy (*In the Boom Boom Room*) is only "a hunk of meat"; and Sergeant Cokes (*Streamers*) finds the world "a vast charnal house." On a more cheerful note, though with scholarly thoroughness, Gerald Berkowitz in "The Metaphor of Paradox in Sondheim's *Company*" (*WVUPP* 25:94–100) shows how the lyrics of Sondheim's songs illustrate the paradoxical theme of *Company* that, in spite of the difficulties of marriage, it supplies a way of coping with life which the bachelor lacks.

Kingsley Widmer's critical biography *Paul Goodman* (TUSAS 358) contains a short section, "Playing Around" (pp. 132–36) describing some of Goodman's 18 plays as produced at Beck and Malina's Living Theatre, not very successfully to be sure, in the main with Goodman as the hero, and showing a lack of dramatic touch, although Goodman, along with his many essays, poems, speeches, and books, such as *Growing Up Absurd,* had been in the process of writing plays for a number of years. In "The One-Person Play: A Form of Contemporary Dramatic Biography" (*MQ* 21:231–40) Philip Bordinat describes a novel form of theatre today. One-person plays of the mid-'70s, *Clarence Darrow, Give 'Em Hell Harry,* and *The Belle of Amherst,* by television writers rather than playwrights have all proved successful, as well as accurate biography in the case of the first two, but questionable for the life of Emily Dickinson. Unlike artists like Ruth Draper and Cornelia Otis Skinner, who portrayed many characters in each performance, or like those creators of certain speeches or events in the life of Twain or of Dickens, the modern monologists present the life story of one character.

Gerald Weales, who can be counted on to give a good account of each theatre season, this year in "American Theatre Watch, 1979–1980" (*GaR* 34:497–508) expresses his opinion of several notables: of Lanford Wilson as "a very conventional dramatist"; of Sam Shepard, whom he admires, as the opposite in his creation of the monologues *Savage/Love* and *Tongues* for and with Joseph Chaikin; of Tennessee Williams as a man who "once did something finer and better" than *Clothes for a Summer Hotel*; of Neil Simon in his "upbeat" phase as less interesting than as the former ebullient nihilist; and of Marsha Norman's *Getting Out* as the good play Weales predicted two years ago before it was brought to New York. For a fuller treatment and better opinion of Wilson, one may turn to Mel Gussow's "Lanford Wilson on Broadway" (*Horizon* 23:30–35), in which a useful summary of Wilson's life and the creation of his plays includes the background which sparked his late successes *5th of July* and *Talley's Folly* as well as his projections for future work.

Yale's periodical, *Theater*, carries many articles on the Off-Broadway and regional theatre scene in late years. In the Spring issue (11,ii) are Kenneth Bernard's "Some Observations on Meredith Monk's *Recent Ruins*" (pp. 88–91), Janice Paran's "Beckett by Baedeker: Mabou Mines' *Mercier and Camier*" (pp. 63–68), and Mark Bly's "Weber on Handke" (pp. 83–87). In the first Bernard reports that Monk's play at La Mama Annex reflects through its archeological concepts the monumental, the enduring, as it mythically excavates a slice of life's processes, leading to a transcendent amalgamation of tortoises and cast of players in a "supra-human hymnal" to time and flow. In the second we learn that Beckett's novel (with considerable similarity to *Waiting for Godot*) as adapted for the stage and presented at the Public Theatre by Mabou Mines, lacks the theatricality of Beckett's drama, and like other imagistic theatre, which asks only that the audience watch rather than think or feel, becomes, while briefly engaging, static through lack of substance. In the third Carl Weber, presently director of New York University's School of the Arts and formerly an assistant to Brecht at the Berliner Ensemble for a decade, explains his recent direction of Handke's *They Are Dying Out* at Yale.

The Summer issue of *Theater* (11,iii) is devoted to "The Greeks." Joel Schechter in "An Interview with Jan Katt" (pp. 18–22) elicits the opinion that the Greek plays are coming into their own because of a new vision of faceless terror in the world. Suzanne Cowan in "Peter Arnott's Marionettes and *The Bacchae*" (pp. 49–53) explains that although Arnott developed his interest in the classics and in puppetry in England, for the past two decades he has given his one-person performances at colleges and festivals all over America. Besides stories on Greek drama, the issue carries Mark Bly's "The Strange Case of *Mary Barnes*" (pp. 104–07), detailing David Edgar's adaptation of the autobiography of a schizophrenic, performed at the Long Wharf Theater in New Haven, a play which admits to the politics of psychiatry and the problem of feminism, as Mary is treated in an anarchic Loingian community of psychotherapists.

Spanning the continent from San Francisco to New York, *Theater*

(12,i) carries reports on original work on both coasts. William Kleb in "Sam Shepard's *True West*" (pp. 65–71) praises San Francisco's Magic Theatre playwright-in-residence who provided two plays to the 1979–80 season—the surreal *Suicide in B*^{b} and *True West*, a realistic and comic story of the relationship of two very different brothers in southern California, praised by audiences and critics, and proof that Shepard can write in different modes. Kenneth Bernard explains in "Some Observations on the Theater of Peter Brook" (pp. 72–78) that the four plays directed by Brook at La Mama should be seen in sequence, since Brook's method is the message. *L'Os* by African writer Birago Diap and Alfred Jarry's *Ubu Roi* portray man's greed; *The Ik*, based on Colin Turnbull's *The Mountain People*, the brutal consequences of greed for a group of native Africans; and *The Conference of the Birds*, based on a 12th-century poem, the transcendence of greed and materialism.

In a remarkable account of a dramatic group's creation of a portrayal of an event in American history, Herbert Blau in "Making History: The Donner Party, Its Crossing" (*TJ* 32:141–56) describes the genesis and production of a play by the KRAKEN group in residence at Oberlin College. The problem of survival in the early '70s in the heartland of America provided interest in the cannibalistic legend of the Donner party in 1846 on the Oregon trail to California.

Minorities and women of late years are the subjects of a number of items in the field of American drama. The Fall/Winter issue of *Theater* (12,i) includes three essays on Latin American theatre. Alisa Solomon in "Theater in Two Americas: The Second Latin American Popular Theater Festival" (pp. 46–54) reports that groups from Puerto Rico, Panama, Colombia, Venezuela, and Arizona performed at the Public Theater in New York for audiences enthusiastic about promoting interchange of the theatre arts among the Americas. Sandra Cypess in "Latin Americans in the Theater and TOLA" (pp. 38–45) explains how Theater of Latin America (TOLA) brings to the United States performers from Chile, Brazil, Peru, and Argentina.

In "Chicano Theater in the Seventies" (pp. 33–37) Nicolas Kanellos sums up the change in Luis Valdez' El Teatro Campesino, originally an innovating agit-prop troupe popularizing the plight of farmworkers and soon spawning many imitators, which moved onto Broadway in 1979 in *Zoot Suit* and into the universities, where it now resides among the educated middle class, far from the grass roots where it started. Kanellos has another article, "Chicano Theatre: A Popular Culture Battleground" (*JPC* 13:541–55) in which he describes how the theatre has been in the forefront of Chicano political and cultural movements, attacking antiMexican stereotypes and reinforcing the Mexican's ethnic identity in the face of the threat of Anglo-American cultural domination. Another piece making somewhat the same point is Loretta Carrillo's "Chicano *Teatro*: The People's Theatre" (*JPC* 13:556–63). According to her, since Valdez's El Teatro Campesino began producing plays in 1965, the number of traveling troupes increased by 1973 to 54, performing the same functions of bettering the Chicano's social position, giving him pride in his Indian-Mexican heritage, and in late years presenting him with intellectual questions of Chicanos as members of the human race.

The *Drama Review* for September (24,iii) is a Jewish Theatre issue "designed to show some of the varieties" of theatre that are an expression of Jewish culture, including the history of troupes in Poland, Russia, and Israel. As for the American scene, Tina Margolis and Susan Weinacht in "Jewish Theatre Festival 1980" (pp. 93–116) describe the origin of several small Jewish theatres and their performances at the First Annual Jewish Theatre Festival at Marymount Manhattan College in June 1980. In "From Vilna to Vaudeville: Minikes and 'Among the Indians' (1895)" by Mark Slobin, a unique vaudeville skit is reproduced, such a skit representing the "low road" of Yiddish entertainment, very popular in its time but mainly unrecorded.

An article about two minorities and their interaction in certain American dramas is Ellen Schiff's "The Inside of the Outsider: Blacks and Jews in Contemporary Drama" (*MR* 21:801–12). Although contemporary black and Jewish playwrights, according to Schiff, have accepted the convention of blacks and Jews in drama as outsiders, they disavow earlier stereotypes, and both explore the parallels between the histories of their peoples. Two plays by Jews and two by blacks illustrate the sensitive interaction of characters of the two races: Howard Sackler's *The Great White Hope*, in which Jack Jefferson's friend and manager is the Jew Goldie; Phillip Hayes Dean's *Thunder in the Index*, in which a black inmate baits a Jewish doctor; Leonard Berkman's *A Shock of Hair and Burning Eyes*, in which

Kitty as an act of Jewish charity tries to rehabilitate a black; and Ed Bullins' *The Taking of Miss Janie*, in which the Jewish villain is a copout, who gets beaten up by a black. In all four the view from inside the outsider is "I'm me"—a person of individual worth.

A minority seldom featured in studies of American drama is the Indian. This year, however, *Three Plays* (Okla.) by Hanay Geiogamah in the New Native American Drama series furnishes an example of the work of an Indian playwright, all of which were premiered by the North American Theater Ensemble, a group organized in 1972 with the help of Ellen Stewart of La Mama. These plays show different aspects of present Indian life—some unpleasant, some humorous, but always with an essentially religious faith in the ongoing process of creation.

Two books and an issue of *Drama Review* deal with women and the American theatre. Janet Brown's *Feminist Drama: Definition and Critical Analysis* (Scarecrow, 1979) is an attempt to bring some descriptive method to bear on existing dramas. Using Kenneth Burke, she arrives at a definition: "When women's struggle for autonomy is a play's central rhetorical motive, that play can be considered a feminist drama." The plays discussed suppose that the struggle of women today is to be individuals in their own right—not in their relationship to men: in each the agent is a woman, her purpose autonomy, the scene an unjust sociosexual hierarchy in which women are powerless. Besides a close analysis of four plays, Brown describes the work of several feminist dramatic groups as it fits or does not fit her definition. Taking a less theoretical approach is Dinah Luise Leavitt, who in *Feminist Theatre Groups* (Jefferson, N.C.: McFarland Pub. Co.) examines four in Minneapolis which provide the basis for analysis of some 90 such groups nationwide, which although local in origin are influenced by the feminist political movement. Leavitt treats the history and future prospects of feminist drama as well as the distinct aesthetic developing through its purpose of effecting social and political change. A third volume, *The Women's Project: Seven New Plays by Women* (New York: Perf. Arts Journal Publications), ed. Julia Miles, includes plays given studio readings or produced at the American Place Theatre, two of the best being Rose Leiman Goldemberg's *Letters Home*, created from the real letters which Sylvia Plath wrote her mother Aurelia, and Joan

Schenkar's *Signs of Life*, which imaginatively brings together Barnum and the Elephant Lady along with Henry James and his sister Alice, both men thinking both ladies are freaks.

Drama Review this June came out with a "Women and Performance" issue, which is concerned with the lives and work of women of diverse accomplishments in the American theatre. Helen Krich Chinoy in "Art versus Business: the Role of Women in American Theatre" (*TDR* 24,ii:3–10) praises the work of playwright Susan Glaspell, actress-director Eva Le Gallienne, producer Cheryl Crawford, teacher and head of the Federal Theatre Project Hallie Flanagan Davis, producer-director Margo Jones, and the leaders of other regional and off-Broadway theatres. Chinoy believes that these women and many others largely rejected the preoccupation with power and money represented by Broadway, putting their values on the social bonding of repertory and experimental group theatres. With high praise, Chinoy concludes that women have created theatres in which the profits are human and the theatres bulwarks of the democratic form of government. Other pieces in the issue describe women in modern American theatre movements: "Ellen Stewart and La Mama" by Ellen Stewart, "Joan Holden and the San Francisco Mime Troupe" by Ruby Cohn, "Laurie Anderson: Performance Artist" by Mel Gordon, "Linda Mussman's Time and Space Limited Theatre" by Jim O'Quinn, and "Anne Bogart's Journeys" by Jessica Abbe. All add evidence to Chinoy's proposal that women contribute originality to the American theatre because of their artistic rather than purely materialistic aims.

Ruth Gordon's autobiographical *Ruth Gordon: An Open Book* (Doubleday) is one of the popularized, anecdotal accounts of a life on the American stage which has some gleanings of pertinent information for students of women in 20th-century American theatre. Carol Billman in "Women and the Family in American Drama" (*ArQ* 36:35–48) makes the point that although Arthur Miller postulated that family dramas are realistic, *man* in society unrealistic, today some plays depict *women* in society as well as in the home —which in the main has not been true in former decades. Whether it is the experimental nature of drama today or the recognition of women as independent and individual, both male and female dramatists, as well as theatre groups, are presenting varied pictures of women today—inside and outside the family.

vii. Reference Works

The most useful volume published this year is Walter J. Meserve's *American Drama to 1900: A Guide to Information Sources* (Gale) which is concerned with the written drama itself rather than with the staging of it. The first of two sections is a listing of general critical, historical, and reference volumes including library collections, indexes, and anthologies. For the works of history and criticism, Meserve has helpful annotations and comments on the contents and worth of many citations. The second section consists of the listing of 34 of the most important playwrights with pertinent critical and biographical scholarship on each. The volume brings together a great deal of information on sources for the study of American playwriting from colonial times to the present century. James H. Maguire in "A Selected Bibliography of Western American Drama" (*WAL* 14:149–63), without defining "Western" or annotating any items, lists alphabetically by author, all but perhaps one appearing to be from this century, playwrights such as Preston Jones from Texas, all of Saroyan's and William Inge's best plays, Maxwell Anderson's *Night Over Taos*, Robert Sherwood's *Petrified Forest*, Rogers and Hammerstein's *Flower Drum Song*, all of which may be Western in one sense, but which would be clarified by definition and annotation.

Modern Drama carries its "Modern Drama Studies: An Annual Bibliography" (23,ii:121–199) by Charles A. Carpenter as usual, with a large section on the American scene. Since moving to Canada several years ago, however, the publication carries fewer studies of American drama—there being none in any of the issues this year. Of some use in obtaining biographical information may be Jeb H. Perry's *Variety Obits: An Index to Obituaries in Variety, 1905–1978*, which includes the date of the obit of those in all areas (except business) of film, TV, stage, minstrelsy, and vaudeville. The respectability being gained by pop culture is evidenced by reference works, papers, and handbooks on the subject. *American Popular Entertainment: Papers and Proceedings of the Conference on the History of American Popular Entertainment* (Greenwood, 1979), ed. Myron Matlaw, includes 25 critical and historical essays and transcripts of skits and songs from the conference held at Lincoln Center in 1977. In *A Guide to Information Sources: American and English Popular Entertainment* (Gale) Don B. Wilmeth writes a section on

"Popular Theatre: English and American." In volume 2 of *Handbook of American Popular Culture* (Greenwood), ed. M. Thomas Inge, experts in all areas of the popular, for example "Circus and Outdoor Entertainment," and "Women in Popular Culture," display their expertise. It may be that in the '80s the postabsurdist, Ontological-Hysteric theatre will give way to the popular. The swing from esoteric to common might be a relief.

University of Florida

19. Black Literature

John M. Reilly

Richard Wright, Ralph Ellison, and Amiri Baraka give shape to the study of black literature, because their works are taken to exemplify the impulse to reconstruct the genres of realism in accordance with the character of Afro-American culture. These writers continue in 1980, as in most years, to be the subject of a hefty number of critical interpretations, but they have further significance also. Past criticism of the major authors serves as precedent for studies of writers more recently included in the critical canon, while the recognition that thematic recapitulation tells us too little about Wright, Ellison, or Baraka produces greater interest in methodology and theory. It can even be argued that the discovery of intriguing problems in 20th-century writers stimulates 19th-century study, and that their example encourages a search for poets and other playwrights who can become comparable reference points in literary history. Not all of the 23 books and over 100 essays mentioned in this report are sophisticated criticism or interpretation, but the majority of them, and certainly all of those I applaud, reveal a sense that Afro-American literary scholarship with its insistent need to reconcile history and aesthetics forms a unique study.

i. Bibliography

Abolition and reform publications flourishing before the Civil War often filled as much as 20 percent of their column space with correspondence. These letters become valuable sources for establishing the intellectual and social contexts of early Afro-American writing. John W. Blassingame and Mae G. Henderson have indexed and annotated the letters from nine publications in *Antislavery Newspapers and Periodicals*, 2 vols. (Hall). The first volume, devoted to the years 1817–45, covers the *Philanthropist, Emancipator, Genius of*

Universal Emancipation, Abolition Intelligencer, African Observer, and *Liberator.* The second volume, for the years 1835-65, indexes the *Liberator, Anti-Slavery Record, Human Rights,* and the *Observer.* The description of each journal includes the original prospectus, a biographical sketch of the editor, and an indication of library holdings. The entire work is indexed by correspondents' names.

Biographical research in secondary sources will be aided by the third edition of *In Black and White: A Guide to Magazine Articles, Newspaper Articles, and Books Concerning More than 15,000 Black Individuals and Groups,* 2 vols. (Gale). Edited by Mary Mace Spradling, this work offers an index to occupations as a means of checking through the alphabetical listings.

In "Nineteenth Century Black Novelists: A Checklist" (*MV* 3,ii: 27-43) James Barbour and Robert E. Fleming concentrate on William Wells Brown, Charles W. Chesnutt, Martin R. Delany, Paul Laurence Dunbar, Sutton E. Griggs, and Frank J. Webb. This revision of a work from 1977 aims to identify the limited body of serious scholarship rather than to trace reputations; therefore, Barbour and Fleming key references to a master list of general studies of fiction and note additional specialized studies for each author. The value of the checklist is that it updates older references such as Darwin T. Turner's Goldentree Bibliography *Afro-American Writers* (1970) and adds some items to the listings in the Hall reference guide to Chesnutt (1977) and the combined volume on Brown and Delany (1979).

Black American Literature Forum continues to provide impressive bibliographies. This year there are two. James V. Hatch, Douglas A. M. Ward, and Joe Weixlmann are responsible for "The Rungs of a Powerful Long Ladder: An Owen Dodson Bibliography" (14:60-68), listing all published writing by and about Dodson. Equally valuable is Janet L. Sims's "Jessie Redmon Fauset (1885-1961): A Selected Annotated Bibliography" (14:147-52). Besides her work in fiction Fauset published extensively in other forms, especially in the *Crisis,* which she served as literary editor from 1919 to 1926. Sims lists these articles chronologically along with Fauset's novels, short fiction, poems, reviews, and translations. The second part of the listing presents selected secondary works, including dissertations, all annotated; and in the third section Sims identifies manuscript holdings.

Ernest Kaiser's column "Recent Books" in *Freedomways* has been noted previously in *ALS* as a record of books related to American blacks, and the annotated listing continues this year (20:60–65,113–23,311–20). Yet a further source deserving mention is the *Afram Newsletter* issued twice yearly under the editorship of Michel Fabre from the Centre d'Etudes Afro-Américaines et des Nouvelles Littératures Anglophones at the University of Paris III (la Sorbonne Nouvelle). The *Newsletter* provides reviews, abstracts, checklists, interviews, and news of conferences on Afro-American, African, and British Commonwealth literatures.

ii. Fiction

a. **W. W. Brown, Chesnutt, J. W. Johnson.** William Wells Brown has such an impressive list of literary "firsts" to his credit that the character of his texts almost seems a secondary matter. The quality of his writing is either overlooked or dismissed as predictably conventional. In "*Clotel*: A Black Romance" (*CLAJ* 23:296–302) Gerald S. Rosselot offers a defense of the first novel by a black American author, arguing that the lack of developed characterization and breathless pace of the plot illustrates Brown's political purpose, taking advantage of the tendency toward didacticism and heavy symbolism in the romance tradition. Rosselot makes an able start, but his approach will yield a conclusive argument only in a longer study.

Sylvia Lyons Render, who contributed significantly to the study of Chesnutt with an edition of *The Short Fiction of Charles W. Chesnutt* (1974), has employed her knowledge of the canon to write an overview, *Charles W. Chesnutt* (TUSAS 373). Render shows little interest in critical interpretation, choosing instead to use her categorical chapters on milieu, characters, themes, style, etc. mainly to tabulate variations (for example, 22 themes) and to observe the function and accuracy of historical reference. That criticism certainly can go further is demonstrated, however, by William L. Andrews in *The Literary Career of Charles W. Chesnutt* (LSU). He locates Chesnutt's models in the writings of Albion Tourgée, Thomas Nelson Page, and Joel Chandler Harris, while showing that Chesnutt's literary purpose develops from a combination of personal experience as a light-complexioned Negro—a marginal man—and a recognition that a predominantly white audience had to be approached by indirection.

The revelation of these complex influences in the process of composition and the reference of each of the published works to prevalent 19th-century fictional types discloses Chesnutt's innovative signature.

P. Jay Delmar adds three articles this year to his previous work on Chesnutt. The most useful, because it contributes detail to the portrayal of artistry is "Character and Structure in Charles W. Chesnutt's *The Marrow of Tradition*" (*ALR* 13:284–89). Here Delmar distinguishes a racial conflict, murder mystery, and love story within the novel, each plot achieving internal coherence by symmetrical balancing of white and black characters. Delmar has written previously about the variety of tragedy in black fiction (see *ALS 1976*, p. 380) and now he expands his point. "Elements of Tragedy in Charles W. Chesnutt's *The Conjure Woman*" (*CLAJ* 23:451–59) traces through three stories the development of the protagonists' own weakness as a cause more important than external factors for reversal of fortunes. Then "Charles W. Chesnutt's 'The Web of Circumstances' and Richard Wright's 'Long Black Song': The Tragedy of Property" (*SSF* 17:178–79) suggests that the tragedy of these stories can be understood as an assertion that racial advancement must be predicated on political power, not economic issues alone.

Critical discussion of James Weldon Johnson's fiction continues to focus, as well it should, on interpretation of the narrator of his novel. Nicholas Canaday in "*The Autobiography of an Ex-Colored Man* and the Tradition of Black Autobiography" (*Obsidian* 6,i–ii:76–80) makes the excellent point that when read against the works of autobiographers such as Frederick Douglass and Booker T. Washington the novel appears as an ironic inversion of conventions. Possibly the most intriguing essay yet written on the subject, however, is "Irony and Symbolic Action in James Weldon Johnson's *The Autobiography of an Ex-Colored Man*" by Joseph T. Skerrett, Jr. (*AQ* 32:540–58). Using Johnson's actual autobiography *Along This Way*, Skerrett discerns Johnson's suppressed feelings of anxiety toward a personal friend who was for a time his alter ego. Those feelings are exorcized and the strategy of avoiding pain by "passing" rejected through the process of objectification required in writing a novel.

b. Toomer, Hurston, Larsen, Schuyler, Fisher, Hughes. Brian Joseph Benson and Mabel Mayle Dillard do an outstanding job of synthesizing sources in *Jean Toomer* (TUSAS 389). Letters and autobiographical writings are used to good effect in establishing the biography, especially the Chicago Gurdjieff period, and the views Toomer expressed on transcendent American identity are presented as the key to the published works of the late 1920s and early 1930s. The 50-page exposition of *Cane*, section-by-section in terms of a circular structure moving from complex to simple and back, gives that work the weight scholars will expect, but Benson and Dillard make it clear they consider Toomer's other writings just as important. The projects they set out for further scholarly work include a thorough biography, a catalogue of all publications, and an edition of letters. Over the years Darwin T. Turner has done much toward completion of related projects, and now with *The Wayward and the Seeking: A Collection of Writings by Jean Toomer* (Howard) he gives us an excellent anthology that reveals the shape and substance of the career. Excluding book-length work, Turner's generic selections are designed to illustrate the psychology and intellectual development before *Cane* and the literary styles Toomer created for each of the genres he chose for expression. The section of autobiographical writing is arranged to construct a coherent story by eliminating repetition; the short fiction presents stories of ego and emotion; most of the poetry comes from the unpublished collection "The Wayward and the Seeking"; dramatic writings represent expressionist work; and the concluding section of aphorisms and maxims presents Toomer as preacher. Turner explains his choices in prefatory notes, and his concluding bibliography describes the Toomer Collection acquired by Fisk University in 1963 but now located in the Beinecke Library at Yale University.

Mark Helbling provides an addendum to Toomer biography in "Jean Toomer and Waldo Frank: A Creative Friendship" (*Phylon* 41:167–78). Helbling sees *Cane* not only as the swan song of black peasantry that Toomer called it, but as the beginning of a quest for new consciousness. The sympathy Toomer received from Frank in that search is documented in detail from correspondence. Frederick L. Rusch's "A Tale of the Country Round: Jean Toomer's Legend 'Monrovia' " (*MELUS* 7,ii:37–46) might serve as a model for critical work on the post-*Cane* writings. Rusch is persuaded of the interest of Toomer's mystical thought but aware that its ineffability blocked successful writing, except in a work like "Monrovia" where Toomer, aided by the possibilities of mythic form, created a symbolic cor-

relative for his subjective feelings. C. O. Ogunyemi's "From a Goat
Path in Africa: Roger Mais and Jean Toomer" (*Obsidian* 5,iii:7–21)
will be of most use to students of the Jamaican novel. Still, it suggests
Toomer's romantic feelings about African heritage.

Lillie P. Howard's *Zora Neale Hurston* (TUSAS 381) gives a
chronological account of the life and times. The chapters on major
works synthesize interpretations to date. This is a basic survey for
quick reference.

Nella Larsen and Jesse Redmon Fauset usually have been classi-
fied as minor writers of the Harlem Renaissance because their subject matter is middle-class domestic life. They may never earn designation as major authors, but certainly a more appreciative judgment
of their work will emerge from contributions such as the Fauset
biliography by Janet L. Sims and critical studies like Claudia Tate's
"Nella Larsen's *Passing*: A Problem of Interpretation" (*BALF* 14:
142–46). Attending to treatment rather than subject matter, Tate
argues that the protrayal of Harlem's Sugar Hill crowd is intentionally romanticized and deliberately associated with language of ambiguity to create a story of psychological intrigue in which the
mulatto condition is a device for suspense. Further study of Larsen
should also be aided by William Bedford Clark's indication of resources in "The Letters of Nella Larsen to Carl Van Vechten: A
Survey" (*RALS* [1978]8:193–99). Clark's description of the contents of the letters notes that Larsen saw herself as a detached observer of absurdity, though she could be stung by criticism and ad-
mitted to writing autobiographically.

In *George S. Schuyler* (TUSAS 349) Michael W. Peplow takes
on the task of recovering for serious critical treatment an author
whose reactionary political views in later life put him at odds with
practically every significant black spokesperson in America. Peplow
succeeds in gaining patient attention by concentrating on the years
1923–33 when Schuyler's most important essays on culture and his
two novels appeared. The essays and the iconoclastic portrayal of
Liberia in *Slaves Today* are explainable as part of Schuyler's effort
to discredit romantic views, but these works retain interest mainly
because they can be associated with the effective satire of racial obsession in *Black No More*. This novel, examined in terms of its satiric
devices and picaresque protagonist, is the central exhibit of the book,
a position that justifies the study and suggests that the recently

stated approval by Ishmael Reed of *Black No More* as an influential science-fiction novel has merit.

Last year Leonard J. Deutsch published a comprehensive survey of Rudolph Fisher's Harlem short stories. In 1980 he adds to that study with "Rudolph Fisher's Unpublished Manuscripts: Description and Commentary" (*Obsidian* 6,i–ii:82–97), a presentation of plots, quotations, and appraisals of the typescripts of four stories in the John Hay Library at Brown University.

Susan L. Blake in "Old John in Harlem: The Urban Folktales of Langston Hughes" (*BALF* 14:100–04) identifies Jesse B. Semple as a migrant descendant of the archetypal folk figure from slavery times. Adapting traditional motifs and patterns of characterization and conflict, Hughes replicates the dramatic relationship of oral storyteller and audience. Blake's analysis of inside and outside plots and the verbal banter between narrator and dramatic speaker neatly explains the folklore dynamics mastered by a skilled, self-conscious writer. The other 1980 essay on Hughes's prose, Brian Lee's " 'Who's Passing for Who?' in the Fiction of Langston Hughes" (*Black Fiction*, pp. 29–40) appears to be concerned with whether or not Hughes tried to write "black," but gives only pedestrian readings by way of argument.

c. **Wright, Motley, Petry.**   Addison Gayle's *Richard Wright: Ordeal of a Native Son* (Doubleday) is neither a critical biography nor a new interpretation of the life. Rather it retells the story of Wright's career from the biographies by Michel Fabre and Constance Webb, laying in quotation from documents obtained under the Freedom of Information Act. These include logs of taps on the telephones of Communist party leaders in the United States, informers' reports on the Franco-American Fellowship founded by Wright in Paris, and background materials prepared for FBI headquarters. Notable among these are Richard Wright's own statement in 1954 to the U. S. Passport Office in Paris and a report that he initiated a meeting with American Embassy staff before the Congress of Black Writers and Artists sponsored by *Présence Africaine* in the fall of 1956. Gayle makes no effort to evaluate or interpret the documents, because, he says, his professional training has not prepared him in the use of such materials. Apparently he is not even prepared to give a full listing of the documents. Reprinting of everything acquired under the FOIA might very well be impossible, but the value of the material to others doing research has been limited by Gayle's (or his publisher's) decision to present it within the conventions of popular biography instead of as the subject of a sharply pointed monograph.

If Gayle's book fails for want of scholarly purpose, then Robert Felgar's *Richard Wright* (TUSAS 386) is undone by its author's hubris. Felgar promises, for example, the "final word" on the controversy about the ending of *Native Son*, then delivers the unremarkable and dubious view that Bigger dies a completely determined creature of his environment. He rejects the poetry and any other works showing traces of Marxism on the simplistic grounds that a class concept in the context of American racism is unrealistic, dismisses the later novels as worthy of only slight attention, and declares that except for *Black Power* the nonfiction is just tendentious. When a work attracts Felgar's critical interest it's because he can interpret it according to Eldridge Cleaver's mythic representation of the sexual basis of racism: Bigger Thomas is the "Supermasculine Menial," Mary Dalton is "the Ultrafeminine," and so forth.

For sound and provocative studies of Wright in 1980 one turns to essays, several of them written by Afro-Americanists whose work has always been of consistently high quality. In the collection of his essays titled *The Second Black Renaissance* (Greenwood) C. W. E. Bigsby includes "The Self and Society: Richard Wright's Dilemma" (pp. 54–84), which describes the struggle to find a language of symbolic perception at the heart of Wright's social and aesthetic concerns. In the light of such a struggle to express a previously unarticulated reality *Native Son* becomes something very different from naturalism, or even protest writing as it is usually understood, for the novel's text appears designed to relate Bigger's movement to a position, similar to his creator's, where he can elude the trap of an alienated personality and sense the connection between himself and others. The point is underlined in Bigsby's interpretation of *The Outsider* as demonstration that the detached self is a natural killer. Bigsby's linking of Wright's intellectual dilemma to his portrayal of character makes suggestions of deeply felt psychological structures in the fiction. Suggestion becomes declarative in Joseph T. Skerrett, Jr.'s "Richard Wright, Writing and Identity" (*Callaloo* 2[1979]:84–94). Skerrett's essential point, that Wright rejected the negative identity racism would have imposed on him and found an active form of rebellion in literature, is not a new idea by any means, but his exposition of the "white death" of Mississippi is so well elaborated that it establishes without question a basis for interpreting Wright's work with reference to projection of psychic burdens. Yet deeper investigation of Wright's psyche through reading of texts occurs in Michel Fabre's brilliant exercise in psychocriticism, "Fantasies and Style in Richard Wright's Fiction" (*NewL* 46, iii:55–81). Exploring the linguistic patterns of episodes that resemble trauma Fabre attempts to decode style to reveal that its bedrock is the persistent influence of unconscious memories surrounding fire, prohibitions, female figures, and violence. Fabre's method of associating image clusters with psychological sources while still allowing for conscious artistry promises an exciting development of the idea that style is the man.

Ian Walker's "Black Nightmare: The Fiction of Richard Wright" (*Black Fiction*, pp. 11–28) comes nowhere near the class of these other essays. Except to diehards the idea that Wright departed from naturalism is not news, and as he troops through the works without recourse to recent criticism Walker throws little light on the nightmare he maintains will explain the shape of Wright's fiction. "Richard Wright and Africa" by Chikwenye Okonjo Ogunyeui (*IFR* 7:1–5) claims that Wright's evident difficulty in understanding Africa is matched by the African reader's problem in comprehending characters formed in the peculiar circumstances of American racial experience. Of the two essays on specific works Takeo Shimizu's "*Uncle Tom's Children*: Eternal Recurrence" (*KAL* 21:33–41) provides a novel interpretation of the stories as a version of expulsion from paradise. In "Blind Eyes, Blind Quests in Richard Wright's *Native Son*" (*CLAJ* 24:48–60) Priscilla R. Ramsey takes up a topic often remarked but never discussed in such detail, so her article becomes a basic source on the thematic significance of the metaphor of blindness.

In "Willard Motley: Making and Unmaking of *Knock on Any Door*" (*The Practice of Fiction*, pp. 71–84) Jerome Klinkowitz amplifies the discussion of Motley's composition in the introduction to his edition of *The Diaries of Willard Motley* (1979). This latest consideration outlines the way the novel—conceived originally as a bold, experimental work—was revised into a commercial property as it passed through the hands of several publishers.

Margaret B. McDowell's intention in "*The Narrows*: A Fuller View of Ann Petry" (*BALF* 14:135–41) is to show the subtlety and complexity of which Petry is capable in a work usually overlooked because it does not square with the assumption that its author is a thoroughgoing naturalist. McDowell's study of images and themes designed to make concrete detail ambiguous and to show the moral inadequacy of historical knowledge is especially effective. On the other hand, Theodore L. Gross in "Ann Petry: The Novelist as Social Critic" (*Black Fiction*, pp. 41–53) is persuaded that not only Ann Petry but all Afro-American authors of the 1920s and 1930s are also naturalists, because the idea of humanity, fated to exist hopelessly within a hostile environment, coincides exactly with their own experiences. On the basis of that absolute, Gross finds the strength of *The Street* to be its setting, *The Narrows* best in its representation of the ghetto, and the other works less credible since they lack scope for oppressive social conditions. Granted, naturalism appeals to black writers, but it has been a function of recent criticism to explain that the writers also resist portrayal of victimization. Gross sees half the picture, which is certainly too little to sustain his general premise.

d. **Ellison, Baldwin, Childress.** *Invisible Man* occupies its prominent place in literary history as a sign of the advent of "modernist" black literature, but it is also significant because its form and style pose important critical questions about works written both before and after 1952. For one thing the departure from social realism evident in Ellison's novel has provoked critics to reexamine that mode. Were authors of so-called protest simply realists, or have our expectations based upon social assumptions obscured understanding of earlier texts? Are the adaptations of the variety of Afro-American character and language evident in *Invisible Man* actually broadly representative of black writing? Robert G. O'Meally in *The Craft of Ralph Ellison* (Harvard) offers help toward these larger questions, though his focus is on Ellison alone. His thesis is that folklore provides the key to the fictional world. In three opening chapters O'Meally outlines the conditions in which Ellison found his popular sources and reports the development in the apprentice writings. The central examination of *Invisible Man* explores the combination of analogues to musical forms and the motifs formed from folklore and literary sources. Entirely properly O'Meally corrects the tendency to abbreviate Ellison's career, and his final chapters treat later stories, observing in those about Hickman the design of a novel in progress. Since several articles on Ellison are also outstanding, this is a banner year for him. C. W. E. Bigsby's "The Flight of Words: The Paradox of Ralph Ellison" (in his *The Second Black Renaissance*, pp. 85–104) claims that the liberating power of the word is potentially a denial of the reality it begins by expressing. Ellison's problem, therefore, is to maintain a balance between experience and language, a dilemma resolved in *Invisible Man* by the challenge to the idea that symbols, such as those embodied in white versions of history or the solipsistic impulses of an alienated black, constitute reality. Laurence B. Holland's "Ellison in Black and White: Confession, Violence and Rhetoric in *Invisible Man*" (*Black Fiction*, pp. 54–73) also focuses on a linguistic contradiction, but one that Holland finds unresolved. The mediating power of fiction translates violence into words, and the words ought to become the basis for positive action; but in Ellison's "confession," as he terms his book, fiction can yield no blueprint for the protagonist because the job of narration has burdened him with ambivalence.

Joseph T. Skerrett, Jr. uses the method of Harold Bloom to study Ellison in relation to his literary paternity. "The Wright Interpretation: Ralph Ellison and the Anxiety of Influence" (*MR* 21:196–212) describes the evasion of Wright's singular influence, with the essays "Richard Wright's Blues" and "Hidden Name and Complex Fate" major landmarks of that progress. In the first, a review of *Black Boy*, Ellison encapsulates Wright in a description that clears the way for his own antithetical view of black culture; in the second he constructs an autobiographical environment in striking contrast to Wright's Mississippi. Robert J. Butler's "Patterns of Movement in Ellison's *Invisible Man*" (*AmerS* 21,i:5–21) finds the basis of the novel in the desire for motion endemic in American culture. The protagonist must be liberated from racial stress signified variously as paralysis and futile circling. His positive movement, like Huckleberry Finn's, is into a frontier of possibilities; thus, the conventions of the American picaresque acquire black particularity. Finally Gillian Thomas and Michael Larsen in "Ralph Ellison's Conjure Doctor" (*ELN* 17:281–88) confirm the functional use of folklore by identifying Peter Wheatstraw as a conjure man and describing the protagonist's bafflement at Wheatstraw's "sounding" as evidence of his alienation from traditional wisdom.

Carolyn Wedin Sylvander's *James Baldwin* (Ungar) appears as a volume in the Modern Literature Series where one expects the summations of plot and biographical fact appropriate to an introductory guide; however, the nature of Baldwin's writing and the skill of Sylvander make a virtue of necessity. Giving attention to the autobiographical writing as the source of themes of love and history, Sylvander persuasively shows that Baldwin has generated both his essays and his fiction from personal experience. The motif emerging from the canon when viewed in this way is a drive toward reconciliation of Baldwin to the extended family of a black audience. Kenneth Kinnamon, who contributes the entry on Baldwin to *American Writers: A Collection of Literary Biographies*, ed. Leonard Unger, supp. 1, part 1 (Scribner's 1979) also identifies personal history as a source of Baldwin's sensitivity to the interrelationship of psychological and social issues. By identifying four sectors of imaginative interest—church, self, city, race—Kinnamon provides in the scope of 24 pages pithy interpretive comments and a neat summation of a career he sees as manifesting an ever-expanding perspective and a still unfulfilled potential. Both Sylvander and Kinnamon include bibliographies of primary and secondary works.

William Wasserstrom's "James Baldwin: Stepping Out on a Promise" (*Black Fiction*, pp. 74–96) ranges over the Cleaver-Baldwin dispute, Baldwin's use of conversion as rebirth, the dilemma of maleness in America, and the relevance of R. D. Laing's conception of a journey through madness. The essay's effectiveness derives from the critic's immense sympathy with Baldwin. A more pointed essay is Charles Scruggs's "The Tale of Two Cities in James Baldwin's *Go Tell It on the Mountain*" (*AL* 52:1–17), which describes the ambivalence of John Grimes in his attempt to choose between the earthly city of chaos and culture and the heavenly city toward which the church temporarily pulls him. This is a strong interpretation of the novel offering the important reminder that Baldwin's consciousness is rooted in religious metaphors. James B. Vopat's "Beyond Sociology? Urban Experience in the Novels of James Baldwin" (*Minority Literature*, pp. 51–58) deserves mention for its notice of other metaphoric structures, particularly the narrow room and the darkness of the movie theater which in Baldwin's distinctive approach to social issues provide the field for individual redemption.

In "'I Wish I Was a Poet': The Character as Artist in Alice Childress's *Like One of the Family*" (*BALF* 14:24–30) Trudier Harris leads us to appreciate the fascinating creation of the day maid Mildred, whose control of her working environment and the vividly imaginative manner in which she relates her experiences to a friend, reveal her as a latter-day oral artist.

e. **Marshall, Morrison, Reed, G. Jones.** John Cooke's "Whose Child? The Fiction of Paule Marshall" (*CLAJ* 24:1–15) relates her search for a political perspective. The length of the search has been in part due to the complexity of Marshall's own cultural inheritance and her predilection for personal plots, but the major problem, according to Cooke, has been to find a way of integrating sexual and political conflicts. This is finally accomplished with the portrayal of Merle Kinbona in *The Chosen Place, The Timeless People*.

Susan L. Blake's eye for the adaptation of folklore in literature results in an engaging examination of Toni Morrison's best-known novel. "Folklore and Community in *Song of Solomon*" (*MELUS* 7, iii:77–82) points out that the title announces a variant of a Gullah folktale. Morrison links it to Milkman, the character pursuing the feeling of community, but the dénouement of the tale and Milkman's story differ. Traditionally the group flies back to Africa, while Morrison's sense of contemporary reality leads her to have Milkman fly alone, into a void. A. Leslie Harris in "Myth as Structure in Toni Morrison's *Song of Solomon*" (*MELUS* 7,iii:69–76) is also concerned with Milkman, though his study of the resonance of symbols leads to the conclusion that the character is reintegrated into a world for which he becomes a defending champion. Despite the apparent disagreement the two essays are usefully read together as a way of exposing the range of imagery in the novel. Barbara Christian's "Community and Nature: The Novels of Toni Morrison" (*JEthS* 7, iv:65–78) also connects the fiction to traditional stories, for her contention is that the novels portray communities where kinship ties are woven into the legends and subconscious and where representations of nature define life.

"Ishmael Reed's Fiction: Da Hoodoo Is Put on America" by Frank McConnell (*Black Fiction*, pp. 136–48) searches for analogies to the shifting voices, changes of diction, and mix of devices in Reed's work. A stand-up comic's monologue, the reconstruction of a given composition in bebop, and the syncretism of voodoo occur in turn to McConnell as correlatives in the development of an increasingly capacious aesthetic. Reed would appreciate the tone of it all.

Another experimentalist, Gayl Jones, is treated by Keith Byerman in "Black Vortex: The Gothic Structure of *Eva's Man*" (*MELUS* 7, iv:93–101). Here the analogy is to the underlying pattern of the Gothic, which Byerman explains as demonic pursuit. The narration of increasingly extreme versions of similar events issues in a concentric, predetermined structure of incidents where males attempt to dominate females by force.

f. **General Criticism of Fiction.** Feminist criticism of Afro-American fiction began as it did in other fields with consideration of literary representations of female experience and characters. That was followed by the resolve to treat women writers as seriously and rigorously as the predominantly male "major figures." Initially these twin purposes may have been impelled by the political desire to give women writers equal consideration with men, or by reasoning that found it unlikely for male authors to be in position to tell the full story of black experience; but the combined study of women as characters and women as authors soon leads to the conclusion that within the general literary history there is a female tradition with its own characteristic projects and styles of writing. Barbara Christian's *Black Women Novelists: The Development of a Tradition, 1892–1976* (Greenwood) is an excellent example of the work that can be done on the premise of differential literary history. The first part of the book examines the ideological sources of black female stereotypes against which authors like Frances Ellen Watkins Harper in *Iola LeRoy, Shadows Uplifted* contended by the creation of a counterstereotype, the tragic mulatta. The second stage of black women's fiction, also treated in the first part of the book, presented writers with the problem of placing their characters in the common life and community, a need satisfied by versions of domestic fiction. The rise of a vital tradition out of these beginnings forms the subject of the second part of Christian's book where she discusses Paule Marshall, Toni Morrison, and Alice Walker—each of whom brings the experience of repression and domination by stereotype directly into fiction as a problem to be met by the characters. A different structural metaphor denominates the work of each author: Marshall's characters are sculpted, Morrison's contemporary fables are wrought out of fantastic realism, and Walker's bits and pieces of material are rescued from oblivion for everyday use as in the sewing of a quilt. The methodological sophistication of the book permits Christian to describe the particularity of the major exhibits while sustaining the idea that together they form an independent literary lineage.

Faith Pullin in "Landscapes of Reality: The Fiction of Contemporary Afro-American Women" (*Black Fiction*, pp. 173–203) is on the same track as Christian, though she begins her account with the cultural nationalism and feminism of Zora Neale Hurston. She also gives considerable weight to the emergence of an interest among authors in their own sexuality. The technical failures Pullin observes she attributes to the difficulty of finding new ways to use language. Valerie Lee's "The Uses of Folktales in Novels by Black Women Writers" (*CLAJ* 23:266–72) announces the interesting topic of folktalk, particularly that about the relations of women and men.

Elizabeth Schultz's "African and Afro-American Roots in Contemporary Afro-American Literature: The Difficult Search for Family Origins" (*SAF* 8,ii:127–45) continues her exploration of how black fiction differs from the mainstream (see *ALS 1979*, p. 410). In this essay she identifies examples of the family novel which contrast with fiction of the immediate post–World War II period. The anguish of rootlessness prevalent in black writing as well as white is supplanted by thematic representation of characters participating in domestic survival rituals.

As I noted earlier transformations of the tradition of realism have become an important critical topic. Sometimes the departure from realism is noted by studies of subject matter as in an essay by Dennis D. Lynch that is now two years old. "Visions of Chicago in Contemporary Black Literature" (*Minority Literature*, pp. 25–32) describes the shift from Willard Motley's unmitigated bleakness which Lynch associates with naturalism, to an existentially inspired description of black urban life in the stories of Cyrus Colter. For Lynch the change is due largely to the authors' choice to focus on the possibilities with black communities rather than upon conflicts with white power. By way of contrast Graham Clarke's "Beyond Realism: Recent Black Fiction and the Language of 'The Real Thing'" (*Black*

Fiction, pp. 204–21) delineates the change by reference to the subversion of the codified system of realism, particularly its dominant
authorial voice, by a dynamic use of language that increasingly finds
its subject in itself. Similarly A. Robert Lee in "Making New: Styles
of Innovation in the Contemporary Black American Novel" (*Black
Fiction,* pp. 222–50) is concerned with the novel of serious experiment free of prescriptive ideology. Clarke's essay is suggestive rather
than conclusive because it has too little technical description of linguistic practice. Lee is successful because his description of the landscape of experimental activity finds its evidence in larger structures.

In the novel of what he calls the Second Black Renaissance C. E.
Bigsby locates a contradiction characteristic of the 1960s. "Judgement Day is Coming! Judgement Day is Coming!" (Bigsby's *Second
Black Renaissance,* pp. 164–81; *Black Fiction,* pp. 149–72) describes
an aborted apocalypse in the works of John A. Williams, William
Melvin Kelley, and John O. Killens. On the one hand, these writers
long for the culmination of racial conflict in open battle; yet they also
betray a feeling that apocalypse may be deferred by the conversion
of America to its professed liberal principles. Bigsby has argued the
point previously in "The Divided Mind of James Baldwin" (*ALS
1979,* p. 405; reprinted in *Second Black Renaissance*), and the contention that black writers almost alone among American authors preserve a faith in liberal social responsibility—or the idea that others
will accept responsibility—provides a central thesis to all of his
essays published in 1980.

iii. Poetry

a. **Wheatley, Douglass, Dunbar.** The two essays from 1980 on
Phillis Wheatley are efforts to place her securely in the milieu of the
18th century. John C. Shields's "Phillis Wheatley and Mather Byles:
A Study in Literary Relationship" (*CLAJ* 23:377–90) points out con-
gruities between Byles's *Poems on Several Occasions* (1744) and
Wheatley's *Poems on Various Subjects* (1733) in the use of heroic
verse, arrangement, and some internal usage. He stops short of describing this as influence, since, as he says, Wheatley's creativity sur-
passes Byles's. Albertha Sistrunk in "Phillis Wheatley: an Eighteenth
Century Black American Poet Revisited" (*CLAJ* 23:391–98) gives a

handbook discussion of Wheatley's subjects and verse form, noting also her sense of a black heritage.

"'Liberty,' A Poem by Frederick Douglass" (*RALS* 8[1978]:103–14) by Thomas Bonner, Jr. reports on one of the earliest artistic works by Douglass yet discovered. He wrote the verse in his notebook on 13 September 1847 while on tour in Cleveland, then revised it to incorporate into a longer poem he delivered in a speech in New York City on 22 October 1847.

Students of Dunbar are disturbed by the appearance of accommodation to the conventions of the plantation tradition in his dialect writings. Emeka Okeke-Exigbo attacks the problem in "Paul Laurence Dunbar and the Afro-American Folk Tradition" (*Obsidian* 6, i–ii:63–74) by identifying a group of "positively Afro-American poems" that show a striking accumulation of the black community's coded references.

b. **S. Brown, Hughes, McKay, Toomer.** The poet-critic Stephen E. Henderson does a superb job in "The Heavy Blues of Sterling Brown: A Study of Craft and Tradition" (*BALF* 14:32–44) explaining the immense skill that produces poems that achieve their effect by the appearance of simple rendition. Henderson shows the depth of reference to the blues in *Southern Road* by indicating echoes of traditional compositions and variations on their form. For the poem "Cabaret" he guides the reader through interlocking levels of perception and commentary to the indictment of neoslavery in the exploitation of musicians, and by the use of diagrams shows the voice levels and duration for performance. Similarly, anaphora within the response pattern of "Memphis Blues" is diagrammed to illustrate the development of the strong rhythms. In sum Henderson reveals that the straightforward verses are remarkable syntheses of a profound knowledge of form and masterful technical ability. Michael Harper, another poet-critic, celebrates Brown's accomplishment in the brief piece, "Sterling Brown, 1901–2001" (*Parnassus* 8,i:294–96). The notebooks of Brown, he says, show him continually at work on the craft and technique by which he merges folk materials and self-conscious artistry.

Donald C. Dickinson, author of *A Bio-Bibliography of Langston Hughes* (1967), contributes the essay on the poet to *American Writ-*

ers: A Collection of Literary Biographies, ed. Leonard Unger, supp.
1, part 1 (Scribner's, 1979). Chronology of the biographical account
reinforces the idea that Hughes's writing was always the product
of his times. Dickinson's judgment that the urban blues show the poet
at his best calls forth a brief discussion of the techniques and the
broken rhythms. Future studies of Hughes, and for that matter Afro-
American literary history, will find invaluable the discussion of
projects and publications in *Arna Bontemps—Langston Hughes, Letters, 1925–1967,* ed. Charles H. Nichols (Dodd, Mead). The correspondence stretched from the year the writers met until Hughes's
death. Nichols selects 500 from about 2,300 extant letters, arranges
them in periods, and supplements them with a brief introduction on
the personalities and an epilogue on their legacy. "Langston Hughes
of Kansas" by Mark Scott (*Kansas History* 3:3–25) brings together
material from published sources to present a narrative of Hughes's
family background starting with his great-grandmother Lucy Langston, a slave in Virginia, whose children included Congressman John
Mercer Langston and Charles, the poet's grandfather. Besides Susan
L. Blake's essay on the Simple stories the other critical work on
Hughes for 1980 is Dona Hoilman's "A Red Southwestern House for
a Black Midwestern Poet" (*CP* 13,ii:55–61), explaining Hughes's
departure from his usual forms to write "A House in Taos" in the
manner of an Indian healing chant.

Marion B. McLeod takes advantage of last year's publication of
a lost manuscript to write "Claude McKay's Russian Interpretation:
The Negroes in America" (*CLAJ* 23:336–51). McLeod points out
important differences from McKay's earlier attitudes toward American black leaders in the book he wrote while in the Soviet Union,
summarizes his call for greater attention to black culture, and suggests that the book raises questions about previous discussions based
upon McKay's autobiography *A Long Way from Home.*

Both of the 1980 essays on Jean Toomer's verse concern his later
poem "Blue Meridian." Frederick L. Rusch, whose excellent study of
"Monrovia" has been noted, presents an equally sound reading in
"The Blue Man: Jean Toomer's Solution to His Problems of Identity"
(*Obsidian* 6,i–ii:38–54). After recounting images of alienation that
appear to express Toomer's sense of alienation in earlier works, including *Cane,* Rusch identifies elements of universalism, ideas the
poet adopted from Melville J. Herskovits' racial theories, and the

signs of cosmic unity he found in mystical experience. From these sources Toomer gained the materials for a utopian poem of racial synthesis that Rusch examines in detail. Bernard W. Bell agrees that the long poem is the zenith of Toomer's quest for identity, and in "Jean Toomer's 'Blue Meridian': The Poet as Prophet of a New Order of Man" (*BALF* 14:77–80) he describes the symbols and Gurdjieffian concepts employed in the creation of an elite new cultural figure. Though they differ in the stress they place on materials assimilated by Toomer, the essays of Rusch and Bell are equally welcome as first-rate interpretations justifying the addition of "Blue Meridian" to the list of poems essential in the study of Afro-American poetics.

c. **Brooks, Tolson, Dodson.** Harry B. Shaw centers his study *Gwendolyn Brooks* (TUSAS 395) on the poet's "awakening" in 1967 to a new mood of possibility in Afro-American life. The energy of the liberation movement and the boldness of younger poets encouraged her to make a totally overt commitment to the idea of the indivisibility of social purpose and aesthetic practice, while the recognition by her peers of the accomplishment manifest in more than two decades of publication led them to establish her as "Surprised Queen" of black poetry. Shaw's organization of the book around categories of social themes follows consistently from this key event. The categories are four: death, both physical and spiritual; the fall from the glory of a memorable black past; the labyrinth of the duplicitous American racial system; and restraint and militance as alternative strategies of survival. Brooks's autobiography *Report from Part One* (1972) and *The World of Gwendolyn Brooks* (1971), the last book of poetry she published with Harper before switching to the black-controlled firm Broadside, are Shaw's chief texts in a discussion that ably sustains the understanding that effective poetry on social themes depends upon literary means. George E. Kent's "Gwendolyn Brooks—Portrait, In Part" (*Callaloo* 2[1979]:74–83) comes from a work-in-progress. This section represents the formation of consciousness in adolescence: Brooks's reading, family occasions, a painful shyness, but also a powerful drive to create that led her to write a poem every day. A product of those teenage years is described and discussed by Erlene Stetson "'Songs After Sunset (1935–1936)': The Unpublished Poetry of Gwendolyn Brooks" (CLAJ 24:87–96). The title refers to a 20-page collection of 33 poems in manuscript at the Lilly Library, Indiana University. In appearance it resembles a copybook of Jacobean times with platonic dedication and compliments, while the textual substance shows debts to Donne, Jonson, and Milton. It begs to be used in a critical biography such as Kent is undertaking.

Mariann Russell, who published an interesting essay on Melvin Tolson's style last year has incorporated that analysis into a full-length study, *Melvin B. Tolson's* Harlem Gallery: A *Literary Analysis* (Missouri). Since *Harlem Gallery* (1965) was preceded by the longer and more representational *Gallery of Harlem Portraits* (1935) Russell devotes a good deal of her study to points of contrast. The earlier poem is placed in the context of the historical Harlem community, complete with references to actual residents. The later poem, more evocative and cerebral, evidences the influence of modernist poetics, which Russell pursues through chapters on milieu, characters, personae, theme, and techniques. One hesitates to say that definitive critical statement has been made about such a complex and little studied poem as *Harlem Gallery,* but certainly the breadth and detail of this discussion make this an essential book.

Owen Dodson is best known as dramatist and novelist, but in "The Alchemy of Owen Dodson" (*BALF* 14:51–52) James V. Hatch arouses interest in his verse by giving an exegesis of "Prisoners," a short poem published for the first time with the article. Specific, if unnamed, references to race infuse a religious poem to relate the central spiritual trials of Christianity and the black condition.

d. **Baraka, Knight.**   Amiri Baraka's interest in poetry has been overshadowed by his reputation as a dramatist and his preference for genres he finds more amenable to political aims; yet he retains importance in literary history as a poet devoted to combat with Western aesthetics. This struggle enters the discussion he has with William J. Harris in "An Interview with Amiri Baraka" (*Greenfield Rev.* 8,iii–iv:19–31). In the present period of his development Baraka sees the movement among poets of the 1950s as a popular front against academicism. The openness of other writers encouraged his own use of personal experience, but he balks at allowing his writing to be called confessional. Similarly he acknowledges influences of Charles Olson and Pound, but adds that events in the world and the example of poets more in tune with popular interests were equally important to him. Henry Blackwell's "Amiri Baraka's Letters to Charles Olson" (*RALS* 10:56–70) describes the 50 pieces of correspondence in the Olson Archives at the University of Connecticut. The letters begin in October 1958 and continue until the date of Malcolm X's assassination in February 1965. The letters, without denying attribution of influence to Olson, offer no support for it.

Patricia Liggins Hill in " 'The Violent Space': The Function of the New Black Aesthetic in Etheridge Knight's Prison Poetry" (*BALF* 14:115–21) studies the pervasive references to separate spaces and emptiness, seeking to relate the imagery to Knight's concern with ways to be free though incarcerated, a need he believes to be equally strong in his black audience. Naturally an imprisoned poet is sensitive to the significance of space, but the basic perception leads to a metaphoric means for Knight to express the more complex idea of the merger of the poet's consciousness with collective subconsciousness.

e. **General Criticism of Poetry.** "The Female Voice in Afro-American and Afro-Caribbean Poetry" (*Umoja* 3[1979]:175–84) by Valerie Lee applies a feminist approach to the practice of verse revealing that women authors, who have regularly sensed the gap between social scientific generalizations and poetic perception, are exploiting subjectivity even further by representing an inward turning by personae. Ruthe T. Sheffey in "Rhetorical Structure in Contemporary Afro-American Poetry" (*CLAJ* 24:97–107) combines Kenneth Burke's scheme of rhetorical analysis with ideas about the influence of African survivals, the model of the King James Bible, and Amiri Baraka's incantations. The result is confusion, though the effort to identity devices and label them with traditional rhetorical terms has interest for relating black poetry to universal practice. C. W. E. Bigsby's "The Black Poet as Cultural Sign" (*Second Black Renaissance*, pp. 257–301) builds a survey of poetry from the past 30 years upon the observation that since Wheatley black poetry has had to find means to express an identity concealed beneath public imagery. The Harlem Renaissance did not end the compromise with audience that grew out of concealment, but in the work of James Weldon Johnson and Langston Hughes it did lay claim to the popular language that flowered in the 1960s. "Black Poetry: A Necessary Ingredient for Survival and Liberation" by Nancy L. Arnez (*JBS* 11,i:3–22) discusses poetry to the extent of proposing ways of emphasizing the vitality of black poetic language and the exemplary role of artists in didactic curricula for black schools.

iv. Drama

a. **Hansberry, Baraka, Bullins.** Steven R. Carter expands his previous discussion of Hansberry's politically informed aesthetics (*ALS 1979*) in "Commitment and Complexity: Lorraine Hansberry's Life in Action" (*MELUS* 7,iii:39–53). This article offers a chronology, quotations from unpublished materials in the collection of Robert Nemiroff, and a discussion of the playwright in relation to social movements.

Lloyd W. Brown's acute study of *Amiri Baraka* (TUSAS 383) could be discussed in several sections of this report, for it shows that Baraka's choice of different genres is an intrinsic function of thematic content. For the plays Brown gives excellent readings of the complex symbolism together with appreciative judgments. He considers only the collected works and published plays, devoting separate chapters to types but tracing in each early cultural rebellion in Greenwich Village, black nationalism, and the recent Marxian socialism. In Brown's view these shifts mirror broad social changes, while beneath them Baraka's antipathy to mainstream socioeconomic values gives consistency to his career. In fact the consistency of attitude is more important for Brown than intellectual constructions, for he finds the theory thin and whenever it moves to pulpit-style declamation, rhetorically ineffective. The hard-headed evaluation of the essays is accompanied by sensitive analysis of the allusive texture of the fiction and the brilliant blend of speech rhythms and evocative imagery in the verse. A contrast to Brown's view of Baraka's political writing can be found in Eric Mottram's "Towards the Alternative: The Prose of LeRoi Jones" (*Black Fiction*, pp. 97–135). Mottram also surveys the evolution of Baraka but gives greater credence and sympathy to the substance of the change, a position that allows him to give a useful exposition of the agitprop dramatic writing. "Les avatars d'Amiri Baraka, citoyen-dramaturge: un montage documentaire" by Michel Fabre (*RFEA* 5,x:285–301) assembles materials demonstrating how deeply significant to his artistic role Baraka sees his Marxist-Leninist politics. "LeRoi Jones' *Dutchman*: Myth and Allegory" by George A. Levesque (*Obsidian* 5,iii[1979]:33–40) adds some detail about metaphoric foreshadowing and implied action to the standard interpretation.

W. D. E. Andrews in "Theatre of Black Reality: The Blues Drama of Ed Bullins" (*SWR* 65:178–90) attributes unique qualities to Bullins' examination of black life patterns. There is, he says, no tradition available because other writers are too ready to see reality in terms of the prevailing cultural philosophy. The survey of several plays then describes Bullins' innovation as a variety of naturalism dialectically contending with vital lyricism.

b. **Childress, Kennedy, Walker, Elder.** "An Unfashionable Tragedy of American Racism: Alice Childress's *Wedding Band*" (*MELUS* 7,iv:57–68) by Rosemary Curb discusses the unflinching realism inherent in a play about the doubled frustration of a character who is a black woman in love with a white man. Curb shows herself equally sensitive when discussing very different sorts of drama in "Fragmented Selves in Adrienne Kennedy's *Funnyhouse of a Negro* and *The Owl Answers*" (*TJ* 32:180–95). Here she lays out the archetypal female obsessions in minds fragmented by the demands of diverse social roles, enumerating the sources of expressionistic conflict in *Funnyhouse* and the ways in which production techniques combine with symbolic imagery in *Owl*. Both of these solid essays also locate the plays within the currents of dramatic history.

Chester J. Fontenot develops his conception of a conflict between linear and mythic conceptions of history (*ALS 1979*) in "Mythic Patterns in *River Niger* and *Ceremonies in Dark Old Men*" (*MELUS* 7,i:41–49). Joseph Walker's play shows the mythic consciousness embattled, Lonne Elder's presents a manifestation of linear history in the memory of the deceased mother overshadowing the lives of her surviving family.

c. **General Criticism of Drama.** C. W. E. Bigsby's treatment of black theatre in his *The Second Black Renaissance*, "Black Drama: The Public Voice" (pp. 207–56) follows his general theme—explor-

ing the permutations of liberalism and the internal contradictions
that arise from a ready acceptance of popular values that are at odds
with the goals of reform or reconstruction. *Raisin in the Sun,* thus,
allows the materialism it intends to reject to dominate the lives of
the characters, and productions of the Negro Ensemble Company
are in danger of appealing exclusively to middle-class intellectuals.
Bigsby even has reservations about the vigor of revolt in *Dutchman,*
which he characterizes as one of the most impressive works in recent
American theatre, and views Ed Bullins' effort to escape compromise
as producing another sort of contradiction of purpose in its reductive
view of human nature.

Kimberly W. Benston's "The Aesthetics of Modern Black Drama:
From *Mimesis* to *Methexis*" (*Theater of Black Americans,* ed. Errol
Hill, Prentice-Hall, vol. 1, pp. 61–78) takes a close view of theoretical writings and recent productions. He finds that since 1964,
the date of Baraka's "The Revolutionary Theater," the conscious effort to reconstruct the theatre has produced a radical shift from the
representational drama in which playwrights battled Western conventions to a participatory theatre that embraces the audience in
ritualistic affirmation. Benston's persuasive findings implicitly counter
Bigsby's argument, largely because Benston makes a more specialized
study, attending especially to the work of Ron Milner, Paul Carter
Harrison, and Carlton Molette II's theatrical work. In "Le nouveau
théâtre noir et la problématique d'une culture populaire afro-
américaine dans le ghetto" (RFEA 5,ix:25–34) Geneviève Fabre explains the evident change in black theatre against the background
of general debate on the nature of Afro-American culture. Artists
who wish to promote it as a complex entity distinct from lower-class
behavior use the theatre as a place for discussion and analysis.

Owen Dodson continues his commentary on theatre in "Who Has
Seen the Wind?: Part III" (*BALF* 14:54–59). This installment of an
examination begun in 1977 and continued last year treats the writing
of Ted Shine, Ossie Davis, and Douglas Turner Ward—"Three Mus-
keteers of Deadly Mirth." Rhett S. Jones in "Community and Commentators: Black Theater and Its Critics" (*BALF* 14:69–76) calls
for criticism that can relate community theatre to the working class,
reporting that many people in black theatre doubt that whites can
write satisfactorily about their projects, though he personally believes

that the discipline of a participant-observer can be learned. Margaret B. Wilkerson's "Critics, Standards and Black Theater" (*Theater of Black Americans*, vol. 2, pp. 120–28) supports Jones's informants by specifying the failure of white critics to understand that theatrical events for blacks have the same participatory value to an audience as the church.

William Cook's "Mom, Dad and God: Values in Black Theater" (*Theater of Black Americans*, vol. 2, pp. 168–84) valorizes the playwright's provision of knowledge about life by undertaking an examination of the ways parents clarify values for their families in works by Hansberry, Baldwin, Bullins, and Joseph Walker. That Cook's sanguine view of the family in drama cannot be generalized any further becomes clear in Rosemary Curb's " 'Goin' Through Changes': Mother-Daughter Confrontations in Three Recent Plays by Young Black Women" (*KFR* 25[1979]:96–102). The influence of feminism in works by J. E. Franklin, Martie Charles, and Elaine Jackson results in plays demanding, from the daughters' viewpoint, a break from maternal direction.

v. Slave Narratives and Autobiography

The outstanding work of 1980 on the outstanding slave narrator is Dickson J. Preston's *Young Frederick Douglass: The Maryland Years* (Johns Hopkins). With the aid of genealogy that establishes February 1818 as the birthdate of Frederick, Preston writes an account of Douglass' black ancestors, the closely knit Baileys who are traceable through five generations on his maternal side. These records and other Talbot County historical documents show that for a slave Douglass had a personally fortunate life. Preston's research, however, does not debunk the portrayal in the *Narrative* of 1845. Rather it establishes a private life for Douglass at least partially distinct from the public persona he created. The point gains support from Preston's indication that in his second and third autobiographies Douglass made an effort to reconcile public and private self-images by amending the record of his childhood. The book is completed by appendices giving a full chronology and the genealogy. *Slave and Citizen: The Life of Frederick Douglass* (Little, Brown) by Nathan Irvin Huggins concentrates exclusively on the public life to retell in popular narrative form the story of a man devoted to the belief that America's special mission required the extirpation of slavery and demanded of its leaders a self-reliance manifest in Douglass' case by refusal to compromise his expansive ideals of freedom from all varieties of bondage.

Raymond Hedin's "Paternal at Last: Booker T. Washington and the Slave Narrative Tradition" (*Callaloo* 2[1979]:95–102) explains that the exslave's desire to act as "father to as many of his people as possible" was Washington's impulse as it was many other narrators'. In Washington's completion of the desire in practical works he came to see Tuskeegee as an extended family and his parental job one of guiding blacks to adulthood. In effect, however, he became more master than father and provoked a resistance that made impossible any successor to his dominant position. To interpret the texts that became keystones in Washington's paternal role Roger J. Bresnahan writes "The Implied Readers of Booker T. Washington's Autobiographies" (*BALF* 14:15–20). Publishing history and internal evidence of differing emphases indicates that *The Story of My Life and Work* (1900) was intended for a rural audience of southern blacks, while *Up From Slavery* (1901) was written for northern whites. Bresnahan applies reader-centered aesthetics to reveal how each work is prestructured so that audiences will discover that their identities require them to support Tuskegee.

Regina Blackburn studies 12 autobiographies for her survey, "In Search of the Black Female Self: African American Women's Autobiographies and Ethnicity" in *Women's Autobiography*, pp. 133–48. The recurrent themes of the works are associated with assigning value to the black self, a task which results in regular use of a scene where the author discovers the significance of her race and the necessity of dealing with self-hatred. The overall purpose of the sampled works is to integrate private and public lives. C. W. E. Bigsby studies a contrasting group of works in "The Public Self: The Black Autobiography" (*Second Black Renaissance*, pp. 182–206), the subgenre of prison-life writing. In these books published between 1964 and 1974 the personal plight is quickly subsumed in the general issues of the black condition as the writers project the paradigm of a new militant identity. The form of the works resembles inspirational Puritan writings with conversion as a central event and the exuberance of rectitude the dominant tone.

vi. Literary History, Criticism

Except for *Negro Historians in the United States* (1958) and *Black Historians: A Critique* (1971), both by Earl E. Thorpe, black historiography has received little scholary attention. Suggestions for analysis appear, however, in two articles from 1980. John David Smith's "DuBois and Phillips—Symbolic Antagonists of the Progressive Era" (*CentR* 24:88–102) works out a contrast between Ulrich B. Phillips and W. E. B. DuBois whose writings prefigure later historical writing. For Smith's purpose the essential difference between the two lies in Phillips' rejection of writings by blacks as dependable sources for his study of a lost civilization and DuBois' neoabolitionist emphasis on the accomplishments of blacks despite the adversity signified by disregard of their writing. August Meier in "Benjamin Quarles and the Historiography of Black America" (*Civil War History* 26:101–16) writes of Quarles's faith in the moral dynamic of history and in the process suggests a contrast with historians using a class analysis and commentators who view America as hopelessly racist. Both Smith and Meier, thus, posit categories that might be refined for further application.

As for the historical study of Afro-American literature itself, a looming problem remains in period definition, and several works are efforts to refine the definition for the Harlem Renaissance. In "The Harlem Renaissance: One Facet of an Unturned Kaleidoscope" (*Toward a New American Literary History*, pp. 195–210) Darwin T. Turner takes pains to explain that the image of jazzed abandon is a misdirection, even though black writers and their friends are largely responsible for its persistence. Following the early models of stage productions like *Shuffle Along* (1921), poetry such as *Weary Blues* (1926), and numerous works of fiction, nightclub scenes came to seem representative of the period. Times were bad for blacks in the jazz age, though, and an undercurrent of melancholy can be found in writing by Wallace Thurman, Countée Cullen, and others. Moreover, it is also true that the emphasis on black celebration in the period was modified both by universal themes and by serious protest. In the light of the prevalent distortions Turner asks whether it makes sense to continue to speak of a renaissance. His answer is decidedly yes, because in the space of a decade more novels were published than in all the years since *Clotel*, the black community theatre emerged, and the foundations laid for the international négritude movement. Charles W. Scruggs also aims to be historically corrective in "Alain Locke and Walter White: Their Struggle for Control of the Harlem Renaissance" (*BALF* 14:91–99). A simple view of the period sees blacks united in a single artistic purpose in which they were dependent upon white patronage. Drawing upon the files of the Locke Collection in the Moorland-Spingarn Research Center at Howard University and the NAACP files at the Library of Congress, Scruggs uncovers incidents of conflict between the leading contenders for actual direction of black publishing. Locke had preconceived ideas of what the literature should be; White wanted to wield influence regardless of the shape of literature. The informative study concludes with the observation that the conflict represents the failure of the renaissance itself, for lofty aesthetic discussion was never successfully integrated with a pragmatic approach to necessities of publication. That Locke's aesthetics, despite the manner of his expression, were not idealist is the point for Ernest Douglas Mason in "Alain Locke's Social Realism" (*Obsidian* 5,iii[1979]: 22–32).

Starting with an examination of a theatre that flourished during the renaissance there are four studies to note as contributions to black theatrical history. Sister M. Francesca Thompson writes in "The Lafayette Players, 1917–1932" (*Theater of Black Americans*, vol. 2, pp. 13–32) about the company that originated through the efforts of the actress Anita Bush, who organized a production of Billie Burke's *The Girl at the Fort* to open at the New Lincoln Theatre on 15 November 1915. By the end of 1917 there were two touring companies. By performing more than 250 plays in 17 years the Lafayette Stock Company laid the foundation of black legitimate theatre. E. Quita Craig takes up the story with *Black Drama of the Federal Theatre Era: Beyond the Formal Horizons* (Mass.). Making use of the recovered archives of the Federal Theatre Project now on permanent loan to George Mason University, Craig examines scripts by Hughes Allison, Theodore Brown, Hall Johnson, and Theodore Ward. She deals with the issue of white-audience expectations in a time of relative ignorance of black culture by asserting that the writers used the dual communication system of inverted meanings. Craig treats production techniques, discusses the search for cultural heritage evident in the texts, and points up the need to recover plays that deserve to be better known. In short, she acquaints us with a forgotten tradition. Ethel Pitts Walker's "The American Negro Theatre" (*Theater of Black Americans*, vol. 2, pp. 49–62) outlines the history of the company founded in 1940 by Abram Hill and Frederick O'Neal. By 1949 A.N.T. had produced 12 original scripts and a total of 19 plays on black life by both black and white authors. After the success of *Anna Lucasta* on Broadway the company abandoned its experimental purpose. Ellen Foreman treats what promises to be the longest-lived company in "The Negro Ensemble Company: A Transcendent Vision" (*Theater of Black Americans*, vol. 2, pp. 72–84). After a chronological outline of the effort to fulfill Douglas Turner Ward's vision of a company that incorporates the best drama of the world into its production schedule, Foreman evaluates the achievement as nothing less than creation of *the* national black theatre company.

There is also to be noted an important contribution to the history of poets' organization in Tom Dent's "Umbra Days" (*BALF* 14:105–08). Dent recollects how he came together with other poets on the Lower East Side of New York City during the 1960s to discuss works-in-progress and give public readings. Participants in what came to be known as the Umbra Workshop included Calvin Herton, David Henderson, Lorenzo Thomas, Archie Shepp, and others, all of them finding common ground in a resolution to work independently of the cynical white literary world. Historically, Dent says, the group represented a stage between protest writing and the literature of separatism. The essay is followed by five pages of contemporary photographs.

Easily the most ambitious criticism of 1980, and the most suggestive theoretical work is Houston A. Baker, Jr.'s *The Journey Back: Issues in Black Literature and Criticism* (Chicago). Baker's announced goal is to devise a method to explain how black narrative texts preserve and communicate culturally unique meanings. Among the early writers he considers are Phillis Wheatley and Gustavus Vassa, whose texts reveal contending systems of meaning, one conventionally white, the other black. Baker shows little enthusiasm for slave narratives because he finds in them a forlorn persona forced to adopt a language invested with alien cultural values, while the indigenous slave culture found its effective expression in oral literature. By the middle of the 20th century, however, the Afro-

American project is entirely literary. Writers of the 1950s sought their "terms of order" with democratically inspired writings—liberalism. In Baker's scheme historical periods gain definition from linguistic practice. For that reason the renaissance gets no special attention, but the creativity of the 1960s and 1970s marks the arrival of an autonomous literature, for in that decade the language is freed from white conceptual restrictions. Baker is critical of the theory of the '60s, but nevertheless finds that it fostered an availability of the collective culture to validate and influence writers. Certainly some of Baker's judgments will be questioned, but his determination to seek the codes that underlie Afro-American literary usage of the common American language announces an approach that generates the sort of engaging questions criticism needs.

In a related project Baker serves as guest editor for a special issue of *Black American Literature Forum* on literary theory. The issue includes his own "A Note on Style and the Anthropology of Art" (14: 30–31), which asserts that art is one system in a network of interrelated cultural systems. Successful criticism, he maintains, requires knowledge of the black style in the components. Jerry W. Ward's "The Black Critic as Reader" (14:21–23) exemplifies the point by distinguishing and then rejoining the reading one does when governed by consciousness of the meaning a text had at a given historical time and the reading of a text in order to study linguistic choices. The Black Aesthetic movement with its insistence on yoking social and literary characteristics of texts also fostered this critical reading. A very different sort of contribution to the theory issue is Amiri Baraka's "Afro-American Literature and the Class Struggle" (14:5–14). This is written on the model of Granville Hicks's *The Great Tradition*, except that Baraka's engagement in the task of announcing a revolutionary trend is so highly personalized that he must constantly digress into vituperation against those who do not fit the select canon.

C. W. E. Bigsby's *The Second Black Renaissance* opens with an introductory essay (pp. 9–53) that locates the source of the historical phenomenon he studies in Richard Wright, who embodied the conflicting passions that come to define the 30-year debate between the demands of the collective and the self. Fluctuations between self-appraisal and assertion of values, between anomie and the sense of shared experience mark the struggle to confront history and then transcend it. "Blueprint for Negro Writing" and *Native Son* are the key texts, the first because it shows awareness of the demands to absorb history and to form the future, the second because it snaps the bonds of naturalism to lay open the core of collective experience personally felt. Besides the introduction to his volume Bigsby's chief exhibit in general literary history is "The Black and White Lazarus: The Revival of the Liberal Tradition" (pp. 139–163), where he explains that, like Jewish writers, blacks have a compelling interest in asserting the responsibility of the individual in society; consequently, black writing takes as given the existence of an attainable social identity and the reality of moral obligations. This is a survival of the liberal tradition that once pervaded all American writing.

For reasons that may indeed have a great deal to do with a liberal faith black writers are preoccupied with history. Barbara Foley in "History, Fiction, and the Ground Between: The Uses of the Documentary Mode in Black Literature" (*PMLA* 95:389–403) schematizes the treatments of history according to whether they render imagined characters and events that have potential analogues in recorded history, or base a fictional text upon a genre of factual writing. As she says, she is providing an anatomy of the uses of the documentary mode. Moreover, she tests its validity in reference to mimetic theory by applying the principles of her description to William Styron's *Confessions of Nat Turner* and Alex Haley's *Roots*. Again this is work that ought to stimulate study. It is no criticism but rather a compliment to say that despite its breadth and systematic approach it raises important questions.

It is appropriate that this report of the critical and scholarly activity in Afro-American literature for 1980 close with reference to an essay that reconsiders an issue that has been discussed since Black Studies became established in the universities. What does it require to be an able critic of Afro-American writing? Must the critic be black? Nathaniel Mackey in "Great White Hope: Jean Wagner Revisited" (*CLAJ* 23:245–65) gives an answer beyond dispute. Wagner's 1962 study, translated into English by Kenneth Douglas as *Black Poets of the United States* (1973) shows a clear preference for religious verse. It is Mackey's contention that this is manifestly the result of biases that Wagner seems unaware he possesses. Jahnheinz Jahn in *Neo-African Literature* (1968) observed previously that Wagner's aesthetic judgments follow his religious attitudes, but

Mackey's fuller discussion of the point becomes conclusive. A literary historian, he says, must learn to move knowledgeably within the network of black cultural systems. In some cases that will mean moving imaginatively out of white culture into black. I might add that in all cases it means working with the sensitivity to the purposes and motives of texts displayed in the number of fine essays and books reviewed here. Mackey presents the issue correctly. It is a matter of providing the literature the good criticism it deserves.

State University of New York at Albany

20. Themes, Topics, Criticism

Jonathan Morse

By the time I finished writing this chapter for last year's *ALS*, I was concerned about what looked like a widening gap between the plodding "Themes and Topics" section and the dashingly sophisticated "Criticism." As it turned out, I need not have worried. Criticism of the formalist sort has been on hold this year, but themes and topics have generated much good work.

i. Themes and Topics

a. **American Studies.** Writing from Germany to William Wetmore Story in Italy, James Russell Lowell said, "I agree with you as to the wants one feels at home. When I look back and think how much in me might have earlier and kindlier developed if I had been reared here, I feel bitter. But on the other hand, I prize my country-breeding, the recollections of my first eight years, my Hosey Biglow experiences as something real, and I mean to make a poem out of them some day that shall be really American." Barbara Novak quotes these words on p. 222 of *Nature and Culture: American Landscape and Painting, 1825–1875* (Oxford), a splendid (and splendidly illustrated) book whose purpose is to define in specific aesthetic terms just what a "really American" art is. Such a definition is an act of historiography as much as of criticism, and Novak has gained historiographic control over her material by considering "the conversion of landscape into art, the evolution of an American culture and its relation to Western art and to culture at large" (p. viii) in terms which have been expanded to the limits of their frames of reference. Novak's study of plant forms in American art, for instance, takes in

This chapter was completed with the aid of a University of Hawaii faculty development award.–*J.M.*

Goethe, Ruskin, Thoreau, and the 19th century's changing ideas of
the place of God in nature—and plant forms are only one of the many
things Novak thinks about. Because I am not an art critic I will not
attempt a detailed analysis of *Nature and Culture*, but I do suggest
that Novak's definitions of American culture may be the most powerful since Henry Nash Smith gave us *Virgin Land* 30 years ago.

Aside from *Nature and Culture*, this has been a good year for
books dealing indirectly with American literature from the historical
and social-scientific point of view. The interdisciplinary perspective
is useful to Peter Conrad when he analyzes four English writers'
descriptions of Niagara Falls and observes that "These versions of
Niagara, ranging from [Anthony] Trollope's prosy estimation of
volume and denomination of safe vantage-points to Brooke's lyrical
impressionism, from Dickens's rhetorical pomp to Wells's ruthless
scientific exploitation of an improvident nature, testify to America's
capacity for self-transformation. Objects in America aren't determined by history or enmeshed by association like those in Europe.
Each observer sees them as if for the first time" (p. 28). Hence (p.
5) "in discovering America you are discovering yourself." And in
Imagining America (Oxford) Conrad uses this idea of self-discovery
to tell the stories of 12 Englishmen who lived and wrote in the United
States, from Frances Trollope to Christopher Isherwood. His technique is an engaging combination of biography, literary criticism,
and pop sociology, thus: "Shambling about in carpet slippers with
uncombed hair and clothes spotted by food stains, peevishly de-
nouncing friends who were a minute late for an appointment, Auden
was a symbolic New Yorker. For, while scrambling people into proximity, that city also separates them, incarcerating each inside his
own fantasies. . . . Emble in *The Age of Anxiety* wonders how you
retrieve some individuality from the urban crowd in which you are
jostled. The answer is to become mildly mad. . . ." (p. 219). Intermittently elaborated for several pages, this observation demonstrates
Conrad's genuine wit, weakness for facile generalization, and tendency to ride ideas into the ground. Another entertaining book on a
related subject, Paul Fussell's *Abroad: British Literary Traveling
Between the Wars* (Oxford), offers an opportunity to contrast American and English scholarly styles. Fussell, writing from Rutgers, is
detailed, overextended (he mentions some American books, such as

Two Years Before the Mast, The 42nd Parallel, and *Appointment in Samarra,* which he obviously hasn't read), a little overawed by his subject (in 1980 he still laughs respectfully at some stale and racist British humor about quaint natives), and at his best with close readings of such established authors as D. H. Lawrence and Evelyn Waugh. Writing from Oxford, Conrad wears his learning without footnotes and is at his best when he is most breezily eclectic.

With its title, its large format, and its many illustrations, Wolfgang Schivelbusch's *The Railway Journey: Trains and Travel in the 19th Century,* trans. Anselm Hollo (Urizen Books, 1979), looks like a coffee-table book. It is actually a Frankfurt-style sociohistory of the ways in which a technological revolution contributed to and grew out of a changing view of the world. Schivelbusch demonstrates, for example, that the view from a train window forced writers to resee the world they described: Goethe, from his coach, took notes on the geology of the region and watched a man climb a tree, but Marcel Proust, in his speeding train, has been reduced to a sensitivity connecting a pair of termini: "'the difference between departure and arrival not as imperceptible but as intense as possible, so that we are conscious of it in its totality, intact, as it existed in our mind when imagination bore us from the place in which we were living right to the very heart of a place we longed to see'" (p. 46). This literary phenomenology is ingenious, but I found Schivelbusch's more directly Marxist analysis more useful for *ALS's* purposes. Why, for instance, do American railroads, unlike European ones, tend to run around natural obstacles rather than over them or through them? Because (pp. 98–100) in the United States 100 years ago land was cheap and labor was expensive. There is a direct connection between physical form and economic function, and this is to say that the shape of a railroad line is a cultural statement. That statement helped keep me alert to all the possibilities inherent in Novak's chapter 8 ("Man's Traces: Axe, Train, Figure"). It also showed me a way to think in terms of American cultural history about some texts that appear to be purely personal, such as the railroad passages in *Walden,* Dickinson's "I like to see it lap the miles," and the second half of *Life on the Mississippi.*

To return to books having a more direct connection with American literature: in *Facing West: The Metaphysics of Indian-Hating and Empire Building* (Minn.) Richard Drinnon touches briefly on the writings of a number of American authors who have thought about our country's racial imperialism, from Thomas Morton to William J. Lederer and Eugene Burdick, who wrote *The Ugly American.* But Drinnon's primary concern is to express his solidarity with the people who are blessed with (in the words of the book's dedication) "lovely dark-brown skin," and as a piece of literary criticism *Facing West* is too simplistic to have much value. On the other hand, Robert Penn Warren offers us scanty and selective factual data in *Jefferson Davis Gets His Citizenship Back* (Kentucky), but his tragic intuitions lead at least to a satisfying meditation on the meaning of American history. Davis, in Warren's view, is an exemplary figure: a representative, like Lincoln, of a moral integrity which is now gone with the wind. There is a sad irony in his being posthumously forced to bear citizenship in a country such as the United States would not have become if only the South had won the Civil War. Warren has always taken a tragically ironic view of humankind, of course, but it is still surprising to note how little his thinking has been changed by the half century that lies between this book and the Confederate nostalgia of *I'll Take My Stand.*

Lewis O. Saum studies *The Popular Mood of Pre-Civil War America* (Greenwood) by examining the letters and diaries of unknown people and comparing what he finds there with the generalizations of conventional great-man historiography. In some cases Saum's evidence fits the standard model; for instance, many of Emily Dickinson's early letters are quite similar, in subject and in choice of clichés, to this barely literate request for deathbed information: "Mother i should have liked to have node whither he was resined to gow Joseph could not tell me exackly whither or not you must tell A to rite to me and let me now all about that gives me eas if he was perfectly resined to gow mother in that triing ower if he was prepared to gow what sweet thoughts to himself and all of his children" (p. 99). But in other cases poular ideas differed from those of the literary class, and here Saum offers a corrective to conventional histories based on high literary evidence. After quoting Perry Miller (pp. 189–90) on the wide popularity of "pseudo-Byronic invocations to Nature" (invocations which play a part in Novak's *Nature and Culture*) Saum counters with the diary of a pioneer who records how the members of his party burst into cheers when they heard a rooster crowing: "a most certain indication that we had passed from a wilderness into some sort of civilization."

Saum's material is organized under two large headings. "Things Spiritual" covers "Providence," "Religion," "Conversion, Revival, and Millennium," and "Death"; "Things Temporal" covers "Self and Society," "Politics and the Nation," "Nature and Art," and "The West." Each chapter is followed by a short conclusion, and an appendix presents Saum's methodological rationale.

Charles C. Alexander's *Here the Country Lies: Nationalism and the Arts in Twentieth-Century America* (Indiana) is a breezily written cultural history which can be recommended to graduate students working up their comprehensive examinations. Alexander is especially good on the critics and commentators. Unfortunately, his mass of detail is held together by a thesis about the development of romantic nationalism and avant-garde modernism out of a revolt against the genteel tradition. This thesis is unexceptionable but unexciting in itself, and in application it tends to limit the book. Let me give two examples.

Alexander completely disregards the Southern Agrarians. These men were genuine nationalists whose ideas extended north of the Mason-Dixon Line, but since their feelings about the genteel tradition mattered less than their feelings about ceremonious manners and dark satanic mills they couldn't be fitted into this book. Alexander's aim is "less for comprehensiveness than for thematic development" (p. xiii), but this major group of thinkers should not have been pushed out of the way by H. L. Mencken and a thesis.

And insofar as Alexander is writing a history of aesthetics, his emphasis on thematic development introduces some distortions. Alexander devotes many pages to the dreary American Scene painters of the 1930s because they had an explicit ideological program; he neglects the great and equally *engagé* photoessayists of the same period because they tended to let their pictures speak for themselves. Margaret Bourke-White shares one line with her husband Erskine Caldwell, who wrote captions for her pictures of chain gangs; Walker Evans, Arthur Rothstein, and Dorothea Lange aren't mentioned at all. On the other hand, John Steuart Curry, a Kansas painter of the O Pioneers school (wheatfields, bulging muscles, facial expressions suitable to a Russian movie about tractors), is mentioned 11 times. This is not to say that Alexander is uncritical; his word for Curry is "mediocre" (p. 181). But to the extent that he undervalues works of art because they lack extraartistic reference he is committing a critical fallacy.

But as a history, not a work of criticism, *Here the Country Lies* is a useful collection of names, dates, and sound opinion, and my only objections here are to a few small matters of detail. *The Little Review* was not an "ephemeral" magazine, for instance (p. 31), and Alexander might profitably have discussed the series of editorials about American culture that Ezra Pound published there. And for $32.50 the Indiana University Press gives you a book with fine print, a flimsy binding, and no illustrations.

Dee Garrison's *Apostles of Culture: The Public Librarian and American Society, 1876–1920* (Free Press, 1979) is an attractive feminist history of the purveyors of America's reading. As a class, American librarians in the third quarter of the 19th century tended to be scholarly men who labored to convert the public's appetite for novels into a taste for nobler things. By the turn of the century American librarians were women, hostess-technicians who endeavored to give the middlebrow public what it wanted. This change—accomplished almost single-handed by the amazing Melvil Dewey, a monomaniacal organizer who surrounded himself with adoring female disciples—has obviously had a major effect on the ways literature is read in the United States, and Garrison has a sharp eye for its good and bad implications.

Finally, a piece of curiosa. *Aaron Burr and the American Literary Imagination* by Charles J. Nolan, Jr. (Greenwood) is a critical survey of the imaginative literature in which Burr has played a part, from Hugh Henry Brackenridge's propaganda play, *The Death of General Montgomery at the Siege of Quebec* (1777), to Gore Vidal's 1973 best-seller. Burr's part turns out to be a very large one: 33 plays and 49 works of fiction, including a 1948 novel "which, mercifully, remains unpublished" (p. 81), plus poems and sermons. This impressive textual bulk allows Nolan to speculate that Burr, as a character in literature, possesses symbolic value: "in his various roles as an American Catiline, Lovelace, and Warwick, he comes to represent aspects of American life that are intensely distressing. . . ." (p. 181).

b. **Regional Studies.**   In *The Brazen Face of History: Studies in the Literary Consciousness of America* (LSU) Lewis P. Simpson writes about figures as diverse as Malcolm Cowley and Benjamin Franklin. But of course the literature of the South is what predominates in this collection, quantitatively and qualitatively. I can especially recommend "Slavery and Modernism" (originally published 1975), which brings a strong reading of literary history to bear on the thesis that "From the complex frustration and defeat of the Old South's attempt to become a unique slave society, the modern southern writer inherited, as did no other American writer of his age, a compelling drama of man and community" (p. 81). In *The Dream of Arcady: Place and Time in Southern Literature* (LSU) Lucinda Hardwick MacKethan undertakes a detailed study of a similar idea. Reading the imagery of escape and nostalgia in nine southern writers whose works cover the period from Reconstruction to the modern era, Mac-Kethan discovers "undercurrents of irony and limitation. . . . Sooner or later in all of them the idyllic vision is subjected to the inescapable moment of awakening, to the inevitable pressure of change. And this is the atmosphere that pertains when an approach that we can identify as being pastoral in its mood and implications is brought to bear by the writers in this study" (pp. 6–7).

J. V. Ridgely's *Nineteenth-Century Southern Literature* (Kentucky) is a short, nontechnical critical history characterized by a chronological and generic (rather than major-figure) organization, a sound critical sense, and a bright prose style. Recommended.

The West sends us three critical studies this year. *The Western: A Collection of Critical Essays*, ed. James K. Folsom (1979), is an addition to Prentice-Hall's "Twentieth Century Views" series and follows its well-known format. The more expensive *Critical Essays on the Western American Novel*, ed. William T. Pilkington (Hall), contains 24 essays to *The Western*'s ten and concentrates in more detail on individual authors. John R. Milton's *The Novel of the American West* (Nebraska) begins by dissociating what Milton calls "the Western" from the commercial "small *w* western," which (p. xv) "deals in stereotyped characters and stock patterns of action . . . exploits the myths of the frontier . . . depends upon a two-sided morality of good and evil, neglecting the many complexities of the human condition . . . [and] is characterized by sameness through hundreds of books. . . ." Milton's attempt to produce a positive definition of the Western, however (chapters 2 and 3, especially pp. 57–60 and 115–16), is an odd mixture of description and stipulation which doesn't get much beyond saying that the Western, unlike the western or the Eastern, is dominated by landscape, derives its themes and plots from medieval origins (romance, morality play), and (p. 115) "[i]n treatment . . . is extensive, constantly engaged in an opening out, from character to action to landscape to a concern with racial consciousness (rather than individual) which is Jungian. . . ." Formally speaking, the problem with this definition is that it confounds two incompatible critical vocabularies. The western's stereotype is detected with the New Critical instrument; the Western's archetype is detected with the Jungian. Perhaps we are looking at different phenomena, perhaps not. Milton does keep scrambling things up this way; in one John Wayne paragraph on p. 109 he goes from the West's dry weather to feelings of freedom to "people with a sense of adventure, perhaps with a touch of masculinity." But most of his book is devoted to practical criticism of such Western writers as Vardis Fisher and Walter Van Tilburg Clark.

The Autobiography of a Yaqui Poet by Refugio Savala, ed. with extensive background material by Kathleen M. Sands (Arizona), is the story of an Indian who lived in the majority culture of the southwestern United States as a manual laborer. His outward life was simply that of a poor man who worked hard, had a drinking problem, and spent a few nights in jail. But Savala moved through this outward life as a poet, and he made coherent sense of his world by shaping it around words. The words are Spanish, English, and Yaqui; the cultural grammar governing them is that of a refugee tribe. Catholic since the early 17th century but having few formal contacts with the Church, officially Mexican but living in unacknowledged asylum from the genocidal Díaz regime, the Arizona Yaquis in the early 20th century should, by all reasonable expectations, have been a demoralized, deracinated people, with nothing before them but extinction. Yet the rhythms of their Christian and preChristian culture endured, and as they endured in Savala they enabled him to make his life a celebration.

c. **Biography.**   Good books are scarce these days, and they are going to get scarcer in the future. That is the depressing message of Thomas Whiteside's "The Blockbuster Complex," a three-part *New Yorker* article (29 Sept., 6 Oct., 13 Oct. 1980), which places the blame for the disappearance of quality on four recent changes in the publishing business: (1) the takeover of independent publishers by conglomerates; (2) the related rise to prominence of a new breed of literary agents, who market a manuscript as part of an entertainment package which also includes T-shirt sales and talk-show appearances; (3) the domination of the retail market by chain bookstores, whose computers keep the books on the shelves for the shortest possible time; and (4) the Supreme Court's 1979 *Thor Power Tool Co.* tax decision, which had the effect of encouraging publishers to liquidate their backlists. These changes are being felt in the campus bookstore as well as in B. Dalton's. As the coordinator of a multisection sophomore survey of American literature, I now have to spend several hours every semester with a copy of *Books in Print*, desperately searching for substitutes for the good books that have disappeared. Perhaps it is circumstances like these that have led to the publication this year of an unusually large number of biographical studies of men of letters from the early 20th century. The biographers are remembering a golden age.

Richard Hauer Costa's *Edmund Wilson: Our Neighbor from Talcottville* (Syracuse) is a memoir of the last ten summers of Wilson's life. Wilson appears to have lived out his *Upstate* period on several parallel tracks: some of his friendships were literary, some were historical, and some were purely personal. That of Costa and his wife was interdisciplinary, to some extent; that is, Costa talked with Wilson about H. G. Wells, Mrs. Costa took Wilson shopping, and Wilson and the Costas spent a number of social evenings together. But the friendship never became intimate, and little of scholarly consequence emerges from this account. What we do get, however, is a vivid picture of the great critic as a sick old man who wore women's tennis shoes, enjoyed *The Yellow Submarine*, drank far too much, refused to wear a pacemaker, and wrote his six pages a day right to the end.

Wilson withdrew his allegiance from communism at the time of the Moscow purges and argued thereafter with Malcolm Cowley, whose loyalty to Stalin lasted longer. How much longer, and why, is a question with some literary interest, for the first (1934) edition of *Exile's Return*, Cowley's study of the American expatriate writers of the 1920s, is a radical polemic, and the second (1951) is not. What happened to Cowley? *The Dream of the Golden Mountains: Remembering the 1930s* (Viking) answers this question in a way that will not satisfy the Cold War generation, for Cowley brings the major portion

of his narrative to a close with the events of 1936: Roosevelt is re-
elected, American radicalism is undercut by the New Deal and the
Popular Front, and Cowley, his heart still with the Communists,
makes a symbolic move from New York to Connecticut. A single
concluding chapter sums up the years from 1936 to 1939, but there
Cowley writes not as an individual but as a spokesman for his disillusioned fellow-radicals.

So *The Dream of the Golden Mountains* is not a typical I-saw-the-
light-on-August-23-1939 confession. What it is is a memoir of one
man's doubts, misgivings, hopes, and dreams, movingly narrated and
full of sharp little details that bring back the 1930s in all their bitter
glory. Because Cowley is now one of our most valuable resources for
20th-century literary history, I wish he had done the academic thing
and footnoted *The Dream of the Golden Mountains*. But I wish much
more fervently that the academic books I have to read for this chapter could be written in real English, like Cowley's.

To move to a name less well-known at the present: Joseph Wood
Krutch was a hypochondriac who didn't have many friends, didn't
write many letters, didn't like teaching, didn't like the plays he reviewed, summed up a decade of intellectual disillusion in *The Modern Temper* (1929) but was most at home on the middlebrow range
of his nature essays, and "[p]erhaps, by the most austere standards
of literary history . . . falls short of deserving a place in the very
first rank of American writers" (p. 230). This is the substance of John
D. Margolis' *Joseph Wood Krutch: A Writer's Life* (Tenn.). A book
with more *raison d'être* is Daniel J. Wilson's *Arthur O. Lovejoy and
the Quest for Intelligibility* (N.Car.), an intellectual biography which
concentrates on the development of Lovejoy's rationalism from its
beginnings to its culmination in *The Great Chain of Being*. Since
Lovejoy was 63 years old when he published his masterpiece, his
ideas had an unusually long foreground, and Wilson delineates this
foreground in plodding but intelligent detail. He tells us about the
family tragedy which killed Lovejoy's mother, for instance, and
speculates cautiously about the possibility of a connection between
that tragedy, Lovejoy's bachelor aloofness, and his lifelong search
for a principle capable of imposing order on the irrationalities of life.
But Wilson explicitly disclaims psychobiography (pp. xii–xiv), and
the main emphasis of his book is on the substance of Lovejoy's ideas.

With William H. Pritchard's *Lives of the Modern Poets* (Oxford) the focus of this section shifts from biography to criticism. In his collection of prefaces to nine poets of the modern canon (Hardy, Yeats, Robinson, Frost, Pound, Eliot, Stevens, Hart Crane, and Williams) Pritchard employs biographical data on the commonsense grounds that "these are interesting in themselves and also for the way they confirm our sense of the poet in his poems" (p. 9), but he is aware that this sense of the poet in his poems will vary from lifework to lifework. The biography of the self-dramatizing Yeats, for instance, must have a critical value different from the biography of the self-effacing Stevens. Pritchard's use of the biographical material is therefore intelligently flexible, and always directed toward helping an educated general reader enjoy the poems.

About the poems Pritchard is conservative. He casts a cold eye on Yeats's occult lore, admits that he finds Hugh Kenner's defense of *The Cantos* "often more entertaining and enlivening than what he's defending" (p. 166), respects even the prosiest lines of *Four Quartets*, concludes with regret that *Paterson* is incoherent, and remarks that reading Stevens criticism is "a bit like going to church, but presumably much more exhilarating and free-breathing than going to church with T. S. Eliot" (p. 205). All nine of Pritchard's prefaces are sympathetic, but he concludes the book with this comparative assessment: "Yeats, Frost, Eliot, and Stevens . . . are the modern poets whose work presents the largest challenge to us, whose poetic presences are the most continuous and inescapable. It was doubtless evident from the individual prefaces that my favorites among them are Frost and Eliot" (p. 296).

In *Prodigal Sons: A Study in Authorship and Authority* (Hopkins) David Wyatt reads a corpus of works by James, Yeats, Hemingway, Faulkner, James Agee, Robert Penn Warren, and Robertson Davies with the paradigmatic aid of the parable of the prodigal son. "In each essay I search for a decisive turn in a career, the moment when an author makes his accommodation with authority and ceases wrestling with his role as a son" (p. xv). Wyatt is occasionally too eager to accept help from Dr. Freud (p. 58, on *The Sun Also Rises*: "Bullfighting is the great orgy of a repressed culture: competence killing potency"), but *Prodigal Sons* as a whole is a very interesting book. Wyatt's readings justify his conclusion that "We have temporarily exhausted the criticism of works and structures; it is time to turn to careers" (p. 150).

But of course the study of careers is already thriving, as this section and the next two theoretical books demonstrate. In *The Forms of Autobiography: Episodes in the History of a Literary Genre* (Yale) William C. Spengemann reads nine autobiographies, two of them American, through this paradigm: "St. Augustine set the problem for all subsequent autobiography: How can the self know itself? By surveying in the memory its completed past actions from an unmoving point above or beyond them? By moving inquisitively through its own memories and ideas to some conclusion about them? Or by performing a sequence of symbolic actions through which the ineffable self can be realized? For these three methods of self-knowledge, Augustine devised three autobiographical forms—historical self-recollection, philosophical self-exploration, and poetic self-expression—from which every subsequent autobiographer would select the one most appropriate to his own situation" (p. 32). Spengemann's readings of his American books—*The Autobiography of Benjamin Franklin*, considered as historical autobiography, and *The Scarlet Letter*, considered as poetic autobiography—are discussed elsewhere in this volume. *The Forms of Autobiography* also deserves comment here, however, as a general method for helping us read autobiographies in interesting, new relations to one another. And Spengemann's 75-page bibliographical essay is very useful. *Autobiography: Essays Theoretical and Critical* (Princeton), ed. James Olney, is a large, good, eclectic collection, about half of which is previously unpublished. Four of the essays deal particularly with American literature: James M. Cox's "Recovering Literature's Lost Ground Through Autobiography" (whose subect is Thomas Jefferson), Robert F. Sayre's "Autobiography and the Making of America," Roger Rosenblatt's "Black Autobiography: Life as the Death Weapon," and Paul John Eakin's "Malcolm X and the Limits of Autobiography." Less detailed than Spengemann's bibliography but equally valuable in its own right is Olney's "Autobiography and the Cultural Moment: A Thematic, Historical, and Bibliographical Introduction."

d. **Postscript.** This elegiac part of the chapter is the place to notice two collections: *The Essays of Mark Van Doren (1924–1972)* (Greenwood), ed. William Claire, and *The Last Decade: Essays and Reviews, 1965–75* (Harcourt, 1979) by Lionel Trilling, ed. Diana Trilling. Van Doren was perhaps the last great American example of the critic as gentleman of letters, and Claire's selection shows him gracefully filling this role to its narrow limits. There is, for example, Van Doren's Introduction to *The Private Reader* (1942), an introduction which Stanley Edgar Hyman called "the most complete and eloquent attack on modern criticism with which I am familiar" (Claire, p. xx). In 1948, when Hyman was writing these words in *The Armed Vision*, "modern criticism" of course meant the New Criticism, and it is understandable that a New Critic might be upset by an essay which says, "Criticism now . . . is nervous in the presence of genius. It prefers the poem whose author can be seen sweating at his job of extending or intensifying an image to the point of systematic dullness, to the end of an admirable aridity. Criticism, itself a puritan for work, can praise only the laborious, can respect poetry only when it groans to overreach itself and become discussable" (p. 7). The New Critic might be upset because, as we can all see by now, Van Doren was right about the New Criticism's predilection for pedantry. But the New Critic might also be upset because Van Doren seems to be rejecting out of hand all that we owe to the New Critics, including such pleasures as learning to enjoy the Metaphysical poets. Van Doren's own critical performance, at any rate, is at its best when it is closest to New Critical practice. Reading by intuition, Van Doren is seduced into extravagant overpraise of some wooden lyrics by his friend Thomas Merton, but it took a strong critical intelligence to be able to say in about 1935 (I am guessing at this date from context; Claire's apparatus is minimal), "[Emily Dickinson] was once in love . . . and the present volume is supposed to be remarkable because a section of it is devoted to the circumstance, but it is more remarkable in its own right as poetry; her love is vastly less interesting than what she said about it" (p. 73).

"When I decided to go into academic life," writes Trilling (p. 13), "my friends thought me naive to the point of absurdity, nor were they wholly wrong—my appointment to an instructorship in Columbia College was pretty openly regarded as an experiment. . . ." Trilling is talking about his Jewishness here, but the experiment that brought him to Columbia was not just a matter of new-found tolerance; it was part of an academic revolution.

In 1911 J. E. Spingarn, the man who invented the term "New Criticism," left his Columbia professorship, so disgusted with his colleagues' timidity that he never returned to the academic world. But after World War I, during Trilling's student days, the academic world began to change. One manifestation of that change at Columbia was John Erskine's General Honors course, which "was directed to showing young men how they might escape from the limitations of their middle-class or their lower-middle-class upbringings by putting before them great models of thought, feeling, and imagination, and great issues which suggested the close interrelation of the private and personal life with the public life, with life in society" ("Some Notes for an Autobiographical Lecture," previously unpublished, p. 234). Trilling and his associates were to continue that revolution, just as other young academics were doing all over the country. But by the 1960s the Trilling generation, having escaped from one set of limitations into another, had become the establishment, and the events of that era made some of those men and women their tragic victims.

A sense of siege therefore permeates some of these last essays, such as "Art, Will, and Necessity" (previously unpublished) and "The Uncertain Future of the Humanistic Educational Ideal," a lecture which, in a near-parody of Trilling's own syrupy prose style, begins, "Partly for Socratic reasons, but chiefly because it is my actual belief, I shall take the view that at the present time in American society, there are few factors to be perceived, if any at all, which make it likely that within the next quarter-century there will be articulated in a convincing and effectual way an educational ideal that has a positive and significant connection with the humanistic traditions of the past" (pp. 160–61). This 1974 address goes on to mourn the death of Great Books programs and to explain their demise with some ideas out of *Sincerity and Authenticity*. In 1968 Trilling had celebrated the "hard, irreducible, stubborn core of biological urgency . . . that culture cannot reach" (*Beyond Culture*; Chace, below, p. 138); now, with General Honors destroyed by the rampaging forces of the id anticulture outside Columbia, Trilling is lost. So it is understandable that this volume is at its best in retrospection. I am thinking of—or, as Trilling would say, I have it in mind to think here of—"A Novel of the Thirties," from which my first quotation comes; "James Joyce in His Letters," a wonderful piece of literary criticism; and the powerful "Whittaker Chambers' Journey." *The Last Decade* lacks the unity of *The Liberal Imagination* and the expansiveness of *The Opposing Self*, and at times it is merely querulous. But it is also a strong book, and a worthy book to mark the end of a career.

The exact value of Trilling's career remains problematic, however. As *The New York Times* noted in its obituary, "He made the life of the mind an exciting experience. Yet, as a critic he founded no school and left no group of disciples closely associated with his name." In *Lionel Trilling: Criticism and Politics* (Stanford) William M. Chace makes the case for Trilling in the best way: by showing us Trilling's mind at work on its evolving subtleties, from the early short stories through "Why We Read Jane Austen," the unfinished last essay. With great literary sensitivity, and a stronger sense of history than Trilling possessed, Chace is able to show us how we ought to value Trilling, in his time and ours. *Lionel Trilling* is a first-rate study in historical criticism.

e. **Feminist Studies.** *The Lost Tradition: Mothers and Daughters in Literature* (Ungar), ed. Cathy N. Davidson and E. M. Broner, is a collection of 24 short essays, plus a bibliography. The American authors who rate chapters to themselves are Emily Dickinson, Edith Wharton, Ellen Glasgow, and Sylvia Plath; another eight essays deal with American writers thematically and historically. This is a notably uneven collection, containing some solid professional work, some pedestrian seminar papers, and a few pages devoted to gushing and cooing ("Thank you for joining me. Thank you for the treasures you are—communicating daughters" [p. 188]). There is also some plain bad writing ("Wharton's novelistic situations flushed out after World War I pertained to the changing role of woman" [p. 149]). In compiling *The Lost Tradition* Davidson and Broner worked under the assumption that scholarship can be "nonhierarchical, a sharing rather than a criticizing" (p. xi). This lazy cant has weakened an otherwise useful book.

Some of the huffing and puffing continues in *Women's Autobiography: Essays in Criticism* (Indiana), ed. Estelle C. Jelinek, where one contribution begins, "Women derive a sense of feminine godhead from their biological connections with one another. This essay attempts to reestablish the sacrality of feminine experience and also to re-mythologize all human experience. . . ." But in general this book does a more efficient job of thinking about its subject, perhaps because organization around a genre allows for more qualifications and definitions than does organization around a theme. At any rate, all 14 of the essays in this collection (the majority of which deal with American authors) are concerned in one way or another with identifying the uniquenesses of women's autobiographies as opposed to autobiographies in general—that is, autobiographies written by men. The rationale is explained simply enough in Jelinek's introduction: "Even if we ignore the subjective biases of critics of autobiography, we find that most of their objective theories are not applicable to women's life studies" (p. 5). Though the contributors to this volume approach the idea of an objective theory of women's autobiography in different ways, they all do agree in practice on its basic validity, and this agreement tends to unify the book's diversity of critical approaches. *Women's Autobiography* is indeed diverse; it includes, for instance, formal criticism of individual authors (James E. Breslin on Gertrude Stein, Marcus K. Billson and Sidonie A. Smith on Lillian Hellman); theme analysis (Regina Blackburn on autobiographies of Afro-American women); historical studies (Carol Edkins on 18th-century Quaker and Puritan spiritual autobiographies); and a politically oriented celebration of a founding mother (Jelinek on Elizabeth Cady Stanton). To my mind, the best of the essays are Patricia Meyer Spacks's "Selves in Hiding" and Suzanne Juhasz' "Towards a Theory of Form in Feminist Autobiography: Kate Millett's *Flying* and *Sita*; Maxine Hong Kingston's *The Woman Warrior*." Spacks probes the self-deprecating and self-glorifying extremes to which she claims women's autobiographies are prone; Juhasz makes a case for a distinctively female psychology of narration.

f. **Science Fiction.**   In his editor's foreword to Oxford's new Science-Fiction Writers series of critical studies Robert Scholes points out that 20th-century critics of fiction have tended to value most highly "individual psychology in characterization, unique stylistic nuance in language, and plausibility in the events presented." These critical criteria, however, are not universally applicable, and they have tended to keep us from reading well "a body of fiction . . . which privileges the type over the individual, the idea over the word, and the unexpected over the plausible event"—that is, SF. Science-Fiction Writers is intended to create a criticism suitable to the genre. "In each volume we will include a general view of the author's life and work, critical interpretations of his or her major contributions to the field of science fiction, and a biographical and bibliographical apparatus. . . ."

In the first volume in the series, *Robert A. Heinlein: America as Science Fiction*, H. Bruce Franklin explains the enormous popularity of Heinlein's right-wing fantasies by correlating their *Tendenzen* with an apocalyptically Marxist reading of American history. It is no accident, in Franklin's view, that Heinlein's 1964 novel *Farnham's Freehold* dealt with a Russian nuclear attack followed by enslavement of the last Americans by black cannibals, for in 1964 the nonviolent civil rights movement came under sustained violent attack, and "Just as the one nation that has ever used nuclear weapons has recurring fantasies about nuclear weapons being used upon it, the nation most notorious for enslaving and oppressing Black people has recurring fantasies about being enslaved and oppressed by Blacks" (p. 157). There is a certain programmatic one-dimensionality about this kind of criticism, but it works well enough in practice with Heinlein's programmatic fiction.

Franklin's subtitle is an oversimplification, but its reverse is certainly true, for science fiction has always been predominantly an American genre. On this fact a number of interesting sociological conclusions can be based. For instance, comparatively speaking, it might be said that "Russian science fiction is . . . conditioned by its response to . . . the official utopianism of the Soviet state; British science fiction owes its repeated visions of castastrophe to the long national history of industrial and imperial decline; German science fiction is replete with visions of the triumph of a master race; and American science fiction derives both the optimism and the ruthlessness of its approach from the frontier experience and the economic subjugation of the West." But "There has as yet been rather little progress toward such a comparative sociology, partly because of the overwhelming influence of American science fiction in the period 1930–1960. . . . [a provincializing influence which is] reflected, for example, in an anthology title like *The Best From the Rest of the World*. . . ." These comments come from pages 30–31 of Patrick Parrinder's *Science Fiction: Its Criticism and Teaching* (Methuen), an appealingly jargon-free piece of genre criticism which (p. xviii) "is intended both to elucidate science fiction's generic identity and to review the various critical (and, in the final chapter, pedagogic) approaches which have been taken to it." What I found most refreshing about this book was its unusual combination of critical sophistication and good English, commitment to the subject, and common sense. Consider, for example, Parrinder's most personal chapter, the one on teaching science fiction. Parrinder is of course happy that his subject is now being taught in American universities, but he is also aware of the mixed motives underlying its presence in the curriculum. It may be true that science fiction is a genre which a priori deserves study just as much as any other genre, but it is also true that chairmen need to fill classrooms and students like easy courses. Academic science-fictionists will have to face the implications of these facts, and the best hope for the long-term survival of their speciality is an attitude of rigorous critical honesty. After quoting the futurologist Alvin Toffler to the effect that SF is literarily worthless but valuable as "a mind-stretching force for the creation of the habit of anticipation," Parrinder speaks for sanity when he observes that "As a 'future-oriented' literature which is readily accessible to the young, science fiction has come to feature very widely in history, philosophy, politics, and sociology courses. . . . Yet the instructor who shares Toffler's attitude is simply exploiting SF for his own ends, rather than adequately and responsibly teaching it. Science fiction *is* a mode of literature, and courses which make use of it, whatever the context, cannot opt out of the business of artistic judgements" (p. 134). Parrinder's ideas are worth quoting at length, if only because his book will probably go unread. Part of Methuen's stimulating but overpriced New Accents series of critical studies, the 166 small pages of *Science Fiction* are being sold in the United States for $6.50 in paperback, $9.95 hardbound.

Patricia S. Warrick's *The Cybernetic Imagination in Science Fiction* (MIT), a study of the image of the computer in SF, is an article which has been padded out to book length with banalities ("The use of computers has grown rapidly because they can accomplish some tasks more effectively than humans," p. 13) and howlers ("Critical debate ignites and flames at the possibility of SF's replacing the realistic novel as the predominant literary form by this century's end," p. 2). A better-written study along the same lines is Walter E. Meyers' entertaining *Aliens and Linguists: Language Study and Science Fiction* (Georgia). Warrick is concerned about her authors' fear of the computer and ignorance of its liberating powers; Meyers wishes, for the sake of a more interesting science fiction, that his authors would think seriously about the linguistic conventions they employ. But neither Warrick nor Meyers is interested in thinking about science fiction in a literary way, and this limits the scope of their studies. Considering a story about a future race of human beings just one one-hundredth of an inch long, for instance, Meyers (p. 41) devotes a paragraph of solidly academic analysis to worrying about how these "micro-Lilliputians" could have deciphered messages from their past. This bothers him, even though he is willing to accept the idea of the micro-Lilliputians. In fact, of course, a recognizably human micro-Lilliputian is a physical impossibility. If you were ten times as tall as you are, you would be 1,000 times as heavy; you cannot change the size without changing the proportions; *Gulliver's Travels* is a lie. The proof of this fact was published by Galileo in 1638, many years before Swift was born, and it offers us a critical choice: either we accept science fiction *as* fiction—size, language, and all; or we act silly and worry selectively about extrinsic details. Perhaps, though, critics of science fiction worry about extrinsic details because the nature of the genre demands that kind of criticism. As Brian Attebery puts it in *The Fantasy Tradition in American Literature: From Irving to Le Guin* (Indiana), "Fantasy . . . needs consistency. Reader and writer are committed to maintaining the illusion for the entire course of the fiction" (p. 2).

Attebery's book is an attempt to prove that a fantasy tradition does exist in the United States and that this tradition "can be considered a long-range attempt at . . . one task: creating an American fairyland" (p. vii). To sustain this thesis in the absence of an American folkloric tradition, Attebery has recourse to a wide variety of critical expedients, from plot summary to Russian-style morphological analysis. The effort is impressive, but the thesis itself seems relatively unimportant. A corpus of literary materials does not make a tradition. But Attebery's many detailed readings are convincing. I liked his treatment of *The Scarlet Letter* as a fairy tale, and it certainly is true that the Scarecrow in *The Wizard of Oz* "is a case of clothes making the man, and doing a pretty good job of it" (p. 100).

Finally, and most ambitiously: Ihab Hassan's *The Right Promethean Fire: Imagination, Science, and Cultural Change* (Illinois) is a wide-ranging meditation about the effects of post-Newtonian science, with its radical new principles of relativity, complemen-

tarity, and indeterminacy, on the ways we will think and perceive in
the future. In the parts where Hassan's "we" applies to literary critics,
Promethean Fire makes some strong points about, e.g., assimilating
deconstructionist "indetermanence" (p. 123) without abandoning the
old humanist belief in the autonomy of the individual consciousness.
When his "we" applies to people-in-general or to Ihab Hassan himself, however, the book begins to look like something that will be
embarrassing to reread when we have grown a few years older. One
warning sign is the book's scrambled ("Mallarméan," p. 21) organization and typography, a self-indulgence which only draws attention
to the recklessness of Hassan's extrapolations from one field of
thought to others; another is Hassan's repeated interruptions of his
formal exposition with great chunks of some truly awful pseudo-
Lawrentian travel writing.

g. Miscellaneous. In *City of Nature: Journeys to Nature in the Age
of American Romanticism* (Delaware) Bernard Rosenthal finds that
the idea of nature in 19th-century American literature has been associated with images of the garden and the city. The uncivilized frontier, by contrast, is not nature but wilderness. Little new here.

George J. Becker's *Realism in Modern Literature* (Ungar) is a
survey of the history and the major European and American documents of the realistic movement. Although it is intended as a supplement to Becker's *Documents of Modern Literary Realism,* this
handbook can be read independently.

Romanticism, Modernism, Postmodernism, one of *Bucknell Review*'s 1980 fascicles (25,ii, ed. Harry R. Garvin), contains two good
essays of interest to *ALS*: David Antin's "Is There a Postmodernism?"
and Marjorie Perloff's reply, "Contemporary/Postmodern: The 'New'
Poetry?" Perloff is willing to believe that there may be such a thing
as postmodernism ("[t]he notion of the poem as language construction in which the free play of possible significations replaces iconic
representation" [p. 172]), but she cautions us against applying the
label to every trendy contemporary. A mild enough request, one
might suppose, but it comes with the effect of a revelation after such
a display of hectoring inanity as this, from Julia Kristeva's "Postmodernism?," p. 140: ". . . in a kind of Dantesque project incorporating
the formal experience of its predecessors, postmodern writing rediscovers *lyricism* (an admission of the subject's ecstasy—*jouissance*) as

well as *epic breadth* (a rhetorical procedure of historical totalization). Through its permanent debate with the event, with politics, with political, sexual, and paranoid dilemmas, this writing is the antidote to (a polar opposite of?) the Ptolemaic universe and its measure."

Essays in Honor of Russel B. Nye, ed. Joseph Waldmeir (Mich. State, 1978), contains essays in all of "the five areas in which Nye has gathered honor to himself over a long and distinguished career —American History . . . American Literature, American Studies, Canadian Culture, and Popular Culture." The essays relevant to *ALS* deal with colonial American theologians (by Norman Grabo), Hawthorne (Hugo McPherson and Milton R. Stern), Henry James (Robert Falk), the Hoosier humorist Kin Hubbard (William McCann), Dos Passos (Linda W. Wagner), and Updike (Waldmeir). In range of quality this is a typical festschrift; that is, for instance, McPherson's "How Hot Is the Scarlet Letter?" reads like a recycled undergraduate lecture, but Stern's "Nathaniel Hawthorne: 'Conservative after Heaven's own fashion'" is a real piece of scholarship.

ii. Criticism

a. **Collections.** Four of the seven essays in *Under the Sign of Saturn* (Farrar), Susan Sontag's first collection of short pieces since 1969, concern this chapter of *ALS*. "On Paul Goodman" and "Remembering Roland Barthes" are primarily eulogies; the former is also an object lesson in the evanescence of topical allusion. (Quick, reader: what was repulsive about "the repulsive martyrdom of Thomas Eagleton"?) But the other two esays are much more consequential. "Fascinating Fascism" uses the format of a review-essay to delineate sharply and convincingly the nature of the fascist aesthetic; "Under the Sign of Saturn," another review-essay, is, despite its necessary incompleteness, the best introduction I have read to the work of Walter Benjamin, a difficult, neurotic, quintessentially middle-European man of letters whose efforts to understand the life in symbols of the early 20th century become more obviously valuable with every passing year. *Under the Sign of Saturn* is worth reading for these essays alone. The original *NYRB* publication of "Fascinating Fascism" was followed by a letter from the single-minded feminist Adrienne Rich, who castigated Sontag for saying negative things about a woman (the Nazi cinematographer Leni Riefenstahl) while failing to discuss Adolf Hitler's maleness. Sontag's reply to Rich (*NYRB* 20 Mar. 1975, pp. 31–32) is quite possibly the best thing Sontag has ever written: deeply felt, rigorous in its refusal to surrender critical honesty to the demands of a party line, and as efficiently devastating as a hydrogen bomb. I wish it could have been reprinted here.

Part of Nature, Part of Us: Modern American Poets (Harvard) is a collection of Helen Vendler's poetry reviews. As we would expect from this critic, the two largest sections in the book (58 and 49 pages, respectively) are devoted to Wallace Stevens and Robert Lowell, but some 40 other poets are discussed at lengths ranging down to a single paragraph. Only one of the essays seems not to have been previously published, and perhaps the missing bibliographical detail is a typographical error. There is no index. The substance of this book should be discussed in chapter 17, but I would like to say some things here about Vendler, reviewing, and criticism.

As compared with the "pure" academic critic, the reviewer has to work closer to her deadline, consider her reading audience's limitations more carefully, and make her critical points in a much more ad hoc fashion, with whatever material comes to hand. This impoverishment of critical resource can be seen in the middlebrow crassness of the *NYTBR*, but the *NYTBR* is only an extreme case of the general American situation with regard to the reviewing of poetry. Because it cannot be assumed that an otherwise educated audience will know anything about poetry, the reviewer with a critical position will unavoidably have to spend time explaining elementary points and rehashing the critical consensus. And even if none of these sad things were true, the review itself would still suffer from a generic limitation. Anchored to the publisher's calendar, the reviewer must grant newness the status of a critical value. She can barely criticize because she can barely do her reading in historical context.

So the reviewer's syllabus must fall more or less short of a critical ideal. Circumstances have prevented Vendler from reviewing John Ashbery or Gary Snyder here, for instance, and have forced her to make the points, once more, that Randall Jarrell was a better critic than poet, W. H. Auden stopped being a major poet some time before he turned 35, and E. E. Cummings never became a major poet because he refused to think. Similarly, Vendler's more controversial opinions (that T. S. Eliot suffered a falling off in poetic power, for instance, or that Robert Lowell didn't) have to be taken here on faith; reviews lack the space for detailed exposition. This is a way of saying that criticism is cumulative, inductive, and synthetic, while reviewing is just the opposite: isolating, deductive, depending on the telling example rather than the encompassing generalization. Because of his gnomic exuberance, the best practitioner of the reviewer's art in this century has been Randall Jarrell. *Part of Nature,* a book which wants to be a work of criticism (you can sense this in Vendler's incidental discussions of other critics), does not challenge Jarrell's *Poetry and the Age* on its own ground. But Vendler's critical intellect is correspondingly more powerful than Jarrell's, and *Part of Nature* is a strong, reliable guide to the poetry of our own more somber age.

Here is Vendler on a poet whose minimalist productions have in the past few years reached the point of anorexia: "[Robert Creeley] remains so much a follower of Williams, without Williams' rebelliousness, verve, and social breadth, that his verse seems, though intermittently attractive, fatally pinched. . . . [H]e purchases composition at the price of momentum and sweep" (pp. 356–57). And here is Linda W. Wagner, writing about the same poet in *American Modern: Essays in Fiction and Poetry* (Kennikat): "One central approach to Creeley's work, all of his work, should have been epistemological. Wittgenstein's premises of knowledge imperfect till trapped in language, and language imperfect trapped as it is in its own game patterns—these were the bases for what I would call Creeley's 'hesitation' stance toward both speaking and expressing meaning. On its most practical level, this hesitancy shows up as short lines in the poems, extremely fragmented syntax, a start-stop rhythm that does accurately reflect Creeley's own normal speech pattern" (p. 180). Vendler is a closer reader than Wagner, and a more accurate writer; she would not commit a critical judgment to a phrase as blurry as " 'hesitation' stance." Wagner, per contra, can be accused of special pleading (how can a reader, as opposed to a listener, be expected to care about Creeley's voice?) and the intentional fallacy. But her own intentions are different from Vendler's. Vendler, as a descendant of the New Critics, reads American poetry for its generic universals; she is interested in its ability to produce the effects that poetry has always produced in all cultures. Wagner reads American poetry (and prose) in cultural terms, as defining and justifying parts of a specifically American and specifically modernist literature. The difference between the two critics is made clear by the titles of their books.

b. **Generic Criticism.** *Ideas and the Novel* (Harcourt), the transcript of four lectures by Mary McCarthy, is full of local insights, but its thesis lacks historical perspective. As of the middle of the 19th century, according to that thesis, "fictions, including the novel, were meeting a new need created by the fact that the horizon had vastly extended while the means of conveying information had not developed to keep pace. . . . The novel was not only a conveyor of factual information. It filled the place of today's round tables and seminars that people watch on television or listen to on the radio and that is [*sic*] the commonest source of their general ideas" (pp. 44–45). But (pp. 3–13) when Henry James invented a form of novel which contained neither ideas nor the circumstantial reality from which ideas are born, he effected a fundamental change in literary history. Thanks to that change, the novel in English has become uncomfortable in the presence of thought.

This is an interesting idea, but it confuses the history of writing with the history of reading. After all, as McCarthy devotes most of her book to pointing out, the great 19th-century novels continue to exert an influence over us, and they do so by forcing us into new relationships with their embodied ideas. Our simultaneous acceptance of novels written according to Jamesian rules must therefore have something to do with a change in reading practice. But this complication is something McCarthy generally fails to consider. She does hint at an explanation broader than simple influence when she discusses the novelist's consciousness of the disparity between the range of reality covered by an idea and the bustling life that goes on outside the margin of thought (pp. 117–19), but the hint remains undeveloped, and all we are left with is the straw man of "the doctrine of progress in the arts" (pp. 119–21). This doctrine, we are told, somehow keeps ideas out of modern novels, except for a period 20 years ago when it didn't (why?), and except for a few contemporary novels and noveloids such as Robert Pirsig's *Zen and the Art of Motorcycle Maintenance* (why?), and except (why?) for the contemporary Jewish novel. After making this nonpoint, *Ideas and the Novel* concludes, just like a bad freshman theme, with a new idea in its last sentence: "If the novel is to be revitalized . . . emergency strategies [like Pirsig's] will have to be employed to disarm and disorient reviewers and teachers of literature, who, as always [why?], are the reader's main foe."

Now, much of this is an apologia for McCarthy's own highly intellectual symposium-novels. It may or may not work as a specific defense argument, but as a general explanation it is unsuccessful. *Ideas and the Novel* also contains some errors of detail. McCarthy's misreading of *The Magic Mountain*, for instance, stems from her notion that the protagonist dies at the end.

Most modern theories of comedy, following the lead of Albert Cook's *The Dark Voyage and the Golden Mean: A Philosophy of Comedy* (1949), have looked at the comic as a social thing. According to this view, comedy is conservative; we laugh at deviations from the social norm, knowing that at the end of the story the deviant will be reconciled with the view of reality that everybody else accepts. But this theory has its limitations. For one thing, as Fred Miller Robinson points out in *The Comedy of Language: Studies in Modern Comic Literature* (Mass.), it refuses to let us acknowledge that "The fictive imaginings of Don Quixote are a joy to us, and we recognize them in ourselves" (p. 10). Cook's theory turns all readers of comedy into Sancho Panzas.

Robinson therefore posits a "metaphysical" theory of comedy, one based on "the distinction between reality and language. It is, after all, our mental processes that tell us that there *is* a reality of which our mental processes do not give us true information. And it is language that expresses that there is a reality which it cannot express" (p. 19). We know only by means of a discontinuity in our ignorance, and we smile an ironic smile when something calls our attention to this funny limitation on ourselves. Robinson elaborates this idea by showing us how the stumbling play of language around its central epistemological void brings about the joyful creativity of *Ulysses*, *As I Lay Dying*, some poems by Stevens, and Beckett's *Watt*. Since Robinson's theory works in a completely different way from Cook's, it does not supersede it but complements it. *The Comedy of Language* is a valuable addition to the existing theory.

Ronald Weber's *The Literature of Fact: Literary Nonfiction in*

American Writing (Ohio) is a compact study of the "nonfiction novel" from its beginnings in the 1940s (*Let Us Now Praise Famous Men; Hiroshima*) through the years of its greatest conspicuousness in the '60s and on up to the present. After characterizing the genre, Weber devotes about two-thirds of his book to detailed criticisms of specific works, then concludes (pp. 164–65) that the books he has discussed "have in their varied ways implications that reach beyond the factual events they reconstruct—implications that cannot be verified as history but known and felt as art. To say this is not to imply [as Tom Wolfe notably did in the '60s] that literary nonfiction is a superior kind of history and certainly not that it is a superior kind of literature. . . . It is quite enough to say that some of the books . . . are works of historical reconstruction and imaginative writing, fact books that yield something of literature's resonant meanings."

One chapter of *The Self-Begetting Novel* (Columbia), a study in Proustianism by Steven G. Kellman, is devoted to an overview of "The Self-Begetting Novel and American Literature." Except perhaps for its mention of the forgotten Clyde Brion Davis (author of a 1938 novel called *"The Great American Novel—"*), this chapter has little value for specialists in American literature.

c. **Language Studies.**   *The State of the Language* (Calif.), ed. Leonard Michaels and Christopher Ricks, is a 600-page collection of essays about contemporary English in almost all of its literary and nonliterary forms. Some of the best-known contributors evidently failed to take their assignments seriously; thus Kingsley Amis blows off steam with an annotated list of malapropisms he has found in print, and Robert M. Adams equates inarticulateness with deconstructionism, links both of these to affirmative action, and floats from there to a prediction of "race warfare, of which the advancing signs are everywhere too prevalent to be enumerated" (p. 585). But between the triviality and the gassiness there is a great deal of interesting material, conventional and unconventional: Alicia Ostriker on body imagery in poems written by women, Mary-Kay Wilmers on the language of novel reviews, Walter Benn Michaels on the location of meaning in contexts rather than texts, and Hugh Kenner on literature and computer language, for instance; not to mention essays about film dubbing, the suppression of infants' imaginative speech

by blue-collar parents, the linguistics of the psychotherapeutic conversation, and Marin County Mellowspeak.

In *Metaphors We Live By* (Chicago) George Lakoff and Mark
Johnson argue that metaphor is not a mere rhetorical decoration but
a fundamental property of language. We learn from our experiences
by organizing them into "experiential gestalts" (p. 117), and metaphor is the language structure which enables us to understand things
with reference to these experiential gestalts. Thus, for instance (ch.
16), if we read the term "argument" in terms of the experiential
gestalts "journey" and "container," we will derive the metaphors "An
argument is a journey" and "An argument is a container." These
metaphors are implicit in such ordinary sentences as "We have now
arrived at a disturbing conclusion" and "That argument *has holes
in it.*" There are mixed metaphors which accommodate both the
"journey" and the "container" vehicles (e.g., "*At this point* our argument doesn't have *much content*"); there are other mixed metaphors
which are immiscible (e.g., "The *direction* of his argument has no
substance"). Analysis of our discourse will convince us that metaphor pervades our language to a far greater extent than we usually
realize, and that in fact it is difficult to conceive of a concept such
as "argument" in nonmetaphoric terms. Generalizing from this discovery, Lakoff and Johnson conclude (p. 185) "that truth is always
relative to a conceptual system, that any human conceptual system
is mostly metaphorical in nature, and that, therefore, there is no fully
objective, unconditional, or absolute truth." And in the last quarter
of *Metaphors We Live By* they elaborate an epistemology of "ex-
perientialism" from this conclusion. According to Lakoff and Johnson, the objectivist account of truth—that a true statement is absolutely meaningful, regardless of its meaningfulness *to* anybody—
cannot account for such phenomena as aesthetic experience. The
contrasting subjectivist account—that experience has no meaning
except what I happen to impose on it in the privacy of my own
mind—is finally (p. 192) a mere "retreat for the emotions. . . ." An
understanding of the metaphoric structure of reality, however, can
harmonize the objectivist and the subjectivist points of view, humanizing the former and giving a basis of value to the latter.

Lakoff and Johnson are willing to test this relativist compromise
under extreme conditions. On pp. 193–94, for instance, they consider

Nazi Germany as a case in which "the conceptual system of a culture" has generated a set of metaphors which are terribly wrong. This, surely, is a situation in which the idea of absolutes deserves thinking about, but Lakoff and Johnson take their ethical stand on behalf of "transcultural concepts and values" which "the world community" can bring to bear, as one metaphor to another, against the aberrant conceptual system. The metaphors in quotation marks are never defined, and the only practical translation I can think of is a 51 percent vote in the United Nations. This is not, I think, a very satisfactory substitute for God. Lakoff and Johnson are guilty of other sophomorisms, including some wide-eyed banalities about love, politics, and (a section heading) "The Importance of Truth in Our Daily Lives." But as a study in linguistic analysis, *Metaphors We Live By* is an attractive book: brightly written, provided with an abundance of interesting examples, and full of provocative insights into the pervasiveness of metaphor in the world.

I can give only brief mention to more technical studies. Linguistics has grown up in several different directions since Saussure and the 19th-century philologists, and Geoffrey Sampson's *Schools of Linguistics* (Stanford) provides a moderately detailed overview. Sampson's *Making Sense* (Oxford) is a continuation, in more technical detail, of the empiricist argument that Sampson started with Noam Chomsky last year in *Liberty and Language* (ALS *1979*, pp. 438–39). Chomsky, meanwhile, continues to buttress the philosophical foundations of his theory in *Rules and Representations* (Columbia), seven lectures which bring linguistics to bear on such fundamental topics as the mind-body problem. *Language and Learning: The Debate Between Jean Piaget and Noam Chomsky* (Harvard), ed. Massimo Piattelli-Palmarini, carries the debate between Chomsky's "innatist" and Piaget's "constructivist" rationalisms beyond linguistics or psychology; in fact, with anthropologists, philosophers, molecular biologists and a mathematician taking part in the post-debate panel discussions, all at a high level of abstraction and each holding forth at length about his own specialty, this symposium volume about the structure of knowledge doesn't fall within any ordinary disciplinary limits. It is of course a formidable volume to read, with its arguments, counterarguments, replies to replies, and extraordinarily wide frame of reference, but Piattelli-Palmarini's editorial interpolations keep things lucid. The title of *Linguistic*

Perspectives on Literature (Routledge), a collection of essays edited by Marvin K. L. Ching, Michael C. Haley, and Ronald F. Lunsford, is self-explanatory. Two essays of particular interest to Americanists are Irene R. Fairley's "Syntactic Deviation and Cohesion," which deals with the structure of five poems by E. E. Cummings, and Samuel Jay Keyser's "Wallace Stevens: Form and Meaning in Four Poems."

d. **Psychological Criticism.** Readers interested in the psychoanalytic structuralism of Jacques Lacan will want to look at *Returning to Freud: Clinical Psychoanalysis in the School of Lacan* (Yale), ed. and trans. Stuart Schneiderman, a volume of clinical studies by Lacan's followers. The most impressive thing in this book is the previously unpublished transcript of one of the master's psychiatric interviews, which is powerful indeed. The rest of the collection does not concern *ALS*, but connoisseurs of the weird may enjoy the tribute from Lacan's personal editor, which reads like a cross between the *Letters of a Portuguese Nun* and an ode to Stalin. The 12 essays in *The Literary Freud: Mechanisms of Defense and the Poetic Will* (Yale), ed. Joseph H. Smith, are more directly concerned with literature, and three in particular should be mentioned here. Shoshana Felman's "On Reading Poetry: Reflections on the Limits and Possibilities of Psychoanalytical Approaches" offers a useful reading of Lacan's "Seminar on 'The Purloined Letter,'" though Felman, a professor of French, is relatively unacquainted with literature in English. John T. Irwin's "Figurations of the Writer's Death: Freud and Hart Crane" is a long, subtle, and rewarding exploration of the ways in which poetic influence is repressed, reworked, and reexpressed in translated form. Harold Bloom's "Freud's Concepts of Defense and the Poetic Will" sets out to analyze *Beyond the Pleasure Principle* as a "High Romantic crisis-poem" (p. 9), using the specialized terminology that Bloom introduced in his study of poetic Oedipalism, *The Anxiety of Influence* (1973), and elaborated in four more books published between 1975 and 1977. By turning his analysis on his own critical progenitor, using for the purpose a language he has done his best to originate ex nihilo, Bloom here works his way toward a resolution of the Oedipus complex underlying his theory. The result is something that looks very much like a completion of Bloom's critical task.

Is There a Text in This Class? The Authority of Interpretive Communities (Harvard) is a collection of Stanley Fish's essays in stylistics and reader-response criticism, from the famous "Literature in the Reader: Affective Stylistics" (1970) to 1979. As Fish points out in his introduction, the earlier essays embody a contradiction: "When someone would charge that an emphasis on the reader leads directly to solipsism and anarchy, I would reply by insisting on the constraints imposed on readers by the text; and when someone would characterize my position as nothing more than the most recent turn of the new-critical screw, I would reply by saying that in my model the reader was freed from the tyranny of the text. . . ." (p. 7). The second half of this defense led Fish into "the most unfortunate sentence I ever wrote. Referring to affective criticism as a 'superior fiction,' I declare[d] that 'it relieves me of the obligation to be right (a standard that simply drops out) and demands only that I be interesting' " (p. 174). The notion of interpretive communities, however, allowed Fish simultaneously to resolve his contradiction and work his way out of his relativism. "Interpretive communities are made up of those who share interpretive strategies not for reading . . . but for writing texts, for constituting their properties and assigning their intentions" (p. 171), and this means (p. 174) that "Within a community . . . a standard of right (and wrong) can always be invoked because it will be invoked against the background of a prior understanding as to what counts as a fact, what is hearable as an argument . . . and so on. . . ." The key phrase, of course, is "*within* a community." The community is alone able to generate and perpetuate norms because it alone can create context. "In a classroom whose authority figures include David Bleich and Norman Holland, a student might very well relate a text to her memories of a favorite aunt, while in other classrooms, dominated by the spirit of Brooks and Warren, any such activity would immediately be dismissed as nonliterary, as something that isn't done" (p. 343).

So Fish remains a relativist of a special kind, one whose relativism is based on the community rather than the individual. Value, under this system, is anything held in common by two or more people. The obvious question is, of course, "What, precisely, *is* a community?", and when Fish considers this question himself he becomes vague to the point of mysticism (see, e.g., p. 173). As a result, Fish's theories have evolved, more than most theories, by means of an

ongoing argument with other critics, a sort of self-institutionalizing
agon. This chapter is not the place to jump into the argument, but
obviously *Is There A Text in This Class?* is a book that should be
looked at. A related collection of essays that I have been unable to
obtain is *Reader-Response Criticism: From Formalism to Post-
Structuralism* (Hopkins), ed. Jane P. Tompkins.

e. **Formalist Studies.** Anglo-American criticism, in Geoffrey H.
Hartman's view, has been stuck since the days of the New Critics in
a humble empiricism which has stunted its intellectual growth. The
New Criticism was, in I. A. Richards' words, practical; it aimed
chiefly to show readers what the texts it called "literature" had to
say. Criticism was not literature; it was only—well, criticism: a mode
of thinking about literature that was hedged in by its own self-
imposed limitations. The French and German critics whose ideas
Hartman has been thinking about, however, have managed to avoid
this trap. Operating out of a continental tradition which considers
criticism a branch of philosophy, they raise the possibility of an un-
trammeled criticism. Yes, criticism depends for its existence on other
texts—but so, when you think about it, does every other verbal expression. We are constituted by textuality, and critical writing is only
a kind of literature which makes explicit its relation to other textuali-
ties. In this respect, it is not only a creative art, it is the most creative
art, because the most liberatingly aware of its own constituting codes.
   Criticism in the Wilderness: The Study of Literature Today
(Yale) is Hartman's detailed statement of this idea. Hartman engages in close readings of primary writers—most notably Emily
Dickinson—and other critics—most notably Carlyle and Walter Benjamin—but the primary effort of this book is to show us by example
and commentary what an absolute criticism looks like. Hartman is
well equipped for this task, for he seems to have read just about
everything. And despite his show-off manner his learning really is
worn lightly, for his combinations and recombinations of old texts
proceed so continuously and creatively that the whole process seems
quite natural. My only objection is that the goal of this large enterprise seems finally trivial. After the reading is done and the decon-
structions have been emplaced, we are left with nothing but an
aggrandizement of the critic as individual personality.
   For the critical utterance, in Hartman's hands, establishes an im-

perial dominance over language, in content and in form. The blurb
for *Criticism in the Wilderness* proclaims that "this eloquent book"
is "written with a general intellectual audience in mind," and it is
true that the famous Hartman prose style, with its puns, allusions, big
words, maudlin personal digressions, and disconnected syntax, has
been brought somewhat under control in this volume. But it still
seems to be directed toward entangling the reader and forcing him
to submit to the critic's ego power. "[T]he spectacle of the polite
critic dealing with an extravagant literature, trying so hard to come
to terms with it in his own tempered language, verges on the ludicrous": this (p. 155) is Hartman's plea for the freedom of his own
critical idiom. It is entirely logical, but the freedom it claims for
itself it takes away from its readers.

Consider Hartman's meditation on Dickinson. Noting that Dickinson used the dash as an all-purpose punctuation mark, Hartman
asks (p. 126), "Why does this formal mark, this hyphen with zero
meaning, have intraverbal force? Perhaps because it both joins and
divides, like a hymen." In fact, of course, (1) a dash is not the same
thing as a hyphen, (2) a hymen can't really be said to join anything,
and (3) as the rest of the paragraph makes clear (though "clear"
isn't the right word) Hartman doesn't have a thought here, he has
an echolalia. Enchanted by the rhyme between "hyphen" and "hymen," he secreted a paragraph of Derrida. This, though, is fair play
under the Hartman rules, for (p. 213) "literary commentary today
is creating texts—a literature—of its own." In E. D. Hirsch's terminology, this would be called an abandonment of significance. That is
an abstract consideration, but it signifies a concrete loss: the loss of
the order that the poem creates out of its own meaning, the loss of our
freedom to read under its law.

What are we to conclude about this? Perhaps, for purposes of
ALS, just two simple things: (1) Geoffrey Hartman is a deeply
learned critic who is forcing us to think out the limits of criticism
in new, sometimes distasteful, always interesting ways. His book
should be read. But (2) that book demonstrates the limits of its own
solipsism. Hartman needs an editor.

In *Destructive Poetics: Heidegger and Modern American Poetry*
(Columbia) Paul A. Bové sets out to perform "a critical destruction
of the Modern critical mind" (p. x) by showing that "Modern poetry,
in its relation to the accumulated past, destroys the language, forms,

tropes, and poems of the 'tradition' projected by Modernist criticism" (p. xi). The poets Bové recruits to his wrecking crew are Whitman, Stevens, and Charles Olson, under the foremanship of Martin Heidegger; their task is to help "[emerge] a theory of literature which sees all language as based on nothing and manifesting itself as fiction emerging out of and reflecting nothing" (p. 92). In this project of carrying deconstruction to its nihilistic limits, other critics are shown up as Laodiceans; thus Paul de Man's "simplifying blindness, that is, his claim that all poetic language is already demystified and not in need of destruction, emerges as an unexamined presupposition. . . ." (p. 32). Bové's own critical practice, however, has not much more destructive power than an Ancient Pistol. Too much time is spent vanquishing straw men such as "the New Critical devaluation of Whitman for his loose, unstructured forms" (p. 131) and "[t]he almost total silence surrounding Olson's work" (p. 217).

The Age of Structuralism: Lévi-Strauss to Foucault (Columbia) by Edith Kurzweil is a sociologically oriented overview of the work of eight French structuralists and antistructuralists, of whom the most important for purposes of *ALS* are Claude Lévi-Strauss, Jacques Lacan, Roland Barthes, and Michel Foucault. Kurzweil sees structuralism as a historically distinct movement which was given its shape by political circumstance, on the one hand, and, on the other hand, by French intellectuals' traditional interdisciplinary interests and common training in philosophy. I found this broad perspective stimulating. As a literary specialist, I would not have interpreted the evolution of Barthes's thought as a "[retreat] from direct social critique to semantic games" (p. 183), but it is salutary for all of us to be reminded that structuralism did originally claim to be not just a way of reading but a way of uniting politics, psychology, and philosophy. Great syntheses like this are part of the French critical tradition, not the American; that is their value for American criticism.

The structuralist era in France began, according to Kurzweil, in 1955, when Lévi-Strauss's intellectual autobiography *Tristes Tropiques* became a best-seller. Within a few years of that event the French intellectual world had become generally familiar with structuralist thinking. In 1968, however, structuralist political slogans lost prestige with the failure of the student revolution; in 1970, Barthes's *S/Z* signaled that structuralist literary formalism had been abandoned by one of its leading practitioners; and in 1971 Lévi-Strauss repudiated the "pseudo-structuralists" who claimed to be building on his ideas. French structuralism, therefore, was the affair of a single generation—a neat, compact thing to think about in historical terms. The history of formalist criticism in America has been less tractable. On the one hand, the deconstructionist era began here in 1966 when Jacques Derrida—little known at that time in France—presented a devastating attack on the idea of structure at a Johns Hopkins symposium. On the other hand, structuralism itself entered the critical mainstream only after the publication of Jonathan Culler's *Structuralist Poetics* in 1975. Meanwhile, the New Criticism, officially dead ever since Northrop Frye wrote its obituary in *Anatomy of Criticism* (1957), is still alive down the hall in the undergraduate classroom. Under these circumstances, writing a history of contemporary American criticism must be a daunting task. But Frank Lentricchia's effort to do so, *After the New Criticism* (Chicago), is a success.

The first half of Lentricchia's long book, subtitled "A Critical Thematics, 1957–1977," deals with five critical methodologies which have dominated the last quarter-century: archetypal criticism on the model of *Anatomy of Criticism*, existentialism, phenomenology, structuralism, and poststructuralism. Given "the scandalously short-lived nature of recent critical movements" (p. 65), Lentricchia keeps his history in steady focus by concentrating on the works of a few major critics. The choice of these figures is conventional (Frye, Sartre, Poulet, Lévi-Strauss, Derrida, etc.); what is original is the way Lentricchia places his subjects in a narrative whose guiding principle (p. xiv) is that "all writing of history is also philosophy of history." This is a sophisticated way of saying that *After the New Criticism* is an argumentative book, less a history in the ordinary sense of the word than an extended logical analysis in the Chicago style. The critical test of such a book is not the ordering power of its chronology but the rigor of its logic and the vigor of its rhetoric, and here Lentricchia succeeds. His historiographic principle allows him to think equally strongly about individual critics and about the presuppositions that underlie their work.

After analyzing his five criticisms, therefore, Lentricchia proceeds to a detailed examination of four critics who represent the current American state of the art: Murray Krieger, E. D. Hirsch, Paul de Man, and Harold Bloom. In Lentricchia's reading, each of these men is, in his own way, an heir of the New Critical formalism which "clos[es] off a literary realm from its practical and diacritical relations with other realms" (p. 351). As against this separation—a separation that postromantic critics have always tended to deplore while simultaneously enforcing by means of such concepts as that of the autotelic text—Lentricchia pleads that "the intertextuality of literary discourse is a sign not only of the necessary historicity of literature but, more importantly, of its fundamental entanglement with all discourses" (loc. cit.). The epistemological model that Lentricchia has in mind here is Michel Foucault's "archaeology of knowledge," but even without Foucault's aid Lentricchia's argument is intuitively a strong one. *After the New Criticism* is a strong book in general. It can be recommended both for its informational content and for its polemic.

A more modest but very useful book is *Structuralism and Since: From Lévi-Strauss to Derrida* (Oxford, 1979), ed. John Sturrock. This collection of essays offers critical introductions to the work of Lévi-Strauss (by Dan Sperber), Barthes (Sturrock), Foucault (Hayden White), Lacan (Malcolm Bowie), and Derrida (Jonathan Culler).

"In everyday speech, we do not usually employ economic discourse in its singularly commercial sense, and we rarely, if ever, use it in the specific sense of economic theorists. . . . In practice, our economic consciousness is so integral to our ordinary thought processes that we constantly think *with* economic terms when we wish to think *about* noneconomic matters which affect moral and aesthetic values. (In German, for instance, the rather common word *Schuld* means both 'indebtedness' and 'guilt.') The splintering of economic discourse from other types of valuation (such as the aesthetic or moral) has created a polarized language. . . ." This structuralist thesis, from pages 72–73 of *The Economics of the Imagination* (Mass.), allows Kurt Heinzelman to elaborate a method of pursuing the concept of value to its source in the philosophical grammar that economics shares with poetry. Along the way Heinzelman reads Ruskin and Thoreau, as we might expect, and devotes a chapter to Williams' *Paterson*. But he has also produced such provocative juxtapositions as this: "The process of Frost's ["Mowing"] demonstrates the mystery of the labor process as described by Marx: 'The process disappears in the product. . . . Labour has incorporated itself with its subject: the former is materialized, the latter transformed. That which in the labourer appeared as movement, now appears in the product as a fixed quality without motion'" (p. 192). I have not done the homework in economics that *The Economics of the Imagination* demands, so I am not in a position to criticize this book. But it seems obvious to me that Heinzelman's readings are fruitful ones.

f. Miscellaneous.   Besides a new edition of his *Literary Disruptions* (Illinois; first ed. 1975) Jerome Klinkowitz has published two small collections of essays this year, both from Iowa State. *The American 1960s: Imaginative Acts in a Decade of Change* is a group of studies in art, literature, and music; *The Practice of Fiction in America: Writers from Hawthorne to the Present* wraps nine writers up in the thesis that "In a sense, all American fiction is experimental" (p. 3). Both collections suffer from this kind of overgeneralization; *The American 1960s*, for instance, finds a deep equivalence between the popularity of Frank O'Hara with one audience and the popularity of Rod McKuen with another, on the grounds that "the poet was now expected to speak directly to the people and their everyday concerns" (p. 34; where have you been all this time, Bill Wordsworth?). But there are many local insights, and Klinkowitz's range of reference is wide.

In *Word-Music: The Aesthetic Aspect of Narrative Fiction* (Rutgers) James Guetti distinguishes the visual tendency of narrative, which expresses itself in sequentiality, from the aural, which expresses itself in repetition or, more generally, in any noncognitive arabesque that interrupts the staidly linear progress of the story. Unfortunately, "whether a narrative is voiced or unvoiced is after all a matter of a reader's perception of it, and obviously there is more to that perception than the nature of the work itself. Which is simply to say that whether we are susceptible to visual or aural energies at a given time depends not only upon the formal dynamics of what we are seeing and hearing but also upon our own perceptual tendencies. . . ." (pp. 67–68). This being the case, *Word-Music* works out to not much more than a demonstration of the sensitivity of Guetti's ear. But Guetti's ear *is* sensitive, and his exercises in practical criticism are worth listening to. The authors to whom he listens in greatest detail are Stevens, Anthony Burgess, Conrad, Stephen Crane, Hemingway, and Faulkner.

iii. Conclusion

A number of good specialist books were published this year, of which Chace's *Lionel Trilling* and Lentricchia's *After the New Criticism* are perhaps the most commendable for scholarly elegance. But the one book I think every Americanist ought to read is Novak's *Nature and Culture.* This book alone raises 1980's level of critical achievement above the average.

University of Hawaii

21. Foreign Scholarship

i. East European Contributions[1]

F. Lyra

For reasons which defy judicious explanation, not a single scholarly publication on American literature has reached me from the Soviet Union for the annual report. This is in striking contrast to the gracious cooperation of Soviet Americanists in the past. Nor could any publications be obtained for review from Bulgaria, Czechoslovakia, and Rumania. In the remaining East European countries contributions covered selectively the whole history of American literature, although studies devoted to the literature of the 20th century dominated, quantitatively as well as qualitatively.

Scholarship on the writing of the pre-independence period is represented only by two short articles, one from Yugoslavia, the other from Hungary. Both pieces display opposing interpretations of the dual character of the influence of Puritanism on American individualism. Brankica Pacić's "Uticaj puritanizma na individualističko shvatanje čoveka u Americi" [The Influence of Puritanism on the Development of the Individualistic View of Man in America] (Zbornik Radova Katedre za Anglistiku, Niš:187–99) covers familiar ground, it partly rehashes interpretations of earlier scholars prior to Sacvan Bercovitch, Michael Kammen, and Larzer Ziff, whose work the author apparently does not know. Due to faulty language, the English summary of the article confuses the author's message. In her paper "The Function of Literature in Colonial America (1607–1750)" (Proceedings of the 7th Congress, vol. 1, pp. 53–57), which seems to be an extract of a larger study, the Hungarian scholar Charlotte Kretzoi deals with the problem of Puritanism and individualism parenthetically. Contrary to Pacić, she maintains that during "the Colonial Period . . . the individual was relegated to the background:

1. The material with English summaries of studies in Hungarian was procured for this report through the generous cooperation of Zoltán Abádi-Nagy of the English Department of Kossuth University, Debrecen.

a step backwards into the Middle Ages as compared with the liberating tendencies of the Renaissance." Such a proposition invites controversy. The substance of her study, however, concerns more significant literary problems. Starting from the assumption that the Puritans had their literary theory, Kretzoi effectively shows that this theory was an endemic product, not just an absorption of the classical doctrine of the plain style. She suggests that the term "puritan style" be used to mark the uniqueness of the Puritans' literary principles. Expanded and supported with textual illustrations and bibliographical documentation, her work might serve as an excellent introduction to colonial New England writing.

Interest in 19th-century American literature in the three countries was only slightly more extensive than that in earlier writing. By sheer coincidence the three studies devoted to that period—one from Yugoslavia, two from Poland—deal mostly with metaphysical aspects in the work of a few American authors. "Man in search of context: methaphysical [sic] conception of man in Emerson, Melville, and Stevens" (Zbornik Radova Katedre za Anglistiku, Niš: 125–37) by Ljiljana Bogoeva is based on Kenneth Burke's idea "that all critical and imaginative works represent stylized strategic answers to questions posed by the situation in which they arose." More specifically, following Lionel Trilling's pronouncement in The Opposing Self that the self has been the central preoccupation of the literature of the last century and a half, characterized by an "adverse imagination of the culture in which it has its being," Bogoeva speculates on the three varieties of the "opposing self" as represented by Emerson, Melville, and Stevens and then analyzes in detail Emerson's concept of the self as revealed in Nature and the Journals. By arguing that his ideas of man were not inconsistent but only different stances within the self, she finds herself in agreement with an identical thesis put forward by Jeffrey L. Duncan in The Power and Form of Emerson's Thought (see ALS 1973, pp. 4–5).

As a spiritual and poetic force Emerson figures prominently in Aleksander Rogalski's study of Emily Dickinson, the first extensive Polish biography of the poet, "Emily Dickinson," in Annetta i Emilia (pp. 137–258). Although Rogalski devotes more than half of his work to Dickinson's life, he manages to draw a comprehensive picture of the variety of forms, styles, and range of subject matter of her poetry. In its interpretation he betrays a bias in favor of her moral

and religious ideas, ascribing them a profundity with which few
critics would entirely agree. At least he admits that many of her
poems allow several readings. In an article, "Metafizyczny nurt w
poezji Emily Dickinson" [The Metaphysical Current in Emily Dickinson's poetry] (*W Drodze* 3:70–80), Rogalski concentrates on the
religious strain in her poetry, stressing Christologial elements.

Studies in 20th-century American prose were with two exceptions confined to post-World War II writers. One of the exceptions
is József Gellén's "Willa Cather and O. E. Rölvaag: Two Ways of
Looking at the Immigrant in Fiction" (*HSE* 13:117–23). The relevance of the theme (Cather and Rølvaag appear rarely in comparative light) and the author's deft generalizations of both novelists'
different perception and creative treatment of the immigrant are
insufficiently backed up by textual exemplification. The other is
Maria Łobzowska's "The Tragic Implications of Henry James's Social Novels" (*Prace Naukowe Uniwersytetu Śląskiego Prace Historyczno-Literackie* 15:37–47). The title promises more than the
article delivers. Opening with the (false) assumption that "there are
scarcely any works analyzing and discussing his social novels," Lob-
zowska sets out to correct the scholars' (supposed) negligence on
eight pages filled with trivial generalizations.

Among the contributions on contemporary American fiction, Zoltán Abády-Nagy's is the most thoughtful. In contrast to the fashionable nihilistic readings of Barthelme, Heller, Vonnegut, and others,
Abády-Nagy demonstrates that "the authors . . . evaluate unwhole-
some modern developments from a broad humanitarian basis. The
very idea of progress is not derided, only its contradictory nature
ascertained, its perverse developments diagnosed and ironically
treated as regressional." In his article "An Ironic Reversal: Progress
as an Entropic Force in Recent American Fiction" (*HSE* 13:85–92)
he argues convincingly that the entropic force gave American novelists "new themes and new ways of artistic rendering." Their satirical
treatment of progress is a manifestation of their desire "to exercise
moral control over progress." For Elżbieta Foeller irony is also a
touchstone for interpreting John Barth's and John Gardner's fiction,
"The Mythical Heroes of John Barth and John Gardner" (Kwartalnik
Neofilologiczny 2:183–97). In her analysis of Barth's novels, *Lost in
the Funhouse* and *Chimera*, Foeller does not move beyond the interpretations of others. Her reading of Gardner's novel *Grendel* and

the narrative poem *Jason and Medeia* is lucid and, as far as I can tell, original. But her implied promise to compare the function of myth in both writers' works has been only partly fulfilled: she notes similarities yet fails to point out the differences.

Surprisingly Carson McCullers has emerged for study. Her novels and stories are well known in Poland, but they are rarely discussed in scholarly periodicals. This year Marzenna Rączkowska's "The Patterns of Love in Carson McCullers' Fiction" (*SAP* 12:169–76) constitutes a welcome break in the negligence, short as it is. But the theme Rączkowska brings to bear on the writer's work is narrow to the point of misreading, although she realizes that pain, solitude, betrayal are as crucial conditions in the existence of McCullers' characters as love is.

Interest in 20th-century American poetry continues to be low. There are only two articles, one devoted to Sylvia Plath, the other to Theodore Roethke. In "The Hate Poems of Sylvia Plath" (*Prace Naukowe Uniwersytetu Śląskiego Prace Historyczno-Literackie* 15: 7–16) Maria Aniśkiewicz-Świderska, following David Holbrook's quasi-psychological approach (see *ALS 1976*, pp. 348–49), perceives "a reversal of values in her poetry," and argues quite successfully that "what is personal and individual in her experience is skillfully transmuted into the culturally symbolic and universal and given external order." An opposite view of Plath's poems is expressed by Agnieszka Salska in "The Poetry of the Disintegrating Self: Theodore Roethke" (*Acta Universitatis Lodziensis*, Seria I, 66:27–42). Salska insists that Plath's confessional poems do not "transcend the limits of personal unhappiness; they fail to show more than herself." As to Roethke's poetry, it is therapeutic, its main purpose is "to prevent the final dissolution of the self."

Krzysztof Andrzejczak's "Początki literatury murzyńskiej w Stanach Zjednoczonych" [The Beginnings of Negro Literature in the United States] (*Acta Universitatis Lodziensis*, Seria I,66:191–217) contributes to the diversity of this year's Polish interest in American literature and nothing else. The article is derivative and surveyish. The author would have rendered greater service had he published it in a popular literary weekly rather than in a scholarly annual of diminutive circulation.

In the study of American drama Peter Egri continues to produce valuable work on O'Neill, thanks to his comparative method. In two publications he examines the points of contact between some of Chekhov's plays and O'Neill's, which he discovers in a number of relationships between the short story and both playwrights' dramas, "A Touch of the Story-Teller: The Dramatic Function of the Short Story Model in Chekhov's Uncle Vanya and O'Neill's A Touch of the Poet" (*HSE* 13:93–113), and "The Reinterpretation of the Chekhovian Mosaic Design in O'Neill's Long Day's Journey Into Night" (*Acta Litteraria* 13,i–ii:29–71). With piercing intelligence Egri analyzes both playwrights' dramas against a wide literary and philosophical background and examines the similarities as well as differences between Chekhov's and O'Neill's techniques in the context of the two authors' views of the world and attitudes to their themes. Equally wide-ranging, though less analytical, is his "The Epic Tradition of the European Drama and the Birth of the American Tragedy" (*Proceedings of the 8th Congress*, vol. 1, pp. 753–59). Egri's main purpose is to test Goethe's views on the difference between the epic and the dramatic motivations of action (progressive, retrogressive, retarding) by applying them to a brief interpretation of O'Neill's *Strange Interlude*. He concludes that, like Brecht, O'Neill was in his later plays "successful in integrating epic and dramatic features . . . into a veritable artistic synthesis."

The two Polish contributions to the study of American drama are of an informative nature. Teresa Pyzik's "Amerykańska warsztatowa krytyka dramatu" [American workshop criticism] (Przegląd Humanistyczny 1:109–16) is a good survey of the subject. Edward Szynal's "Arthur Miller's Reputation in Poland Between 1946 and 1966" (*Acta Universitatis Wratislaviensis Anglica Wratislaviensis 7* [1979]:89–99) reviews Miller's Polish reception in literary magazines and periodicals. Szynal has studied the ideological and literary background which shaped Miller's reception, and he presents a sensible account of the Polish critics' conception of Miller's art in general and their controversial reactions to the 38 stagings of the particular plays: *All My Sons* (six), *The Crucible* (seven), *A View from the Bridge* (ten), *Death of a Salesman* (ten), *After the Fall* (one), *Incident at Vichy* (four).

American literary criticism is only sporadically submitted to scrutiny in East European countries outside the Soviet Union. This year Ratomir Ristić comments on Eliot in "T. S. Eliot i knjizevna interpretacija" [T. S. Eliot and the Art of Interpretation] (*Zbornik*

Radova Katedre za Anglistiku, Niš 201–11). In the soundly documented study the Yugoslav scholar takes issue with Eliot's view that the duty of the critic is to compare and analyze and not to interpret the meaning of a poem. In Ristić's opinion, "Eliot seems to forget that by comparing and analyzing, the critic illuminates (Eliot's favourite word), i.e., explains the meanings which cannot be grasped without much effort." On the other hand Ristić approves of Eliot's skepticism about the value of interpreting poetry by exploring its origins, which "may help us better understand the poet but not his poetry." Two articles on American criticism were published in Poland, one by Irena Przemecka, "Negro Critics on Negro Literature" (*SAP* 12:151–56), which deals inconclusively with the question of black writers' racial and aesthetic identity, the other by Stanislaw Dąbrowski, "William K. Wimsatt o wykładni jako ocenie" [William K. Wimsatt on Explication as Criticism] (*Teksty* 1:144–59), which is a toughly reasoned devastating attack on Wimsatt's system of critical values in general and his "Explication as Criticism" (in *The Verbal Icon*) in particular. Dąbrowski accuses Wimsatt of chaotic reasoning and lapses in aesthetic judgment and thought; he even disapproves of Wimsatt's respect for Croce. His greatest errors, Dąbrowski says, are his inability to differentiate between literary explication and literary criticism and his identification of criticism with evaluation.

Enikö Bollobás's essay "Speech Acts in Literature" (*HSE* 13:39–47) provides a reasonable pretext to avoid ending this report on Dąbrowski's vitriolic note. Bollobás has tested John L. Austin's and John Searle's philosophies of language on a large body (too large in my opinion) of American fiction, poetry, and drama, from Mark Twain through Pound, Fitzgerald, and William Carlos Williams to representatives of the Black Mountain School. (It should be noted that the speech-act theory has been critically modified by Stanley Fish in this year's *Is There a Text in This Class?*) Bollobás uses Austin's and Searle's ideas with tactful restraint, which is the more commendable as the proliferation of epigonic criticism on the one hand and aesthetic doctrinairism on the other tend to diminsh the value of the pluralistic approach to literary studies.

University of Warsaw

ii. French Contributions

Marc Chénetier

As I take over this section from Maurice Couturier, may I be allowed
to pay this friend a brief tribute for the work accomplished over
the years, and ask the readers of this year's report their forgiveness
for the let-down occasioned by the switch? Maurice Couturier unfortunately ended last year's report on what has become a bitter
note: deploring Sartre's death, he hoped "Barthes would remain
with us for a long time." The latter's untimely demise in 1980 sent
a long ripple of mourning through all lovers of literature and literary
criticism and scholarship.

This year the abundance of French production can hardly be
said to have abated, as the growth of magazines and reviews dealing
with American literature seems to confirm itself as time goes by.

a. **Bibliography.** Jean-Marie Bonnet has put together a "dossier
critique" on Edgar Allan Poe (1955–75) for the benefit of French
readers in an issue of *Romantisme* (27:129–38). The differences between American and French "readings" of Poe are highlighted.

There has been a reprint of Jacques-Fernand Cahen's *La Littérature Américaine* in the celebrated "aide-mémoire" collection of
the Presses Universitaires de France (Que Sais-Je?) after years of
being out of print. Issuing a seventh edition with too little revision
creates such misstatements as including McCullers, Mailer, Capote,
Salinger, Ellison, Kerouac, etc. as the "young generation." The need
for a revised edition is obvious.

Elements that may complete the extensive Afro-American Bibliography compiled last year by Michel and Geneviève Fabre can be
found this year in numbers 10 to 13 of the *AFRAM Newsletter* put
out by M. Fabre's research center (Recherches Afro-Américaines)
at the University of Paris III. Bibliographies on Stein, Capote and
the American theatre will also be found at the end of the specialized
issues of magazines listed below.

b. **18th- and 19th-Century Literature.** In a new series which Liliane
Abensour and Françoise Charras have, darkly indeed, entitled "Le

Choix du Noir" (Paris: Editions J.M. Place), these two colleagues
have transplanted and presented Charles Brockden Brown's *Edgar
Huntly* under the title *Edgar Huntly ou Les Mémoires d'un Somnam-
bule.* Another of Brown's books is announced, as well as some of
Hawthorne's writings.

Melville is the subject of Régis Durand's article "Melville et ses
signes: violence première" (Régis Durand, ed. *Le Discours de la
Violence,* pp. 19–34), which is a part of his remarkable 1980 book:
Melville: Signes et Métaphores (Lausanne: L'Age d'Homme). To
the six parts of his study (La Fiction et ses Abords, Jeux de l'Imaginaire et du Symbolique, La Métaphore Sans Limites, Stratégies et
Modèles dans *Moby-Dick* et *The Confidence Man,* Le Roi Captif
(on *Pierre*) and Pour Lire Melville), Durand has added a stimulating
translation of the unpublished fragment "John Marr." Fed by contemporary theory (Lacan, Derrida, Deleuze) this study takes us
resolutely away from the rut of endless metaphysical interpretations,
toward a central interrogation on evasive and illusory meaning. The
metaphorical process in Melville is, according to Durand, the exponent of an unstable, troubled and fragmented vision, alien to the
everlasting quest for a transcendental signified which most Melville
scholarship postulates. From a neighboring perspective Michel
Granger has written "Le Discours Cétologique et le Corps dans
Moby-Dick" as a chapter of *Corps Création,* pp. 13–24.

Moving back in time and back towards interpretation and meaning, Jean Béranger, in his own edition of *Le Facteur Religieux en
Amérique du Nord* studies the "Interprétation et Utilisation de
l'Apocalypse par Jonathan Edwards" (pp. 31–48) while, in the same
volume, Bernard Chevignard comments upon Warville and Crévecoeur ("Une Apocalypse sécularisée: le Quakerisme selon Brissot
de Warville et St John de Crévecoeur," pp. 49–68). Jean Béranger
had published an excerpt from J. M. Bonnet's thesis last year (see
ALS 1979) in another publication of the Centre de Recherches
Anglo-Américaines. The whole of this dissertation is now available
from Ann Arbor (Univ. Microfilms): *The Emergence of Literary
Criticism in America, 1783–1836.* Moving further away from colonial
times, Jean Cazemajou in *Le Facteur Religieux* analyzes the double
reflexion on "Apocalypse and Utopia in American Literature at the
end of the nineteenth century" (pp. 69–84). The dialectics of catas-
trophic information and speculation on the one hand and millenial

hopes on the other activates, he writes, the thought of writers in the 1890s. Joaquin Miller, Donnelly, Twain, Howells, and Bellamy provide his illustrations. Jean Cazemajou, a specialist of Stephen Crane, has also published "L'Autre Visage de Stephen Crane: le 'comédien'" (*EA* 76:88–104) in which he argues for a little-known aspect of Crane's personality usually eclipsed by the gloom of his naturalistic outlook.

On Henry James, reminders are in order: in 1979, Jean Perrot published an article unreported in last year's review: "Henry James: Stratégie Littéraire et Constitution de l'Image de Lettres" (*Littérature* 33[1979]:37–57). Also in 1979, in *Le Discours de la Violence*, Nancy Blake, whose dissertation on Henry James should be defended in 1981, published "Hystérie, Langue et Violence dans *Les Ailes de la Colombe*" (*The Wings of the Dove*) (pp. 35–46).

Finally, to close this section, I must mention a book and an article which, although they deal with material that is not always considered as "literary," actually matters to anybody concerned with artistic expression in words, from the philological scholar of sources to the analyst of intertextuality and levels of discourse within a literary text: Michel Oriano's book on the songs of lumbermen, tramps, and cowboys (*Les Travailleurs de la Frontière*, Paris: Payot) and Monique Lecomte's analysis of workers' songs of protest: "De la Violence à l'Ordre: les chants de revendication ouvrière (1865–1900)," in *Le Discours de la Violence* (pp. 165–92).

This last foray into "minority" or submerged cultures invites me to continue dealing with margins here, either racial or ethnic, or those of alien worlds and visions. Three publications dominate the field this year in France: a collection of essays edited by Michel Fabre, *Regards sur la Littérature Noire Américaine/French Approaches to Black American Literature* (Paris: Publications de la Sorbonne Nouvelle) features articles by Gérard Cordesse ("the Two Models in Toomer's *Cane*, pp. 9–43), Michel Fabre ("Richard Wright's 'The Man Who Killed a Shadow,' A Study in Compulsion," pp. 44–64), Simone Vauthier ("Of African Queens and Afro-American Princes: Miscegenation in *Old Hepsy*," pp. 65–107), G. Balmir ("Le Chant Spirituel et le Chant Sermon," pp. 109–53) and a collective essay authored by Fabre's seminar "Réactions Francaises à la Littérature Noire Américaine."

One of the full-length books published in France in 1980 deals with the presence of Mexican-Americans in American literature. Marcienne Rocard, whose dissertation on the subject won high praise, has entitled her study *Les Fils du Soleil: La Minorité Mexicaine à travers la Littérature des Etats-Unis* (Paris: Maisonneuve). The cultural dilemma of the Mexican-American and the double image of his identity that prevails both in his own production and in that of the "anglos" is at the center of the problem as m. Rocard sees it. This is a theme which she also develops in her article "Le Paradoxe du Mexicain-Américain: étranger dans son pays," to be found in a special issue of *RFEA* (9:203–40) dedicated to "L'Etranger—'the other, the alien'—dans la culture Américaine" and edited by J. Cazemajou. In this article (pp. 59–66) the evolution of the Mexican-American's dilemma is illustrated through the respective presentations of the "poncho," the "pachuco" and the "chicano." Most articles in this special issue deal with aspects of the problem that are nonliterary, but Geneviève Fabre's "Le Nouveau Théâtre Noir et la Problématique d'une Culture Populaire Afro-Américaine dans le Ghetto" (pp. 25–34) shows how the new black theatre has entered the debate that opposes such as believe "black culture is to be considered mostly as a lower-class culture—a 'culture of poverty'—and those who approach it as a diversified, complex, and distinct entity." Fabre concludes that "the theatre shows the creative process through which a culture evolves both from the reality of black experience and from the symbolic quality of the political imagination." On the border between literature and lexicology, Henri Bejoint shows "the evolution in the attitude of the American society towards 'ethnopaulisms,' which have recently been included in dictionaries from which they used to be barred." This remarkable article is entitled "La Représentation de l'étranger dans le lexique américain" (pp. 107–16).

From a somewhat different point of view, Geneviève Hily-Mane has devoted two of her recent articles on Hemingway to the relationship of this author to foreign languages in general ("Hemingway et les Langues Etrangères," Reims: *L'Ailleurs dans la Littérature Anglo-Américaine*) and to Swahili in particular ("Hemingway et le Swahili," Ghana: *Actes du Colloque de Cape Coast*).

Finally, the absolutely alien terrain of science fiction and utopia have provided interesting grounds for analysis. Jean Raynaud, whose "doctorat d'Etat" (Univ. of Paris III) on the theory of science fiction was defended in 1980, has also published two articles in *Inter-*

férences (Univ. de Haute-Bretagne): "Utopie et Science-Fiction" (10:96–126) and "Science-Fiction and New Fiction" (10:88–95). John Dean assigns three objectives to his "Strangely Familiar Forms: Exploitations of Romance in American Science-Fiction and Fantasy" (*RFEA* 9:149–58): "To clarify the relationships existing between 'romance', fantasy and science-fiction in modern American literature; to explore the basis of this relationship in Hawthorne, Melville and Poe"; and finally "to show the aesthetic value of the relationships entertained with romance by four fantasy and science fiction novels: *The Compleat Enchanter, Forbidden Planet, The Wind Whales of Ishmaël,* and *Merlin's Mirror.*"

c. 20th-Century Poetry. A colloquium organized in Amiens by the Centre d'Etudes Américaines of the Université de Picardie has given birth to a volume entitled *Amérique, Ecriture, Argent,* containing two articles centered on Ezra Pound. Jean-Michel Rabaté, encouraged by Pound himself to pun on the theme, has given the poet a sterling reference ("Pound/£") in order to explore the relationship entertained by Pound with currency and monetary signs. The links between signs and value, symbolic and ideological rates of exchange, the overwhelming presence of usury in Pound's thought and the conspicuous absence of added value provide the main articulations of this article. The libidinal and sexual prolongations of the theme are not omitted in a piece that wonderfully exemplifies the most intelligent use to which contemporary theories may be put. Jacques Darras, editor of this volume, follows an itinerary: "De Pound à *Paterson* par Pleynet" (pp. 17–28). A Freudian thread links Pound and Williams, running through an article largely based on Marcellin Pleynet's "La Compromission Poétique" (*Art et Littérature,* Paris: Le Seuil, 1977). Economic theory is seen as more or less explicitly integrated to the work of the two poets and the notion of poetic "investment" is of course at the heart of Darras' discussion. Darras edits a magazine (*In'Hui,* Amiens) which also published several translations of American poets in 1979. Translation of poetry is becoming quite active these days in France and we may expect quite a few collections of American poetry in translation next year, particularly Patchen and Williams.

Le Discours de la Violence contains an interesting analysis by Jean-Philippe Lecourt: "Langage et Violence chez Theodore

Roethke" (pp. 137–64). The focus here is on the particular oscillation between deconstruction and reconstruction to be found in Roethke's writing and the temptation of a "reterritorialization" that would be both Oedipian and linguistic in scope; the "rage" with which Roethke says he is "eating himself up" finds here clear articulations.

Finally, Marc Chénetier's "thèse d'Etat" on Vachel Lindsay (*L'Obsession des Signes: L'Esthétique de Vachel Lindsay*, Univ. of Paris III) is now available from Ann Arbor (Univ. Microfilms). It attempts to destroy the clichés of the "jingleman" and the "jazz poet" as dominant images and to underline and analyze the visual components of Lindsay's imagination and poetic praxis, as well as the modernity of a poet obsessed with semiotic processes. Chénetier has also published this year an article on Vachel Lindsay's motion picture analyses, the first ever (1915) written in book form: "Vachel Lindsay as Movie Critic," *Amerikastudien*, 24:i:81–98.

d. **Drama.**   The year 1980 has been particularly rich in the field of theatre studies in this country; outside of the special issue of *RFEA* mentioned below (10) and entirely dedicated to the theatre in America, several articles have come out. Marie-Claire Pasquier, who edited the special issue, has also published two articles (on Tennessee Williams and Edward Albee) in *Encyclopaedia Universalis*. *Regards sur la Littérature* contains an article by Geneviève Fabre on "Le Théâtre d'Ed Bullins et la Rhétorique du Blues" (pp. 155–201). "The Free Southern Theatre: 1963–1979," also by Geneviève Fabre (*Amst* 25:270–78) "attempts to give an account of the FST, a radical theatre group that performed in the South of the United States, but also of the many problems and contradictions it faced during the 15 years of its existence." In a similar vein, Liliane Kerjan, author of a well-known book on Albee, gives an overall view of "les théâtres populaires aux Etats-Unis en 1979" (*Situations Contemporaines du théâtre populaire en Amérique, Paris: Klincksieck, pp. 21–46). *RFEA* already carried one article on the theatre: Jean Normand's "Le poète image de l'étranger: l'Orphée de Tennessee Williams" (9:117–26), in which Normand contended that most of Williams' characters are avatars of Orpheus. Number 10 of this review is entitled "Les Théâtres de l'Amérique," a plural justified by the diversity of the types analyzed. In "Metatheatre" (pp. 187–98), C. W. E. Bigsby tries to apply some concepts of "post-modernism" to the American theatre, and particularly self-consciousness. Most of his analysis is concerned with Albee's theatre. In "Une Nouvelle Théâtralité: La Performance" (pp. 199–206), Régis Durand argues that "performance" is not a new "genre," but "a new attitude which privileges the notion of process"; his examples run from Spalding Gray and Elizabeth Lecompte to Meredith Monk and Joan La Barbara. Herbert Blau's long life in the theatre finds its usual lucid, brilliant, and warm expression in a semi-autobiographical text entitled "A Dove in My Chimney" (pp. 209–16). Four useful interviews are gathered in this issue: one of Joseph Chaikin ("The Actor Still Present," pp. 217–22), one of Meredith Monk by M. C. Pasquier ("The Sybil," pp. 223–26), one of Robert Wilson by Claude Grimal ("A Propos d'Edison," pp. 227–30) and one of Ron Jenkins on the "Mudhead Masks" by Liliane Kerjan (pp. 255–58). Françoise Kourilisky, author of *Le Théâtre aux Etats-Unis* (1967) sends a "Lettre de New York" (pp. 231–33), in which she tells of her own work on Jane Bowles's *In the Summer House*. Michel Rémy and Jean Marie Bonnet describe in "La Présence Américaine au Festival Mondial de Théâtre de Nancy" (pp. 235–48) the various aspects of American participation in the Festival which Jack Lang, now French Minister of Culture, launched in 1962. Their archives put forward three trends: "militant theatre," "theatre of the body," and "political theatre." Yves-Charles Grandjeat writes briefly (pp. 249–54) of "Le Théâtre Chicano en marge de Zoot-Suit: Dixième Festival Tenaz" and analyzes the tenth festival of Chicano theatres organized in June 1979 by the Teatro Nacional de Aztlan. Geneviève Fabre has yet another article in this issue (pp. 259–70) on Ntozake Shange's choreographic poem and drama "For Colored Girls Who Have Considered Suicide When the Rainbow is Enuf," where she tries "to account for the continuity in the Afro-American dramatic tradition as well as for some new directions offered by the drama of the 1970s." For Liliane Kerjan ("Sam Shepard et l'invisibile espace," pp. 271–83), Shepard "beguiles our disbelief" and "with his emphasis on language" may be "the alternative American theatre." Michel Fabre, finally, has concocted a "montage documentaire" entitled "Les avatars d'Amiri Baraka, citoyendramaturge" (pp. 285–94), in which he asks a number of questions on Baraka's shifts in ideology and examines them in relation to his aesthetics. An excellent bibliography (recent items only) completes this special issue on the theatre in America.

Marie-Claire Pasquier wonders whether Gertrude Stein's theatre is "post-modern" (*Delta* 10:43–60), questioning in the process, the validity of the adjective itself. From *Doctor Faustus Lights the Lights* to *Four Saints in Three Acts*, however, she traces the presence of elements that may justify a "post-modern reading" of the plays.

e. **Twentieth Century Fiction.** This section is, as usual, the most "crowded": the French seem in general to have more of a soft spot for American fiction than for either poetry or drama, and the scholarly production of 1980 reflects this state of things. A long tradition has accorded one of the first places to William Faulkner and this year seems to bear it out, all the more so as Faulkner was on the "agrégation" syllabus for 1980–81. This fact prompted *RANAM*, under the enlightened direction of one of the best Faulkner specialists, André Bleikasten, to put out a special issue (No. 13) dedicated entirely to *Requiem for a Nun*. Six articles, of diverse interest, deal respectively with "Genèse et avatars de *Requiem for a Nun* (Michel Gresset, pp. 5–37); "Le Sud dans les prologues de *Requiem for a Nun* (Jean Rouberol, pp. 38–47); "Naissance d'un sujet collectif: Jefferson" (Jacqes Pothier, pp. 46–63), where the three chapters of introduction are shown to be the basis for the constitution of a collective identity; "Nun out of Habit: Nancy Mannigoe, Gavin Stevens and *Requiem for a Nun* (Noel Polk, pp. 64–75); "L'Education de Temple Drake" (André Bleikasten, pp. 76–89); and "The Rebounding Images of Faulkner's *Sanctuary* and *Requiem for a Nun*" (Patrick Samway, pp. 90–111).

André Bleikasten has published "Pan Pierrot, ou les premiers masques de Faulkner" (*RLC* 53[1979]:299–310). Etienne de Planchard has a sociologically informative article on "Créoles et quarteronnes ou le rôle des femmes dans la critique sociale et politique de G. W. Cable" (*Caliban* 17:149–56).

A variety of articles have been published on authors of the '20s and '30s. Elizabeth Béranger, a specialist of Djuna Barnes, has two new essays: "La Femme Invisible: Introduction à l'écriture de Djuna Barnes" in *Caliban* (17:99–110) and in *Le Facteur Religieux:* "*Nightwood* ou l'Anti-Millénium" (pp. 107–20). The first revolves around the now-frequent question of whether there are determining signs in feminine writing, a question that was at the center of Elizabeth

Béranger's earlier work. The second aims at showing that *Nightwood* is an "apocalyptic text." A "prophetic tone" and "hyperbolic writing" unite to the point of incoherence. The narrative, for E. Béranger, "inverts the message of hope" transmitted by an "apocalyptic discourse."

Sinclair, Steinbeck, and Dreiser present facets of a "family tradition" of realism. Robert Sihol in "Steinbeck et la Crise de 1929: *The Grapes of Wrath* et le Sujet Collectif" (GRENA); André Muraire in "L'Apocalypse selon Sinclair" (*Le Facteur Religieux*, pp. 85–106); and Michel Labarde in "Superstition, Religion et Religiosité dans les trois ouvrages autobiographiques de Théodore Dreiser: *A Hoosier Holiday, Newspaper Days* et *Dawn*" (*Le Facteur Religieux*, pp. 207–27) severally underline little-known or neglected aspects of writers whose supposed straightforward grappling with reality is shown to be relative.

Nancy Blake is the editor of the tenth number of *Delta*, centered on Gertrude Stein. Blake's own essay, "Here and Now with Gertrude Stein" (pp. 1–10) introduces this number in three parts. "Gertrude Stein and Us" includes "Ring a Ring o'Roses: Le Cercle Enchanté de Gertrude Stein," by Jean Marcet (pp. 11–18), where homophony is systematically explored; "Melanctha and Metonymy," by Millicent Bell (pp. 19–32), an essay which concludes that "perhaps the governing theme of 'Melanctha' is the irreconcilable disparity between individuals"; "La Musique de Gertrude Stein," by Claude Grimal (pp. 33–42), one of the translators of Stein into French; and the drama article by Pasquier mentioned above. Part 2—"Reading Gertrude Stein"—is made up of three articles which all rely on very close textual reading. Noëlle Batt's "Gertrude Stein ou la composition faite sens: *An Exercise in Analysis*; an Analysis of the Exercise" (pp. 61–89) deals with metrical structure, a misshapen dramatic structure, and a formal structure of exchange and a structure of self-generation, concluding that the configuration of the text itself becomes its meaning. Gérard Cordesse in "Sur les Falaises de Stein: la lecture-limite" (pp. 89–102) reinstates the necessity for a reading that incorporates communication, defining the critic's primary functions as a sorting out of lines, a triumph over noise and a clear demonstration of the powers of language. "La Théâtralité" ("the dramatic quality") of language in Gertrude Stein is the theme of Jacky Martin's article (pp. 103–20). The third section ("Writing writing") consists in a semifictional take-off on Gertrude Stein by Harry Blake, who mixes invention ("Biddle-Making Gertrude Stein") and critical notations (pp. 121–28), and an extended bibliography.

Moving closer to our period, let us mention, in stride, a marvelously clear and pedagogical theoretical piece by André Bleikasten, which may well serve as our introduction to critical productions on contemporary texts: "The Paradox of the True Lie: On the Fictionality of Fiction" (*Amst* 25:406–17) has it that "the assumptions behind most postmodern novels are . . . indebted to postromantic idealism" and that, "far from being a radical departure from modernism, postmodernism has been so far little more than the actualization of its disruptive potentialities." Bleikasten concludes that even for the most adventurous practitioners of new fiction, "writing fictions is still an attempt to encounter the world, and even their seemingly perverse impulse to expose them *as* fictions points paradoxically to an irrepressible concern for truth."

Paying our respects to the recently departed dean of contemporary fiction in the United States, I will first briefly mention the existence of two articles on the work of Henry Miller; one due to Jean-Michel Rabaté, who, with his customary acumen and culture, studies "L'idéologie entre violence symbolique et viol imaginaire: Broch et Miller" (*Le Discours de la Violence*, pp. 73–98) and the other by François Lecercle (*Corps Création*) entitled "Il n'y a rien— "There is nothing"–La fantasmatique du Corps dans *Tropic of Capricorn.*" But the number and variety of articles on recent American fiction is embarrassing as far as logical presentation is concerned: one might as well go alphabetically as borrow any other means of organization. However, if one may postulate a movement that progressively drifts away from modernism and/or realism, the respective studies of Joyce Carol Oates, Saul Bellow, and John Updike seem bound to take precedence. A study of "Le Discours de la Violence dans la Fiction de Joyce Carol Oates" is due to Judith Heerswinghels (*Le Discours de la Violence*, pp. 47–72). For her, the world of Oates is in the tradition of the grotesque, akin to an art of the monstrous and of deformity which "compels us to perceive the defects of our system." A publication of the University of Reims (*Aspects du Sacré dans la Littérature Anglo-Américaine*) published a study by Elizabeth Boulot called "Désacralisation et profanation du sacré dans *Couples* de John Updike" (pp. 131–46) and one by

Colette Gerbaud on Saul Bellow: "Aventure(s) et Sacré dans *Les Aventures d'Augie March*" (pp. 107–30). There is another article on Bellow in *Le Facteur Religieux*: Elyette Labarthe, "L'Apocalypse selon Saul Bellow" (pp. 121–42).

A hinge figure in many aspects, Truman Capote is the theme of the 11th number of *Delta*, edited by Régis Durand. Mostly centered on *In Cold Blood* and *Other Voices, Other Rooms*, this 100-page number makes for interesting and varied reading. Robert C. Davis in "*Other Voices, Other Rooms* and the Ocularity of American Fiction" (pp. 1–14) conducts a Freudian and Lacanian analysis of the text. Fabienne Durand-Bogaert studies "death and stasis" in the same book (pp. 15–24) and detects "the death of the labour of the sign" at the center of a thematically death-oriented text. J. M. Rabaté's short contribution (pp. 25–30), "Being read to by a boy, waiting for rain," is a pleasantly written text which explores the relationships of Joël and the Law. The last text to deal with this book is Nancy Blake's "Southern Gothic or Medieval Quest?" (pp. 31–47), where she explores the links the text entertains with the legends of the Grail inasmuch as the latter deals fundamentally with the unacceptable nature of paternity.

Dianne Grantham opens the second part with "*In Cold Blood: Ambiguïtés*" (pp. 49–68) in which the status of the real in Capote's tale is analyzed, not always convincingly. More traditional in his approach, J. M. Bonnet writes in "*In Cold Blood* et le roman policier" (pp. 69–74) that both this book and the related genre are "a staging, a spectacle, an exorcism." Bonnet is the author of the bibliography that closes this collection of essays, while Régis Durand concludes the analytical part with "Le Retour de la Fiction" (pp. 75–88), a reflection on the texts published in the New York magazine *Interview* between June 1979 and 1980.

Régis Durand has published two similar articles on Capote and Barthelme: one of them ("On Conversing: In/On Writing," *Sub-Stance* 27:47–51) extends his reflection on these two authors to the work of William Gaddis. The other in *Amérique, Ecriture, Argent* ("Notes sur les Voix et les Transactions dans le roman américain contemporain," pp. 29–38) links the notions of voice and money, of transaction and signature. In the same publication is another article dealing with the work of Donald Barthelme: Jean Bissière's "Donald Barthelme: Good Old Money" (pp. 39–50). In Barthelme's use of money as theme, Bissière sees the "frame of transactional psychology." Indeed, most of the team which had produced the special issues of *Delta, Trema,* and *Revue Française d'Etudes Américaines* on contemporary fiction these last years has, this year, produced new critical material in a more dispersed manner. Another member of André LeVot's research team, Pierre Gault, has published "Le narrateur et les autres dans *The Blood Oranges*" (*RFEA* 9:137-48), while Marc Chénetier wrote the Hawkes and Barth articles for *Encyclopaedia Universalis,* and Maurice Couturier the Nabokov article. Sylvie Mathé's analysis of enunciation and the narrator's psychology and stategy in *Second Skin* was published this year ("Mon évocation à travers un verre doré": L'énonciation dans *Cassandra,*" *Poétique* 44:504-14).

A bulky *Cahier de l'Herne* which came out in 1979 on Gothicism (*Le Romantisme Noir,* ed. L. Abensour and F. Charras; Paris: l'Herne) contained an article by Marc Chénetier ("Le Monstre et les Discours," pp. 351-56) dealing with the discursive struggles taking place at the heart of Richard Brautigan's *The Hawkline Monster.* Another collection of studies of discourse (*Le Discours de la Violence*) contained another essay by the same author dealing with the "Gonzo Journalism" of Hunter Thompson: "Las Vegas Parano: L'Expressionisme de Hunter Thompson" (pp. 99-116) in which Chénetier studies the formal and rhetorical devices and figures by which Thompson represents paroxysm. In the same volume there is, to conclude this list of articles on contemporary fiction, a brilliant essay by Claudine Thomas on Thomas Pynchon: "Une Parabole du Pouvoir: lecture de *The Crying of Lot 49*" (pp. 117-36). Entropy and the play with codes within the narrative are not the only themes broached here: the devices of symbolic exchange are studied on the level of syntax and formal manipulation in a most convincing manner.

It should be mentioned also that several texts of fiction have found their way into French this year in *Bas de Casse* (Paris), a new magazine dedicated to fiction and poetry. Grace Paley and Robert Coover have had texts translated in the first three issues. Other texts by Barthelme, Baumbach, and Coover are announced for the next issues.

To conclude this presentation of the 1980 vintage, let me allude to three pieces of work which may stand as symbols of the work done in France this year: studies in a lighter vein, they are nonetheless methodologically very sophisticated. Rolande Diot has studied

Benchley's word plays in "De l'Aliénation à l'Altérité: les jeux de Benchley sur les signes du monde" (*RFEA* 9:127–36) and shown how Benchley's "Little Man" follows an itinerary that could be described as a farcical, neosurrealistic search for a "Semiology of Chaosmos." Meanwhile, Robert Silhol has dedicated a part of his sociological and pschoanalytical talent to an examination of . . . *Love Story*: "*Love Story* as a Metaphor of War: A research on the sociological conditons of the production of literature" (*RFEA* 9: 159–72).

Last, but not least, the humorous note spread by its editor, Daniel Royot, through the fourth issue of *RFEA* dedicated in 1977 to "American Humor" is taken up in his recently published dissertation: *L'Humour Américain, Des Puritains aux Yankees (1620–1860)* (Presses Universitaires de Lyon). Although not directly literary in scope, this book may well be worth the literary reader's while: it will constantly remind him that literary reading, study, and analysis are and should always remain a pleasure, and prevent him from taking the impact of his own endeavors too seriously. However important the work furnished in the field of American literature in France this year, it is a rewarding thing to realize that most of its authors, while generally rather at ease with critical tools of great sophistication, most of the time keep enough distance from them, creating their own systems of analysis and mostly not letting themselves get "enslaved by another man's." Even though psychoanalysis, in its Lacanian version, has gained considerable ground in recent years, along with a number of other "deconstructionist" techniques, our own analysis leads us to think that a return to ideological, historical, and value judgments may well accompany, supplement, reinforce, and prolong theoretical renewal in the years to come.

Université d'Orléans

iii. German Contributions

Hans Galinsky

In 1980 German publications dropped in number from around 130 to around 105. Reversing last year's trend, book-length monographs decreased considerably, whereas essays contributed to collections, encyclopedias, or periodicals remained almost stable, with some of them formidably increasing in length. Explorations of literary theory and comparative and didactic studies kept rising, while the structuralist-semiotic viewpoint has advanced still further and ideology criticism has maintained its popularity. The historical view, though adopted more rarely, is still alive. The change of *Amerikastudien* from a biannual to a quarterly has meant a welcome speed-up of article publication.

a. **Literary History—General.** Theme-oriented studies cutting across several periods of American literature were just as frequent as genre-centered or general ones. The first, *Kleinstück Festschrift*, is of particularly broad thematic scope. It concerns the "constitution" of reality in English-language literatures of the world. Of the 18 essays included, only three treat American works. Their authors are as disparate as Thomas Bailey Aldrich, W. D. Howells, and Arthur Miller. They will be reviewed in their particular period sections below. Of less extensive thematic frame is *Geschichtsdrama*, ed. Elfriede Neubuhr, Wege der Forschung 485 (Darmstadt: Wissenschafliche Buchgesellschaft). This collection contains 17 essays on the theory and practice of historical drama. From a comparative angle not an American dramatist but a novelist, Twain, and his *Personal Recollections of Joan of Arc* are of interest. Combined with the geographical land and spiritual theme of the "wilderness," the historical topic secures a much wider and more specifically American variation in Ursula Brumm's *Geschichte und Wildnis in der amerikanischen Literatur*, Grundlagen der Anglistik und Amerikanistik 11 (Berlin: Schmidt). She brings her wonted expertise to the treatment of a basic topic of American theology and literature. Her method is inductive and deliberately selective. "Beginnings in the Wilderness" are exemplified by Bradford's *Of Plymouth Plantation*, Johnson's *Wonder-Working Providence*, and Cotton Mather's spiritual biographies. "Fictionalizing the Historical: Independence and Self-Definition" finds its spokesmen in Cooper (*The Last of the Mohicans*) and Hawthorne ("Endicott and the Red Cross," "The Gray Champion," and *The Scarlet Letter*). "Difficulties with History: Europe, the Civil War, and the Frontier" are viewed from five angles: (1) "Heritage, desired but burdened with guilt" shows up, in the shape of the European past, with Hawthorne (*The Marble Faun, English*

Notebooks, Dr. Grimshawe's Secret), and James's "A Passionate Pilgrim," *The Sense of the Past*; (2) "Pilgrimages to the Past" are undertaken by Twain (*A Connecticut Yankee in King Arthur's Court*), Melville (*Billy Budd, Clarel*) and Henry Adams (*Mont-Saint-Michel and Chartres*); (3) "The Civil War as 'Unwritten War'" is represented by Hale's "The Man Without a Country"; (4) "The Frontier in History and Literature" rests on Turner's "The Significance of the Frontier in American History," and on Cather's *O Pioneers!*; (5) "History as an Element of Consciousness" unfolds in Faulkner's *Sartoris*, "Was," "The Bear," and *Absalom, Absalom!*. Interpretation is both intrinsic and extrinsic. Confining itself to prose works, the selection stresses the Puritan tradition and eastern writers, but Twain, Turner, Cather, and Faulkner add western and (deep-) southern perspectives. Though intended as an introduction of students and teachers to "basics of Americanistics," this is a seminal product of research.

A general frame other than "history" is established by "world literature." In the category of general reference works a special service has been rendered by several Austrian and German Americanists. Sonja Bahn, Renate von Bardeleben, Gudrun Grabher, Klaus-Jürgen Popp, and Sepp Tiefenthaler have contributed new items or revised older contributions to the second edition of *Lexikon der Weltliteratur*, vol. 2: *Werke*, ed. Gero von Wilpert (Stuttgart: Kröner). Among the new descriptive and interpretive entries the ones on Albee, Baldwin, Barth, Burroughs, Capote, Ellison, Kopit, Kosinski, Malamud, Arthur Miller, Plath, Roth, Singer, Vonnegut, and Welty are particularly informative. For a similar service users of reference books on children's and young people's literature are indebted to Walter Kühnel. He wrote a concise article on animal storyteller Ernest Thomson Seton, British-born Canadian and later American resident, for *Lexikon der Kinderand Jugendliteratur*, ed. Klaus Doderer et al. (Weinheim: Beltz).

Not reader-oriented but methodological and interdisciplinary is the general frame which Manfred Markus' article "Linguistik und Literaturwissenschaft: Tempus und Aspekt in Englisch als interdisziplinäres Problem" (*GRM* 30:1–24) sets up for his literary examples drawn from various periods of English and American literatures. The past tense as functioning in the introductory chapter of Dreiser's *Sister Carrie*, the increasing use of the historic present with Hawthorne ("Wakefield," "The New Adam and Eve"), Poe ("The Mask of the Red Death"), and Bierce ("An Occurrence at Owl-Creek Bridge") are analyzed. Markus concludes that "like Bunyan Hawthorne obviously used the present to emphasize the timeless moral significance of the epic event." The use of the tenses, the relative frequency of their simple and their expanded forms, as a device to characterize the four "narrators" of *The Sound and the Fury* by way of their "different attitudes toward time" is equally well observed but more examples will be needed to convince Faulkner's critical readers.

Like "world literature" and "linguistics," "ethnicity" supplies a general concept to which Werner Sollors relates American literature in "Literature and Ethnicity," an article contributed to the *Harvard Encyclopedia of American Ethnic Groups*, ed. Stephan Thernstrom (Harvard-Belknap), pp. 647–65. It falls into six sections: (1) "The Roots of Ethnicity: Etymology and Definitions"; (2) " 'Promised Land and Melting Pot': Typology and Ethnicity"; (3) "Red, Black and White: Ethnicity and History"; (4) " 'The Divided Heart': Classic Ethnic Literature and Realism"; (5) "Ethnicity and Literary Form"; and (6) "Ethnicity in American Literature: Rosebud or MacGuffin?" Each section abounds in illustrative examples ranging from the 17th to the 20th centuries, and in the case of Spanish-American analogs taking in the 16th century as well. Section 5 is of special interest as it includes the "creation of exuberant multilingual forms" and "humor or irony" in their relations to ethnicity.

Not as an example or as part of a larger whole but for its own sake and as a generic whole does American litreature function in a genre-centered work, Günther Ahrends' *Die amerikanische Kurzgeschichte: Theorie und Entwicklung* (SuL 107). Ahrends is the first German Americanist to concentrate exclusively on the American short story instead of on the British or, more rarely, Anglo-Irish one as well, and to regard its theory and practice, its past and present. In the first part of his book he outlines the history of the theory, of its normative and descriptive branches. For spokesmen of the former he chooses only practitioners of the genre (Poe through Wharton), for examples of the latter predominantly practitioners (Hawthorne through Oates) and a few academic critics. In the second, larger, part he relates the history of the genre's practice from Irving through Cheever and Oates. Afro-Americans are represented by Wright and

Baldwin. Understood as an account of a "development," this part divides into "Conditions of Origin," "Myth, Allegory and Symbolism," "The Beginnings of Realism," "The Analysis of Consciousness and of Society," "Formal Experiments and Return to Myth." There is an extensive bibliography. The presentation balances between a detailed analysis of individual short stories and a cursory report on the history of the genre. As usual, conditions of origin exclude the colonial tradition of shorter prose narratives but include 19th-century folktales and tall tales.

Once again do American authors serve as paradigmatic means to larger ends in two genre-centered collections of essays. Drama-centered is *The Languages of Theater*, ed. Ortrun Zuber (Oxford: Pergamon Press). Franz H. Link has contributed to it "Translation, Adaptation and Interpretation of Dramatic Texts" (pp. 24–50). Translation from contemporary language to previous stages of the same language is demonstrated by the archaisms in T. S. Eliot's *Murder in the Cathedral*. Translation into and from a foreign language is exemplified by Eva Hesse's German rendering of Pound's American rendering of Sophocles' *Women of Trachis*. As for (stage) adaptation, adapting to different places of performance is illustrated by Eliot's play as originally written for performance at the Canterbury Festival. Setting as factor in stage adaptations of dramatic texts is shown by the "very detailed descriptions" in O'Neill plays, by Jo Mielziner's setting for Williams' *A Streetcar Named Desire* and, contrastively, by Wilder's almost bare stage. Acting as another factor is discussed with reference to Anna Magnani "as the best actress for Serafina in Williams' *Rose Tattoo*." As to interpretation, "rewriting" as one of its modes is represented by O'Neill's *Mourning Becomes Electra*, a myth transfer into end-of-Civil War and postbellum New England, and by Williams' *Cat on a Hot Tin Roof*, its different endings offering "different interpretations of the story." Thus the usefulness of American drama as a storehouse of illustrative material for systematic approaches of drama in general is amply proven.

The other genre-directed collection, encompassing essays on American authors, concerns poetry. *Poetic Knowledge* assembles American, British, French, German, and Italian contributions on poetry of these five countries and of Ireland. The ones which relate to American poetry, with one partial exception, are devoted to 20th-

century, pre- and post-1945, poets. Therefore they will be reviewed
below.

a–1. **Colonial, Revolutionary, and 19th Century.** When not viewed
as part of a multiperiod study such as Brumm's, Colonial literature
proved attractive not for its own sake but either for its documentary
value as a source to be tapped by historians of education and society or for its impact on fields of later American life. Peter Wagner's "A Note on Puritans and Children in early colonial New
England" (*Amst* 25:47–62) is of interest here not for its specific
generational conclusions but for its use, in part, of sermons, e.g., by
Richard and Eleazar Mather and Thomas Hooker; tracts, e.g., by
John Wilson; epic poetry by Wigglesworth; letters from Thomas
Shepard, Jr.; diaries (Sewall), and historiography (John Norton,
Samuel Willard, Cotton Mather). The discrepancy between ideals
set forth in exhortations and complaints on the one hand and
actual practice on the other is emphasized, occasionaly even overemphasized. Ursula Brumm's "Die Puritaner im amerikanischen
Bewußtsein," *Jahrbuch 1979* (Berlin: Berliner Wissenschaftliche
Gesellschaft), pp. 118–28, surveys American reactions, especially
20th-century ones, to 17th-century New England Puritanism while
Gustav H. Blanke's "Early Theories about the Nature and Origin of
the Indians, and the Advent of Mormonism" (*Amst* 25:243–68) follows the gradual crystallization of a cluster of ideas resulting in
politico-religious action. Brumm's method of presentation surveys
confrontations of the descendants, 18th-, 19th-, and 20th-century
Americans, with their Puritan heritage and highlights the 20th-
century ones. Denigrators, especially among intellectuals and literary authors, come to the fore in a detailed representative sketch
of Mencken. Scholarly attitudes find their pioneer spokesman in Perry
Miller, with Sacvan Bercovitch standing for further developments
and modifications of Miller's basic effort. Brumm's essay serves as a
concise and lively guide through a complex issue. In Blanke's erudite
article Colonial literature's views of the native American and his
origins figure in references to early explorers Thomas Hariot and
Arthur Barlow, Pilgrim father Edward Winslow, colonial returnee
Thomas Lechford, colonial theologians John Eliot, Roger Williams,
Increase and Cotton Mather, Judge Samuel Sewall, and utopian
writer Joseph Morgan (*The History of the Kingdom of Basaruah*).

Their views are related to European primitivist and antiprimitivist theories of the 16th, 17th, and early 18th centuries, especially to pseudobiblical genealogies, of which the most influential one links the American Indians to the ten lost tribes of Israel. Blanke's study carries over into the Revolutionary and the Early Republican period by including Dr. Benjamin Rush, Freneau, theologians Charles Crawford, Jonathan Edwards, Jr., Ezra Stiles, Joseph Belknap, and others as well as "first 'Zionist' Mordecai M. Noah, editor of *The New York Enquirer*." Thus it examines not only the role played by the origin of the Indians in Christian millenarianism but also the support given by it and Jewish Messianism to American nationalism. This second role is found to climax in Joseph Smith's *The Book of Mormon*. Aside from the author of this inclusive study, no German Americanist has taken up a subject concerned exclusively with Revolutionary or Early Republican literature.

Once more, at least inclusively, does the latter figure in a book-length monograph dealing with the 19th century as a whole. Franz H. Link, in *Geschichte der amerikanischen Erzählkunst im 19.Jahrhundert* (SuL 112), is the first German to attempt, in a single-handed effort, a comprehensive presentation of America's "narrative art" from Brown through Norris. Link covers the whole area, i.e., romance, novel, and short story, with essay, sketch, and tale or story for the short story's reflective, descriptive, and narrative predecessors. Travelog, biography, and autobiography remain at the periphery of this form-centered account. It has a multinational, British, French, and German slant in that it includes non-American origins of, affinities with, and influences on, American works and takes in their reception abroad. Link's basic method is that of the close text-analyzing reader of selected works of chosen authors, 13 in all. The choice is determined by artistic merit. Hence it is oriented toward literary products, to the exclusion of such processes of literary production as will lead to major works not until the 20th century. Consequently it is the authors of the Anglo-American mainstream, not the emergent "ethnics" like Sealsfield, Chesnutt, or Cahan that occupy Link's attention. Within the mainstream, however, developments, foreshadowing variations or culminations in later works of the 19th or 20th centuries are by no means overlooked. "The Gothic Novel" (Brown), "Romantic Narrative Art" (Irving, Cooper), "Narrative Art of the American Renaissance" (Poe, Hawthorne, Melville),

"Indigenous Realism" (Harte, Twain), "Moral Realism" (James, Howells), "New Realism" (Bierce, Crane, Norris) comprise six chapters, with the "American Renaissance" one receiving by far the largest share. Omissions of authors or particular works of included ones are accounted for in the introduction. A firm attitude as to questions of aesthetic and religious values permeates this 400-page history. The sheer power of its unified panoramic view bids fair to remain a challenge to scholars attempting to tackle the same demanding subject.

Of the fiction writers prominent in Link's book only Poe and Melville are also explored in articles. Two of them concern Poe but for their comparative slant they will be reviewed in section *b*. In Helmbrecht Breinig's "The Symbol of Complexity: 'I and My Chimney' and Its Significance in the Context of Melville's Later Writings" (*Anglia* 98:51–67) the chief accent is "on religious symbolism," "because here the muddle can clearly be shown to be planned and meaningful, and because from here a discussion of Melville's concept of art can get under way most easily." Breinig succeeds in achieving his aim and also explains the political symbolism, upholding as he does its "contradictoriness." It is found to lie in the narrator's comparison of the chimney to a "truncated pyramid." The latter is convincingly linked to the "unfinished pyramid" "on the reverse of the Great Seal of the United States." According to Breinig "the chimney is not so much a complex symbol but a symbol of complexity, a symbol of symbolic creation, as it were." The demonstration of the story's "significance in the context of Melville's later writings" could stand expansion. Likewise not only for its own sake but also related to a larger topic does a story by Melville's younger contemporary Aldrich come up for interpretation in Volker Bischoff's "Zur Form und Funktion literarischer Illusionsbildung in Th. B. Aldrichs Kurzgeschichte 'Marjorie Daw'," *Kleinstück Festschrift*, pp. 231–48. In the frame of "literature and reality" he investigates the creation, by the epistolary form, of a dual illusion, that of the reader due to the author, and that of Flemming caused by Delaney. Its destruction is dual, too, due to the surprise ending and the prior abandonment of the epistolary technique. Bischoff infers an authorial intention to "ironize the conventional creation of illusion." For the story's contemporary reader, however, the title figure lives on, as is evidenced by Eunice E. Comstock's poem, "Marjorie Daw." For explanation

Bischoff quotes Howells' comment that she "has outlived myriads of heroines whose reality has never been impeached by their authors," because her creator had "conditioned her so that to any mood she shall be easily imaginable." Bischoff interprets this as agreement between the author's presentation and the genteel-age reader's expectation of idealization, especially of womanhood. He rightly stresses the cancellation of this agreement by the surprise ending, thus reassessing Aldrich's place in his age, and turning against both the period's laudatory view, and the later depreciation, nay, almost total neglect of this story.

From peripheral place in Bischoff's essay Howells advances to central position in Rolf Meyn's "Aspekte der Realismus-Theorie William Dean Howells' und das Problem von Wirklichkeitsstruktur und Wirklichkeitsdeutung in seinem Roman *A Modern Instance*," *Kleinstück Festschrift*, pp. 249–70. It outlines Howells' fortunes in literary criticism, mainly American, develops his theory of realism as in part derived from his critiques of American and foreign realists, and compares the theory to the practice as followed in *A Modern Instance*. Here reality is constituted by a "moralist disguised as satirist," measuring morality by Christian norms, by an ironist siding against their pronouncer (Atherton), and by a constructor of character-experienced reality which "does not originate any more only from motivations, dispositions or social conditions but in part dissolves in a chain of accidents." Meyn finds a discrepancy between the norms presented, and between (1) the authorial tone implied, and (2) the importance of fateful chance chaotically obstructing the realizations of the norms. On the strength of these observations Howells appears to him as "a representative of a modern literary tradition extending up to the generation of the Hellers and Keseys." To fully substantiate this claim the existence of an absurd element in *A Modern Instance* would require scrutiny. The overall theme of the literary constitution of reality returns by way of "new problems of verisimilitude" in Hans-Joachim Lang's "Paradoxes of Utopian Consciousness: From *Looking Backward* to *Young West*" (*Amst* 25: 231–42). The shift from the contrast between "here and now" and "no-place and everlasting present time," i.e., the change from "spatial to temporal utopias," is found to yield problems for the paradoxical time-traveler's consciousness. They climax in a crisis of identity. In this context of "fables of identity" Irving's "Rip Van Winkle,"

William Austin's "Peter Rugg, the Missing Man," and William James's *Principles of Psychology* incorporating the Ansel Bourne case help us see the mind of Edward Bellamy's Julian West more distinctly. He differs in that his identity crisis is solved by conversion along Puritan typological lines, with the old beloved, Edith Bartlett, serving as type, and the new, Edith Leete, functioning as antitype. Solomon Schindler's *Young West, A Sequel to Edward Bellamy's Celebrated Novel "Looking Backward"* (1894) takes up again the motif of the utopian time-traveler's psyche. In the success story of West, Jr. the unhappiness story of West, Sr. is embedded. The germ of the pessimistic end to the time-traveler's identity crisis is discovered in Schindler's "Dr. Leete's Letter to Julian West." Lang links it to a personal squabble in Boston's "National Movement" founded in the heyday of *Looking Backward's* influence. With its conclusions neatly enumerated, this article, for all its scholarship and concise style, is the most entertaining of the whole year's crop.

Lang's study approached the turn of the century and, with its reference to H. G. Wells's *A Modern Utopia*, transcended it. Another specimen of the time-travel mode, not a prospective one like the futurity novel, but a retrospective one, the autobiography is the subject of Edda Kerschgens' *Das gespaltene Ich: 100 Jahre afroamerikanischer Autobiographie: Strukturuntersuchungen zu den Autobiographien von Frederick Douglass, Booker T. Washington und W. E. B. DuBois*, NSAA 20 (Lang). It also links the two centuries, and this on a chronologically larger scale. The 12 works analyzed reach from 1845, the date of *Narrative of the Life of Frederick Douglass, an American Slave*, to 1968, the year *The Autobiography of W. E. B. DuBois* was published. In an appendix to the first of the monograph's five parts the author retraces even 18th-century beginnings of the genre "Afro-American autobiography." She sets out to demonstrate (1) "the reflex of Afro-American history" and (2) the development of the personal identity problem in these writings of three leaders. The split into " two souls, two thoughts" (DuBois) is held to be the "dominant structural principle" of all of the works selected. Irony is found to serve as their common tone. They are also thought to agree in their "rejection of American types of Christianity," in a "skeptical view of the manifestations of democratic American principles," and in their didactic intention. The value of this book lies in its systematic comparison of three representative works against a background of 200 years of American history.

The 19th century also meets the 20th in the only article concerned with the poetry of the former illuminating the poetry of the latter. Nineteenth-century drama, however, goes just as unnoticed as its 18th-century forerunner. Armin Paul Frank in "Emerson and Stevens: The Poem as Hibernal Architecture" (*Poetic Knowledge*, pp. 141–48, 150–51) compares Emerson's "Snow-storm" and Stevens' "Man and Bottle," "both being concerned with the concept of art as a destructive-creative force presented in the image—in the one case dominant, in the other, subservient—of the snowstorm." The result is brilliantly formulated: "Stevens' ideal poet is, at best, half of Emerson's: a sayer, not a seer, a namer, not a knower." Emerson's "Seashore," Whitman's "Out of the Cradle Endlessly Rocking" (1881 version), and Stevens' "The Idea of Order at Key West" are juxtaposed to the effect that "Emerson's poetry is one of idealistic transcendence, Whitman's of materialistic transcendence, and Stevens' of linguistic transcendence."

a–2. **20th-Century Poetry, Drama, and Fiction to 1945.** Pound has remained the experts' domain. Supported by Roman Jakobson's differentiation of the metaphoric and the metonymic mode of discourse and by the ascription of the latter to aphasics, Max Nänny in "Context, Contiguity and Contact in Ezra Pound's *Personae*" (*ELH* 47: 386–98) asserts "that Pound's mental makeup and predilections as well as his innovating strategies of reforming an excessively metaphorical poetic tradition pushed him close to the metonymic pole." For evidence, he tests Pound's *Personae* poems in their New York edition of 1926 along pragmatic, syntactic, and semantic lines. Results of this application of discourse theory are enlightening. They may become useful to the future establishment of a critical text of Pound's work. Nänny's predominantly interpretive essay is rounded out by Hans-Joachim Zimmermann's review article " 'an armour against utter consternation' " (*Archiv* 217:111–21). With its subtitle "Neuere Literatur zu Ezra Pound" it points the way to a much-needed critical survey of recent editions, of guides to *Selected Poems* (1977) and *Personae*, 1926 (1969), of book-length studies in the complete or single poetical and poetological works, of collections of critical essays, of checklists and biographies. The survey also embraces Pound's literary and music criticism and other prose as well as facsimiles and reprints of important sources consulted by him. Investigations of his influence and his era supplement this critical panorama. Its final section is saved up for *The Cantos*, both editions and studies. The critic's attention centers on books from around 1969 through 1978. Articles are excluded. Even so, this is a circumspect presentation of a rapidly expanding research area.

To receive commentary as well as translation is a rare feat in the annals of German academic responses to American poetry. Annemarie and Franz H. Link's *H.D. (Hilda Doolittle), 'Trilogie': Übersetzt und Kommentiert*, vol. 1, vol. 2, Annotations and Commentary (Freiburg i.Br.:Published by the translators, 1978) was overlooked at the time. This extraordinary effort blends two translators' sense of equivalencies with two commentators' erudition, which Norman H. Pearson had allowed to benefit from his own comments on H. D.'s text. Scholars may consult a copy deposited at Yale's Beinecke Library. Like Pound and H. D., Eliot will invite explicating skill. Willi Erzgräber proves his in "Zu T. S. Eliots 'The Waste Land,' V.60–76" (*Archiv* 217:369–74). Elizabeth Drew's conjecture in 1954, "Maybe there's a hint of *The Hound of Heaven*, and that the 'nails' associate the Osiris myth with the Crucifixion" (*T. S. Eliot: The Design of his Poetry*, p. 75) grows more plausible by Erzgräber's suggestion that "Dog" (v.74) stands for God anagrammatically reversed and retaining capitalization. The Dog's qualification as "friend to men" is taken as an allusion to St. John 15:13–15. Belief in a natural regeneration as suggested by the prevalent mythological interpretation of the passage is thought to be an attempted "repression of guilt," a "way out," "annihilated by Christ." The attitude of the speaker toward the Christian tradition is understood as hypocrisy shared with the apostrophied "hypocrite lecteur." This reviewer might add that the substitution of Dog for God, the crucial point of Erzgräber's conjecture, should have come easy to Eliot, a native American, by way of the well-known substitution of "doggone" for "goddam." Like Pound research Eliot study has produced a useful state-of-research report. Armin Paul Frank's review essay (*Anglia* 98:536–43) focuses on Eliot's early years and emphasizes biographical inquiry.

Interest in women members of this most productive generation of the 1880s extends from poet H. D. to dramatist Susan Glaspell. Gerhard Bach's *Susan Glaspell und die Provincetown Players: Die Anfänge des modernen amerikanischen Dramas und Theaters* (Lang) was overlooked last year. It is the first German book-length study of her in the context of the Provincetown Players. Their place in the Little Theater Movement, and its intra- and extra-American affiliations, the reception and the characteristics of their repertoire, and the share of George Cram Cook in the integration and disintegration of the group receive adequate treatment. This first part of the monograph is valuable for its use of previously unresearched material of the New York Public Library. In the second part, which inquires into Glaspell's plays, her development from negligible short-story writer to, next to O'Neill, the group's leading playwright, her interrelations with other group authors, e.g., Djuna Barnes and Floyd Dell, stand out more clearly than the ones with O'Neill. Not young O'Neill of the Provincetown Players but the author of the last plays interests Josef Oswald. *The Discordant, Broken, Faithless Rhythm of Our Time: Eine Analyse der späten Dramen Eugene O'Neills* (NSAA 21), like Bach's book, fixes on stage plays but unlike Bach's it stresses their theatrical aspects less than their literary ones. It analyzes a phenomenon asserted to be central to them, i.e., the lack of a transcendent determining entity. Proof rests on the "merely formal use" of religious, especially Christian, terms and patterns, the way drama content includes religious substance, and "the repudiation of any secular substitutes for God." This lack is also inferred from "the reduction of human interaction," "a fundamental revaluation of language and its communicative properties," "incapability to love and work" as well as "the confinement in a temporal continuum." "Search for escape" is the common denominator for "philosophical detachment," "a life of 'as if'," "artificially induced states of ecstasy," "pipe dreams, alcohol, drugs, and suicide." None of these features is new to O'Neill students. What is new, however, is their systematic and methodical analysis across all of the pertinent five plays, and their interpretation as thematic and formal correspondences to the dramatist's ontological stance.

The fiction of the period attracts somewhat more frequent yet less comprehensive treatment. In "Identität und Rolle in Theodore Dreiser's *Sister Carrie*, Teil I: Rollenverhalten, Identität und soziale Struktur" (*LJGG* 21:253–82) Kurt Müller starts from recent research on theatre imagery permeating *Sister Carrie*. He extends it along the lines of role theory, and successfully demonstrates "the dialectic relationship of social role and personal identity" as "the central structuring element of the novel." In the New York phase of Hurstwood's development he reveals below Dreiser's naturalistic image of man a hard unadapted core of a self-understanding in terms of individual pride and dignity. Integrating Riesman's social typology with role theory, Müller interprets Hurstwood's attitude as representative of the inner-directed type of American socioeconomic development localized in the Chicago of the novel. Hurstwood's fate in New York is seen as arising from the confrontation of this type with a transitional one, anticipating the outer-directed type. A final verdict on this reinterpretation of a naturalistic classic has to be suspended until the publication of promised part 2, which will deal with Carrie Meeber's "structure of character."

Upton Sinclair has been a favorite subject of Dieter Herms for years. His "Afterword" to the second, revised, German edition of *The Jungle* (*Der Dschungel*, Frankfurt: Zweitausendeins, pp. 479–84) and a brief article, "From West Point Cadet to Presidential Agent: Popular Literature Elements in Upton Sinclair" (*Upton Sinclair Quarterly* 4:12–19) make up this year's vintage. The article approaches Sinclair from an angle deserving the attention of social psychologists of literary reception.

Of the generation of the 1890s and 1900s Hemingway alone keeps fascinating at least one scholar. But even he restricts himself to the roles of retrospective editor and introducer. *Hemingway heute,* ed. Horst Weber, Wege der Forschung, 546 (Darmstadt: Wissenschaftliche Buchgesellschaft) contains 18 previously published essays of American, British, French, Russian, and German critics. Only the editor's preface and introduction are new. In accordance with the series of which it forms a part, this 422-page volume traces "ways of research." Its appended bibliography reduces this veritable maze of Hemingway research to manageable proportions by concentrating on American, British, French, and German publications, mainly of the 1960s and 1970s. Weber's critical review of them follows three lines, (1) critical reception by a contemporary British fiction writer (V. Woolf) and several literary scholars, (2) explorations of values, religious, philosophical, and moral, embodied in the fiction, (3) examination of literary modes of "mastering reality." Weber's essay

"Hemingway heute" marks a return to the significance of Hemingway's earlier prose.

A link between the fiction of the 1930s and its post-1945 successor has been established by Arno Heller's "Zur Nachwirkung der 'Southern Agrarians' im neueren Roman des amerikanischen Südens," *Americana-Austriaca*, 5, ed. Klaus Lanzinger (Wien: Braumüller), pp. 64–84. Dealing with the effect of *I'll Take My Stand* on the more recent novel of the South, it defines the main ideas of this "ideological self-understanding" and pursues their transformation into fiction. Its first stage, the historical novel, i.e., the Civil War novel, of the 1930s is sketched, with Tate's *The Fathers* being analyzed at some length. Heller elaborates "thematic" and "ideological" affinities of Faulkner's Yoknapatawpha novels with the southern Agrarians but he is aware of those works' "transitional" character. It is said to mark "the transition from a prevailingly description-oriented and ideologically motivated literature to an epistemologically deepened literature of consciousness." As for R. P. Warren, pre-1945 novels like *Night Rider* and *At Heaven's Gate* are thought to be still indebted to agrarian ideas. *All the King's Men*, however, in the figure of Jack Burden is felt to transcend "the negative and retrospective agrarian criticism of the *New South*" by "a more acute philosophical and psychological diagnosis of the agrarian conflict." According to Heller, *The Cave* continues this process of "internalizing Warren's agrarian critique," while the shift from communal to individual disintegration sets off the early work of McCullers and Capote. Increasingly tenuous links with the Agrarians are ascribed to O'Connor's works, especially *The Violent Bear It Away*, to Styron's *Lie Down in Darkness* and *Set This House on Fire*, to Price's *A Long Happy Life* and *A Generous Man*, to Welty's *Losing Battles* and *The Optimist's Daughter* as well as to Percy's *The Moviegoer* and *The Last Gentleman*. Cases of "existential malaise" are placed in the South, but they are not of the South. Indeed, this is an interesting line of argument.

a–3. **General and Fiction since 1945.** No general view of the period has been attempted. Of the literary genres only fiction can boast of two synoptic studies. One cultivates the ethnic part of the field and includes nonfiction as well, another confines itself to a nonethnic group of writers, the postmodernists. Both studies were undertaken

by Kurt Dittmar. "Partikularistische Gestaltungszüge in der zeitgenössischen jüdisch-amerikanischen Prosaliteratur" (*Amst* 25:7–46)
testifies to Dittmar's familiarity with 20th-century Jewish-American
literature and its context. It had already characterized last year's
book *Assimilation and Dissimilation, 1900–1970* (see *ALS 1979*, p.
497) and now continues in Dittmar's advance beyond 1970. The
universalizing, "humanistic," trend of the Bellow, Malamud, and
Roth type of Jewish-American fiction, tending to render the particular, "the social and spiritual problems of [Jewish] marginality," a
paradigm of the human condition, is shown up as leading with Roth
to a parody on "cultural philosemitism." It is contrasted with a par-
ticularistic tendency to reflection on, and presentation of, the essential otherness of the Jew. This turn to a religious ethnocentricity is
exemplified most prominently by Cynthia Ozick, less so by Arthur A.
Cohen and Hugh Nissenson, with Chaim Potok for analog in the
popular novel. In autobiography Herbert Gold, Ronald Sanders, and
Mark J. Mirsky indicate the same new trend. It is suggested to be
due to (1) the Near-East crisis and its "solidarity effect" on American Jews, (2) the "struggle of ethnic groups for social influence"
in a situation of diminishing upward mobility chances, (3) a Jewish
variety of counterculture in its turn against the mainstream. Finally
Dittmar compares American prospects of this ethnocentric type to
those in Israel. Theme and execution make this article one of the
best of the year. Shifting his ground from the ethnicity to the "literary reality" topic, Dittmar returns to the 1970s in "Realität und
Fiktion in der zeitgenössischen amerikanischen Erzählliteratur,"
(*Kleinstück Festschrift*, pp. 401–28). Because of the vogue of this
subject he can limit himself to a useful review essay on literary critics,
anthologists, and postmodernist author-critics trying to name, define,
and explain changes in fiction from mimetic to antimimetic or ami-
metic modes, often relating them to changes in science (Einstein,
Planck, Heisenberg), the arts (aleatorism), pseudocommunication
in the mass-media, and, much earlier, philosophy (Nietzsche). Dittmar illustrates his conclusions with an interpretation of Bellow's *The
Victim* (1947) and Vonnegut's *Breakfast of Champions* (1973). As
in the preceding essay the analysis stresses events and figures. References to William H. Gass's dictum "the novelist . . . will keep us
kindly imprisoned in his language" and to echolalia in Vonnegut
excepted, the role of language in these processes of "derealization"

is not diagnosed yet. A comparison with Gerhard Hoffman's methodology-centered article on a similar topic is instructive.

Not synoptic and concerned with a limited time span but focusing on two novelists, the one born in 1899, the other 20 years older, and branching out into the English and French history of an Italian dramatic form type, Kordula Rose-Werle's *Harlekinade* rests on a solid comparatist basis. Therefore it will be reviewed in *b*. The female contribution continues with four of the six publications which single out one post-1945 novelist each. With one exception, an essay on Nabokov, all of them are concerned with fiction writers of the generation of the 1930s. Here as in post-1945 poetry criticism, Austrian Americanists are particularly productive. Authors selected comprise Barth, Elkin, Updike, Kosinski, and Oates.

In "Das Spiel des *Unreliable Narrator* in Nabokovs *Lolita*" (*Amst* 25:418–31) Renate Hof attempts to prove Humbert Humbert unreliable. As Nänny's (*a–2*) her armory is applied linguistics, with reception aesthetics and game and role theory added. Adhering to the principle that "judg[ment] on a specific behavior" can be eventually inferred only from the interaction of all of the semantic relations of the narrative text, she finds that the narrator of *Lolita* "is not only the expression of a paradox, grotesque situation but at the same time a parodistic means to resolve the paradoxes—if the reader sees through the rules of the game in progress." To effect the reader's distancing from the narrator's perspective she distinguishes the level of narration from that of action, and the different situations on them. The distance achieved, the (implied) author's irony can be recognized because the author enables the reader to see through the "games" of the narrator. There is sound sense in her thesis that "only by contrasting the different speech-situations in this text can we grasp the subtle contradictions which reveal the narrator's unreliability as a form of self-deception."

Like Nabokov, Barth upholds his fascination. Heide Ziegler's three articles "John Barth's *Sot-Weed Factor* Revisited: The Meaning of Form" (*Amst* 25:199–206), "John Barth's 'Echo': The Story in Love with Its Author" (*IFR* 7:90–93), and "An Interview with John Barth" (*Granta*, NS 1:169–77) afford ample evidence. Since the second article is easily available to foreign readers, only the other two require comment here. The first explores the importance of form, i.e., of parody, in the *The Sot-Weed Factor*. As imitation it is tied to an earlier work by necessity, as play of the imagination it is free. With its dual nature parody provides an "emblem of the postmodern imagination." In terms of content this duality leads to a story of twins, of identity and role, in terms of form to a past recorded and a past as material for authorial game-playing. "Fictional and historical events alike" are "treat[ed] as stories." The function of language in this process should be regarded, though. In the "Interview," actually a short part of an interview on 9 and 16 November 1976, combined with a longer part of another in September 1979, attention gradually shifts from *The Sot-Weed Factor* to *Letters*. Thanks to his sophisticated interviewer Barth is stimulated to expatiate on "the past('s) relation to the present" in his fiction, "a special relationship between the fictional and the factual," "the Platonic Form" as the target of Bray's effort "to create the perfect novel," and "the tragic view of characterization in that we cannot, no matter how hard we try, make real people by language."

Unlike Barth, his exact contemporary, Elkin, has not yet gained a frequent hearing in German scholarship. Doris G. Bargen's *The Fiction of Stanley Elkin*, Studien und Texte zur Amerikanistik, Studien 8 (Lang) makes up for it by devoting a whole book to him, the first on Elkin published in Germany. Biography and critical reception, literary contexts ("Metafiction and Black Humor," "American-Jewish Writing") and four theme-oriented chapters ("Modern Man in Consumer Culture," "From Jewish Peddler to American Franchiser," "The Problem of Communication between the Hero and his Audience," "Modern Man in Search for the Primitive") make up an entertaining, though painstakingly researched monograph. Like Ziegler, Bargen reprints interviews ("as edited by Stanley Elkin"). A useful bibliography incorporates a checklist of reviews of his fiction. Best of all, Bargen is responsive to Elkin's humor.

In "John Updike: From *Rabbit, Run* to *Marry Me*," (*Stürzl Festschrift*, pp. 477–506), young Austrian Americanist Dorothea Steiner considers *The Poorhouse Fair* as "'prolog'," "The Coup" as "'epilog'" of Updike's career of "'master of the American middle-class domestic scene'." Within this frame she investigates his first novel's message and relates it to his fiction from *Rabbit, Run* to *Marry Me*. Finding Updike's statement on the former as "foundation of his work" only "half-right" in that it disregards "the central position" of woman in it, she establishes a "thematic triad" of freedom—God—woman as "the continuity underlying his work." Supportive analyses, chiefly of plot and figures, of *Rabbit, Run* and *Rabbit Redux* are less penetrating than that of *Marry Me*. It is here that genre criticism, both historical and occasionally psychoanalytical, comes to grips with the "romance" promised the reader in the novel's subtitle. The continuity of the triadic theme, and the pervasiveness of the playful element, the toying with letter symbolism and its functionality, are convincingly demonstrated.

Steiner's compatriot Sepp L. Tiefenthaler, whose essay on Kosinsky was reviewed in *ALS 1979*, has extended his observations to a book-length monograph. *Jerzy Kosinski: Eine Einführung in sein Werk*, Abhandlungen zur Kunst-, Musik- und Literaturwissenschaft 305 (Bonn: Bouvier) is a pilot study of this author in any German-speaking country. Intended as an "introduction," it opens with a sketch of Kosinski's life, and advances via his two nonfictional pieces to his fictional works up to *Passion Play*. "Thematic Procedures" as first part of its longest, third, chapter concerns itself with the unifying features of his literary achievement while the second part, "Analysis and Interpretation," takes up each work of fiction separately. Of them the analysis of *The Painted Bird* is particularly perceptive as regards the function of natural scenery, archetypal characterization of figures, and narrative mode. Anticipatory symptoms of growing interest in more experimental devices of narration are accurately gauged. *Steps* is rightly judged as their culmination whereas a turning away from innovation is felt to be typical of the later novels. Likewise a nonnative speaker of English, Tiefenthaler can project himself into Kosinski's linguistic sensibilities and in this respect see him akin with such other Slav latecomers to the English language as Conrad and Nabokov.

The third Austrian service to the study of post-1945 fiction, although briefly touching upon her author's poetry as well, is rendered by Brigitte Scheer-Schäzler's "Die Rhetorik der Gewalt: Zur Prosa von Joyce Carol Oates" (*Merkur* 34:721–29). Oates's "passion for precision and completeness" is found to be "parallel[ed]" by American journalism (muckrakers Steffens and Phillips) and contemporary literature (Mailer, Terkel, Tom Wolfe). Oates's "indictment of violence" is paid special attention. Examples are taken from *Expensive People, Them, Do With Me What You Will*, and "Concerning the Case of Bobby T" (*The Goddess and Other Women*). Violence

imagined but exceeded by violence in reality is considered to raise
the general problem of "fictionality vs. reality" and the place of
storytelling within this problem. Oates's fiction is understood as supplying an answer to it. Her literary practice as in part "re-imagining"
Kafka and others, as well as her literary criticism (*The Edge of
Impossibility*; *New Heaven, New Earth*) are thought to have been
influenced by her profession of university teacher of English. For
principal stimulation, however, Scheer-Schäzler relies on Oates's own
explanation of her writing as release from a pressure to externalize
dreams, personal yet likely to be shared by any human being. Prominent among these dreams is that of force as a means to solve problems of the void of the modern psyche, especially the female one.
The physical image, for psychic states, of pressure and explosion, of
matter and energy is traced through "Matter and Energy" (*The
Wheel of Love, Them*, and *Love and Its Derangements*, a collection
of her poems. Oates's strength is held to lie in the short story rather
than the novel. *All the Good People I've Left Behind*, a short-story
collection, is singled out for proof in an article which is the most suc-
cinct of all in this section.

a-4. **Drama and Poetry since 1945.** Response to post-1945 drama
shrinks to three essays consisting of a detailed analysis of one particular aspect of Arthur Miller's early plays and two survey articles
on the "radical" and "alternative" types of present-day drama. The
former essay reflects the gradual rise of women's studies, the latter
ones signal the continuation of an ideological trend of literary research noticeable ever since the early 1970s. In "Die Rolle der Frau
in Arthur Millers frühen Dramen: Untersuchungen zu seinem Kon-
zept gesellschaftlicher Wirklichkeit," (*Kleinstück Festschrift*, pp.
307–22), Hedwig Bock puts her finger on a contradiction in Miller's
imaginative construction of social reality: he posits "a kind of responsibility. Man for man" (*All My Sons*) as a "basic presupposition
for the functioning of a democratic society," but "excludes women
from participatory determination and responsibility." For evidence
she points to occasional traits like fathers' pride in boys, women's
clumsiness in handling modern gadgets, and the Xantippe stereotype
impersonated by Sue Bayliss (*All My Sons*). More pervasive is the
recurrence of the two roles of mother and whore. Bock assigns Kate
and Ann Deever (*All My Sons*), Linda (*Death of a Salesman*), and

Abigail (*The Crucible*) to the one category, The Woman, Letta, and Miss Forsyth (*Death of a Salesman*), and Abigail (*The Crucible*) to the other. Authorial skill of character motivation is said to decline as regards Elizabeth and Abigail. Excepting references to Freudian impact, the question of for what reasons Miller's dramatic construction of social reality assigns women to these very categories is excluded. So are nature and function of ethnic women such as Tituba (*The Crucible*).

The drama of the 1970s turns up in two articles by Dieter Herms, "Current Trends in US Alternative Theatre," *Tot Lering en Vermaak: 9 Manieren voor 10 Jaar Vormingstheater*, ed. Dina van Berlaer-Hellemans and Marianne Van Kerkhoven (Antwerp: Soethoudt), pp. 49–63, and "Radical Theatre in the 1970's" (*Amst* 25:280–292). As the two essays often overlap in content and judgments, this reviewer may concentrate on the second. Like the first it is based on information and assessments presented in Herms's and his collaborators' publications (noticed in *ALS 1973*, pp. 447, 448; *1976*, p. 442; *1979*, pp. 499–500). But both articles also expand the scope of inquiry. The second combines the increasingly significant element of ethnic theatre, the Chicano one, with other alternative theatre groups under the common denominator of "radical theatre." The unifying view underlying the assessment of all of these activities can be inferred from Herms's summarizing statement: "But when the short wave [of guerilla street theatre] subsided, these groups [the Teatro Campesino, the San Francisco Mime Troupe, and the Bread and Puppet Theater] emerged stronger than before, artistically and politically." The picture of Chicano theatre widens so as to include the activities of El Teatro de la Esperanza and its performances of *Guadalupe* and *La Victima*. The work of the Bread and Puppet Theater is supplemented by glimpses of the repertoire of the New York Caravan Street Theater, i.e., the *Bremer Stadt-musikanten* and *Sacco and Vanzetti*. "The trend towards the authentic history play" is said to be common to all of these theatre groups. Herms's characterization of their work stresses the ideological features but does not neglect the formal ones. The use of as-yet-unpublished material, the numerous bibliographical references, and the attention given the language of the Chicano plays including their use of caló open up a new field of contemporary drama and theatre research.

Slightly more intense than the appeal of post-1945 drama is that of poetry. As in 1979, a relatively strong response, though this time not the only one, stems from Austria. Leo Truchlar's "Das Kalkül der Vision: John Ashbery als Lyriker," (*Stürzl Festschrift*, pp. 507–23), and Waltraud Mitgutsch's "Gary Snyder's Poetry: A Fusion of East and West," (discussed below), single out one poet each of the generation of the late 1920s and early 1930s. Franz H. Link joins these two critics with an essay on Ashbery's exact contemporary W. S. Merwin. He had shown up briefly as early as 1968 in Hans Galinsky's *Wegbereiter moderner amerikanischer Lyrik* while Snyder ten years later figured with Faas (see *ALS 1978*, p. 460) as well as shortly after with Schiffer (*ALS 1979*, p. 505). Ashbery, however, seems a newcomer to researchers in German-speaking countries, although he started publication almost 30 years ago. Truchlar's "attempted appreciation" proceeds by quotation collage. Half of the ten chapters reprint poetological texts from two older American and two younger German poets (Poe, Stevens; Günter Eich, Hans Magnus Enzensberger) as well as a statement on the short review essay by contemporary American poet-critic Laurence Lieberman. Motif-like, they prelude themes sounded in Truchlar's own "approximation" of Ashbery. Similarly quotes from Ashbery's poetics in chapters 3 and 4 prelude Truchlar's comments on Ashbery's work from 1953 through 1977. They illumine "the central thematic complexes" of "consciousness and temporality." The comparative slant provided by Eich and Enzensberger is particularly enlightening. Unlike Ashbery, Snyder does not need an introduction any more. Since Mitgutsch interprets his poetry as "a fusion of East and West," the aspect of comparative literature is incisive. Hence this essay and, also due to its comparative affiliations, another essay which at least in part once more concerns Ashbery will be reserved for section *b*. So will an essay on Robert Duncan because of its accent on poetics.

Without a primary angle on comparison or poetics is Link's "W. S. Merwin: Metaphysiker des Schweigens" (*LJGG* 21:303–20). He reprints 20 poems selected as representative of the three phases Link makes out in Merwin's career. The first, that of acquisition of technical mastery, is said to extend from *A Mask for Janus* through *The Drunk in the Furnace*, the second marked by the "expression of a personal style" is understood to range from *The Moving Target* through *Writings to an Unfinished Accompaniment* while a third phase apparently reflecting "the mellowness of a late style" is felt to start with *The Compass Flower* (1977). Each of the chosen poems is briefly interpreted as indicating a "relationship with reality" "in the different stages of [Merwin's] development." The language of the poems is shown to "mirror" this "relationship." It is Merwin the "metaphysician of silence" who finally emerges from this first, selective, analysis of more than 25 years of his poetry. The analysis, primarily intrinsic, admits such biographical and literary-historical data as Merwin's concern with Zen Buddhism and his allusions to other poets, both American and foreign. A large subject has been thrown open circumspectly.

b. **Literary Criticism and Theory. Comparative and Didactic Studies.** Whereas literary criticism and theory exercised less appeal, that of comparative and didactic studies intensified. In the former field two general topics, the value of literary works (including autobiographies) about art and artists as documentary sources of literary theory, and problems of literary reception have been examined. Alfred Weber's "Poetologische Gedichte und Künstlererzählungen als Dokumente der Poetik," *Anglistentag; Vorträge und Protokolle*, ed. Kuno Schuhmann, TUB Dokumentation Kongresse und Tagungen (Berlin: Technische Universität), pp. 67–96, defines a personal and a thematic criterion for material suitable to be evaluated for a projected, mainly American, history of the first-mentioned topic. Weber senses the difficulty that goes with deriving discursive statements on poetics from completely or partly imaginative treatments of art and artists. He is right in stressing the significance of such research for a more intensive illumination of the poetics of an author, a period, an age or a literature as a whole. Alphabetically arranged, a "first, tentative checklist" of 315 18th-through-20th-century authors of stories and novels about art and artists is appended. An annotated bibliography is in preparation. The discussion following the original delivery of this article as a conference paper is printed in an appendix. Reception problems are discussed in Hartmut Heuermann's "Kognitive Dissonanz als Phänomen der literarischen Rezeption: Zur Übertragung und Anwendung einer sozialpsychologischen Theorie auf die Literaturwissenschaft" (*Archiv* 217:134–50). Heuermann asks to what extent American communication theories and American literary criticism that responded to them can be applied to German literary scholarship. The material for Heuermann's article consists of collected and selectively quoted reactions of German readers to short stories, among them such a post-Modern American specimen as J. P. Donleavy's "At Longitude and Latitude" (*Meet My Maker the Mad Molecule*). Scholarly informants on literary author-reader communication include American literary critics M. H. Abrams (ed., *Literature and Belief*) and Robert Scholes (*Structural Fabulation*), several social psychologists, e.g., R. P. Abelson, J. S. Adams, J. O. Friedman and W. McGuire. The title of Heuermann's essay explicitly refers to Leon Festinger's *A Theory of Cognitive Dissonance*. Heuermann answers his topical questions as an adherent to empirical methods in social psychology and as a believer in the basic identity of human reactions to empirical and fictional social reality. Therefore Irving L. Janis et al., *Personality and Persuability* is thought to be particularly relevant to students of literary reception. Final judgment will have to await the announced complete publication of Heuermann's informants' response data.

As for the more specific topics, Ulrich Horstmann's "Mythos der Bemächtigung: Ammerkungen zur Ästhetik des Ralph Waldo Emerson" (*Amst* 25:175–97) substitutes Emerson the "artificial" mythmaker for Emerson the rational thinker. He tries to justify this substitution by critically examining previous researchers' three ways of coming to terms with the "irrationalisms" in Emerson's world-view: (1) "surrender" of one's own claim to a rational perception of that view, (2) "rigorous rationalizations of the irrational," (3) "evasion into the empirics" of tracing the sources of Emerson's ideas. These approaches are asserted to have failed. Emerson the mythmaker is detected by applying criteria of French structuralists Lévi-Strauss and Barthes to his writings. The myth is supposed to be that of man "seizing" (or usurping) nature in accordance with the Judeo-Christian tradition rooted in the command of Genesis. Emerson's myth is seen in line with the 19th-century's colonizing imperialism. Art serves as "a kind of trailblazer for an anthropocentric usurpation that has lost all sensitiveness of the dignity and autonomy of the natural object." A much less active countermyth, however, is also observable. In it "nature's inaccessibility" is "remembered," and art functions in that myth as effecting a Kantian state of disinterested pleasure. Horstmann's radical revision of the prevailing image of Emerson feels supported by Perry Miller's skepticism of a history-of-ideas approach toward Emerson's thought. Horstmann dates it toward the end of that approach. As a matter of fact, the pertinent essay was published as early as 1940.

With Rolf Meyn's *Die "Rote Dekade": Studien zur Literaturkritik und Romanliteratur der dreissiger Jahre in den USA* (Hamburg: Hamburger Buchagentur) attention shifts to literary criticism and literary practice of the 1930s. Both had already attracted Hansen (*ALS 1977*, p. 489; *ALS 1979*, p. 483) and Diedrich (*ALS 1979*, p. 494). From the former he differs by combining literary theory with literary practice, from the latter by not restricting himself to Afro-American writers. In part 1 he describes the "left drift" in American literature represented by the "Red Decade's discussion of literary theory." In part 2 he examines the range of proletarian fiction and novels of social realism. The "Epilog" looks beyond the decade to new developments. Both parts are connected by a state-of-research report on the Red Decade to enrich a monograph packed with information. The poetics of a single author, evolving through several decades after the Red one, are explored in Reinhold Schiffer's "Robert Duncan: The Poetics and Poetry of Syncretic Hermeticism" (*Poetic Knowledge*, pp. 160–65). Considering him a "secularized mythologist," Schiffer is aware of the diversity of Duncan's mythological sources but fixes upon Eros as their unifying principle. Thus Schiffer's essay is primarily a poetics, not a comparative, study. Texts commented upon stem from *Caterpillar Anthology* and *The Truth and Life of Myth in Poetry*. Duncan's poetics, building on what Schiffer calls a "parallelism between theogony and genesis of the poem," is shown to yield a poetic practice which uses "the collage of the numinous." "A Poem Slow Beginning" and "Moving the Image" serve for examples. The comparatist in Schiffer, by adducing Blake, drives home a decisive difference: "For all the evocations of a mystical brotherhood in poetry, he [Duncan] is no visionary of the transcendental. Blake's authors in eternity are Duncan's authors in fictions." From a poet-theorist of the 1940s to 1970s we move to a literary scholar-theorist of the 1960s and 1970s in Brigitte Scheer-Schäzler's "From New Criticism to Paracriticism: Some Comments on the Work of Ihab Hassan," (*Americana-Austriaca* 5:117–32). The evolution of his writings are held to reflect "the major trends in postwar American literary criticism." This evolution is defined in terms of "existentialist," "apocalyptic utopian" and "Orphist." Its range could be marked by a criticism of literature widening to a criticism of culture and eventually expanding to a criticism of consciousness. Of Hassan's books *Radical Innocence, The Literature of Silence,* and *Paracriticisms* serve for illustrations. As influences on the ideas of this latest of his books Marcuse and Buckminster Fuller are suggested while a "formal model" is found in the collage. Hassan's strengths and weaknesses are clearly stated, convincingly explained, and fairly assessed. As one of the first Scheer-Schäzler had drawn attention to Cage's experimental prose (*ALS 1977*, p. 485). It is the practicing musician as well as the musical and literary theorist that Wolfgang Max Faust returns to in "Das Wort, die Musik, das Schweigen—Notizen zu John Cage" (*Sprache im technischen Zeitalter* 20:161–72). He follows Cage as a "discoverer of silence in music and literature" from "piece 4'33"" (1952), the "Lecture on Nothing," the "Lecture on Something," and "Mestotics" in *M. Writings '67–'72* to *Il treno di John Cage* (1978). Music and literature as integrating silence are thought to be meant for an individual anarchism overcoming the capitalist system from within nonaggressively. The international, especially French and Canadian context (Maurice Blanchot and Roland Barthes; Marshall McLuhan) is touched upon briefly. From single post-Modern literary and cultural theorists one returns to a group and period phenomenon: the post-Modern decades of the 1960s and 1970s. Gerhard Hoffmann's essay "The Foregrounded Situation: New Narrative Strategies in Postmodern American Fiction," *The American Identity: Fusion and Fragmentation,* ed. Robert Kroes, *European Contributions to American Studies* 3 (Amsterdam: Amerika Instituut, Universiteit van Amsterdam), pp. 289–343, explores his topic against the background of postmodernism as "an international and general cultural phenomenon." He aims to devise "new concepts of criticism" adequate to the new products. He assumes "that any change in the basic structure of the experience of reality can, and in most cases actually does, have consequences on how the construction of meaning is achieved in literature at the situational basis." Leaning on a host of secondary sources, which seems to miss out only Hannah Arendt and Teilhard de Chardin, he delineates "the general social and cultural situation of contemporary man" with reference to "Culture and Society," "Culture and the Self," "Epistemological Change: The Sciences and Literature," "The Epistemological Void and the Modern Aesthetic Construct" and " 'Situationalism' as an Aspect of the Episteme of Postmodernism." The keyword "situation" as applied to culture, moral evaluation, and the narrative text is defined as "an experiential and imaginative structure which is common to all experiences of reality and all fictional complements to it." The term as used in general literary theory becomes of special relevance in the sections devoted to John Barth ("Parody and the Narrative Situation"), John Hawkes ("The Paradoxical Situation"), Richard Brautigan ("The Ideology of the Situation") and Thomas Pynchon ("'Abstract' situation and analogical, logical and serial narrative structures"). Related to it, the post-Modern attitude toward "symbol and meaning" is discussed with regard to Barth, Hawkes, and Pynchon. The "deconstruction and reconstruction of the imaginative fictional world" is held "to extend possibilities" to the "Fantastic," and its "Satiric, Grotesque and Comic Perspectives." This thoughtful article unites a general diagnosis of culture and literature with a theory of post-Modern fiction and an analysis of its representative works.

Comparative and didactic studies have multiplied so enormously that choice, however difficult, of representative specimens is imperative. Their continuing growth signals scholars' progressive grasp of the truth that (1) what often looks indigenously American or European has in fact been transplanted and metamorphosed, (2) American like any literary art cannot be adequately understood without relation to the other arts, and (3) American literature is consolidating its place in German classroom teaching. American roots in ancient Greek and Roman literature surface in Viktor Link's *Die Tradition der aussermenschlichen Erzählperspektive in der englischen und amerikanischen Literatur* (AF 147). He traces American and English extrahuman narrative perspective, as far as animal perspective is concerned, to Lucian's dialog "Mycillus or the Cock" and to Apuleius' *The Golden Ass*. Supported by Locke's epistemology and Henry James's literary theory and practice, multisubjectivity-oriented perspectivism is demonstrated to underlie "animal" and "thing" viewpoints of narration. An extensive bibliography helps pursue them and their "vegetable" analogs across American literature from late 18th-century American magazine stories and early 19th-century edifying tracts via Cooper's *Le Mouchoir* and the anonymous *History of a Sewing Machine* (1867) to Twain's *A Dog's Tale* and *A Horse's Tale*. A virtual terra incognita has been opened up. Only Greek literature's, Homer's, shadow falls across 20th-century Ameri-

can poetry in Klaus Martens' "Language as Heuristic Process: The
Ulysses Motif in Stevens and Ashbery" (*Poetic Knowledge*, pp. 152–
59). With Stevens it is a Dante-mediated shadow. Differing from
Homer's hero, Stevens' in "The Sail of Ulysses," according to Martens,
"knows no turning back," while closer to Dante's hero he "proves a
discoverer of knowledge; but unlike the former, he discovers knowledge only through the act of meditation." In Stevens' "Prologues to
What is Possible" the hero's voyage becomes "the uncovering of the
world by language." In the 1970s Ashbery's "Business Personals"
compares the poet with Ulysses, both being "tricksters" or "*artistes*,"
using "superior skill" in overcoming the dangers in their sailings
through their times. Also solely Greek literature figures, though not
as an influence but a point of comparison, in Katrina Bachinger's
"The Platonic Mr. P.," Part I of "The Unwritten Tales of Edgar Allan
Poe: A Nineteenth Century Artist Who Might Have Been a Twentieth" (*Stürzl Festschrift*, pp. 3–27). She analyzes cosmogonic ideas
in *Eureka* and compares them to cosmogonic thought in pre-Socratic
and in late Antique philosophy, especially Plotinus' *Enneads*. As
to "origin" and "composition" his cosmos is found to "anticipate in
many important features their equivalents in *Eureka*." Differences,
e.g., "the degree to which Poe's universe was subject to change," are
asserted to be due to Stoic influences. From sources of Poe's cosmogony inquiry turns to its links with "his literary theory and practice." The former are explored also in the essay's second part, "Poe's
'Half-Closed' Vision" (*ibid.*, pp. 28–43). The latter are reserved for
treatment in this second part. According to Bachinger "out of the
analogy between a composition and a universe and that between an
author and the Godhead come many of the characteristic qualities
in Poe's writing. . . . But Poe does not seem to have overcome the
Plotinus in his creative soul, much though he did in his cosmogony."
She sees her thesis proved by "MS. Found in a Bottle," *The Narrative
of Arthur Gordon Pym*, and especially "The Fall of the House of
Usher." Her conclusion that "Poe's tale, although modeled on his
cosmogony, comes to a Plotinic end, when it might, on the basis of
his own arguments, have foreshadowed "Finnegan's Wake" or "Waiting for Godot" seems premature. Emphasis on the cosmogonic ideas
and reference to Plotinus will surely be taken up by future research.

The ancient Roman and Germanic heritage in the Arlechino and
Harlequin figures of Italian and French Renaissance theatre is

studied for its filtering through the British and American 18th–19th-century stage and for its impact on post-1945 American fiction in Kordula Rose-Werle's *Harlekinade*. The view of vaudeville as middle-class continuation of *commedia dell' arte* is basic to this monograph. As for Salinger, it examines "A Perfect Day for Bananafish," *Franny and Zooey, Raise High the Roof-beam, Carpenters,* and *Seymour an Introduction,* and "Hapworth 16, 1924." The "vaudeville origin" of the Glass family, *Franny and Zooey* as harlequinade, with Franny as Columbine and Zooey as Harlequin, and Seymour interpreted as contemporary modification of Pierrot furnish the main topics. With reference to the last, Rose-Werle pleads only for affinities, not for influence. The sections "Humor and Melancholy" and "Genius and Disease" contain particularly sound arguments for the Seymour-Pierrot and the Buddy-Clown metamorphoses. As for Nabokov, naturally *Look at the Harlequins!* but also the earlier *Speak, Memory: An Autobiography Revisited* supply the material for a perceptive interpretation of a remembered great-aunt's childhood advice "look at the Harlequins!" operating as leitmotif. The last chapter "The End of a Narrator" is competently argued.

Provençal literature as donor to 20th-century American literature forms the background of yet another modern metamorphosis. In "Pound's Imagist Alba: Myth as Cognitive Method" (*Poetic Knowledge,* pp. 128–40) Link relates Pound's "Aube of the West Dawn. Venetian June" and "Alba" to the Provence tradition of the "secular" and the "spiritual alba," to an Italian Cinquecento echo of the latter, and to other instances of Pound's interest in that tradition. Link's historical, analytical, and comparative method yields proof that " 'Alba' is a translation of 'Aube of the West Dawn' into imagism. In the earlier poem the mystic experience is expressed in terms of myth, in the later poem in terms of the Image." In the light of this "translation" Pound's "The Garret" is identified as another "imagist alba" in a deceptively contemporary setting. This poem like the other two is convincingly interpreted as revealed knowledge, "as an epiphany of shared reality."

The wide field of American-British literary interrelations reveals 19th-century American fiction as donor and 20th-century American drama as recipient and transformant. Uwe Böker's "Drei versteckte Briefe: Die produktive Rezeption von E. A. Poe's 'The Purloined Letter' in der englischen Detektivliteratur vor 1865 (mit besonderer

Berücksichtigung von Wilkie Collins und Andrew Forrester)" (*ArAA* 5:241–53) compares three stories crystallized around the same motif: Poe's "The Purloined Letter" (1844), Collins' "A Stolen Letter" (1854–56), and Forrester's "Arrested on Suspicion" (1863). Evidence of British borrowing is mostly internal, in Forrester's case also external. Both borrowers take over plot features and domesticate them in Victorian middle-class England, with Forrester borrowing from Poe's "The Gold Bug" as well. Both cut down on Poe's poetological and epistemological reflections and increase the narrative element. Forrester's protagonist Pendrath, a detached mathematician, is closer to Poe's Dupin than is Collins' emotional attorney and first person narrator. In *Anglo-amerikanische Shakespeare-Bearbeitungen des 20.Jahrhunderts*, ed. Horst Priessnitz, Ars interpretandi 9 (Darmstadt: Wissenschaftliche Buchgesellschaft), the editor draws up a flexible typology of British, Anglo-Irish, and American adaptations and rewritings. In " 'Haply, for I am black . . .': Politische Aspekte in den *Othello*–Bearbeitungen von Donald Howarth, Paul Ableman und Charles Marowitz" (*ibid.*, pp. 307–25) Priessnitz touches upon American 19th-century adaptations of *Othello*. Of pertinent 20th-century American works, contributors to this volume of essays select only four, post–1945 examples for description and explanation of deviation from Shakespearean models. Dieter Schulz treats of "Elmer Rice, *Cue for Passion*, Paul Baker, *Hamlet ESP*" (pp. 293–306), Norbert H. Platz investigates "Barbara Garson, *MacBird!*" (pp. 385–98). The latter contribution is a reprint from a 1976 publication (see *ALS 1976*, pp. 441–42). Less the adapting author than the radical theatre producer is the subject of Wilhelm Hortmann's "Illumination und Absurdität: Zu *William Shakespeare's 'Naked' Hamlet* von Joseph Papp" (pp. 275–92). Of these essays on *Hamlet* adaptations Schulz's is particularly methodical and due to its double topic instructively comparative. Rice's adoption of Ernest Jones's psychoanalytical interpretation, and his transformation of the Danish court setting into a California middle-class milieu are studied as to (1) their consequences for Rice's modification of Shakespeare's play as a whole, (2) the contemporary context of the 1950s (the play premiered in 1958), (3) "two tendencies characteristic of modern drama as a whole, i.e., resistance to tragedy, and the epic theatre." With Hamlet's "marvelous sensitivity" (Baker's own words), nay, "extrasensory perception" (ESP) for its center and collage for its "structuring principle" Baker's very different adaptation is analyzed with equal skill and assessed with increased severity. Hortmann's description of Papp's adaptation proceeds in terms of Papp's career, his production of *William Shakespeare's 'Naked' Hamlet* and of its critical reception. Not the Americanness of this theatrical phenomenon but its significance as an index to a trend in the international theatre is Hortmann's focus on this play. Therefore British and especially German plays and their productions are drawn in for comparison. Symptomatic of a radical tendency toward exposing the absurdity of modern life, it legitimately exploits "classic" works traditionally meant to "illuminate" life as meaningful.

Not the modern American dramatist or producer-dramatist but the British poet functions as recipient in the "Excerpts from Ted Hughes' Critical Writings" which Ekbert Faas assembles in "Appendix I" of his *Ted Hughes: The Unaccommodated Universe, With Selected Critical Writings by Ted Hughes & Two Interviews* (Black Sparrow). Here is made available valuable material for future studies of the critical and perhaps creative impact on a major contemporary British author of Emily Dickinson, Isaac Bashevis Singer, and the late Sylvia Plath, his wife.

The neighboring area of Anglo-Polish literature and its relations with American literature is visited in an affinity, not an influence study by Ferdinand Schunck. "Conrad, Hawthorne und die Tradition archetypischen Erzählens" (*Archiv* 217:374–83) distills affinities of form and world-view chiefly from "Young Goodman Brown" and "Heart of Darkness." Both stories are interpreted as journeys of initiation into evil, with their stages clearly marked. Differences in the reactions of Hawthorne's Brown and Conrad's Marlow after their return from "wilderness" to "civilization" are not concealed. The comparison is work-centered. Extrinsic factors, especially religious and moral traditions accounting for analogies and disparities, are not entirely neglected. Late 17th-century North American and late 19th-century African phases of European colonization, and corresponding culture clashes come in for brief attention. Influence of Hawthorne on Conrad via the latter's Melville and James interests is neither asserted nor excluded. After Brumm's, Ahrends', and Link's explications in their thematic, genre, and period histories Schunck's is the year's fourth attempt to elucidate Hawthorne's intriguing tale. Schunck's comparative method, based on C. G. Jung and Joseph Campbell, and its findings will provoke further discussion.

American-German crosscurrents are studied in two publications only. Thomas W. Buschhorn's "Die Resonanz der Neuen Welt: Amerikanische Stimmen zu Sudermann" is a German-language contribution of an American resident in Germany to *Hermann Sudermann: Werk und Wirkung*, ed. Walter T. Rix (Würzburg: Könighausen & Neumann), pp. 333–43. Leaning on contemporary newspaper and periodical criticism, and on American, chiefly German-American, writers' views, e.g. Mencken's *Prejudices: First Series*, Huneker's *Iconoclasts* and *Ivory Apes and Peacocks*, and Edith Wharton's *A Backward Glance*, the essay draws attention to the American translation, reputation, and influence of a once internationally acclaimed German dramatist and fiction writer. Equally informative, though in a different respect, is *USA und Deutschland: Amerikanische Kulturpolitik, 1942–1949. Bibliographie—Materialien—Dokumente*, ed. Michael Hoenisch, Klaus Kämpfe, Karl-Heinz Pütz, Materialien 15 (Berlin: John F. Kennedy-Institut). It supplements Borchers' and Vowe's monograph restricted to selected periodicals of 1945–49 (see *ALS 1979*, p. 510). It combines a selective bibliography (pp. 1–119) with reprints of documents and related material (pp. 120–350). In both parts the sections on American literature and theatre are of special relevance. So are the printings of interviews with two persons actively involved at the time. Tape-recorded in 1979, they are heavily retrospective.

Norwegian-American literary relations are represented by Dos Passos' borrowings from Ibsen. Hartwig Isernhagen's "The Boyg: A Note on Dos Passos and Ibsen," (*Arcadia* 15:44–48) restores "boyg" to its rightful place (instead of its false substitute "bogy") in "The Bitter Drink" portrait of Veblen in *The Big Money*. The novelist's own statement in 1916 that "The Great Boyg happens in Ibsen's play *Peer Gynt*" lays the basis for an ingenious study in Dos Passos-Ibsen relations. In *August Strindberg und Edward Albee: Eine vergleichende Analyse moderner Ehedramen* (Mit einem Exkurs über Friedrich Dürrenmatts *Play Strindberg*), EurH, ser. 18, vol. 23, Manfred Treib traces the indebtedness of Albee's *Who's Afraid of Virginia Woolf?* to Strindberg's *The Dance of Death* along thematic and structural lines. The representative value of the results for modern "marriage plays" is tested (1) in the frame of Albee's other plays such as *A Delicate Balance* and *The American Dream* on the one hand, (2) with reference to Dürrenmatt's adaptation of *The Dance of Death* in his *Play Strindberg* on the other.

We move from Euro-American contacts to Asian-American ones in Waltraud Mitgutsch's "Gary Snyder's Poetry: A Fusion of East and West" (*Stürzl Festschrift*, pp. 424–54). Snyder's concept of nature comes not from the classic writers of the New England Renaissance but from Amerindian folklore and Buddhist thought. The latter, as she explores it, proves complex indeed.

Ulrich Bachteler's *Die Darstellung von Werken der Malerei in der amerikanischen Lyrik des 20.Jahrhunderts* (Frankfurt: Rita Fischer) focuses on the "Bildgedicht" in pre- and post-1945 American poetry. A considerable range of poets reflected an exposure to art, both old and new: Ezra Pound, W. C. Williams, W. D. Snodgrass, Paul Engle, Nancy Sullivan, John Berryman, and others.

Didactic interest fuses with interest in a comparative approach toward American literature when imagology, the foreign study of another country's image, focuses on America's image. Its self-image is the subject of Aribert Schroeder's "Der Lincoln-Mythos: Zur Kategorie des Autostereotyps im amerikakundlichen Unterricht der Sekundarstufe II" (*Anglistik & Englischunterricht* 10:70–87). Of pre-1945 poetry Cummings' meets not only this interest but also a linguistic one. In Klaus-Dieter Gottschalk's "E. E. Cummings: Orientale II. Eine Gedichtanalyse zur Einführung in die Linguistik" (*Perspektive: textextern. Akten des 14.Linguistischen Kolloquiums Bochum 1979*, ed. Gerhard Tschauder and Edda Weigand, LArb 89, vol. 2, pp. 149–60) a Cummings poem serves as introduction to the linguistic method of textual analysis. Several of his poems receive attention in Ute Schütze's "Motivation und ästhetische Sensibilisierung im Lyrikunterricht der Klasse 12: Dargestellt an Gedichten von E. E. Cummings" (*Anglistik & Englischunterricht* 11:97–114) and in Helmut Slogsnat's "Eine Sonettfolge als Index epochaler Prozesse" (ibid., pp. 115–64). Much less form- and history-oriented is the didactic interest in the poetry of the 1960s. In Erwin Otto's "Allen Ginsbergs 'Wichita Vortex Sutra' als Gegenstand der Amerikastudien" (*ibid.*, 10:88–100). The poem is handled as a paradigm of how a modern literary text may serve a critical geocultural and sociocultural study of the United States.

The enthusiasm of didactics for the 20th century persists in the
choice of specimens from drama. Here almost only post-1945 works
are analyzed. Two out of 18 essays contributed to the collection *Das
moderne Drama im Englischunterricht der Sekundarstufe II*, ed.
Horst Groene and Berthold Schik, Scriptor Taschenbücher S 152
(Königstein: Scriptor) concern American plays. Schik takes up "The
American Dream: Traum und Alptraum in modernen amerikanischen
Drama" (pp. 33–54), Jürgen Wolter discusses "Society and the Individual: Die Geschichte der Vereinigten Staaten im modernen
amerikanischen Drama" (pp. 55–75). Schik selects Albee's *The
American Dream*, an obvious choice, Wolter makes a less obvious
one, Kopit's *Indians*, and, for briefer reference only, a most obvious
one, Miller's *The Crucible*. They complement each other in that
Albee and Miller present the white man's image of his 20th-century
present while Kopit develops the white man's image of America's
oldest ethnic minority.

As for the narrative genre, the didactic angle as usual is on the
short story. In Peter Bruck's "William Melvin Kelley's 'The Only
Man on Liberty Street' als Ausgangspunkt für eine Unterrichts-
sequenz zur afro-amerikanischen Kurzgeschichte" (*ArAA* 5:255–69),
it blends with the continuing interest in ethnic-minority literature.
Bruck distances himself from the 'misuse' of the Afro-American short
story "as a social document." His sequence of selected texts has arranged them in such a way that they primarily appeal to "the emotive
dimension of teaching." In this sequence figure the title story and "A
Good Long Sidewalk," another story of Kelley's, as well as John A.
Williams' "The Figure Eight." Choice and interpretation of these
works mark the turn from a "pseudo-intellectual" to an emotive and
empathetic approach. Even the tough subject of postmodernist fiction is tackled in didactic publications. An introduction to its short-
fiction genre is provided by Joseph C. Schöpp's "Donald Barthelme:
Leseanleitungen und Leseübungen" (*LWU* 13:34–46). In a sequence
of graded difficulty, Barthelme's "The Balloon" (from *Unspeakable
Practices, Unnatural Acts*), "The Glass Mountain," (from *City Life*),
"The Sandman" and "Sentence" (both from *Sadness*), Schöpp reminds the reader of language as a self-referential system and of fiction as language-made art, in this way language becoming its own
message. He is aware that fiction with language for its theme and
processes of its generation will shock the reader out of his com-

placency, i.e., out of his habits appropriate to mimetic literature; but he is not blind to the danger that continuous shocks will lead to monotony of texts and indifference of readers. This well-reasoned article is one of the best in this rapidly expanding field of didactics.

With the strength of its synchronic, and the relative weakness of its diachronic view of American culture and its literature, didactics more often than ever before reflects and accentuates the same characteristics of the year's German literary scholarship on the research level.

Johannes Gutenberg Universität, Mainz

iv. Italian Contributions

Gaetano Prampolini

In 1979 Professor Anzilotti—whose seven year service as contributor of *ALS* deserves the gratitude of all Italian Americanists and whose splendid reports will provide guidelines and inspiration for his immediate successor—wondered if that year's ratio of 21 contributions in book form to seven shorter ones meant the setting in of a new mode of production. The 1980 output shows a reversion to the trend of previous years: books have come down to the average figure of ten; noteworthy essays, articles and notes have risen to the unprecedented figure of 50, two-thirds of these being concentrated in three periodicals—a double issue of *Studi americani*, antedated to 1977–78 and of uncommonly good quality; two issues of *Letterature d'America*, a newly founded quarterly whose interesting program will deal with the literatures in English, Spanish, and Portuguese of the whole continent; and a special English language number of *Dismisura*, devoted to contemporary literature. Judging from sheer quantity, studies of American literature in Italy seem very thriving indeed. Their quality, however, varies within the customary, predictable range. Although most types of critical approaches are being used, those wholly or partially derived from linguistics, structuralism, semiotics and neorhetoric appear to be gaining ground, especially among young scholars. As it favors a greater closeness to the literary text, this proves in some cases a very fecund orientation—and is therefore a most welcome one. In many others, though, what strikes the reader is not so much the full mastery of procedures as the hasty assimilation of a terminology to be used as a trendy jargon. While all periods and genres have received attention, a greater share of it has gone to 20th-century poetry and to fiction (both 19th century and contemporary). Whitman, Melville, Stephen Crane, and Pound figure as the most studied of the major writers.

The interest in American literature before 1800 is witnessed this year by only three items, all of them on Puritan writers—one on Edward Taylor and two on Jonathan Edwards. In "Edward Taylor fra teologia e poesia" (*Studi di letteratura inglese e americana*, Milano: Opera Univ. dell'Univ. Cattolica, pp. 107–26), an essay clearly written but apparently uninformed about the developments of Taylor studies since 1972, Anna Maria Pellegrini, after apportioning the metaphysical and emblematistic components in some of the earlier *Preparatory Meditations* and insisting on the searing effects increasingly wrought by the imperatives of theological orthodoxy on Taylor's poetical gifts (however limited), comes to the trite conclusion that the poet's proper collocation is in the wake of the English metaphysical school. Like Pellegrini, Angelo Cecchini's essay on "Jonathan Edwards' System of Theology and Its 'Contemporariness' " (*Studi filosofici e pedagogici* 2[1978]:81–106) may be useful as a primer on its topic, inasmuch as it is a concise exposition of the main lines of Edwards' theological thought. As to the claim for the relevance of Edwards' ideas in our time, the author is far from convincing—he himself admits to have based his argument on "sweeping generalizations." Marcella de Nichilo's familiarity with Edwards' canon (both printed and manuscript), and with the studies which have accumulated around it, is as impressive as is important the topic of her *Realtà e immagine: L'estetica nei sermoni di Jonathan Edwards* (L'Aquila: L.U. Japadre), the first full-length book in Italian on this writer. It is a pity therefore that instead of a close discussion of the questions implied in its title, this 360-page thickly set volume offers an encyclopedic kind of treatment of Edwards, his life, his historical background, his culture, his intellectual development and his writings, with prolix expositions of and quotations from these as well as Edwardsian scholarship. A drastic editing would probably have helped eliminate the inconclusiveness and haziness that now impair a great deal of what de Nichilo has to say on Edwards' typology and "aesthetics" as well as on a variety of stimulating subjects such as Edwards' innovations in the rhetoric of sermon, his meta-phorical system, "pre-Romanticism" and influence on later American writers.

Three books and almost a score of shorter contributions make the crop of studies on poetry considerably richer than in previous years. In *Inventari di poesia: Walt Whitman e la poesia del Novecento* (Urbino: Quatro Venti) Alfredo Rizzardi has gathered together pieces of varying length he had been publishing since 1963—along with the essay on Whitman noticed in *ALS 1976*, the introductions to his own versions of Pound's *Pisan Cantos* and Williams' *Paterson*, a study of MacLeish's poetical achievement and two articles occasioned by the translations of books of verse by Robert Creeley and Thomas Merton. Some of these essays deserve a distinguished place in the history of American studies in Italy, presenting as they did major works by major poets to the understanding and appreciation of the Italians; the book as a whole renders a faithful image of the method of one of the most attentive and acute students—and also one of the most sensitive and successful translators—of American poetry in Italy. Precise and lucid in positioning each poet in relation to historical circumstances, cultural milieu, and literary tradition, Rizzardi's essays always manage to bring into sharp focus those moments when a poet's vision and technical skill perfectly fuse and find unique embodiment in language. Since Tommaso Pisanti's *L'immagine e il furore* (Napoli: Liguori) also consists of materials already published (and mostly noticed in ALS—cf. issues 1973, 1975, 1977), the only new book-length study of a poet is Angelo Cecchini's *Il trionfo di "Eros" su "Thanatos": "The Dream Songs" di John Berryman* (Pisa: ETS). The author's main thesis in this impassioned and fervidly reasoned (although at times carelessly written) essay, is that *The Dream Songs* have as their fundamental theme the conflict between Eros and Thanatos and, furthermore, that Berryman—consciously rejecting Freud's pessimism—succeeded in staging what he saw as the hard-won victory of Eros over Thanatos within himself. To prove all this, Cecchini explores the semantic complexity of the "Songs" that are crucial to his argument, using heuristic tools derived from Freud's works. Whatever may be the validity of the overall thesis, the analyses of the poems reveal a great deal of interpretative acumen and should be noted by future students. The essay, on the other hand, loses cogency and clarity toward the con-

clusion, where Cecchini, in his contention that Berryman both subsumes and subverts a whole literary and cultural tradition, banks too
heavily on such broad generalities from Leslie Fiedler and R. W. B.
Lewis as the Americans' "shrinking from paternity" and "the American Adam."

Three of the shorter contributions deal with 19th-century poets.
In "E. A. Poe e due canzoni femministe dell'Ottocento" (SA 23-24:
7-26) Alessandro Portelli resorts to a considerable amount of soph-
istry in trying to make Poe's ideas square with his own rather
platitudinous remarks on the reciprocal influences of highbrow,
written literature and popular, oral tradition: as a matter of fact,
of the two feminist songs under discussion, the one that has really
anything to do with Poe is "A Strike," an anonymous parody of "The
Raven" published in 1889. In " 'Come Up From the Fields Father':
lettura di una strip whitmaniana" (SGym 33,ii:955–85) Maria Vit-
toria D'Amico chooses to read this Drum Tap poem as a "mass culture product ante litteram" and specifies how easily a cartoonist
could transmute it into a comic strip by just heeding the many cues
offered by the text. The author's assumption that in this particular
poem Whitman was experimenting with an "alternative" mode of
expression so as to convey his democratic and pacifistic message to
the widest possible audience seems questionable, but this unusual
kind of reading does succeed in highlighting the kitsch side of Whitman's work. In "The Craftsmanship of Timelessness: A Linguistic
Investigation of Leaves of Grass" (SA 23–24:87–110), a dense and
stimulating essay which owes its conceptual framework and terminology to generative-transformational linguistics. Paola Ludovici's
concern is with Whitman's experimentation with language as it mani-
fests itself in violations of the phrase structure rules of English. In
particular, she concentrates on those utterances characterized by deletion of the verb: it is so that Whitman achieves timelessness, a
necessary feature of his transcendental vision of the world; but abolition of time specifications may endanger communication in many
ways. Whitman's awareness of this inescapable dilemma, the author
suggests in her rather undeveloped conclusion, accounts for the
"randomness" which marks the occurrence of that type of utterance.

Turning to 20th-century poetry, it is only becoming to start with
an essay on Pound. Although longish and overdetailed, Caterina
Ricciardi's "Pound traduce Pound: Frammenti del Canto XLIX in

'versione toscana'" (*LetA* 1,ii:67–106) is a well-grounded analysis of some lines of Canto 49 that Pound turned into Italian as guidelines for his translator Luigi Berti, who was corresponding with him in 1942. The essay clearly shows how the poet's linguistic choices and syntactic and rhythmic solutions are consonant with his pronouncements on the art of translation, mainly with his principle of essential condensation; this in turn provides keys for the interpretation of Pound's original lines. The letters of Pound to Berti quoted by Ricciardi appear also in *Ezra Pound, Lettere: 1907–1958* (Milano: Feltrinelli), a selection which includes some 40 hitherto-unpublished letters (most of them written to Italian correspondents, a good many in Italian). In a brief preface editor Aldo Tagliaferri stresses the importance of Pound's letters for an understanding of the evolution of both his poetics and politics, and also sketches an interpretation of Pound's career in psychoanalytical terms. With a "No, the late Mr Eliot was a symbolist," Donald Davie denied in 1970 that Eliot might be chiefly considered an imagist; Fausto Fiumi, in "Sul simbolismo di T. S. Eliot" (*SA* 23–24:245–303), verifies Davie's pronouncement, but also corrects it—by insisting throughout that in Eliot's thought and verse symbolism and imagism are to be seen not as mutually exclusive alternatives but as coexisting and complementary aspects. The essay culminates in a painstaking comparative discussion of Eliot's and Paul Valery's poetics: several central concepts of the former are shown to have their precise counterparts in the latter's writings; but there are also divergences—a capital one, indicative of the ultimate diversity of the two poets' goals, concerns the degree of "purity" each postulated for the language of poetry. Well-informed and rich in judicious observations, this study makes rewarding reading if one does not grow too impatient with its meandering progress and Fiumi's narcissistic prose. Current views on Hart Crane's conception of reality and on his language are likely to be modified by Barbara Nugnes's driving and penetrating "L'amoroso vuoto: considerazioni sulla natura e sul linguaggio nella poesia di Hart Crane" (*SpM* 12[1979]:70–86). Drawing her evidence mostly from *Key West* poems usually neglected by Crane students (although written at the same time as *The Bridge*) and corroborating it with an enlightening analysis of "O Carib Isle!", Nugnes points up how nature as Crane presents it is the realm of the inhuman. But while the poet's reason accepts the stark truth of a universe utterly indifferent and unresponsive to man's feelings and longings, the poet's heart rebels against it and, fascinated by nature's very "Otherness" (being absolute "Absence"), cannot resist loving and celebrating her as its only possible god. Preference for the oxymoronic and for ambiguous, obscure, even asemantic, language can then be viewed as Crane's attempt both to imitate the impenetrable self-contained-ness of the natural world and express his own ambivalent attitude toward it. A helpful guide to the reading of *Tender Buttons* is sup-plied by Marina Camboni's "Le poesie oggetto di Gertrude Stein" (SA 22–24:305–22). The author redefines, in the more rigorous terms of linguistics, the nature, aims, and results of Stein's experimenta-tions with language, recalls how "in assigning a deictic rather than a referential function to words," in trying to dissociate words from their usual referents, Stein was well aware of an analogous orienta-tion in contemporary painting (Cézanne, Picasso, the Cubists), and finally analyzes some representative "Tender Buttons" to illustrate tersely the functioning of the three fundamental procedures the writer employed in the composition of her "paintings in words."

The *Letterature d'America* issue (1,iv–v) dedicated to the lit-erature of *negritude* in the Americas contains three essays on the Harlem Renaissance. Although the one that deals with Jean Toomer's *Cane* is not primarily on poetry, the thematic concern with "cultural dualism" and "the search for identity" shared by all essays suggests a common treatment here. In the best of the three, "*Cane* di Jean Toomer: dualismo culturale e gioco oppositivo delle immagini" (pp. 167–92), Clara Bartocci acutely interprets the epigraph of the book as the generative nucleus of the whole text and shows how, in *Cane*, themes are reinforced by a network of lexical and conceptual anti-theses running through the whole structure and through individual stories and poems as well. Stefania Piccinato in "Il legato africano: ambiguità tra mito e storia in alcuni esempi della Harlem Renais-sance" (pp. 119–44) examines poems by James W. Johnson, Claude McKay, Toomer, and Countee Cullen to prove that in the attitude of the black poets of the 1920s toward Africa there coexist celebration and elegy, a proud sense of belonging and a painful sense of estrange-ment, and that this very ambivalence reflects the black American's awareness of the double cultural displacement he has to reckon with in his quest for identity. But the wording of the essay is not very lucid and, at times, the author strains the texts to yield meanings serviceable to her argument. A tendency to "overreading" also mars some of Paola Russo's otherwise perceptive analyses in "La tecnica delle antitesi nella poesia nera degli anni '20: Claude McKay e Countee Cullen" (pp. 145–66). Moreover, what Russo calls "the technique of antitheses"—while no doubt at work *within* some of the poems she examines—does not seem appropriate as overall description for the phenomenon under study: the fact that her two black poets express black American outlooks and values within forms and conventions adopted from English (white) literature should perhaps have been more simply and more correctly presented as an instance of the tradition-innovation dialectic.

Close readings of individual poems are provided by Dorith Ofri-Scheps and by Susan M. Scott. Elegantly reasoned and written in a clearcut style, Ofri-Sheps's "E. E. Cummings: A Paradox of Non-Difficulty" (*SA* 23–24:323–43) offers a model analysis of "quick i the death of thing": by poring over the phonemic, rhythmic, metric and syntactic structures of this poem and by skillfully unravelling the implications of their interplay, the author makes us realize the subtleness of Cummings' method and how rightfully the poem, being a rejoicing over Resurrection, occupies a pivotal position in *Xaîpe*. In "Wallace Stevens' 'An Ordinary Evening in New Haven': An Analysis" (*Dismisura* 39–50:98–111) Scott's attention is limited to the semantic level only, to following out the poet's "never ending meditation" on the elusive nature of reality and imagination: her clarifying comments make us aware of the importance of this last of Stevens' long poems as a recapitulation of one of the central themes in his work.

Five items concern poetry since 1945. Of these, two appear in *Dismisura* 39–50: Rolando Anzilotti's restrained and penetrating "On Lowell's *The Dolphin*: Facing Oneself" (pp. 2–6), the Italian version of which received notice in *ALS 1979*, and Paul Vangelisti's "'Where the Deer and the Antelope Play': Avantgarde Magazines in the U.S." (pp. 7–10), a cursory and yet usefully informative inventory of the major publications in the field of contemporary experimentalism (verse, visual and sound poetry). In a brief and perceptive introduction to her own translation of Lawrence Ferlinghetti's *The Mexican Night, Travel Journal* (*Notte Messicana*; Roma: Newton Compton) Barbara Lanati interprets the title of this work and recalls the reasons—existential, political and literary—that led the poet to Mexico, suggesting that while his journey ends up in total failure, his journal stands as the honest record of a positive, even if frustrating, process of self-discovery. Gabriella Morisco in *Almanacco dello Specchio* 9 (Milano: Mondadori) also writes a brief introduction to her fine versions of poems from Elizabeth Bishop's *Geography III*, but what she has to say on this poet is more amply committed to "La geografia poetica di Elizabeth Bishop" (*SpM* 12 [1979]:121–48). Here Morisco takes into account themes and tone, language and creative method, and stresses in particular the manifold roles geography plays in Bishop's poetry—as stimulus to inspiration, theme in itself, source of symbols and metaphors, and (especially in later verse) as starting point for an inward journey toward subliminal truths. Although occasionally indulging in paraphrase, the essay provides a comprehensive and reliable description of the poet's achievement. At the beginning of "*Of Woman Born*: non una stanza ma una cultura" (*LetA* 1,ii:103–34) Marina Camboni affirms that in her 1976 prose book Adrienne Rich transforms and synthesizes structural and stylistic traits of the journal, the biography, the psychological and the anthropological essay to inaugurate a new kind of *écriture*, apt to express a feminine/feminist outlook. This claim, however, is not supported by adequate evidence, since most of the essay is devoted to an impassioned and very sympathetic discussion of the ideas Rich sets forth.

For scope, learning, and insight Sergio Perosa's *Vie della narrativa americana* (Torino: Einaudi) deserves priority of mention among the studies on fiction. Originally published in 1965, this volume of essays written at different times and for different purposes, but all bearing on one central problem, now reappears thoroughly revised, updated in its bibliographical references, and substantially enlarged. What gives unity to the book is Perosa's concern with what he terms "the tradition of the new"—that search for new forms and techniques, that impulse toward experimentation, which has been an essential trait of American fiction since the second half of the 19th century. A little less than two-thirds of the volume deals with the fiction of this period, through analyses of specific works and discussions of a wider compass, while 20th-century fiction receives a briefer, "panoramic," treatment, inasmuch as its course reveals the continuing dialectic of principles and methods inherited from the previous period. The two chapters on James, the key figure in Perosa's tradition, and the two on the 1890s—that seething crucible of contradictions and innovations where, Perosa affirms, is the true beginning of 20th-century fiction—can be reckoned therefore as the fundamental ones. Chapters 3–4 (largely coinciding with part 1 of Perosa's *Henry James and the Experimental Novel,* [see *ALS 1978,* pp. 100–101]) follow out the theoretical elaboration of James's most crucial and influential innovations as well as their applications to the novels he wrote from the later 1880s to the eve of his major phase; chapters 5–6 elucidate the transformations naturalistic premises undergo in the hands of Crane, Garland, Norris, and London, as each of them, in his own peculiar way, comes to the awareness that only in being faithful to his subjective vision and through impressionistic, even "visionary," writing can the novelist best serve truth. But the whole book—the only weak part of which is perhaps the appendix (where not all the writers Perosa chooses as samples of post-World-War-II fiction obtain satisfactory characterizations)—is teeming with acute and stimulating suggestions: e.g., the definition of *The Confidence-Man* as the first American "anatomy" (Melville's anatomy of evil) or the interpretation of James's *The Sacred Fount* as both metafiction and an anticipation of the mid-20th-century antinovel.

On fiction there are three more contributions in book form— three monographs varying a great deal in quality, each offering the first Italian extended treatment of its subject. In *Una strada nel bosco: Scrittura e coscienza in Djuna Barnes* (Vicenza: Neri Pozza) Alide Cagidemetrio does perform what her title announces: it is indeed "a path into the wood" of Barnes's *écriture* and vision that she describes—a fascinating, most revealing and at times breathtaking path, though one not always easy to follow, especially for readers who happen not to be familiar with the as yet rather esoteric thought of Blanchot, Bataille, and Kristeva, in whose terms and style the author couches some of her most probing arguments. But once this is said, one as readily realizes that in this book difficulties pertain essentially to subject matter and to the depth at which this is treated, and also that its aphoristic and metaphorical style, while helping convey the author's earnest and discriminating sympathy for her writer, is part of a strategy of presentation more economical than any that could have been devised. In fact, this book is centered on *Nightwood,* and it is through the study of this novel only that Cagidemetrio manages to draw her complex and very convincing picture of Barnes as significant exponent of modernism in fiction, as a unique voice in women's literature and, above all, as an investigator of almost preternatural clear-sightedness into the recesses of the unconscious. Also in Leo Marchetti's *La narrativa di Kurt Vonnegut jr.* (Pescara: Coop. Libraria Univ. Abruzzese) the author's sympathy for his writer is clear. Clarity, however, is not an outstanding quality of this 100-page book. On the one hand, Marchetti's awkward and idiosyncratic language (critical and general) is a constant source of perplexities for the reader; on the other, the chosen strategy of treating simultaneously Vonnegut's themes (his critique of modern America, human history, and culture in defense of the inalienable rights of the self) and Vonnegut's forms (his evolution from dystopic novel through fantasy to more or less fashionable experimentations) does not prove a wise one. The result is an apparently aimless, repetitious wandering through Vonnegut's fiction and not an organic introduction to it. A volume in a series of short monographs meant for the general reader, Franco Palmieri's *Isaac Bashevis Singer* (Firenze: La Nuova Italia), is the sorry outcome of improvisation: chaotic, full of irrelevancies and factual errors, so badly written as often to prove meaningless, it could be ignored altogether here, were it not for the inclusion of a hitherto unpublished interview, sprightly and wideranging, of Singer by Lisa Billig.

Melville is the only romantic fiction writer treated this year in essay form: three items concern as many of his works. Strictly related to a forthcoming study by the same author on the same novel, Donatella Izzo's *"Typee* o della ambiguità" (*Paragone* 368:21–39) is a remarkable essay, solidly grounded in textual evidence and praiseworthy for cogency and agility. Reading her text in terms of the opposition civilization/nature, and of other antitheses deriving from this (such as sea/island, open/closed space, mobility/immobility, etc.), Izzo demonstrates not only how Tom's journey to the Typees can be interpreted as both a progressive *iter* toward knowledge and a regressive *iter* toward the innocent infancy of man and history, but, more inclusively, how ambiguity is the ruling principle on which *Typee* has been intentionally structured. The hermeneutical importance of this essay thus resides in seeing how Melville's first work, far from being simply an autobiographical tale of adventures, partakes of a basic epistemological concern of the American renaissance—and also, in the coincidence of opposite meanings it dramatizes, reflects the original ambivalence of the American experience. In his well-informed essay "*Moby-Dick; or, The Whale*: analisi di un titolo" (*SA* 23–24:27–61) Mario Corona ingeniously and exhaustively examines the title of Melville's masterpiece as "diabolically" charged with hidden meanings, finally coming to the conclusion that it contains simultaneously, in a coded manner, all the themes in the book (adventure, cosmic mystery, phallism, diabolism) as well as the author's conceptual position in regard to reality and nature. Leonardo Terzo's sociologically oriented "Lettura di 'Bartleby'" (*SA* 23–24:63–86) presents an attentive, if not very original, reading of this tale, in which the scrivener, in his very impenetrable and disturbing "otherness," is seen as the "provocative enigma" whose function is to unveil and measure the selfishness, self-complacency, hypocrisy and cowardliness of the lawyer, who in turn is seen as representative of and spokesman for degraded middle-class values.

Five items concern, instead, major fiction writers of the later 19th century. In his preface to the reprint of a selection of Henry James's tales translated by the late Carlo Izzo (*La panchina della desolazione e altri racconti*, Milano: Bompiani), Agostino Lombardo manages to compress within 17 pages, lucidly and forcefully, the essential things a reader should keep in mind about the writer's vision, method, and achievement. In "Mark Twain alle soglie della fantascienza" (*SA* 23–24:177–212) Maria Ornella Marotti rejects the views of "The Enchanted Sea-Wilderness" and "The Great Dark"—the two unfinished tales from the *Which Was the Dream?* volume of *The Mark Twain Papers* she analyzes—as simply expressions of the later Mark Twain's abhorrence of "the machine" and "the mob" or as symbols of his despair. She argues that, in their multiple dichotomies and ironical inversions, they dramatize instead Mark Twain's fundamental ambivalence about the topics which were at the center of his meditation in the 1890s. And it is significant, she finds, that it is in texts such as these that, by manipulating the conventions of the tall tale, the writer arrives at a form "at the threshold of S/F," which can embody his serious concern with the future of man. Despite some prolixities and a certain clumsiness in describing the narrative techniques employed in the two tales, Marotti makes her case rather convincingly. Stephen Crane's first important work is the object of close study in two essays also published in *SA* 23–24: Biancamaria Pisapia's "Stephen Crane: la 'lunga logica' di *Maggie*" (pp. 111–38) and Paola Cabibbo's "Linguaggio e metalinguaggio teatrale in *Maggie*" (pp. 139–75). The former closes and the latter opens on the same note, both critics finding that "absence" (of syntagmatic continuity, narrative consequentiality, climactic scenes, etc.) is the dominant element in their text: this is but one of the several, inevitable, areas of concurrence or overlapping in these essays; and yet, they differ a great deal from each other in method, objects, and results. Pisapia adopts a rather "mild" structural approach to go, somewhat diffusely, over such essential aspects of *Maggie* as its revolutionary narrative structure (elliptical and paratactical), the Bowery as closed and inescapable environment, the irony arising from asyndetic juxtaposition of disparate cultural codes, the parody of popular forms of sentimental literature and the critique of their effects. In its general drift the essay appears to be in keeping with established lines of interpretation so that its merit resides, rather, in a number of valuable insights scattered throughout. Thoroughgoing and much more sophisticated in her structuralism, Cabibbo concentrates on the theatrical dimension of *Maggie*. Deriving her interpretive model from the codes of drama, she points out, for instance, how the 19 chapters function like Brechtian *tableaux*, or how "real" spaces are presented as scenic space—and her analysis of spatial functions, in their multiple levels and complex interplay, clearly evidences what a powerful generator of meaning space is in *Maggie*. Chapter 8 receives special attention as it is, in the author's words, "the system of paraphrase of the text," reflecting "by inverted reduplication" Maggie's story, the thematic and technical novelty of *Maggie* and the attitude—aesthetically distanced, actively and critically participative—Crane requires of his reader. Cabibbo's demonstration impeccably proves that "*le pluriel du texte*" does in fact permit her kind of reading. While leaving practically nothing to add on the specific aspect it deals with, her essay throws light on Crane's nonmimetic procedures as well as the significance of *Maggie* as an early instance of narrative discontinuity. Heather Gardner's "Frank Norris: *The Octopus*" (SA 23–24: 213–43) is a comprehensive discussion of Norris' most important novel. After refuting the previous critical interpretations that tended to show how its principal message came either from the populist or anarchist vision of Norris, Gardner convincingly argues that the writer was simply an American progressive, and that *The Octopus* is "the mirror of the ideology that prevailed in the United States at the beginning of the century."

With "La 'Beatrice' di Edith Wharton" (*LetA* 1,ii:43–66) Emanuela Dal Fabbro ushers us into *entre deux guerres* fiction about which, surprisingly enough, relatively few essays have been written this year. In her tightly reasoned examination of the Wharton manuscript entitled "Beatrice Palmato" Dal Fabbro argues that the plot summary and the only finished fragment of which it consists must not be seen, respectively, as an outline and a completed part of the same whole, but as two disparate, though concomitant, conceptions. Whereas the plot summary adumbrates a ghost story in the thematic line of Shelley's *The Cenci*, the fragment brings about a total reversal of Shelley's view and treatment of incest and appears to be —Dal Fabbro sagaciously points out through a subtle textual analysis —the conclusive stage in a search for a definition of feminine identity, developing since Wharton's earliest writings and charged with autobiographical implications. With the precision and the ease of a true authority Sergio Perosa in his introduction to the Italian translation of *The Notebooks of F. Scott Fitzgerald* (*I taccuini*; Torino: Einaudi) reminds the reader of the extraordinary value of this volume as the writer's "stock-taking" at the time of his crack-up, as his literary "reservoir" and "workshop," but also as a record—no less revelatory for being fragmentary and desultory—of Fitzgerald's relationship with Zelda and Hemingway. The function of a seemingly digressive and insignificant episode in Hemingway's *A Farewell to Arms* is gracefully elucidated by Marina Gradoli in her note on "Count Greffi's Birthday Parties" (*Dismisura* 39–50:112–14): it is from the old Italian count that Frederic Henry, at a critical point of his *Bildung*, receives confirmation that in risking death and defeat (and not in trying to preserve oneself) lies the only possibility of life and redemption. In the year of his death Henry Miller figures as the subject of two articles, but neither serves him too well: in his superficial and naively commendatory "La rivolta di Henry Miller" (*OPL* 26,7:31–36) Wolfango Rossani offers trite remarks on the importance of the writer as social and moral iconoclast; in Stefano Poponi's "Henry Miller e il mondo del divenire" (*Paragone* 368:53–62) abundant, intertwined and, on the whole, abstruse references to Deleuze's concept of "difference" as well as to Nietzsche's Dionysian aesthetics and to psychoanalysis (this, very mechanistically applied) end by obfuscating, rather than clarifying the topic, i.e., the centrality of "becoming" (and related notions like flux, masking, appearance, deception) in Miller's views of reality and of writing.

A spirited, provocative, and at times amusing survey of post-World-War-II fiction, using religious categories to group writers, giving an insider's account of the origins of the innovative trend and questioning the meaning and "morality" of "obtrusive techniques" employed in new fiction, is offered by John Gardner in "A Writer's View of Contemporary American Fiction" (*Dismisura* 39–50:11–31), an essay which, to all effects, reads like a preparatory draft of Gardner's *On Moral Fiction* (see ALS *1978*, p. 431). In her study of madness as a central theme in the novels of the 1960s ("Strategie della follia nel romanzo americano degli anni Sessanta," *Studi di letteratura inglese e americana*, pp. 9–55) Gianfranca Balestra distinguishes novels where madness respectively appears in connection with the woman's condition, in the context of a critique of society and its repressive mechanisms, as a metaphor of reality or an escape from rationality, and examines Plath's *The Bell Jar*, Kesey's *One Flew Over the Cuckoo's Nest*, and Pynchon's *The Crying of Lot 49* as representative of each of the three types. The topic is not very original, but the essay, if lengthy, is highly readable and contains some fine observations, especially on the technical problems a writer has to solve in rendering psychotic states.

Three articles deal with individual writers. In "James Purdy's Short Stories" (SA 23–24:345–62), though offering no really new insights (except perhaps in the interpretation of "Sermon" as Purdy's "most explicit illustration of his view of the human condition" and also as "the manifesto of [his] conception of the author and his relation to his public"), Jane Wilkinson proves perceptively alert to the symbolic meanings of recurrent images, settings, and characters. On the whole, her essay makes a sound introduction to Purdy's fictional world. Jerome H. Stern's "The Interfaces of *Gravity's Rainbow*" (*Dismisura* 39–50:51–57) focuses on Pynchon's concept of "interface" as both a structural principle (suggesting a plurality and interaction of meanings) and a pervasive image in his novel. Life for Pynchon is richest, most fully felt—the author maintains—whenever rational oppositions are fused and transcended: the novel's artistic power is thus to be found in the writer's ability to bring together the many paradoxes of reality, fusing them in what Stern aptly calls an "apotheosis of transformation." In "Ishmael Reed: strategie di uno '*storyteller*' " (*LetA* 1,iv–v:215–32) Fedora Giordano likens the writer to a "man of words" of Afroamerican oral tradition and his works to performances by a traditional storyteller involving the audience in active participation. From the title one may expect this essay to be centered on the analysis of storytelling strategies, but more than half of it is devoted to an exposition of the contents of Reed's books.

Two items on N. Scott Momaday's *House Made of Dawn* bear witness to the interest growing around the literature of the "American Indians." In his introduction to the Italian version of the novel (*Casa fatta di alba*, Milano: Guanda [1979]) Franco Meli delineates the writer's concerns and achievement and offers a sensible reading of *House Made of Dawn*, rightly stressing in particular the crucial importance of the language motif in view of both literal and symbolic meanings of Abel's story. Gaetano Prampolini's "On N. Scott Momaday's *House Made of Dawn*" (*Dismisura* 39–50:58–75) begins by investigating the function of the second of Tosamah's sermons within the whole semantic structure; then, in turn, contrasts the meanings that landscape, animal life, and progress take on in Momaday's novel and in Willa Cather's *My Ántonia*, defines the extent of Momaday's indebtedness to Faulkner's style and narrative techniques, and tries to prove how parallelism is the structuring principle everywhere at work in the novel. The essay ends by suggesting an analogy between Momaday and the fiction writers of the Southern Renaissance—one resting on affinities in narrative method and poetics but ultimately on the historical experience of defeat shared by the cultures they respectively belong to.

Incisive questions elicit informative answers from two prominent writers in two interviews that also appear in *Dismisura* 39–50. In "On His Sexual Triad. A Conversation with Stefano Tani [which took place in 1976]" (pp. 32–37) John Hawkes talks at length of *Travesty* and comments on themes, characters, and image patterns recurrent throughout his work. In "On *The Surface of Earth*" (pp. 38–50), edited by Liana Borghi from a class discussion taped at the Salzburg Seminar in 1977, Reynolds Price expatiates on his writing habits, southern history and mind, but chiefly on characters (especially female), structure, style, and the autobiographical matrix of his latest novel.

Not much work has been done this year on drama. What we have, however, is well done and interesting. The bulk of Ruggero Bianchi's 521-page *Autobiografia dell'avanguardia: Il teatro sperimentale americano alle soglie degli anni Ottanta* (Torino: Tirrenia-Stampatori) consists of the answers given by the leaders of 22 theatre groups active in New York and San Francisco during the interviews Bianchi had with them in 1978–1979. To produce the effect of "self-analysis" implied in the title, Bianchi effaces himself as interviewer by suppressing his own questions and arranging the answers as if they were independent pronouncements. One may wonder whether this method really achieves the objectivity looked for by Bianchi: in any case, the book (to which an impressive bibliography is appended) is an extremely rich source of information on one aspect of contemporary American theatre as yet largely unknown in Italy. A first assessment of it—convincing though necessarily provisional— is offered in an introductory essay where Bianchi indicates common trends in the work of the various groups and suggests that what distinguishes the avant-garde theatre of the 1970s from that of the 1960s is greater theoretical awareness, emphasis on experimentation as the true essence of theatre, but also the rejection of direct political commitment. In "Agit-prop Theater of the Thirties" (*Dismisura* 39–50:81–92), after shrewdly pointing out how the uniqueness of each performance, the participants' attitude toward the event and the sociopolitical homogeneity of actors and audience are the main distinctive traits of this type of theatre as compared to both traditional drama and political mass-spectacles, Annamaria Pinazzi outlines the history of Agit-prop in the United States, placing special emphasis on the substantial changes in purposes, themes and modes of production that finally caused it to dissolve into conventional forms of professional theatre. In a lively interview given in 1976 to Antonella Siniscalco (*Dismisura* 39–50:93–97) Edward Albee looks back to and comments on the various phases of his career.

American writers traveling or sojourning in a foreign country peg out for the Americanists of that country a very inviting and at times more accessible field of study—one covered this year in Italy by one book and three essays. Giovanni Cecchin's purpose in *Con Hemingway e Dos Passos sui campi di battaglia italiani della Grande Guerra*

(Milano: Mursia) is to identify closely persons, places, and events connected with Dos Passos' and—mainly—Hemingway's service in Italy during World War I. His research through the American Red Cross archives and through journals, interviews, and documents of every kind is formidably extensive and minute, and traces a vividly detailed picture of life in the frontline and behind it. Much guess-work is involved in verifying passages of Hemingway's fiction and Dos Passos' letters and diaries. Cecchin's curiosity indulges too much in this, and the book, though impressive with the information dis-played, is bound to be a disappointment if one expects it to discuss how Hemingway transforms facts into fiction. In a 28-page pamphlet (*Viaggiatori americani a Livorno nella prima metà dell'Ottocento*, Pisa: ETS) Algerina Neri culls from letters, memoirs, and journals the most telling (and sometimes curious) reactions of ten Americans —the most famous of whom are Elizabeth Ann Seton, James F. Cooper, and Bayard Taylor—who visited Leghorn from 1803 to 1847. The last two essays of this group appear both in *Studi di fiologia e letteratura* [Univ. di Genova] 5, and both take Pound's residence in Rapallo as their starting point. Massimo Bacigalupo's "Linea ligure angloamericana: Pound, Yeats" (pp. 477–533) combines exegesis and reminiscence to provide a number of fine insights into Pound's activity in Italy. The author's long familiarity with Pound's *oeuvre* is shown by the ease with which he explicates individual lines and references; his essay, scholarly and well written, though somewhat rambling, touches upon such different subjects as Pound's version of Cavalcanti, his friendship and literary association with Yeats, and emphasizes the central role played by Ligurian landscape in the physical and symbolic geography of the *Cantos*. In "*L'Indice*: Ezra Pound e gli anni '30 in una rivista genovese" (pp. 395–427) Laura Barile illustrates Pound's contribution to a little magazine published in Genoa from 1930 to 1931. The poet's pronouncements (in Italian) may frequently sound incoherent and naive, yet they appear re-freshingly alive, irreverent, and informative when set against the background of the stifling provincialism in which they were con-ceived.

Three more essays may be grouped together under a "compara-tive studies" heading. With "La penna del pittore: artisti-scrittori dell'Ottocento americano" (*LetA* 1,ii:5–41) Andrea Mariani takes another step in his study of the relationship between literature and art in America by soberly evaluating the writings of four early 19th-century painters. Very little of literary merit is shown in S. J. Copley's letters, Washington Allston's poems, Thomas Cole's and A. B. Durand's verse; the important thing—Mariani propounds in his conclusion—is that these men helped establish that figure of writer-artist that was to become so prominent in American culture from the second half of the century on. In her "Dossi, Poe e il gusto del macabro" (*Otto-Novecento* 4,v–vi:58–67) Antonia Tonucci Mazza tries to trace Poe's influence on the 19th-century Lombard writer Carlo Dossi, whose early work presents some predilection for macabre and morbid themes of death. Since no external evidence can be found of Dossi ever reading Poe, and the internal evidence is very small and based on affinities, analogues, and coincidences, Mazza's conclusion that "Dossi is to be included in the list of the earliest Italian readers of Poe" remains arbitrary or, at least, questionable. An unfairly neglected episode in the history of Eliot's fortune in Italy is exhaustively and intelligently studied by Barbara Nugnes in "T. S. Eliot e Mario Luzi un caso di affinita" (*RLMC* 33,ii:129–55). The thematic and stylistic development of this major Italian poet in the postwar years had long been regarded as somewhat idiosyncratic: solidly resting on the comparison of significant passages, Nugnes's investigation not only reveals the startling analogies between the two poets' visions and values but also demonstrates the quality and extent of Luzi's indebtedness at a crucial point of his literary growth to Eliot's ideas and poetic achievement.

The final mention goes to a reference book: *Dizionario della letteratura mondiale del 900* (3 vols., Roma: Edizioni Paoline), the American literature section of which, directed by Rolando Anzilotti, consists of 295 entries concerning all the major and most of the minor writers of this century (including the majority of those who have won their renown since 1965). Mostly written by Italian specialists, the entries vary in length and also in quality, but the standard seems consistently higher than in the average enterprise of this kind. After basic biographical information on the writer each entry offers a description and an evaluation of his work and is followed by a bibliography updated to 1979—virtually complete for primary sources and obviously selective for the secondary ones.

Università di Firenze

v. Japanese Contributions

Hiroko Sato

In 1980 Japanese scholars of American literature were as prolific as ever. The present report is by no means a complete list of their products but a commentary on their major achievements. The most impressive production of the year is the three-volume collection of critical essays on American literature, *Bungaku to Amerika* [*Literature and America*] (Tokyo:Nan'undo), published in celebration of the 60th birthday of Kenzaburo Ohashi, the president of the American Literature Society of Japan. This voluminous work (about 1,200 pages altogether) is representative of the range of interest, quality, and methods of scholars of American literature in this country. The 19 contributors of the first volume are the most recent of Ohashi's students at the University of Tokyo; some of them are still in the graduate school, while others have just started their teaching careers. It is a remarkable event that those young students, who have previously published their accomplishments only in privately printed magazines, are given a chance to present the results of their research to the wider public. Most of these scholars choose as the objects of their study works of major writers, such as Poe, Melville, Twain, Crane, West, Steinbeck, Faulkner, and Bellow, but some ambitiously deal with such postmodernist writers as Thomas Pynchon, while others try to gain wider cultural perspective through considering the writings of Benjamin Franklin, Henry David Thoreau, and Walt Whitman. Though most of the contributors of this volume are still nebulous in their critical ideas and methods, some articles show that their writers have already found subjects of interest and their own methods to apply to them. Takaki Hiraishi's article on Melville's "Bartleby the Scrivener," " 'Bartleby' to Hampuku no Genri ['Bartleby' and the Principle of Repetition]" (pp. 63–73), for example, is an attempt to account for the artistic success of the story from a technical point of view. Hiraishi notices that Melville uses the technique of repetition, which is a cliché of the 19th-century novel effective in creating "flat people," on several levels such as actions, situations, and language, and so succeeds in emphasizing the mysteriousness of the protagonist, impervious to understanding, in contrast with the flat people around him, each with one easily recognizable characteristic.

Yasuki Saeki ambitiously applies Wolfgang Iser's theory of the "reader" and tries to reconstruct Faulkner's *The Sound and the Fury* in the whole context of the Yoknapatawpha Saga, in "Fukuzai suru Nendaiki [A Hidden Chronicle]" (pp. 144–59). Two essays on Thomas Pynchon, Yoichiro Miyamoto's "Meikyu no V[V in a Labyrinth]" (pp. 239–53) and Yoshiaki Sato's "Chitsujo to Konton no Arina de [In the Arena of Order and Chaos]" (pp. 254–65), attract our attention because of their authors' fresh sensibility, not yet marred by the toilsome work of interpretation, which enables them to feel an instinctive affinity with the world of this difficult author. Miyamoto insists that Pynchon defies interpretation (applying Susan Sontag's definition of "interpretation"), and that in V Pynchon creates a universe which no traditional interpretation, however brilliant, such as that of Tony Tanner (*City of Words*), will ever be able to grasp. Miyamoto points out that effectiveness of Pynchon's use of the disruption of identity and paranoiac psychology, and his circuitous way of narrating in creating that universe. Sato goes a step further and defines Pynchon's standpoint as being in the arena where order (the world of meaning) and chaos (that of nonmeaning) engage in a deadly conflict. This conflict, a symbol of modern civilization, is presented by Pynchon's use of metaphors and analogies throughout his novels from V to *Gravity's Rainbow*. The first volume concludes with an article by Kenzaburo Ohashi himself, based on his final lecture at the University of Tokyo on his retirement in March 1980. Titled "Faulkner no Hoho [Faulkner's Methods]" (pp. 266–80), this essay indicates what Ohashi has done, is doing, and will be doing as the most-noted and prolific Faulknerian in Japan. (The publication of the third and last volume of his *Faulkner Studies* [volume 1 in 1977 and volume 2 in 1979] is being awaited with great expectation.)

The second volume of *Literature and America* includes 25 articles by Ohashi's former students who are now rising scholars and teachers of American literature. Their ways of approach and choice of subjects are wider and more varied than those of the contributors of the first volume. Some of them try comparisons: Haruko Kimura juxtaposes the critical principles of Poe and Margaret Fuller and tries to show the excellence of Fuller as a literary critic in "Poe to [and] Fuller" (pp. 4–24), while Koichi Ikeda searches for common images in the works of Longfellow, Whittier, and Hawthorne in

"Mori to Rohan [Woods and Hearth]" (pp. 28–42). Hiroshi Narasaki tries an even wider topic in his "Gendai Amerika Shosetsu ni okeru Isho [Design in Contemporary American Novel]" (pp. 374–88). However, perhaps because of the limited space allowed (no more than 20 pages), the most convincing essays are those which deal with one work from a very restricted point of view. In *"Billy Budd* Shiron [On *Billy Budd*]" (pp. 77–89) Taro Shimada contends that Melville started to write the novella not in 1888, as has generally been believed since Jay Leyda's *Melville Log*, but sometime in the 1870s. Referring to Captain Vere's controversial attitude toward Billy's execution and to various interpretations of Billy's final words, Shimada also points out that, through gradual changes, Melville comes to accept the necessity of the sacrifice of an individual for the sake of the order and peace of a society. Shimada's demonstration of the development of Melville's philosophy, using his letters, poems such as "The House-Top," and the underlined parts in the books he read around that time as supporting materials, is quite convincing. Hirotada Ohara shows how just the choice of names of characters multiplies and deepens the significance of a story in *"Winesburg, Ohio* no 'Te' Saiko [A Reconsideration of 'Hands' in *Winesburg, Ohio*]" (pp. 180–97). Two names assumed by the protagonist, Adolph Meyers and Wing Biddlebaum, emphasize his isolated state, for both Meyers and Biddlebaum not only suggest German origin (an immigrant in America) but Jewishness, while the latter also refers to John Biddle, the British religious fanatic. "Wing" itself suggests the airy dexterity of his hands. On the other hand, the name of his persecutor, Henry Bradford, originates from William Bradford (the Puritan) and Henry Ford (the capitalist and Jew-hater). Ohara argues that Anderson's intention in writing this story goes beyond the expression of grotesqueness of the human mind; he creates a segment of the modern world which can be regarded as representative of how manual laborers are persecuted and alienated. In *"The Wild Palms* Shiron [On *The Wild Palms*]" (pp. 298–314) Fumiyo Hayashi asserts that *The Wild Palms* is one of the most important novels by Faulkner and argues that the two stories are indispensable to each other as they illustrate two aspects of the relationship between man and woman. Hayashi diagrams the relationships of the characters, such as Charlotte and the convict versus Harry, valuing Harry's acceptance of prison life as a symbolic gesture of his love for Char-

lotte and comparing his attitude with that of the evasive Ike Mc-
Caslin. Hayashi points out that Faulkner places this novel outside of
Yoknapatawpha County because he wants to examine the question
fully, without being restricted by the social and historical set-up of
the imaginary region.

Twenty distinguished scholars who are Ohashi's friends and contemporaries are the contributors to the last and most substantial vol-
ume of this collection. Most of their names are already familiar to the
readers of *ALS*; to name a few, Iwao Iwamoto [*Malamud* (1979)],
Yokichi Miyamoto [*American Authors and Japanese Readers* (1977)],
Masayuki Sakamoto [*Writers of American Renaissance* (1974) and
Hawthorne (1977)], and Toshio Yagi [*Poe* (1978)]. These noted
Americanists seem to be at the height of their powers in these short
essays. Some of the articles are examples of textual criticism; Hikaru
Saito compares two editions (the first and New York editions) of
James's *The Portrait of a Lady* and discusses the merits and demerits
of the revision in "*Aru Fujin no Shozo* Kaitei ni okeru Hitotsu no
Gimon [A Question on the Revision of *The Portrait of a Lady*]" (pp.
240–51), while Masaji Onoe's "*The Sound and the Fury* to [and]
T. S. Eliot" (pp. 329–51) not only shows the influence of T. S. Eliot
on Faulkner, but also throws light on some obscure passages in Faulkner's novel. Several articles add new facts to the history of American
literature. "Sedai no Kyokaisen [A Borderline between Generations]"
(pp. 270–81), by Fukuo Hashimoto, deals with the relationship between the Lost Generation and its predecessor, symbolized by Hemingway's writing of *The Torrents of Spring*, and the circuitous way
of transmitting literary heritage. Kenji Inoue in "Steinbeck to Jin-
shuteki Henken [Steinbeck and Racial Prejudice]" (pp. 390–403)
takes up a thus-far-ignored side of the novelist. Kichinosuke Ohashi's
"*American Spectator* to [and] Sherwood Anderson" (pp. 282–96),
which throws light on the relationship between the literary newspaper and Anderson and Dreiser, is a fruit of his lifelong study of
Anderson, while another product of his wide-ranging research,
"*Amerika Proretaria Shishu* to Sherwood Anderson [*American Proletarian Poetry* and Sherwood Anderson]" (a study of the influence
of American socialistic poetry on Japanese intellectuals), published
in 23 installments in *Eigo Seinen* (*The Rising Generation*), was
completed in October and will be published in book form in 1981.

Toshio Watanabe's survey of the history of Mark Twain criticism
(pp. 222–39) is also a survey of the history of literary criticism in
America. In "Mark Twain no Tanjo [The Birth of Mark Twain]"
(pp. 204–21) Shunsuke Kamei analyzes the construction, contents,
and language of *Roughing It* to show that all the elements which
later flowered in Mark Twain's major works had already existed in
this chaotic earlier autobiographical work. This article and "Recon-
sidering Mark Twain" (*Eigo Seinen* 125:484–86), which deals with
The Gilded Age, seem to be two parts of a larger study of the writer.
Shizuo Suyama's "Eugene O'Neill: *The Iceman Cometh*" (pp. 297–
312) is a very stimulating essay and a good illustration of what Japanese traditional intuitive literary criticism is like. After examining
critical comments on the play by Rosamond Gilder, Eric Bentley,
Mary McCarthy, Doris Falk, Robert Brustein, and others and pointing out their defects, Suyama denies Hicky's madness and tells us
how this fact makes the world of the play futile and desolate, and
what a trying experience it must be to the audience to witness the
revelation. Among three essays on Faulkner, Shozo Kajima's "Kakuju
ni yoru Heiko [Balance by Development]" (pp. 352–77) is outstanding for his solid scholarship and logical presentation of his ideas.
Kajima, whose translation of *Light in August* is generally acclaimed,
exemplifies by this novel how Faulkner's novel came to take its
present form through finding a balance while simultaneously stretching the branches of the narrative in various directions. Hidekatsu
Nojima's "June Miller: Meikyu no Onna Noto [A Note on Women
in a Labyrinth]" (pp. 404–23) is a part of a larger work (which will
be published in book form in 1981); it is an inspiring study of mysterious conflicts between the sexes and of how the impact of these
conflicts instigates the creative power of a writer and affects the
world he creates. Hisao Kanaseki, the author of the delightful book
American Indian Poetry (1977), here contributes an essay on Robert
Bly. In "Fushigi no Kuni no Shijin: Robert Bly [A Poet in Wonder-
land: Robert Bly]" (pp. 460–78) Kanaseki demonstrates the effect
of Bly's plain, antipoetic language and the beauty of Bly's poetry
with appropriate quotations.

A handy reference book on American literature came out this
year. *The Compact History of American Literature* (Tokyo: Aratake
Shuppan), ed. Iwao Iwamoto and Masayuki Sakamoto, is accurate

in information and judicious in judgment; it will be a great help to college students interested in American literature. Another book of reference worth mentioning is *Amerika Joryusakka Gunzo* [*American Literary Women*] (Kyoto: Shinshindo), ed. Rikutaro Fukuda. This book gives biographical facts, explanatory notes on major works, and suggestions for further research, with bibliography, on 30 American women writers and poets from Anne Bradstreet to Erica Jong.

Though entirely different in nature, two books on American culture attract our attention. One is Toshio Watanabe's *Franklin to Amerika Bungaku* [*Franklin and American Literature*] (Tokyo: Kenkyusha). Well aware of, and partially sympathetic to, the derogatory image of Franklin created by D. H. Lawrence, Watanabe nevertheless carefully evolves his own image of this versatile man of the Enlightenment by comparing him with Jonathan Edwards and Mark Twain and shows how Franklin's philosophy of life has affected American society until the present day. This book, seemingly a biography of a single man, is in reality an illuminating study of American culture as a whole. The other is an enchanting book by Hisao Kanaseki titled *Navaho no Sunae* [*Sand Paintings by the Navajo*] (Tokyo: Ozawa Shoten). In this collection of essays on American poetry and art, Kanaseki successfully presents the essence of American culture, while also giving his personal impressions.

Among books on individual writers and poets, three scholarly works are quite outstanding. Four years after the publication of the scholarly feat, *A Sinclair Lewis Lexicon* (1976), Hiroshige Yoshida brought out *Huckleberry Finn Kenkyu* [*A Study of "Huckleberry Finn"—Study Notes, Style, Glossary*] (Tokyo: Shinozaki Shorin). In this book Yoshida's interest lies in the linguistic aspect of the novel, and parts 2 and 3, "Style and Dialectic Element" and "Glossary," are valuable contributions to the study of Mark Twain in Japan. *Emily Dickinson no Giho* [*The Art of Emily Dickinson*] (Tokyo: Kirihara Shoten), by Takao Furukawa, is a good example of how artistic intuition is combined with a keen analytical mind to create a solid critical work. Himself a poet, Furukawa's analysis of Emily Dickinson's art is supported by his instinctive affinity with the poet. Supporting his theory of her poetics, and of the structure and techniques of her poetry with appropriate examples, he tries to present Emily Dickinson as a poet always mindful of the artistic effect of her poetry. Hisao Aoki's *Erskine Caldwell Kenkyu Josetsu* [*An Introduction to a*

Study of Erskine Caldwell] (Tokyo: Wako Shuppan) is a well-documented study of the now almost forgotten novelist.

Two periodicals brought out special issues on American literature. *Eureka* (June Special Issue; Tokyo: Seidosha), featuring contemporary American poetry, discusses works by such poets as Pound, Stevens, Williams, Cummings, Roethke, Olson, Creeley, and Bly. Noted scholars and poets like Junnosuke Sawasaki, Yozo Tokunaga, Shinichi Niikura, Yuzuru Katagiri, Yu Suwa, and Hisao Kanaseki are the contributors, and the charm and power of contemporary American poetry are fully exhibited in this special issue. Studies of children's literature have been a fad for some time in this country, and this tendency must have been the reason for the issue of *Jido Bungei* [*Children's Literature*] (Tokyo: Nihon Jido Bungeika Kyokai) featuring American children's literature. Works by such writers as Laura Ingalls Wilder, Frances Burnett, Louisa May Alcott, Susan Coolidge, and Mark Twain are examined.

Innumerable articles on American literature appeared in various scholarly magazines and periodicals, so let it suffice to name just a few outstanding ones in widely circulated periodicals. Among the writings on the writers of the American Renaissance, two articles are especially significant. Midori Yamamoto's "Thoreau's *A Week on the Concord and Merrimack Rivers*: Structural and Thematic Unity" (*The American Review* 14:112–40) is an attempt to endow Thoreau's descriptions of nature with philosophic significance. Masayuki Sakamoto in "From Land to the Sea—the Formation of the Ishmael Figure" (*Eigo Seinen* 126: 114–18) presents the creative process of the alienated protagonist through an analysis of the works preceding *Moby-Dick*. An impressive study of Henry James's *The Golden Bowl* by Yoshimi Kudo, "Point of View, Consciousness and Language—On Henry James' *The Golden Bowl*" (*Eigo Seinen* 126:122–24,200–202, 250–53), is a psychological approach to this difficult novel. Takeshi Morita in "Turning Point for Deepening: *The Town*—On the Snopes Trilogy" (*Eigo Seinen* 126: 322–24), through a thorough analysis of *The Town*, points out how Faulkner's attitude toward Flem Snopes changes from hatred to sympathy around the middle of the novel, reflecting a deepening of the author's understanding of human nature. Women writers as well as the writers of minority groups are popular as usual. "Women in American Literature at the Turn of the Century: Continuity and Change" (*The American Review* 14:

163–82), by Takashi Sasaki, deals with Katharine Ferguson, Dreiser, and Kate Chopin and surveys the process of the formation of an ideal image of woman. Another Sasaki essay, "Challenge to the Taboo: A Study of the Ending of *The Awakening*" (*Studies in American Literature* 17: 74–86), presents an interesting interpretation of the ending of the novel, rejecting the interpretations of Seyersted and Spangler. Tadatoshi Saito's "American Pluralism and the American Negro—with Emphasis on Ralph Ellison and James Baldwin" (*The American Review* 14: 24–38) and Sataye Shinoda's "An Introductory Account of Japanese American Literature" (*The American Review* 14: 63–89) are both contributions to an issue of this journal featuring "Pluralism in America." Shinoda's article, with an accurate chronological table of the historical and literary events concerning Japanese Americans, is a valuable introductory study of a thus-far-ignored part of American literature. Shigeo Hamano's "On Anzia Yezierska's *Bread Giver*" (*Tohoku Studies in American Literature* 4:27–40) gives a glimpse into the world of Jewish writers in the early part of this century. Comparatively few articles were written on plays and theater this year. Shinako Kusuhara's "The Forerunner of the American Avant-garde Theater—On the Living Theater" (*Eigo Seinen* 126:458–62) is, though, an informative historical survey of various theatrical activities preceding the revolutionary movement in the 1960s.

Translations of American books have not been limited to creative works. Two books, though not written by Americans, of great influence on critical studies of American literature have been translated. Northrop Frye's *Anatomy of Criticism* (Tokyo: Hosei University Press) and Tony Tanner's *City of Words* (Tokyo: Hakusuisha) have been translated by groups of able and learned scholars. The long-overdue translation of Frye's classical work will be a stimulant in the field of literary criticism, while Tanner's forceful book will heighten the interest in American postmodernist writers. Just to mention the names of two creative works translated this year will be sufficient to show how eager the Japanese public is to absorb American literature: Donald Barthelme's *Come Back, Dr. Caligari* (Tokyo: Kokusho Kankokai) and *Genius and Lust: Mailer on Miller* (Tokyo: TBS Britanica).

Tokyo Woman's Christian University

vi. Scandinavian Contributions

Rolf Lundén

It is difficult to draw general conclusions from such a limited number of contributions as the Scandinavian scholars produced during 1980. However, certain trends are visible: an uncommonly large proportion of the contributions was devoted to poetry this year, and the interest in American women writers continued to grow. As during the last few years, scholars tended to focus on 20th-century American literature, and to devote only scant attention to earlier periods.

The only piece this year to deal with American literature before 1900 was P. T. Barry's "Physical Descriptions in the International Tales of Henry James" (*OL* 35:47–58). Discussing six early tales ("A Passionate Pilgrim," "The Madonna of the Future," "Madame de Mauves," "Four Meetings," "An International Episode," and "A Bundle of Letters"), Barry holds that James's physical descriptions of his characters are so similar from one story to another that they become types, representing the main divergencies between European and American culture. Americans are depicted in hard, straight lines indicative of dullness but also of intellectual honesty and moral integrity. The soft, diffused light and the curved line are characteristic of the portraits of Europeans, presenting the richness of European culture but also revealing its moral degeneration.

In an imprecise, repetitive article, "The Clash of American Dreams in Carl Sandburg's Poetry" (*MSpr* 74:3–20), Ingegerd Friberg applies Leo Marx's machine-in-the-garden thesis to Sandburg's poetry. According to Friberg, there is in Sandburg's poems nostalgia for the country coupled with an ambivalent attitude toward the city. The city is simultaneously destructive and dynamically progressive. Friberg argues that Sandburg, in socialism, finally reaches a reconciliation of the tension between the pastoral and the urban way of life; the Machine in the Garden can be a postive force only if the people are not made its victims.

Another contribution dealing with poetry was Roger D. Sell's *Robert Frost: Four Studies* (AAAH 57,ii). These loosely related articles are all concerned with the lesser known of Frost's works. The first study, "The Early Years: Towards a Literary Biography," shows how many of Frost's philosophical and literary convictions were developed as early as shortly after the turn of the century. Sell studies the early prose Frost wrote for poultry journals and a high school bulletin and the short stories he wrote for his children—pieces which have not been given much scholarly attention before—and makes clear, among other things, how Frost's masterly ear for conversational tone was well adapted even at this early stage of his career. Another study in the volume, " 'In an Art Factory' and 'The Guardeen': Two Unpublished Plays," traces the history of creation of the plays and convincingly investigates their autobiographical background. The two remaining, less convincing, studies are called "Expansion and Contraction: Children and Adults" and "Socio-cultural Differentiation and Freedom."

Like Sandburg, Hart Crane expressed an ambivalent attitude toward the city and the machine culture characterizing the United States. This ambivalence is one of Helge Normann Nilsen's focal points in *Hart Crane's Divided Vision, An Analysis of* The Bridge (Oslo: Universitetsforlaget). According to Nilsen, Crane, inspired by Whitman and Waldo Frank, developed a faith in a sense of "the Whole," a synthetic faith that envisaged a "unification of the American experience in which evil and darkness are included and transcended." Crane's main expression of this belief was *The Bridge*, which was to present a revelation of spiritual unity in America. But Crane's utopianism is also characterized by a divided attitude toward the synthesis of America. His optimistic, affirmative view of life is coexisting with disbelief and black disillusionment; his faith in the divine whole is balanced against his suspicion that this future unification is only an illusion. The predominant part of Nilsen's book is devoted to a perceptive close reading of Crane's text. The study makes maybe a bit too much of the importance of Waldo Frank's thought upon Crane's philosophy of life, for the seeming parallels may be a case of "kindred spirits."

Helge Normann Nilsen feels that, on the whole, Waldo Frank is being neglected today. In "The Status of Waldo Frank in American Letters" (*AmerSS* 12:27–32) he argues that the attention should be redirected toward those parts of Frank's work which remain significant. What makes Frank worth remembering, Nilsen states, is his "inclusive vision" of America as a potential organic whole, divinely fashioned, which may be revealed in a new art and a new culture.

Helge Normann Nilsen has also directed his attention to the art of Saul Bellow in "Helt eller klovn? Omkring noen uløste konflikter i Saul Bellows forfatterskap" [Hero or Clown? On Some Unresolved Conflicts in the Art of Saul Bellow] (*Edda*, pp. 93–102). While Nilsen accepts the ambivalence of Hart Crane's outlook as an integral part of his art, he looks upon a similar divided vision in Bellow's later novels as evidence that Bellow has not come to terms with himself and his art. In works like *Seize the Day, Henderson the Rain King*, and *Herzog*, Nilsen argues, there is a lack of integration between the character of the protagonist and his actions, between the growth of the story and the dénouement, between Bellow's serious intention and his undercutting parody.

In his comprehensive analysis, *John Barth's* Giles Goat-Boy, *A Study* (Jyväskylä: Univ. of Jyväskylä) Douglas Robinson is also concerned with the paradoxical tensions of a work of art. Moving from language through setting and myth to philosophy, Robinson makes a thorough and illuminating investigation of a series of dialectical tensions between parody and allegory. Following the theories of Lord Raglan and Joseph Campbell, Robinson traces, for instance, the hero myth and how Barth parodies this allegorical pattern. He also shows how the novel's allegorical characters are grouped in paradoxical pairs and how the protagonist in his assignments must come to an understanding of several paradoxical concepts. Robinson tersely states that "paradoxically, Barth both believes and does not believe that the universe and the mind of man are characterized by paradox." He holds that the ultimate vision of *Giles Goat-Boy* is that in the midst of the tragedy of life we are given the joy of art, and we are asked to accept both, "with our right to joy and our ironic privilege mutually checked, and mutually affirmed."

Ruth Sherry's article " 'For the Union Dead': A Bostonian's Notes" (*AmerSS* 12:33–38) explains numerous geographical phenomena in Lowell's poem and how this physical background contributes to its symbolic meaning.

The interest in women writers has grown fast in Scandinavian universities, and even though the main concern is with indigenous writing, American women writers have also received a share of the attention. In a somewhat simplistic article, "Women Writers in American Literary History" (*AmerSS* 12:39–47), Linda Ricketts Sørbø argues that women writers are conspicuously underrepresented and underrated in histories and anthologies of American literature.

As is often the case when you have an axe to grind, Sørbø overstates her argument. Granted even though there have been many instances of "phallic criticism," Dickinson, Fuller, Jewett, Stein and others have not been quite as ill treated as Sørbø insists. In conclusion, Sørbø shows that since the beginning of the 1970s the attitude toward women writers has changed for the better, and that there is hope for the future that American women writers will get the fair treatment that they deserve.

The mother-daughter relationship is a very prevalent and fundamental issue in literature today. In "Mothers and Daughters in Recent North American Literature" (*Edda*, pp. 23–31) Tiina Nunnally and Fran Hopenwasser Petersen have selected eight contemporary works for analysis: Maxine Hong Kingston's *The Woman Warrior*, Gail Godwin's *The Odd Woman*, Margaret Atwood's *Lady Oracle*, Toni Morrison's *The Bluest Eye*, Marge Piercy's *Small Changes*, Kate Millett's *Flying*, Tillie Olsen's *Tell Me a Riddle*, and Lisa Alther's *Kinflicks*. Nunnally and Petersen have chosen to look at the relationship first from the point of view of the daughters, and how they fear becoming like their mothers at the same time as they desperately seek their mothers' approval, and secondly from the angle of the mothers, and how they struggle with their bitterness and how they face the rejection of their daughters.

In Leif Sjöberg's interview with Joyce Carol Oates, "Samtal med Joyce Carol Oates" (*Artes* 6:13–32), the conversation moves from the complementary roles of science and art, to Oates's denial that there is a widening gap between serious and popular culture, to her preference for fiction that combines the naturalistic with the symbolic. Good fiction, according to Oates, should have a depth of vision, a certain scope, interest in various levels of society, compassion for many kinds of people, historical awareness, and an interest in contemporary history, and finally a consciousness of the forces which interplay in politics, religion, economy, and morals.

University of Uppsala

22. General Reference Works

J. Albert Robbins

The year's supply of reference works is not particularly distinguished. The most general is one which Professor Woodress noticed in *ALS 1979.* I shall comment on it briefly, for it was published (at least the copyright page says it was published) in 1980, the subject year of this *ALS.* I grew up with "Thrall and Hibbard," as we called it, and it is fitting for such a worthy book to be revised and updated periodically. So, the work of William Flint Thrall and Addison Hibbard is now refurbished as the 4th edition by the late C. Hugh Holman and still called *A Handbook to Literature* (Bobbs-Merrill). It is one of the most useful volumes a scholar can have within reach on his shelf. The range of information is great: terms of prosody, literary types, critical terms, -isms from Aestheticism to Vorticism, literary periods —even some terms used in film criticism. Occasionally one is surprised at gaps (nothing on social realism or objectivism, for example), but these are few. The back matter includes a useful chronology and lists of major prizes and awards. Long life to "Thrall and Hibbard and Holman"!

The Gale people in Detroit continue to produce reference works of many kinds, the most useful this year an enlargement of their DLB series (Dictionary of Literary Biography). (A more exact title would be Dictionary of American Literary Biography. Or could the publishers be planning to cover British writers if the library market for such volumes remains firm?) We have noticed the first three (DLB 1 and 2 in *ALS 1978,* p. 491; DLB 3 in *ALS 1979,* p. 534). This year there are four: *American Writers in Paris, 1920–1939* (DLB 4, ed. by Karen Lane Rood); *American Poets Since World War II* in two parts (DLB 5, edited by Donald J. Greiner); and *American Novelists Since World War II,* Second Series (DLB 6, edited by James E. Kibler, Jr.). The latter has a cumulative index.

As to totals, these four 1980 tomes add 1705 large format, double-columned pages to the series, covering a total of 302 authors. Of these, 99 are in the Paris volume, 133 in the two volumes on poets, and 70 in the 2nd series on novelists. If you want the four volumes, they cost $210 at list price. Entries (including essays and selective bibliographies) vary from 1½ pages for a distinctly minor person to 25 for a major writer. The essays are a blend of biography, commentary on major works, and general criticism.

American Writers in Paris is fascinating, because it brings together with words and pictures 99 Americans who converged upon Paris and made it, one often feels, a larger cultural colony than could have been found anywhere in the States. One note of warning: don't expect definitive and inclusive dates of Paris sojourns. The sketch of John Gould Fletcher, for example, notes that his first visit in 1913 lasted seven weeks but gives no sense of how long other visits in 1923, 1925, and 1930 lasted. Another question that occurs is this: will some authors treated partially here (such as Hemingway) get full treatment in later volumes? The answer is yes.

In *ALS 1978* (p. 491) I noticed the inauguration of a new Gale series, *Twentieth-Century Literary Criticism*: excerpts of criticism grouped by the subject-author. It is international, so in a given volume half or less than half of the entries are American, but it is a time-saver for the scholar or teacher in a hurry. During 1980 Gale gave us TCLC 3. It might be useful to note that CLC (*Contemporary Literary Criticism*) covers authors living from 1960 to the present, and that TCLC treats authors who died between 1900 and 1960.

John Somer and Barbara E. Cooper have compiled a useful bibliography that should be useful to those dealing with the contemporary age, *American & British Literature, 1945–1975: An Annotated Bibliography of Contemporary Scholarship* (Kansas). The title is silent on one relevant matter: the compilation treats books only; no articles. The principal portion of the work is arranged by General Studies, Drama, Fiction and Prose, Poetry, and Critical Theory. Annotations touch upon central thesis or purpose of the book, mention special features, and give a selective list of subject authors—all briefly, in notes of up to 75 words each. The citations would have been more useful if the number of pages in each book had been indicated. An index leads one to authors of the books, writers treated, and such subject areas as existentialism, religion, experimental literature, and self. A substantial group of 356 bibliographies, handbooks, and guides (without annotation) conclude the compilation. Library card catalogs or the *National Union Catalog* provide a quick access by author; but if one is seeking materials by subject or theme, the search is far harder. The volume particularly addresses itself to the latter need.

Last year (*ALS 1979*, pp. 534–35) Professor Woodress commented on Vol. 1 of *American Women Writers: A Critical Reference Guide from Colonial Times to the Present*, edited by Lina Mainiero (Ungar, 1979). Vol. 2 of the four volume work appeared in 1980. The more I examine the work, the more its utility seems to be for brief discussions of minor and obscure women authors. Here are facts and references on such people as Alice Bradley Haven and Margaret Thompson Janvier; but I would not go to this work for more substantial women authors. Here, for example, the sketch of Shirley Jackson runs to just under 1000 words; while in the Gale volume, *American Novelists Since World War II*, Second Series (see above) the essay runs to over 4500 words. Such a work as this has its uses. The comparisons just made are intended to be factual, not critical.

David Kirby's *America's Hive of Honey, or Foreign Influences on American Fiction through Henry James: Essays & Bibliographies* (Scarecrow) looks upon foreign influences as biographical (Dante, Spenser, Cervantes, Shakespeare, Milton, and so on) and temporal (the Classics, the Bible, the Middle Ages, the Renaissance, and so on) or as movements (romantics, realists, and naturalists). Each chapter has a brief preface, followed by citations of books and articles under major-author headings with descriptive annotations.

A familiar reference work since 1950 has been *Poetry Explication: A Checklist of Interpretation Since 1925 of British and American Poems, Past and Present*. It is now in its third edition, edited by Joseph M. Kuntz and Nancy C. Martinez (G. K. Hall). One would expect a great increase in items since the second edition in 1962 and there is. The second edition recorded approximately 5,600 citations; the third edition, I estimate, has about 12,500. The checklist not only covers a wide range of periodicals; it also analyzes a large number of critical books on poetry. This is a reference tool deserving a third edition and, in due course, a fourth.

G. K. Hall has issued four studies of specialized areas in publishing. The first is a directory of *Boston Printers, Publishers, and Booksellers, 1640–1800*, edited by Benjamin Franklin V—a substantial volume of 545 pages. Some of these career biographies are brief, but some run to several pages—up to 7½ pages for the principal publisher of the age, Isaiah Thomas. The second is a livelier study of *Publishers for Mass Entertainment in Nineteenth Century America,* edited by Madeleine B. Stern. Hers is the fascinating realm of "cheap" literature—the dime novels, the melodramatic formulaic tales that satisfied a universal hunger for romance, adventure, patriotism and—face it—good "clean" violence. A few major houses are here, such as Harper and Holt; but most are specialist firms—such familiar names as Beadle, Samuel French, Frank Leslie, Roberts Brothers, Street & Smith, and others less well known. The informational sketches are enlivened by photographs of pictorial covers—Beadle's Dime Novel No. 1 of course (Ann S. Stephens' *Malaeska, The Indian Wife of the White Hunter*); *Pauline, The Female Spy; The Red Revenger: Or, The Pirate King of the Floridas;* and *Buffalo Bill and the White Spectre; Or, The Mysterious Medicine Man of Spirit Lake.* Mary Lystad (whose training has been in social psychology) is herself an author of children's books. Her *From Dr. Mather to Dr. Seuss: 200 Years of American Books for Children* is a chronological study which seeks patterns in "socializing children, and of definitions of social values." In another field L. W. Curry claims to include more authors and titles in his *Science Fiction and Fantasy Authors: A Bibliography of First Printings of Their Fiction and Selected Nonfiction* (1979) than any previous compilations. This large, 571-page volume seems to have the collector in mind, but it has uses for the Sci-Fi scholar as well.

The title of *Guide to Marxist Literary Criticism,* by Chris Bullock and David Peck (Indiana) is a misnomer. It is not an expository but a bibliographical guide. The major sections cover genres and national literatures (British, United States, and English-Canadian). Annotations, when present, are minimal. The "Topic [that is, topical] Index" is a useful guide to such subjects as aesthetics, modernism, politics and literature, socialist realism, and women and literature. The compilers have included non-Marxist items on Marxist works and writers, and non-Marxist critics whose work has furthered the development of Marxist criticism.

Finally, *Southwestern American Literature, A Bibliography,* edited by John Q. Anderson, Edwin W. Gaston, Jr., and James W. Lee (Swallow), is a substantial volume of close to 450 pages, of which one third is devoted to five topics (Land, People, Work, Art, and Ethos) and two-thirds to individual authors. The definition of "southwestern" includes the southernmost tier of states east of California: Arizona, New Mexico, Texas, and Oklahoma. Of the over 400 authors included I found only some 7% familiar: good southwesterners such as Will Rogers, John Lomax, Tom Lea, and J. Frank Dobie; as well as others I do not associate with the southwest: Terry Southern, Lew Wallace, John Berryman, and Joseph Wood Krutch. A work which will have little appeal outside the region it documents.

Author Index

Subject Index